TOOLS OF
TITANS

TOOLS OF
TITANS

THE TACTICS, ROUTINES, AND HABITS OF BILLIONAIRES, ICONS, AND WORLD-CLASS PERFORMERS

TIM FERRISS

FOREWORD BY ARNOLD SCHWARZENEGGER
ILLUSTRATIONS BY REMIE GEOFFROI

Houghton Mifflin Harcourt
BOSTON   NEW YORK
2016

PUBLISHER'S LEGAL DISCLAIMER

This book presents a wide range of opinions about a variety of topics related to health and well-being, including certain ideas, treatments, and procedures that may be hazardous or illegal if undertaken without proper medical supervision. These opinions reflect the research and ideas of the author or those whose ideas the author presents, but are not intended to substitute for the services of a trained healthcare practitioner. Consult with your health care practitioner before engaging in any diet, drug, or exercise regimen. The author and the publisher disclaim responsibility for any adverse effects resulting directly or indirectly from information contained in this book.

TIM'S DISCLAIMER

Please don't do anything stupid and kill yourself. It would make us both quite unhappy. Consult a doctor, lawyer, and common-sense specialist before doing anything in this book.

CREDITS

DEDICATION

First, gratitude to you all, my "companions on the path," as James Fadiman would say.

Second, a portion of author royalties will be donated to these worthwhile causes:

>> **After-School All-Stars (AFTERSCHOOLALLSTARS.ORG),** which provides comprehensive after-school programs for keeping children safe and helping them to succeed in both school and life.

>> **DonorsChoose.org,** which makes it easy for anyone to help a high-need classroom, moving us closer to a nation where all students have the tools they need for a great education.

>> **Scientific research at institutions such as the Johns Hopkins University School of Medicine,** where entheogens are being studied for applications to treatment-resistant depression, end-of-life anxiety (in terminal cancer patients), and other debilitating conditions.

Third, for all the seekers, may you find much more than you're looking for. Perhaps this book will help.

FOREWORD

I am not a self-made man.

Every time I give a speech at a business conference, or speak to college students, or do a Reddit AMA, someone says it.

"Governor/Governator/Arnold/Arnie/Schwarzie/Schnitzel (depending on where I am), as a self-made man, what's your blueprint for success?"

They're always shocked when I thank them for the compliment but say, "I am not a self-made man. I got a lot of help."

It is true that I grew up in Austria without plumbing. It is true that I moved to America alone with just a gym bag. And it is true that I worked as a bricklayer and invested in real estate to become a millionaire before I ever swung the sword in *Conan the Barbarian*.

But it is not true that I am self-made. Like everyone, to get to where I am, I stood on the shoulders of giants.

My life was built on a foundation of parents, coaches, and teachers; of kind souls who lent couches or gym back rooms where I could sleep; of mentors who shared wisdom and advice; of idols who motivated me from the pages of magazines (and, as my life grew, from personal interaction).

I had a big vision, and I had fire in my belly. But I would never have gotten anywhere without my mother helping me with my homework (and smacking me when I wasn't ready to study), without my father telling me to "be useful," without teachers who explained how to sell, or without coaches who taught me the fundamentals of weight lifting.

If I had never seen a magazine with Reg Park on the cover and read about his transition from Mr. Universe to playing Hercules on the big screen, I might still be yodeling in the Austrian Alps. I knew I wanted to leave Austria, and I knew that America was exactly where I belonged, but Reg put fuel on the fire and gave me my blueprint.

Joe Weider brought me to America and took me under his wing, promoting my bodybuilding career and teaching me about business. Lucille Ball took a huge chance and called me to guest star in a special that was my first big break in Hollywood. And in 2003, without the help of 4,206,284 Californians, I would never have been elected Governor of the great state of California.

So how can I ever claim to be self-made? To accept that mantle discounts every person and every piece of advice that got me here. And it gives the wrong impression — that you can do it alone.

I couldn't. And odds are, you can't either.

We all need fuel. Without the assistance, advice, and inspiration of others, the gears of our mind grind to a halt, and we're stuck with nowhere to go.

I have been blessed to find mentors and idols at every step of my life, and I've been lucky to meet many of them. From Joe Weider to Nelson Mandela, from Mikhail Gorbachev to Muhammad Ali, from Andy Warhol to George H.W. Bush, I have never been shy about seeking wisdom from others to pour fuel on my fire.

You have probably listened to Tim's podcasts. (I particularly recommend the one with the charming bodybuilder with the Austrian accent.) He has used his platform to bring you the wisdom of a diverse cast of characters in business, entertainment, and sports. I bet you've learned something from them — and oftentimes, I bet you picked up something you didn't expect.

Whether it's a morning routine, or a philosophy or training tip, or just motivation to get through your day, there isn't a person on this planet who doesn't benefit from a little outside help.

I've always treated the world as my classroom, soaking up lessons and stories to fuel my path forward. I hope you do the same.

The worst thing you can ever do is think that you know enough.

Never stop learning. Ever.

That's why you bought this book. You know that wherever you are in life, there will be moments when you need outside motivation and insight. There will be times when you don't have the answer, or the drive, and you're forced to look beyond yourself.

You can admit that you can't do it alone. I certainly can't. No one can.

Now, turn the page and learn something.

— Arnold Schwarzenegger

ON THE SHOULDERS OF GIANTS

I am not the expert. I'm the experimenter, the scribe, and the guide.

If you find anything amazing in this book, it's thanks to the brilliant minds who acted as teachers, resources, critics, contributors, proofreaders, and references. If you find anything ridiculous in this book, it's because I didn't heed their advice or made a mistake.

Though indebted to hundreds of people, I wish to thank here the many guests who have appeared on my podcast and who grace the pages of this book, listed in alphabetical order:

Scott Adams (p. 261)

James Altucher (p. 246)

Sophia Amoruso (p. 376)

Marc Andreessen (p. 170)

Sekou Andrews (p. 642)

Patrick Arnold (p. 35)

Peter Attia (p. 59)

Glenn Beck (p. 553)

Scott Belsky (p. 359)

Richard Betts (p. 563)

Mike Birbiglia (p. 566)

Alex Blumberg (p. 303)

Amelia Boone (p. 2)

Justin Boreta (p. 356)

Tara Brach (p. 555)

Brené Brown (p. 586)

Bryan Callen (p. 483)

Shay Carl (p. 441)

Dan Carlin (p. 285)

Ed Catmull (p. 309)

Margaret Cho (p. 538)

Paulo Coelho (p. 511)

Ed Cooke (p. 517)

Kevin Costner (p. 451)

Whitney Cummings (p. 477)

Dominic D'Agostino (p. 21)

Alain de Botton (p. 486)

Joe De Sena (p. 38)

Mike Del Ponte (p. 299)

Peter Diamandis (p. 369)

Tracy DiNunzio (p. 313)

Jack Dorsey (p. 509)

Stephen J. Dubner (p. 574)

Dan Engle (page 109)

James Fadiman (p. 100)

Jon Favreau (p. 592)

Jamie Foxx (p. 604)

Chris Fussell (p. 435)

Cal Fussman (p. 495)

Adam Gazzaley (p. 135)

Malcolm Gladwell (p. 572)

Seth Godin (p. 237)

Evan Goldberg (page 531)

Marc Goodman (p. 424)

Laird Hamilton (p. 92)

Sam Harris (p. 454)

Wim Hof (p. 41)

Reid Hoffman (p. 228)

Ryan Holiday (p. 334)

Chase Jarvis (p. 280)

Daymond John (p. 323)

Bryan Johnson (p. 609)

Sebastian Junger (p. 420)

Noah Kagan (p. 325)

Samy Kamkar (p. 427)

Kaskade (p. 329)

Sam Kass (p. 558)

Kevin Kelly (p. 470)

Brian Koppelman (p. 613)

Tim Kreider (p. 489)

Paul Levesque (p. 128)

Phil Libin (p. 315)

Will MacAskill (p. 446)

Brian MacKenzie (p. 92)

Justin Mager (p. 72)

Nicholas McCarthy (p. 208)

Gen. Stan McChrystal (p. 435)

Jane McGonigal (p. 132)

BJ Miller (p. 400)

Matt Mullenweg (p. 202)

Casey Neistat (p. 217)

Jason Nemer (p. 46)

Edward Norton (p. 561)

B.J. Novak (p. 378)

Alexis Ohanian (p. 194)

Amanda Palmer (p. 520)

Rhonda Patrick (p. 6)

Caroline Paul (p. 459)

Martin Polanco (p. 109)

Charles Poliquin (p. 74)

Maria Popova (p. 406)

Rolf Potts (p. 362)

Naval Ravikant (p. 546)

Gabby Reece (p. 92)

Tony Robbins (p. 210)

Robert Rodriguez (p. 628)

Seth Rogen (p. 531)

Kevin Rose (p. 340)

Rick Rubin (p. 502)

Chris Sacca (p. 164)

Arnold Schwarzenegger (p. 176)

Ramit Sethi (p. 287)

Mike Shinoda (p. 352)

Jason Silva (p. 589)

Derek Sivers (p. 184)

Joshua Skenes (p. 500)

Christopher Sommer (p. 9)

Morgan Spurlock (p. 221)

Kelly Starrett (p. 122)

Neil Strauss (p. 347)

Cheryl Strayed (p. 515)

Chade-Meng Tan (p. 154)

Peter Thiel (p. 232)

Pavel Tsatsouline (p. 85)

Luis von Ahn (p. 331)

Josh Waitzkin (p. 577)

Eric Weinstein (p. 523)

Shaun White (p. 271)

Jocko Willink (p. 412)

Rainn Wilson (p. 543)

Chris Young (p. 318)

Andrew Zimmern (p. 540)

CONTENTS

PART 2 : WEALTHY

NON-PROFILE CHAPTERS

PART 3 : WISE

READ THIS FIRST—
HOW TO USE THIS BOOK

"Out on the edge you see all kinds of things you can't see from the center.
Big, undreamed-of things—the people on the edge see them first."

—Kurt Vonnegut

"Routine, in an intelligent man, is a sign of ambition."

—W.H. Auden

I'm a compulsive note-taker.

To wit, I have recorded nearly every workout since age 18 or so. Roughly 8 feet of shelf space in my home is occupied by spine upon spine of notebook upon notebook. That, mind you, is one subject. It extends to dozens. Some people would call this OCD, and many would consider it a manic wild goose chase. I view it simply: It is the collection of my life's recipes.

My goal is to learn things once and use them forever.

For instance, let's say I stumble upon a picture of myself from June 5, 2007, and I think, "I really wish I looked like that again." No problem. I'll crack open a dusty volume from 2007, review the 8 weeks of training and food logs preceding June 5, repeat them, and—voilà—end up looking nearly the same as my younger self (minus the hair). It's not always that easy, but it often is.

This book, like my others, is a compendium of recipes for high performance that I gathered for my own use. There's one big difference, though—I never planned on publishing this one.

_____

As I write this, I'm sitting in a café in Paris overlooking the Luxembourg Garden, just off of Rue Saint-Jacques. Rue Saint-Jacques is likely the oldest road in Paris, and it has a rich literary history. Victor Hugo lived a few blocks from where I'm sitting. Gertrude Stein drank coffee and F. Scott Fitzgerald socialized within a stone's throw. Hemingway wandered up and down the sidewalks, his books percolating in his mind, wine no doubt percolating in his blood.

I came to France to take a break from *everything*. No social media, no email, no social commitments, no set plans . . . except one project. The month had been set aside to review all of the lessons I'd learned from nearly 200 world-class performers I'd interviewed on *The Tim Ferriss Show*, which recently passed 100,000,000 downloads. The guests included chess prodigies, movie stars, four-star generals, pro athletes, and hedge fund managers. It was a motley crew.

More than a handful of them had since become collaborators in business and creative projects, spanning from investments to indie film. As a result, I'd absorbed a lot of their wisdom outside of our recordings, whether over workouts, wine-infused jam sessions, text message exchanges, dinners, or late-night phone calls. In every case, I'd gotten to know them well beyond the superficial headlines in the media.

My life had already improved in every area as a result of the lessons I could remember. But that was the tip of the iceberg. The majority of the gems were still lodged in thousands of pages of transcripts and hand-scribbled notes. More than anything, I longed for the chance to distill everything into a playbook.

So, I'd set aside an entire month for review (and, if I'm being honest, *pain au chocolat*), to put together the ultimate CliffsNotes for myself. It would be the notebook to end all notebooks. Something that could help me in minutes but be read for a lifetime.

That was the lofty goal, at least, and I wasn't sure what the result would be.

Within weeks of starting, the experience exceeded all expectations. No matter the situation I found myself in, something in this book was able to help. Now, when I'm feeling stuck, trapped, desperate, angry, conflicted, or simply unclear, the first thing I do is flip through these pages with a strong cup of coffee in hand. So far, the needed medicine has popped out within 20 minutes of revisiting these friends, who will now become your friends. Need a reassuring pat on the back? There's someone for that. An unapologetic slap in the face? Plenty of people for that, too. Someone to explain why your fears are unfounded . . . or why your excuses are bullshit? Done.

There are a lot of powerful quotes, but this book is much more than a compilation of quotes. It is a toolkit for changing your life.

There are many books full of interviews. This is different, because I don't view myself as an interviewer. I view myself as an experimenter. If I can't test something or replicate results in the messy reality of everyday life, I'm not interested. Everything in these pages has been vetted, explored, and applied to my own life in some fashion. I've used dozens of these tactics and philosophies in high-stakes negotiations, high-risk environments, or large business dealings. The lessons have made me millions of dollars and saved me years of wasted effort and frustration. They work when you need them most.

Some applications are obvious at first glance, while others are subtle and will provoke a "Holy shit, *now* I get it!" realization weeks later, while you're daydreaming in the shower or about to fall asleep.

Many of the one-liners teach volumes. Some summarize excellence in an entire field in one sentence. As Josh Waitzkin (page 577), chess prodigy and the inspiration behind *Searching for Bobby Fischer*, might put it, these bite-sized learnings are a way to "learn the macro from the micro." The process of piecing them together was revelatory. If I thought I saw "the Matrix" before, I was mistaken, or I was only seeing 10% of it. Still, even that 10% — "islands" of notes on individual mentors — had already changed my life and helped me 10x my results. But after revisiting more than a hundred minds as part of the same fabric, things got very interesting very quickly. For the movie nerds among you, it was like the end of *The Sixth Sense* or *The Usual Suspects*: "The red door knob! The fucking Kobayashi coffee cup! How did I not notice that?! It was right in front of me the whole time!"

To help you see the same, I've done my best to weave patterns together throughout the book, noting where guests have complementary habits, beliefs, and recommendations.

The completed jigsaw puzzle is much greater than the sum of its parts.

WHAT MAKES THESE PEOPLE DIFFERENT?

"Judge a man by his questions rather than his answers."

—**Pierre-Marc-Gaston**

These world-class performers don't have superpowers.

The rules they've *crafted* for themselves allow the bending of reality to such an extent that it may seem that way, but they've learned how to do this, and so can you. These "rules" are often uncommon habits and bigger questions.

In a surprising number of cases, the power is in the absurd. The more absurd, the more "impossible" the question, the more profound the answers. Take, for instance, a question that serial billionaire Peter Thiel likes to ask himself and others:

"If you have a 10-year plan of how to get [somewhere], you should ask: Why can't you do this in 6 months?"

For purposes of illustration here, I might reword that to:

"What might you do to accomplish your 10-year goals in the next 6 months, if you had a gun against your head?"

Now, let's pause. Do I expect you to take 10 seconds to ponder this and then magically accomplish 10 years' worth of dreams in the next few months? No, I don't. But I do expect that the question will productively break your mind, like a butterfly shattering a chrysalis to emerge with new capabilities. The "normal" systems you have in place, the social rules you've forced upon yourself, the standard frameworks—they don't work when answering a question like this. You are forced to shed artificial constraints, like shedding a skin, to realize that you had the ability to renegotiate your reality all along. It just takes practice.

My suggestion is that you spend real time with the questions you find most ridiculous in this book. Thirty minutes of stream-of-consciousness journaling (page 224) could change your life.

On top of that, while the world is a gold mine, you need to go digging in other people's heads to unearth riches. Questions are your pickaxes and competitive advantage. This book will give you an arsenal to choose from.

PERFORMANCE-ENHANCING DETAILS

When organizing all of the material for myself, I didn't want an onerous 37-step program.

I wanted low-hanging fruit with immediate returns. Think of the bite-sized rules within these pages as PEDs — performance-enhancing details. They can be added to any training regimen (read here: different careers, personal preferences, unique responsibilities, etc.) to pour gasoline on the fire of progress.

Fortunately, 10x results don't always require 10x effort. Big changes can come in small packages. To dramatically change your life, you don't need to run a 100-mile race, get a PhD, or completely reinvent yourself. It's the small things, done consistently, that are the big things (e.g., "red teaming" once per quarter, Tara Brach's guided meditations, strategic fasting or exogenous ketones, etc.).

"Tool" is defined broadly in this book. It includes routines, books, common self-talk, supplements, favorite questions, and much more.

WHAT DO THEY HAVE IN COMMON?

In this book, you'll naturally look for common habits and recommendations, and you should. Here are a few patterns, some odder than others:

>> More than 80% of the interviewees have some form of daily mindfulness or meditation practice

>> A surprising number of males (not females) over 45 never eat breakfast, or eat only the scantiest of fare (e.g., Laird Hamilton, page 92; Malcolm Gladwell, page 572; General Stanley McChrystal, page 435)

>> Many use the ChiliPad device for cooling at bedtime

>> Rave reviews of the books *Sapiens*, *Poor Charlie's Almanack*, *Influence*, and *Man's Search for Meaning*, among others

>> The habit of listening to single songs on repeat for focus (page 507)

>> Nearly everyone has done some form of "spec" work (completing projects on their own time and dime, then submitting them to prospective buyers)

>> The belief that "failure is not durable" (see Robert Rodriguez, page 628) or variants thereof

>> Almost every guest has been able to take obvious "weaknesses" and turn them into huge competitive advantages (see Arnold Schwarzenegger, page 176)

Of course, I will help you connect these dots, but that's less than half of the value of this book. Some of the most encouraging workarounds are found in the outliers. I want you to look for the black sheep who fit your unique idiosyncrasies. Keep an eye out for the non-traditional paths, like Shay Carl's journey from manual laborer to YouTube star to co-founder of a startup sold for nearly $1 billion (page 441). The variation is the consistency. As a software engineer might say, "That's not a bug. It's a feature!"

Borrow liberally, combine uniquely, and create your own bespoke blueprint.

THIS BOOK IS A BUFFET — HERE'S HOW TO GET THE MOST OUT OF IT

RULE #1: SKIP LIBERALLY.

I want you to skip anything that doesn't grab you. This book should be fun to read, and it's a buffet to choose from. Don't suffer through anything. If you hate shrimp, don't eat the goddamn shrimp. Treat it as a choose-your-own-adventure guide, as that's how I've written it. My goal is for each reader to like 50%, love 25%, and never forget 10%. Here's why: For the millions who've heard the podcast, and the dozens who proofread this book, the 50/25/10 highlights are *completely* different for *every* person. It's blown my mind.

I've even had multiple guests in this book — people who are the best at what they do — proofread the same profile, answering my question of "Which 10% would you absolutely keep, and which 10% would you absolutely cut?" Oftentimes, the 10% "must keep" of one person was the *exact* "must cut" of someone else! This is not one-size-fits-all. I expect you to discard plenty. Read what you enjoy.

RULE #2: SKIP, BUT DO SO INTELLIGENTLY.

All that said, take a brief mental note of anything you skip. Perhaps put a little dot in the corner of the page or highlight the headline.

Perhaps it's skipping and glossing over precisely these topics or questions that has created blind spots, bottlenecks, and unresolved issues in your life? That was certainly true for me.

If you decide to flip past something, note it, return to it later at some point, and ask yourself, "Why did I skip this?" Did it offend you? Seem beneath you? Seem too difficult? And did you arrive at that by thinking it through, or is it a reflection of biases inherited from your parents and others? Very often, "our" beliefs are not our own.

This type of practice is how you *create* yourself, instead of seeking to *discover* yourself. There is value in the latter, but it's mostly past-tense: It's a rear-view mirror. Looking out the windshield is how you get where you want to go.

JUST REMEMBER TWO PRINCIPLES

I was recently standing in Place Louis Aragon, a shaded outdoor nook on the River Seine, having a picnic with writing students from the Paris American Academy. One woman pulled me aside and asked what I hoped to convey in this book, at the core. Seconds later, we were pulled back into the fray, as the attendees were all taking turns talking about the circuitous paths that brought them there that day. Nearly everyone had a story of wanting to come to Paris for years — in some cases, 30 to 40 years — but assuming it was impossible.

Listening to their stories, I pulled out a scrap of paper and jotted down my answer to her question. In this book, at its core, I want to convey the following:

1   **Success, however you define it, is achievable if you collect the right field-tested beliefs and habits.** Someone else has done your version of "success" before, and often, *many* have done something similar. "But," you might ask, "what about a first, like colonizing Mars?" There are

still recipes. Look at empire building of other types, look at the biggest decisions in the life of Robert Moses (read *The Power Broker*), or simply find someone who stepped up to do great things that were deemed impossible at the time (e.g., Walt Disney). There is shared DNA you can borrow.

2 **The superheroes you have in your mind (idols, icons, titans, billionaires, etc.) are nearly all walking flaws who've maximized 1 or 2 strengths.** Humans are imperfect creatures. You don't "succeed" because you have no weaknesses; you succeed because you find your unique strengths and focus on developing habits around them. To make this crystal-clear, I've deliberately included two sections in this book (pages 197 and 616) that will make you think: "Wow, Tim Ferriss is a mess. How the hell does he ever get anything done?" Everyone is fighting a battle you know nothing about. The heroes in this book are no different. Everyone struggles. Take solace in that.

A FEW IMPORTANT NOTES ON FORMAT

STRUCTURE

This book is comprised of three sections: Healthy, Wealthy, and Wise. Of course, there is tremendous overlap across the sections, as the pieces are interdependent. In fact, you could think of the three as a tripod upon which life is balanced. One needs all three to have any sustainable success or happiness. "Wealthy," in the context of this book, also means much more than money. It extends to abundance in time, relationships, and more.

My original intention with *The 4-Hour Workweek* (4HWW), *The 4-Hour Body* (4HB), and *The 4-Hour Chef* (4HC) was to create a trilogy themed after Ben Franklin's famous quote: "Early to bed and early to rise, makes a man healthy, wealthy, and wise."

People constantly ask me, "What would you put in *The 4-Hour Workweek* if you were to write it again? How would you update it?" Ditto for 4HB and 4HC. *Tools of Titans* contains most of the answers for all three.

EXTENDED QUOTES

Before writing this book, I called Mason Currey, author of *Daily Rituals*, which profiles the rituals of 161 creatives like Franz Kafka and Pablo Picasso. I asked him what his best decisions were related to the book. Mason responded with, "[I] let my subjects' voices come through as much as possible, and I think that was one of things that I did 'right.' Often, it wasn't the details of their routine/habits, so much as how they talked about them that was interesting."

This is a critical observation and exactly why most "books of quotes" fail to have any real impact.

Take, for example, a one-liner like "What's on the other side of fear? Nothing." from Jamie Foxx. It's memorable, and you might guess at the profound underlying meaning. I'd still wager you'd forget it within a week. But, what if I made it infinitely more powerful by including Jamie's own explanation of why he uses that maxim to teach his kids confidence? The context and original language teaches you how to THINK like a world-class performer, not just regurgitate quotes. That is the key meta-skill we're aiming for. To that end, you'll see a lot of extended quotes and stories.

I've occasionally **bolded** lines within quotes. This is my emphasis, not the guest's.

How to Read Quotes—The Micro

. . . = Portion of dialogue omitted

[words in brackets] = additional information that wasn't part of the interview but may be necessary to understand what's being discussed, or related info or recommendations from yours truly

How to Read Quotes—The Macro

One of my podcast guests, also one of the smartest people I know, was shocked when I showed him his raw transcript. "Wow," he said. "I generally like to think of myself as a decently smart guy, but I use past, present, and future tense like they're the same fucking thing. It makes me sound like a complete moron."

Transcripts can be unforgiving. I've read my own, so I know how bad it can be.

In the heat of the moment, grammar can go out the window, to be replaced by false starts and sentence fragments. Everyone starts an ungodly number of sentences with "And" or "So." I and millions of others tend to use "and I was like" instead of "and I said." Many of us mix up plural and singular. This all works fine in conversation, but it can hiccup on the printed page.

Quotations have therefore been edited in some cases for clarity, space, and as a courtesy to guests and readers alike. I did my best to preserve the spirit and point of quotes, while making them as smart and readable as possible. Sometimes I keep it fast and loose to preserve the kinetic energy and emotion of the moment. Other times, I smooth out the edges, including my own stammering.

If anything sounds silly or off, assume it was my mistake. Everyone in this book is amazing, and I've done my best to showcase that.

PATTERNS

Where guests have related recommendations or philosophies, I've noted them in parentheses. For instance, if Jane Doe tells a story about the value of testing higher prices, I might add "(see Marc Andreessen, page 170)," since his answer to "If you could have a billboard anywhere, what would you put on it?" was "Raise prices," which he explains in depth.

HUMOR!

I've included ample doses of the ridiculous. First of all, if we're serious all the time, we'll wear out before we get the truly serious stuff done. Second, if this book were all stern looks and no winks, all productivity and no grab-assing, you'd remember very little. I agree with Tony Robbins (page 210) that information without emotion isn't retained.

Look up "von Restorff effect" and "primacy and recency effect" for more science, but this book has been deliberately constructed to maximize your retention. Which leads us to . . .

SPIRIT ANIMALS

Yes, spirit animals. There wasn't room for photographs in this book, but I wanted some sort of illustrations to keep things fun. It seemed like a lost cause, but then — after a glass or four of wine — I recalled that one of my guests, Alexis Ohanian (page 194), likes to ask potential hires, "What's your spirit animal?" Eureka! So, you'll see thumbnail spirit animals for anyone who would humor me and play along. The best part? *Dozens* of people took the question *very* seriously. Extended explanations, emotional changes of heart, and Venn diagrams ensued. Questions poured in: "Would a mythological creature be acceptable?" "Can I be a plant instead?" Alas, I couldn't get a hold of everyone in time for publication, so drawings are sprinkled throughout like Scooby snacks. In a book full of practicality, treat these like little rainbows of absurdity. People had fun with it.

NON-PROFILE CONTENT AND TIM FERRISS CHAPTERS

In all sections, there are multiple non-profile pieces by guests and yours truly. These are typically intended to expand upon key principles and tools mentioned by multiple people.

URLS, WEBSITES, AND SOCIAL MEDIA

I've omitted most URLs, as outdated URLs are nothing but frustrating for everyone. For nearly anything mentioned, assume that I've chosen wording that will allow you to find it easily on Google or Amazon.

All full podcast episodes can be found at fourhourworkweek.com/podcast. Just search the guest's name, and the extended audio, complete show notes, links, and resources will pop up like warm toast on a cold morning.

In nearly every guest's profile, I indicate where you can best interact with them on social media: TW = Twitter, FB = Facebook, IG = Instagram, SC = Snapchat, and LI = LinkedIn.

YOUR SEND-OFF — THE 3 TOOLS THAT ALLOW ALL THE REST

Siddhartha by Hermann Hesse is recommended by many guests in this book. There is one specific takeaway that Naval Ravikant (page 546) has reinforced with me several times on our long walks over coffee. The protagonist, Siddhartha, a monk who looks like a beggar, has come to the city and falls in love with a famous courtesan named Kamala. He attempts to court her, and she asks, "What do you have?" A well-known merchant similarly asks, "What can you give that you have learned?" His answer is the same in both cases, so I've included the latter story here. Siddhartha ultimately acquires all that he wants.

MERCHANT: ". . . If you are without possessions, how can you give?"

SIDDHARTHA: "Everyone gives what he has. The soldier gives strength, the merchant goods, the teacher instruction, the farmer rice, the fisherman fish."

MERCHANT: "Very well, and what can you give? What have you learned that you can give?"

SIDDHARTHA: **"I can think, I can wait, I can fast."**

MERCHANT: "Is that all?"

SIDDHARTHA: "I think that is all."

MERCHANT: "And of what use are they? For example, fasting, what good is that?"

SIDDHARTHA: "It is of great value, sir. If a man has nothing to eat, fasting is the most intelligent thing he can do. If, for instance, Siddhartha had not learned to fast, he would have had to seek some kind of work today, either with you, or elsewhere, for hunger would have driven him. But, as it is, Siddhartha can wait calmly. He is not impatient, he is not in need, he can ward off hunger for a long time and laugh at it. "

I think of Siddhartha's answers often and in the following terms:

"I can think" → Having good rules for decision-making, and having good questions you can ask yourself and others.

"I can wait" → Being able to plan long-term, play the long game, and not misallocate your resources.

"I can fast" → Being able to withstand difficulties and disaster. Training yourself to be uncommonly resilient and have a high pain tolerance.

This book will help you to develop all three.

I created *Tools of Titans* because it's the book that I've wanted my entire life. I hope you enjoy reading it as much as I enjoyed writing it.

Pura vida,

Tim Ferriss
Paris, France

HEALTHY

"When I let go of what I am, I become what I might be."

— *Lao Tzu*

"It is no measure of health to be well adjusted
to a profoundly sick society."

— *J. Krishnamurti*

"In the end, winning is sleeping better."

— *Jodie Foster*

" I'm not the strongest. I'm not the fastest. But I'm really good at suffering. **"**

AMELIA BOONE

Amelia Boone (TW: @AMELIABOONE, AMELIABOONERACING.COM) has been called "the Michael Jordan of obstacle course racing" (OCR) and is widely considered the world's most decorated obstacle racer. Since the inception of the sport, she's amassed more than 30 victories and 50 podiums. In the 2012 World's Toughest Mudder competition, which lasts 24 hours (she covered 90 miles and ~300 obstacles), she finished second OVERALL out of more than 1,000 competitors, 80% of whom were male. The one person who beat her finished just 8 minutes ahead of her. Her major victories include the Spartan Race World Championship and the Spartan Race Elite Point Series, and she is the only three-time winner of the World's Toughest Mudder (2012, 2014, and 2015). She won the 2014 championship 8 weeks after knee surgery. Amelia is also a three-time finisher of the Death Race, a full-time attorney at Apple, and she dabbles in ultra running (qualified for the Western States 100) in all of her spare time.

Spirit animal: Carp

✳ What would you put on a billboard?
"No one owes you anything."

✳ Amelia's best $100 or less purchase?
Manuka honey bandages. Amelia has scars all over her shoulders and back from barbed-wire wounds.

✳ Most-gifted or recommended book
  House of Leaves by Mark Danielewski: "This is a book that you have to hold, because there are parts of it where you need to turn it upside down to read it. There are certain pages where, you are reading it, and it turns in a circle. . . . This is a book that's an entire sensory experience."

AMELIA'S TIPS AND TACTICS

» **Hydrolyzed gelatin + beet root powder:** I've consumed gelatin for connective tissue repair in the past. I've never stuck with it long term because gelatin takes on a seagull poo–like texture when mixed into cold water. Amelia saved my palate and joints by introducing me to the Great Lakes hydrolyzed version (green label), which blends easily and smoothly. Add a tablespoon of beet root powder like BeetElite to stave off any cow-hoof flavor, and it's a whole new game. Amelia uses BeetElite pre-race and pre-training for its endurance benefits, but I'm much harder-core: I use it to make tart, low-carb gummy bears when fat Tim has carb cravings.

» **RumbleRoller:** Think foam roller meets monster-truck tire. Foam rollers have historically done very little for me, but this torture device had an immediate positive impact on my recovery. (It also helps you sleep if used before bed.) Warning: Start slow. I tried to copy Amelia and did 20-plus minutes my first session. The next day, I felt like I'd been put in a sleeping bag and swung against a tree for a few hours.

≫ **Rolling your foot on top of a golf ball** on the floor to increase "hamstring" flexibility. This is infinitely more helpful than a lacrosse ball. Put a towel on the floor underneath the golf ball, lest you shoot your dog's eye out.

≫ **Concept2 SkiErg** for training when your lower body is injured. After knee surgery, Amelia used this low-impact machine to maintain cardiovascular endurance and prepare for the 2014 World's Toughest Mudder, which she won 8 weeks post-op. Kelly Starrett (page 122) is also a big fan of this device.

≫ **Dry needling:** I'd never heard of this before meeting Amelia. "[In acupuncture] the goal is not to feel the needle. In dry-needling, you are sticking the needle in the muscle belly and trying to get it to twitch, and the twitch is the release." It's used for super-tight, over-contracted muscles, and the needles are not left in. Unless you're a masochist, don't have this done on your calves.

≫ **Sauna for endurance:** Amelia has found using a sauna improves her endurance, a concept that has since been confirmed by several other athletes, including cyclist David Zabriskie, seven-time U.S. National Time Trial Championship winner. He considers sauna training a more practical replacement for high-altitude simulation tents. In the 2005 Tour de France, Dave won the Stage 1 time trial, making him the first American to win stages in all three Grand Tours. Zabriskie beat Lance Armstrong by seconds, clocking an average speed of 54.676 kilometers per hour (!). I now use a sauna at least four times per week. To figure out the best protocols, I asked another podcast guest, Rhonda Patrick. Her response is on page 7.

✳ **Who do you think of when you hear the word "successful"?**
"Triple H is a great example [of someone who's transitioned extremely well from athlete to business executive]. So, Paul Levesque." (See page 128.)

RANDOM FACTS

»   Amelia eats Pop-Tarts as part of her ritual pre-competition breakfast.

»   Her record for unbroken double-unders (passing a jump rope under your feet twice with one jump) is 423, and is thus able to impress all CrossFitters. Unbeknownst to them, she was a state jump rope champion in third grade. Also unbeknownst to them, she ended at 423 because she had to pee so badly that she peed her pants.

»   Amelia loves doing training runs in the rain and cold, as she knows her competition is probably opting out. This is an example of "rehearsing the worst-case scenario" to become more resilient (see page 474).

»   She is a gifted a cappella singer and was part of the Greenleafs group at Washington University in St. Louis.

RHONDA PERCIAVALLE PATRICK, PhD

Rhonda Perciavalle Patrick, PhD (TW/FB/IG: @FOUNDMYFITNESS, FOUNDMYFITNESS.COM) has worked alongside notables including Dr. Bruce Ames, the inventor of the Ames mutagenicity test and the 23rd most-cited scientist across *all* fields between 1973 and 1984. Dr. Patrick also conducts clinical trials, performed aging research at the Salk Institute for Biological Studies, and did graduate research at St. Jude Children's Research Hospital, where she focused on cancer, mitochondrial metabolism, and apoptosis. More recently, Dr. Patrick has published papers on a mechanism by which vitamin D is able to regulate the production of serotonin in the brain and the various implications this may have for early-life deficiency and relevance for neuropsychiatric disorders.

Spirit animal: Coywolf

THE TOOTH FAIRY MIGHT SAVE YOUR LIFE (OR YOUR KIDS' LIVES)

Dr. Patrick introduced me to using teeth for stem-cell banking. If you are having your wisdom teeth removed, or if your kids are losing their baby teeth (which have a particularly high concentration of dental pulp stem cells), consider using a company like StemSave or National Dental Pulp Laboratory to preserve them for later use. These companies will send your oral surgeon a kit, and then freeze the biological matter using liquid nitrogen. Costs vary, but are roughly $625 for setup and then $125 per year for storage and maintenance.

Mesenchymal stem cells can later be harvested from the dental pulp of teeth for useful (e.g., bone, cartilage, muscle, blood vessels, etc.), life-changing (e.g., motor neurons for repairing damaged spinal cord), or potentially life-saving (e.g., traumatic brain injury) treatments using your own biological raw materials.

HEAT IS THE NEW BLACK

"Hyperthermic conditioning" (calculated heat exposure) can help you to increase growth hormone (GH) levels and substantially improve endurance. I now take ~20-minute sauna sessions post-workout or post-stretching at least four times per week, typically at roughly 160 to 170°F. If nothing else, it seems to dramatically decrease DOMS (delayed-onset muscle soreness).

Focusing on endurance and growth hormone, here are some observations from Dr. Patrick:

>>> "One study has demonstrated that a 30-minute sauna session twice a week for 3 weeks post-workout increased the time it took for study participants to run until exhaustion by 32% compared to baseline. The 32% increase in running endurance found in this particular study was accompanied by a 7.1% increase in plasma volume and 3.5% increase in red blood cell count."

>>> "Two 20-minute sauna sessions at 80°C (176°F) separated by a 30-minute cooling period elevated growth hormone levels two-fold over baseline. Whereas, two 15-minute dry-heat sessions at 100°C (212°F) separated by a 30-minute cooling period resulted in a five-fold increase in growth hormone. . . . The growth hormone effects generally persist for a couple of hours post-sauna."

TF: Hot baths can also significantly increase GH over baseline, and both sauna and hot baths have been shown to cause a massive release in prolactin, which plays a role in wound healing. I usually stay in a hot bath or sauna for about 20 minutes, which is long enough to significantly elevate my heart rate. I push a few minutes past dynorphin release, which usually makes one feel dysphoric and want to get out (but *not* to dizziness or lightheadedness). Generally, I'll listen to an audiobook like *The Graveyard Book* by Neil Gaiman during the heat, then cool off for 5 to 10 minutes using an ice bath (I put 40 pounds of ice in a large bath to get it to roughly 45°F; more details on page 43) and/or by drinking ice water. I'll repeat this cycle 2 to 4 times.

* Three people Dr. Patrick has learned from or followed closely in the last year
Dr. Bruce Ames, Dr. Satchin Panda (professor at the Salk Institute in San Diego, California), Dr. Jennifer Doudna (professor of biochemistry and molecular biology at UC Berkeley).

> **"** If the best in the world are stretching their asses off in order to get strong, why aren't you? **"**

CHRISTOPHER SOMMER

Christopher Sommer (IG/FB: @GYMNASTICBODIES, GYMNASTICBODIES .COM) is a former U.S. National Team gymnastics coach and founder of GymnasticBodies, a training system that I've tested for the last 8 months (no affiliation). As a world-renowned coach, Sommer is known for building his students into some of the strongest, most powerful athletes in the world. During his extensive 40-year coaching career, Coach Sommer took meticulous notes on his training techniques — his wins and failures — so that he could translate the best elements into a superior exercise system for both high-level and beginner athletes. His four decades of careful observation led to the birth of Gymnastics Strength Training (GST).

Spirit animal: Falcon

BACK STORY

The combination of GST and AcroYoga (page 52) has completely remodeled my body in the last year. I'm more flexible and mobile at age 39 than I was at age 20. I'm going to skip explaining a lot (e.g., Maltese, Stalder press handstand) that is best seen in video or pictures, though I'll describe the most critical (starting on page 53). Google is your friend.

ON WORKING ON YOUR WEAKNESSES

"If you want to be a stud later, you have to be a pud now."

Coach first told me this when I was complaining about slow progress with shoulder extension (imagine clasping your hands together behind your back, arms straight, then raising your arms without bending at the waist). **When in doubt, work on the deficiencies you're most embarrassed by.** My biggest weaknesses are shoulder extension and bridging using the thoracic spine (versus lower-back arch). After improving them 10% over 3 to 4 weeks—going from "making coach vomit" to merely "making coach laugh"—a host of physical issues that plagued me for years completely disappeared. To assess your biggest weaknesses, start by finding a Functional Movement Screen (FMS) near you. Related from Sommer: "You're not responsible for the hand of cards you were dealt. You're responsible for maxing out what you were given."

"FLEXIBILITY" VERSUS "MOBILITY"

Sommer's distinction between "flexibility" and "mobility" is the most concrete and clear I've heard. **"Flexibility" can be passive, whereas "mobility" requires that you can demonstrate strength throughout the entire range of motion, including the end ranges.** See the J-curl and pike pulse exercises on pages 15 and 18 for two examples of mobility, which can be also be thought of as "active flexibility." The pike pulse is a particularly clear demonstration, as it tests "compression strength" in a range that most people never experience.

CONSISTENCY OVER INTENSITY

"Slow down. Where's the fire?" This is Coach's constant reminder that certain adaptations take weeks or months of consistent stimuli (see page 160).

If you rush, the reward is injuries. In GST, there are surprising stair steps after long periods of zero progress. Roughly six months into doing his "hamstring series" with minor gains, I seemingly doubled my max ranges overnight. This was completely unsurprising to Sommer.

> "I used to tell my athletes there are stupid gymnasts, and there are old gymnasts, but there are no old, stupid gymnasts because they're all dead."

"DIET AND EXERCISE" → "EAT AND TRAIN"

Coach Sommer dislikes the fitness fixation on "diet and exercise." He finds it much more productive to focus on "eat and train." One is aesthetic, and the other is functional. The former may not have a clear goal, the latter always does.

THEY FAILED WARMUP!

Coach describing his first-ever seminar for non-gymnast adults, in roughly 2007:

"We've got all of these beasts there [advanced lifters], and they're strong. I tried to do my entry-level plyometric group work and some floor work with them. The stronger the athlete, the faster they went down: knees, lower back, ankles . . . from baby stuff. We're not talking anything hard. We're talking about standing in place, and, with knees straight, being able to bounce down the floor using just your calves.

"No way. Their tissues couldn't take it. They hadn't done anything like it. [To show you] how bad mobility was, we had 15 minutes on the schedule to stretch. Nothing intricate, nothing intense — just an easy, basic stretch. Get them loosened up for the day. That stretch took an hour and a half to complete. There were bodies lying everywhere. It was like I was in Vietnam or filming a war movie. I turned to my staff, and I'm like, 'What the fuck am I supposed to do now? They failed warmup. They failed *warmup.*'"

WHY THOSE OLYMPIC BOYS HAVE GIGANTIC BICEPS

Male Olympic gymnasts don't have biceps the size of their waists from curls. It comes largely from straight-arm work, especially Maltese work on rings.

But how on earth can you practice a Maltese as a novice? I use a 50/50 pulley system to cut my body-weight resistance in half, which is similar to the Ring Thing (Power Monkey Fitness) or generic "dream machine" that Jason Nemer (page 46) loves using. I combine this with "power levers," strap-on metal gauntlets that allow me to attach the ring ropes to my forearms anywhere between the elbow and the fist. This allows me to use progressive resistance, starting near the elbow and moving out to the hand. The best versions are currently only available in Europe, but there are vaguely similar "iron cross trainers" available in the U.S.

3 MOVEMENTS EVERYONE SHOULD PRACTICE

>> **J-Curl** (page 15)

>> **Shoulder Extension:** Lift a dowel behind your back (standing), or sit on the floor and walk your hands backward behind your hips.

>> **Thoracic Bridge:** Elevate your feet enough to feel the bulk of the stretch in the upper back and shoulders, not the lower back. The feet might be 3+ feet off the ground. Ensure you can concentrate on *straightening* your arms (and legs, if possible), holding the position, and breathing.

GOOD GOALS FOR ADULT NON-GYMNASTS

The following goals incorporate many different aspects of strength and mobility into single movements:

Beginner: J-Curl
Intermediate: Straddle Press Handstand [**TF:** I'm working on this]
Advanced: Stalder Press Handstand

SOMETIMES, YOU JUST NEED A VIBRATOR

Coach Sommer introduced me to a Russian medical massage specialist who recommended I use the plug-in (not cordless) model of the Hitachi Magic Wand on its high setting. I've never experienced such heights of ecstasy. Thanks, Vladmir!

Just kidding. In this case, it's for relaxing hypertonic muscles (i.e., muscles that are tense even though they shouldn't be). Just place the wand on your muscle belly (not insertion points) for 20 to 30 seconds, which is often all it takes at the proper hertz. Tension headaches or a stiff neck? It's great for relaxing the occipitals at the base of the skull. Warning: Having Hitachi Magic Wands lying out around your house can go terribly wrong — or terribly right. Good luck explaining your "hypertonic muscles." As one friend said to me, "I think my wife has that same problem. . . ."

GYMNAST STRONG

Unusual and Effective Bodyweight Exercises

In less than eight weeks of following Coach Sommer's protocols, I saw unbelievable improvement in areas I'd largely given up on.

Try a few of my favorite exercises, and you'll quickly realize that gymnasts use muscles you didn't even know you had.

QL Walk — An Unusual Warmup

Coach Sommer borrowed this exercise from power lifter Donnie Thompson, who calls it the "butt walk." Donnie "Super D" Thompson is the first person to hit a power lifting total of more than 3,000 pounds (bench press + deadlift + squat). The QL walk is intended to get your glutes and quadratus lumborum (QL) firing, the latter of which Donnie calls "an angry troll in your back":

1. Sit down on a mat (or gravel, if you want to turn your ass into hamburger meat). Legs are extended in front of you, ankles can be touching or slightly apart, and your back should be straight. I keep legs together. This is "pike" position, which I'll refer to quite a bit in this book.

2. Lift a kettlebell or dumbbell to your collarbones (think front squat). I weigh 170 pounds and use 30 to 60 pounds. I hold the kettlebell "horns," but Donnie prefers to support it from underneath.

3. Keeping your legs straight (no bend at the knee), walk your butt cheeks — left, right, left, right — across the floor. I typically go 10 to 15 feet.

4. Reverse direction and go backward 10 to 15 feet. That's it.

Jefferson Curl (J-Curl)

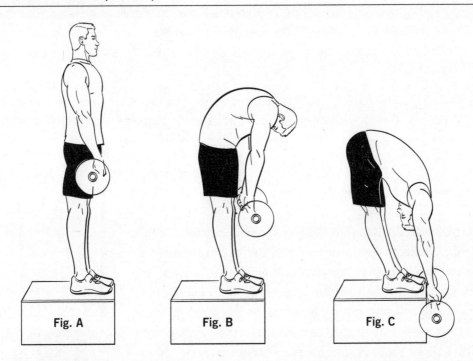

Fig. A   Fig. B   Fig. C

Think of this as a controlled, slowly rounded, stiff-legged deadlift. From Sommer: "Progress slowly and patiently. Do not rush. For this type of loaded mobility work, never allow yourself to strain, grind out reps, or force range of motion. Smooth, controlled movement is the order of the day." The ultimate goal is body weight on a bar, but start with 15 pounds. I currently use only 50 to 60 pounds. This can perform miracles for thoracic, or mid-back, mobility, all while helping the hamstrings in the pike position. When I asked Coach Sommer how often I should do these, he said, "We do these like breathing." In other words, at a minimum, J-Curls are done at the beginning of every primary workout.

1. Begin by standing up straight, legs locked, holding a bar waist-high with your arms shoulder width apart. **(fig. A)** Think dead-lift top position.

2. Tuck your chin tightly against your chest (keep it tucked for the entire movement) and slowly bend over, one vertebra at a time, from the neck down. **(fig. B)** Keep your arms straight and the bar close to your legs.

Lower until you can't stretch any farther. As you become more flexible, stand on a box (I use a Rogue plyo box), with the goal of passing your wrists below your toes. Keep your legs as perpendicular to the ground as possible, and try to not push your hips back until your head is below your waist.

3. Slowly stand back up, rolling one vertebra at a time. Your chin should be the last thing to come up. **(fig. C)** That's 1 rep. Repeat for a total of 5 to 10 reps.

Dips with RTO (Ring Turn Out)

So you can do 10 to 20 regular dips? Fantastic. I challenge you to do 5 slow dips on rings with proper turnout at the top ("support position"). Imagine the lines of the knuckles pointing to 10 and 2 o'clock at the apex. Perform this without piking (bending at the hips) or leaning your torso forward. This requires the brachialis to work like a mofo at the top, and it requires good shoulder extension at the bottom—my nemesis. Curse me, then thank me in 8 weeks. If you can't do 15 regular dips, consider starting with **push-ups with RTO**, which Kelly Starrett (page 122) first showed me. For the push-ups, ensure that you use the hollow and protracted position from cast wall walks on page 19.

Hinge Rows

This is an excellent low-risk option for smashing your mid-traps and external rotator cuff muscles, which are used for handstands and just about everything in gymnastics. Visualize popping up like Dracula in a coffin, then hitting a double bicep pose. The catch: Your hands are holding rings the entire time. Once you can do 20 reps of hinge rows, Google "lat flys" and progress to those.

1. Set up a pair of rings to hang about a foot above your head when you're sitting on the floor.

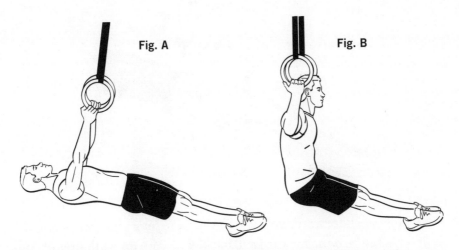

Fig. A   Fig. B

2. While sitting on the floor, grab the rings. Keeping your heels on the floor, lie back, and — arms straight — lift your hips off the ground. Focus on making your body (head to heel) ramrod straight. **(fig. A)**

3. Sit up (pike) until your head is between the rings and hit that double-bicep pose. The bends at your waist and elbows should be about 90 degrees. **(fig. B)**

4. Slowly lower yourself back down. Repeat 5 to 15 times.

Ag Walks with Rear Support

These are hugely productive and a major wakeup call for most people. 99% of you will realize you have no shoulder flexibility or strength in this critical position.

1. Get some furniture sliders ($5 to $15). These look like drink coasters and are used to move furniture around without scratching the floor.

2. Sit down in pike position and put your heels on the furniture sliders (which I now always pack for travel workouts).

3. Put your hands on the floor by your hips and — arms straight — lift your hips off the ground. Try to make your body perfectly straight from shoulder to heel, just as in the hinge rows.

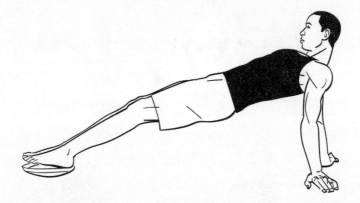

4. Easy? Now walk forward with your hands, pushing your feet along the floor. This can be done forward and backward. Aim for 5 minutes of constant movement, but feel free to start with 60 seconds (you'll see). Pro tip: This is a great way to freak people out when done at 2 a.m. in hotel hallways.

Pike Pulses

When one of my meathead friends is laughing at my GST exercises, I have them attempt this. It usually ends with a head shake and a puzzled "Holy fuck."

1. Sit in pike position in the middle of the floor. Point your toes and keep your knees locked.

2. Walk your hands out on the floor, as far toward (or past) your feet as you can.

3. Now, try to lift your heels 1 to 4 inches, which is 1 repetition or "pulse." For 99% of you, this will be completely impossible and you'll feel like an ice statue. Ratchet back and put your hands midway between hip and knee. See how you do and then move your hands forward enough to allow only 15 to 20 pulses.

If you did really well, now try it with your lower back against a wall. What happened?! Sorry, killer, you weren't actually pulsing, you were rocking back and forth like a cradle. Do it against the wall to keep yourself honest.

Cast Wall Walk

If you have no gymnastics background, this one will be fun/terrible. I use cast wall walks as a workout finisher and recommend you do the same, as you'll be worthless afterward. First, let's define the position you need to maintain.

Torso "Hollow": Sit on a chair, back straight, with your hands on your knees. Now, try to bring your sternum (chest bone) to your belly button; "shorten" your torso by 3 to 4 inches by contracting and pulling in your abs. You'll maintain this position throughout the entire exercise. No lower-back arch or sag permitted.

Shoulders "Protracted": Keep your torso "hollow" per the above. Now, pretend you're hugging a telephone pole. Your shoulders should be well in front of your chest, sternum pulled back strongly. Straighten your arms but maintain this position. Next, **without losing any of the aforementioned**, lift your arms overhead as high as you can. There you go. Now we can begin.

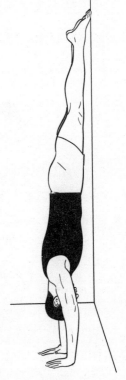

1. Get into a handstand position against a wall, nose facing toward the wall. **(fig. A)**

2. Keeping your body in one line, slowly walk your hands out and your feet down the wall simultaneously. **(fig. B)** Keep your knees straight and walk with your ankles. The steps should be small.

3. Reach the bottom with your feet on the floor in a push-up position. **(fig. C)** Correct your form to be maximally hollow and protracted.

Fig. A

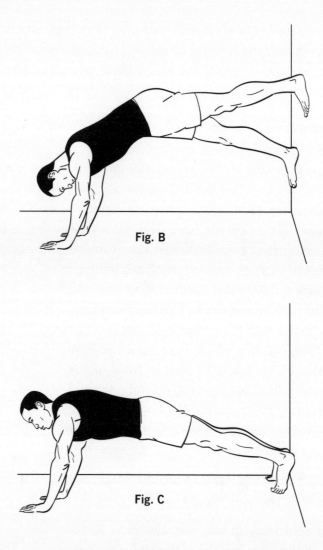

Fig. B

Fig. C

4. Reverse and go back up the wall, returning to handstand position. That is 1 rep, my friend.

Target is 10 reps, but stop this one at least a few reps before muscular failure. Otherwise, woe unto your face when gravity opens a can of whoop-ass on your flattened head.

DOMINIC D'AGOSTINO

Dr. Dominic "Dom" D'Agostino (TW: @DominicDAgosti2, KETONUTRITION.ORG) is an associate professor in the Department of Molecular Pharmacology and Physiology at the University of South Florida Morsani College of Medicine, and a senior research scientist at the Institute for Human and Machine Cognition (IHMC). He has also deadlifted 500 pounds for 10 reps after a 7-day fast.

He's a beast and — no big surprise — he's a good buddy of Dr. Peter Attia, my MD friend (page 59) who consumed "jet fuel" in search of optimal athletic performance. The primary focus of Dom's laboratory is developing and testing metabolic therapies, including ketogenic diets, ketone esters, and ketone supplements to induce nutritional/therapeutic ketosis, and low-toxicity metabolic-based drugs. Much of his work is related to metabolic therapies and nutritional strategies for peak performance and resilience in extreme environments. His research is supported by the Office of Naval Research, Department of Defense, private organizations, and foundations.

Spirit animal: Beaver

LITTLE-KNOWN FACTS

>>> Back around 1995, Dom gifted Tony Robbins's (page 210) *Personal Power* audio set to all of his undergrad lifting buddies. Two contacted him years later to thank him for changing their lives.

>>> After my first podcast with Dom, Whole Foods Markets around the country sold out of Wild Planet canned sardines.

PREFACE

This profile is one of several that might save your life, and it has certainly changed mine. As such, it deviates from the usual format to act as more of a mini-primer on all things ketosis. There is a lot of diet talk, but the supplements and fasting can be treated as separate tools—no bacon or heavy cream required. For ease of reading, some of the concepts are slightly simplified for a lay audience. My current personal regimen is included.

FIRST, SOME BASICS

>>> **The ketogenic diet,** often nicknamed "keto," is a high-fat diet that mimics fasting physiology. Your brain and body begin to use ketones (derived from stored or ingested fat) for energy instead of blood sugar (glucose)—a state called ketosis. The diet was originally developed to treat epileptic children, but there are many variations, including the Atkins diet. You can achieve ketosis through fasting, diet, exogenous ketones, or a combination.

>>> **How do you know when you're in ketosis?** The most reliable way is to use a device called the Precision Xtra by Abbott. This can measure both glucose and blood levels of beta-hydroxybutyrate (BHB). Once you reach 0.5 mmol—millimolars, a concentration—you can consider yourself lightly "in ketosis." I tend to feel increased mental clarity at 1 mmol or higher.

>>> **The primary resource, as you'll come back to this:** Dom's top go-to resource for the ketogenic diet, including FAQs, meal plans, and more is ketogenic-diet-resource.com.

"I like to promote mild to moderate ketosis for health and longevity, which is between 1 to 3 mmol."

TF: These levels help protect DNA from damage, among other benefits.

WHY CONSIDER KETOSIS OR SUPPLEMENTAL KETONES?

>>> **Fat loss and body recomposition**

>>> **Potent anti-cancer effects**

>>> **Better use of oxygen:** Dom can hold his breath for two times his normal duration when in deep ketosis (2 minutes → 4 minutes). I observed the same. Essentially, you can derive more energy per oxygen molecule with ketone metabolism. This oxygen utilization advantage is why some elite cyclists are experimenting with keto. This also helps performance at high altitudes, if you're going from sea level to mountains, for instance.

>>> **Maintain or increase strength:** In a study with 12 subjects, Dom demonstrated that even advanced weight lifters could maintain or increase strength, performance, and hypertrophy after 2 weeks of keto-adaptation, consuming 75 to 80% of calories from fat (supplemented with MCT and coconut oils) and restricting carbohydrates to 22 to 25 g per day. Ketones have an anti-catabolic protein-sparing and anti-inflammatory effect.

>>> **Lyme disease:** (Caveat: This is a personal experience, not a double-blind study.) Reaching deep ketosis (for me, 3 to 6 mmol) through fasting, then continuing with calorie-restricted keto for a week, completely eradicated symptoms of Lyme disease when all else failed. It was the only thing that helped after my first course of antibiotics. It produced a night-and-day difference: a 10-time improvement in my mental performance and clarity. I suspect this relates to mitochondrial "rehab" and the anti-inflammatory effects of ketones. More than a year has passed and the symptoms have not returned, despite following the *non*-ketogenic Slow-Carb Diet (see page 81) 90% of the time.

WHY CONSIDER FASTING?

Dom has discussed the idea of a therapeutic **"purge fast"** with his colleague Dr. Thomas Seyfried of Boston College. Per Dom: **"If you don't have cancer and you do a therapeutic fast 1 to 3 times per year, you could purge any precancerous cells that may be living in your body."**

If you're over the age of 40, cancer is one of the four types of diseases (see Dr. Peter Attia on page 59) that will kill you with 80% certainty, so this seems like smart insurance.

There is also evidence to suggest — skipping the scientific detail — that fasts of 3 days or longer can effectively "reboot" your immune system via stem cell–based regeneration. **Dom suggests a 5-day fast 2 to 3 times per year.**

Dom has done 7-day fasts before, while lecturing at the University of South Florida. On day 7, he went into class with his glucose between 35 and 45 mg/dL, and his ketones around 5 mmol. Then, before breaking the fast, he went to the gym and deadlifted 500 pounds for 10 reps, followed by 1 rep of 585 pounds. Dom was inspired to do his first 7-day fast by George Cahill, a researcher at Harvard Medical School, who'd conducted a fascinating study published in 1970* wherein he fasted people for 40 days.

Fasting doesn't need to make you miserable and weak. In fact, it can have quite the opposite effect. But let's start with how *not* to do it. . . .

SOME PERSONAL BACKGROUND

I did my first extended fast as a last resort. Lyme disease had decimated me and put me at 10% capacity for nearly 9 months. My joints hurt so much that it took 5 to 10 minutes to get out of bed, and my short-term memory worsened to the point that I began to forget good friends' names. Adding inputs (e.g., drugs, IV treatments, etc.) didn't seem to help, so I decided to try removing all inputs, including food. I did my homework, found the best-reviewed fasting clinics in the U.S., and headed off.

My first 7-day fast was excruciating. It was medically supervised at a clinic, where we also had room and board. Patients were permitted to consume nothing but distilled water. Tap water, toothpaste, and even bathing were advised against. No exercise or leaving the facility were permitted for liability reasons.

---

*Cahill, George F. "Starvation in Man." *New England Journal of Medicine* 282 (1970): 668–675.

From days 3 to 4, my lower back pain was so extreme that I remained on my bed in the fetal position. The doctors told me this was "toxins" being released, which I didn't accept. I insisted on blood testing instead, and the explanation for the lower-back pain was simple: My kidneys were getting hammered by sky-high uric acid levels. I wasn't allowed to exercise (not even brisk walking), so it was taking forever to get into ketosis. My body was breaking down muscle tissue so the liver could convert it into glucose, and uric acid was a by-product. On top of this, since patients were limited to distilled water, nearly all the fasters (about 40 in total) couldn't sleep due to electrolyte depletion and subsequent cholinergic responses (e.g., rapid heart rate when trying to sleep). Nonetheless, I noticed benefits: Long-standing skin issues disappeared after a few days, as did chronic joint pain.

On the morning of day 7, I woke up to blood spilling out of my mouthguard. I had been dreaming of strawberry shortcake (seriously) and chewed the fucker so hard that my gums split open. *Basta.*

I broke my fast with stewed pork—against doctor's orders—and decided two things: Fasting was very interesting, but this wasn't how I would do it.

WAIT . . . SO WHAT'S THE FASTING YOU PRACTICE?
In the last 2 years, I've done a lot of fasting experiments, focusing on real science instead of old wives' tales (e.g., you must break your fast with shredded cabbage and beets). **I now aim for a 3-day fast once per month and a 5- to 7-day fast once per quarter.** I would like to do one 14- to 30-day fast per year, but the logistics have proven too inconvenient.

The longest fast I've done to date was 10 days. During that fast, I added vitamin C IVs and hyperbaric oxygen (2.4 ATA x 60 minutes) 3 times per week. I did DEXA body scans every 2 to 3 days for tracking and also consumed roughly 1.5 g of BCAAs upon waking and roughly 3 g of BCAAs intra-workout. After a 10-day fast, I had lost *zero* muscle mass. In contrast, I lost nearly 12 pounds of muscle in that first 7-day fast.

How and why the difference?

First, I allowed trace amounts of BCAAs and 300 to 500 calories of pure fat per day on my "fast."

Second, I got into ketosis as quickly as possible to skip muscle wasting. I can now do this in under 24 hours instead of 3 to 4 days. The more often you enter keto, the faster the transition takes place. There appears to be a biological "muscle memory" related to monocarboxylate transporters and other things beyond my pay grade. Fasting is key, which is why the keto protocol used at Johns Hopkins for children with drug-resistant seizures begins with fasting.

Here's my protocol for my usual monthly 3-day fast from Thursday dinner to Sunday dinner:

>> On Wednesday and Thursday, plan phone calls for Friday. Determine how you can be productive via cell phone for 4 hours. This will make sense shortly.

>> Have a low-carb dinner around 6 p.m. on Thursday.

>> On Friday, Saturday, and Sunday mornings, sleep as late as possible. The point is to let sleep do some of the work for you.

>> Consume exogenous ketones or MCT oil upon waking and 2 more times throughout the day at 3- to 4-hour intervals. I primarily use KetoCaNa and caprylic acid (C8), like Brain Octane. The exogenous ketones help "fill the gap" for the 1 to 3 days that you might suffer carb withdrawal. Once you're in deep ketosis and using body fat, they can be omitted.

>> On Friday (and Saturday if needed), drink some caffeine and prepare to WALK. Be out the door no later than 30 minutes after waking. I grab a cold liter of water or Smartwater out of my fridge, add a dash of pure, unsweetened lemon juice to attenuate boredom, add a few pinches of salt to prevent misery/headaches/cramping, and head out. I sip this as I walk and make phone calls. Podcasts also work. Once you finish your water, fill it up or buy another. Add a little salt, keep walking, and keep drinking. It's brisk walking — NOT intense exercise — and constant hydration that are key. I have friends who've tried running or high-intensity weight training instead, and it does *not* work for reasons I won't bore you with. I told them, "Try brisk walking and tons of water for 3 to 4 hours. I bet you'll be at 0.7 mmol the next morning." One of them texted me the next morning: "Holy shit. 0.7 mmol."

>>> Each day of fasting, feel free to consume exogenous ketones or fat (e.g., coconut oil in tea or coffee) as you like, up to 4 tablespoons. I will often reward myself at the end of each fasting afternoon with an iced coffee with a bit of coconut cream in it. Truth be told, I will sometimes allow myself a SeaSnax packet of nori sheets. Oooh, the decadence.

>>> Break your fast on Sunday night. Enjoy it. For a 14-day or longer fast, you need to think about refeeding carefully. But for a 3-day fast, I don't think what you eat matters much. I've done steak, I've done salads, I've done greasy burritos. Evolutionarily, it makes no sense that a starving hominid would need to find shredded cabbage or some such nonsense to save himself from death. Eat what you find to eat.

ONCE YOU'RE IN KETO, HOW CAN YOU KEEP IT GOING WITHOUT FASTING?

The short answer is: Eat a boatload of fat (~1.5 to 2.5 g per *kilogram* of body weight), next-to-no carbs, and moderate protein (1 to 1.5 g per kilogram of body weight) each day. We'll look at Dom's typical meals and day in a minute, but a few critical notes first:

>>> High protein and low fat doesn't work. Your liver will convert excess amino acids into glucose and shut down ketogenesis. Fat as 70 to 85% of calories is required.

>>> This doesn't mean you always have to eat rib eye steaks. A chicken breast by itself will kick you out of ketosis, but a chicken breast cut up into a green leafy salad with a lot of olive oil, feta cheese, and some Bulletproof Coffee (for example) can keep you in ketosis. One of the challenges of keto is the amount of fat one needs to consume to maintain it. Roughly 70 to 80% of your total calories need to come from fat. Rather than trying to incorporate fat bombs into all meals (one does get tired of fatty steak, eggs, and cheese over and over again), Dom will both drink fat between meals (e.g., coconut milk — not water — in coffee) and add in supplemental "ice cream," detailed on page 29.

>>> Dom noticed that dairy can cause lipid profile issues (e.g., can spike LDL) and has started to minimize things like cream and cheese. I experienced the same. It's easy to eat a disgusting amount of cheese to stay in keto. Consider coconut milk (Aroy-D Pure Coconut Milk) instead. Dom doesn't worry about elevated LDL as long as other blood markers aren't out of whack (high CRP, low HDL, etc.). From Dom: "The thing that I focus on most is triglycerides. If your triglycerides are elevated, that means your body is just not adapting to the ketogenic diet. Some people's triglycerides are elevated even when their calories are restricted. That's a sign that the ketogenic diet is not for you. . . . It's not a one-size-fits-all diet."

All that preamble out of way, here's what Big Dom eats. Keep in mind that he weighs roughly 100 kg (220 lbs), so scale as needed:

Breakfast

4 eggs (cooked in a combo of butter and coconut oil)
1 can of sardines packed in olive oil (such as Wild Planet brand)
½ can oysters (Crown Prince brand. Note: Carbs on the label are from non-glycemic phytoplankton)
Some asparagus or other vegetable

TF: Both Dom and I travel with boxes of sardines, oysters, and bulk macadamia nuts.

"Lunch"

Instead of lunch, Dom will consume a lot of MCT throughout the day via Quest Nutrition MCT Oil Power. He will also make a Thermos of coffee with a half stick of butter and 1 to 2 scoops of MCT powder, which he sips throughout the day, totaling about 3 cups of coffee.

Dinner

"One trick I've learned is that before dinner, which is my main meal of the day, I'll have a bowl of soup, usually broccoli cream soup or cream of mushroom soup. I use concentrated coconut milk in place of the dairy cream. I thin it out [with a bit of water] so it's not super dense in calories. After eating that, the amount of food that I want to consume is cut in half."

Dom's dinner is always some kind of large salad, typically made up of:

Mixed greens and spinach together
Extra-virgin olive oil
Artichokes
Avocado
MCT oil
A little bit of Parmesan or feta cheese
A moderate amount — about 50 g — of chicken, beef, or fish. He uses the fattiest versions he can get and increases the protein in the salad to 70 to 80 g if he had a workout that day.

In addition to the salad, Dom will make some other vegetable like Brussels sprouts, asparagus, collard greens, etc., cooked in butter and coconut oil. He views vegetables as "fat delivery systems."

Dom's Recipe for Keto Ice Cream

Dom's "ice cream" recipe contains roughly 100 g of fat, or 900 kcal of keto goodness. It can save the day if your dinner is lacking fat (remember to hit 70 to 85% of total calories from fat!):

2 cups sour cream (I like Straus Creamery brand) or unsweetened coconut cream (*not* coconut water)
1 tablespoon dark chocolate baking cocoa
1–2 pinches of sea salt (my favorite is flaky Maldon)
1–2 pinches of cinnamon
A small dash of stevia (Dom buys NOW Foods organic stevia in bulk)
Optional: 1/3–1/2 cup blueberries, if Dom hasn't had carbs all day, or if he has worked out

Stir that all into a thick mousse and stick it in the freezer until it takes on an ice cream–like consistency. Once you've removed it and are ready to dig in, you can eat it straight or add toppings:

>>> Make whipped cream using heavy cream (nearly 100% fat) and a bit of stevia.

>>> Drizzle on 1 tablespoon of heated coconut oil (especially if the "bomb" has the blueberries in it) and mix it all in, which produces the mouth-feel of crunchy chocolate chips.

The keto diet calls for around 300 g of fat per day at Dom's body weight of 100 kg (220 lbs). This dessert helps up the ante dramatically. It's also delicious. Dom's wife does not follow a ketogenic diet, but even she loves this dessert.

Dom's Tip for Vegetarians

"MRM Veggie Elite Performance Protein — the chocolate mocha is very good. If you take roughly one scoop and mix it with coconut milk, throw in a half an avocado, pour in some MCT oil — the C8 oil — the [shake] that I made up has 70% of the calories from fat and 20% of the calories from protein, 10% of the calories from carbohydrates."

DOM'S GO-TO SUPPLEMENTS

>>> Quest Nutrition MCT Oil Powder and Quest Nutrition Coconut Oil Powder

>>> Kettle & Fire Bone Broth — 2 to 3 times per week

>>> Idebenone "is another product that I take [400 mg] when I fly or before hard exercise. I think of idebenone as a version of coenzyme Q10. It's more absorbable and gets to the mitochondria easier. It's like a mitochondrial antioxidant."

>>> Magnesium daily. "Magnesium citrate, magnesium chloride, and magnesium glycinate . . . When I started the ketogenic diet, I started getting cramps. Now that I'm supplementing, I don't get any cramps. . . . If I had one go-to magnesium, it would be this magnesium citrate powder called Natural Calm."

>>> Scivation XTEND Perform branched-chain amino acids (BCAAs): leucine, isoleucine, and valine in a 2 to 1 to 1 combination, leucine

being the predominant branch chain amino acid in the formula. "Leucine is a powerful activator of mTOR, which is a good thing; activating mTOR in skeletal muscle is really important in a short workout. I use the product pre-workout and intra-workout."

»» KetoCaNa and KetoForce

»» Prüvit KETO//OS — Creamy exogenous ketones, tastes great

»» Kegenix — More of a tangy Kool-Aid flavor

Both Prüvit and Kegenix are based on a BHB + MCT patent Dom's lab developed, which is owned by his university.

MORE ON FASTING AND CANCER TREATMENT

"Fasting before chemotherapy is definitely something that should be implemented in our oncology wards," says Dom. He adds, "Fasting essentially slows (sometimes stops) rapidly dividing cells and triggers an 'energetic crisis' that makes cancer cells selectively vulnerable to chemo and radiation." There are good studies to support this.*

One of my friends is in full remission from advanced testicular cancer. Others in his chemo cohort were laid out for 2 to 3 days in bed after chemo sessions, but he fasted for 3 days before sessions and was running 10 miles the next morning. Fasting sensitizes cancer cells to chemo, as mentioned, but it also helps normal cells resist the toxicity. This isn't appropriate for all patients, especially those with extreme cachexia (muscle wasting), but it is applicable to many.

In cases of cachexia, some selective androgen receptor modulators (SARMs), which are designed to have the anabolic tissue-building potency of testoster-

---

* Safdie FM, Dorff T, Quinn D, Fontana L, Wei M, Lee C, Cohen P, Longo VD. "Fasting and cancer treatment in humans: A case series report." *Aging (Albany NY)* 1.12 (2009): 988–1007. Dorff TB, Groshen S, Garcia A, Shah M, Tsao-Wei D, Pham H, Cheng CW, Brandhorst S, Cohen P, Wei M, Longo V, Quinn DI. "Safety and feasibility of fasting in combination with platinum-based chemotherapy." *BMC Cancer*, 16.360 (2016). Bianchi G, Martella R, Ravera S, Marini C, Capitanio S, Orengo A, Emionite L, Lavarello C, Amaro A, Petretto A, Pfeffer U, Sambuceti G, Pistoia V, Raffaghello L, Longo VD. "Fasting induces anti-Warburg effect that increases respiration but reduces ATP-synthesis to promote apoptosis in colon cancer models." *Oncotarget* 6.14 (2015): 11806–19. Lee C, Raffaghello L, Brandhorst S, Safdie FM, Bianchi G, Martin-Montalvo A, Pistoia V, Wei M, Hwang S, Merlino A, Emionite L, de Cabo R, Longo VD. "Fasting cycles retard growth of tumors and sensitize a range of cancer cell types to chemotherapy." *Science Translational Medicine* 4.124 (2012): 124ra27.

one (and other anabolic steroids) without the androgenic (i.e., secondary hormonal) effects, could be helpful. Dom is also researching the use of BCAAs. He has had ~50% increase in survival in cancerous rats by adding the branched-chain amino acids to a ketogenic diet. Just as promising, the animals maintained their body weight.

In one study, treating mice with aggressive metastatic brain cancer using keto and hyperbaric oxygen treatment (HBOT), Dom, Dr. Seyfried, and other scientists were able to increase the average survival time from 31.2 days (standard diet) to 55.5 days. For the HBOT protocol, Dom used 2.5 Atmospheres (2.5 ATA) for 60 minutes on Monday, Wednesday, and Friday. Including pressurization and depressurization, each session lasted about 90 minutes.

Even in a worst-case scenario — if a patient is intubated and on their last legs — one could potentially add exogenous ketones to an IV alongside (or in place of) glucose, as exogenous ketones have been demonstrated to have a significant tumor-suppressing or -shrinking effect, *even in the presence of dietary carbohydrates*. To me, the last italicized part is the most remarkable.

If you think the ketogenic diet is for lunatics, exogenous ketones only require mixing a scoop in water and swigging it down.

5 THINGS IN CASE OF LATE-STAGE EMERGENCY

Here are the 5 things Dom would do if he were diagnosed with one of the worst-case scenarios — late-stage glioblastoma (GBM), an aggressive brain cancer.

Some of Dom's colleagues are opposed to the "standard of care" protocols, like chemotherapy. Based on the literature, Dom feels these are warranted in situations involving testicular cancer, leukemia, lymphoma, and stage 1 and 2 breast cancer. Outside of those examples, "it makes little sense to treat cancer with something we know is a powerful carcinogen (chemotherapy)."

Dom's 5 picks all appear to work through overlapping mechanisms. This means that there is a synergy in using them together. The whole is greater than the sum of its parts. 1 + 1 + 1 + 1 + 1 = 10, let's say, not 5. I've starred those on the following list that I've experimented with myself.

>>> ***Ketogenic diet** as base therapy. This is the foundation.

>>> ***Intermittent fasting:** 1 meal per day within a daily 4-hour window

>>> ***Ketone supplementation 2 to 4 times per day:** His objective would be to elevate his BHB levels 1 to 2 mmol above his baseline, achieved by the aforementioned two. In other words, if he were running at ~1.5 mmol using a 1-meal-per-day modified Atkins diet, he would take enough supplemental ketones to consistently achieve 2.5 to 3.5 mmol. The easiest options are KetoCaNa and/or Quest Nutrition MCT Oil Powder. Combining them, you're "approaching the potency of a ketone ester developed for military applications." The powdered MCT increases gut tolerability 2 to 3 times versus oil, so you can consume more of it.

>>> ***Metformin:** He would titrate the daily dosage (i.e., start low and gradually increase) until he reached GI distress (diarrhea or reflux), then dial it back slightly. This would give him his upper tolerable limit, which ranges from 1500 to 3000 mg/day for most people.

>>> **DCA (dichloroacetic acid):** For reasons not completely understood, and under some circumstances, DCA can kill cancer cells at dosages relatively non-toxic to normal cells. Dom would start with 10 mg per kilogram of body weight (he weighs ~100 kilograms) and titrate up, not exceeding 50 mg per kilogram, as you can start to experience peripheral neuropathy at that level (thiamine [B_1] can reduce neuropathy). Clinical trials use around 20 mg per kilogram. DCA appears to work well on all diets, including high-carbohydrate.

I asked another MD I trust the same question ("What would you do if you had late-stage GBM?"), without sharing Dom's answers. His anonymized answer is below. I've again starred those I'm experimenting with.

"If I (meaning [name omitted], freak of all time) had GBM I would do the following:

1. No radiation

2. *Calorie-restricted keto diet with support from exogenous BHB

3. *Metformin at 2 or 2.5 g/day

4. DCA

5. *Hyperbaric oxygen

6. Rapamycin in modest, intermittent doses

7. Sequence the tumor to see if a checkpoint inhibitor (a type of immuno-therapy) could be effective

"Not sure I could recommend this to anyone, though."

* Dom's most-gifted or recommended books

Cancer as a Metabolic Disease by Thomas Seyfried: required reading for all of Dom's students

Tripping Over the Truth by Travis Christofferson: Dom has gifted this to seven or eight people over the last year

The Language of God: A Scientist Presents Evidence for Belief by Francis Collins

* Recommended to watch

"The Gut Is Not Like Las Vegas: What Happens in the Gut Does Not Stay in the Gut," presentation by Alessio Fasano

* A fantastic idea I wish would expand nationwide

KetoPet Sanctuary (KPS): Funded by the Epigenix Foundation, KPS goes out of its way to rescue dogs with incurable, terminal cancer. Their goal isn't to provide hospice-like treatment for terminal dogs. Of course, they care for and love the animals, but instead of writing off the canine companions to their fate, KPS provides groundbreaking human-grade metabolic-based cancer therapy for dogs.

PATRICK ARNOLD

Patrick Arnold (FB: @PROTOTYPENUTRITION, PROTOTYPENUTRITION .COM), widely considered the "father of prohormones," is the organic chemist who introduced androstenedione (remember Mark McGwire?) and other compounds into the dietary supplement world. He also created the designer steroid known as THG, or "The Clear." THG and two other anabolic steroids that Patrick manufactured (best known: norboletone) weren't banned at the time of their creation. These hard-to-detect drugs were at the heart of the BALCO doping scandal involving Barry Bonds and others. These days, Patrick is innovating in the legal world of ketone supplementation, including breakthroughs for military and commercial applications.

THE NEW PERFORMANCE ENHANCERS

No big surprise, I'm fascinated by all performance-enhancing drugs, which have been used since before the first Olympiad. On the legal side, here are two of Patrick's creations that I've found useful:

"Ur Spray" Ursolic Acid

Ursolic acid helps with body recomposition. The benefits are summarized nicely in the title of one study: "Ursolic Acid Increases Skeletal Muscle and Brown Fat and Decreases Diet-Induced Obesity, Glucose Intolerance and Fatty Liver Disease."* It can't be ingested in pill form, as it will be destroyed by first-pass (liver) metabolism; nor can be it be injected, as it doesn't mix with oil. This led Patrick to create a topical alcohol suspension, as ursolic acid is neither hydrophilic nor hydrophobic. Tricky stuff. Ur Spray is sold on his Prototype Nutrition site.

Funny side note: The dose is 50 sprays for approximately 249 mg of active ursolic acid. That's a lot of pumping. Some other guests' wives have complained about late-night bathroom *Pssshhh! Pssshhhh! Pssshhh!* sessions that seem to go on forever.

Patrick Arnold's Pre-Workout "Shake"

If you are in ketosis, drinking exogenous ketones pre- and intra-workout can substitute for carbs. As Patrick elaborates: "It's pretty amazing. I've given it to people who tell me, 'I'm on the ketogenic diet, and I work out and I feel like crap.' I say, 'Try this,' and they say, 'Wow! I didn't get tired. My body had all the fuel it needed.'

"My friend Ian Danney's company, Optimum EFX, has a product called Amino Matrix. It's very expensive but since I've worked with him — we make some of his products — I get it for free. It's basically a full spectrum of essential amino acids, branched-chain amino acids with some other things thrown in there: lipoic acid, citrulline malate, and a few other things.

"I mix that with about 45 ml of KetoForce, which is the [liquid exogenous ketones] you're not supposed to drink straight (see the "jet fuel" story on

---

*Kunkel SD, Elmore CJ, Bongers KS, Ebert SM, Fox DK, Dyle MC, et al. "Ursolic acid increases skeletal muscle and brown fat and decreases diet-induced obesity, glucose intolerance and fatty liver disease." *PLoS ONE* 7(6) (2012): e39332 doi:10.1371/journal.pone.0039332.

page 60). If you mix it with the Amino Matrix, which is very tart, it buffers the alkalinity of the KetoForce and it ends up tasting quite good."

TF: A tablespoon of lemon juice (in the water you use to dilute KetoForce) will also work for buffering. If KetoForce is too odd for your stomach, try the powdered KetoCaNa, also developed by Patrick, which I often use before aerobic exercise.

METFORMIN FOR LIFE EXTENSION

Both Patrick Arnold and his frequent collaborator, Dominic D'Agostino, PhD (page 21), are interested in metformin, which is not their creation. Dom considers it the most promising of the anti-aging drugs from a scientific standpoint, and I would estimate that a dozen of the people in this book use it.

In type 2 diabetics (to whom it's prescribed), metformin decreases the liver's ability to make and deposit glucose into the bloodstream. Metformin also dampens the signaling pathways associated with cancer growth proliferation. Rats with metastatic cancer in Dom's studies have increased survival rates by 40 to 50%. It mimics calorie restriction and fasting in many respects. Some researchers believe it could damage mitochondria, but nonetheless, many MDs and technologists are taking metformin prophylactically to prevent cancer.

Dom did a test where he took 1 g of metformin daily for 12 weeks, and had blood work done throughout. His diet and exercise didn't change. In his "post" test, his triglycerides were the lowest they had ever been, his HDL was around 98 (bumping up from 80), and his C-reactive protein wasn't even measurable. The only side effect he saw was that his testosterone was lower, and that came back into normal range once he stopped taking metformin.

JOE DE SENA

Joe De Sena (TW/FB/IG: @SPARTANRACE, SPARTAN.COM) is the co-founder of the Death Race, Spartan Race (more than 1 million competitors), and more. He has completed the famously grueling Iditarod dog-sledding race . . . by foot. He also finished the Badwater Ultramarathon (135 miles at over 120°F/49°C), Vermont 100, and Lake Placid Ironman — all in the same week. The man is a maniac, and he's a very strategic businessman. I first met him through Summit Series (summit.co). He keeps inviting me to visit him in Vermont, and I refuse because I'm afraid.

Spirit animal: Wolf

WHY HE STARTED TACKLING INSANE EVENTS WHILE WORKING ON WALL STREET

"You make and lose $30K, $40K in minutes screwing up an order or having customers tell you that they are no longer going to deal with you. It was very stressful business. [I wanted] to get back to the core of life.... [A friend] said, 'Well, you could die. There is this one — the Iditarod in Alaska. They do it in the middle of the winter, it is by foot, and it is 30 below. But, you have to —' 'Sign me up. I have to do it.' **I had to get back to this place where you just want water, food, and shelter. All the craziness of my life — this Wall Street life I had taken on — would go away, would melt away.**"

ON THE ORIGINS OF THE DEATH RACE

"And what if I created — with a buddy of mine — this race that purposely broke these people? Not the way the races I had done or a marathon does, but where I would actually drive the participants crazy? Not tell them when it is starting, not tell them when it is ending, not giving them water, giving them buses during the middle of the race and saying, 'You could quit here. Just get on the bus. This is not for you. You are too weak,' ... and that was the beginning of my race business."

TIM: "How do you break people?"

JOE: "Well, I don't think they knew what they were getting into, because we had never done it before. One guy — I remember specifically — started crying and he was like, 'I am a really good runner. I just do not know how to chop wood.' Broken. Because no one knew. We did not tell them. So, Doug Lewis, who is an Olympic-level downhill skier, is 15, 18 hours into this thing and he is cracking. He is broken and he turns to me and says, 'I made the Olympics. I trained my whole life. I am a pretty tough guy.' He goes, 'This is fucking crazy.' That moment, we knew we had a winner."

FUNNY ANECDOTE FROM AMELIA BOONE

Amelia Boone (page 2) has finished the Death Race three times and sent this to me:

"Hurricane Irene washed out a bridge on his property. A 1-ton metal I-beam had been stuck in the water for a few years, and the state was going to fine him some obscene amount if he didn't remove it. It would have cost him tens of thousands of dollars to have it removed, so instead, he had his winter Death Racers get in the river in January and remove it for him. It took us probably 8 hours. I came away with second-degree frostbite in most of my toes, as did many others. And the hilarious part? People paid HIM to experience that (the race entrance fee) AND he avoided fines and the cost of removal. Fucking genius."

RANDOM TIDBITS FROM FOLLOW-UP CONVERSATIONS

» Joe, like Jocko [Willink, page 412], believes that you shouldn't need caffeine or alcohol. He also thinks, "You should sweat like you're being chased by the police daily."

» When people tell Joe to stop and smell the roses, his first response is, "Who is maintaining the roses?"

* Do you have any quotes you live your life by or think of often?
"It could always be worse."

WIM "THE ICEMAN" HOF

Wim Hof (TW/IG: @Iceman_Hof, icemanwimhof.com) is a Dutch world record holder nicknamed "The Iceman." He is the creator of the Wim Hof Method and holds more than 20 world records. Wim is an outlier of daredevils, as he routinely asks scientists to measure and validate his feats. Here are just a few examples:

» In 2007, he climbed past the "death zone" altitude on Mount Everest (~7,500 meters) wearing nothing but shorts and shoes.

» In 2009, Wim completed a full marathon above the Arctic Circle in Finland, once again only in shorts, despite temperatures close to –20°C (–4°F).

» Wim has set multiple records for ice bath endurance, with his best time at nearly 2 hours.

» In 2011, he ran a full marathon in the Namib Desert without water. He can also run at altitude without suffering altitude sickness.

WARNING: NEVER DO BREATHING EXERCISES IN WATER OR BEFORE TRAINING IN WATER. SHALLOW-WATER BLACKOUTS CAN BE FATAL, AND YOU WILL NOT FEEL THE ONSET UNTIL IT'S TOO LATE.

Wim Hof breathing should never be done near water. Joshua Waitzkin (page 577), another podcast guest with decades of free-diving experience, suffered a shallow-water blackout at a public pool in New York City and was underwater for an additional 3 minutes before being pulled out by a lifeguard. He remained unconscious for an additional 20 minutes, and was then hospitalized for 3 days and subjected to a barrage of tests to assess the damage, including potential brain damage. He could have died extremely easily. So, to reiterate: Do not practice this type of breath work in combination with water immersion. There will be no warning sign before you lose consciousness. M'kay?

A MIND-BLOWING EXPERIMENT

Before I describe the exercise, I shall repeat my usual refrain: Don't be stupid and hurt yourself, please. Use a very soft surface in case you face plant.

1. Do a set of push-ups and end a few repetitions short of failure. Record the number.

2. Rest at least 30 minutes.

3. Do ~40 repetitions of the following breathing exercise: Max inhale (raise chest) and "let go" exhale (drop chest sharply). The let-go exhale can be thought of as a short "*hah*." If you're doing this correctly, after 20 to 30 reps you might feel loose, mild lightheadedness, and a little bit of tingling. The tingling is often felt in the hands first.

4. On the last breathing cycle, breathe in completely, exhale completely, then do another set of push-ups. More often than not, people will experience a sharp increase in the max number of push-ups, even though their lungs are empty.

COLD IS A GREAT PURIFYING FORCE

Wim, surfing king Laird Hamilton (page 92), and Tony Robbins (page 210) all use cold exposure as a tool. It can improve immune function, increase fat loss (partially by increasing levels of the hormone adiponectin), and dramatically elevate mood. In fact, Van Gogh was prescribed cold baths twice daily in a psychiatric ward after severing his own ear.

> "All the problems I have in the daily world subside when I do [cold exposure]. Exposing myself to the worthy cold . . . it is a great cleaning purifying force."

Wim takes cold to terrifying extremes (his retinas froze once while swimming in a lake under sheets of ice), but you can start with a cold water "finish" to showers. Simply make the last 30 to 60 seconds of your shower pure cold. Among others in this book, Naval Ravikant (page 546), Joshua Waitzkin (page 577), and I now do this. Josh does it with his tiny son, Jack, who he's trained to say "It's so good!" when it feels unbearable.

Below is my current cold regimen, often alternated with heat, which we covered on page 7. My full "workout" process then, is 1) pre-workout BCAA, 2) workout, 3) post-exercise whey protein, 4) immediate heat (~20 minutes) followed by 5) cold (5 to 10 minutes). I repeat the hot-cold cycle 2 to 4 times.

My post-workout cold routine is as follows:

» Put ~40 pounds of ice (this will depend on your bathtub size) into a bathtub, and then fill with water. That order avoids splashing and speeds things up. Instacart is helpful for ice delivery, or buy a garage freezer just for bags of ice, which is far easier than fancy ice-making or cooling contraptions.

» 15 to 20 minutes later, when the water reaches ~45°F, it is ready for use. I drop a $5 immersion thermometer from Carolina Biological Supply Company in the water for tracking. Coach Sommer (page 9) uses the low 50s°F for his athletes.

>> After heat, I enter the ice bath, keeping my hands out of the water. This allows me to stay in for longer, as capillary density is high in the hands. Hands go under for the last 3 to 5 minutes.

THE MAGIC DIET

I expected a mutant such as Wim to have dietary tricks. When I asked him about his typical dinners, his answer made me laugh: "I like pasta, and I like a couple of beers, too. Yeah!" How can he function on this food? Genetics might play a role, but he also rarely eats before 6 p.m. and tends to eat one single meal per day. To use the lingo of the cool kids: He has practiced intermittent fasting for decades now.

HEART-TO-HEART HUGS

When I first trained with Wim in person in Malibu, California, I noticed he hugged differently than most people. He throws his left arm over the person's shoulder, putting his head to the right of theirs. I asked someone on his team if he was left-handed.

"No. He just wants to hug heart-to-heart with everyone."

I love this, and several friends in this book now do this on special occasions. Just be forewarned: It throws people off, just like offering someone your left hand to shake, so best to explain (just tap your heart and say "heart to heart"). This also helps to avoid headbutts.

WIM + DOM = INTERESTING

During that same training session, I went from my normal 45-second breath hold time to 4 minutes and 45 seconds with no perceptible side effects. Several months later, while in deep ketosis (6+ mmol) after 8 days of fasting, I did the same exercises in a hyperbaric oxygen chamber at 2.4 ATA. The result? I held my breath for a staggering 7 minutes and 30 seconds before stopping in fear of my brain melting. In case you miraculously missed my warning at the beginning of this profile (page 42), read it. If you read it, please reread it. For more on ketosis and fasting, see Dominic D'Agostino on page 21.

RICK RUBIN'S BARREL SAUNA

Here are the specs for Rick Rubin's (page 502) barrel sauna, which is a slightly smaller version of what Laird Hamilton (page 92) has. There are two long benches along the walls, and it can easily seat 6 to 8 people. It is about 7 feet in diameter and height.

I have an exact duplicate in my backyard, which I often use 1 to 2 times daily, as it only takes 5 to 15 minutes to warm up. How on earth is it so fast? The heater is 3 to 4 times larger than it should be for the cubic footage. This is done on purpose, but it will freak out suppliers who are hesitant to combine a small sauna with a large heater. Put them together at your own risk!

The sauna and heater components are typically sold separately. This book will likely give Dundalk, the sauna company I used, the "hug of death" — they'll be overwhelmed with requests and cease to be a viable option. I've provided a few alternatives below. Prices obviously change over time.

Sauna

Dundalk 7' x 8' Red Cedar Barrel Sauna with Window and Heavy Duty Fold Up Benches and Extra Wood for Heater Guard (Door Hinged on Left) — Cost ~$6,500 (unassembled)
dundalkleisurecraft.com

Other suppliers with decent reviews worth considering:
almostheaven.com
barrel-sauna.com
leisureliving.ca

Heater

Model NC-12 with SC-9 control and 1-phase relay box, plus 2 boxes of rocks (what I have) — Cost ~$2,000
sauna.com/nordic-sauna-heaters
leisureliving.ca

JASON NEMER

Jason Nemer (IG: @JASONNEMER, ACROYOGA.ORG) is a cofounder of AcroYoga, which blends the spiritual wisdom of yoga, the loving-kindness of Thai massage, and the dynamic power of acrobatics. Jason was a two-time U.S. Junior National champion in sports acrobatics and represented the U.S. at the World Championships in Beijing in 1991. He performed acrobatics in the opening ceremonies of the 1996 Olympics. AcroYoga now has certified teachers in more than 60 countries and hundreds of thousands of practitioners.

Spirit animal: Bunny

BACK STORY

In 2015, I sat next to Jason at a dinner party at a friend's house in L.A. Somehow, my lower-back pain — which had been plaguing me — came up, and he offered to "fly" me on the spot. Having no idea what that was, I agreed and ended up getting spun around in the air on his feet for about 15 minutes. It was surreal and seemed to defy the laws of physics. Two things worth noting: I weighed ~180 pounds and he weighs ~160 (he's done the same with someone ~280 and 6′7″), and my back no longer hurt after the upside-down traction.

In the past, I'd always been repelled by yoga: too much mumbo-jumbo, too little excitement. AcroYoga is a different beast. You'll endure the occasional Sanskrit, but it's otherwise like a combination of body-weight strength training, dance (the "base" is the lead, and the "flier" follows), roughhousing (lots of wipeouts), and hip rehab (after ten sessions, my lower body felt 10 years younger).

It's also the ultimate movement-based Prozac. In a culture where physical touch is taboo, this allows you to experience sensual but not sexual connection, all while getting incredibly strong and flexible. Last but not least, I laugh at least 50% of the time in all training sessions. It's a wonderful balance to all the "serious" training that I do. If you'd like to see me both basing and flying, as well as teaching some basic techniques, just search "acroyoga" on youtube.com/timferriss.

ODDS AND ENDS
Duck Shit Oolong Tea

Jason brought this delicious tea for us to drink during recording. It's sometimes called "duck shit fragrance tea." Supposedly, long ago in a region in China, the local populace wanted to keep this amazing tea for themselves, so they nicknamed it "duck shit" tea. Smart move. It was played down for centuries, until being rediscovered as very much non–duck shit flavored. Jason gets his from Quantitea (quantitea.com).

Jason has traveled the world for the last 6 years, never staying in one place more than 3 weeks. He travels with next to no luggage but insists on carrying a ukulele and a donkey's load worth of tea.

FeetUp (Shoulder Stand Device) or Substitutes

The limiting factor for most people learning handstands is the wrists. This weakest link prevents you from getting enough upside-down practice. The FeetUp device addresses this—imagine a small padded toilet seat cushion mounted on a low stool. You stick your head through it, rest your shoulders on the padding, grab the two handles, and kick up into a headstand or handstand, with your shoulders supporting your weight. This allows you to work on alignment, tightness, positional drills (tuck, pike, straddle, etc.) in higher volume. The FeetUp is Jason's preference, but it's hard to find in the U.S. (en.feetup.eu). The BodyLift Yoga Headstand and Yogacise Bench are similar, or search for "yoga headstand bench."

A Saying from One of Jason's Mentors, Chinese Master Acrobat Lu Yi

"Mo' extension!" (more extension). In a handstand, you should push your shoulders as near (or past) your ears as possible. If you've ever done shrugs with dumbbells, imagine doing that with your arms overhead, and avoid arching your back. Also, the first knuckle (fist knuckle) of the index finger is prone to lifting off the ground in handstand practice. Jason calls this "the naughty knuckle."

For Instagram inspiration, check out these profiles:

@theacrobear
@duo_die_acrobatics
@acrospherics
@cheeracro_
@acropediaorg
@mike.aidala
@yogacro
@lux_seattleacro

To find AcroYoga classes, teachers, and movements:

AcroYoga.org

Facebook—Search your city's name and "acroyoga." The AcroYoga Berlin page, for example, has 3,650 playmates and training partners ready for you.

Acromaps.com
Acropedia.org (techniques)

✳ What do you believe that other people think is insane?

It's Jason's follow-up that I love the most, but this gives context:

"That you can trust people. You can trust a lot of people. You don't have to live in fear of strangers. Strangers are just people you haven't flown yet. It seems crazy to me that, in many cultures, we teach our children to fear and not talk to strangers. I've been all over the world. My mom was not happy when I was going to go to the Middle East for the first time. I was actually in Boston, about to lead a teacher training, when the Boston Marathon bombing happened. I had 15 students who were on lockdown for 24 hours.

"I got on the phone to my mom and I said 'Look, Mom, you think Israel is dangerous. I'm in Boston. You cannot hide from danger.' But I don't think that's a reason to not trust people. I've traveled the world in some very sketchy places and I've never had anything bad happen to me.

"I assume the best in people. I assume that I can trust them until they prove me wrong. When you do this practice enough, trusting is like a muscle that you flex. It doesn't mean that I'm a cowboy with it. I have really good credit assessment."

TIM: "Hold on — you said nothing bad has happened to you. How much of that is simply seeing things in the most positive light? Because you had your throwing knives [stolen by customs officers] in Panama. So shit happens, I'm imagining."

Jason laughed, was quiet for a second, then answered:

"One of the things that happened to me that was really amazing — I had all of my objects liberated from me. . . . Basically, I didn't want to work in restaurants [anymore], and I'm like, 'I'm a yogi. I'm going to do this. I don't care how hard it is. I love this.' *Boom*. So I was living in my van.

"My 30th birthday, my friend throws me a party. That night I got a book on Buddhism, a case of coconuts, and I hung out with my friends. The next day, my van's gone. My home is gone. Everything is gone. So I go crack a coconut and start reading about Buddhism because . . . what the fuck else am I gonna do? And page 4 is talking about homelessness and wandering. I think, 'That's what I'm going to do.' And that started my nomadic traveling. If I had stayed in San

Francisco and tried to make it as a yoga teacher, AcroYoga wouldn't be a world-wide practice.

"Let go of what's not working and really assess what is working and 'what can I be excited about?' It's not that bad things don't happen to me. I don't label a lot of things good/bad. [Instead, I ask] can I evolve from this? What do I want now? Where is my center now?"

✳ Most-gifted or recommended books

The Prophet by Kahlil Gibran: "I love really condensed, *shakti* [empowerment]-filled, energy-filled statements — something that you can read in a few minutes or you can read for your whole life." [**TF:** This little tome is fewer than 100 pages long. Spend the extra $5 for the version with the author's illustrations.]

Tao Te Ching by Lao Tzu: Jason travels with this book. "Oftentimes before meditation, I'll just open it randomly to a page. I read about something and then just have that be what I steep in as I sit." (See Rick Rubin, page 502, and Joshua Waitzkin, page 577.) When I asked Jason via text which translation he liked, he joked *"Tao de Chinga tu madre"* (ah, my friends), and then specified: Stephen Mitchell.

✳ Jason's best $100 or less purchase

Jason loves disc (Frisbee) golf and travels with discs. In particular, Innova's Roc mid-range disc and his "go-to driver," the TeeBird. He plays the game, but he also, on rare occasions, lets a disc go:

"I correct people when they get really serious because there are people who have caddies. For real. Those people think it's a sport. It's a pastime, no matter how hard you work at it. It's a piece of plastic, and you're throwing it around. . . .

"But to watch a disc fly for about a minute, it's magical. . . . In yoga, there's this philosophy, *svaha*. I call it 'Fuck it, let go.' . . . I like to throw Frisbees off of really high objects. And when I'm in these very ceremonial places like Machu Picchu, it's like, 'What am I releasing?' So it's an intentional act."

✳ What would you put on a billboard?

"**Play!** Play more. I feel like people are so serious, and it doesn't take much for people to drop back into the wisdom of a childlike playfulness. If I had to prescribe two things to improve health and happiness in the world, it'd be movement and play. Because you can't really play without moving, so they're intertwined.

"Treadmills kill your spirit. There are reasons and times to do treadmills, but if that is your only way of moving your body, you're selling yourself short. There are much cooler ways to move your body, way more fun things, and I just happened to have the good fortune to learn a lot of these really cool things. So play."

PARTING THOUGHTS: DON'T OVERCOMPARTMENTALIZE

On theoretical yoga versus applied yoga: "I also feel that there's a ceiling on yoga, and the ceiling is: You have all this amazing knowledge and all this amazing practice, but **how are you bringing that into the world? What happens when you're in traffic? How are you with your mom? Do you talk to your mom? Do you tell her the truth?**"

ACROYOGA—THAI AND FLY

AcroYoga is a blend of three complementary disciplines: yoga, acrobatics, and therapeutics.

The therapeutics were brought into the fold by Jenny Sauer-Klein, the other cofounder of AcroYoga (along with Jason Nemer, page 46), and resemble suspended Thai massage. So much so that it's often referred to as "Thai and fly."

I've seen Jason blow high-level acrobats' minds (even those from Cirque du Soleil) with Folded Leaf (page 55), perhaps the easiest of all AcroYoga therapeutic poses. Be forewarned that it's sometimes jokingly referred to as "Leaf Blower," as it puts face close to groin. If your partner's not ready to be inches from your crotch, Hippie Twist (page 54) is a Disney-friendly alternative.

To intro you to the "Acro" world, I'll share a few of my favorite moves from therapeutic flying. They are much safer than acrobatics, which require a teacher and spotters.

In 5 minutes or so, I've used the following to fix lower-back pain in at least six of the people featured in this book. "I haven't felt this type of release and relaxation in years . . . or ever" is a common response. Take it SLOW and enjoy! If it's uncomfortable, you're not doing it right. Do this on a mat or grass, and I suggest practicing the moves in the order listed.

Anything in quotation marks is what I'd say as a base (the person on their back) teaching a first-time flyer (the person getting inverted). Good rule for Acro and for life: **Tell people what you *want*, not what you don't want, and keep it simple.** In other words, say "Stronger elbows" and not "Don't bend your arms." Say "Softer feet" and not "Stop poking my abs with your toes."

There are a million ways to teach Acro basics well, of course. The following is my personal preference.

Before Inverting Anyone

FLYER: Practice on the ground what you'll be doing in the air.

1. Sit on the ground, legs straight and spread (90 degrees is fine), back as straight as possible. This is a "pike straddle" position. The angle between your torso and thighs should be 90 degrees. **This bend at the hips is super critical, as it provides a "shelf" foothold for the base's feet.** Put your hands on top of your hip crease, including the first 1 to 2 inches below. I'll say: "That is where my feet are going to be."

2. Now, bring your feet in, soles together, into "butterfly" stretch position. The space in between your legs should look something like a diamond. For you yoga people who love Sanskrit, it's *baddha-konasana*. The *asana* suffix just means "pose." This all meant nothing to me when I first started learning, so I called it *"butter-kanasa"* for months.

3. Keeping that butterfly position, now reach behind your back and grab your elbows. If you can't do that, grab your forearms.

BASE: Load test your legs.

1. Get on your back and put your legs straight up in the air. This is an "L-base" position.

2. Have your flyer cross their arms so that their forearms are on their chest. Have them place their forearms across both of your feet and lean onto you, putting weight on your legs. How does it feel?

3. Don't let your toes drift toward your face, which will make things strenuous. Keep the hip angle at 90 degrees, if possible.

4. If your hamstrings are very tight, you can fold a yoga mat or towel and put it under your lower back. The elevation will help.

Hippie Twist

1. **BASE:** Lie down. **FLYER:** Stand right by the base's hips, feet twice shoulder width apart.

2. **BASE:** Put your slightly turned-out feet on flyer's hip creases.

3. **BASE:** Tell flyer, "Put your hands on my knees." **(fig. A)**

4. "Look in my eyes, take a deep breath. As you exhale, bend forward and I'll catch your shoulders. Keep your hands on my knees but let your arms bend." And, if needed, "Aim to put the top of your head on my stomach."

5. **BASE:** Meet flyer's shoulders with arms straight and fingers pointing up, and lift flyer into the air. **(fig. B)**

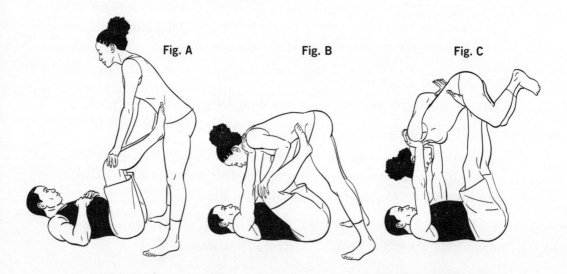

Fig. A   Fig. B   Fig. C

6. "Keep your legs wide and your feet heavy. Toes to the ground." **FLYER:** Keep a strong bend at your hips. Most flyers lift their legs, losing the "shelf," which can lead to a fall. Another cue: "Keep your feet as close to the floor as possible."

7. "Let your upper body be heavy and legs be super heavy."

8. "Now, reach behind your back and grab your own elbows, if you can. Grabbing forearms or wrists is also fine."

9. "Bring the soles of your feet together to butterfly stretch. **(fig. C)** Now, bring your toes down enough that you can see them." This ensures the proper "shelf."

10. **BASE:** Arms and legs should be straight. "Deep inhale, and exhale."
    BASE: On the exhale, slowly bend one leg to twist the flyer at the waist. Return to all straight. Repeat the breath and twist to the other side. Repeat 4 to 6 reps total.

Folded Leaf and Leaf Hugger

Repeat steps 1 to 7 of Hippie Twist (opposite).

8. **BASE:** Tell flyer, "Now, relax your arms completely and put the tops your hands on the floor. I'll help." Lightly grab flyer's wrists and place their hands well behind their hips. **(fig. D)** Flyer should not be supporting any weight. Flyer's legs should be wide and heavy, as close to the floor as possible without straining. This is Folded Leaf position.

9. **BASE:** Reach your hands under the flyer's armpits and underhook, landing your hands on the upper back. **(see inset)**

10. **BASE:** Bend your legs to lightly rest the flyer's ribcage on your shins. **(fig. E)** This creates a safer angle for the flyer's shoulders.

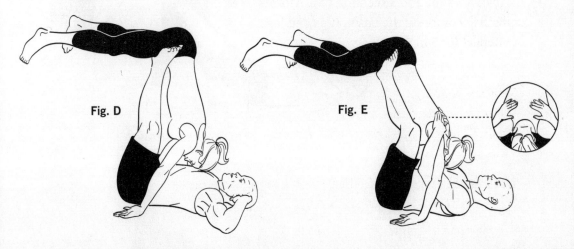

Fig. D   Fig. E

11. **BASE** and **FLYER**: Inhale together. **BASE**: Extend the flyer back with your bent legs as your arms traction the flyer's upper body back in opposition. This is Leaf Hugger.

12. **BASE**: Return to legs straight, releasing traction on the flyer's back, then repeat for 2 to 4 reps.

Leg Love — "Gravity Boots"

At the end of an AcroYoga session, the base's legs are typically fried. This is when "Leg Love" comes in — the flyer helping to decompress and restore the base's legs and hips. There are dozens upon dozens of techniques (e.g., "Bus Driver"), but this one gives a fantastic bang for the buck. Since I've never heard a name for it, I'll call it "Gravity Boots," as the effect is similar.

Even used independent of AcroYoga, this exercise has therapeutic value.

1. **BASE**: Lie on your back, legs straight and spread a few feet.

2. **FLYER**: Stand between base's legs and pick up their feet, holding onto the lower Achilles and top of the heel. Base should completely relax and not help.

3. **FLYER**: Stagger your stance, turn the base's feet inward — like a pigeon-toe stance — behind your hips (**see inset**), and then lean back for 2 to 5 seconds. (**fig. A**) This will decompress the base's hips and legs. Repeat for 3 to 5 reps.

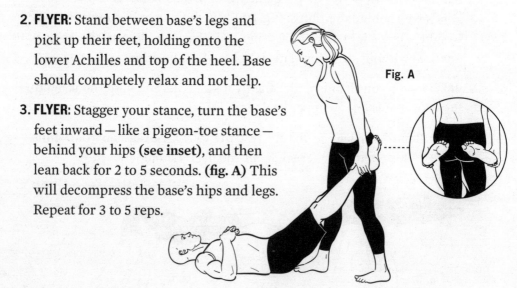

Fig. A

DECONSTRUCTING SPORTS AND SKILLS WITH QUESTIONS

As Tony Robbins would say, "The quality of your questions determines the quality of your life."

When I was interviewing athletes and coaches from 2008 to 2010, digging up non-obvious tactics for *The 4-Hour Body*, I sent different combinations of the following questions to dozens of experts. These can be modified for any skill or topic, not just sports. Just replace [SPORT] with what you want to learn, and track down your mentors. You can often find past gold and silver medalists willing to answer these via Skype for $50 to $100 per hour, which is an incredible steal and could save you years of wasted effort.

- » Who is good at [SPORT] despite being poorly built for it? Who's good at this who shouldn't be?

- » Who are the most controversial or unorthodox athletes or trainers in [SPORT]? Why? What do you think of them?

- » Who are the most impressive lesser-known teachers?

- » What makes you different? Who trained you or influenced you?

- » Have you trained others to do this? Have they replicated your results?

>> What are the biggest mistakes and myths you see in [SPORT] training? What are the biggest wastes of time?

>> What are your favorite instructional books or resources on the subject? If people had to teach themselves, what would you suggest they use?

>> If you were to train me for 12 weeks for a [FILL IN THE BLANK] competition and had a million dollars on the line, what would the training look like? What if I trained for 8 weeks?

In the case of basketball, I added four more to the above. The following questions were emailed to Rick Torbett, the founder of Better Basketball:

>> What are the biggest mistakes novices make when shooting or practicing shooting? What are the biggest misuses of time?

>> What mistakes are most common, even at the pro level?

>> What are your key principles for better, more consistent shooting? What are they for foul shots (free throws) vs. 3-pointers?

>> What does the progression of exercises look like?

I received his email responses and, 2 days later, hit 9 out of 10 free throws for the first time in my life. Then, on Christmas Eve, I went bowling and realized that many of the basketball principles (e.g., determining eye dominance to move your vertical "center line") applied to the lane, too. I scored 124, my first time over 100 and an Everest above my usual 50 to 70. Upon returning home, I immediately went outside and sank the first two 3-pointers of my life. That's a hell of a lot of fun. It all starts with good questions.

DR. PETER ATTIA

Peter Attia, MD (TW: @PETERATTIAMD, EATINGACADEMY.COM) is a former ultra-endurance athlete (e.g., swimming races of 25 miles), compulsive self-experimenter, and one of the most fascinating human beings I know. He is one of my go-to doctors for anything performance- or longevity-related. Peter earned his MD from Stanford University and holds a BSc in mechanical engineering and applied mathematics from Queen's University in Kingston, Ontario. He did his residency in general surgery at the Johns Hopkins Hospital, and conducted research at the National Cancer Institute under Dr. Steven Rosenberg, where Peter focused on the role of regulatory T cells in cancer regression and other immune-based therapies for cancer.

PETER'S BREAKFAST

"It usually starts with nothing, and then I usually do a second course — because I'm a little hungry — and I'll have a little bit more nothing. I usually top it off with a bit of nothing."

Peter rarely eats breakfast and has experimented with many forms of intermittent fasting, ranging from one meal a day (i.e., 23 hours of fasting per day) to more typical 16/8 and 18/6 patterns of eating (i.e., 16 or 18 hours of fasting and only eating in an 8- or 6-hour window). Going 16 hours without eating generally provides the right balance of autophagy (look it up) and anabolism (muscle building).

RANDOM BITS

>>> Peter spent 3 straight years in nutritional ketosis, and maintained a high level of performance not only in ultra–long distance cycling and swimming, but also in strength (e.g., flipping a 450-pound tire 6 times in 16 seconds). He still enters ketosis at least once per week as a result of fasting (one primary meal per day at ~6 to 8 p.m.), and he feels he is at his best on a ketogenic diet. His main reason for moving away from it was a craving for more fruits and vegetables.

>>> Peter is obsessed with many things, including watches (like the Omega Speedmaster Professional, Caliber 321, which has been around since the 1950s) and professional-grade car racing simulators. The simulator Peter owns uses iRacing software, but the hardware (seated cockpit, steering wheel, hydraulics, etc.) is all custom-built, so it doesn't have a name. His favorite car to drive is the Formula Renault 2000.

WHY PETER AND I GET ALONG

Peter explains the joy of drinking his first experimental batch of synthetic (exogenous) ketones:

"The first one I tried was the beta-hydroxybutyrate ester, which a very good friend of mine sent me [Dominic D'Agostino, page 21], and I had been told these things taste horrible. I had talked to two people who had consumed them before, and these are stoic, military dudes. These weren't 6-year-old kids. They said, 'Oh, man, that's the worst-tasting stuff on earth.' So I knew that, but I think that piece of information was fleeting in the excitement when the box came. I tore open the box, and there was also a note in there that explained a somewhat palatable cocktail that you could mix — how you could mix this with ten other things. I just disregarded that and took out the 50-ml flask.

"I chugged it, and I remember it was like 6:00 in the morning, because my wife was still sleeping. First of all, you drink it, and it tasted like how I imagine jet fuel or diesel would taste. If you've ever smelled distillate, it's this horrible odor, and you can sort of imagine what it would taste like. This is what it tasted like, and so my first thought was, 'Goddamn, what if I go blind? What if there's methanol in here? What did I just do?' And then my next thought was just, 'Oh my god, you're gagging. I mean, you're really gagging. If you puke this stuff up, you're gonna have to lick up your puke. It's just gonna be a disaster.' And so I'm retching and gagging and trying not to wake up the family and trying not to spew my ketone esters all over the kitchen. It took around 20 minutes for me to get out and do my bike ride, which was the whole purpose of that experiment."

TOOLS OF THE TRADE
Peter wears a Dexcom G5 continuous glucose monitor to track his glucose levels 24/7, which are displayed on his iPhone. His real goal, if he could wave a magic wand, is to keep his average glucose and glucose variability low. Outside of a lab, this approximates minimizing your insulin "area under the curve" (AUC). To accomplish this, Peter aims to keep his average glucose (per 24-hour period) at 84 to 88 mg/dl and his standard deviation below 15. The Dexcom displays all of this. Peter calibrates the Dexcom 2 to 3 times per day with a OneTouch Ultra 2 glucometer, which requires less blood and appears more accurate than the Precision Xtra that I use for ketone measurement.

GLUTE MEDIUS WORKOUT
"Modern man is weakest and most unstable in the lateral plane. Having a very strong gluteus medius, tensor fasciae latae, and vastus medialis is essential for complete knee-hip alignment and longevity of performance."

Peter once visited me in San Francisco and we went to the gym together. In between sets of deadlifts and various chalk-laden macho moves, I glanced over and saw Peter in a centerfold pose doing what looked like a Jane Fonda work-out. Once I finished laughing, he explained that he avoided knee surgery thanks to this exercise set, taught to him by speed guru Ryan Flaherty and kinesiologist Brian Dorfman (Brian also helped him avoid shoulder surgery after a torn labrum).

I tried his "reverse thighmaster" series and was dumbstruck by how weak my glute medius was. It was excruciating, and I felt and looked like an idiot. (See Coach Sommer's quote, "If you want to be a stud . . ." on page 10.) For each of the following 7 moves, start with 10 to 15 reps each. Once you can do 20 reps for all 7 consecutively, consider adding weight to your ankles.

You'll likely feel quite smug and self-satisfied for the first few, but remember: No rest until all 7 are done and no rest in between exercises.

For all of these — keep your big toe below your heel (think pigeon-toed) to ensure you're targeting the right muscles, and perform this series 2 times per week.

#1 — Up/Down

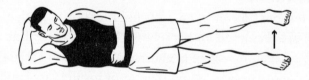

Lie down on your side and use your arm to support your head. Keeping your legs straight, lift your top leg and lower it, keeping your foot internally rotated as described above. Don't lift the foot very high. The max angle at your crotch should not exceed 30 degrees. Higher reduces the tension and defeats the purpose.

For exercises #2–4, maintain a roughly 12-inch distance between your ankles at the bottom. Maximize tension on the glute medius and only move your leg in a horizontal plane. Ensure the ankle doesn't dip when kicking behind you, for instance. In the first 1 or 2 workouts, aim to find the leg height that is *hardest* for you. It's usually 12 to 18 inches from the lower ankle. Remember to keep toe below heel.

#2 — Front Kick/Swing
Kick your top leg out to 45 degrees at the hip (as shown at right). Think "cabaret."

#3 — Back Swing
Swing your leg back as far as possible without arching your back.

#4 — Full Front and Back Swing
Swing your leg forward and then back (the previous two combined), with no pause at the midline.

#5 — Clockwise Circles
Paint an 18-inch-diameter circle with your heel. Remember, at the bottom of the circle, your ankles should be roughly 12 inches apart. If you let the ankles get within inches of each other, you're cheating.

#6 — Counterclockwise Circles
Repeat in the other direction.

#7 — Bicycle Motion
Pedal as if you were using a bicycle.

Easy peasy, Japanesey? Switch sides and repeat.

PLANK CIRCLES ON SWISS BALL
The goal of this separate exercise is to create scapular (shoulder blade) movement and rotation. Scapular mobility is one of the keys to upper-body function and longevity. The target muscles are the teres minor, infraspinatus, supraspinatus, subscapularis, and rhomboid.

The setup is simple: Get into a plank position with your elbows propped on a Swiss ball, forearms pointing straight ahead. Don't sag between the shoulder blades or at the lower back (keep the "hollow" and "protracted" positions described on page 19). Start with the legs wide for stability, and you can narrow the feet as you get stronger. Keeping your body in this position, use your forearms to move the ball as described below. One set consists of 10 to 15 reps of each of the following with no rest in between:

1. Clockwise circles

2. Counter-clockwise circles

3. Forward and backward (i.e., sliding the elbows forward 6 to 12 inches and then back to your ribs)

When you're doing this correctly, you should feel your entire shoulder blades (scapulae) moving.

Peter will do 3 total sets per workout, 2 times per week. He will superset these with "Wolverines" (Google it) on a cable machine. If done correctly, Wolverines target the rhomboids more than the deltoids.

5 BLOOD TESTS PETER GENERALLY RECOMMENDS

"Of course, the answers depend on the individual and the risks each person faces (cardiovascular disease, cancer, etc.) based on family history and genetics, but—broadly speaking—looking through the lens of preventing death, these five tests are very important."

1 **APOE Genotype:** "This informs my thinking on a person's risk for Alzheimer's disease (AD). The gene is far from causal, meaning, having it does not cause AD, but it increases risk anywhere from a bit to a lot, depending on which variant you have and how many copies you have. For what it's worth, the apoE phenotype (i.e., the actual amount of the lipoprotein in circulation in your body) is more predictive of AD than the gene and is obviously a better marker to track, however [a test is] not yet commercially available. Stand by, though. I'm working on it."

2 **LDL Particle Number via NMR** (technology that can count the number of lipoproteins in the blood): "This counts all of the LDL particles, which are the dominant particles that traffic cholesterol in the body, both to and from the heart and to and from the liver. We know [that] the higher the number of these particles, the greater your risk of cardiovascular disease."

3 **Lp(a) ("L-P-little-A") via NMR:** "The Lp(a) particle is perhaps the most atherogenic particle in the body, and while it's included in the total of LDL particle numbers, I want to know if somebody has an elevated Lp(a) particle number, because that, in and of itself, independent of the total LDL particle number, is an enormous predictor of risk. It's something we have to act on, but we do so indirectly. In other words, diet and drugs don't seem to have any effect on that number, so we pull the lever harder on other things. Nearly 10% of people have inherited an elevated level of Lp(a), and it is hands down the most common risk for hereditary atherosclerosis. The bad news is that most doctors don't screen for it; the good news is that knowing you have it can save your life, and a drug (in a class called "apo(a) antisense" drugs) to treat it directly will be around in approximately 3 or 4 years."

4 **OGTT (Oral Glucose Tolerance Test):** "In this test, you drink a glucose concoction and then look at insulin and glucose response at 60 minutes and 120 minutes. The 1-hour mark is where you may see the early warning signs with elevated glucose levels (or anything over 40 to 50 on insulin), which can represent hyperinsulinemia, a harbinger of metabolic problems. In fact, the 1-hour insulin response may be the most important metabolic indicator of your propensity to hyperinsulinemia and insulin resistance, even in the presence of normal 'traditional' markers such as HbA1C."

5 **IGF-I (Insulin-like Growth Factor-I):** "This is a pretty strong driver of cancer. Diet choices (e.g., ketogenic diet, caloric restriction, intermittent fasting) can help keep IGF-1 levels low, if such a strategy is warranted."

KETOSIS WARNING SIGNS

"Keto works well for many people, but it's not ideal for all. It's also not clear why some people do well for long periods of time, while others seem to derive max benefit from cycling. If certain markers get elevated (e.g., C-reactive protein, uric acid, homocysteine, and LDL particle numbers), it's likely that the diet is not working properly for that person and requires tweaking or removal. Some patients who suffer from significant LDL particle number increases on keto can reverse the trend by limiting saturated fat to fewer than 25 g and replacing the required fat calories with monounsaturated fats (e.g., macadamia nut oil, olive oil, limited avocado oil)."

BEFORE YOU GET COMPREHENSIVE WORK DONE, DECIDE WHAT YOUR THRESHOLD OF ACTION IS

"The likelihood of doing comprehensive testing and finding everything 'normal' is low, so don't have testing done unless you're willing to accept the uncertainty that comes from needing to make decisions (or not) with incomplete — and at times conflicting — information. Before you check your APOE gene, for example, you should know what you'll do if you have one or two copies of the '4' allele."

TF: Decide beforehand — and not reactively when emotions run high — what types of findings are worth acting upon or ignoring, and what your "if/then" actions will be.

THE DANGERS OF BLOOD TEST "SNAPSHOTS"

It's important to get blood tests often enough to trend, and to repeat/confirm scary results before taking dramatic action. This has been echoed by other guests who have appeared on my podcast like Justin Mager, MD (page 72), and Charles Poliquin (page 74):

"In 2005, I swam from Catalina Island to L.A., and I had my friend Mark Lewis, who's an anesthesiologist, draw my blood around 10 minutes before I got in the water on Catalina Island and then 10 minutes after I got out of the water in L.A., 10.5 hours later. It was a real epiphany for me, because I had developed something called systemic inflammatory response syndrome, SIRS, which is something that we typically see in hospitalized patients who have horrible infections or who have been in really bad trauma: gunshot, car accident, that sort of thing.

"My platelets went from a normal level to 6 times normal. My white blood cell count went from normal to — I don't know — 5 times normal. All of these huge changes occurred in my blood, so that you couldn't distinguish me from someone who had just been shot. . . .

"I've always been hesitant to treat a patient for any snapshot, no matter how bad it looks. For example, I saw a guy recently whose morning cortisol level was something like 5 times the normal level. So, you might think, wow, this guy's got an adrenal tumor, right? But a little follow-up question and I realized that at 3 a.m. that morning, a few hours before this blood draw, the water heater blew up in his house. The normal level of morning cortisol assumes a guy sleeps through the night. He had to de-flood his house."

4 BULLETS TO DODGE

> "If you're over 40 and don't smoke, there's about a 70 to 80% chance you'll die from one of four diseases: heart disease, cerebrovascular disease, cancer, or neurodegenerative disease."

"There are really two pieces to longevity. The first is delaying death as long as possible by delaying the onset of chronic disease (the 'big four' above). We call that the defensive play. The second is enhancing life, the offensive play. On that defensive play, there are basically four diseases that are going to kill you. In other words, if you're 40 years old and you care about this, you're probably not going to die in a car accident or homicide, because you're out of that demographic. You're less likely to die of X, Y, and Z. It turns out that when you look at the mortality tables, there's an 80% chance you're going to die from cardiovascular disease, cerebrovascular disease, cancer, or neurodegenerative disease, period.

"If you remember nothing else, remember this: If you're in your 40s or beyond and you care about living longer, which immediately puts you in a selection bias category, there's an 80% chance you're going to die of [one of] those four diseases. So any strategy toward increasing longevity has to be geared toward reducing the risk of those diseases as much as is humanly possible.

"[For those who don't know,] cerebrovascular disease would be stroke, and there's two ways you can have a stroke. One is through an occlusion; the other one is through bleeding, usually due to elevated blood pressure and things like that. Neurodegenerative disease, as its name suggests, is degeneration in the brain. The most common cause of that is Alzheimer's dementia, and Alzheimer's is one of the top ten causes of death in the United States.

"[Studies] suggest to me that there's something about highly refined carbohydrates and sugars — and potentially protein, though it might be for a different reason — that seems to raise insulin, which we know, by extension, raises insulin-like growth factor (IGF). And we know that IGF is driving not just aging but also certainly driving a lot of cancers, though not all of them."

SUPPLEMENTS THAT PETER DOES *NOT* TAKE

Peter consumes a fair selection of supplements based on his own blood work, so it's highly personalized. He does not take, however, a number of the common ones:

>> **Multivitamin:** "They're the worst of both worlds. They contain a bunch of what you don't really need and don't contain enough of what you do need. It poses an unnecessary risk with no up side."

>> **Vitamins A and E:** He's not convinced he needs more than what he absorbs through whole foods.

>> **Vitamin K:** "If you eat leafy green vegetables, you're getting enough. K2 might be a different story for some people, depending on their diet."

>> **Vitamin C:** "Most of us get sufficient amounts in our diet, and while megadoses might be interesting, especially for combatting viral illnesses, it's not bioavailable enough in oral form."

He is a proponent of magnesium supplementation. Our ability to buffer magnesium with healthy kidneys is very high. He takes 600 to 800 mg per day, alternating between mag sulfate and mag oxide. He also takes calcium carbonate 2 times per week. Two of his favored brands are Jarrow Formulas and NOW Foods.

THE LOGIC OF LOW-DOSE LITHIUM

Based on conversations with Peter, I now take low-dose lithium in the form of 5 mg of lithium orotate. The more I read epidemiological studies, the more I've come to think of lithium as an essential, or conditionally essential, element. 1 to 5 mg is enough to effectively ensure you are getting the high range of what is naturally occurring in groundwater in the U.S. As a primer, I suggest reading the *New York Times* piece, "Should We All Take a Bit of Lithium?"* From that article:

> Although it seems strange that the microscopic amounts of lithium found in groundwater could have any substantial medical impact, the more scientists look for such effects, the more they seem to discover. Evidence is slowly accumulating that relatively tiny doses of lithium can have beneficial effects. They appear to decrease suicide rates significantly and may even promote brain health and improve mood.

And from Peter: "Lithium is actually really, really safe at low doses—basically anything below about 150 mg—if you have normal kidney function. It's one of those drugs that got such a bad rap with the large doses that were sometimes needed to treat recalcitrant monotherapy bipolar disorder, but those doses—easily approaching 1200 mg—have nothing in common with the logic above."

MORE COMEDY — LONG AGO, WHEN PETER WENT FROM 170 TO 210 POUNDS, GAINING MOSTLY FAT

"Frankly, I just got aggravated beyond words. We joke about it now, but at the time I literally said to my wife, 'I'm going to go get a gastric bypass.' And she said, 'You are the most ridiculous human being who's ever lived. We're going to have to talk about our marriage, if that's what you're considering at the weight of 210 pounds.' I actually did go and see the top bariatrician in the city of San Diego, and it's kind of weird story because, even though I was obviously overweight, I was the thinnest person in the waiting room by a long shot. It put it in perspective. [I thought to myself,] 'Peter, you think you've got problems. I mean, these people each weigh 400 pounds.' And when it was my turn to see the doctor, the nurse took me up to the scale and weighed me. We got on the scale, and I'm like 210. She says, 'Ah, this is fantastic. Are you here for a follow-up?'"

---

*Anna Fels. "Should We All Take a Bit of Lithium?" *The New York Times* (Sept. 13, 2014).

ON DROPPING RUNNING AND PICKING UP WEIGHTS

"Nothing breaks my heart more than seeing that person who's struggling to lose weight who thinks that they need to run 20 miles a week. They have no desire to do it, their knees hurt, they hate it, and they're not losing weight. And I'd like to say, 'Well, I've got great news for you. You don't ever need to run another step a day in your life, because there's no value in that.'

"There is value in exercise, though, and I think that the most important type of exercise, especially in terms of bang for your buck, is going to be really high-intensity, heavy strength training. Strength training aids everything from glucose disposal and metabolic health to mitochondrial density and orthopedic stability. That last one might not mean much when you're a 30-something young buck, but when you're in your 70s, that's the difference between a broken hip and a walk in the park."

PETER'S PATH TO MEDITATION

10% Happier by Dan Harris is the book that got Peter meditating regularly. After limited success with open monitoring or mindfulness meditation, he was introduced to Transcendental Meditation by a friend, Dan Loeb, billionaire and founder of Third Point LLC, a $17 billion asset management firm.

* **Most-gifted or recommended books**

Surely You're Joking, Mr. Feynman! by Richard Feynman

Mistakes Were Made (But Not by Me) by Carol Tavris and Elliot Aronson. The latter is a book about cognitive dissonance that looks at common weaknesses and biases in human thinking. Peter wants to ensure he goes through life without being too sure of himself, and this book helps him to recalibrate.

* **Peter's best $100 or less purchase?**

Peter has a monthly daddy/daughter date with his 8-year-old daughter. The below came up at the tail-end of one outing:

"We were walking back to the hotel, and one of those rickshaw guys came up with a fully lit-up bike. I would normally never even think about hopping a ride on one of those things, but I could just see this look in her eye: 'Wow, this bike has lights all over it.' [So we hopped on.] This guy gave us a ride back, which probably cost $20, so not even $100. And, believe me, it's $20 more than we should have spent to just walk back, but the look on her face was worth every dollar I have. I just got a little cheesy and cliché because old dads are like that, but that's the best $20 I've spent in a long time."

✳ Who do you think of when you hear the word "successful"?

Peter mentioned several people, including his friend John Griffin, a hedge fund manager in New York, but I'd like to highlight his last answer: his brother. Peter's brother Paul (TW: @PapaAlphaBlog) is a federal prosecutor, a great athlete, and father of 4 kids under the age of 5. He thinks an enormous amount about being a better federal prosecutor, and thinks just as much about how to be a better father. Peter elaborates:

"Success is: Do your kids remember you for being the best dad? Not the dad who gave them everything, but will they be able to tell you anything one day? Will they able to call you out of the blue, any day, no matter what? Are you the first person they want to ask for advice? And at the same time, can you hit it out of the park in whatever it is you decide to do, as a lawyer, as a doctor, as a stockbroker, as a whatever?"

JUSTIN MAGER, MD

Dr. Justin Mager has helped me with dozens of my "human guinea pig" experiments, complete with blood testing and next-generation tracking. He's brilliant and hilarious. Justin appeared on the podcast with Kelly Starrett (page 122), a mutual friend and collaborator. When we ended the episode, I asked my usual "Where should people check you out?" Justin's answer was, "My honest parting comment is not to check me out, just fucking look in the mirror and check yourself out. My aspiration is to go underground and be a ghost." Love this guy.

"WE'RE NOT AN OBJECT, WE'RE A PROCESS"

"We want to judge things as good or bad. . . . So, there's this idea that inflammation is bad, [thus the opposite] is good. High cholesterol bad, low cholesterol good. [But] you have to understand what blood testing actually represents. First of all, it's a snapshot. It's a moment in time, and we're not an object, we're a process."

"OPTIMAL" DEPENDS ON WHAT YOU'RE OPTIMIZING FOR

"[For instance], there's some literature that suggests that if you have high LDL cholesterol, you can actually build more lean body mass at a faster rate. So, if you're in a strength-building phase, it actually might be to your advantage to actually have that present . . . you need to know context. You [also] have to understand what the marker actually represents, not just [have] a judgment of whether it's good or bad."

HEY, DOC, WHAT DOES CHOLESTEROL DO?

"I like to ask that to physicians, especially if they're antagonizing me about my practice methods. I say, 'Hey, what does cholesterol do?' and it's interesting, because a lot of them will take a step back and they'll fumble, because they're so indoctrinated into the algorithm of 'All I really need to do is identify high cholesterol and treat it' versus understanding what purpose it serves in the human body."

TF: There is a big difference between understanding something (what you want in a physician) and simply knowing its name or labeling it. This is also one of the lessons that Nobel Prize winner Richard Feynman's father taught him. The story is contained in *Surely You're Joking, Mr. Feynman!*, the most-gifted book of several people in this book, as well as in a wonderful short documentary called *The Pleasure of Finding Things Out*.

> **"**The rule is: The basics are the basics, and you can't beat the basics.**"**

> **"**What you put in your mouth is a stressor, and what you say — what comes out of your mouth — is also a stressor.**"**

CHARLES POLIQUIN

Charles Poliquin (TW/FB: @STRENGTHSENSEI, STRENGTHSENSEI.COM) is one of the best-known strength coaches in the world. He has trained elite athletes from nearly 20 different sports, including Olympic gold medalists, NFL All-Pros, NHL All-Stars and Stanley Cup champions, and IFBB bodybuilding champions. His clients include America's first-ever Olympic gold medalist in women's wrestling, Helen Maroulis, long-jump gold medalist Dwight Phillips, NHL MVP Chris Pronger, and MLB batting champion Edgar Martínez, among many others. Poliquin has authored more than 600 articles on strength training, and his work has been translated into 24 different languages. He has written 8 books, including a short gem entitled *Arm Size and Strength: The Ultimate Guide.*

Spirit animal: Siberian tiger

JUST BECAUSE YOU EXERCISE DOESN'T MEAN YOU DESERVE SUGAR WATER

"The most important thing I've learned about nutrition is you need to deserve your carbs . . . to deserve [hundreds of kcal of carbs] post-exercise, you need to be sub-10% body fat. And the quickest way to know if you have sub-10 body fat as a male is: Can I see the lineal alba [vertical separation] on your abs? In other words, can I see all ab rows? One ab row doesn't count; you've got to see them all. In other words, **you have to have penis skin on your abs.**"

TF: One female reader responded on social media with "What if it's someone else's penis skin?" Might be a workaround.

"I've got some athletes who do best on 70% carbs, 20% protein, 10% fat. But they deserve their carbohydrates. They've got a great pancreas, they're insulin-sensitive, blah, blah, blah, they've got a lot of muscle mass. But some athletes, they're allowed 10 licks of a dried prune every 6 months. That's all they deserve and that's all they'll get. And after 6 months, they're actually allowed to look at calendar pictures of cakes once a week."

TF: For a low-carb post-workout option, see goat whey on page 84 (Portable Fuel).

HOW DO YOU IDENTIFY A GOOD STRENGTH COACH?

"A good strength coach should get a female, no matter what her body fat is, to be able to do 12 chin-ups in 12 weeks."

CHARLES'S TYPICAL BREAKFAST

Charles takes breakfast seriously. His typical combo includes some type of wild meat (typically pan fried in Meyenberg goat butter), nuts, and sometimes berries or avocados:

"**I really like macadamia nuts, but I vary that so I don't develop intolerances.** . . . On the road, one of the reasons I stay at the Marriott worldwide is it's the only place that will serve steak and eggs." When traveling, of course, things can be harder: "In Manchester [UK], for example, there was no way I could get steak and eggs for breakfast, so my assistant and I bought sardines. So we had sardines and Brazil nuts for breakfast the next day. I don't negotiate on that. For me, I either have meat, fish, or seafood and some nuts."

TF: I bolded the above, as I have many friends who've been tested for food intolerances and called me with: "I'm intolerant to navy beans! Egg whites, too!" Such results don't necessarily mean you have genetics that disallow these foods. There's a decent likelihood that A) you've simply been consuming too much of the same food and provoked a correctable autoimmune response, or B) the lab has made an error. I've seen labs return *every* patient (dozens) in a given week as intolerant to egg whites. Lab errors happen, equipment malfunctions, and people make mistakes. The moral of the story: Vary your food sources and confirm any scary test results with a second test.

FOR LOOSE SKIN OR STRETCH MARKS

"There's an herb called gotu kola that—I learned this from Dr. Mauro Di Pasquale, who was one of my early mentors—will get rid of what we call unnecessary scar tissue or unnecessary connective tissue. The truth of the matter, though, is that you will see zero progress for the loose skin for 6 months. So people say it's not worth it, but I tell people, just keep doing it for 6 months. And then it's almost like overnight. . . .

"There are some compounding pharmacists who will make you a gotu kola bioabsorbable cream. That works a lot faster. I would say if you can find a compounding pharmacist who will do that, and it's a biologically active form, you could get the same results in about 2 to 3 months."

TF: I asked Charles about oral sources, and he suggested one dropperful of Gaia Herbs Gotu Kola Leaf liquid extract per day, which also improves tendon repair and cognitive function.

4 TESTS TO CHECK EVERY 8 WEEKS

Charles recommends checking these biomarkers every 8 weeks:

1. Morning (fasting) insulin

2. Morning (fasting) glucose: "One thing I insist on is that they always [do this test] exactly 12 hours after the last bite. Why? Because I want pre- and post-measures that are valid. Your morning glucose could be all over the place because you fasted an extra 2 hours, and it's not valid."

   TF: This is a hugely important point. Standardize as many variables as possible. For instance, I will do blood tests on the same day of the week, and attempt to hydrate equally, typically by drinking 1–2 liters of water and ensuring my pee is clear. Imagine that you do one blood test on Thursday, then your follow-up tests on a Monday after a weekend of booze, which can elevate liver enzymes. The values aren't comparable. It's also a good idea to avoid hard workouts for the 24 hours prior to your blood tests, if possible, so you don't get a false read on inflammatory markers. Control thy variables!

3. **Reactive insulin test:** "I think the reactive insulin test is the most underrated test in health." (Dr. Peter Attia also includes this as "OGTT (Oral Glucose Tolerance Test)" in his top 5 tests; see page 65 for more details.)

4. **HbA1c** (usually read as "hemoglobin A1c"): "**They say that, basically, you age at the rate you produce insulin.** HbA1c will tell me what was the average insulin over the last 3 months. . . . I've found over the years that, actually, the amount of magnesium, supplemental magnesium, you consume, is the fastest way to drop that value. So magnesium is probably one of the best anti-aging minerals."

MORE ON MAGNESIUM

"I think the best magnesium out there is magnesium threonate, if I were to pick one. But I prefer taking different chelates. [**TF:** Dominic D'Agostino also takes magnesium; see page 30 for his thoughts.] So I use glycinate, I use orotate. If you look at the physiology behind it, and there's a lot of good research that's really easy to find, every form of magnesium tends to go to a specific tissue. So for example, magnesium glycinate has a preference for liver and muscle tissue; magnesium orotate tends to work more in the vascular system. Magnesium threonate is more of a GABA inducer, therefore it improves sleep. Personally, I take 2 g of magnesium threonate at the last meal before going to bed, and I use various forms of chelates like magnesium glycerophosphate from GabaMag [made by Trilogy Nutritional Supplements]."

Another go-to recipe for sleep: glutamine and physician-prescribed probiotics (vary the brands) before bed.

ON GOOD DOCTORS

"The length of time they spend with you on your first visit is probably your best indicator [of their quality]."

TO INCREASE T, DECREASE C

"As a rule . . . **the best thing to increase testosterone is to lower cortisol.** Because the same raw material that makes testosterone and cortisol is called pregnenolone. Under conditions of stress, your body is wired to eventually go toward the cortisol pathway."

TF: If you've ever laid down in bed exhausted, then felt wired and been unable to sleep, cortisol might be a factor. To mitigate this "tired and wired" phenomenon — as well as reduce glucose levels — before bed, I take phosphatidylserine and N-acetyl cysteine (NAC). For me, this also has a noticeable impact on lowering anxiety the following day.

"The best educator on HRT (Hormone Replacement Therapy) is Thierry Hertoghe from Belgium."

✱ "Back squat, front squat, or overhead squat, if you had to choose one for your athletes?"
"The front squat. I have a lot of statistical data on that. Because it is impossible to cheat on the front squat. I'm talking ass-to-the-grass front squat, meaning you leave a stain in the carpet in the bottom position. In my opinion, for athletic purposes, all squats should be done that way. . . . They should [perform] it the way the Olympic lifters do it. So hands slightly wider than shoulder width, elbows up as high as you can, and actually the **elbows in**. That locks the bar into right in front of your throat. If you find the exercise comfortable, you're not doing it correctly. You should feel some restriction in the neck when you front squat properly."

(See Kelly Starrett's thoughts on squats on page 124.)

STEP #1 IN A SQUAT WARMUP

"There's a lot of research that shows that mobility in the ankle is what decreases the probability of any lower extremity injuries, whether it's an ACL tear or hamstring pull or groin tear or whatever. So the first thing I would do [in a warmup prior to squatting] is go on a calf machine and stretch the calves, and then go down and statically stretch for 8 seconds. I'd finish off with voluntary contraction, because it resets the pattern for strength. Research is clear: If you do static stretching and you don't finish with a contraction, you're more likely to get an injury."

TF: This, along with Paul Levesque's recommendation, prompted me to take Cossack squats seriously (see page 87). I pay more attention to my calves now than ever before, both for injury prevention and upper-leg flexibility (see Christopher Sommer, page 9).

ACTIVATING THE HAMSTRINGS

I once took a Kinetic Chain Enhancement seminar under Charles, in which he tore my arms apart with ART (Active Release Techniques) and doubled my shoulder internal-rotation ROM in minutes (see *The 4-Hour Body*). He also taught us the "muscle-tendon technique" — how to activate the hamstrings, among other muscles, by using simple cross-fiber friction near the insertion points. For instance, to immediately increase your strength output in a set of hamstring curls, you could lie on the floor and have someone use a knife hand — think "judo chop" edge — to rapidly rub back and forth on each of the dotted lines in this illustration for 8 to 10 seconds each. For reasons that exceed the space we have, start at the gluteal fold (butt fold) lines for hamstring curls, but start with lines just below the knee for deadlifts.

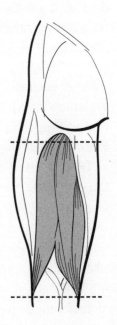

✳ **Most-gifted or recommended books**

59 Seconds: Change Your Life in Under a Minute by Richard Wiseman (for stress reduction)

The 4-Hour Workweek
The ONE Thing: The Surprisingly Simple Truth Behind Extraordinary Results by Gary Keller

"So after reading [*The 4-Hour Workweek* and *The ONE Thing*], when I'm at home, I work 2 and a half to 4 hours max. I take the month of July off. I take the first 2 weeks of August off. I don't work from the month of December until about end of January, and a week a month I take off."

∗ Charles's best $100 or less purchase
"It was a gift, so I'm not sure what the price was, but it can't be that high. It's called a Bamboo Bench [made by German personal trainer Bernd Stoesslein]. It has this half-moon shape [it attaches to any bench] where your spine rests. So when you do pressing movements, you can drop the elbows much farther than with a regular bench. It allows for a freer scapular movement, it allows for a greater range of motion when you lift, and it allows pain-free upper body pressing."

∗ Who do you think of when you hear the word "successful"?
Winston Churchill. "This guy had balls. He stood up to Hitler, he rallied the United Kingdom, he refused to surrender. He's a Nobel Prize winner in literature. Very few people know that."

TF: Fun note — after Charles said this on my podcast, the owner of Winston Churchill's former home reached out to invite him to visit.

THE SLOW-CARB DIET® CHEAT SHEET

Many people lose hope when trying to lose weight.

Fortunately, it need not be complicated. Though I regularly fast and enter ketosis, the Slow-Carb Diet (SCD) has been my default diet for more than a decade. It works almost beyond belief and affects much more than appearance. From one reader:

"I just wanted to sincerely thank Tim for taking the time to research and write *The 4-Hour Body*. My mom, in her late 60s, lost 45 pounds and got off her high blood pressure meds that she had been on for 20+ years. She did all this in about 3 months. This means that I get to have her around for a long time."

The basic rules are simple, all followed 6 days per week:

Rule #1: Avoid "white" starchy carbohydrates (or those that can be white). This means all bread, pasta, rice, potatoes, and grains (yes, including quinoa). If you have to ask, don't eat it.

Rule #2: Eat the same few meals over and over again, especially for breakfast and lunch. Good news: You already do this. You're just picking new default meals. If you want to keep it simple, split your plate into thirds: protein, veggies, and beans/legumes.

Rule #3: Don't drink calories. Exception: 1 to 2 glasses of dry red wine per night is allowed, although this can cause some peri-/post-menopausal women to plateau.

Rule #4: Don't eat fruit. (Fructose → glycerol phosphate → more body fat, more or less.) Avocado and tomatoes are allowed.

Rule #5: Whenever possible, measure your progress in body fat percentage, NOT total pounds. The scale can deceive and derail you. For instance, it's common to gain muscle while simultaneously losing fat on the SCD. That's exactly what you want, but the scale number won't move, and you will get frustrated. In place of the scale, I use DEXA scans, a BodyMetrix home ultrasound device, or calipers with a gym professional (I recommend the Jackson-Pollock 7-point method).

And then:

Rule #6: Take one day off per week and go nuts. I choose and recommend Saturday. This is "cheat day," which a lot of readers also call "Faturday." For biochemical and psychological reasons, it's important not to hold back. Some readers keep a "to-eat" list during the week, which reminds them that they're only giving up vices for 6 days at a time.

Comprehensive step-by-step details, including Q&As and troubleshooting, can be found in *The 4-Hour Body*, but the preceding outline is often enough to lose 20 pounds in a month, and drop 2 clothing sizes. Dozens of readers have lost 100–200 pounds on the SCD.

MY 6-PIECE GYM IN A BAG

I take these 6 items with me whenever I travel. In some cases, I buy several sets, which live in trunks stored at hotels in my most common locations, like L.A. and NYC. For the cost of checking luggage on a few flights, I can have my "kit" waiting in a few cities and avoid check-in lines.

1. **Voodoo Floss ($20 to $30):** This looks like a rubber ACE bandage. It is used to wrap and compress stiff or injured body parts. It's small enough to fit in a jacket pocket, yet it often decreases pain and increases ROM more than fancy injections and $200/hour therapy. I use Voodoo Floss 1 to 2 times per day on my elbows and forearms during hard gymnastics training. Source: Kelly Starrett (page 122).

2. **Furniture Sliders ($5 to $15):** I've used these to freak out guests in hotels around the world. I'll put them under my heels for a move called "Ag walks with rear support" (page 17), which I do up and down hallways on the carpet. Source: Christopher Sommer (page 9).

3. **RumbleRoller:** Think foam roller meets monster truck tire. (See details on page 3.) Source: Amelia Boone (page 2).

4. **Bed of Needles:** Technically, I bought a Nayoya Acupressure Mat. There is a competitor (same same but different) called Bed of Nails, both available on Amazon. This type of roll-out needle mat, which is covered with "needles" that look like cleat spikes, was recommended to me by Andrii Bondarenko (IG: @andrii_bondarenko), one of Cirque du Soleil's one-armed-handstand prodigies. His former Ukrainian sport acrobatics coach had athletes use these for up to an hour a day. I find that 5 to 10

minutes in the morning can seemingly perform miracles, particularly for back pain. For one lat tear, this device was the only healing modality that got me back to training.

5. **Tera's Whey Goat Whey Protein:** If you are lactose-sensitive, this can be a godsend. Even for those who tolerate dairy well, many (like me) find it easier to digest. I use a simple mason jar for mixing. If it's too goaty for you—I find it very neutral—consider adding a tablespoon of beet root powder from BeetElite or another brand. Source: Charles Poliquin (page 74).

6. **Mini-parallettes:** Anyone who's seen gymnastics knows of the parallel bars. Anyone who's been to a CrossFit gym knows about the miniature versions called "parallettes," typically made out of PVC pipes. What many haven't seen are the Vita Vibe MP12 ultra-light mini-parallettes that are small enough to fit in carry-on luggage. They are only high enough to clear your knuckles and are perfect for L-sits, planche leans, and handstand training. This is much easier on the wrists than flat hand work. Famed neuroscientist Adam Gazzaley, PhD (page 135), first introduced me to good at-home "p-bars."

PAVEL TSATSOULINE

Pavel Tsatsouline (TW/FB: @BeStrongFirst, StrongFirst.com) is Chairman of StrongFirst, Inc., a worldwide school of strength. He is a former physical training instructor for Spetsnaz, the Soviet special forces, and is currently a subject matter expert to the U.S. Marine Corps, the U.S. Secret Service, and the U.S. Navy SEALs. He is widely credited with introducing the now-ubiquitous kettlebell to the United States and is the author of *Kettlebell: Simple & Sinister*.

SOUND CHECK

Before interviews, I always check equipment with the same question. It's intended to get people talking for at least 10 seconds. This is what happened with Pavel:

TIM: "Pavel, if you don't mind, tell me about what you had for breakfast this morning as a sound check."

PAVEL: "Sound check. Breakfast: Coffee."

I thought this was so funny that I stuck it at the beginning of the episode. Many fans listen to it over and over again for laughs.

TWO WARMUPS: HALOS AND COSSACK SQUATS

If you're looking for brief, high-return warmups, here are two to consider.

Halos

Grasp a weight with both hands and rotate it around your head to loosen up the shoulder girdle. I use a 25- to 45-pound kettlebell or plate for this and perform 5 *slow* reps in each direction. Start light.

Cossack Squat

When everything else failed, Cossack squats with a kettlebell (as shown below) roughly doubled my ankle mobility, which had a chain of positive effects. Keep your heels on the ground throughout, keep your knees in line with your toes, and keep your hips as low as possible when switching sides. I do 5 to 6 reps per side for 2 to 3 sets, often supersetting with Eric Cressey's "walking Spiderman" warmup.

BASIC TENETS FOR STRENGTH

» "Strength is the mother quality of all physical qualities."

» "Strength is a skill, and, as such, it must be practiced."

» "Lift heavy, not hard."

» "Anything more than 5 reps is bodybuilding. . . . If you want to be strong, you want to keep your reps at 5 and under."

» "If you are training for strength, you want to try and avoid the burn altogether. The burn is your enemy."

» "Training is something that should be enjoyed."

The last quote isn't a motivational throwaway line. It's literal. If you're training for maximal strength, you should feel better after your workout than you did when you walked in. There is a huge neural component.

EFFORTLESS SUPERHUMAN

Pavel introduced me to track coach Barry Ross. Ross had read a study performed by Peter Weyand at Harvard concluding that the key to a sprinter's success is their relative strength: specifically, how much force he or she puts into the ground per pound of body weight. Then Ross read Pavel's prescription for increasing strength with minimal muscle gain: deadlifts with heavy weights, low reps, low volume, and a de-emphasized negative. Barry put two and two together and developed a deadlift-based program to create world-class sprinters. One of his early prodigies was Allyson Felix. His deadlift-based protocol utilizes partial range of motion and no negative/eccentric (lowering). I followed this protocol over a period of ~8 weeks and describe this at length in *The 4-Hour Body*, so I'll only provide the simplified basics here:

> **The Basic Technique:** Deadlift to your knees and then drop the bar. I used a "sumo-style" stance, but conventional is fine.
>
> **Format:** 2 to 3 sets of 2 to 3 reps each, each set followed by plyometrics (e.g., sprinting 10 to 20 meters, 6 to 8 box jumps, etc.), then at least 5 minutes of rest. My best gains came from 10-minute rests, which aren't uncommon among power athletes.
>
> **Frequency:** I did this twice weekly, on Mondays and Fridays. The total "time under tension" during sets is less than 5 minutes per week.
>
> **Results:** I added more than 120 pounds to my max deadlift in ~8 weeks and gained less than 10 pounds of additional mass. For relative strength, I've never experienced anything like it. Think you're too old, or too X for deadlifts? Pavel's father took up this lift in his 70s. He pulled more than 400 pounds without a belt a few years later, setting several American records in the process.

THE "BREATHING LADDER"

Have terrible endurance? Here's a strategy from Pavel's colleague, fitness instructor Rob Lawrence. For kettlebell swings, sprints, or any exercise that makes you feel gassed, decide beforehand that you're going to rest from one set to the next for a certain number of breaths (i.e., you get to do 5, 10, 30, or however many in between). This is going to discipline you to slow your breathing and stop overtaxing your nervous system. This control will help your endurance, even before biochemical adaptations.

Amelia Boone (page 2) uses the breathing ladder with burpees as a warmup. She will do ascending sets of burpees, from 1 rep to 10. In other words, she'll do 1 burpee, take 1 breath, 2 burpees, 2 breaths, and so on until she does 10 burpees and 10 breaths.

3 HIGH-YIELD EXERCISES — PAVEL'S "SIMPLE & SINISTER" KETTLEBELL PROGRAM

>>> One-arm swing

>>> Turkish get-up (TGU)

>>> Goblet squat

Do these three exercises in some form every day, and you are guaranteed to get a great return on your investment. The TGU is also excellent for diagnosing deficiencies.

THE HOLLOW POSITION ISN'T JUST FOR GYMNASTICS

If you want to master pull-ups, you need to develop your "hollow position" (see page 19). This, plus turning my toes inward (engaging obliques more fully), helped me to do strict military pull-ups (neck to the bar with pause) with 24 kg on the feet. To see the hollow position in action, watch any gymnast on rings: The tail is tucked in and the body looks like a dish. Pavel's tip: Try to bring your tailbone and your navel closer to each other.

"WHEN IN DOUBT, TRAIN YOUR GRIP AND YOUR CORE"

"Strengthening your midsection and your grip will automatically increase your strength in any lift. With the abs, the effect is partly due to greater intra-abdominal pressure and partly to improved stability. With the grip, you are taking advantage of the neurological phenomenon of *irradiation* — tension 'radiates' from the gripping muscles into other muscles.

"The most direct route to elite grip strength is IronMind's Captains of Crush Grippers [which are available up to 365-pound resistance]. Among effective midsection exercises are 'power breathing,' hollow rocks, Janda sit-ups, hanging leg raises, and 'hard-style planks.' To do the last, hold a plank for 10 seconds under max contraction, not for several minutes. Hold it like you're about to be kicked and breathe 'behind the shield' of your tensed midsection. For a challenge, consider putting your feet on the wall, a few inches from the floor."

For reps and sets, do 3 to 5 sets of 3 to 5 reps in dynamic (moving) exercises or hold ~10 seconds for static exercises. Take 3 to 5 minutes of rest in between sets for both.

Or, as Pavel would say, "Better yet, grease the groove." That leads us to the next principle.

"GREASE THE GROOVE" FOR STRENGTH ENDURANCE AND STRENGTH

"To increase your pull-up numbers, start doing half the reps you're capable of (e.g., sets of 4 if your personal best is 8) in repeated sets throughout the day. Simply accumulate reps with at least 15 minutes between sets, and adjust the daily volume to always feel fresh."

Using GTG for several months, Pavel's father-in-law went from 10 to 20 strict pull-ups at age 64 — and he could not do that many when he was a young Marine. The minimum of 15 minutes' rest is necessary for creatine phosphate hypercompensation.

"Whereas most **strength-endurance** programs work by training one to tolerate more lactic acid, GTG instead trains one to produce less acid. It increases the quantity and quality of mitochondria in fast-twitch muscle fibers and makes them more aerobic."

If you are "greasing the groove" for a **maximal strength** movement, do not exceed 5 reps per set. In this case, the method works through a different mechanism (for the nerds: *synaptic facilitation* and *myelination*). Let's say you're working up to a single perfect rep of a one-armed push-up. In your progression, you might do one-armed push-ups with feet on the floor and hands on the edge of a table or counter. If 6 reps is your max, you would do GTG sets of no more than 2 to 3 reps.

MY FAVORITE ODD STRETCH — WINDMILLS

Kettlebell windmills (or "high windmills") are incredible for hip rehab and "prehab." The standing position is similar to yoga's *trikonasana*, but you support 70 to 80% of your weight on one leg while you keep a kettlebell overhead. YouTube is your friend.

A FAVORITE QUOTE

From *Enter the Dragon*: "Sparta, Rome, the knights of Europe, the samurai . . . worshipped strength. Because it is strength that makes all other values possible."

"CALM IS CONTAGIOUS"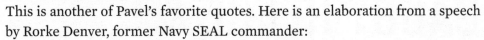

This is another of Pavel's favorite quotes. Here is an elaboration from a speech by Rorke Denver, former Navy SEAL commander:

"A master chief, the senior enlisted rank in the Navy — who was like a god to us — told us he was giving us an invaluable piece of advice that he'd learned from another master chief during the Vietnam War. He said, 'This is the best thing you're ever going to learn in SEAL training.' We were excited to learn what it was, and he told us that when you're a leader, people are going to mimic your behavior, at a minimum. . . . It's a guarantee. So here's the key piece of advice, this is all he said: 'Calm is contagious.' "

* Most-gifted or recommended book

"Most people exist between the on and off switch. They are unable to turn on and put out high power, and they are unable to turn off completely and enjoy true rest. To learn how to control your on and off switch, read the book *Psych* by Dr. Judd Biasiotto. He is one of the most successful power lifters in history, having squatted over 600 pounds at a bodyweight of 132 . . . drug free, at the age of 44, after back surgery."

LAIRD HAMILTON, GABBY REECE & BRIAN MacKENZIE

Laird Hamilton (TW/FB: @LAIRDLIFE, LAIRDHAMILTON.COM) is widely considered the greatest big wave surfer of all time. He is credited with the creation of tow-in surfing (using a Jet Ski to pull surfers into enormous waves), as well as the rebirth of stand-up paddle boarding. Hamilton has starred in multiple surfing films and was the centerpiece of *Riding Giants*, a documentary about big wave surfing.

Gabrielle Reece (TW/IG: @GABBYREECE, GABRIELLEREECE.COM) has been named one of the "20 Most Influential Women in Sports" by *Women's Sports & Fitness* and is best known for her success in volleyball. Reece led the Women's Beach Volleyball League in kills for four consecutive seasons. She parlayed that into a successful modeling career and then starred as a trainer on *The Biggest Loser*. Her crossover success led to her becoming the first female athlete to ever design a shoe for Nike. *Rolling Stone* has placed her on their "Wonder Women" list.

Brian MacKenzie (TW/IG: @IAMUNSCARED) is the founder of Cross-Fit Endurance and the author of the *New York Times* best-selling book *Unbreakable Runner*. Brian has created controversy by suggesting a counterintuitively minimalist approach to distance running. He challenges

Spirit animals: Laird = Killer whale; Gabby = Hawk; Brian = Raven

not only high-mileage runs, but also high-carb diets, and he utilizes intense strength training to conquer everything from 5K runs to ultra-marathons. He was prominently featured in *The 4-Hour Body*, where he described how to prepare for a marathon in 8 to 12 weeks. Brian has been featured in *Runner's World*, *Men's Journal*, *ESPN*, *Outside*, and *The Economist*.

―――――――――――

BACK STORY

Laird was one of my surfing teachers in my TV series, *The Tim Ferriss Experiment*, which was shot by ZPZ, the production company behind Anthony Bourdain's *No Reservations*, *Parts Unknown*, etc.

My interview with Laird, Gabby, and Brian took place at Laird and Gabby's kitchen table in Malibu, immediately after a workout. I felt as high as a kite. Brian had brought me to experience how Laird trains in his customized pool, which is 13 feet deep at the deep end and has stairs built into the floor. It also features underwater speakers for music and a slack line about 2 feet above the surface. I'd been invited by Brian before but always demurred out of fear of drowning. That morning, I bit the bullet and nervously joined 6 to 10 other guys to repeat the following cycle for roughly 90 minutes: underwater training with dumbbells, ice bath for at least 3 minutes, then 220°F sauna for 15 minutes. The entire gang does this workout twice a week, alternating with twice-weekly dry land weight-training sessions. They cheer each other on, and it's wonderful. Assholes don't last long.

THE "WARMUP" FOR TOUGH GUYS

Top professional athletes occasionally visit Laird to test-drive his famed pool workout. If a big musclehead comes in with an attitude, he'll suggest they go "warm up" with Gabby. This is code. Gabby proceeds to casually annihilate them, leaving them bug-eyed, full of terror, and exhausted. Once they've been force-fed enough humble pie, Laird will ask "Okay, are you ready to start the workout?" As Brian has put it: "The water goes, 'Oh, mighty and aggressive? Perfect. I'll just drown you.'"

WHAT WE DRANK

Pre-workout: Laird made everyone coffee, which he mixed with his own mocha-flavored "superfood creamer" (lairdsuperfood.com). It lights you up like a Christmas tree.

Post-workout: Fresh-squeezed turmeric root, chaga mushroom, liquid pepper extract, raw honey, apple cider vinegar, and water (dilute to taste). Laird sometimes combines the turmeric with KeVita kombucha to reduce any residual bitterness.

GEAR IN THE POOL

Cressi Big Eyes 2-lens diving mask. Goggles will come off.

PSOAS RELEASE — NOT SUPPOSED TO FEEL GOOD

Laird routinely releases his psoas — deep muscles that connect the lower back and the hip — by getting on the ground and lying on top of either a kettlebell handle or the edge of a 25-pound Olympic weight-lifting plate.

THE MAN BOOK CLUB

Laird has what Gabby calls the "man book club." The regulars who come to his house to train — which includes super celebs, world-record-setting free divers, and hugely successful CEOs — can suggest a nonfiction book of the month and everyone will read it for discussion. Rick Rubin is a frequent contributor. Here are two that made the cut just prior to our interview:

Natural Born Heroes by Christopher McDougall
Deep Survival by Laurence Gonzales, which Laird calls "an incredible book about fear and dealing with fear."

PRACTICE GOING FIRST

GABBY: "I always say that I'll go first. . . . That means if I'm checking out at the store, I'll say hello first. If I'm coming across somebody and make eye contact, I'll smile first. [I wish] people would experiment with that in their life a little bit: Be first, because — not all times, but most times — it comes in your favor. The response is pretty amazing. . . . I was at the park the other day with the kids.

Oh, my God. Hurricane Harbor [water park]. It's like hell. There were these two women a little bit older than me. We couldn't be more different, right? And I walked by them, and I just looked at them and smiled. The smile came to their face so instantly. They're ready, but you have to go first, because now we're being trained in this world [to opt out] — nobody's going first anymore."

TF: People are nicer than they look, but you have to go first. This made me think of a line from fictional character Raylan Givens in the TV series *Justified*: "If you run into an asshole in the morning, you ran into an asshole. If you run into assholes all day, you're the asshole." I will often write "GO FIRST" in my morning journal as a daily prompt.

Side note: Derek Sivers (page 184) listened to this episode and Gabby's "go first" principle was one of his favorite takeaways.

EARLY KITEBOARDING EXPERIMENTS, BEFORE IT WAS POPULAR

"We were the first ones to get the French non-restartable kites . . . where you release the guy and he just flies until he craps and then it's over. Sometimes you'd be like 2 miles out to sea with a giant quilt. **Have you ever tried to swim with a quilt? It's very hard.** Like a giant quilt . . . and a lunch tray. Literally, the board looks like a lunch tray [and] you're 2 miles out, and you're looking at the shore and you're like: 'This is not a good day for me.'"

WHERE CAN LISTENERS FIND YOU?

I ask this at the end of all of my interviews, so guests can mention social media, websites, etc. Laird answered without hesitation: "The Pacific Ocean."

THE INSPIRATION OF DON WILDMAN

BRIAN, *discussing Don Wildman and his incredible physical prowess at the age of 82:* "Well, Don Wildman did 80 days of snowboarding last year. I just went heli snowboarding with him 1 or 2 months ago in Alaska. I mean, heli boarding is a rigorous activity, a week straight of 15, 16 runs a day. The third, fourth day, you're wobbling, [but] not a word out of the gunslinger. . . . I can take pretty much almost anybody on a bicycle unless you're like a professional bicyclist, and he will hammer you."

GABBY: "The other thing Don does that's very genius . . . is he solicits people to be in his group because no man can really do it alone. So he always has these guys around him, most of them quite a bit younger. **So the energy goes into the pot, and everybody rolls.**" [**TF:** Rick Rubin also talks about Don on page 506.]

"A LONELY PLACE IS AN UNMOTIVATED PLACE"

This line from Laird underscored everything I saw around him. He has a tightly bonded tribe around him, and scheduled group exercise appears to be the glue that keeps the group together. If you spend a lot of time thinking of the "how" and "what" of exercise (exercises, programming, etc.), as I do, you might consider asking yourself, "What if I had to choose all of my exercise based on 'Who?' first? What would I do if exercise were only allowed with other people?" This is how I ended up diving into AcroYoga (page 52).

PARENTING ADVICE

Laird and Gabby, married since 1997, have very close and affectionate relationships with their three kids. I've observed them over and over again. There is a lot of physical touch, and the pervasive feeling is one of warmth. It's lovely to be around. The following parenting tidbits are taken from different points in the conversation.

LAIRD: "Loving your children can override a lot of wrongs. [Even if you get some of the specifics wrong or make missteps.]"

GABBY: "We're inclusive, and we treat them like adults. We've always spoken to them like adults. . . .

"As a parent, you have to learn to say sorry because you blew it. . . . Sometimes you can go, 'Hey, you know what? I am extra tired today and my fuse is short. I am being unfair to you, and I'm sorry.' You have to learn that you're imperfect and open that door. . . . I always [ask] my girls, 'Do you feel loved enough?' . . . and they say, 'Oh, come on, Mom.' But I think you should ask. . . .

"I tell my kids to learn how to say, 'I'm sorry, that doesn't work for me.' I've learned a lot from being around men. I respect a lot of traits. You can deliver a message without emotion. Usually, women, in order to finally stand up for themselves, they have to kind of be ramped up, and then it just comes out ballistic, instead of, 'No, that doesn't work for me.' And [I also teach them] not to then second guess [themselves] after they've laid that line down. I think that that's really important. And if you have gifts and talents, whatever they are, don't feel guilty and bad or weird about it. . . .

"I always tell kids, 'If you're on the team, you're lucky, and if you're the best one, you're the luckiest.'"

GABBY ON LEARNING ASSERTION

"As a woman, we're taught as young girls, 'Hey, be nice. Nice girls act like this,' so it takes a long time to get to a place of 'I'm going to do things, say things, and believe in things that people aren't going to like, and I'm going to be okay with that.' Men do that much more easily, and it takes women a very long time. The only [female] athletes I've seen that do it very easily are generally the youngest girl [in a family] with all older brothers."

(See Caroline Paul, page 459.)

ON THE MALE/FEMALE DYNAMIC IN RELATIONSHIPS

LAIRD: "[Of 10,000 successful couples studied], there's only one thing that everybody had in common, no matter what the dynamic. What is it? The man respected the woman. The number one thing."

GABBY: "But can I say one thing? I know all those dynamics differ — the woman's the breadwinner, the man's the breadwinner, she's dominant, he's dominant, whatever — but ultimately, more times than not, if the woman can refrain from trying to change or mother her partner, she has a greater opportunity of putting herself in a position where the guy will respect her. A man needs support. I mean, I love you guys and you're all strong, but you're very fragile, and you need to be supported and [for us to] help you fully realize your voice, whatever that is.

"Laird said to me the first couple of years we were together — unfortunately, his mom passed away the second year we were together — 'I had a mom, and she died.' He made it very clear . . . that's off the table. Women by nature, we can't help it, we're nurturers, right? So sometimes that seeps over into, 'Hey, honey, that joke was kind of inappropriate at the dinner table, and you're talking kind of loud,' and all that. And because the man's trying to be loving, they pacify us and change all the ways we want them to, and then we don't want them. So it's a great thing to just say, 'Hey, I'm going to pick a partner when I feel like our value systems are similar, and we may get there very differently, but . . . how we wind up on some of the big items is the same.'"

ON WEIGHING SACRIFICES BASED ON THE INDIVIDUAL —
WHAT'S EASY FOR YOU ISN'T WHAT'S EASY FOR SOMEONE ELSE

GABBY: "For a man to say, 'I'm going to really try to be with one woman,' they're giving you . . . most of what they've got. They're giving you like 80%. For a woman, maybe she's giving you 35% [to be monogamous]. . . . Or let's say I was very shy and I came out and was having a very nice conversation with you. Maybe I'm giving you 200% because of my nature. So I think it's also starting to understand who they are, that they're giving how they can give, and receiving it that way. . . ."

ON FIXING PHYSICAL WEAKNESSES

LAIRD: "All you flexible people should go bang some iron, and all you big weight lifters should go do some yoga. . . . We always gravitate toward our strengths because we want to be in our glory."

ADVICE TO BEAT-UP FORMER ATHLETES?

BRIAN: "More humility. That's why I thought it was so important that you come up here. It wasn't, 'Oh, I need to dose Tim with humility.' No, it was, 'Hey, come see what it's like to apply something that you can do for the rest of your life.'"

TF: By "more humility," I took Brian to mean considering scary options with an open beginner's mind. I'm so thrilled I took the risk of embarrassment to train with Laird and the gang. First, it showed me an intense but sustainable method of training, which includes ingredients I often neglect (social cohesion, training outdoors, etc.). Second, it made me believe I am capable of much more than I thought.

ADVICE FOR YOUR 30-YEAR-OLD SELF?

GABBY: "Not to take anything personally, but also **don't hold yourself back**. I think this is a trait of a female more than of a male. We have a tendency sometimes to sit on our talents and potential because we don't want to offend anyone or be singled out. . . . I heard a great story. I had a coach once, who was an assistant coach to the men's USA volleyball team. One game [they needed one point], and the coach looked straight at Karch Kiraly and said, 'I need you to put this ball away and for you to win this game,' and it was like, *boom* — 'Okay.' And then Karch did it.

"[Then the same coach] was coaching women at a very high level, and he did the same thing to the athlete who was 'the one.' It didn't work because . . . [it's] a singling-out that we [women] have a hard time with, instead of understanding that you can be singled out . . . for the greater good."

LAIRD: "Stop drinking now. Stop drinking right now and patent all your ideas . . . and exercise compassion every day."

JAMES FADIMAN

James Fadiman, PhD (PSYCHEDELICSRESEARCH@GMAIL.COM, JAMES FADIMAN.COM), has been involved with psychedelic research since the 1960s. He did his undergraduate work at Harvard and his graduate work at Stanford, where he collaborated with the Harvard Group, the West Coast Research Group in Menlo Park, and Ken Kesey. He is the author of *The Psychedelic Explorer's Guide* and is often referred to as America's wisest and most respected authority on psychedelics and their use.

PREFACE

Some of my loved ones would insist that the most important work I've done in the last 4 years has involved studying and judiciously using psychedelics. As just one example, ~90% of the latent anger and resentment I'd had for more than 25 years was eradicated after 48 hours of "medicine work" 2 years ago, for reasons still not entirely clear, and my hair-trigger habits of decades have not returned.

NOTE: I do think the pharmacological risks of these compounds are exaggerated, but their legal side effects are not. In the U.S., most classic psychedelics (LSD, psilocybin in "magic mushrooms," peyote, etc.) are in the same legal class as heroin (Schedule I) and carry similar penalties. And although the LD50—lethal dose for 50% of the population, a common measure of toxicity—is unbelievably high or practically non-existent for most psychedelics, things can go horribly wrong in uncontrolled environments (e.g., walking in front of oncoming traffic), and they can greatly exacerbate pre-existing mental health conditions. I watched one family friend go from "normal" to schizophrenic (his family had a history of it) after frequent LSD use. Of course, I wouldn't want you to go to jail or hurt yourself, so only use psychedelics in legal contexts with professional medical supervision. For a legal alternative, see Dan Engle's discussion of flotation tanks on page 110.

WHAT ARE PSYCHEDELICS?

The word *psychedelic* (Greek for "mind-revealing") is generally used to refer to compounds that can reliably separate you from your ego and occasion mystical or transcendental experiences. The best formal definition of "psychedelics" I've found is that of N. Crowley in *The British Journal of Psychiatry* ("A role for psychedelics in psychiatry?"):

> The difference between psychedelics (entheogens) and other psychotropic drugs is that entheogens work as "non-specific amplifiers of the psyche," inducing an altered or non-ordinary state of consciousness (Grof, 2000). The content and nature of the experiences are not thought to be artificial

products of their pharmacological interaction with the brain ("toxic psychoses") but authentic expressions of the psyche revealing its functioning on levels not ordinarily available for observation and study.

Many psychedelics (psilocybin, mescaline, etc.) have been used ceremonially for hundreds or thousands of years by indigenous cultures. More recently, universities around the world have begun testing these molecules for addressing treatment-resistant depression, removing end-of-life anxiety in terminal cancer patients, ending nicotine addiction, and more. Roland Griffiths, PhD, a professor at Johns Hopkins medical school, shares a typical upshot from one early study: "Most of the [36] volunteers looked back on their experience up to 14 months later and rated it as the most, or one of the five most, personally meaningful and spiritually significant of their lives." For volunteers with children, the experience was often put above, or on par with, the birth of their first child.

From a psychopharmacological perspective, many psychedelics resemble a naturally occurring molecule called DMT and act as 5-HT2A (serotonin) or NDMA receptor agonists, but there are exceptions, and the mechanisms of action remain poorly understood. This is part of the reason that I'm helping fund scientific studies at places like Johns Hopkins and UCSF.

Although marijuana, ketamine, and MDMA have compelling medical applications, I don't consider them psychedelics. Jim explains our shared distinction, using MDMA as an example: "It's not exactly a psychedelic because **you don't leave your identity behind**, but it is the single best way to overcome intractable post-traumatic stress disorder."

The noun "entheogen," meaning "generating the divine within," has become a popular alternative to the term "psychedelic."

MY GOOD FRIEND

I have a good friend, let's call him Slim Berriss, who's devised a schedule for himself that combines practical microdosing and pre-planned 1- to 2-day treks into deeper territory. For him, this blend provides a structured approach for increasing everyday well-being, developing empathy, and intensively exploring the "other." Here is what it looks like:

Microdosing of ibogaine hydrochloride twice weekly, on Mondays and Fridays. The dosage is 4 mg, or roughly 1/200 or less of the full ceremonial dosage at Slim's bodyweight of 80 kg. He dislikes LSD and finds psilocybin in mushrooms hard to dose accurately. Woe unto he who "microdoses" and gets hit like a freight train while checking in luggage at an airport (poor Slim). The encapsulated ibogaine was gifted to him to solve this problem.

Moderate dosing of psilocybin (2.2 to 3.5 g), as ground mushrooms in chocolate, once every 6 to 8 weeks. His highly individual experience falls somewhere in the 150 to 200 mcg description of LSD by Jim later in this piece. Slim is supervised by an experienced sitter.

Higher-dose ayahuasca once every 3 to 6 months for 2 consecutive nights. The effects could be compared (though very different experiences) to 500+ mcg of LSD. Slim is supervised by 1 to 2 experienced sitters in a close-knit group of 4 to 6 people maximum. **NOTE:** In the 4 weeks prior to these sessions, he does not consume any ibogaine or psilocybin.

Note that not all psychedelics are for all people. Jim, for instance, doesn't use ayahuasca. On our walk in a canyon in San Francisco, he said to me, "I feel like the plant [aya] has its own agenda." I'd have to agree with him, but that could fill an entirely separate book. Be sure to read Dan Engle and Martin Polanco's profiles on page 109, which explore ayahuasca and ibogaine, specifically.

ORIGINS AND DANGEROUS BOOKS

"There are two great beings who invented psychedelics: God and Sasha Shulgin. I think Sasha may have invented more, but there are literally hundreds that he played with and looked at." Sasha wrote two books about his creations and experiments:

Pihkal: A Chemical Love Story (Pihkal = Phenethylamines I Have Known and Loved)

Tihkal: The Continuation (Tihkal = Tryptamines I Have Known and Loved)

The two volumes are filled with instructions for how to synthesize these various molecules. He said he put these books out so that the government couldn't stop people from experimenting. Personally, I prefer the whole-plant sources that have been used for millennia.

What Does It Feel Like?

"If you are depressed, you are living in the past. If you are anxious, you are living in the future. If you are at peace, you are living in the present."

—Lao Tzu

Most of us have had the experience of sitting at a computer with 20 open tabs. *How did this happen? Didn't I just clean this up last week?* Then you get a warning of "Startup disk almost full." So you delete a few videos as damage control, but . . . why is everything still running so damned slowly? Oh, Dropbox is syncing. Slack has 17 new notifications. Microsoft needs *another* "critical" update? There are 20 applications running on top of 20 windows, fracturing your ability to focus. 60 minutes later, you've done a lot of *stuff*, tapped the keyboard a lot, and burned a ton of energy, but you couldn't say what you've achieved. Feeling rushed and frustrated, overwhelm begins to set in. Time to go get another coffee . . .

Life can feel this way. Finances, taxes, relationships, wedding invitations, car check-ups, Facebook, groceries . . . "Startup disk almost full."

For me, moderate to high dose of psilocybin with supervision serves as a hard reboot. It closes all the windows, "force quits" all the applications, flushes the cache, installs upgrades, and — when I'm back to "normal" — restores my 30,000-foot view. It removes the noise, giving me a crystal clear view of the most critical priorities and decisions. The first time I used psilocybin at sufficiently high doses, the anxiolytic — anxiety decreasing — effect lasted 3 to 6 months. This catalyzes not only insight but action.

Sounds great, right? It can be, but that result is far from guaranteed. Psychedelics usually give you what you need, not what you want. To get to pleasure, you often need to claw through pain first.

DOSES AND EFFECTS — FROM NIAGARA FALLS TO A CASUAL STROLL

NOTE: The below dosages are specified by Jim. They are listed from high to low and are specific to LSD, but the effects correlate to many psychedelics. Here's framing context from Jim: "These substances, unlike almost every other kind of medication, have very different effects at different dose levels. It is almost as if they were different substances."

Heroic dose: Ethnobotanist Terence McKenna coined the term "heroic dose," which is often equated to 5 or more grams of mushrooms or more than 400 mcg of LSD. James doesn't recommend this brute-force dosing, which McKenna described as "sufficient to flatten the most resistant ego." Jim feels that you don't remember anything, nor do you bring anything back, at this dose. "It's kind of like: You want to go swimming? How about going over Niagara Falls?"

400 mcg is where you have a transcendental or mystical experience. At this dose or higher, it is critical to have qualified supervision in the form of a guide. "Transcendental" here roughly means "the feeling or the awareness that you are connected not only to other people but to other things and to living systems." More on this later.

200 mcg can be used for psychotherapy, self-exploration, deep inner work, and healing.

100 mcg is useful for creative problem solving with non-personal matters (e.g., physics, biomechanics, or architecture). A number of Nobel Prize laureates in chemistry, biology, and elsewhere attribute breakthroughs to LSD.

Jim once worked on a study involving large companies and research institutes trying to solve incredibly difficult problems like new circuit board designs. Volunteers were given psychedelics, and 44 out of the 48 problems were "solved," meaning resulted in a patent, product, or publication. Jim attributes this to enhanced focus and pattern recognition. Low enough doses (i.e., 100 mcg of LSD or 200 mg of mescaline) can immensely increase the capacity to solve problems.

"We said, 'You may come to this study, and we'll give you the most creative day of your life. But you have to have a problem which obsesses you that you have been working on for a couple of months and that you've failed [to solve].' . . . We wanted them to have . . . an emotional 'money in the game.' [We gave] them psychedelics and [had them] relax with music and eye shades for a couple of hours. And then, right at the peak, we bring them out and say, 'You may work on your problem' . . . what was wonderful is nobody did any personal therapeutic work because that's not what they came for. And out of the 48 problems that people came in with, 44 had solutions."

50 mcg is considered a "concert dose" or "museum dose." Self-explanatory.

10 to 15 mcg is a "microdose." Described by Jim: "Everything is just a little better. You know at the end of a day when you say, 'Wow, that was a really good day'? That's what most people report on microdosing. They're a little bit nicer."

He elaborates: "What I'm finding is that microdoses of LSD or mushrooms may be very helpful for depression because **they make you feel better enough that you do something about what's wrong with your life.** We've made [depression] an illness. It may be the body's way of saying, 'You better deal with something, because it's making you really sad.'

"[A microdose of psychedelics is] actually a low enough dose that it could be called 'sub-perceptual,' which means you don't necessarily see any differences in the outside world. As one person said to me, 'The rocks don't glitter even a little, and the flowers don't turn and watch you.'"

Albert Hofmann, the inventor of LSD, considered microdosing the most neglected area of research. Hofmann microdosed LSD often for the last few decades of his life. He remained sharp until he died at 101. He would take it when he was walking among trees. In Jim's opinion, microdosing psychedelics does a far better job than a whole class of drugs we now call "cognitive enhancers," most of which are simply derivatives of speed.

Oddly, there are consistent reports of microdosing having a lag effect. I've experienced this myself, and it's the reason for Slim Berriss's Monday/Friday spacing of ibogaine. Many microdosers, including one executive who runs a large corporation with manufacturing in five countries, have said, "The second day is better."

WHICH USERS HAVE THE MOST DURABLE POSITIVE EFFECTS?

In short, it's those who experience a "transcendental experience." Remember that squirrelly term?

Jim describes this as "the feeling or the awareness that you are connected not only to other people, but to other things and living systems and to the air you breathe. We tend to think we're kind of encapsulated. . . . Obviously, the air I am breathing comes from all over the world, and some of it's a billion years old. Every 8 years, I get almost all new cells from something. Everything I eat is connected to me. Everyone I meet is connected to me. Right now you and I are sitting outside, and our feet our touching the ground. We're connected to the ground. **Now, that's all easy to say intellectually and even poetically. But when you actually experience that you're part of this larger system, one of the things that you become aware of is that your ego — your personal identity — is not that big a part of you.**

"What I learned was — and this is from my own personal experience in 1961 — 'Jim Fadiman' is a subset of me, and the *me* is very, very large and a lot smarter and knows a lot more than 'Jim Fadiman.'"

He saw a similar shift in subjects during his dissertation research, and they very often laughed during these realizations:

"In a very deep way, and it isn't the giggles of marijuana. **It's the laughter of 'how could I have forgotten who I really am?'** And then, much later in the day, when they're reintegrating and finding that they are surprisingly still in the same body they came in with . . . one person said very beautifully, **'I was back in the prison of all of the things that hold me back, but I could see that the door was locked from the inside.'"**

DON'T RUSH THE EXPERIENCE, DON'T CHEAPEN THE EXPERIENCE

"There's something called *Salvia [divinorum]*, and the wonderful thing about salvia is it has nothing to do chemically with anything else I've just talked about. . . . It's been used in Mexico historically for who knows how many thousands of years for divination, for finding out things. And, again, we seem to be able as Americans to take almost anything that is indigenous and screw it up in some way. So people smoke salvia and have a short, intense, sometimes meaningful experience. That isn't how it's [traditionally] used. It's chewed, which means it takes about an hour, and it comes on slowly. It's a totally different experience."

TF: Please note that *Salvia divinorum* is illegal in either case. The point is that mode of administration matters.

ON "SITTERS"

A "sitter" is someone who supervises a psychedelic experience, ensuring safety and comfort. Jim's book (*The Psychedelic Explorer's Guide*) offers comprehensive guidelines for this role, but in simple terms: "A good sitter is someone you trust. A great sitter is someone who loves you and you trust. A superlative sitter is someone who doesn't have any agenda of their own. They don't want you to see a certain thing. They don't want you to be a certain way. They don't want you to discover a certain thing." With or without psychedelics, sounds like good criteria for close friends, too.

ON THE IMPORTANCE OF "PRE" AND "POST" WORK

There's a saying in the psychedelic world: **"If you get the answer, you should hang up the phone."** In other words, when you get the message you need, you shouldn't keep asking (i.e., having more experiences), at least until you've done some homework assignments, or used the clarity gained to make meaningful changes. It's easy to use the medicine as a crutch and avoid doing your own work, as the compounds themselves help in the short term as antidepressants.

Compulsive users generally neglect critical preparation and post-session integration work. MDMA is a wonderful tool for releasing people from PTSD, for instance, but the success can usually be attributed, in large part, to preparing for the experience with a psychotherapist, having two guides (male and female), and spending a lot of time talking and integrating after the experience. There's no point in going to a motivational seminar if you're not going to take any next steps.

MARTIN POLANCO & DAN ENGLE

Martin Polanco, MD (TW: @Martin_Polanco7, CrossroadsIbogaine .com), is the founder and program director of Crossroads Treatment Center, based in Rosarito, Mexico. Crossroads specializes in helping patients conquer powerful addictions (such as heroin or cocaine) using the African hallucinogen ibogaine and 5-MeO-DMT, also referred to as "the God molecule."

Dan Engle, MD (TW: @drdanengle, drdanengle.com), is board-certified in psychiatry and neurology. He combines functional medicine with integrative psychiatry to enhance regenerative health and peak performance. His prior experience includes traumatic brain injury research and working in the Peruvian jungle with plant medicines such as ayahuasca.

In this profile, we discuss several psychedelics, including one legal option: flotation therapy. Ibogaine and 5-MeO-DMT are detailed at some length, as they're both used at Martin's clinic. Ibogaine is the only compound I've seen that can eliminate 90%+ of the physical withdrawal symptoms of heroin addiction in one fell swoop. It's also one of the few psychedelics that can kill you, so I cover it at the end.

Spirit animal: Martin = Gummy bear

✳ **What would you put on a billboard?**

DAN: "Be curious."

FLOTATION TANK AS "PSYCHEDELIC"

DAN: "I'm just about as excited about flotation therapy as I am about psychedelics, because not everybody is going to do a psychedelic. Maybe it's not in everybody's best interests to do it . . . but everybody can float. When prepped well and done consistently over time, it can still be an extraordinary 'psychedelic' arena. By this, I essentially mean coming back to a deeper connection with one's self."

TF: "Flotation therapy," in simple terms, is floating in a roughly 98.6°F hot tub with a lid over it. It's completely dark, there is no sound, and there are 800 to 1,200 pounds of Epsom salt in the water to make you float on the surface, feeling weightless. It can be thought of as a sensory-deprivation tank.

If you can't handle at least 60 minutes in a flotation tank, you aren't ready to have an unstoppable psychedelic experience. As one guide for the latter put it to me: "I can start the music, but I can't make it stop." In contrast, if you get twitchy during a float, you can step out. Use this environment as training. Lab-verified lucid dreaming (Google "Lucid Dreaming 101 Ferriss") is also useful for developing navigational skills for psychedelics, but lying in salt water requires less work.

When possible, I now try to float twice per week — Monday and Friday. After 2 weeks, I feel like I normally would after a month of daily meditating, even if I'm not meditating.

DAN: "[Floating in an isolation tank] is the first time that we've been without sensory experience, sensory environmental stimuli, since we were conceived. There is no sound, no sight, no temperature gradient, and no gravity. So all of the brain's searching and gating information from the environment is relaxed. Everything that was in the background — kind of 'behind the curtain' — can now be exposed. When done consistently over time, it's essentially like meditation on steroids. It starts to recalibrate the entire neuroendocrine system. People who are running in stress mode or sympathetic overdrive start to relax that over time, and you get this bleed-over effect into everyday life. It's not just what happens in the tank. It continues outside of the tank. You see heart rate normalize, hypertension normalize, cortisol normalize. Pain starts to re-solve. Metabolic issues start to resolve.

"Anxiety, insomnia, and mental chattering can be significantly improved in [2 to 3 times per week for a total of] anywhere between 3 and 7 sessions. For pain, it's normally 7 to 10 sessions. I recommend doing a 2-hour float if people are able."

TF: According to Dan, most people get exponentially more benefit from a sin-gle 2-hour session than 2 separate 1-hour sessions. Nonetheless, 2-hour floats still make me fidgety, so I routinely do 1-hour sessions.

Keeping it simple, Dan suggests you start with 2 to 3 floats inside of 1 month. "I've never had anybody come back and say 'Yeah, that didn't work.'"

AYAHUASCA OR "LA PURGA" (THE PURGE)

This Amazonian brew is one of Dan's specialties. The experience generally lasts 4 to 7 hours.

If you think of psilocybin, LSD, or peyote as different types of alcohol—say vodka, red wine, and Scotch—ayahuasca is more like a cocktail. This makes it hard to standardize. Just as in an Old Fashioned, there are core ingredients. In this case, they are the DMT-containing chacruna leaf and the ayahuasca vine itself, which contains an MAO inhibitor that makes the chacruna DMT orally bioavailable. Different *ayahuasqueros* (ayahuasca shamans) will then add their own ingredients to the brew, sometimes including powerful or even dangerous plants like toé (similar to the North American Datura plant, containing scopol-amine). No session is quite the same as any other.

For me, ayahuasca has been unique among psychedelics for many reasons.

In my second-ever session, for example, I had the scariest experience of my life. It involved uncontrolled grand mal seizures on a floor for 2 hours, among other things. I awoke to rug burns all over my face and hands, and I was un-tethered from reality for the next 48 hours. Thankfully I had hired someone to watch me 24/7 during and after the weekend. He was able to baby-sit and pre-vent insane ideas from becoming life-destroying actions. His repeated advice was "If it's really true today, it will still be true tomorrow."

I haven't had this extreme a reaction since, but it happened.

And such a response, while not typical, is also not *that* uncommon. You might wonder: Why would I ever use ayahuasca again after that? Here's why: Over subsequent weeks, I realized that some of most critical relationships in my life had been completely repaired. I saw things differently, reacted differently, and interacted differently, as if I had been reprogrammed. Those changes all persist to this day. So, there's a huge potential upside but equally huge potential downside if taken lightly or done with the wrong people.

I mention this cautionary tale because ayahuasca has become terribly trendy. It's THE thing to talk about at cocktail parties, and I shudder every time I hear something along the lines of "I'm going to my friend's place in Manhattan for an aya ceremony this Sunday night. She mail-ordered some brew from Hawaii, and we're doing it together. It's going to be amazing." There are now hundreds of new-age folks — out-there yoga instructors, didgeridoo players, whatever — who decide to "play shaman" based on reading a few books, watching a few YouTube videos, or having experienced a few ceremonies themselves. I consider this all psychological Russian roulette.

My suggestion is that you treat ayahuasca as if you are planning to have a brain tumor removed by a brain surgeon. Spiritually, this is effectively what you're attempting.

In such a case, you would spend months, if possible, researching all of the best doctors. You would treat it like a life-and-death decision because of what could go wrong if it were done incorrectly. From my direct experiences, I feel like ayahuasca warrants this level of caution, respect, preparation, and due diligence. Martin elaborates:

"That's why it's so critical to have preparation before the experience and then a period of integration afterward, because you are in this opened-up and receptive state and more suggestible. Whatever habits you incorporate in the weeks afterward can stick, and these can be good or bad."

DAN: "Ayahuasca is traditionally done in a group ceremony setting, but it's a very solo, inward journey. Typically, it's done in the dark, in the jungle. You go through deep, psychological healing, oftentimes pre-verbal healing around traumatic issues that [occurred] between birth and age 4. From a developmental psychological perspective, this is when most of the long-term personality traits are formed. You gain a witness perspective, the fear centers relax, the trauma is brought back up onto the screen of the mind . . . you oftentimes get this replay of very early things and can have a corrective experience. . . .

"Through that, I can [personally] see the network of interrelated factors and potentials. My mind starts to understand how things have affected me, how things are affecting the world, [and] potentially the next step for me to take in my journey."

TF: Ayahuasca is sometimes called *la purga* ("the purge"), because participants often experience uncontrolled vomiting or defecating. I've never experienced either, but all of my companions have at least vomited. I was concerned at one point that I wasn't "doing it right" or getting maximum benefit, and the shaman assured me that purging is not a good measure of how valuable the experience is. He had only purged twice in 10 years.

DAN: "It is very successful in helping people transition from chronic depression into what would be called *euthymia*, or normal mood. Many people don't even know what having a normal mood feels like; but optimism, faith, courage, strength, [and] personal empowerment are some of its qualities."

TF: Ayahuasca is classically described as very "visionary," or rich in visual hallucinations, though some people have more mental or kinesthetic experiences. I tend to go through it in three stages: visual (often overwhelming), mental (intellectually able to engage and see solutions or answers), then physical. More often than not, I will cycle through these three phases during each long *icaro*, or song, that is sung. For the best approximation, search for Jan Kounen's "Ayahuasca Visions" on YouTube.

5-MEO-DMT

Martin uses 5-MeO-DMT with his patients after treating them with ibogaine and iboga. DMT is sometimes referred to as the "spirit molecule," and its variant 5-MeO-DMT is called the "God molecule." 5-MeO-DMT is found in the venom of a desert toad and is vaporized and inhaled (not taken orally; it's toxic if ingested). It is a short 5- to 15-minute experience.

To put it in context, here is what the schedule might look like for a heroin addict at Martin's clinic:

Pre-care for several weeks: Improving diet and exercise, weaning off psychiatric meds, etc.

Monday of treatment week: Comprehensive medical tests in Mexico; heroin addicts are switched to morphine.

Wednesday night: IV of saline and electrolytes, then encapsulated ibogaine, dosed at 10 to 12 mg per kg of body weight. Patients are hooked up to continuous cardiac monitoring throughout. The IV catheter is kept in with a hep-lock, in case atropine needs to be administered for an abnormally slow heartbeat (bradycardia).

Thursday: Patients typically haven't slept, and this is nicknamed the "gray day." Addicts sometimes have residual withdrawal symptoms and feel as though they're not benefitting.

Friday: Patients begin to feel better and regain their feet. If any residual withdrawal symptoms persist, iboga (300 mg capsule, then more if needed), which contains ibogaine and other alkaloids, is used.

Saturday: 5-MeO-DMT administered.

Post-care: 2 to 3 weeks in San Diego (recommended but optional).

MARTIN: "DMT is found in ayahuasca, whereas the 5-MeO-DMT is naturally found in certain plants and in the venom of the Sonoran Desert toad (also known as the Colorado River toad), which lives in northern Mexico and southern Arizona. Its venom is thought to have been used ceremonially for hundreds, if not thousands, of years by Mexican indigenous cultures to induce states of mystical consciousness.

"What we like about this medicine, and what is particularly useful for drug addiction, is that it reliably occasions mystical experiences. In our patients, about 75% report experiencing an intense and profound sense of awe, divine presence, peace, joy, and bliss that transcends time and space. People often describe their 5-MeO experience as one of the peak transformational and spiritual moments of their entire lives.

"In the body, 5-MeO-DMT acts on the serotonin 1A and 2A receptor sites, which have been linked to mystical experiences in other psychedelics such as LSD and psilocybin. However, compared to classic psychedelics, 5-MeO appears to induce these experiences more consistently, and with greater potency and shorter duration. Interestingly, 5-MeO is also shown to have anti-inflammatory, immune-regulating, and pain-reducing effects because of its action at the sigma-1 receptor. Our patients often report a reduction or elimination of pain as a result of their experience. Frequently people will stretch or move their bodies during sessions to work out physical and emotional tension that they may not have been aware of.

"By incorporating 5-MeO-DMT into the treatment program, we can help patients who have had the ibogaine experience to feel a certain sense of release from the material that came up, as well as motivation and inspiration to move on with their life. Ibogaine can bring up a lot from the subconscious and people are overwhelmed after the experience. In a recent overview article of the research on using psychedelics to treat addiction, the depth of one's mystical experience was the greatest predictor of long-term success. When we added the 5-MeO-DMT to our ibogaine protocol, we saw better outcomes in our patients versus ibogaine alone."

TF: 5-MeO-DMT was not classified as a Schedule 1 substance in the U.S. until 2011, and its use is legal in Mexico.

DAN: "It's extraordinarily strong in its flavor and acts as a rocket ship back to God. . . . It does take you back to source consciousness."

MARTIN: "[Addicts] realize that they are divine beings, and when you have this realization that you're indestructible and infinite and divine, it's very hard to put a needle in your arm and continue using."

TF: I have used 5-MeO-DMT but prefer edible, longer-acting psychedelics. I don't worry much about 5-MeO addiction, but the rapid onset and short duration is closer in profile to substances I want to avoid (such as crack). I feel it's too user-friendly for my convenience-seeking personality. I like the fact that most edible whole-plant options make one slightly nauseous, have a 4- to 8-hour or longer effect, and if you consume too much, you will almost certainly vomit. I view these characteristics as built-in safety mechanisms. Different strokes for different folks.

IBOGA/IBOGAINE

Okay, now we'll cover the big gun.

MARTIN: "Iboga is an obscure psychedelic that doesn't have a long history of recreational use, because it is not a recreational experience. It is probably the least recreational psychedelic. . . . It's an African psychedelic that has been used for decades to treat opiate addiction and other types of substance-abuse disorders."

TF: "Iboga" refers to the plant, specifically a root bark, that has been taken

NOTE: Traditional ceremonial doses of ibogaine/iboga, while incredibly promising for eliminating opiate (e.g., heroin) addiction in record time, can also produce fatal cardiac effects in roughly 1 out of every 300 people. Even certain antibiotics interact with ibogaine/iboga and can cause arrhythmias.

For this reason, both Dan and Martin generally reserve its use for dire-straits addicts, who are likely—without a successful intervention—to die prematurely from drug use or related violence. Based on notes from non-addict friends who've done "full-ride" iboga and microdosing, microdosing twice weekly appears to provide at least 50% of the anxiolytic (anxiety-reducing) benefits with a tiny fraction of the risk.

as a rite of passage by the Bwiti followers in Gabon for centuries. Ibogaine is the primary alkaloid found in iboga. Both act as dissociatives. The effects are similar but not identical. The difference is akin to using white willow bark for inflammation versus its refined version, aspirin. Martin's clinic uses ibogaine to detox patients and iboga as a "booster," or supplementary medication, after the treatment.

Interestingly, ibogaine appears to cause hallucinations that are mediated via muscarinic cholinergic pathways involved in dreaming and memory, as well as through the kappa-opioid receptors (activated also by the plant *Salvia divinorum*), rather than via serotonin receptors.

MARTIN: "Who is a good candidate for ibogaine and who isn't? I get requests from people who just want to explore their psyche, or they have depression, or they want to deal with some childhood trauma. I often direct them toward ayahuasca, because I do think that ibogaine is the big gun and it is generally best used for [treatment of] addictions. That's not to say that people who don't have addictions don't derive benefit from it, but I do think that there are other modalities that they should explore first that are less risky."

DAN: "Just because something is effective doesn't mean somebody is ready for it. . . . Iboga is like Everest. It's climbing a huge mountain. Never going hiking and then starting with Everest is a bad idea.

"[It] is such an ego-focused medicine. It will ride the psyche relentlessly until a person has no choice but to essentially give up and give in to the experience. They can then surrender to the greater experience of becoming who they thought they could be, or who they were maybe scared to be, freed from the limitation of something like addiction. . . .

"Iboga is four to five orders of magnitude [superior to] anything in the general psychiatric rehab arena [for treating opiate addicts]. You have the same level of success with using MDMA-assisted therapy to treat chronic post-traumatic stress disorder (PTSD). That's why MDMA is going into Phase III trials. Psilocybin is similarly going into Phase III trials because you have such a high success rate with people going through [cancer-related] end-of-life transitions being relieved of anxiety, and really being able to walk through death with dignity and strength."

TF: Phase III trials are critically important for rescheduling psychedelics, which would make them prescribable by qualified physicians. As noted earlier, nearly all psychedelics are currently Schedule I drugs, defined by "high potential for abuse" and "no currently accepted medical treatment use in the U.S." These substances are largely non-addictive, so the abuse claim is unfounded, but this is difficult to prove in long-term human studies given current legal constraints. Therefore, the more efficient path to "prescription-legal" is demonstrating a clear medical application for conditions such as treatment-resistant depression or end-of-life anxiety in terminal cancer patients. Since quitting the investment game (see page 384), I've redirected much of my financial focus to this area.

Funny aside: During the 1972 presidential race, Hunter S. Thompson claimed that Democratic primary candidate Edmund Muskie was addicted to ibogaine. Hunter made the whole thing up but used it to spin the media into a tizzy.

THE IBOGA/IBOGAINE EXPERIENCE

The typical ibogaine experience is long-lasting—up to 36 hours total—and has three major phases. It tends to keep patients awake for several days. Martin explains:

First Phase

"The first [phase] is a visionary component, which can last anywhere from 3 to 12 hours, and these hallucinations are perceived almost like watching a movie of your life.

"It's a life review, and people report that in the back of their eyelids they have gigantic screens where they see images from their childhood. They see opportunities they missed, people they've hurt, and unfinished business that they need to resolve. I think being confronted with who they really are, and not being able to look away, can be difficult. Patients who are using opiates are generally trying to numb themselves. They don't want to think; they don't want to feel. Ibogaine really forces them to have that discussion. Look what you've done, look where you will end up if you continue using. So it is not a fun experience.

"Many cases of addiction are linked to post-traumatic stress disorder. This can also be resolved with ibogaine because it allows a person to go back to that traumatic event and experience it without any emotional pain. One is able to go back and let go of the experience, come to terms with the experience, or just re-contextualize the experience.

"Like Dr. Engle was saying, a lot of trauma that happens is pre-verbal. . . . The brain stores this as an emotional charge because there are no words associated with the experience. Ibogaine allows them to go back and see what happened, almost as if they were floating in the room as an observer. Because they're seeing this experience through the eyes of an adult, it allows them to put it in a different context.

"Other imagery that comes up during the ibogaine experience is related to the sentience or intelligence of plant life, the creation and the fate of the universe, and our own mortality. There are certain images that can be disturbing to patients. You do see spirits and images of dead people. In Africa, they say ibogaine is a 'controlled-death experience.' So you go into the land of the dead, and you're given information by your ancestors, which you can then take back into this world and apply to your life."

Second Phase

"The second phase is a phase of introspection and this can last up to 24 hours. Opiate withdrawal is pretty much gone [at this point], as well as the craving. Ibogaine has a very potent antidepressant effect, so people who take it feel an elevated mood for a period of time afterward.

"In terms of the differences between ibogaine and ayahuasca, I think that introspective life review is more pronounced with ibogaine, although only 70% of people have it. So a full 30% experience no visions at all. I don't know the statistics with ayahuasca, but it might be more reliably psychedelic in that regard than ibogaine."

Third Phase

"The third phase, which takes place after the clinical experience, is referred to as the 'temporary freedom' or the 'window of opportunity,' as noribogaine, a metabolite of ibogaine, continues to do its work for up to 3 months, making it easier for new patterns and habits to take effect. This is referred to as the 'integration phase,' where a person takes action to fuel the necessary positive changes that were revealed through the experience. It is important to take advantage of the learning and growth opportunities in this phase, and to develop habits that will help sustain self-control once noribogaine flushes out."

BIOCHEMICALLY, WHY IS IBOGAINE SO ODDLY EFFECTIVE?

"[Ibogaine isn't] just masking the withdrawal like a substitution drug would. For example, if somebody on heroin takes methadone, they won't have withdrawal for a period of time, but as soon as the methadone leaves the system, the withdrawal comes back. This is not something that happens on ibogaine. You take ibogaine, and the withdrawal is gone — 90% of the withdrawal is completely gone. That's telling us that the ibogaine is actually changing the receptor to the way it was before the person started using. It's actually restructuring and healing it. Ibogaine appears to affect almost every major class of neurotransmitter, primarily via opioid, NMDA, serotonin, sigma, and nicotinic receptors. A prominent ibogaine researcher, Dr. Kenneth Alper [of New York University School of Medicine], has stated in presentations that certain aspects of ibogaine defy traditional paradigms in pharmacology."

TF: I have noticed that microdosing seemed to increase my happiness "set point" by 5 to 10%, to peg a number on my subjective experience. This persists for several days after consumption. Preliminarily, the effect appears to relate to upregulation of mu-opioid receptors. From one study: ". . . in vivo evidence has been provided for the possible interaction of ibogaine with μ-opioid receptor following its metabolism to noribogaine."*

---

*Bhargava, Hemendra N., Ying-Jun Cao, and Guo-Min Zhao. "Effects of ibogaine and noribogaine on the antinociceptive action of μ-, δ-and κ-opioid receptor agonists in mice." *Brain research* 752, no. 1 (1997): 234–238.

MARTIN: "[In treating chemical dependency] it's opiate-specific. We have seen some benefits for certain psychiatric medications, but not for benzodiazepine or alcohol withdrawal. These two withdrawals are actually dangerous. When somebody gets the shakes, it's DT (delirium tremens) and that can be deadly. So, it's a very delicate process and somebody who's physically addicted to alcohol should not take ibogaine. They need to detox first, and then they can take ibogaine for the psychological and the anti-addictive benefits."

HOLD THE GOLD — KEEP IT CLOSE TO YOUR CHEST

Following powerful healing experiences with psychedelics, Dan's strong recommendation is **"Hold the gold."** He explains:

"Keep that experience really close and private. When it feels right to share, share it with people who are very sensitive to the fact that you just went on a strong life-altering journey, and who are going to be supportive of that.

"[Pick people who are] not going to ridicule it or judge it or persecute it, because all of that flavors your primary experience. So many people, when they have a big experience, want to go share it, and sometimes the response they get isn't always supportive. That alters the healing that they just received."

RESOURCES

Heffter Research Institute (heffter.org): I've interacted most with this organization. Founded and run primarily by PhDs and MDs, Heffter facilitates cutting-edge research at universities like Johns Hopkins, NYU, University of Zurich, and others.

MAPS (maps.org): Founded in 1986, the Multidisciplinary Association for Psychedelic Studies (MAPS) is a 501(c)(3) non-profit research and educational organization that develops medical, legal, and cultural contexts for people to benefit from the careful uses of psychedelics and marijuana.

ICEERS (iceers.org): Based in Spain, the International Center for Ethnobotanical Education, Research, and Service has the primary goal of bridging the ethnobotanical knowledge of indigenous cultures (primarily iboga and ayahuasca) with Western science and therapeutic practice.

GITA (ibogainealliance.org): The Global Ibogaine Therapy Alliance is an international group of ibogaine providers, researchers, and advocates. They recently published the first established standard of care guidelines for ibogaine treatment.

RELATED AND RECOMMENDED BOOKS

Singing to the Plants: A Guide to Mestizo Shamanism in the Upper Amazon by Stephan V. Beyer. This book did not come up in the podcast, but it is the most comprehensive book related to ayahuasca that I've found.

The Cosmic Serpent by Jeremy Narby

Autobiography of a Yogi by Paramahansa Yogananda. This was one of the more impactful books that Dan read while living in the jungle. Steve Jobs had this book passed out to attendees at his funeral.

The Journey Home: Autobiography of an American Swami by Radhanath Swami

Ibogaine Explained by Peter Frank

Tryptamine Palace: 5-MeO-DMT and the Sonoran Desert Toad by James Oroc. Martin considers this a fantastic read because it looks at the 5-MeO-DMT experience from a Buddhist and Hindu perspective.

The Toad and the Jaguar by Ralph Metzner. A quick read on 5-MeO-DMT from a pioneer in psychedelic therapy and research.

KELLY STARRETT

Dr. Kelly Starrett (TW/IG: @MOBILITYWOD, MOBILITYWOD.COM) is one of my favorite performance coaches. He has trained CrossFit athletes for more than 150,000 hours and 11 years at San Francisco CrossFit, which he founded with his wife in 2005. It is one of the first 50 CrossFit affiliates, out of a current 10,000+, in the world. Kelly's clients include Olympic gold medalists, Tour de France cyclists, world record holders in Olympic lifting and powerlifting, CrossFit Games medalists, professional ballet dancers, and elite military personnel. He is a treasure trove of one-liners and the author of the *New York Times* bestseller *Becoming a Supple Leopard.*

Spirit animal: Lion with three lotuses

BEHIND THE SCENES

» Just before recording our second podcast together, Kelly offered me a cup of coffee. Once I'd downed it, he showed me the bottle: It was a cold brew concentrate that you're supposed to dilute. I'd just consumed about five cups of coffee. Kelly calls it his "cup of fear." We hit RECORD and I immediately started to sweat like I was being chased by hyenas.

» Kelly has done standing backflips at a lean 230 pounds. At the same weight, he completed an ultra-marathon with no training runs longer than 5K, courtesy of Brian MacKenzie (page 92). Kelly has also power cleaned 365 pounds, but he has a bum wrist and catches the weight with one arm bent across his chest like a salute.

» He drinks an incredible amount of water, and he drops a small pinch of salt in his water when he can. Why? The bigger risk isn't dehydration but hyponatremia, or dangerously low concentrations of sodium in the blood. From a 2005 study by CSD Almond et al in the *New England Journal of Medicine*: "Hyponatremia has emerged as an important cause of race-related death and life-threatening illness among marathon runners."[*]

» Kelly is a legitimate fantasy and sci-fi nerd. He knows *Dune* by Frank Herbert and *The Diamond Age* by Neal Stephenson inside and out. For whatever reasons, many men in this book like precisely these two fiction books. Kelly has daughters and texted me about the latter book, which follows a young female protagonist: "How do you raise girls that are of the system but crush the system while rebuilding a better one?"

---

[*]Almond, Christopher SD, Andrew Y. Shin, Elizabeth B. Fortescue, Rebekah C. Mannix, David Wypij, Bryce A. Binstadt, Christine N. Duncan et al. "Hyponatremia among runners in the Boston Marathon." *New England Journal of Medicine* 352, no. 15 (2005): 1550–1556.

BONER OR NO BONER?

> "Men, if you wake up and you don't have a boner, there's
> a problem. Yes or no? One or zero? Boner, no boner?"

TF: "Quantified self" tracking doesn't need to be complicated. It's easy to miss the flashing red signal in front of your face while chasing the cutting edge of blood testing, genomics, etc. For men, the "boner or no boner" test is a simple but excellent indicator of sleep quality, hormonal health (GH, FSH, testosterone), circadian rhythm timing, and more.

THE CAMPFIRE SQUAT TEST

"If you can't squat all the way down to the ground with your feet and knees together, then you are missing full hip and ankle range of motion. This is the mechanism causing your hip impingement, plantar fasciitis, torn Achilles, pulled calf, etc. That is the fucking problem, and you should be obsessing about [fixing] this."

> "The most dangerous sport to middle-aged men is
> a track workout [because the body is working with
> high force production at unfamiliar (end) ranges of
> motion]."

ON THE OVERHEAD SQUAT

"[Greg] Glassman [the founder of CrossFit] valued it as one of the most important capacities. In fact, one of the earliest, best CrossFit workouts—I think it's called 'Nancy'—is run 400 meters, and then overhead squat 95 pounds 15 times. So innocuous, right? Then [repeat that sequence] 5 times. What you're going to see really quickly is, everyone can fake it for 3. But then, as you start to fatigue, or your positions aren't robust, you bounce off the tent. You no longer have access to compensation. The world gets really small, and then you really start suffering. . . .

"All we're doing when we say 'overhead squat' is I'm saying: 'Show me can squat with your torso upright.' And that looks a lot like sport, doesn't it? If you have to lean forward really far to do that, then it says you have incomplete hip and ankle function and you don't know how to create stability in your trunk."

TF: Doing light-weight overhead squats with a narrow stance, in combination with Cossack squats (page 87), for 3 months is what helped me get 99% toward passing the "campfire test" above. My left ankle is still sadly bone on bone.

"IF YOU CAN'T BREATHE, YOU DON'T KNOW THY POSITION."

In other words, if you can't breathe in a given position, you haven't mastered it.

THE TOP MOBILIZATIONS TO DO EVERY DAY

"Here are a few things you should probably do every day:

1. Everyone can benefit from something that looks like the cow stretch (also sometimes called "cat-camel" in yoga classes). It's a low-level static stretch that gets you into this extension pattern, and out of the other pattern of sitting in the rounded flexion position.

2. Spend as much time in a lunge as you can. [**TF:** One simple way to check this box prior to workouts is Eric Cressey's "walking Spiderman" exercise. I touch my inside elbow to the ground before switching sides. This is also a game-changer for hip flexibility in AcroYoga.]

3. 'Smash' your gut (i.e., roll on it) for downregulation before bed with a medicine ball. [**TF:** This really works as a sleep aid. My favorite tool was actually designed by Kelly, the MobilityWOD Supernova (120 mm). Amelia Boone (page 2) always travels with one.]

4. Internal shoulder rotation is so crucial. Doing the Burgener warmup will help show you if you have full internal rotation of your shoulder.

All of these things have to be normal."

"THROWING COMPRESSION SOCKS ON [POST-WORKOUT] IS A GAME-CHANGING EXPERIENCE."
Kelly currently like SKINS brand.

SLEEP HYGIENE

Dark means DARK. "They've done studies where they shine a laser on the back of someone's knee, and people pick it up. It's light. You cannot have your phone in your room. You cannot have a TV in your room. It needs to be black, black as night."

Soft is the solution for bedding. "Today's modern human needs to sleep on a soft mattress. Ideally, you would be sleeping in a hammock. You should be waking up in the morning feeling amazing without having to loosen up your lower back. Most athletes and people are extension-sensitive because of excessive sitting and extension-biased training (e.g., running, jumping, squatting). Sleeping on a hard bed actually puts you into extension, which is the exact opposite of what you want if you're extension-sensitive. Yes, you'd ideally be able to sleep on the floor and wake up feeling great, but we are not those people anymore due to excess sitting and inactivity.

Kelly's Mattress Checklist

» The softest mattress you can get your hands on is ideal, but avoid those made solely of memory foam, as it locks you into extension.

» Lie on a bed at a mattress store for 5 minutes. If you have to cross your feet, your bed is too hard. [**TF:** Kelly found a Stearns and Foster model works well for him.]

» If you need to put a pillow under your legs to put you into flexion, then you need a softer bed. You should also focus on opening up hip extension.

PULSE OXIMETER GO/NO-GO

Kelly uses Restwise software alongside pulse oximeters (for measuring blood oxygen saturation) in the morning to determine whether his athletes should exercise or not. Their technology answers the question (and provides the clever tagline) "Am I training too hard or not hard enough?" The company claims 62 world championships won by athletes using the system. There are many subtleties to the system, but here a basic observation: If your pulse ox reading is 1 to 2 points lower than normal, it can indicate lung inflammation and the onset of a cold. It's best to postpone training in such cases.

GO-TO MULTIVITAMIN

The whole-food based Nutriforce WODPak (Nutriforce Sports).

ONE TACTIC FOR CHRONIC PAIN — USE A CLOSE COUSIN OF THE MOVEMENT THAT INJURED YOU

"Movement and pain get mapped. If you experience pain during a given movement for a month, for instance, it's a chronic pain condition. Your brain starts to map the pain pathway with the movement motor pathway and those become conjoined. The brain starts to remember the movement that created pain (got you injured), and even if there is no trauma, every time you move that particular way, you still get the pain sensation. So, one of the ways that we're able to help people get out of chronic pain is to give them a new motor program (e.g., don't squat with your knees in)."

GO "ZERO DROP" FOR YOUR KIDS

Get your kids (and yourself) flat "zero drop" shoes, where the toes and heel are an equal distance from the ground. I wear Vans for this reason, my favorite model being Vans Classic Slip-On skate shoe (unisex, gum sole) in black. These can be used for hiking in a pinch, or worn to a business meeting when traveling light. Kelly elaborates on the rationale of zero drop: "Don't systematically shorten your kids' heel cords (Achilles) with bad shoes. It results in crappy ankle range of motion in the future. Get your kids Vans, Chuck Taylors, or similar shoes. Have them in flat shoes or barefoot as much as possible."

"When you make it, the job gets harder."

PAUL LEVESQUE (TRIPLE H)

Paul Levesque, more popularly known as Triple H (TW/FB/IG: @TRIPLEH), is a 14-time world champion in World Wrestling Entertainment (WWE). He is also the Executive Vice President of talent, live events, and creative at the WWE.

Spirit animal: Lion

BEHIND THE SCENES

Paul has three kids, and business and family duties run late. He typically trains in the gym between 10 p.m. and 1 a.m. with Joe DeFranco, who appeared in *The 4-Hour Body* in the "Hacking the NFL Combine" section. Paul wakes up at ~6 a.m. and starts it all over again. One of his common warmup movements is an unweighted version of Cossack squats (page 87).

> "Kids don't do what you say. They do what they see.
> How you live your life is their example."

THE KETO "FRAPPUCCINO"

He often works with bodybuilder Dave "Jumbo" Palumbo on diet in preparation for WrestleMania, WWE's largest event of the year (more than 100,000 live attendees in 2016). Dave has Paul follow the ketogenic diet, and Paul has developed a healthy "frappuccino" that suits his needs:

"I use [Palumbo's] protein powder, by Species Nutrition. Every morning, I roll downstairs and: 2 scoops of whey protein [Isolyze], ice, a bunch of powdered Starbucks coffee, some macadamia nut oil, and I make a shake. That's the start."

OVERCOMING JET LAG

During his peak travel period, Paul traveled 260+ days per year, performing in a different city each night. Here is one of his rules:

"When I landed, I would check into the hotel. The second we checked in, I'd ask them: 'Is the gym open? Can I go train?' Even if it was to get on a bike and ride for 15 minutes to reset things. I learned early that it seemed any time I did that, I didn't get jet lag."

TF: This absolutely seems to work, even if done at 1 a.m. and for 3 to 5 minutes. I don't know the physiological mechanism, but I use it.

IS THAT A DREAM OR A GOAL?

"[Evander Holyfield] said that his coach at one point told him, something like his very first day, 'You could be the next Muhammad Ali. Do you wanna do that?' Evander said he had to ask his mom. He went home, he came back and said, 'I wanna do that.' The coach said, 'Okay. Is that a dream or a goal? Because there's a difference.'

"I'd never heard it said that way, but it stuck with me. So much so that I've said it to my kid now: 'Is that a dream, or a goal? Because a dream is something you fantasize about that will probably never happen. A goal is something you set a plan for, work toward, and achieve. I always looked at my stuff that way. The people who were successful models to me were people who had structured goals and then put a plan in place to get to those things. I think that's what impressed me about Arnold [Schwarzenegger]. It's what impressed me about my father-in-law [Vince McMahon].'"

WORRYING ABOUT IT NOW ISN'T GOING TO CHANGE A DAMN THING

"I'm friends with Floyd Mayweather, and I was walking him to the ring one time, I think when he fought Marquez. I wanted to watch some of the undercard, and we got there early. Then his guys came and got me and said, 'Floyd just wanted to say hi before he starts getting ready, chat with you for a few minutes.' So Steph — my wife — and I went backstage, we get in his locker room, and he's lying down on the couch watching a basketball game. He said, 'Hi, have a seat.' We're talking a little bit, but I'm trying to be ultra-respectful of him. He's about to go into this massive fight.

"The second there's a lull in the conversation, I say, 'All right, man. We're gonna get outta your hair and head back, and we'll come back here when it's time for us to get ready for your deal.' And he's like, 'Man, you don't gotta take off. You can sit down. I'm enjoying the conversation.' He's completely relaxed.

"So at another lull in the conversation, I say, 'We're gonna run, Floyd. I don't wanna be in your way,' and he says, 'Hunter, I'm telling you: I'm just chilling, watching the game.' I said, 'You're not wound up about this at all?' and he goes, 'Why would I be wound up? I'm either ready or I'm not. Worrying about it right now ain't gonna change a damn thing. Right? Whatever's gonna happen is gonna happen. I've either done everything I can to be ready for this, or I haven't.'"

TF: Whitney Cummings (page 477) told me something similar, on big standup specials: "My work isn't done tonight. My work was done 3 months ago, and I just have to show up."

ONE LESSON FROM HIS EARLY MENTOR, KILLER KOWALSKI

"There are a lot of things that he said to me then that I find myself telling the young guys now. . . . For example, if you don't do something well, don't do it unless you want to spend the time to improve it. Still, to this day, I see a lot of guys do stuff in the ring and think, 'He doesn't do that well, but he does it all the time.' You shouldn't do that."

TF: This led me to ask myself, usually during my quarterly 80/20 reviews of stress points, etc., "What am I continuing to do myself that I'm not good at?" Improve it, eliminate it, or delegate it.

"I've learned an important trick: To develop foresight, you need to practice hindsight.**"**

"The opposite of play isn't work. It's depression.**"**

JANE McGONIGAL

Jane McGonigal, PhD (TW: @AVANTGAME, JANEMCGONIGAL.COM), is a research affiliate at the Institute for the Future and the author of the *New York Times* bestseller *Reality Is Broken: Why Games Make Us Better and How They Can Change the World*. Her work has been featured in *The Economist, Wired*, and the *New York Times*. She has been called one of the "Top Ten Innovators to Watch" by *BusinessWeek* and one of the "100 Most Creative People in Business" by *Fast Company*. Her TED talks on games have been viewed more than 10 million times.

Spirit animal: Coconut octopus

TETRIS AS THERAPY

Have trouble getting to sleep? Try 10 minutes of Tetris. Recent research has demonstrated that Tetris — or Candy Crush Saga or Bejeweled — can help over-write negative visualization, which has applications for addiction (such as over-eating), preventing PTSD, and, in my case, onset insomnia. As Jane explains, due to the visually intensive, problem-solving characteristics of these games:

"You see visual flashbacks [e.g., the blocks falling or the pieces swapping]. They occupy the visual processing center of your brain so that you cannot imagine the thing that you're craving [or obsessing over, which are also highly visual]. This effect can last 3 or 4 hours. It also turns out that if you play Tetris after witnessing a traumatic event [ideally within 6 hours, but it's been demon-strated at 24 hours], it prevents flashbacks and lowers symptoms of post-traumatic stress disorder."

LITTLE-KNOWN FACT

I've interviewed two people who have identical twins: Jane McGonigal and Caroline Paul (page 459). Both have experienced real-time "spooky action at a distance": feeling or perceiving what their twin is experiencing.

* **Recommended documentaries**
  G4M3RS: A Documentary (can be found for free on YouTube)
  The King of Kong
  TF: The latter is also one of Kevin Kelly's (page 470) favorite documenta-ries of all time.

* **Most-gifted or recommended books**
  Finite and Infinite Games by James Carse
  Suffering Is Optional by Cheri Huber
  TF: Cheri also has a podcast, *Open Air*.

* **Best recent purchase of under $100?**
  BabyBjörn baby carrier.

* Do you have any quotes that you live your life by or think of often?

"'Any useful statement about the future should at first seem ridiculous' by Jim Dator. Also, 'When it comes to the future, it's far more important to be imaginative than to be right' by Alvin Toffler. Both are famous futurists. These quotes remind me that world-changing ideas will seem absurd to most people, and that the most useful work I can be doing is to push the envelope of what is considered possible. If what I'm doing sounds reasonable to most people, then I'm not working in a space that is creative and innovative enough!"

* What is something you believe that other people think is crazy?

"That you should never publicly criticize anyone or anything unless it is a matter of morals or ethics. Anything negative you say could at the very least ruin someone's day, or worse, break someone's heart, or simply change someone from being a future ally of yours to someone who will never forget that you were unkind or unfairly critical. It's so common today to complain or criticize others' work on social media, or dogpile on someone for a perceived offense. I won't do it. It's not my job to be the world's critic, and I'd rather not rule out any future allies."

ADAM GAZZALEY

Dr. Adam Gazzaley (FB/TW: @ADAMGAZZ, NEUROSCAPE.UCSF.EDU) earned his MD and a PhD in Neuroscience at the Mount Sinai School of Medicine in New York, then did postdoctoral training in cognitive neuroscience at UC Berkeley. He is now the director of the Gazzaley Lab at UC San Francisco, a cognitive neuroscience laboratory.

Dr. Gazzaley is co-founder and chief science advisor of Akili Interactive, a company developing therapeutic video games, and is also a cofounder and chief scientist of JAZZ Venture Partners, a venture capital firm investing in experiential technology to improve human performance. Additionally, he is a scientific advisor to more than a dozen technology companies, including Apple, GE, Magic Leap, and Nielsen.

Spirit animal: Silver fox

BEHIND THE SCENES

Adam has a bet over virtual reality with Kevin Rose (page 340). Adam is bullish and Kevin is bearish. The prize: a bottle of 25-year-old Suntory Hibiki whisky, which you have to fly to Japan to track down. They'd go and drink it together, so, as Kevin put it, it's a win-win bet.

HUMANS USE ONLY 10% OF THEIR BRAINS? NOT QUITE . . .

"The most complex structure in the entire universe doesn't have just a vacant parking lot waiting for someone to drive in and start building. It's all used all the time, and in complex ways that we don't always understand."

HOW HE HIRES FOR COVETED SPOTS IN HIS LAB

"I don't really have a tight methodology for how I do that. A lot of it is that connection you get with someone when they're talking about what they do, what excites them. That's usually where I start: **'What do you think about that really gets you excited?'** Because I'm more interested in what drives someone and motivates them and makes them want to get out of bed in the morning than a list of classic résumé check-boxes."

ALL WORK AND NO PLAY MAKES JACK A DULL BOY

Since 2008, Adam has hosted a party for diverse friends of his (usually 40 to 80 people) the first Friday of every month, called First Friday. He has vetted every type of alcohol imaginable for these events, and his current favorite is rye whiskey. His recommendation in our conversation was **Whistle Pig rye**.

"Ryes are an interesting whiskey because they really were the dominant form of American whiskey pre-Prohibition, because the industry was more northern — Pennsylvania, Vermont, New York, etc. — where rye did really well. And then, with Prohibition and the move south with corn, bourbon exploded, which is still, by far, dominant. But rye is coming back, and I love it."

✳ **Favorite documentary**

Carl Sagan's *Cosmos* series inspired Adam to become a scientist, which is true for many of the top-tier scientists I've met and interviewed. [**TF:** Neil deGrasse Tyson has a revised version of *Cosmos* that is also spectacular.]

"It was a really powerful, friendly way of being introduced to the complexities and wonders that were gripping to me as a kid. I watched it with my dad. It was great bonding for us. The way [Sagan] delivered it was just captivating, and it was really what sealed the deal for me that I wanted to be a scientist."

* Advice to your 30-year-old self?

"I would say to have no fear. I mean, you've got one chance here to do amazing things, and being afraid of being wrong or making a mistake or fumbling is just not how you do something of impact. You just have to be fearless."

As context, Adam said the following earlier in our conversation: "I want to do fundamental breakthroughs, if possible. If you have that mindset, if that's how you challenge yourself, that that's what you want to do with your life, with your small amount of time that you have here to make a difference, then **the only way to do it is to do the type of research that other people would think of as risky or even foolhardy. That's just part of the game.**"

5 TOOLS FOR FASTER AND BETTER SLEEP

As a former lifelong insomniac, I've tried everything to fall asleep faster and remain asleep longer.

Here are five tricks that work. I deliberately omitted melatonin and prescription medications, which I don't use unless adjusting to large time zone differences. I use the following in the order listed, starting 60 to 90 minutes before bed. Omit what you don't like and try what you do.

(Optional) If I Have a Partner with Me, Acro Basing

I'll put them in Folded Leaf and base them for a few minutes (detailed on page 55). After a day of sitting, this will push the head of my femur back to where it should be in the hip. This isn't undone by the next step.

Decompress the Spine

I learned daily decompression from Jerzy Gregorek, a 60-something-year-old emigré from Poland and world record holder in Olympic weight lifting. He also wrote *The Happy Body*, which contains the morning mobility work that both Naval Ravikant (page 546, who introduced us) and I do on a near-daily basis. Jerzy considers hanging upside down mandatory after load-bearing training sessions. Keep in mind that Jerzy, at around 135 pounds body weight, can still throw hundreds of pounds overhead and land in a perfect ass-to-heels snatch position. Take off a little weight, and he can do the same on a wobble board

(Indo Board). He's unapologetically and refreshingly no-bullshit. Before my first training session with him, we sat down to have tea (he only drinks Mariage Frères Marco Polo black tea) and discuss goals. Midway through, he narrowed his eyes and looked me over. He reached across the table, pinched my tit, and announced, "You're too fat." My kinda guy.

Below are three options, listed in *increasing* order of safety. My protocol for any of them is 2 to 3 sets of 5 to 7 seconds and no more:

1. **Teeter EZ-Up Gravity Boots:** This is my default and I often hold onto weights (20 to 50 pounds) to increase traction, but gravity boots can be fatal if misused, as you'll fall on your neck. Do us all a favor and don't die. Definitely skip this if you can't easily do a strict pull-up or touch your toes with straight legs.

2. **Inversion table:** I don't use one myself, but several Special Operations friends swear by daily use. These are advertised on infomercials and are infinitely less likely to kill you than gravity boots.

3. **The Lynx Portable Back Stretcher or Teeter P3 Back Stretcher:** This is a portable gadget roughly the size of a large camera tripod. I use this several times a week, when it's too much hassle (after a late dinner) or risk (after booze) to hang upside down in gravity boots. It allows you to lock in your ankles, lie down, and use a dip-like movement to unlock lower back tightness. This is the fastest of the three options, but it doesn't allow you to relax your upper (thoracic/cervical) back. If you have a human with you, the "Leg Love" on page 56 is a great substitute.

ChiliPad

This was first introduced to me by Kelly Starrett (page 122) and Rick Rubin (page 502). Rick and I both set it to the coldest temperature possible about 1 hour prior to bed.

Let's paint a familiar scene. A man and a woman are sleeping in bed under the same set of sheets and blankets. The woman's temperature is running at roughly 700°F, giving off the heat of a pizza oven. The guy gets sweaty and kicks one leg out and on top of the sheets. Then he gets cold 10 minutes later and puts the leg underneath, repeating this cycle ad nauseam. He might even yank the covers like a child, upsetting the woman. It's a huge headache for everybody. Sleep temperature is highly individualized.

The ChiliPad allows you to put an extremely thin—almost imperceptibly thin—sheet underneath your normal sheets that circulates water through a bedside contraption at a very precise temperature of your choosing. There are versions with two zones, so two people side by side can choose different numbers. Maybe your magic sleeping temperature is 55°F. Or 61°F, or 75°F? If you're cold, you can increase the temperature of the ChiliPad underneath you instead of throwing a thick blanket on top that's going to make your partner sweat to death. It can modulate between 55 and 110°F. Experiment and find your silver bullet.

Several of my close friends in Silicon Valley sheepishly admitted that, of all the advice I've ever given in my books and podcasts, the ChiliPad had the biggest impact on their quality of life. Several others have said the same about honey + ACV, described next.

Honey + Apple Cider Vinegar or Yogi Soothing Caramel Bedtime Tea or California Poppy Extract

Your mileage may vary, but usually at least one of these will work.

Honey + ACV: My go-to tranquilizer beverage is simple: 2 tablespoons of apple cider vinegar (I use Bragg brand) and 1 tablespoon honey, stirred into 1 cup of hot water. This was taught to me by the late and great Seth Roberts, PhD. Some of his readers also noticed large and immediate strength improvements in exercise after a few days of using this pre-bed cocktail.

Yogi Soothing Caramel Bedtime Tea: If you're trying to avoid sugar (honey), this is an alternative. The packaging of this tea is targeted toward women to a comical degree. I recall dismissing it when an ex-girlfriend first offered me some, thinking it was for menstrual cramps. A few nights later, little Timmy found himself alone craving a hot beverage with flavor. I grabbed the caramel, let it brew for 5 minutes, and polished it off. 10 minutes later, I start getting wobbly, and then I felt like Leonardo DiCaprio in the pay phone scene from *The Wolf of Wall Street*. In the most awkward fashion possible, I dragged my ass to the bedroom and fell asleep. It was around 9 p.m. Note: This tea appears to affect only 30% of my readers this way.

California Poppy Extract: If both honey + ACV and Yogi Bedtime Tea fail, try plan C: a few drops of California poppy extract in warm water. Yogi Bedtime Tea does contain California poppy extract, but taking it directly allows you to increase the dose.

Visual Overwriting

"Visual overwriting" is what I do right before bed to crowd out anything replaying or looping in my mind that will inhibit sleep (e.g., email, to-do lists, an argument, "I should have said . . ."). Here are two specific tools that I've found effective:

10 minutes of Tetris before bed: This recommendation is from Jane McGonigal, PhD (page 132). The free version works fine.

OR

Short and uplifting episodic television: I'll offer just one recommendation here: *Escape to River Cottage*, Season One. I've watched this series multiple times. If you've ever fantasized about saying "Fuck it," quitting your job, and going back to the land, buy this as a present for yourself. If you've ever dreamed of getting out of the city and moving to Montana or God-knows-where rural Utopia, procuring your own food and so on, then this is your Scooby snack. It's endearingly retro, like a warm quilt from Mom, and host/chef Hugh Fearnley-Whittingstall will make you want to grow tomatoes, even if you hate tomatoes. And catch eels, too. Don't forget the eels.

Into the Darkness

Sleep Master sleep mask and Mack's Pillow Soft Silicone Putty (ear plugs): The Sleep Master sleep mask — great product, terrible name. I've tried dozens of sleep masks, and this is my favorite. It was introduced to me by Jeffrey Zurofsky, who was an integral piece of *The 4-Hour Chef*, where he appeared as "JZ." Some of you may recall our "food marathon," which involved 26.2 dishes in 26 different locations in Manhattan in less than 24 hours. But I digress . . . The most important feature of this mask is that it goes *over* your ears, not on top of them. This may seem minor, but it's a huge design improvement: It quiets things down, it doesn't irritate your ears, and it doesn't move around. Furthermore, it uses Velcro instead of elastic to secure the contraption to your head.

Mack's Silicone Putty can be used for blocking out snores, water (for swimming), or just about anything irritating. Comfortable even for side sleepers, they're soft on your ears, hard on noise.

Marpac Dohm DS "sound conditioner" white noise machine: If earplugs bother you — and they occasionally bother me — use a Marpac Dohm DS dual-speed sound conditioner white noise machine. This was introduced to me by readers, and it tunes out everything from traffic (why I bought it) to loud neighbors, leaky faucets, and fidgety dogs. It currently has nearly 10,000 reviews on Amazon and ~75% are 5 stars. If you want to MacGyver it, a cheap fan (needs to be loud-ish) pointing away from you can get close.

5 MORNING RITUALS THAT HELP ME WIN THE DAY

And then . . . you wake up. Now what?

After asking 100+ interviewees about morning routines, I've tested a lot and figured out what works for me.

Here are five things that I attempt to do every morning. Realistically, if I hit three out of five, I consider myself having won the morning. And if you win the morning, you win the day. I'm probably not the first person to say this, but it's how I frame the importance of the first 60 to 90 minutes of the day. They facilitate or handicap the next 12+ hours. I've deliberately set a low bar for "win."

These will probably seem like small things, but just remember: The small things are the big things.

#1 — Make Your Bed (<3 minutes)

In 2011 in Toronto, I chanced upon a former monk named Dandapani (Dandapani.org) at an event called Mastermind Talks. I was going through a very scattered period in my life and felt like my energy was traveling a millimeter outward in a million directions. For grounding, he convinced me to start making my bed.

If a monk with three dots on his forehead is too much for you, I would say first: Open your mind, you savage. Second, I would quote legendary Naval Admiral William McRaven, who has commanded at every level within the Special Operations community, including acting as head of Joint Special Operations

Command (JSOC) during the Osama bin Laden raid. From his University of Texas at Austin commencement speech:

"If you make your bed every morning, you will have accomplished the first task of the day. It will give you a small sense of pride, and it will encourage you to do another task and another and another. By the end of the day, that one task completed will have turned into many tasks completed. Making your bed will also reinforce the fact that little things in life matter."

What is "making your bed" to me? I use the sweep-it-under-the-rug approach. The goal is visual tidiness, not Four Seasons. I don't tuck in the sheets. I have a large blanket or duvet, and I'll use that to cover the sheets, smoothing it out. Then, I place the pillows symmetrically underneath or on top of the blanket, and I'm done. That's it. It's very simple. If you work from home, this serves double duty, especially if you work in or near your bedroom. If you see an external distraction (speaking personally), you end up creating an internally distracted state. Noah Kagan (page 325) and I "make" our beds even when at hotels.

Life is also unpredictable. There are many unexpected problems that will pop up, and I've found that two things help me sail choppy water during the day. Both are done in the morning: A) read a few pages of stoicism, like Marcus Aurelius's *Meditations*, and B) control at least a few things you can control. I'll elaborate.

First, for A, here is one Marcus Aurelius quote on my refrigerator that often does the trick (bolding mine):

"When you wake up in the morning, tell yourself: The people I deal with today will be meddling, ungrateful, arrogant, dishonest, jealous, and surly. They are like this because they can't tell good from evil. But I have seen the beauty of good, and the ugliness of evil, and have recognized that the wrongdoer has a nature related to my own — not of the same blood or birth, but the same mind, and possessing a share of the divine. And so **none of them can hurt me.**" (For more on stoicism, see page 474.)

Now, B) control what you can control. **No matter how shitty your day is, no matter how catastrophic it might become, you can make your bed. And that gives you the feeling, at least it gives me the feeling, even in a disastrous day, that I've held on to the cliff ledge by a fingernail and I haven't fallen. There is** at least one thing I've controlled, there is something that has maintained one hand on the driver's wheel of life. At the end of the day, the last experience you have is coming back to something that you've accomplished. It's hard for me to overstate how important this ritual has become, but number one: Make your bed.

#2 — Meditate (10 to 20 minutes)

I cover different options on page 149. At least 80% of all guests profiled in this book have a daily mindfulness practice of some type. Sometimes I will do "Happy Body" mobility exercises from Jerzy Gregorek (introduced to me by Naval Ravikant, page 546) in place of meditation.

When I'm done, I walk into the kitchen and flip a switch to near-boil water (about 85% of the full dial) using a cheap Adagio utiliTEA electric kettle. This is for tea (in step 4).

#3 — Do 5 to 10 Reps of *Something* (<1 minute)

I started doing this after numerous exchanges with the 4:45 a.m.–rising Jocko Willink (page 412). He trains before most people wake, and I train when most people are getting ready for bed (like Triple H on page 128).

The 5 to 10 reps here are not a workout. They are intended to "state prime" and wake me up. Getting into my body, even for 30 seconds, has a dramatic effect on my mood and quiets mental chatter. My preferred exercise is push-ups with ring turn out (RTO) (see page 16), as it nicely lights up the nervous system. I'll often take a 30- to 60-second pure cold shower after this, à la Tony Robbins (page 210).

#4 — Prepare "Titanium Tea" (this name was a joke, but it stuck) (2 to 3 minutes)

I prepare loose-leaf tea in a Rishi glass teapot but you could use a French press. The below combo is excellent for cognition and fat loss, and I use about 1 flat teaspoon of each:

Pu-erh aged black tea

Dragon well green tea (or other green tea)

Turmeric and ginger shavings (often also Rishi brand)

Add the hot water to your mixture and let it steep for 1 to 2 minutes. Some tea purists will get very upset and say, "Damn it, Ferriss, you should really do your homework, because the steeping temperatures for those teas are all different. And the first steeping should be 15 seconds!" This is all true, and I can do the fancy stuff, but when I'm groggy in the morning, I don't give a shit and like my uppers simple. Explore the complexities of tea on the weekends. Roughly 185°F is fine.

Separately, add one of the following to your drinking mug: 1 to 2 tablespoons of coconut oil, which is about 60 to 70% MCTs (medium-chain triglycerides) by weight or 1 scoop of Quest MCT Oil Powder, which will give the tea a creamy consistency.

Pour your tea into your mug, stir to mix, and enjoy. In my case, I grab my tea, a glass of cold water, and then take a seat at my comfy acacia wood kitchen table for the next step.

#5 — Morning Pages or 5-Minute Journal (5 to 10 minutes)

Next up is journaling, which is not a "Dear Diary" situation.

I use two types of journaling and alternate between them: Morning Pages and The 5-Minute Journal (5MJ). The former I use primarily for getting unstuck or problem solving (what should I do?); the latter I use for prioritizing and gratitude (how should I focus and execute?). I cover the Morning Pages extensively on page 224, so I'll only describe the 5MJ here.

The 5MJ is simplicity itself and hits a lot of birds with one stone: 5 minutes in the morning of answering a few prompts, and then 5 minutes in the evening doing the same. Each prompt has three lines for three answers.

To be answered in the morning:

I am grateful for . . . 1. _____ 2. _____ 3. _____

What would make today great? 1. _____ 2. _____ 3. _____

Daily affirmations. I am . . . 1. _____ 2. _____ 3. _____

To be filled in at night:

3 amazing things that happened today... 1. _____ **2.** _____
3. _____ (This is similar to Peter Diamandis's "three wins" practice; see page 373.)

How could I have made today better? 1. _____ 2. _____ 3. _____

The bolded lines are the most critical for me. I'm already a checklist and execution machine. It's easy to obsess over pushing the ball forward as a type-A personality, which leads to being constantly future-focused. If anxiety is a focus on the future, practicing appreciation, even for 2 to 3 minutes, is counter-balancing medicine. The 5MJ forces me to think about what I have, as opposed to what I'm pursuing.

When you answer "I am grateful for . . . ," I recommend considering four different categories. Otherwise, you will go on autopilot and repeat the same items day after day (e.g., "my healthy family," "my loving dog," etc.). I certainly did this, and it defeats the purpose. What are you grateful for in the below four categories? I ask myself this every morning as I fill out the 5MJ, and I pick my favorite three for that day:

» An old relationship that really helped you, or that you valued highly.

» An opportunity you have today. Perhaps that's just an opportunity to call one of your parents, or an opportunity to go to work. It doesn't have to be something large.

» Something great that happened yesterday, whether you experienced or witnessed it.

» Something simple near you or within sight. This was a recommendation from Tony Robbins. The gratitude points shouldn't all be "my career" and other abstract items. Temper those with something simple and concrete — a beautiful cloud outside the window, the coffee that you're drinking, the pen that you're using, or whatever it might be.

I use Intelligent Change's bound 5-Minute Journal and suggest it for convenience, but you can practice in your own notebook. It's fun and good therapy to review your p.m. "amazing things" answers at least once a month.

Got it? My morning routine looks longer on paper than it takes in reality.

Of course, there are days when life intervenes, and you have emergencies to deal with. Do I always hit all five? Absolutely not. That's 30% of the time, at best.

But you can always knock off at least one, and if you tick off three, I find the likelihood of the day being a home run infinitely greater.

MIND TRAINING 101

"We do not rise to the level of our expectations. We fall to the level of our training."

—Archilochus

The Most Consistent Pattern of All

More than 80% of the world-class performers I've interviewed have some form of daily meditation or mindfulness practice. Both can be thought of as "cultivating a present-state awareness that helps you to be nonreactive." This applies to everyone from Arnold Schwarzenegger (page 176) to Justin Boreta of The Glitch Mob (page 356), and from elite athletes like Amelia Boone (page 2) to writers like Maria Popova (page 406). It's the most consistent pattern of them all.

It is a "meta-skill" that improves everything else. You're starting your day by practicing focus when it *doesn't* matter (sitting on a couch for 10 minutes) so that you can focus better later when it *does* matter (negotiation, conversation with a loved one, max deadlift, mind-melding with a Vulcan, etc.).

If you want better results with less stress, fewer "I should have said X" mental loops, etc., meditation acts as a warm bath for the mind. Perhaps you're a world-conquering machine with elite focus, but you might need to CTFO (chill the fuck out) a few minutes a day before you BTFO (burn the fuck out).

Meditation allows me to step back and gain a "witness perspective" (as with psychedelics), so that I'm observing my thoughts instead of being tumbled by them. I can step out of the washing machine and calmly look inside it.

Most of our waking hours, we feel as though we're in a trench on the front lines with bullets whizzing past our heads. Through 20 minutes of consistent meditation, I can become the commander, looking out at the battlefield from a hilltop. I'm able to look at a map of the territory and make high-level decisions. "These guys shouldn't even be fighting over here. What the hell is Regiment B doing over there? Call them out. We need more troops around the ridge. For objectives, we should be going after A, B, and C in that order. Ignore all the other so-called emergencies until those are handled. Great. Now, deep breath, and . . . execute."

The Buffet of Options

If I could only choose one physical exercise for the body, it would probably be the hex-bar deadlift or two-handed kettlebell swing. If I could only choose one exercise for the mind, it would be 10 to 20 minutes of meditation at least once daily.

There are many options. Oddly, in polling readers, substantially more men end up at Transcendental Meditation (TM), and substantially more women end up at vipassana. Go figure. I currently use both in a roughly 60/40 split. But each person needs to find the shoe that fits.

How to figure out what works best for you? Try one or more of the following. I have used each successfully and so have hundreds (and often thousands) of my fans:

1. **Use an app like Headspace or Calm.** Headspace's free "Take10" will guide you for 10 minutes a day for 10 days. A number of my guests also use Headspace to help them get to sleep. Some of my listeners in the media, like Rich Feloni of *Business Insider*, have written entire feature-length pieces on how this app has changed their lives. Amelia Boone uses both Headspace and Calm, depending on the circumstances. I prefer the narrator for Headspace (Andy Puddicombe), but Calm features background sounds of nature that soothe the nerves.

2. **Listen to a guided meditation from Sam Harris (page 454) or Tara Brach (page 555).** Maria Popova of BrainPickings.org (page 406) listens to the same recording every morning — Tara Brach's Smile Guided Meditation recording from the summer of 2010.

3. **Take a TM course (tm.org).** It will probably cost $1,000 or more, but this option offers a coach and accountability. For me, this is what kicked off more than 2 years of consistent meditation. I'm not a fan of everything the TM organization does, but their training is practical and tactical. Rick Rubin and Chase Jarvis convinced me to bite the bullet on the cost when I was going through a particularly hard period in my life. I'm glad they did. The social pressure of having a teacher for 4 consecutive days was exactly the incentive I needed to meditate consistently enough to establish the habit. Rick and Chase both effectively said, "You can afford it, and it might help. What do you really have to lose?" In this particular case, I was penny wise and pound foolish for a long time. I was also afraid of "losing my edge," as if meditation would make me less aggressive or driven. That was unfounded; meditation simply helps you channel drive toward the few things that matter, rather than every moving target and imaginary opponent that pops up.

4. **If you want to try mantra-based meditation without a course, you can sit and silently repeat one two-syllable word (I've used "na-ture" before) for 10 to 20 minutes first thing in the morning.** TM purists would call this heresy, but you can still see results. Aim for physical comfort. No crossed legs or yoga-like contortion required. The default is sitting reasonably straight on a chair with your feet on the floor, hands on your thighs or in your lap, and back supported.

5. **Try one or more of Chade-Meng Tan's suggested exercises, starting on page 154.** They are simple and brilliant. I practice a few times per week, often in the sauna.

How Long Does It Take to See Results?

Macro

Commit to at least one 7-day cycle. I hate to say it, but I think less is worthless. There appears to be a binary not-boiling/boiling phase shift. If your doctor prescribes a week of antibiotics and you only take the medication for 3 days, the infection isn't fixed and you're back to square one. I believe there is a minimum effective dose for meditation, and it's around 7 days.

If you need a kick in the ass, consider using accountability partners or betting through a service like Coach.me or Stickk.com.

Complete 7 sessions before you get ambitious with length. 10 minutes is plenty. Do NOT start with 30- to 60-minute sessions, or you'll quit before hitting the phase shift. Start small and rig the game so you can win.

The Dalai Lama was once asked how long it took for noticeably *life-changing* effects, to which he replied succinctly: "Around 50 hours." That really ain't much, and it might be less. Based on a number of recent studies, a mere 100 minutes of cumulative "sitting" time appears sufficient to produce subjectively significant changes.

Curiously, for some outliers like Arnold Schwarzenegger (page 176), it appears that one year of diligent practice can provide a lifetime of recalibration, even if you never meditate again.

Micro

In my own sessions of 20 minutes, 15 minutes is letting the mud in the water settle, and the last 5 minutes are really where I feel the most benefit. For me, it's much like training to failure with weight lifting. The benefits are derived from the last few reps, but you need all the preceding reps to get there.

But what if you think of your to-do list, past arguments, or porn for 19.5 minutes out of 20? Do you get an F in meditation? No. If you spend even a second noticing this wandering and bringing your attention back to your mantra (or whatever), that is a "successful" session. As Tara Brach pointed out to me, the muscle you're working is bringing your attention *back* to something. My sessions are 99% monkey mind, but it's the other 1% that matters. **If you're getting frustrated, your standards are too high or your sessions are too long.** Once again, for 7 days, rig the game so you can win. The goal is not to "quiet the mind," which will give your brain a hyperactive tantrum; the goal is to observe your thoughts. If you're replaying some bullshit in your head and notice it, just say, "Thinking, thinking" to yourself and return to your focus.

Done consistently, my reward for meditating is getting 30% to 50% more done in a day with 50% less stress. Why? Because I have already done a warmup in recovering from distraction: my morning sit. If I later get distracted or interrupted during work hours, I can return to my primary task far more quickly and completely. (Tech nerd side note: Momentum extension for Chrome is also very helpful.)

In Closing

"Give me six hours to chop down a tree and I'll spend the first four sharpening the axe."

—**Abraham Lincoln**

Whacking trees with a blunt axe is no way to go through life.

Try it for 7 days and sharpen your mind.

As Rick Rubin and Chase Jarvis asked me: What do you have to lose?

THREE TIPS FROM A GOOGLE PIONEER

Chade-Meng "Meng" Tan (TW/FB: @CHADEMENG, CHADEMENG.COM) is a Google pioneer, award-winning engineer, and best-selling author. Meng was Google employee #107 and led the creation of a groundbreaking mindfulness-based emotional intelligence course for employees called Search Inside Yourself, which regularly had a waitlist of 6 months. Meng's work has been endorsed by President Carter, Eric Schmidt of Google, and the Dalai Lama. He is the co-chair of One Billion Acts of Peace, which was nominated for the Nobel Peace Prize in 2015. His book, *Joy on Demand*, is one of the most practical books on meditation that I've found.

Enter Meng

How do you sustain your meditation practice up to the point that it becomes so compelling that it's self-sustaining? I have three suggestions:

I. Have a Buddy

I learned this from my dear friend and mentor, Norman Fischer, whom we jokingly call the "Zen Abbot of Google." We use the gym analogy. Going to the gym alone is hard, but if you have a "gym buddy" whom you commit to going with, you're much more likely to go regularly. Partly because you have company, and partly because this arrangement helps you encourage each other and hold each other accountable (what I jokingly call "mutual harassment").

Spirit animal: Chinese dragon

We suggest finding a "mindfulness buddy" and committing to a 15-minute conversation every week, covering at least these two topics:

a. How am I doing with my commitment to my practice?
b. What has arisen in my life that relates to my practice?

We also suggest ending the conversation with the question, "How did this conversation go?"

We instituted this in our mindfulness-based emotional intelligence program (Search Inside Yourself) and found it very effective.

2. Do Less Than You Can

I learned this from Mingyur Rinpoche, whose book, *The Joy of Living*, I most highly recommend. The idea is to do less formal practice than you are capable of. For example, if you can sit in mindfulness for 5 minutes before it feels like a chore, then don't sit for 5 minutes, just do 3 or 4 minutes, perhaps a few times a day. The reason is to keep the practice from becoming a burden. If mindfulness practice feels like a chore, it's not sustainable.

My friend Yvonne Ginsberg likes to say, "Meditation is an indulgence." I think her insight beautifully captures the core of Rinpoche's idea. Don't sit for so long that it becomes burdensome. Sit often, for short periods, and your mindfulness practice may soon feel like an indulgence.

3. Take One Breath a Day

I may be the laziest mindfulness instructor in the world because I tell my students that all they need to commit to is one mindful breath a day. Just one. Breathe in and breathe out mindfully, and your commitment for the day is fulfilled. Everything else is a bonus.

There are two reasons why one breath is important. The first is momentum. If you commit to one breath a day, you can easily fulfill this commitment and preserve the momentum of your practice. Later, when you feel ready for more, you can pick it back up easily. You can say you don't have 10 minutes today to meditate, but you cannot say you have no time for one breath, so making it a daily practice is extremely doable.

The second reason is having the intention to meditate is *itself* a meditation. This practice encourages you to arise an intention to do something kind and beneficial for yourself daily, and over time, that self-directed kindness becomes a valuable mental habit. When self-directed kindness is strong, mindfulness becomes easier.

Remember, my friends, never underestimate the power of one breath. Mental fitness and joy on demand both start here, with one breath.

My Two Favorite Exercises from Meng, in His Own Words

I. Just Note Gone

There is a simple practice that can greatly enhance your ability to notice the absence of pain [whether physical, mental, or emotional], though it isn't only concerned with pain.

With "Just Note Gone" we train the mind to notice that something previously experienced is no more. For example, at the end of a breath, notice that the breath is over. Gone. As a sound fades away, notice when it is over. Gone. At the end of a thought, notice that the thought is over. Gone. At the end of an experience of emotion — joy, anger, sadness, or anything else — notice it is over. Gone.

This practice is, without a doubt, one of the most important meditation practices of all time. Meditation master Shinzen Young said that if he were allowed to teach only one focus technique and no other, it would be this one. Here are the instructions for the informal practice of Just Note Gone, from Shinzen's article "The Power of Gone."

———————

Whenever all *or part* of a sensory experience suddenly disappears, note that. By note I mean clearly acknowledge when you detect the transition point between all of it being present and at least some of it no longer being present.

If you wish, you can use a mental label to help you note. The label for any such sudden ending is "Gone."

If nothing vanishes for a while, that's fine. Just hang out until something does. If you start worrying about the fact that nothing is ending, note each time *that* thought ends. That's a "Gone." If you have a lot of mental sentences, you'll have a lot of mental periods — full stops, Gones!

———————————

So what? Why should we care about whether we can detect the moment when a particular burst of mental talk, or a particular external sound, or a particular body sensation suddenly subsides?

As a first step in answering this question, let's start with an admittedly extreme example.

Suppose you had to go through some horrible experience that involved physical pain, emotional distress, mental confusion, and perceptual disorientation all at once. Where could you turn for safety? Where could you turn for comfort? Where could you turn for meaning?

Turning toward your body won't help. There's nothing but pain and fear there. Turning toward your mind won't help. There's nothing but confusion and uncertainty there. Turning toward sight and sound won't help. There's nothing but turmoil and chaos there.

Under such extreme duress, is there anywhere you could turn to find relief? Yes.

You could concentrate intently on the fact that each sensory insult passes. In other words, you could reverse the normal habit of turning to each new arising and instead turn to each new passing. Micro-relief is constantly available.

2. Loving-Kindness and the Happiest Day in 7 Years

In many of my public talks, I guide a very simple 10-second exercise. I tell the audience members to each identify two human beings in the room and just think, "I wish for this person to be happy, and I wish for that person to be happy." That is it. I remind them to not do or say anything, just think — this is an entirely thinking exercise. The entire exercise is just 10 seconds' worth of thinking.

Everybody emerges from this exercise smiling, happier than 10 seconds before. This is the **joy of loving-kindness**. It turns out that being on the giving end of a kind thought is rewarding in and of itself. . . . All other things being equal, to increase your happiness, all you have to do is randomly wish for somebody else to be happy. That is all. It basically takes no time and no effort.

How far can you push this joy of loving-kindness? One time, I gave a public talk in a meditation center called Spirit Rock in California. As usual, I guided the audience in this 10-second exercise, and just for fun, I assigned them homework. I was speaking on a Monday evening, and the next day, Tuesday, was a work day, so I told the audience to do this exercise for Tuesday: Once an hour, every hour, randomly identify two people walking past your office and secretly wish for each of them to be happy. You don't have to do or say anything — just think, "I wish for this person to be happy." And since nobody knows what you're thinking, it's not embarrassing — you can do this exercise entirely in stealth. And after 10 seconds of doing that, go back to work. That's all. On Wednesday morning that week, I received an email from a total stranger, Jane (not her real name). Jane told me, "I hate my job. I hate coming to work every single day. But I attended your talk on Monday, did the homework on Tuesday, and Tuesday was my happiest day in 7 years."

Happiest day in 7 years. And what did it take to achieve that? It took 10 seconds of secretly wishing for two other people to be happy for 8 repetitions, a total of 80 seconds of thinking. That, my friends, is the awesome power of loving-kindness.

INFORMAL PRACTICE: WISHING FOR RANDOM PEOPLE TO BE HAPPY

During working hours or school hours, randomly identify two people who walk past you or who are standing or sitting around you. Secretly wish for them to be happy. Just think to yourself, "I wish for this person to be happy, and I wish for that person to be happy." That is the entire practice. Don't do anything; don't say anything; just think. This is entirely a thinking exercise.

If you prefer, you can do this at any time of the day for any amount of time. You can also do it at any other place. If there is nobody present, you can bring someone to mind for the purpose of this exercise.

FORMAL PRACTICE: ATTENDING TO THE JOY OF LOVING-KINDNESS

Sit in any posture that allows you to be alert and relaxed at the same time, whatever that means to you. You may keep your eyes open or closed.

Repeat this cycle once per minute: Bring to mind someone for whom you can very easily feel loving-kindness. Wish for him or her to be happy. The joy of loving-kindness may arise, and if that happens, bring full attention to the joy until it fades away. For the rest of the minute, just rest the mind.

When the next minute begins, start the cycle again, for a total of 3 minutes.

You can do this for however many minutes you choose. You don't have to stick to a once-per-minute regimen — feel free to rest your mind for as long as you want between each cycle. The timing is not important; the only thing that is important is attending to the joy of loving-kindness, that is all.

———————

TF: I tend to do a single 3- to 5-minute session at night, thinking of three people I want to be happy, often two current friends and one old friend I haven't seen in years. A mere three days into doing this in Paris, while working on this book, I found myself wondering throughout the day, "Why am I so happy?" Part of the reason I think it's so effective is that meditation is normally a very "me"-focused activity, and you easily get caught in the whirlpool of thinking about your "stuff." This loving-kindness drill takes the focus off of you entirely — which, for me, immediately resolves at least 90% of the mental chatter.

COACH SOMMER — THE SINGLE DECISION

We all get frustrated.

I am particularly prone to frustration when I see little or no progress after several weeks of practicing something new.

Despite Coach Sommer's (page 9) regular reminders about connective-tissue adaptations taking 200 to 210 days, after a few weeks of flailing with "straddle L extensions," I was at my wits' end. Even after the third workout, I had renamed them "frog spaz" in my workout journal because that's what I resembled while doing them: a frog being electrocuted.

Each week, I sent Coach Sommer videos of my workouts via Dropbox. In my accompanying notes at one point, I expressed how discouraging it was to make zero tangible progress with this exercise. Below is his email response, which I immediately saved to Evernote to review often.

It's all great, but I've bolded my favorite part.

Hi Tim,

Patience. Far too soon to expect strength improvements. Strength improvements [for a movement like this] take a minimum of 6 weeks. Any perceived improvements prior to that are simply the result of improved synaptic facilitation. In plain English, the central nervous system simply became more efficient at that particular movement with practice. This is, however, not to be confused with actual strength gains.

Dealing with the temporary frustration of not making progress is an integral part of the path towards excellence. In fact, it is essential and something that every single elite athlete has had to learn to deal with. If the pursuit of excellence was easy, everyone would do it. In fact, this impatience in dealing with frustration is the primary reason that most people fail to achieve their goals. Unreasonable expectations timewise, resulting in unnecessary frustration, due to a perceived feeling of failure. Achieving the extraordinary is not a linear process.

The secret is to show up, do the work, and go home.

A blue collar work ethic married to indomitable will. It is literally that simple. Nothing interferes. Nothing can sway you from your purpose. Once the decision is made, simply refuse to budge. Refuse to compromise.

And accept that quality long-term results require quality long-term focus. No emotion. No drama. No beating yourself up over small bumps in the road. Learn to enjoy and appreciate the process. This is especially important because you are going to spend far more time on the actual journey than with those all too brief moments of triumph at the end.

Certainly celebrate the moments of triumph when they occur. More importantly, learn from defeats when they happen. In fact, if you are not encountering defeat on a fairly regular basis, you are not trying hard enough. And absolutely refuse to accept less than your best.

Throw out a timeline. It will take what it takes.

If the commitment is to a long-term goal and not to a series of smaller intermediate goals, then only one decision needs to be made and adhered to. Clear, simple, straightforward. Much easier to maintain than having to make small decision after small decision to stay the course when dealing with each step along the way. This provides far too many opportunities to inadvertently drift from your chosen goal. The single decision is one of the most powerful tools in the toolbox.

2
WEALTHY

"If you set your goals ridiculously high and it's a failure,
you will fail above everyone else's success."

— *James Cameron*

"If you find yourself in a fair fight, you didn't
plan your mission properly."

— *Colonel David Hackworth*

"Not my circus. Not my monkeys."

— *Polish proverb*

"It may be lucky, but it's not an accident."

CHRIS SACCA

Chris Sacca (TW/FB/IG/SC: @SACCA, LOWERCASECAPITAL.COM) is an early-stage investor in dozens of companies, including Twitter, Uber, Instagram, Kickstarter, and Twilio. He was the cover story of *Forbes*'s Midas issue in 2015 thanks to what will likely be the most successful venture capital fund in history, Lowercase I of Lowercase Capital. (Get the name? It took me embarrassingly long.) Previously, Chris was Head of Special Initiatives at Google Inc., and he is currently a recurring guest Shark on ABC's *Shark Tank*.

Spirit animal: Animal crackers

RANDOM BITS

» I first met Chris in 2008 at a barbecue organized by Kevin Rose (page 340). For my entire life, I'd had a phobia of swimming and an acute fear of drowning. This came up over wine, and Chris said, "I have the answer to your prayers." He introduced me to Total Immersion swimming by Terry Laughlin, and in less than 10 days of solo training, I went from a 2-length maximum (of a 25-yard pool) to swimming more than 40 lengths per workout in sets of 2 and 4. It blew my mind, and now I swim for fun.

» Chris is one of the people who generously mentored me in the startup investing game. The other majors include Naval Ravikant (page 546), Kevin Rose (page 340), and Mike Maples, who got me started (see the Real-World MBA on page 250).

» Chris mentioned several books when he appeared on my podcast, including *I Seem to Be a Verb* by Buckminster Fuller. 48 hours later, used copies were selling for $999 on Amazon.

ARE YOU PLAYING OFFENSE OR DEFENSE?

Despite the fact that people refer to Chris as a "Silicon Valley investor," he hasn't lived in San Francisco since 2007. Instead, he bought a cabin in rural Truckee, Tahoe's less-expensive neighbor, and moved to prime skiing and hiking country. It is no tech hotbed. Back then, Chris hadn't yet made real money in the investing game, but he had a rationale for buying the getaway:

"I wanted to go on offense. I wanted to have the time to focus, to learn the things I wanted to learn, to build what I wanted to build, and to really invest in relationships that I wanted to grow, rather than just doing a day of coffee after coffee after coffee."

TF: He no longer felt compelled to take meetings he didn't want. There were no more early-morning coffee dates and late-night social dinners he didn't want to attend. Rather, Chris invited specific founders to spend weekends at "the jam pad" and "the jam tub" (the hot tub outside). He considers the cabin the best investment he's ever made:

"Everyone loves coming to the mountains. Over the years, that's helped me build lasting friendships. Some of those have been the catalysts for my investments in Uber, Twitter, and others. I've even had a body-hacking, grill-manning, best-selling author stay there a few times. [**TF:** I also embarrassed myself with Euro-style Speedos.] I borrow the cash for a 3-bedroom house and get a lifetime's worth of pals and a hugely successful business in return? Best trade ever."

Chris elaborates: "Generally, what all of this comes down to is whether you are on offense or defense. I think that as you survey the challenges in your lives, it's just: **Which of those did you assign yourself, and which of those are you doing to please someone else? Your inbox is a to-do list to which anyone in the world can add an action item.** I needed to get out of my inbox and back to my own to-do list."

GO TO AS MANY HIGHER-LEVEL MEETINGS AS POSSIBLE

TIM: "If working in a startup environment, what should one do or focus on to learn and improve as much as possible?"

CHRIS: "Go to all the meetings you can, even if you're not invited to them, and figure out how to be helpful. If people wonder why you're there, just start taking notes. Read all the other notes you can find on the company, and gain a general knowledge that your very limited job function may not offer you. Just make yourself useful and helpful by doing so. That's worked for me in a few different environments, and I encourage you to try it."

TF: Chris was well known at Google for showing up to meetings with anyone, including the co-founders. Even if attendees looked at each other puzzled, Chris would sit down and let them know he'd be taking notes for them. It worked. He got a front-row seat to the highest levels of Google and soon became a fixture in those meetings.

COWBOY SHIRTS

Chris is known for wearing somewhat ridiculous cowboy shirts. They've become his signature style. Here's a bit more context, from a *Forbes* profile of Chris by Alex Konrad: "Steve Jobs had his black turtleneck. Chris Sacca has his embroidered cowboy shirt. He bought his first one, impulsively, at the Reno airport en route to a speech, and the reaction prompted him to buy out half the store on his return." He likes the brands Scully and Rockmount. A good place to look at a wide selection is VintageWesternWear.com.

A shirt might seem like a small thing, but Chris realized early on that being a successful investor isn't simply knowing which companies to invest in. Part of the process is ensuring founders know who *you* are. If a single shirt can create seemingly unending media mentions and doesn't hurt your reputation, it's low-hanging fruit. On top of that: "It also saved me a lot of time thinking about what to wear and a lot of money that would've been wasted on suits."

WHEN THE GOING GETS TOUGH — "TONIGHT, I WILL BE IN MY BED."

In 2009, Chris did a charity bicycle ride with the Trek Travel team from Santa Barbara, California, to Charleston, North Carolina:

"I had a phrase I kept repeating in my head over and over again, which was, 'Tonight, I will be in my bed. Tonight, I will be in my bed. Tonight, I will be in my bed.' . . . It was something I repeated to remind me that the pain of what I was going through was temporary and that, no matter what, at the end of that day, I would be in my bed that night."

ON THE ADVANTAGE OF CULTIVATING BEGINNER'S MIND

"**Experience often deeply embeds the assumptions that need to be questioned in the first place.** When you have a lot of experience with something, you don't notice the things that are new about it. You don't notice the idiosyncrasies that need to be tweaked. You don't notice where the gaps are, what's missing, or what's not really working."

TF: Just like Malcolm Gladwell's dad (see page 573) and Alex Blumberg (page 303), Chris is incredibly smart about asking the "dumb" questions hiding in plain sight.

EMPATHY ISN'T JUST GOOD FOR LIFE, IT'S GOOD FOR BUSINESS

"As a builder, as an entrepreneur, how can you create something for someone else if you don't have even enough glancing familiarity with them to imagine the world through their eyes?"

SWEET AND SOUR SUMMERS

"There is something my parents did, and it was pretty unique. My brother and I refer to it as 'The Sweet and Sour Summer.' My parents would send us, for the first half of the summer, to an internship with a relative or a friend of the family who had an interesting job. So, at 12, I went and interned with my godbrother, who is a lobbyist in D.C. I would go along with him to pitch congressmen. I had one tie, and I was a pretty good writer. I'd write up one-page summaries of these bills we were pitching, and I'd literally sit there with these congressmen with these filthy mouths — you know, the old Alabaman senator and stuff like that — and watch the pitch happen. It was awesome. I learned so much and developed so much confidence, and really honed my storytelling skills.

"But then, from there, I would come home and work in a construction outfit, in a nasty, nasty job. I mean, hosing off the equipment that had been used to fix septic systems, gassing shit up, dragging shit around in the yard, filling up propane tanks. Just being the junior guy on the totem pole, and quite literally getting my ass kicked by whichever parolee was angry at me that day. I think it was part of their master plan, which was: There's a world of cool opportunities out there for you, but let's build within you a sense of not just work ethic, but also, a little kick in the ass about why you don't wanna end up in one of those *real* jobs. . . ."

TIM: "You had the introduction to the godbrother, for the lobbying. Did your parents also help organize the sour part of each summer?"

CHRIS: "The guy who ran that construction company is my dad's best friend, and he was under strict orders to make sure we had the roughest day there."

"GOOD STORIES ALWAYS BEAT GOOD SPREADSHEETS"

"Whether you are raising money, pitching your product to customers, selling the company, or recruiting employees, never forget that underneath all the math and the MBA bullshit talk, we are all still emotionally driven human beings. We want to attach ourselves to narratives. We don't act because of equations. We follow our beliefs. We get behind leaders who stir our feelings. In the early days of your venture, if you find someone diving too deep into the numbers, that means they are struggling to find a reason to deeply care about you."

"BE YOUR UNAPOLOGETICALLY WEIRD SELF"

"I gave a commencement speech in Minnesota few years ago [at the Carlson School of Management]. The core of it was to **be your unapologetically weird self.** I think authenticity is one of the most lacking things out there these days."

An excerpt from that speech: "Weirdness is why we adore our friends. . . . Weirdness is what bonds us to our colleagues. Weirdness is what sets us apart, gets us hired. Be your unapologetically weird self. In fact, being weird may even find you the ultimate happiness."

TF: As an example — mullet wigs.

CHRIS: "If you could bring one thing to make for an amazing party night, it's wigs, seriously. Go to Amazon right now and order 50 mullet wigs. Mullet wigs change everything."

MARC ANDREESSEN

Marc Andreessen (TW: @PMARCA, A16Z.COM) is a legendary figure in Silicon Valley, and his creations have changed the world. Even in the epicenter of tech, it's hard to find a more fascinating icon. Marc co-created the highly influential Mosaic browser, the first widely used graphical web browser. He also co-founded Netscape, which later sold to AOL for $4.2 billion. He then co-founded Loudcloud, which sold as Opsware to Hewlett-Packard for $1.6 billion. He's considered one of the founding fathers of the modern Internet, alongside pioneers like Tim Berners-Lee, who launched the Uniform Resource Locator (URL), Hypertext Transfer Protocol (HTTP), and early HTML standards.

This all makes him one of the few humans ever to create software categories used by more than a billion people *and* establish multiple billion-dollar companies. Marc is now co-founder and general partner of venture capital firm Andreessen Horowitz, where he has become one of the most influential and dominant tech investors on the planet.

"RAISE PRICES"

This was Marc's response to "If you could have a billboard anywhere, what would it say?" He'd put it right in the heart of San Francisco, and here's the reason:

"The number-one theme that companies have when they really struggle is they are not charging enough for their product. It has become conventional wisdom in Silicon Valley that the way to succeed is to price your product as low as possible, under the theory that if it's low-priced, everybody can buy it, and that's how you get to volume," he said. "And we just see over and over and over again people failing with that, because they get into a problem called 'too hungry to eat.' They don't charge enough for their product to be able to afford the sales and marketing required to actually get anybody to buy it. Is your product any good if people won't pay more for it?"

DON'T FETISHIZE FAILURE

"I'm old-fashioned. Where I come from, people like to succeed. . . . When I was a founder, when I first started out, we didn't have the word 'pivot.' We didn't have a fancy word for it. We just called it a fuck-up.

"We do see companies that, literally, every time we meet them, they've pivoted. Every time, they're off to something new, and it's like watching a rabbit go through a maze or something. They're never going to converge on anything because they're never going to put the time into actually figuring it out and getting it right."

(See Peter Thiel's thoughts on failure on page 233.)

THE "NERDS AT NIGHT" TEST

How does Marc look for new opportunities? He has dozens of tools, but one of his heuristics is simple:

"We call our test 'What do the nerds do on nights and weekends?' Their day job is Oracle, Salesforce.com, Adobe or Apple or Intel or one of these companies, or an insurance company, bank [or they're a student]. Whatever. That's fine. They go do whatever they need to do to make a living. The question is: What's the hobby? What's the thing at night or on the weekend? Then things get really interesting."

STRESS-TESTING IDEAS WITH A "RED TEAM"

"Each of our GPs [general partners] has the ability to pull the trigger on a deal without a vote or without consensus. If the person closest to the deal has a very strong degree of positive commitment and enthusiasm about it, then we should do that investment, even if everybody else in the room thinks it's the stupidest thing they've ever heard . . . however, you don't get to do that completely on your own without stress-testing. If necessary, we create a 'red team.' We'll formally create the countervailing force to argue the other side."

TF: To avoid the potential problem of newer hires getting battered more than senior folks, Marc and his founding partner, Ben Horowitz, make a point of smashing each other. "Whenever [Ben] brings in a deal, I just beat the shit out of it. I might think it's the best idea I've ever heard of, but I'll just trash the crap out of it and try to get everybody else to pile on. And then, at the end of it, if he's still pounding the table saying, 'No, no, this is the thing . . .' then we say we're all in. We're all behind you. . . . **It's a 'disagree and commit' kind of culture.** By the way, he does the same thing to me. It's the torture test."

TF: Where can you create a "red team" in your life to stress-test your most treasured beliefs? (See Samy Kamkar, page 427; Stan McChrystal, page 435; and Jocko Willink, page 412.)

ALWAYS FORWARD

I'll let the below exchange speak for itself. This philosophy pairs well with the 21-Day No Complaint experiment that I've written about before on my blog (fourhourblog.com):

TIM: "What advice would you give to Marc, the 20-something, at Netscape?"

MARC: "I've never for a moment even thought about that. I don't do replays well. The question I'll never answer is, 'What would you have done differently had you known X?' I never, ever play that game because you didn't know X.

"If you've ever read the Elvis Cole novels by the great crime novelist Robert Crais — Elvis Cole is this kind of postmodern, L.A. private detective. They're great novels, and he's got this partner, Joe Pike. He's my favorite fictional character, maybe of all time. He's a former Marine Force Recon guy, so a lot like your friend Jocko. And in the novels, Joe Pike always wears the same outfit every day. He wears jeans, he wears a sweatshirt with the sleeves cut off, and

mirrored aviator sunglasses. He's got bright red arrows tattooed on his ⌐
pointing forward. And, basically, his entire thing is 'forward.'"

TIM: "So that's how you feel?"

MARC: "Forward, like: We don't stop. We don't slow down. We don't revisit past decisions. We don't second guess. So, honestly, that question, I have no idea how to answer."

TIM: "I think you just did."

MARC: "Okay, good. Onward."

"STRONG VIEWS, LOOSELY HELD"

For a long time, this phrase was in Marc's Twitter bio. I asked him to explain the meaning:

"Most people go through life and never develop strong views on things, or specifically go along and buy into the consensus. One of the things I think you want to look for as both a founder and as an investor is things that are out of consensus, something very much opposed to the conventional wisdom.... Then, if you're going to start a company around that, if you're going to invest in that, you better have strong conviction because you're making a very big bet of time or money or both. [But] what happens when the world changes? What happens when something else happens?"

TF: That's where "loosely held" comes in. People everywhere hate changing their minds, but you need to be able to adapt in light of new information. Many of my friends in this book will fight you tooth and nail over a topic, perhaps making dinner company nervously glance around, but as soon as you cite better information or a better logic, they'll concede and say something like, "You're totally right. I never thought about that."

TWO RULES TO LIVE BY

Marc and I are both huge fans of Steve Martin's autobiography, *Born Standing Up: A Comic's Life.* Marc highlighted one takeaway:

"He says the key to success is, 'Be so good they can't ignore you.'"

TF: Marc has another guiding tenet: "Smart people should make things." He says: "If you just have those two principles — that's a pretty good way to orient."

WHAT DOES YOUR IDEAL DAY LOOK LIKE?

"The perfect day is caffeine for 10 hours, alcohol for 4. It balances everything out perfectly."

TF: This was said jokingly, but it's surprisingly similar to my approach during crunch time. My preferred late-night "Silicon Valley speedball" for writing deadlines is a combination of Cruz de Malta yerba mate tea and 2 to 3 glasses of Malbec red wine. Not mixed but alternated. I sip the tea over hours with a traditional *bombilla* straw, taking a swig of the nectar of the gods every 5 to 10 minutes. Pro tip: Your writing does *not* get better after the third glass.

DON'T OVERESTIMATE THE PEOPLE ON PEDESTALS

"Get inside the heads of the people who made things in the past and what they were actually like, and then realize that they're not that different from you. At the time they got started, they were kind of just like you . . . so there's nothing stopping any of the rest of us from doing the same thing."

TF: Both Marc and Brian Chesky, CEO of Airbnb, have read and recommend Neal Gabler's biography of Walt Disney. Marc also mentioned a Steve Jobs quote in our conversation, which is printed in full below. It was recorded in a 1995 interview conducted by the Santa Clara Valley Historical Association, while Jobs was still at NeXT:

"Life can be much broader, once you discover one simple fact, and that is that **everything around you that you call 'life' was made up by people that were no smarter than you**. And you can change it, you can influence it, you can build your own things that other people can use. Once you learn that, you'll never be the same again."

STUDY THE OPPOSITES

In addition to studying his competition in tech and early-stage investing, Marc studies value investors on the completely opposite side of the spectrum, such as Warren Buffett and Seth Klarman. This doesn't mean they invest in the same types of companies; rather, the synergy is related to first principles.

TIM [joking]: "You're not going to invest in See's Candies [one of Buffett's investments]?"

MARC: "No. No. Absolutely not. Furthermore, every time I hear a story like

See's Candies, I want to go find the new scientific superfood candy company that's going to blow them right out of the water. We're wired completely opposite in that sense. Basically, he's betting against change. We're betting for change. When he makes a mistake, it's because something changes that he didn't expect. When we make a mistake, it's because something doesn't change that we thought would. We could not be more different in that way. But what both schools have in common is an orientation toward, I would say, original thinking in really being able to view things as they are as opposed to what everybody says about them, or the way they're believed to be."

SHORT AND SWEET

I followed Marc on Twitter well before we met in person. Here are a few of my favorite tweets of his, many related to the above points:

"My goal is not to fail fast. My goal is to succeed over the long run. They are not the same thing."

"To do original work: It's not necessary to know something nobody else knows. It is necessary to believe something few other people believe."

"Andy Grove had the answer: For every metric, there should be another 'paired' metric that addresses adverse consequences of the first metric."

"Show me an incumbent bigco failing to adapt to change, I'll show you top execs paid huge cash compensation for quarterly and annual goals."

"Every billionaire suffers from the same problem. Nobody around them ever says, 'Hey, that stupid idea you just had is really stupid.' "

" 'Far more money has been lost by investors trying to anticipate corrections, than has been lost in corrections themselves.' — Peter Lynch"

ARNOLD SCHWARZENEGGER

Arnold Schwarzenegger (FB: @ARNOLD, TW/IG: @SCHWARZENEGGER, SCHWARZENEGGER.COM) was born in Thal, Austria in 1947, and by the age of 20 dominated the sport of competitive bodybuilding, becoming the youngest person ever to win the Mr. Universe title. With his sights set on Hollywood, he emigrated to America in 1968 and went on to win five Mr. Universe titles and seven Mr. Olympia titles before retiring from competitve bodybuilding to dedicate himself to acting. Schwarzenegger, who worked under the pseudonym Arnold Strong in his first feature, had his big break in 1982 with *Conan the Barbarian*. To date, his films have grossed more than $3 billion worldwide.

He gratefully served the people of California as the state's 38th governor from 2003 to 2010. Notably, Schwarzenegger made California a world leader in renewable energy and combating climate change with the Global Warming Solutions Act of 2006, became the first governor in decades to invest in rebuilding California's critical infrastructure with his Strategic Growth Plan, and instituted dynamic political reforms that stopped the century-old practice of gerrymandering by creating an independent redistricting commission and brought political leaders closer to the center by creating an open primary system.

Schwarzenegger acts as chairman of the After-School All-Stars, a nationwide after-school program, and he continues his policy work through the USC Schwarzenegger Institute for State and Global Policy, which seeks to advance his vision of post-partisanship, where leaders put people over political parties and work together to find the best ideas and solutions to benefit the people they serve.

BEHIND THE SCENES

» Arnold is a huge chess fan and plays daily. He rotates through different partners and keeps annual score cards. By the end of a year, some of them have tallies in the thousands of games. One of his favorite documentaries is *Brooklyn Castle*, a film about chess in inner-city schools.

» When I first met Arnold and we sat down at his kitchen table, I didn't know how to address him and nervously asked. He replied: "Well, you can address me any way you want. You can call me Governator, Governor, schnitzel, Arnold, anything. But I think Arnold will be right."

» I used a Zoom H6 recorder for primary audio, but I had a backup recorder (Zoom H4n) for our first interview. Arnold asked "What's this for?" to which I replied, "Backup, in case the primary fails." He tapped his head and looked at his team, seated around the room. Having backup audio makes a good impression. Cal Fussman (page 495) got the same response from Richard Branson, as no busy person wants to take 1 to 3 hours for an interview that never gets published.

"I WASN'T THERE TO COMPETE. I WAS THERE TO WIN."

I brought up of a photo of Arnold at age 19, just before he won his first big competition, Junior Mr. Europe. I asked, "Your face was so confident compared to every other competitor. Where did that confidence come from?" He replied:

"My confidence came from my vision. . . . **I am a big believer that if you have a very clear vision of where you want to go, then the rest of it is much easier.** Because you always know why you are training 5 hours a day, you always know why you are pushing and going through the pain barrier, and why you have to eat more, and why you have to struggle more, and why you have to be more disciplined. . . . I felt that I could win it, and that was what I was there for. **I wasn't there to compete. I was there to win.**"

EUROPEAN BRICK LAYING

In 1971, Arnold started a brick laying company with his best friend, Franco Columbu, an Italian powerlifting, boxing, and bodybuilding champion who'd lived in Germany. At the time, anything "European" was exotic and assumed to be better (e.g., the Swedish massage craze), so they put ads in the L.A. *Times* for "European bricklayers and masonry experts, marble experts. Building chimneys and fireplaces the European style."

"Franco would play the bad guy, and I played the good guy. We would go to someone's house and then someone would say, 'Well, look at my patio. It's all cracked. Can you guys put a new patio in here?' I would say 'yes' and then we would run out and get the tape measure, but it would be a tape measure with centimeters. No one in those days could at all figure out anything with centimeters. We would be measuring up and I would say '4 meters and 82 centimeters.' They had no idea what we were talking about. We were writing up dollars and amounts and square centimeters and square meters. Then I would go to the guy and say, 'It's $5,000,' and the guy would be in a state of shock. He'd say, 'It's $5,000? This is outrageous.' I'd say, 'What did you expect?' and he'd say, 'I expected like $2,000 or $3,000.' I'd say, 'Let me talk to my guy because he's really the masonry expert, but I can beat him down for you a little bit. Let me soften the meat.' Then I would go to Franco and we would start arguing in German. '[Content in German]!!!' This would be going on and on, and he was screaming back at me in Italian. Then, all of a sudden, he would calm down, and I would go to the guy and say, 'Phew . . . okay, here it is. I could get him as low as $3,800. Can you go with that?' He says, 'Thank you very much. I really think that you're a great man' and blah, blah, blah and all this stuff. I'd say, 'Give us half down right now and we'll go right away and get the cement and the bricks and everything we need for here and we'll start working on Monday.' The guy was ecstatic. He gave us the money and we immediately went to the bank and cashed the check. We had to make sure the money was in the bank account, and then we went out and got the cement, the wheelbarrow, and all the stuff that we needed and went to work. We worked like that for 2 years very successfully."

TF: The "content in German" is really fun to listen to. Most people, myself included, had never heard Arnold speak in his native German, let alone shout insults in German. It's fantastic. Just jump to 29:30 in the full episode at fourhourworkweek.com/arnold

"DID YOU HURT YOUR KNEE?" AND OTHER PSYCHOLOGICAL WARFARE

"By the time I came to America and started competing over here [I would say to my competitors something like], 'Let me ask you something, do you have any knee injuries or something like that?' Then they would look at me and say, 'No, why? I have no knee injury at all . . . my knees feel great. Why are you asking?' I said, 'Well because your thighs look a little slimmer to me. I thought maybe you can't squat, or maybe there's some problem with leg extension.' And then I'd see him for all 2 hours in the gym, always going in front of the mirror and checking out his thighs. . . . People are vulnerable about those things. Naturally, when you have a competition, you use all this. You ask people if they were sick for a while. They look a little leaner. Or 'Did you take any salty foods lately? Because it looks like you have water retention, and it looks like you're not as ripped as you looked a week or so ago.' It throws people off in an unbelievable way."

HOW ARNOLD MADE MILLIONS BEFORE HE BECAME A MOVIE STAR

"[Early on] I did not rely on my movie career to make a living. That was my intention, because I saw over the years, the people that worked out in the gym and that I met in the acting classes, they were all very vulnerable because they didn't have any money, and they had to take anything that was offered to them because that was their living. I didn't want to get into that situation. I felt if I was smart with real estate and took my little money that I made in bodybuilding and in seminars and selling my courses through the mail, I could save up enough to put down money for an apartment building. I realized in the 1970s that the inflation rate was very high and therefore an investment like that is unbeatable. Buildings that I would buy for $500K within the year were $800K and I put only maybe $100K down, so you made 300% on your money. . . . I quickly developed and traded up my buildings and bought more apartment buildings and office buildings on Main Street down in Santa Monica and so on. . . . I benefited from [a magic decade] and I became a millionaire from my real estate investments. That was before my career took off in show business and acting, which was after *Conan the Barbarian*."

TF: This makes me think of one of my favorite negotiating maxims: "In negotiation, he who cares the least wins." He could ignore bit parts because he had cash flow from his real estate investments. On a related note, Arnold makes films or stars in them, but he doesn't invest in them. He's offset the potential volatility of his own career by investing primarily in real estate. I've taken a similar approach to date, focusing on two ends of the spectrum: early-stage tech startups (extremely volatile) and real estate that I'm happy to hold forever, if need be.

NEVER AUDITION — OWN OR CREATE A UNIQUE NICHE

"I never auditioned. Never. I would never go out for the regular parts because I was not a regular-looking guy, so my idea always was: Everyone is going to look the same, and everyone is trying to be the blond guy in California, going to Hollywood interviews and looking somewhat athletic and cute and all this. **How can I carve myself out a niche that only I have?** . . . Of course, the naysayers were there, and they said, 'Well, you know the time [for bodybuilders] has passed. It was 20 years ago. You look too big, you're too monstrous, too muscular, you will never get in the movies.' That's what producers said in the beginning in Hollywood. That's also what agents and managers said. 'I doubt you're going to be successful. . . . Today's idols are Dustin Hoffman, Al Pacino, Woody Allen, all little guys. Those are the sex symbols. Look at you. You weigh 250 pounds or something like that. That time is over.' But I felt very strongly and had a very clear vision that the time would come that someone would appreciate that. . . . [Eventually] the very things that the agents and the managers and the studio executives said would be a total obstacle became an asset, and my career started taking off."

TF: Arnold was able to use his biggest "flaws" as his biggest assets, in part because he could bide his time and didn't have to rush to make rent. He shared an illustrative anecdote from the *Terminator* set: "Jim Cameron said if we wouldn't have had Schwarzenegger, then we couldn't have done the movie, because only he sounded like a machine."

ARNOLD'S MOST PERSONALLY PROFITABLE FILM WAS . . . *TWINS*?

"*Twins* came together because I felt very strongly that I had a very humorous side, and that if someone would be patient enough and willing to work with me as a director, that they would be able to bring that humor out of me."

Arnold loved *Ghostbusters*, so he pursued the director, Ivan Reitman. Since most people felt a comedy with Schwarzenegger would flop, that was a blind spot they could capitalize on:

"We sat around at a restaurant, and we made a deal on a napkin: 'We're going to make the movie for free. We don't want to get any salaries and we get a big back end. Ivan gave it to Tom Pollock, who was then running Universal Studios. Tom Pollock said 'This is great, and we can make this movie for $16.5M if you guys don't take a salary and you get a big back end [profit participation]. We're going to give you 37%' or whatever for Danny [DeVito], Ivan, and me [to divide among ourselves]. We worked out the percentage [our salaries would have been of the production budget] . . . and that's how we ended up dividing up the pot amongst ourselves. Let me tell you, I made more money on that movie than any other movie, and the gift keeps on giving. It's just wonderful. Tom Pollock, after the movie came out, he says, 'All I can tell you is that this is what you guys did to me.' Then he turned around and bent over and pulled his pockets out. 'You've fucked me and cleaned me out.' It was very funny. He said he'd never make that deal again. The movie was a huge hit. It came out just before Christmas. Throughout Christmas and New Year's, it made $3 to $4M every day, which in today's terms would be, of course, double or triple. It was just huge and went up to $129M domestically, and I think worldwide it was $269M or something like that."

TF: This reminded me of the deal that George Lucas crafted for *Star Wars*, in which the studio effectively said, "Toys? Yeah, sure, whatever. You can have the toys." That was a multi-billion-dollar mistake that gave Lucas infinite financing for life (an estimated 8,000,000,000+ *units* sold to date). When deal-making, ask yourself: Can I trade a short-term, incremental gain for a potential longer-term, game-changing upside? Is there an element here that might be far more valuable in 5 to 10 years (e.g., ebook rights 10 years ago)? Might there be rights or options I can explicitly "carve out" and keep? If you can cap the downside (time, capital, etc.) and have the confidence, take uncrowded bets on yourself. You only need one winning lottery ticket.

MEDITATE FOR A YEAR, GET BENEFITS FOR LIFE?

When Arnold's movie career first began to gel, he was inundated with new opportunities and options. For the first time, he felt overly worried and anxious, due to pressures he'd never felt before. By sheer coincidence, he met a Transcendental Meditation teacher at the beach. "He says, 'Oh, Arnold, it is not uncommon. It is very common. A lot of people go through this. This is why people use Transcendental Meditation as one way of dealing with the problem.' He was very good in selling it, because he didn't say that it was the only answer. He said it's just one of many." The man encouraged Arnold to go to Westwood, in L.A., to take a class the following Thursday.

"I went up there, took a class, and I went home after that and tried it. I said to myself, 'I've got to give it a shot.' I did 20 minutes in the morning and 20 minutes at night, and I would say within 14 days, 3 weeks, I got to the point where I could really disconnect my mind and stay and find a few seconds of this connection and rejuvenate the mind and learn how to focus more and to calm down. I saw the effect right away. I was much more calm about all of the challenges that were facing me. I continued doing that for a year. By that time, I felt that, 'I think I have mastered this. I think that now I don't feel overwhelmed anymore.'

"**Even today, I still benefit from that because I don't merge and bring things together and see everything as one big problem.** I take them one challenge at a time. When I go and I study my script for a movie, then that time of day when I study my script, I don't let anything else interfere. I just concentrate on that. The other thing that I've learned is that there are many forms of meditation in the world. Like when I study and work really hard, where it takes the ultimate amount of concentration, I can only do it for 45 minutes, maybe an hour.

"I also figured out that I could use my workouts as a form of meditation because I concentrate so much on the muscle, I have my mind inside the bicep when I do my curls. I have my mind inside the pectoral muscles when I do my bench press. I'm really inside, and it's like I gain a form of meditation, because you have no chance of thinking or concentrating on anything else at that time."

✳ Who do you think of when you hear the word "successful"?
He mentioned several people, including Warren Buffett, Elon Musk, Nelson Mandela, and Muhammad Ali, but his final addition stuck out:

"**Cincinnatus.** He was an emperor in the Roman Empire. Cincinnati, the city, by the way, is named after him because he was a big idol of George Washington's. He is a great example of success because he was asked to reluctantly step into power and become the emperor and to help, because Rome was about to get annihilated by all the wars and battles. He was a farmer. Powerful guy. He went and took on the challenge, took over Rome, took over the army, and won the war. After they won the war, he felt he'd done his mission and was asked to go and be the emperor, and he gave the ring back and went back to farming. He didn't only do this once. He did it twice. When they tried to overthrow the empire from within, they asked him back and he came back. He cleaned up the mess through great, great leadership. He had tremendous leadership quality in bringing people together. And again, he gave the ring back and went back to farming."

DEREK SIVERS

Derek Sivers (TW/FB: @SIVERS, SIVERS.ORG) is one of my favorite humans, and I often call him for advice. Think of him as a philosopher-king programmer, master teacher, and merry prankster. Originally a professional musician and circus clown (he did the latter to counterbalance being introverted), Derek created CD Baby in 1998. It became the largest seller of independent music online, with $100 million in sales for 150,000 musicians.

In 2008, Derek sold CD Baby for $22 million, giving the proceeds to a charitable trust for music education. He is a frequent speaker at TED conferences, with more than 5 million views of his talks. In addition to publishing 33 books via his company Wood Egg, he is the author of *Anything You Want*, a collection of short life lessons that I've read at least a dozen times. I still have an early draft with highlights and notes.

BEHIND THE SCENES

>>> Derek has read, reviewed, and rank-ordered 200+ books at sivers
.org/books. They're automatically sorted from best to worst. He is a
huge fan of Charlie Munger, Warren Buffett's business partner, and
introduced me to the book *Seeking Wisdom: From Darwin to Munger*,
by Peter Bevelin.

>>> He read *Awaken the Giant Within* by Tony Robbins (page 210) when
he was 18, and it changed his life.

>>> I posted the following on Facebook while writing this chapter: "I
might need to do a second volume of my next book, 100% dedicated
to the knowledge bombs of Derek Sivers. So much good stuff. Hard to
cut." The most upvoted comment was from Kevin O., who said, "Put
a link to the podcast and have them listen. It's less than two hours,
and it will change their life. Tim, you and Derek got me from call center worker to location-independent freelancer with more negotiation
power for income and benefits [than] I previously imagined. You both
also taught me the value of 'enough' and contentment and appreciation, as well as achievement." That made my week, and I hope this
makes yours: fourhourworkweek.com/derek

"IF [MORE] INFORMATION WAS THE ANSWER, THEN WE'D ALL BE BILLIONAIRES WITH PERFECT ABS."

TF: It's not what you know, it's what you do consistently. (See Tony Robbins,
page 210.)

"HOW TO THRIVE IN AN UNKNOWABLE FUTURE? CHOOSE THE PLAN WITH THE MOST OPTIONS. THE BEST PLAN IS THE ONE THAT LETS YOU CHANGE YOUR PLANS."

TF: This is one of Derek's "Directives," which are his one-line rules for life, distilled from hundreds of books and decades of lessons learned. Others include
"Be expensive" (see Marc Andreessen, page 170), "Expect disaster" (see
Tony Robbins, page 210), and "Own as little as possible" (see Jason Nemer,
page 46, and Kevin Kelly, page 470).

٭ Who do you think of when you hear the word "successful"?

"The first answer to any question isn't much fun because it's just automatic. What's the first painting that comes to mind? *Mona Lisa*. Name a genius. Einstein. Who's a composer? Mozart.

"This is the subject of the book *Thinking, Fast and Slow* by Daniel Kahneman. There's the instant, unconscious, automatic thinking and then there's the slower, conscious, rational, deliberate thinking. I'm really, really into the slower thinking, breaking my automatic responses to the things in my life and slowly thinking through a more deliberate response instead. Then for the things in life where an automatic response is useful, I can create a new one consciously.

"What if you asked, **'When you think of the word "successful," who's the *third* person that comes to mind? Why are they actually more successful than the first person that came to mind?'** In that case, the first would be Richard Branson, because he's the stereotype. He's like the *Mona Lisa* of success to me. Honestly, *you* might be my second answer, but we could talk about that a different time. My third and real answer, after thinking it through, is that we can't know without knowing a person's aims.

"What if Richard Branson set out to live a quiet life, but like a compulsive gambler, he just can't stop creating companies? Then that changes everything, and we can't call him successful anymore."

TF: This is genius. Ricardo Semler, CEO and majority owner of the Brazil-based Semco Partners, practices asking "Why?" three times. This is true when questioning his own motives, or when tackling big projects. The rationale is identical to Derek's.

FOR PEOPLE STARTING OUT — SAY "YES"

When Derek was 18, he was living in Boston, attending the Berklee College of Music.

"I'm in this band where the bass player, one day in rehearsal, says, 'Hey man, my agent just offered me this gig — it's like $75 to play at a pig show in Vermont.' He rolls his eyes, and he says, 'I'm not gonna do it, do you want the gig?' I'm like, 'Fuck yeah, a paying gig?! Oh, my God! Yes!' So, I took the gig to go up to Burlington, Vermont.

"And, I think it was a $58 round-trip bus ticket. I get to this pig show, I strap my acoustic guitar on, and I walked around a pig show playing music. I did that for about 3 hours, and took the bus home, and the next day, the booking agent called me up, and said, 'Hey, yeah, so you did a really good job at the pig show. . . .'

"So many opportunities, and 10 years of stage experience, came from that one piddly little pig show. . . . When you're earlier in your career, I think the best strategy is to just say 'yes' to everything. Every little gig. You just never know what are the lottery tickets."

THE STANDARD PACE IS FOR CHUMPS

"Kimo Williams is this large, black man, a musician who attended Berklee School of Music and then stayed there to teach for a while. . . . What he taught me got me to graduate in half the time it would [normally] take. He said, 'I think you can graduate Berklee School of Music in two years instead of four. The standard pace is for chumps. The school has to organize its curricula around the lowest common denominator, so that almost no one is left out. They have to slow down, so everybody can catch up. But,' he said, 'you're smarter than that.' He said, 'I think you could just buy the books for those, [skip the classes] and then contact the department head to take the final exam to get credit.'"

DON'T BE A DONKEY

TIM: "What advice would you give to your 30-year-old self?"

DEREK: "Don't be a donkey."

TIM: "And what does that mean?"

DEREK: "Well, I meet a lot of 30-year-olds who are trying to pursue many different directions at once, but not making progress in any, right? They get frustrated that the world wants them to pick one thing, because they want to do them all: 'Why do I have to choose? I don't know what to choose!' But the problem is, if you're thinking short-term, then [you act as though] if you don't do them all this week, they won't happen. The solution is to think long-term. To realize that you can do one of these things for a few years, and then do another one for a few years, and then another. You've probably heard the fable, I think it's 'Buridan's ass,' about a donkey who is standing halfway between a pile of hay and a bucket of water. He just keeps looking left to the hay, and right to the water, trying to decide. Hay or water, hay or water? He's unable to decide, so he eventually falls over and dies of both hunger and thirst. A donkey can't think of the future. If he did, he'd realize he could clearly go first to drink the water, then go eat the hay.

"So, my advice to my 30-year-old self is, don't be a donkey. You can do everything you want to do. You just need foresight and patience."

BUSINESS MODELS CAN BE SIMPLE: YOU DON'T NEED TO CONSTANTLY "PIVOT"

Derek tells the story of the sophisticated origins of CD Baby's business model and pricing:

"I was living in Woodstock, New York, at the time, and there was a cute, tiny record store in town that sold consignment CDs of local musicians on the counter. So, I walked in there one day, and I said, 'Hey, how does it work if I wanna sell my CD here?' And she said, 'Well, you set the selling price at whatever you want. We just keep a flat $4 per CD sold, and then just come by every week, and we'll pay you.' So, I went home to my new website that night and wrote 'You set your selling price at what you want, we'll just keep a flat $4 per CD sold, and we'll pay you every week.' And then, I realized that it took about 45 minutes for me to set up a new album into the system, because I had to lay the album art on the scanner, Photoshop it and crop it, fix the musicians' spelling mistakes in their own bio, and all that kinda stuff.

"I thought 45 minutes of my time, that's worth about $25. That shows you what I was valuing my time at in those days. So, I'll charge a $25 setup fee to sign up for this thing. And, then, oooh . . . in my head, $25 and $35 don't feel very different when it comes to cost. $10 is different, and $50 is different, but $25, $35 — that occupies the same space in the mind. So you know what? I'm gonna make it $35, that will let me give anyone a discount any time they ask. If somebody's on the phone and upset, I'll say, 'You know what? Let me give you a discount.' So, I added in that little buffer so I could give people a discount, which they love. **So $35 setup fee, $4 per CD sold, and then, Tim, for the next 10 years, that was it. That was my entire business model, generated in 5 minutes by walking down to the local record store and asking what they do."**

ONCE YOU HAVE SOME SUCCESS — IF IT'S NOT A "HELL, YES!" IT'S A "NO"

This mantra of Derek's quickly became one of my favorite rules of thumb, and it led me to take an indefinite "startup vacation" starting in late 2015. I elaborate on this on page 385, but here's the origin story:

"It was time to book the ticket [for a trip he'd committed to long ago], and I was thinking, 'Ugh. I don't really want to go to Australia right now. I'm busy with other stuff.' . . . I was on the phone with my friend Amber Rubarth, who's a brilliant musician, and I was lamenting about this. She's the one who pointed out, 'It sounds like, from where you are, your decision is not between yes and no. You need to figure out whether you're feeling like, "Fuck yeah!" or "No."'

"Because most of us say yes to too much stuff, and then, we let these little, mediocre things fill our lives. . . . The problem is, when that occasional, 'Oh my God, hell yeah!' thing comes along, you don't have enough time to give it the attention that you should, because you've said yes to too much other little, half-ass stuff, right? Once I started applying this, my life just opened up."

"BUSY" = OUT OF CONTROL

"Every time people contact me, they say, 'Look, I know you must be incredibly busy . . .' and I always think, 'No, I'm not.' Because I'm in control of my time. I'm on top of it. 'Busy,' to me, seems to imply 'out of control.' Like, 'Oh my God, I'm so busy. I don't have any time for this shit!' To me, that sounds like a person who's got no control over their life."

TF: Lack of time is lack of priorities. If I'm "busy," it is because I've made choices that put me in that position, so I've forbidden myself to reply to "How are you?" with "Busy." I have no right to complain. Instead, if I'm too busy, it's a cue to reexamine my systems and rules.

✱ What would you put on a billboard?

"I really admire those places, like Vermont and São Paulo, Brazil, that ban billboards. But, I know that that wasn't really what you were asking. So, my better answer is, I think I would make a billboard that says, '**It Won't Make You Happy**,' and I would place it outside any big shopping mall or car dealer. You know what would be a fun project, actually? To buy and train thousands of parrots to say, 'It won't make you happy!' and then let them loose in the shopping malls and superstores around the world. That's my life mission. Anybody in? Anybody with me? Let's do it."

TAKE 45 MINUTES INSTEAD OF 43 — IS YOUR RED FACE WORTH IT?

"I've always been very Type-A, so a friend of mine got me into cycling when I was living in L.A. I lived right on the beach in Santa Monica, where there's this great bike path in the sand that goes for, I think, 25 miles. I'd go onto the bike path, and I would [go] head down and push it — just red-faced huffing, all the way, pushing it as hard as I could. I would go all the way down to one end of the bike path and back, and then head home, and I'd set my little timer when doing this. . . .

"I noticed it was always 43 minutes. That's what it took me to go as fast as I could on that bike path. But I noticed that, over time, I was starting to feel less psyched about going out on the bike path. Because mentally, when I would think of it, it would feel like pain and hard work. . . . So, then I thought, 'You know, it's not cool for me to associate negative stuff with going on the bike ride. Why don't I just chill? For once, I'm gonna go on the same bike ride, and I'm not going to be a complete snail, but I'll go at half of my normal pace.' I got on my bike, and it was just pleasant.

"I went on the same bike ride, and I noticed that I was standing up, and I was looking around more. I looked into the ocean, and I saw there were these dolphins jumping in the ocean, and I went down to Marina del Rey, to my turnaround point, and I noticed in Marina del Rey, that there was a pelican that was flying above me. I looked up. I was like, 'Hey, a pelican!' and he shit in my mouth.

"So, the point is: I had such a nice time. It was purely pleasant. There was no red face, there was no huffing. And when I got back to my usual stopping place, I looked at my watch, and it said 45 minutes. I thought, 'How the hell could that have been 45 minutes, as opposed to my usual 43? There's no way.' But it was right: 45 minutes. That was a profound lesson that changed the way I've approached my life ever since. . . .

"We could do the math, [but] whatever, 93-something-percent of my huffing and puffing, and all that red face and all that stress was only for an extra 2 minutes. It was basically for nothing. . . . [So,] for life, I think of all of this maximiza-tion — getting the maximum dollar out of everything, the maximum out of every second, the maximum out of every minute — you don't need to stress about any of this stuff. Honestly, that's been my approach ever since. I do things, but I stop before anything gets stressful. . . .

"You notice this internal 'Argh.' That's my cue. I treat that like physical pain. What am I doing? I need to stop doing that thing that hurts. What is that? And, it usually means that I'm just pushing too hard, or doing things that I don't re-ally want to be doing."

ON LACK OF MORNING ROUTINES

"Not only do I not have morning rituals, but there's really nothing that I do every day, except for eating or some form of writing. Here's why: I get really, re-ally, really into one thing at a time. For example, a year ago I discovered a new approach to programming my PostgreSQL database that made all of my code a lot easier. I spent 5 months — every waking hour — just completely immersed in this one thing.

"Then after 5 months, I finished that project. I took a week and I went hiking in Milford Sound in New Zealand. Totally offline. When I got back from that, I was so zen-nature-boy that I spent the next couple of weeks just reading books outside."

✱ What's something you believe that other people think is crazy?
"Oh, that's easy. I've got a lot of unpopular opinions. I believe alcohol tastes bad, and so do olives. I've never tried coffee, but I don't like the smell. I believe all au-dio books should be read and recorded by people from Iceland, because they've got the best accent. I believe it would be wonderful to move to a new country every 6 months for the rest of my life. **I believe you shouldn't start a business unless people are asking you to.** I believe I'm below average. It's a deliberate, cultivated belief to compensate for our tendency to think we're above average. I believe the movie *Scott Pilgrim vs. the World* is a masterpiece. I believe that mu-sic and people don't mix; that music should be appreciated alone without see-ing or knowing who the musicians are and without other people around. Just listening to music for its own sake, not listening to the people around you and not filtered through what you know about the musician's personal life."

TREAT LIFE AS A SERIES OF EXPERIMENTS

"My recommendation is to do little tests. Try a few months of living the life you think you want, but leave yourself an exit plan, being open to the big chance that you might not like it after actually trying it. . . . The best book about this subject is *Stumbling on Happiness* by Daniel Gilbert. His recommendation is to talk to a few people who are currently where you think you want to be and ask them for the pros and cons. Then trust their opinion since they're right in it, not just remembering or imagining."

"EVEN WHEN EVERYTHING IS GOING TERRIBLY, AND I HAVE NO REASON TO BE CONFIDENT, I JUST DECIDE TO BE."

"There's this beautiful Kurt Vonnegut quote that's just a throwaway line in the middle of one of his books, that says, 'We are whatever we pretend to be.'"

THE MOST SUCCESSFUL EMAIL DEREK EVER WROTE

At its largest, Derek spent roughly 4 hours on CD Baby *every six months*. He had systematized everything to run without him. Derek is both successful and fulfilled because he never hesitates to challenge the status quo, to test assumptions. It doesn't have to take much, and his below email illustrates this beautifully.

Enter Derek

When you make a business, you're making a little world where you control the laws. It doesn't matter how things are done everywhere else. In your little world, you can make it like it should be.

When I first built CD Baby, every order had an automated email that let the customer know when the CD was actually shipped. At first, it was just the normal, "Your order has shipped today. Please let us know if it doesn't arrive. Thank you for your business."

After a few months, that felt really incongruent with my mission to make people smile. I knew could do better. So I took 20 minutes and wrote this goofy little thing:

Your CD has been gently taken from our CD Baby shelves with sterilized contamination-free gloves and placed onto a satin pillow.

A team of 50 employees inspected your CD and polished it to make sure it was in the best possible condition before mailing.

Our packing specialist from Japan lit a candle and a hush fell over the crowd as he put your CD into the finest gold-lined box that money can buy.

We all had a wonderful celebration afterwards and the whole party marched down the street to the post office where the entire town of Portland waved "Bon Voyage!" to your package, on its way to you, in our private CD Baby jet on this day, Friday, June 6th.

I hope you had a wonderful time shopping at CD Baby. We sure did. Your picture is on our wall as "Customer of the Year." We're all exhausted but can't wait for you to come back to CDBABY.COM!!

That one silly email, sent out with every order, has been so loved that if you search Google for "private CD Baby jet" you'll get more than 20,000 results. Each one is somebody who got the email and loved it enough to post on their website and tell all their friends.

That one goofy email created thousands of new customers.

When you're thinking of how to make your business bigger, it's tempting to try to think all the big thoughts, the world-changing, massive-action plans.

But please know that it's often the tiny details that really thrill someone enough to make them tell all their friends about you.

ALEXIS OHANIAN

Alexis Ohanian (TW/IG: @ALEXISOHANIAN, ALEXISOHANIAN.COM) is perhaps best known for being a co-founder of Reddit and Hipmunk. He was in the very first class of Y Combinator, arguably the world's most selective startup "accelerator," where he is now a partner. He is an investor or advisor in more than 100 startups, an activist for digital rights (e.g., SOPA/PIPA), and the best-selling author of *Without Their Permission*.

Spirit animal: Black bear

"YOU ARE A ROUNDING ERROR"

"[I had] an executive at Yahoo! who brought me and Steve in [for a potential acquisition discussion] — this was early in Reddit — and told us we were a rounding error because our traffic was so small. . . . I put, 'You are a rounding error,' on our wall in the Reddit office after that meeting as a wall of negative reinforcement for me. That ended up being kind of valuable for me and helpful, and I still am grateful to this day that he was such a dick, because it was so motivating. But I don't want to be that guy."

(See Amanda Palmer's quote, "Take the pain and wear it like a shirt" on page 521.)

TF: Reddit is now a global top-50 website.

YOU HAVE TO GIVE A LOT OF DAMNS

"[Our site] made [users] laugh sometimes because we had jokes in the error messages, that kind of thing. I ask people, . . . 'Give me an example of something that you've built into your product or your service that you're especially proud of, that's one of these touch points for someone to just go, "Wow . . . if you can inject this life into your software, into the copy, into the whatever, you can connect with people." ' I mean, people still fucking tweet about our error message on Hipmunk, and it's an error message. Why are they doing that? Because it gave them a moment of levity while they were doing something that they expected to be pretty boring, like searching for a flight.

"Founders have to realize the bar is set so low because most companies stopped giving a fuck so long ago. . . . It's something that I really expect other founders to do, and it ends up being pretty easy. Compared to building out the actual site or architecting the back end, this doesn't require a few years of programming expertise. **It just requires you to gives lots of damns, which not enough people do.**"

A DAMN-GIVING ASSIGNMENT OF LESS THAN 15 MINUTES

Improve a notification email from your business (e.g., subscription confirmation, order confirmation, whatever):

"Invest that little bit of time to make it a little bit more human or — depending on your brand — a little funnier, a little more different, or a little more whatever. It'll be worth it, and that's my challenge."

(See Derek Sivers's best email ever on page 192.)

* One of his questions for founders who apply to Y Combinator:
"What are you doing that the world doesn't realize is a really big fucking deal?"

GIVING FEEDBACK TO FOUNDERS — HOW DO YOU EXPRESS SKEPTICISM?

Alexis has many approaches, of course, but I liked this example of what Cal Fussman (page 495) might call "letting the silence do the work": "I really think a lot can be conveyed with a raised eyebrow."

ORGANIZATIONS ALEXIS INTRODUCED ME TO:

Electronic Frontier Foundation (eff.org) is the leading nonprofit organization defending civil liberties in the digital world.

Fight for the Future (fightforthefuture.org) is dedicated to protecting and expanding the Internet's transformative power in our lives by creating civic campaigns that are engaging for millions of people.

"PRODUCTIVITY" TRICKS FOR THE NEUROTIC, MANIC-DEPRESSIVE, AND CRAZY (LIKE ME)

This chapter was one of the harder for me to write. I drafted a portion, then I'd let it sit for months. Feeling guilty, I'd spend a few more hours on it, then repeat my procrastination. As a result, the lessons are spread out over a few years.

Eventually, it was the below quote that helped me finish this piece, which I hope will be as helpful to you as it is embarrassing for me.

> "The moment that you feel that, just possibly, you're walking down the street naked, exposing too much of your heart and your mind and what exists on the inside, showing too much of yourself. That's the moment you may be starting to get it right."
>
> **—Neil Gaiman, University of the Arts commencement speech**

So, here goes, and I hope it aids at least a few of you.

Reality Check

Not long ago, I had a birthday party.

A dozen friends and I gathered for several days of wonderful sun, beach, and catching up. On the last day, I didn't get up until 11:30 a.m., knowing full well that the last remaining friends were leaving at 12 noon.

I was afraid of being alone.

Like a child, I hid my head under the covers (literally) and hit snooze until reality couldn't be postponed any further.

But . . . why am I telling you this?

The Dangerous Myths of "Successful" People

We all like to appear "successful" (a nebulous term at best) and the media like to portray standouts as superheroes.

Sometimes, these dramatic stories of overcoming the odds are inspiring. More often, they lead to an unhealthy knee-jerk conclusion:

"Well . . . maybe they [entrepreneur/artist/creator painted as superhero] can do it, but I'm just a normal guy/girl. . . ." This chapter is intended to give you a behind-the-scenes look at my own life. Though I've occasionally done profiles like "A Day In The Life" with Morgan Spurlock's crew, I rarely let journalists follow me for a "normal" day.

Why?

Because I'm no superhero. I'm not even a consistent "normal."

In 2013, I hit a rough patch of three months, during which I:

>> Cried while watching *Rudy*.

>> Repeatedly hit snooze for 1 to 3 HOURS past my planned wake time, because I simply didn't want to face the day.

>> Considered giving everything away and moving to Montreal, Seville, or Iceland. Location varies based on what I imagine escaping.

>> Saw a therapist for the first time, as I was convinced that I was doomed to lifelong pessimism.

>>> Used gentlemanly (ahem) websites to "relax" during the day when I clearly had urgent and important shit to do.*

>>> Took my daily caffeine intake (read: self-medication) so high that my "resting" pulse was 120+ beats per minute. 8 to 10 cups of coffee per day at minimum.

>>> Wore the same pair of jeans for a week straight just to have a much-needed constant during weeks of chaos.

Seems pretty dysfunctional, right?

But, in the last 8 weeks of that same period, I also:

>>> Increased my passive income 20%+.

>>> Bought my dream house.

>>> Meditated twice per day for 20 minutes per session, without fail. That marked the first time I'd been able to meditate consistently.

>>> Ended up cutting my caffeine intake to next-to-nothing (in the last 4 weeks): usually pu-erh tea in the morning and green tea in the afternoon.

>>> With the help of my blog readers, raised $100,000+ for charity: water for my birthday.

>>> Raised $250,000 in 53 minutes for a startup called Shyp.

>>> Signed one of the most exciting business deals of my last 10 years — my TV show, *The Tim Ferriss Experiment*.

>>> Added roughly 20 pounds of muscle after learning the pain and joy of high-rep front squats (and topical DHEA) courtesy of Patrick Arnold (page 35).

>>> Transformed my bloodwork.

---

* Any guy who claims he's never done this shouldn't be trusted.

>> Realized — once again — that manic-depressive symptoms are just part of entrepreneurship.

>> Came to feel closer to all my immediate family members.

The Point

Most "superheroes" are nothing of the sort. They're weird, neurotic creatures who do big things DESPITE lots of self-defeating habits and self-talk.

Personally, I suck at efficiency (doing things quickly). To compensate and cope, here's my 8-step process for maximizing efficacy (doing the right things):

1. Wake up at least 1 hour before you have to be at a computer screen. Email is the mind-killer.

2. Make a cup of tea (I like pu-erh) and sit down with a pen/pencil and paper.

3. Write down the 3 to 5 things — and no more — that are making you the most anxious or uncomfortable. They're often things that have been punted from one day's to-do list to the next, to the next, to the next, and so on. Most important usually equals most uncomfortable, with some chance of rejection or conflict.

4. For each item, ask yourself: **"If this were the only thing I accomplished today, would I be satisfied with my day?" "Will moving this forward make all the other to-dos unimportant or easier to knock off later?" Put another way: "What, if done, will make all of the rest easier or irrelevant?"**

5. Look only at the items you've answered "yes" to for at least one of these questions.

6. Block out at 2 to 3 hours to focus on ONE of them for today. Let the rest of the urgent but less important stuff slide. It will still be there tomorrow.

7. TO BE CLEAR: Block out at 2 to 3 HOURS to focus on ONE of them

for today. This is ONE BLOCK OF TIME. Cobbling together 10 minutes here and there to add up to 120 minutes does not work. No phone calls or social media allowed.

8. If you get distracted or start procrastinating, don't freak out and downward-spiral; just gently come back to your ONE to-do.

Congratulations! That's it.

This is the only way I can create big outcomes despite my never-ending impulse to procrastinate, nap, and otherwise fritter away days with bullshit. If I have 10 important things to do in a day, it's 100% certain *nothing important* will get done that day. On the other hand, I can usually handle one must-do item and block out my lesser behaviors for 2 to 3 hours a day.

It doesn't take much to seem superhuman and appear "successful" to nearly everyone around you. In fact, you just need one rule: **What you do** is more important than **how you do** everything else, and doing something **well** does **not** make it **important**.

If you consistently feel the counterproductive need for volume and doing lots of *stuff*, put these on a Post-it note:

Being busy is a form of laziness — lazy thinking and indiscriminate action.
Being busy is most often used as a guise for avoiding the few critically important but uncomfortable actions.

And when — despite your best efforts — you feel like you're losing at the game of life, remember: Even the best of the best sometimes feel this way. When I'm in the pit of despair, I recall what iconic writer Kurt Vonnegut said about his process: "When I write, I feel like an armless, legless man with a crayon in his mouth."

Don't overestimate the world and underestimate yourself. You are better than you think.

And you are not alone.

"When you can write well, you can think well."

"Everyone is interesting. If you're ever bored in a conversation, the problem's with you, not the other person."

MATT MULLENWEG

Matt Mullenweg (TW/IG: @PHOTOMATT, MA.TT) has been named one of *BusinessWeek*'s 25 Most Influential People on the Web, but I think that's an understatement. He is best known as the original lead developer of WordPress, which now powers more than 25% of the entire web. If you've visited sites like *Wall Street Journal*, *Forbes*, TED, NFL, or Reuters (or my li'l website), you've seen WordPress in action. Matt is also the CEO of Automattic, which is valued at more than $1 billion and has a fully distributed team of 500 employees around the world. I'm honored to be an advisor.

When he appeared on my podcast, I attempted to get him drunk on sipping tequila (Casa Dragones Blanco; he also likes Don Julio 1942) and make him curse, both of which are hard.

Spirit animal: Mantis shrimp

BEHIND THE SCENES

» Matt truly doesn't curse. I once heard him say — I kid you not — "That's really bad butt," to which I responded "What? You're trying to get around 'bad ass'? No, you're not allowed to do that."

» We're both big fans of Peter Drucker and his book *The Effective Executive*, as well as Alain de Botton's (page 486) *How Proust Can Change Your Life*.

» Matt wrote the majority of the code for WordPress over a year of "polyphasic" sleep: roughly 4 hours of waking, followed by 20 to 30 minutes of sleep, repeated indefinitely. This is nicknamed the "Uberman" protocol. Why did he stop? "I got a girlfriend."

» We have traveled to many countries together. He takes all the photos, and I try and learn the language to translate. On one flight to Greece in 2008, I was all wound up about people pirating *The 4-Hour Workweek* online. He asked me "Why are you upset?" which threw me off. Wasn't it obvious? He followed up with "The people who download your book as a bad PDF aren't your customers. They would never buy it in the first place. Look at it as free advertising." And with a 30-second intervention, he eliminated my worrying about it.

» Matt is one of the people I most try to emulate. He is exceptionally calm and logical under pressure. I've seen him face multiple data-center collapses with near-indifference, calmly sipping beer before another billiards shot. What should I tell a hugely influential journalist asking about it? "Tell him we're on it." Then he sunk another ball. He's the epitome of "getting upset won't help things." I frequently ask myself "What would Matt do?" or "What would Matt say to me?"

DON'T BE A DOG — THINK "WHAT IF?"

"From the early days of WordPress, we would always think: 'Okay, if we do X today, what does that result in tomorrow, a year from now, ten years from now?' The metaphor I think of the most — because it's simple — is the dog chasing the car. What does the dog do if he catches the car? He doesn't have a plan for it. So I find it just as often on the entrepreneurial side. People don't plan for success."

ON LOSING A $400,000 CHECK

Matt constantly misplaces things.

"I have a meeting and I spend 10 minutes looking for my wallet because I just stuck it someplace. It's in the fridge or something. I don't know. I'm always losing something. Actually, I lost one of our initial investment checks. It was a check for $400,000."

TIM: "That's not good to lose."

MATT: "It was investor Phil Black, who's still on the board today, and he wrote a paper check, like the kind you would use at the grocery store or for normal things. The most money I'd ever seen in my life. I was 20 years old. I was like: 'What is this?' I expected it to be a check like a Publishers Clearing House, you know? Like the size of a table."

TIM: "Right, that you could surf like a floating carpet from *Aladdin* down to the bank."

MATT: "Luckily, the other investors wired their money because I misplaced this check. And I was thinking, 'Oh, my goodness, what do I do in this situation?' Because obviously, he could stop the check, but then he's just entrusted me with $400,000 and I've lost it. Do I tell him? Do I not tell him? Is he going to notice at some point? And months passed. Literally months passed. He doesn't say anything, I don't say anything."

TIM: "Because you didn't want to ask him."

MATT: "I didn't ask him. And I'm going back to Houston for Thanksgiving, and I open the book I'm reading and I had used it as a bookmark. And it kind of fell out of the book on the plane. I was like: 'Oh, my goodness!'"

THE TAIL END

On a hike in San Francisco, Matt recommended I read "The Tail End" by Tim Urban on the *Wait But Why* blog — if you only read one article this month, make it that one. It uses diagrams to underscore how short life really is. Here's just one gem: "It turns out that when I graduated from high school, I had already used up 93% of my in-person parent time. I'm now enjoying the last 5% of that time. We're in the tail end." Might be time for you (and me) to rethink our personal priorities. On a related and sad note, Matt's father passed away unexpectedly weeks after he recommended this article to me. Matt was at his bedside.

QWERTY IS FOR JUNIOR VARSITY

The normal QWERTY keyboard layout was designed to slow down human operators to avoid jams. That time has passed, so try the Dvorak layout instead, which is easier on your tendons and helps prevent carpal tunnel syndrome. Read *The Dvorak Zine* (dvzine.org). Colemak is even more efficient, if you dare. Within Automattic, Matt has held speed-typing challenges, where the loser has to switch to the winner's layout. So far, Dvorak has always beaten QWERTY.

ON GETTING THE MA.TT DOMAIN NAME

"I had to wire money [several grand] to Trinidad and Tobago. I was in the Bank of America, and they said, 'Sir, are you sure about this?' I was like, 'Yeah, yeah, it's fine. I read it on the Internet.'"

TOOLS OF THE TRADE

Here are some of Matt's go-to tech enablers:

P2 (WordPress theme) for replacing email — p2theme.com
Slack for replacing IM — slack.com
Momentum: Chrome extension to help you focus.
Wunderlist: To-do management app/tool to help you get stuff done.
Telegram: a messaging app with really good encryption
Calm.com for meditation

HOW MATT GOT IN SHAPE

He committed to one push-up before bed. Yes, just one push-up:

"No matter how late you're running, no matter what's going on in the world, you can't argue against doing one push-up. Come on. There's no excuse. I often find I just need to get over that initial hump with something that's almost embarrassingly small as a goal, and then that can become a habit."

TF: Remember Chade-Meng Tan's "one breath" on page 155? Same idea.

FULLY TEXT, FULLY DISTRIBUTED

Automattic has more than 500 employees and is fully distributed across more than 50 countries. They have almost no in-person or phone meetings. There is no "headquarters," so to speak. They skip the offices, hire the best talent worldwide, and spend the savings on $250 per month co-working stipends and other benefits.

"The interview process is as much like the actual work as possible. It's all [email or] text chat, because that's how we primarily communicate. It also prevents you from any subconscious bias."

TIM: "What do you look for or disqualify against?"

MATT: "I look for a passion, attention to detail, drive beyond the things that they need to do. I'm totally down with quirky."

TIM: "What questions do you ask to get an indication of those things?"

MATT: "So at this point [in the early stages] all I'm doing is looking at emails. So literally there's no chat, no anything. It's purely based on the care and effort that they put into this email. We've tried forms and things they fill out before, and we've gone back to just a freeform email because I want to see what kind of attachment they use. I want to see who their email client is. I want to see if you can tell they've copied and pasted things because of different text and different font sizes. All of those are indicators, and not any one of them [alone].

"You know something I can say, you asked about what we look for in candidates: clarity of writing. I think clarity of writing indicates clarity of thinking."

TF: I highly recommend reading "The CEO of Automattic on Holding 'Auditions' to Build a Strong Team" from the April 2014 issue of the *Harvard Business Review* (find it on hbr.org).

WORDS THAT WORK

Matt pays incredible attention to word choice and ordering (diction and syntax). He loves studying "code poets" — coders who have elegant, poetic style — but he does the same with spoken language. He recommended I read the book *Words That Work*, written by Republican political strategist Frank Luntz. It's brilliant. Matt added, "If someone likes that book, then I might point them to George Lakoff. He has a great seminal work from the 1980s called *Women, Fire, and Dangerous Things*." He loves books about framing and language.

✻ Advice to your 20-year-old self?

"Slow down. I think a lot of the mistakes of my youth were mistakes of ambition, not mistakes of sloth. So just slowing down, whether that's meditating, whether that's taking time for yourself away from screens, whether that's really focusing in on who you're talking to or who you're with."

104 CHICKEN McNUGGETS

"The Super Bowl was in Houston, Texas [in 2004]. I lived like a mile from Reliant Stadium. For the Super Bowl, McDonalds did a special where you could get 20 McNuggets for around $4, and I was super broke at the time. So I thought: 'Man, I'm just gonna stock up on these,' the way you might get ramen or cans of Campbell's, which I would do when they went on sale. I'd always buy a bunch of them.

"So I just like got a bunch of McNuggets and then—I love McNuggets—I had to sweet-talk the person so they gave me lots of extra sweet and sour sauce."

TIM: "Oh, my God."

MATT: "And the McDonalds sweet and sour sauce is not like sweet and sour sauce anywhere else in the world. All sweet and sour sauce is red, and for some reason theirs is brown. I don't know why. You might."

TIM: "It's been genetically engineered to be as addictive as possible? I don't know."

MATT: "It's so good. So I just start popping them, and next thing I knew it was 104."

TIM: "It wasn't even a bet or anything? You just rampaged through 104?"

MATT: "While watching the Super Bowl."

NICHOLAS McCARTHY

Nicholas McCarthy (TW: @NMcCarthyPiano, nicholasmccarthy
.co.uk) was born in 1989 without his right hand, and started to play the
piano at the age of 14. He was told he would never succeed as a concert
pianist. The doubters were wrong. His graduation from the prestigious
Royal College of Music in London in 2012 appeared in press around the
world, as he became the only one-handed pianist to graduate from the
Royal College of Music in its 130-year history.

Nicholas has now performed extensively throughout the world, including playing alongside Coldplay and giving a rendition of the Paralym-
pic Anthem in front of an in-person audience of 86,000 people and half a
billion worldwide TV viewers. His first album, entitled *Solo*, features 17
pieces of left-hand repertoire spanning three centuries and has been released around the world to great acclaim.

FRANZ LISZT

I'm embarrassed to admit that I'd never heard of Liszt before my conversation with Nicholas. Now, he's part of my regular listening. Search YouTube for "Best of Liszt" (Halidon Music):

"Franz Liszt is one of the great romantic composers of piano literature. He was really held as the super-virtuoso of the 19th century."

✳ Lesser-known musicians to explore?

"The concert(s) of the Argentinian pianist Martha Argerich. She is just super-human. She is quite elderly now, but she still plays. She's coming to the BBC Proms this year. She has cult status in our world."

TF: I now routinely listen to her. To have your mind explode, search "Tchaikovsky Piano Concerto No 1 FULL Argerich Charles Dutoit" and check out minute 31.

PLAYING THE LONG GAME

Nicholas explains why he decided to specialize in left-hand repertoire, instead of also using his right "little hand," a very short extension of his forearm from the elbow:

"It was what my teacher at the time said: 'You don't want to become a gimmick.' Especially with all the TV talent shows, which were just coming about then. It was at the start of *Britain's Got Talent.* . . . I'm so relieved I took her advice, because I would've been that gimmick who maybe made a quick buck over two years, but I certainly wouldn't have the respect that I have now as a pianist, and I certainly wouldn't have had the career that I've had to date and that I look forward to continuing until I'm in my 60s."

✳ Nicholas's best $100 or less purchase?

Neal's Yard aromatherapy diffuser, which he uses every day when at home: "I find [geranium] relaxes me, but at the same time keeps me perked up enough to be able to work."

TF: I started using geranium oil shortly after our podcast, when working on early brainstorming and drafting for this book. Lacking a diffuser, I started by dabbing a bit on my wrists and then rubbing it on my neck near my ears. Placebo or not, I felt noticeably more stamina. I later purchased an InnoGear 200 ml aromatherapy diffuser in "wood grain" (most diffusers look cheap otherwise) for home use.

TONY ROBBINS

Tony Robbins (TW/FB/IG: @TONYROBBINS, TONYROBBINS.COM) is the world's most famous performance coach. He's advised everyone from Bill Clinton and Serena Williams to Leonardo DiCaprio and Oprah (who calls him "superhuman"). Tony Robbins has consulted or advised international leaders including Nelson Mandela, Mikhail Gorbachev, Margaret Thatcher, François Mitterrand, Princess Diana, Mother Teresa, and three U.S. presidents. Robbins has also developed and produced five award-winning television infomercials that have continuously aired — on average — every 30 minutes, 24 hours a day, somewhere in North America, since 1989.

BACK STORY

I first read Tony Robbins's *Unlimited Power* in high school, when it was recommended by a straight-A student. Then, just out of college, I listened to a used cassette set of *Personal Power II* during my commute in my mom's hand-me-down minivan. It catalyzed my first real business, which led to many of the adventures (and misadventures) in *The 4-Hour Workweek*. People say, "Don't meet your heroes" because it nearly always ends in disappointment. With Tony, however, it's been the opposite: The more I get to know him, the more he impresses me.

LITTLE-KNOWN FACT

The first Instagram pic I ever posted (@timferriss) was of Tony literally palming my entire face. His hands are like catcher's mitts.

"I DIDN'T SURVIVE, I *PREPARED*."

Nelson Mandela's answer when Tony asked him, "Sir, how did you survive all those years in prison?"

IS THERE A QUOTE THAT GUIDES YOUR LIFE?

"It's a belief: **Life is always happening** *for* **us, not** *to* **us.** It's our job to find out where the benefit is. If we do, life is magnificent."

SHORT AND SWEET

"'Stressed' is the achiever word for 'fear.'"

"Losers react, leaders anticipate."

"Mastery doesn't come from an infographic. What you *know* doesn't mean shit. What do you *do* consistently?"

THE BEST INVESTMENT HE'S EVER MADE?

$35 for a 3-hour Jim Rohn seminar, attended at age 17. He agonized over the $35 decision, as he was making $40 a week as a janitor, but Jim gave Tony's life direction. Decades later, when Tony asked Warren Buffett what his all-time best investment was, the answer was a Dale Carnegie public speaking course, taken at age 20. Prior to that, Buffett would vomit before public speaking. After the course—and this is the critical piece—Buffett immediately went to the University of Omaha and asked to teach, as he didn't want to lapse back into his old behaviors. As Tony recounted, Buffett told him, "Investing in yourself is the most important investment you'll ever make in your life. . . . There's no financial investment that'll ever match it, because if you develop more skill, more ability, more insight, more capacity, that's what's going to really provide economic freedom. . . . It's those skill sets that really make that happen." This echoes what Jim Rohn famously said, "If you let your learning lead to knowledge, you become a fool. If you let your learning lead to action, you become wealthy."

QUALITY QUESTIONS CREATE A QUALITY LIFE

Tony sometimes phrases this as, "The quality of your life is the quality of your questions." Questions determine your focus. Most people—and I'm certainly guilty of this at times—spend their lives focusing on negativity (e.g., "How could he say that to me?!") and therefore the wrong priorities.

A FOCUS ON "ME" = SUFFERING

"This brain inside our heads is a 2 million-year-old brain. . . . It's ancient, old survival software that is running you a good deal of time. Whenever you're suffering, that survival software is there. **The reason you're suffering is you're focused on yourself.** People tell me, 'I'm not suffering that way. I'm worrying about my kids. My kids are not what they need to be.' No, the reason [these people are] upset is they feel they failed their kids. It's still about them. . . . Suffering comes from three thought patterns: loss, less, never."

   TF: The bolded portion above, combined with another friend's advice, changed my life. It took a while for me to connect the dots. I don't think I'm a complete narcissist (too bald and pale for that), but I still wondered how to put this into a concrete daily practice. Then, I learned the dead simple "loving-kindness meditation" exercise from my friend Chade-Meng Tan (page 157), which had a profound effect after just 3 to 4 days. Try it.

STATE → STORY → STRATEGY

I learned this from my first Tony Robbins event, Unleash the Power Within (UPW), which Tony invited me to after our first podcast. Perhaps more than any other lesson from Tony, I've thought about this the most in the last year. If you were to look at my daily journal right now, you'd see that I've scribbled "STATE → STORY → STRATEGY" at the top of each page for the next several weeks. It's a reminder to check the boxes in that order.

   Tony believes that, in a lowered emotional state, we only see the problems, not solutions. Let's say you wake up feeling tired and overwhelmed. You sit down to brainstorm strategies to solve your issues, but it comes to naught, and you feel even worse afterward. This is because you started in a negative state, then attempted strategy but didn't succeed (due to tunnel vision on the problems), and then likely told yourself self-defeating stories (e.g., "I always do this. Why am I so wound up I can't even think straight?"). To fix this, he encourages you to "prime" your **state** first. The biochemistry will help you proactively tell yourself an enabling **story**. Only then do you think on **strategy**, as you'll see the options instead of dead ends.

"Priming" my state is often as simple as doing 5 to 10 push-ups or getting 20 minutes of sun exposure (see Rick Rubin, page 502). Even though I do my most intense exercise at night, I've started doing 1–2 minutes of calisthenics — or kettlebell swings (see Justin Boreta, page 356) — in the morning to set my state for the day. Tony's own priming process is included below.

I now often ask myself, "Is this really a problem I need to *think* my way out of? Or is it possible I just need to fix my biochemistry?" I've wasted a lot of time journaling on "problems" when I just needed to eat breakfast sooner, do 10 push-ups, or get an extra hour of sleep. Sometimes, you think you have to figure out your life's purpose, but you really just need some macadamia nuts and a cold fucking shower.

MORNING "PRIMING" INSTEAD OF MEDITATION

Upon waking, Tony immediately goes into his priming routine, which is intended to produce a rapid change in his physiology: "To me, if you want a primetime life, you've got to prime daily." There are many tools that I've seen Tony use over the years, several of which I've adopted for myself, including:

» Cold-water plunge (I use a quick cold shower, which could be just 30 to 60 seconds)

» Tony follows this with breathing exercises. He does 3 sets of 30 reps. His seated technique is similar to the rapid nasal "breath of fire" in yoga, but he adds in rapid overhead extension of the arms on the inhale, with the elbows dropping down the rib cage on the exhale.

» Alternative: "Breath walking." This is vintage Tony, but I still use it quite often when traveling. Simply walk for a few minutes, using a breathing cycle of 4 short inhales through the nose, then 4 short exhales through the mouth.

Following something like the above, Tony does 9 to 10 minutes of what some might consider meditation. To him, however, the objective is very different: It's about cueing and prompting enabling emotions for the rest of the day. His 9 to 10 minutes are broken into thirds. Here is an abbreviated synopsis:

The first 3 minutes: "Feeling totally grateful for three things. I make sure that one of them is very, very simple: the wind on my face, the reflection of the clouds that I just saw. But I don't just think gratitude. I let gratitude fill my soul, because when you're grateful, we all know there's no anger. It's impossible to be angry and grateful simultaneously. When you're grateful, there is no fear. You can't be fearful and grateful simultaneously."

The second 3 minutes: "Total focus on feeling the presence of God, if you will, however you want to language that for yourself. But this inner presence coming in, and feeling it heal everything in my body, in my mind, my emotions, my relationships, my finances. I see it as solving anything that needs to be solved. I experience the strengthening of my gratitude, of my conviction, of my passion. . . ."

The last 3 minutes: "Focusing on three things that I'm going to make happen, my 'three to thrive.' . . . **See it as though it's already been done, feel the emotions, etc. . . .**

"And, as I've always said, there's no excuse not to do 10 minutes. If you don't have 10 minutes, you don't have a life."

This reminded me of something I've heard from many adept meditators (such as Russell Simmons) in various forms: "If you don't have 20 minutes to delve into yourself through meditation, then that means you really need 2 hours."

FOUR COMMONALITIES ACROSS THE BEST INVESTORS

Tony has interviewed and developed friendships with some of the best investors in the world, including Paul Tudor Jones (who he's coached for more than 10 years), Ray Dalio, Carl Icahn, David Swensen, Kyle Bass, and many more. These are the hard-to-interview "unicorns" who consistently beat the market, despite the fact that it's called impossible. Tony wrote a book based on his learnings (*Money: Master the Game*), and here are few of the patterns he identified:

1 **Capping the downside:** "Every single one of those [people] is obsessed with *not* losing money. I mean, a level of obsession that's mind-boggling." On Richard Branson: "His first question to every business is, 'What's the downside? And how do I protect against it?' Like when he did his piece with Virgin [air travel] — that's a big risk to start an airline — he went to Boeing and negotiated a deal that [he] could send the planes back if it didn't work, and he wasn't liable."

TF: Branson also tested with little or no risk. In *Losing My Virginity*, which had a huge impact on me around college graduation, he described his very first flight: "We were trying to catch a flight to Puerto Rico, but the local Puerto Rican scheduled flight was canceled. The airport terminal was full of stranded passengers. I made a few calls to charter companies, and agreed to charter a plane for $2,000 to Puerto Rico. I divided the price by the number of seats, borrowed a blackboard, and wrote VIRGIN AIRWAYS: $39 SINGLE FLIGHT TO PUERTO RICO. I walked around the airport terminal and soon filled every seat on the charter plane. As we landed in Puerto Rico, a passenger turned to me and said: 'Virgin Airways isn't too bad — smarten up the service a little and you could be in business.'"

Back to Tony, "cap the downside" also applies to thinking long-term about fees and middlemen: "If three of my friends [and I] all put aside the same amount of money, and we all get a 7% return, but my buddy's getting fees of 3%, my other buddy's 2%, and I'm 1%, and all three of us put $1 million in or $100,000 . . . the person with 3% of fees ends up with 65% less money [in the long-term]. . . ."

2 **Asymmetrical risks and rewards:** "Every single one of them is obsessed with asymmetrical risk and reward. . . . It simply means they're looking to use the least amount of risk to get the max amount of upside, and that's what they live for. . . . [They don't believe they] have to take huge risks for huge rewards. **Say, 'How do I get no risk and get huge rewards?' and because you ask a question continuously and you believe [there's an] answer, you get it.**"

TF: Here's a wild example. Kyle Bass at one point bought $1 million worth of nickels (roughly 20 million coins). Why? Because their face value was 5 cents and their scrap metal value was 6.8 cents at the time. That's an immediate gain of $360,000. Nicely done.

3 **Asset allocation: "They absolutely, beyond a shadow of a doubt, know they're going to be wrong** . . . so they set up an asset allocation system that will make them successful. They all agree asset allocation is the single most important investment decision." In *Money: Master the Game*, Ray Dalio elaborated for Tony: "When people think they've got

a balanced portfolio, stocks are three times more volatile than bonds. So when you're 50/50, you're really 90/10. You really are massively at risk, and that's why when the markets go down, you get eaten alive. . . . Whatever asset class you invest in, I promise you, in your lifetime, it will drop no less than 50% and more likely 70% at some point. That is why you absolutely must diversify."

4 **Contribution:** "And the last one that I found: almost all of them were real givers, not just givers on the surface . . . but really passionate about giving. . . . It was really real."

    TF: One great example is the Robin Hood Foundation, conceived of by Paul Tudor Jones, which fights poverty in New York City.

✳ Who comes to mind when I say the word "punchable"?

For a few dozen podcast episodes, I asked the question: "When you think of the word 'punchable,' whose face is the first that comes to mind?" Nine times out of ten, it fell flat, and I've since stopped asking it. But in my interview with Tony, all of those flops were redeemed. He took a long pause and then said, "Punchable. Oh, my gosh. Well, I had an interesting meeting with President Obama . . ." and proceeded to describe a closed-session conversation with President Obama (you can hear the full story at 42:15 in episode #38). It was one of those "God, I really hope my audio equipment is working" moments. He closed it with "So, I don't know if I'd say 'punch,' but 'shake' him."

✳ Most-gifted or recommended books

    Man's Search for Meaning by Viktor Frankl
    The Fourth Turning by William Strauss (Also, *Generations* by William
        Strauss, which was gifted to Tony by Bill Clinton)
    Mindset by Carol Dweck (for parenting)
    As a Man Thinketh by James Allen (see Shay Carl, page 441)

CASEY NEISTAT

Casey Neistat (TW/IG: @CaseyNeistat, youtube.com/caseyneistat) is a New York–based filmmaker and YouTuber. Casey ran away from home at 15 and had his first child at 17. He went on welfare to get free milk and diapers and never asked his parents for money again.

His online films have been viewed nearly 300 million times in the last 5 years. He is the writer, director, editor, and star of the series *The Neistat Brothers* on HBO and won the John Cassavetes Award at the 2011 Independent Spirit Awards for the film *Daddy Longlegs*. His main body of work consists of dozens of short films he has released exclusively on the Internet, including regular contributions to the critically acclaimed *New York Times* Op-Docs series. He is also the founder of Beme, a startup aiming to make creating and sharing video dead simple.

Spirit animal: Sled dog

ALL YOU NEED TO KNOW IS FROM WORLD WAR II

"I always say I got all my understanding of how business and life works from studying the Second World War."

Aside from *The Autobiography of Malcolm X*, Casey's favorite book is *The Second World War* by John Keegan. He's read this massive tome three times, cover to cover. He remembers showing up to work and getting in trouble because he was tired from staying up all night reading this textbook.

The Life and Death of Colonel Blimp is Casey's favorite movie, made during World War II. Wes Anderson studied this film, and you can see a lot of his adapted style in this movie.

✷ Favorite documentary

Little Dieter Needs to Fly by Werner Herzog is Casey's favorite documentary, made in 1997. This is about a U.S. fighter pilot in Vietnam who gets shot down in his very first mission, and is trapped as a POW for a number of years. This documentary will bring you to your knees. Any time you are having a bad day (or you think you have it hard), watch this movie and you will understand what it means to survive. (See Jocko Willink, page 412.)

FOLLOW WHAT ANGERS YOU

Casey made the short film *Bike Lanes* in 2011, and it became his first viral hit. He was given a summons from a New York City police officer for riding his bike outside of the bike lane, which isn't an actual infraction. Instead of going to court, fighting the $50 summons, and wasting half a day in the process, Casey redirected his anger and made a movie that expressed his frustration in a clever way.

Casey begins the movie by repeating what the cop told him: He has to stay in the bike lane for safety and legal reasons, no matter what. Casey proceeds to ride his bike around NYC, crashing into everything that is in the bike lanes preventing people from following this rule. The film's grand finale is Casey crashing into a police car that was truly parked in the middle of a bike lane.

His movie went tremendously viral and was seen around 5 million times in its first day. At one point, Mayor Bloomberg had to respond to a question about the video in a press conference. When in doubt about your next creative project, follow your anger (see Whitney Cummings, page 477, and James Altucher, page 246).

WHAT'S THE MOST OUTRAGEOUS THING YOU CAN DO?

Make It Count, at close to 20 million views, is Casey's all-time most popular video on YouTube. The catalyst: He'd built a successful career in advertising by 2011 but was extremely bored. He was in the middle of a three-commercial deal with Nike: "The first two movies were right down the line, what you'd expect. I had big, huge, $100-million athletes in them. They were very well received. I loved making them. But when it came time to make the third movie, I was really burnt out from the process.

"At the ninth hour, I called my editor up and said, 'Hey, let's not make this advertisement. Instead, let's do something I've always wanted to do, which is: Let's just take the entire production budget and travel the world until we run out of money, and we'll record that. We'll make some sort of movie about that.' And he said, 'You're crazy, but sure.'"

The *Make It Count* video literally opens with scrolling text that says, "Nike asked me to make a movie about what it means to make it count. Instead of making their movie, I spent the entire budget traveling around the world with my friend Max. We'd keep going until the money ran out. It took 10 days." They covered 15 countries.

Make It Count became a video about chasing what matters to you. This was the entire message and point of the campaign to begin with. *Make It Count* ended up being Nike's most watched video on the Internet for several years.

TF: How can you make your bucket-list dreams pay for themselves by sharing them? This is, in effect, how I've crafted my entire career since 2004. It's modeled after Ben Franklin's excellent advice: "If you would not be forgotten as soon as you are dead and rotten, either write things worth reading, or do things worth writing."

THE YOUTUBE INFLECTION POINT

Casey's subscriber count and success on YouTube hockey-sticked when he decided on his 34th birthday to vlog (video blog) daily. Shay Carl (page 441) had the same experience.

PHILOSOPHY AND DAILY ROUTINE

"You realize that you will never be the best-looking person in the room. You'll never be the smartest person in the room. You'll never be the most educated, the most well-versed. You can never compete on those levels. But what you can always compete on, the true egalitarian aspect to success, is hard work. You can always work harder than the next guy."

Casey walks the talk. He wakes up at 4:30 a.m., 7 days a week, and he immediately finishes his vlog edit from the night before.

>>> The edit usually gets done between 6:30 a.m. and 7 a.m.

>>> 7 a.m. to 7:45 a.m. is for processing, uploading, and designing the video.

>>> The video goes live at exactly 8 a.m., 7 days a week.

Casey works out immediately after 8 a.m., which usually involves running (8 to 12 miles) or the gym. He likes listening to the Jonny Famous playlist on Spotify.

He goes into the office by 9:30 a.m. after his workout. He works in his office all day, and tries to get out by 6:30 p.m. to race home and give his baby a bath. He will then hang out with his wife for about an hour until she goes to bed around 9 p.m.

After his wife goes to bed, he sits down and edits until he passes out at his computer, usually around 1 a.m. Casey usually sleeps on the couch until 4:30 a.m., and then he starts the process all over again.

* Who do you think of when you hear the word "successful"?
"My grandmother. She passed away at 92. She's my hero, she's my muse, she's my everything. She started tap dancing when she was 6 years old. She was a little fat girl and her parents made her do something to lose the weight, so she started tap dancing, and she loved it. She fell in love with something at age 6 and she didn't stop tap dancing until the day before she died at age 92. She died on a Monday morning, and the first thing we had to do was call her 100 students to say she wasn't going to make class that day.

"What is the ultimate quantification of success? For me, it's not how much time you spend doing what you love. It's how little time you spend doing what you hate. And this woman spent all day, every day doing what she loved."

MORGAN SPURLOCK

Morgan Spurlock (TW: @MORGANSPURLOCK, MORGANSPURLOCK.COM) is an Oscar-nominated documentary filmmaker based in New York. He is a prolific writer, director, producer, and human guinea pig. His first film, *Super Size Me*, premiered at the Sundance Film Festival in 2004, winning Best Directing honors. The film went on to garner an Academy Award nomination for best feature documentary.

Since then, Morgan has directed, produced, and/or distributed the critically acclaimed CNN series *Morgan Spurlock: Inside Man*, the FX series *30 Days*, and the films *Where in the World Is Osama Bin Laden?*, *Freakonomics*, *The Greatest Movie Ever Sold*, and many others.

Morgan's latest project is a tech startup called Clect (clect.com), which is a community and one-stop marketplace where people can browse, sell, and buy collectibles of any type imaginable (Star Wars, Smurfs, comics, a Millennium Falcon made from motorcycle parts, etc.).

Spirit animal: Rhino

"ONCE YOU GET FANCY, FANCY GETS BROKEN."

TF: This was related to gear, but it can be extended to much more.

HOW *SUPER SIZE ME* CAME TO BE

"I was sitting on my mom's couch in a spectacular tryptophan haze, when a news story came on about these two girls who were suing McDonald's. These girls said, 'We're fat, we're sick, and it's your fault.' I thought, 'Come on, that's crazy. You're going to sue somebody for selling you food that you bought, that you ate, and then blame them for it? How can you do that?' Then a spokesperson for McDonald's came on and said, 'You can't link our food to these girls being sick. You can't link our food to these girls being obese. Our food is healthy. It's nutritious. It's good for you.' I thought, 'I don't know if you can say that either. . . . If it's that good for me, then shouldn't I be able to eat it for 30 days straight with no side effects?' And I was like: 'That's it.'"

TF: Is there a common saying, or some public pronouncement, that you can disprove by making art about it? By doing a test? What makes you angry? (See Casey Neistat, page 217, and Whitney Cummings, page 477.)

ON CHEERING FOR YOURSELF FIRST

"Touré is a great writer-commentator. He told me a story [about going to Kanye West's house] once . . . and inside Kanye's house, there's a big, giant poster of Kanye right inside the living room. Touré asked, 'Kanye, why do you have a giant picture of you on the wall?' and Kanye goes, 'Well, I got to cheer for me before anyone else can cheer for me.' I thought, 'There is some fantastic logic. That's a good response.'"

STORY TRUMPS CINEMATOGRAPHY

Advice to aspiring filmmakers: "You can sacrifice quality for a great story. . . . I'll watch shaky camera footage now . . . so long as it's a great story and I'm engaged."

"WATCHING HIM LIGHT IS LIKE WATCHING A MONKEY FUCK A FOOTBALL." — JAMES CAMERON

This is one of Morgan's favorite one-liners attributed to James Cameron, from a *New Yorker* profile of Cameron, "Man of Extremes." I actually met Jim briefly through Peter Diamandis (page 369), as we went on a zero G flight (zero gravity parabolic flight) together. As part of the experience, which was a fundraiser for the XPRIZE, we all got crew shirts from the first *Avatar* production. The shirts have just three lines on them in huge font: HOPE IS NOT A STRATEGY. LUCK IS NOT A FACTOR. FEAR IS NOT AN OPTION. I still wear the T-shirt for motivation during big projects, as I did for the final deadline sprint for *The 4-Hour Body*.

DON'T BE AFRAID TO SHOW YOUR SCARS

"A friend of mine, a few years ago, gave me some good advice. He said, '**You can't be afraid to show your scars.**' That's who you are, and he said you have to continue to stay true to that. I think that was some of the best advice I ever got."

* **Most-gifted or recommended book?**

    The Living Gita: The Complete Bhagavad Gita — A Commentary for Modern Readers by Sri Swami Satchidananda

* **Favorite documentaries**

    The Fog of War (Errol Morris) — Many guests recommend this. It's incredible and has an unbelievable 98% average on Rotten Tomatoes.
    Brother's Keeper (Joe Berlinger and Bruce Sinofsky)
    Hoop Dreams (Steve James)
    Enron: Smartest Guys in the Room and *Going Clear: Scientology and the Prison of Belief* (Alex Gibney)

WHAT MY MORNING JOURNAL LOOKS LIKE

History is littered with examples of successful (and unsuccessful) people who kept daily journals, ranging from Marcus Aurelius to Ben Franklin, and from Mark Twain to George Lucas.

But what on earth did they write about?

Perhaps you've seen excerpts of their private journals and thought to yourself, "Goddamn, that reads like the Gettysburg Address!" and become demoralized.

In this chapter, I'll show you what my raw morning journal looks like and describe its function.

Why?

Because it's messy, and seeing the mess can be encouraging. It's easy to imagine our heroes as unflappable juggernauts, who conquer insecurity with a majestic mental karate chop every morning. This is, of course, a fantasy. Most people you see on magazine covers have plenty of mornings when they'd rather hide under the covers all day long.

If you want to be wealthy — as measured in money, time, relationships, ease of sleep, or otherwise — "spiritual windshield wipers" will help you get there with fewer accidents and less headache. Let me explain. . . .

The Daily Struggle

Nearly every morning, I sit down with a hot cocktail of turmeric, ginger, pu-erh tea, and green tea. Next, I crack open *The Artist's Way: Morning Pages Journal* by Julia Cameron.

The original *Artist's Way* was first recommended to me by screenwriter and producer Brian Koppelman (page 613), so he's to thank for this practice in my life. But I largely skipped the original—perhaps unfairly—as more book consumption didn't interest me. I often use reading to procrastinate. What I needed was a daily and meditative practice of production, like a tea ceremony. So, voilà, I bought the journal. This "companion" provides plenty of context to be used by itself.

To be clear, I don't journal to "be productive." I don't do it to find great ideas, or to put down prose I can later publish. The pages aren't intended for anyone but me.

Morning pages are, as author Julia Cameron puts it, **"spiritual windshield wipers."** It's the most cost-effective therapy I've ever found. To quote her further, from page viii:

"Once we get those muddy, maddening, confusing thoughts [nebulous worries, jitters, and preoccupations] on the page, we face our day with clearer eyes."

Please reread the above quote. It may be the most important aspect of trapping thought on paper (i.e., writing) you'll ever encounter. Even if you consider yourself a terrible writer, writing can be viewed as a *tool*. There are huge benefits to writing, even if no one—yourself included—ever reads what you write. In other words, *the process matters more than the product*.

Below is one of my real entries, which I've typed out for easier readability.

SUNDAY, DEC. 28, NEW YORK

Woke up at 7:30 a.m., before everyone else. Feels great.

It's a Sunday, so I feel I can take it slow, which is probably the reason it feels great.

Why should Monday or Tuesday be any different? There are still people waiting regardless. Let them wait.

It's funny how we work and aim and strive to get to a point where people wait for us, not the other way around. Cue Get Shorty!

And yet, when we arrive at this vaunted point, the masses of people (often rightly) incessantly knocking on the door, one after another, causes far more stress than when you were a mere peon (sp)! [I was unsure of spelling.]

Is it because of the 100x more inbound, which decreases a feeling of self-directed free will? A feeling that you're constantly choosing from someone else's buffet instead of cooking your own food?

Or is it because you *feel* you must be defensive and protect what you have: time, money, relationships, space, etc.?

For someone who's "won" through a lifetime of offense, of attacking, playing the defensive game conflicts with the core of who they are.

So . . . What's the Point Again?

There are two ways to interpret the above journal entry, and they're not mutually exclusive:

I. I'm trying to figure things out, and this might help.

For instance: I've identified conflicts between goals (become "successful" in some respect) and related side-effects (100x more inbound), which negate the benefits. I've also noted that my big wins in life have come from being aggressive, much like iconic coach Dan Gable, whose epic rants in the hard-to-find doc *Competitor Supreme* are worth finding. But the fetters of even moderate success makes one feel like they have to play defense, or manage instead of conquer. This runs counter to my DNA, which leads to unhappiness. Therefore, I need to divest myself of assets that require "protecting," or I need to better delegate this responsibility.

That all sounds pleasantly analytical. Aren't we smart? But perhaps the real value is that . . .

2. I'm just caging my monkey mind on paper so I can get on with my fucking day.

If you take nothing from this chapter but #2 above and the next few lines, I'll consider my mission accomplished.

Morning pages don't need to solve your problems. They simply need to get them out of your head, where they'll otherwise bounce around all day like a bullet ricocheting inside your skull.

Could bitching and moaning on paper for 5 minutes each morning change your life?

As crazy as it seems, I believe the answer is yes.

REID HOFFMAN

Reid Hoffman (LI/TW: @REIDHOFFMAN, REIDHOFFMAN.ORG) is often referred to as "The Oracle of Silicon Valley" by tech insiders, who look at his company-building and investing track record (Facebook, Airbnb, Flickr, etc.) with awe. Reid is co-founder and executive chairman of LinkedIn, which has more than 300 million users and was sold to Microsoft for $26.2 billion in cash. He was previously executive vice president at PayPal, which was purchased by eBay for $1.5 billion. He has a master's degree in philosophy from Oxford, where he was a Marshall Scholar.

BEHIND THE SCENES

≫ Reid, along with Matt Mullenweg (page 202), is one of the calmest people I've ever met. His former chief of staff has told stories of Reid responding to an insult with "I'm perfectly willing to accept that" and moving on.

≫ Reid was nicknamed "firefighter in chief" at PayPal by then-CEO Peter Thiel.

≫ Reid and I are both on the advisory board of QuestBridge, where he is the chair. QuestBridge supplies more exceptional low-income talent (i.e., kids) to top universities than all other nonprofits combined. QuestBridge has created a single standardized college application that's accepted by more than 30 top universities like Stanford, MIT, Amherst, and Yale. This allows them to do some very innovative things, such as give away laptops and have the giveaway forms double as college applications. They then offer scholarships to many kids who could otherwise not even think of college. Did you know that roughly $3 billion available for scholarships goes wasted each year? It's not a funding problem: It's a sourcing problem. What Billy Beane of the Oakland A's and *Moneyball* fame was to baseball, QuestBridge is to college education.

HOW REID DEVELOPED THE ABILITY TO DECONSTRUCT PROBLEMS AND INTERACT WITH MANY STAKEHOLDERS AT ONCE (CREDIT CARD PROCESSORS, BANKS, REGULATORS, ETC.)

"I think the most fundamental was, as a child, I played a lot of Avalon Hill board games, and each board game is actually a complex set of rules and circumstances." Reid also read Carl von Clausewitz and Sun Tzu as a boy, which informed his strategic thinking.

FOR THE PHILOSOPHY-PHOBIC, ONE PHILOSOPHER TO START WITH

Reid recommends studying Ludwig Wittgenstein, about whom he's taught a course at Oxford. "One of the bedrocks of modern analytic philosophy is to think of [language] . . . if you're trying to talk to someone else about some problem, and you're trying to make progress, how do you make language as positive an instrument as possible? What are the ways that language can work, and what are the ways that language doesn't work?"

TF: One of my all-time favorite quotes from dear Ludwig is: "The limits of my language mean the limits of my world." (*Die Grenzen meiner Sprache bedeuten die Grenzen meiner Welt.*)

IT DOESN'T ALWAYS HAVE TO BE HARD

"I have come to learn that part of the business strategy is to **solve the simplest, easiest, and most valuable problem**. And actually, in fact, **part of doing strategy**

is to solve the easiest problem, so part of the reason why you work on software and bits is that atoms [physical products] are actually very difficult."

TF: The bolded lines are key elements that I'm prone to under-examining. In doing an 80/20 analysis of your activities (simply put: determining which 20% of activities/tasks produce 80% of the results you want), you typically end up with a short list. Make "easy" your next criterion. **Which of these highest-value activities is the easiest for me to do?** You can build an entire career on 80/20 analysis and asking this question.

GIVE THE MIND AN OVERNIGHT TASK

On a daily basis, Reid jots down problems in a notebook that he wants his mind to work on overnight. Bolding below is mine, as I think the wording is important. Note "might have" instead of "have," etc.:

"What are the kinds of key things that might be **constraints on a solution,** or might be the **attributes of a solution,** and **what are tools or assets I might have?** . . . I actually think most of our thinking, of course, is subconscious. Part of what I'm trying to do is allow the fact that we have this kind of relaxation, rejuvenation period in sleeping, to essentially possibly bubble up the thoughts and solutions to it."

He might write down "a key thing that I want to think about: a product design, a strategy, a solution to a problem that one of my portfolio companies is looking at," or something else he wants to solve creatively before an upcoming meeting.

Josh Waitzkin (page 577) has a near-identical habit, but he's particular about when he writes things down—right after dinner and not before bed. To Josh, the pre-sleep gestation period of a few hours is important, as he doesn't want to be *consciously* thinking about the problem when he gets under the sheets.

Josh and Reid also mirror each other upon waking. Ideally, Reid budgets 60 minutes for the following: "The very first thing I do when I get up, almost always, is to sit down and work on that problem [I've set the day before] because that's when I'm freshest. I'm not distracted by phone calls and responses to things, and so forth. It's the most *tabula rasa*—blank slate—moment that I have. I use that to maximize my creativity on a particular project. I'll usually do it before I shower, because frequently, if I go into the shower, I'll continue to think about it."

TF: Reid and Josh's descriptions led me to put the following quote at the top of my notebook: "Never go to sleep without a request to your subconscious." — Thomas Edison

ADDITIONAL LESSONS FROM BEN CASNOCHA (FB: CASNOCHA), REID'S FORMER CHIEF OF STAFF

Reid's First Principle Is Speed

"We agreed I was going to make judgment calls on a range of issues on his behalf without checking with him. He told me, '**In order to move fast, I expect you'll make some foot faults. I'm okay with an error rate of 10 to 20% — times when I would have made a different decision in a given situation — if it means you can move fast.**' I felt empowered to make decisions with this ratio in mind, and it was incredibly liberating."

TF: "Foot faults" is a metaphor here. "Foot fault" literally refers to a penalty in tennis when you serve with improper foot placement, often due to rushing.

On Vetting the Best Employees or Partners

"How do you know if you have A-players on your project team? You know it if they don't just accept the strategy you hand them. They should suggest modifications to the plan based on their closeness to the details."

Reid Seeks a Single Reason for a Potentially Expensive Action — Not a Blended Reason

"For example, we were once discussing whether it'd make sense for him to travel to China. There was the LinkedIn expansion activity in China, some fun intellectual events happening, the launch of *The Start-Up of You* [Reid's book] in Chinese. [There were] a variety of possible good reasons to go, but none justified a trip in and of itself. He said, '**There needs to be one decisive reason, and then the worthiness of the trip needs to be measured against that one reason. If I go, then we can backfill into the schedule all the other secondary activities. But if I go for a blended reason, I'll almost surely come back and feel like it was a waste of time.**'"

PETER THIEL

Peter Thiel (TW: @PETERTHIEL, WITH 1 TWEET AND 130K+ FOLLOW-ERS; FOUNDERSFUND.COM) is a serial company founder (PayPal, Palantir), billionaire investor (the first outside investor in Facebook and more than a hundred others), and author of the book *Zero to One*. His teachings on differentiation, value creation, and competition alone have helped me make some of the best investment decisions of my life (such as Uber, Alibaba, and more).

BACK STORY

>> Peter is known as a master debater. When he appeared on my podcast, he answered questions submitted by my fans, which were upvoted on Facebook. Notice how often he reframes the question (examines whether the question is the right question) before answering. In several cases, how he dissects wording is as interesting as his answers.

>> The "tools" in this profile are Peter's thinking, and his macro-level beliefs that guide thousands of smaller decisions. His answers are worth reading a few times each, asking yourself afterward, "If I believed this, how would it affect my decisions in the next week? Over the next 6 to 12 months?"

✴ What do you wish you had known about business 20 years ago?

"If you go back 20 or 25 years, **I wish I would have known that there was no need to wait.** I went to college. I went to law school. I worked in law and banking, though not for terribly long. But not until I started PayPal did I fully realize that you don't have to wait to start something. **So if you're planning to do something with your life, if you have a 10-year plan of how to get there, you should ask: Why can't you do this in 6 months?** Sometimes, you have to actually go through the complex, 10-year trajectory. But it's at least worth asking whether that's the story you're telling yourself, or whether that's the reality."

✴ How important is failure in business?

"I think failure is massively overrated. Most businesses fail for more than one reason. So when a business fails, you often don't learn anything at all because the failure was overdetermined. [**TF:** *Overdetermined*: "To determine, account for, or cause (something) in more than one way or with more conditions than are necessary."] You will think it failed for Reason 1, but it failed for Reasons 1 through 5. And so the next business you start will fail for Reason 2, and then for 3 and so on.

"I think people actually do not learn very much from failure. I think it ends up being quite damaging and demoralizing to people in the long run, and my sense is that the death of every business is a tragedy. It's not some sort of beautiful aesthetic where there's a lot of carnage, but that's how progress happens, and it's not some sort of educational imperative. So I think failure is neither a Darwinian nor an educational imperative. Failure is always simply a tragedy."

✴ What are the biggest tech trends that you see defining the future?

"I don't like talking in terms of tech 'trends' because I think, once you have a trend, you have many people doing it. And once you have many people doing something, you have lots of competition and little differentiation. You, generally, never want to be part of a popular trend. You do not want to be the fourth online pet food company in the late 1990s. You do not want to be the twelfth thin-panel solar company in the last decade. And you don't want to be the nth company of any particular trend. So I think trends are often things to avoid. What I prefer over trends is a sense of mission. That you are working on a unique problem that people are not solving elsewhere.

"When Elon Musk started SpaceX, they set out the mission to go to Mars. You may agree or disagree with that as a mission statement, but it was a problem that was not going to be solved outside of SpaceX. All of the people working there knew that, and it motivated them tremendously."

TF: Peter has written elsewhere, "The next Bill Gates will not build an operating system. The next Larry Page or Sergey Brin won't make a search engine. And the next Mark Zuckerberg won't create a social network. If you are copying these guys, you aren't learning from them."

* How would you reply to someone who says that your position on college and higher education is hypocritical since you, yourself, went to Stanford for both undergraduate and law school?

[Context: Many people see Peter as "anti-college" due to his Thiel Fellowship, which "gives $100,000 to young people who want to build new things instead of sitting in a classroom."]

"I think some people will always find objections of one sort or another. Had I not gone to Stanford or law school, people would object and say I had no idea what I was missing. So I think they're likely to complain in any event. But I would say my view is not hypocritical because I have never made the claim that there's a one size fits all. So if I said that nobody should go to college, that might be hypocritical. But what I have said is that not everybody should do the same thing. There is something very odd about a society where the most talented people all get tracked toward the same elite colleges, where they end up studying the same small number of subjects and going into the same small number of careers.

"That strikes me as sort of a lack of diversity in our thinking about the kinds of things people should be doing. It's very limiting for our society as well as for those students. I certainly think I was very much guilty of this myself, if I look back on my Stanford undergraduate and law school years. It's possible I would do it again. But if I had to do something over, I would think about it much harder. **I would ask questions. Why am I doing this? Am I doing this just because I have good grades and test scores and because I think it's prestigious? Or am I doing this because I'm extremely passionate about practicing law?**

"I think there are good answers, and there are bad answers. And my retrospective on my early 20s is that I was way too focused on the wrong answers at the time."

✻ What do you think the future of education looks like?
[**TF:** I include this mostly for the very first line and his reframe.]

"I don't like the word 'education' because it is such an extraordinary abstraction. I'm very much in favor of learning. I'm much more skeptical of credentialing or the abstraction called 'education.' So there are all of these granular questions like: What is it that we're learning? Why are you learning it? Are you going to college because it's a 4-year party? Is it a consumption decision? Is it an investment decision where you're investing in your future? Is it insurance? Or is it a tournament where you're just beating other people? And are elite universities really like Studio 54 where it's like an exclusive nightclub? I think if we move beyond the education bubble that we're living in today, the future will be one in which people can speak about these things more clearly."

(Listen to his entire riff on this in episode #28 at 17:24.)

✻ What one thing would you most like to change about yourself or improve on?
"It's always hard to answer this, since it sort of begs the question of why I haven't already improved on it. But I would say that when I look back on my younger self, I was insanely tracked, insanely competitive. And when you're very competitive, you get good at the thing you're competing with people on. But it comes at the expense of losing out on many other things.

"If you're a competitive chess player, you might get very good at chess but neglect to develop other things because you're focused on beating your competitors, rather than on doing something that's important or valuable. So I've become, I think, much more self-aware over the years about the problematic nature of a lot of the competition. There have been rivalries that we get caught up in. And I would not pretend to have extricated myself from this altogether. **So I think, every day, it's something to reflect on and think about 'How do I become less competitive in order that I can become more successful?'"**

✻ You studied philosophy as an undergraduate. What does philosophy have to do with business? And how has your study of philosophy helped you in your investing and career today?
"I'm not sure how much the formal study of philosophy matters, but I think the

fundamental philosophical question is one that's important for all of us, and it's always this question of 'What do people agree merely by convention, and what is the truth?' There's a consensus of things that people believe to be true. Maybe the conventions are right, and maybe they're not. And we never want to let a convention be a shortcut for truth. **We always need to ask: Is this true? And this is always what I get at with this indirect question: 'Tell me something that's true that very few people agree with you on.'**"

TF: Peter will also sometimes ask potential hires, "What problem do you face every day that nobody has solved yet?" or "What is a great company no one has started?" I will sometimes pose a bastardized version of his "something few people agree with you on" question to podcast guests: "What do you believe that other people think is insane?"

3 OF 7 QUESTIONS

There are 7 questions that Peter recommends all startup founders ask themselves. Grab *Zero to One* for all of them, but here are the 3 I revisit often:

The Monopoly Question: Are you starting with a big share of a small market?

The Secret Question: Have you identified a unique opportunity that others don't see?

The Distribution Question: Do you have a way to not just create but deliver your product?

> **"** It's always the hard part that creates value. **"**

> **"** You are more powerful than you think you are. Act accordingly. **"**

SETH GODIN

Seth Godin (TW: @THISISSETHSBLOG, SETHGODIN.COM) is the author of 18 best-selling books that have been translated into more than 35 languages. He writes about the way ideas spread, marketing, strategic quitting, leadership, and challenging the status quo in all areas. His books include *Linchpin*, *Tribes*, *The Dip*, *Purple Cow*, and *What to Do When It's Your Turn (and It's Always Your Turn)*.

Seth has founded several companies, including Yoyodyne and Squidoo. His blog (which you can find by typing "Seth" into Google) is one of the most popular in the world. In 2013, Godin was inducted into the Direct Marketing Hall of Fame. Recently, Godin turned the book publishing world on its ear by launching a series of four books via Kickstarter. The campaign reached its goal in just three hours and became the most successful book project in Kickstarter history.

Spirit animal: Loon

"Trust and attention — these are the scarce items
in a post-scarcity world."

"We can't out-obedience the competition."

TF: I like this so much that I wanted to mention it twice. More context next time.

BE A MEANINGFUL SPECIFIC INSTEAD OF A WANDERING GENERALITY

On saying "no" and declining things: "The phone rings, and lots of people want a thing. If it doesn't align with the thing that is your mission, and you say 'yes,' now [your mission is] their mission. There's nothing wrong with being a wandering generality instead of a meaningful specific, but don't expect to make the change you [hope] to make if that's what you do.

"MONEY IS A STORY . . . AND IT'S BETTER TO TELL A STORY ABOUT MONEY YOU'RE HAPPY WITH."

"Once you have enough for beans and rice and taking care of your family and a few other things, money is a story. You can tell yourself any story you want about money, and it's better to tell yourself a story about money that you can happily live with."

IF YOU GENERATE ENOUGH BAD IDEAS, A FEW GOOD ONES TEND TO SHOW UP

"People who have trouble coming up with good ideas, if they're telling you the truth, will tell you they don't have very many bad ideas. But people who have plenty of good ideas, if they're telling you the truth, will say they have even more bad ideas. **So the goal isn't to get good ideas; the goal is to get bad ideas. Because once you get enough bad ideas, then some good ones have to show up.**"

(See James Altucher on page 246.)

WHAT YOU TRACK DETERMINES YOUR LENS — CHOOSE CAREFULLY

"Those of us who are lucky enough to live in a world where we have enough and we have a roof and we have food — we find ourselves caught in this cycle of keeping track of the wrong things. Keeping track of how many times we've been rejected. Keeping track of how many times it didn't work. Keeping track of all the times someone has broken our heart or double-crossed us or let us down. Of course, we can keep track of those things, but why? Why keep track of them? Are they making us better?

"Wouldn't it make more sense to keep track of the other stuff? To keep track of all the times it worked? All the times we took a risk? All the times we were able to brighten someone else's day? When we start doing that, we can redefine ourselves as people who are able to make an impact on the world. **It took me a bunch of cycles to figure out that the narrative was up to me.**

"If a narrative isn't working, well then, really, why are you using it? The narrative isn't done to you; the narrative is something that you choose. Once we can dig deep and find a different narrative, then we ought to be able to change the game."

"STORIES LET US LIE TO OURSELVES AND THOSE LIES SATISFY OUR DESIRES"

TF: The stories we tell ourselves can sometimes be self-defeating. One of the refrains that I've adopted for myself, which I wrote in my journal after some deep "plant medicine" work (see James Fadiman, page 100, for more on that) is "Don't retreat into story."

TRY SITTING AT A DIFFERENT TABLE

"If you think hard about one's life, most people spend most of their time on defense, in reactive mode, in playing with the cards they got instead of moving to a different table with different cards. Instead of seeking to change other people, they are willing to be changed. Part of the arc of what I'm trying to teach is: Everyone who can hear this has more power than they think they do. The question is, what are you going to do with that power?"

CAN YOU PUSH SOMETHING DOWNHILL?

"If you think about how hard it is to push a business uphill, particularly when you're just getting started, one answer is to say: 'Why don't you just start a different business, a business you can push downhill?'

"My friend Lynn Gordon is a brilliant thinker and designer, and for years, she was in the business of designing toys and soft goods for moms with toddlers. Every toy company in America was mean to her, rejected her, had nothing to do with her. I said: 'Lynn, it's simple. Toy companies don't like toy designers. They're not organized to do business with toy designers. They're not hoping toy designers will come to them.' I said, 'Come with me into the book business. Because every day, there are underpaid, really smart people in the book business who wake up waiting for the next idea to come across their desk. They're eager to buy what you have to sell.' And within two months, she did the 52® activity decks and [ultimately] sold more than 5 million decks of cards."

FIRST, TEN PEOPLE

Seth has published roughly 6,500 posts on his blog since 2002. Which blog post would he point people to first, if he had to pick one?

"The blog post I point people to the most is called 'First, Ten,' and it is a simple theory of marketing that says: tell ten people, show ten people, share it with ten people; ten people who already trust you and already like you. If they don't tell anybody else, it's not that good and you should start over. If they do tell other people, you're on your way."

TO CREATE SOMETHING GREAT (OR EVENTUALLY HUGE), START EXTREMELY SMALL

"My suggestion is, whenever possible, ask yourself: What's the smallest possible footprint I can get away with? What is the smallest possible project that is worth my time? What is the smallest group of people who I could make a difference for, or to? Because smallest is achievable. Smallest feels risky. Because if you pick smallest and you fail, now you've really screwed up.

"We want to pick big. Infinity is our friend. Infinity is safe. Infinity gives us a place to hide. So, I want to encourage people instead to look for the small. To be on one medium in a place where people can find you. To have one sort of interaction with one tribe, with one group where you don't have a lot of lifeboats."

(See "1,000 True Fans" on page 289.)

"NO ONE GETS A SUZUKI TATTOO. YOU CAN DECIDE THAT YOU WANT TO BE TATTOO-WORTHY."

Seth on Suzuki versus Harley-Davidson, the latter of which has deliberately created an aspirational brand.

"I QUANTIFY ALMOST NOTHING IN MY LIFE"

I sometimes fear I'll lose my edge if I stop measuring everything. This line was freeing for me to hear, as Seth has been an idol of sorts for years. He inspired me to start "cycling off" of quantification, much like I cycle off of supplements for at least 1 week every 2 months (example: I took July 2016 off of tracking weight/body fat, social media, website, and newsletter stats).

I like to study what Seth *doesn't* do as much as what he does. Seth has no comments on his blog, he doesn't pay attention to analytics, and he doesn't use Twitter or Facebook (except to rebroadcast his daily blog posts, which is automated). In a world of tool obsession and FOMO (fear of missing out) on the next social platform, Seth doesn't appear to care. He simply focuses on putting out good and short daily posts, he ignores the rest, and he continues to thrive. There are no real rules, so make rules that work for you.

QUICK TAKES
Breakfast
"Breakfast is one more decision I don't make, so it's a frozen banana, hemp powder, almond milk, a dried plum, and some walnuts in the blender."

Cooking Lessons
"My wife got me a Chris Schlesinger cooking class, and it was the only cooking class I'd ever taken. In 20 minutes, I learned more about cooking than I think I've learned before or since. Because Chris basically taught me how to think about what you were trying to do and basically said, **A) You should taste the food as you go, which a surprisingly small number of people do; and B) salt and olive oil actually are cheating and they're secret weapons and they always work.**"

Audiogon
Seth is an audiophile. He particularly enjoys focusing on analog and, in many ways, anachronistic equipment still made by hand. Audiogon is a website "where you can find people who buy things new and sell them 6 months later in perfect condition."

PARENTING ADVICE

"What could possibly be more important than your kid? Please don't play the busy card. If you spend 2 hours a day without an electronic device, looking your kid in the eye, talking to them and solving interesting problems, you will raise a different kid than someone who doesn't do that. That's one of the reasons why I cook dinner every night. Because what a wonderful, semi-distracted environment in which the kid can tell you the truth. For you to have low-stakes but superimportant conversations with someone who's important to you."

ON EDUCATION AND TEACHING KIDS

"Sooner or later, parents have to take responsibility for putting their kids into a system that is indebting them and teaching them to be cogs in an economy that doesn't want cogs anymore. Parents get to decide . . . [and] from 3 p.m. to 10 p.m., those kids are getting homeschooled. And they're either getting home-schooled and watching *The Flintstones*, or they're getting homeschooled and learning something useful.

"I think we need to teach kids two things: 1) how to lead, and 2) how to solve interesting problems. Because the fact is, there are plenty of countries on Earth where there are people who are willing to be obedient and work harder for less money than us. **So we cannot out-obedience the competition.** Therefore, we have to out-lead or out-solve the other people. . . .

"The way you teach your kids to solve interesting problems is to give them interesting problems to solve. And then, don't criticize them when they fail. Because kids aren't stupid. If they get in trouble every time they try to solve an interesting problem, they'll just go back to getting an A by memorizing what's in the textbook. I spend an enormous amount of time with kids . . . I think that it's a privilege to be able to look a trusting, energetic, smart 11-year-old in the eye and tell him the truth. And what we can say to that 11-year-old is: 'I really don't care how you did on your vocabulary test. I care about whether you have something to say.'"

✳ What's something you believe that other people think is crazy?

"Deep down, I am certain that **people are plastic in the positive sense: flexible and able to grow. I think almost everything is made, not born, and that makes people uncomfortable because it puts them on the hook**, but I truly believe it."

* Seth's favorite audiobooks, which he listens to repeatedly

TF: First I'll provide the list, then his recommended uses.

Goals: Setting and Achieving Them on Schedule, How to Stay Motivated, and *Secrets of Closing the Sale* by Zig Ziglar: "Zig is your grandfather and my grandfather. He's Tony Robbins's grandfather. None of us would be here if it weren't for Zig."

Works of Pema Chödrön: "Almost the flip side. I'm so much better at [protracted difficult periods] because of Pema and because of meditation and because of knowing how to sit with it and not insist that the tension go away."

Leap First: "Inspired by [Zig and Pema], and some work I did, I did this book for charity; it's a short audiobook and you can get it at Sounds True.

The Art of Possibility by Rosamund Stone Zander and Benjamin Zander: "…. which is very hard to find on audio and is totally worth seeking out."

The War of Art by Steven Pressfield: "Also hard to find on audio. I find Steve's voice to be fascinating, and even before I knew him, I was fascinated by listening to him speak his own work. *The War of Art* is one of those books, at least for me when I finally was exposed to it, I said, 'Why wasn't I informed? Why did it take this long for this book to land on my desk?' . . . You need to be clear with yourself about what you are afraid of, why you are afraid, and whether you care enough to dance with that fear because it will never go away."

Just Kids by Patti Smith: "This is the single best audiobook ever recorded by Patti Smith. It is not going to change the way you do business, but it might change the way you live. It's about love and loss and art."

Debt by David Graeber: "I recommend it in audio because David is sometimes repetitive and a little elliptical but in audio it's all okay because you can just listen to it again."

TIM: "Which of these, going from Zig to Pema and onward down to debt with David, which of these do you think I should start with, or which one would you suggest I start with?"

SETH: "For me, if you are feeling stuck, it's all about *The War of Art* and *The*

Art of Possibility. If you are feeling stressed, it's about Pema. If you need to see a path that is more colored than the one you're already on, which is pretty Technicolor, then it's Zig. And if you just want to cry a little, it's *Just Kids*, and then *Debt* is the one that is closest to reading a book. I don't think many people should listen to *Debt* ten times."

✳ Seth's best purchase of $100 or less?

"You could become obsessed with **artisanal bean-to-bar chocolate**. Not that one should, but one could. So I did, and I worked my way up the ladder. About a year ago, I was going to start my own chocolate company because it's not that hard. Then I bumped into a few brands that were doing it better than I ever could. . . . There are two chocolate companies I want to highlight: **Rogue** [from western Massachusetts] and **Askinosie**. And I'm actually an advisor to a new acumen company called **Cacao Hunters** in Colombia."

✳ What advice would you give your 30-year-old self?

"I had so many bumps starting when I was 30 years old. They lasted for 9 years, and I wouldn't tell my 30-year-old self anything. **Because if I hadn't had those bumps, I wouldn't be me, and I'm glad I'm me.**"

PET OBSESSIONS — COFFEE AND VODKA

Seth doesn't drink coffee or alcohol. Nonetheless, he enjoys making elaborate espresso and vodka for his family and guests. Odd side obsessions are a common trait of nearly everyone in this book, and I find Seth's description hilarious. His vodka recipe is also simply delicious:

"The coffee thing, we'll start there. I don't drink coffee. I wish I did. I need a vice. But I like making it. I like — without being one of those people who is measuring everything, because that's not my shtick — to have an intuitive sense of what makes a good pull of espresso. I used to have a fancy Slayer machine, which is this super digital hunk of a device that did not belong in anyone's kitchen, particularly mine. So when it started acting up, I was able to sell it for a fair price and switched, in the completely opposite direction, to a Swiss-made, 17-year-old, totally manual machine. You've got to pull a handle.

"And I roast my own beans, which is key. Marco Arment [co-founder of Tumblr, creator of Instapaper and Overcast] taught me that. Roasting your own beans is more important than any other thing you can do, if you want to make coffee. I think there's a metaphor there. I know there's a metaphor there. Which is, you can spend a lot of time trying to fix stuff later but starting with the right raw materials makes a huge difference."

TIM: "Then, vodka . . ."

SETH: "There's a place near my house called [Blue Hill at] Stone Barns Center, which used to be the Rockefellers' summer house. It's a nice restaurant. At the bar — I don't drink either, but I'm told that at the bar — they serve honey oatmeal vodka. I reverse engineered the recipe, and it's not a still, but I make it in my basement. The recipe, for those who are interested, is you take a bottle of vodka — you don't want the supercheap stuff but you don't want the expensive stuff because that's a little bit of a rip-off — you pour it over a pound of just plain old oatmeal, uncooked, and half a jar of honey. You let it sit in the fridge for 2 weeks, stirring it now and then. Then you strain it back into the original bottle and you're done."

* Final words of advice?

"Send someone a thank-you note tomorrow."

"We all have, let's say, two or three dozen massive pain points in our lives that everyone can relate to. I try to basically write about those, and then I try to write about how I attempted to recover from them.**"**

JAMES ALTUCHER

James Altucher (TW: @JALTUCHER, JAMESALTUCHER.COM) is an American hedge fund manager, entrepreneur, and best-selling author. He has founded or co-founded more than 20 companies, including Reset and Stockpickr. 17 failed, and 3 of them made him tens of millions. He is the author of 17 books, including *The Power of No*. I've never seen anyone build a large, committed readership faster than James.

Spirit animal: Mouse

TF: To me, the quote on the previous page explains how James went from unknown to millions of readers faster than most writers gain a thousand readers. James made his specialty exploring his own pain and fear, and he shows the light at the end of the tunnel without ignoring the darkness in the middle. This is refreshing in a world of rah-rah positive-thinking "gurus" who are all forced smiles and high-fives.

Some of my most popular blog posts since 2007 have been the least time-consuming but the most uncomfortable. To produce these, I usually ask myself: "What am I embarrassed to be struggling with? And what am I doing about it?"

IF YOU CAN'T GENERATE 10 IDEAS, GENERATE 20

James recommends the habit of writing down 10 ideas each morning in a waiter's pad or tiny notebook. This exercise is for developing your "idea muscle" and confidence for creativity on demand, so regular practice is more important than the topics:

"What if [you] just can't come up with 10 ideas? Here's the magic trick: If you can't come up with 10 ideas, come up with 20 ideas. . . . You are putting too much pressure on yourself. Perfectionism is the ENEMY of the idea muscle . . . it's your brain trying to protect you from harm, from coming up with an idea that is embarrassing and stupid and could cause you to suffer pain. The way you shut [this] off is by forcing [the brain] to come up with bad ideas.

"So let's say you've written down 5 ideas for books and they are all pretty good. And now you are stuck. . . . Well, let's come up with some bad ideas. Here's one: *Dorothy and the Wizard of Wall Street*. Dorothy is in a hurricane in Kansas and she lands right at the corner of Broadway and Wall Street in New York City and she has to make her way all the way down Wall Street to find 'The Wizard of Wall Street' (Lloyd Blankfein, CEO of Goldman Sachs) in order to get home to Kansas. Instead, he offers her a job to be a high-frequency trader. What a bad idea! OK, now go on to the next 15 ideas.

"I [then] divide my paper into two columns. On one column is the list of ideas. On the other column is the list of FIRST STEPS. Remember, only the first step. Because you have no idea where that first step will take you. One of my favorite examples: Richard Branson didn't like the service on airlines he was flying, so he had an idea: 'I'm going to start a new airline.' How the heck can a magazine publisher start an airline from scratch with no money? His first step:

He called Boeing to see if they had an airplane he could lease. No idea is so big that you can't take the first step. If the first step seems too hard, make it simpler. And don't worry again if the idea is bad. This is all practice."

TF: If you can't get 10 good ideas, get 20 ideas. This mantra has proven very valuable. About a year ago, I brainstormed a list of "The craziest things I could do" while sitting at a *Wired* conference listening to out-of-the-box thinkers like iconic photographer Platon. After a few bullets (e.g., "Give away all my money," "Sell all my belongings," "Go offline completely for 6 months"), I got stuck. So, in true James fashion, I decided to drop my standards and go nuts. Things got deep into "bad idea" territory quickly, even including "Cut off both feet" (WTF?). But the list grew and grew, and one of them was "Take an indefinite startup vacation," which ended up being one of the most important ideas of the last 5 years of my life (see page 384 for more).

SAMPLE LISTS FOR JAMES'S "DAILY 10" PRACTICE

Not all of James's idea lists are business-related. In fact, few are. He elaborates: "It's hard to come up with more than 3,000 business ideas a year. I'm lucky if I come up with a few business ideas. The key is to have fun with it, or else you don't do it."

In his words, but condensed for space, here are some examples of the types of lists James makes:

10 old ideas I can make new

10 ridiculous things I would invent (e.g., the smart toilet)

10 books I can write (*The Choose Yourself Guide to an Alternative Education*, etc).

10 business ideas for Google/Amazon/Twitter/etc.

10 people I can send ideas to

10 podcast ideas or videos I can shoot (e.g., *Lunch with James*, a video podcast where I just have lunch with people over Skype and we chat)

10 industries where I can remove the middleman

10 things I disagree with that everyone else assumes is religion (college, home ownership, voting, doctors, etc.)

10 ways to take old posts of mine and make books out of them

10 people I want to be friends with (then figure out the first step to contact them)

10 things I learned yesterday

10 things I can do differently today

10 ways I can save time

10 things I learned from X, where X is someone I've recently spoken with or read a book by or about. I've written posts on this about the Beatles, Mick Jagger, Steve Jobs, Charles Bukowski, the Dalai Lama, Superman, Freakonomics, etc.

10 things I'm interested in getting better at (and then 10 ways I can get better at each one)

10 things I was interested in as a kid that might be fun to explore now (Like, maybe I can write that "Son of Dr. Strange" comic I've always been planning. And now I need 10 plot ideas.)

10 ways I might try to solve a problem I have This has saved me with the IRS countless times. Unfortunately, the Department of Motor Vehicles is impervious to my superpowers.

SHORT AND SWEET

On the Value of Selective Ignorance, After Working at a Newspaper

"You're basically told, 'Find the thing that's going to scare people the most and write about it.' . . . It's like every day is Halloween at the newspaper. I avoid newspapers." **TF:** Many productive people do the same, including Nassim Taleb.

The World Doesn't Need Your Explanation. On Saying "No":

"I don't give explanations anymore, and I'll catch myself when I start giving explanations like 'Oh, I'm sorry, I can't make it. I have a doctor's appointment that day. I'm really sick. I broke my leg over the weekend' or something. I just say, 'I can't do it. I hope everything is well.'"

Haven't Found Your Overarching, Single Purpose? Maybe You Don't Have To.

"Forget purpose. It's okay to be happy without one. The quest for a single purpose has ruined many lives."

HOW TO CREATE A REAL-WORLD MBA

It's fun to think about getting an MBA.

They're attractive for many reasons: developing new business skills, developing a better business network, or — most often — taking what is effectively a 2-year vacation that looks good on a résumé.

In 2001, and again in 2004, I wanted to do all three things.

This short chapter will share my experience with MBA programs and how I created my own. My hope is that it will make you think about real-world experiments versus theoretical training, untested assumptions (especially about risk tolerance), and the good game of business as a whole. There is no need to spend $60K per year to apply the principles I'll be discussing.

Last caveat: Nothing here is intended to portray me as an investing expert, which I am not.

Beginnings

Ah, Stanford Graduate School of Business (GSB). Stanford, with its palm tree–lined avenues and red terra cotta roofing, always held a unique place in my mind.

But my fantasies of attending GSB reached a fever pitch when I sat in on a class called Entrepreneurship and Venture Capital taught by Peter Wendell, who had led early-stage investments in companies such as Intuit.

Within 30 minutes, Pete had taught me more about the real world of venture capital inside baseball than all of the books I'd read on the subject.

I was ecstatic and ready to apply to GSB. Who wouldn't be?

So I enthusiastically began a process I would repeat twice: downloading the application to get started, taking the full campus tour, and sitting in on other classes.

It was the other classes that got my knickers in a twist. Some were incredible, taught by all-stars who'd done it all, but many, many others were taught by PhD theoreticians who used big words and lots of PowerPoint slides. One teacher spent 45 minutes on slide after slide of equations that could be summed up with, "If you build a crappy product, people won't buy it." No one needed to prove that to me, let alone drown me in calculus to do so.

At the end of that class, I turned to my student guide for the tour and asked him how it compared to other classes. He answered: "Oh, this is easily my favorite."

That was the death of business school for me.

How to Make a Small Fortune

By 2005, I was done chasing my tail with business school, but I still itched to learn more about venture capital (VC). In 2007, I started having more frequent lunches with the brilliant Mike Maples, who had been a co-founder of Motive Communications (IPO to $260 million market cap) and a founding executive of Tivoli (sold to IBM for $750 million). He is now a founding partner of Floodgate Fund.

Our conversations usually bounced among a few topics, including physical performance, marketing campaigns (I'd just launched *The 4-Hour Workweek*), and a focus of his at the time: "angel investing."

Compared to traditional VC, angel investing involves putting relatively small amounts of money — often from $10K to $50K — into early-stage startups. In Mike's world, "early-stage" could mean two engineers with a prototype for a website, or it could mean a successful serial entrepreneur with a new idea. The angels usually have relevant business experience and are considered "smart money." In other words, their advice and introductions are just as valuable as the money they put in.

After several lunches with Mike, I'd found my business school.

I decided to make a 2-year "Tim Ferriss Fund" that would replace Stanford business school. I wouldn't go through the formal steps to create a legally viable fund; I would simply set a plan and invest my own capital as if I had such a fund.

Stanford GSB isn't cheap. I rounded it down to ~$60K per year in 2007, for a total of $120K over 2 years. For the Tim Ferriss Fund, I would aim to intelligently spend $120K over 2 years on angel investing in $10K to $20K chunks, meaning 6 to 12 companies in total. The goal of this "business school" would be to learn as much as possible about startup finance, deal structuring, rapid product design, acquisition conversations, etc., as possible.

But curriculum was just part of business school. The other part was getting to know the "students," preferably the most astute movers and shakers in the startup investing world. Business school = curriculum + network.

The most important characteristic of my personal MBA: I planned on "losing" $120K.

I went into the Tim Ferriss Fund viewing the $120K as a sunk tuition cost, but expecting that the lessons learned and people met would be worth that $120K investment over time. The 2-year plan was to methodically spend $120K for the learning experience, not for the ROI.

Please note that I would not suggest mimicking this approach with angel investing, unless:

1. You have a clear informational advantage (insider access) that gives you a competitive edge. I live in the nexus of Silicon Valley and know many top CEOs and investors, so I have better sources of information than the vast majority of the world. I rarely invest in public companies precisely because I know that professionals have more tools and leverage than I do.

2. You are 100% comfortable losing your "MBA" funds. You should only gamble with what you're very comfortable losing. If the prospective financial loss drives you to even mild desperation or depression, you shouldn't do it.

3. You have started and/or managed successful businesses in the past.

4. You limit angel investment funds to 10 to 15% or less of your liquid assets. I subscribe to the Nassim Taleb "barbell" school of investment, which I implement as 90% in conservative asset classes like cash-like equivalents and the remaining 10% in speculative investments that can capitalize on positive "black swans."

Even if the above criteria are met, people overestimate their risk tolerance. Even if you have only $100 to invest, this is important to explore. In 2007, I had one wealth manager ask me, "What is your risk tolerance?" and I answered honestly: "I have no idea." It threw him off.

I then asked him for the average of his clients' responses. He said, "Most answer that they would not panic up to about 20% down in one quarter."

My follow-up question was: "When do most actually panic and start selling low?" His answer: "When they're down 5% in one quarter."

Unless you've lost 20% in a quarter, it's practically impossible to predict your response. Also, you might be fine losing $20 out of $100 but freak out when you're down $20K out of $100K. The absolute number can matter as much as the percentage.

As Cus D'Amato, Mike Tyson's legendary first trainer, famously said: "Everyone has a plan until they get punched in the face." To would-be angel investors, I suggest the following: Go to a casino or racetrack and don't leave until you've spent 20% of a typical investment and watched it disappear.

Let's say you're planning on making $25K worth of investments. I'd ask you to then purposefully lose $5K over the course of at least 3 hours, and certainly not all at once. It's important that you slowly bleed losses as you attempt to learn the game, to exert some control over something you can't control. If you can remain unaffected after slowly losing your $5K (or 20% of your planned typical investment), consider making your first angel investment.

But proceed with caution. Even among brilliant people in the startup world, there is an expression: "If you want to make a small fortune, start with a large fortune and angel invest."

The First Deal and First Lesson

So what did I do? I immediately went out and broke my own rules like a dummy.

There was a very promising startup that, based on using Alexa ranking correlations to valuations (beware of this approach), was more than 5 times undervalued! Even if it hit a "base hit" like a $25 million exit, I could easily recoup my planned $120K!

I got very excited and cut a check for $50K. "That's a bit aggressive for a first deal, don't you think?" Mike asked me over coffee. Not a chance. My intuition was loud and clear. I was convinced, based on other investors and all of the excitement surrounding the deal, that this company was on the cusp of exploding.

This startup was on life support within 2 years and dead shortly thereafter, so I lost that $50K. Oops.

Following the Rules

Lesson #1: If you've formulated intelligent rules, follow your own f*cking rules.

Below are a few that subsequently worked well for me. Note that I don't need to satisfy all of them, but I do want to satisfy most of them:

>> If it has a single founder, the founder must be technical. Two technical co-founders are ideal.

>> I must be eager to use the product myself. This rules out many great companies, but I want a verified market I understand.

>> Related to the previous point: consumer-facing product/service (e.g., Uber, Twitter, Facebook, etc.) or small-business focused product/service (e.g., Shopify), not big enterprise software. These are companies whose valuations I can directly impact through my platform, promotion to my audience, introductions to journalists, etc.

>> More than 100K active users OR serial founder(s) with past exits OR more than 10K paying customers. Whenever possible, I want to pour gasoline on the fire, not start the fire.

>> More than 10% month-on-month activity growth.

>> Clean "cap table," minimal previous financing (or none), no bridge rounds.

>> U.S.–based companies or companies willing to create U.S.–based investable entities. Shopify started in Canada, for instance.

>> Have the founders ever had crappy service jobs, like waiting tables or bussing at restaurants? If so, they tend to stay grounded for longer. Less entitlement and megalomania usually means better decisions and better drinking company, as this stuff normally takes quite a few years.

By the end of 2010, following these rules, I was fortunate to have had two successful exits.

The first, Daily Burn, was acquired by IAC. This guaranteed that I would not lose money on my 2-year fund, assuming I didn't piss the proceeds away. Relevant side note on Daily Burn: They checked the boxes on my checklist, but the majority of the investors (but not all) I asked to participate declined because the co-founders lived in Alabama and Colorado instead of a tech hub. Mike Maples explained a simple rule of thumb to me at the time, and I've applied it to many deals since: **Breaking your rules to co-invest with well-known investors is usually a bad idea, but following your rules when others reject a startup can work out extremely well.**

The second exit might seem odd. Remember that *learning* was my main reason for doing the real-world MBA in the first place.

My second exit was *my own company*! Using what I learned through angel investing about deal structures and the acquisition process, I became less intimidated by the idea of "selling" a company. It need not be complicated, as I learned, and BrainQUICKEN was sold in late 2009. This means the ROI on my personal MBA was, based on those two alone, well over twice my "tuition."

Now, that might seem like a paltry sum to some people ($120K–200K for two years of effort?), but it's important to note two things:

1. Selling my company completely freed up my time to focus on other things, such as *The 4-Hour Body*, which hit #1 on the *New York Times* bestseller list and created thousands of opportunities.

2. Two exits is not where the story ends. That was just the beginning.

Startup investments can be illiquid and locked up for 7 to 10 years. This is why the "fund life" of most venture capital funds is 10 years. That is how long it takes most big successes to reach IPO or get acquired. In other words, you might not know if you're good or bad at angel investing, right or wrong in your bets, for a LONG time.

So, what are some of the other bets I made between 2007 and 2009? Some of them ended up being later-stage than Seed or Series A, as I began getting invited to such deals:

> » Shopify (IPO — advisor)

> » Uber (TBD but looking to be my biggest of all)

> » Facebook (IPO)

> » Twitter (IPO)

> » Alibaba at $9/share (IPO)

As I write this in 2016, I've had 6 to 10 additional successful exits, and I've also been able to sell some private stock on the "secondary market." When startups raise new rounds of financing, this is sometimes offered to existing shareholders.

It's worth mentioning that I had to adjust my investment approach from 2008 to 2010 due to my $50K slip-up and the self-imposed limit of $120K of starting capital.

I adopted the additional rules below, which — while seemingly arbitrary — helped me to filter out 90% of deals and not lose money. I used these until roughly 2010, at which point I had more capital and A) preferred to invest cash instead of time (easier to scale), and B) could use slightly different rules, as I had a bigger safety net.

Even if you have no interest in the startup game, you should have an interest in formally deciding on rules that make damaging, bad decisions hard. Here are a few that helped me.

If each startup exits at 5 times its current Series A valuation, it should be able to cover two-thirds of your fund capital.

Most of your startups will fail, so the successes need to make up for losses.

Let's say there's a startup that's offered you $15K worth of investment, and they're going to have a $1.5 million "post-money" valuation after the round of financing. If we're using the "two-thirds" rule, and your fund (like mine from 2007 to 2009) is $120K, you shouldn't invest $15K in this startup, as 15K x 5 = $75K. Two-thirds of $120K is $80K, so you'd either have to invest slightly more, lower the valuation, or add in advising (expanded upon below) and get more equity in return. This isn't even accounting for dilution, which is beyond the scope of this book but likely in most cases.

If a startup exits at 3 times its current valuation, it should allow you to walk away with $300k.

This was one of my preferred methods for qualifying or disqualifying a startup. As much as I might love someone, I can't take another part-time job for 7 to 10 years for a $50K payoff.

Let's say a startup ends up with a $3 million post-money valuation. If I help them more than triple the value of their company to $10 million, how much do I walk away with if there are no more rounds of funding? If it works out to $50K, it isn't worth it for me. If, considering the time invested, I could earn 5 times that doing other things, it makes no sense to do the deal.

Move from Investor → Investor/Advisor → Advisor

Let's assume you have committed to spending $60K per year on angel investments, just as I did without really knowing what I was signing up for. This means two things:

1. You aren't going to be able to satisfy the previous rules of "covering two-thirds of the fund" or "making $300K at 3x" for many companies. Perhaps you'll make 3 to 6 investments.

2. 3 to 6 investments generally doesn't work in angel investing, where most pros assume that 9 out of 10 will fail.

It's therefore nearly impossible for you to get a good statistical spread with $60K per year. The math just doesn't work. The math especially doesn't work if you screw it up like I did by getting overexcited and dropping $50K on your first investment.

Here's how I did a course correction and dealt with this problem:

First, I invested very small amounts in a few select startups, ideally those in close-knit "seed accelerator" (formerly called "incubator") networks like Y Combinator and Techstars. Then, I did my best to deliver above and beyond the value of my investment. In other words, I wanted the founders to ask themselves, "Why the hell is this guy helping us so much for a ridiculously small amount of equity?" This was critical for establishing a reputation as a major value-add, someone who helped a lot for very little.

Second, leaning on this burgeoning reputation, I began negotiating blended agreements with startups involving some investment, but additional advisory equity as a requirement. "Advising" equity is equity that I get over time (say, $\frac{1}{24}$ of the total each month for 2 years) but don't have to pay for. The startup can cancel at any time if I'm not performing.

Third and last, I made the jump to pure advising. After the end of the first year of the Tim Ferriss Fund, more than 70% of my startup "investments" were made with time rather than cash. In the last 6 months of the fund, I wrote only one check for a startup.

Moving gradually from pure investing to pure advising allowed me to reduce the total amount of capital invested, increase equity percentages, and make the $120K work, despite my early mistakes. This approach also, I believe, produced better results for the startups.

Ultimately, startups became my golden goose, and when CB Insights analyzed the top 1,000 angel investors in 2014, they placed me in sixth place. The irony is that I've now stopped angel investing completely, even though it will ultimately make me 10 times what I've made in publishing and everything else. Why? That's on page page 384.

But enough damn tech talk. Let's look at some other options for you.

Creating Your Own Graduate Program

How might you create your own MBA or other graduate program? Here are three examples with hypothetical costs, which obviously depend on the program:

Master of Arts in Creative Writing — $12K/year

How could you spend (or sacrifice) $12K a year to become a world-class creative writer? If you make $75K per year, this could mean that you join a writers' group and negotiate Mondays off work (to focus on drafting a novel or screenplay) in exchange for a $10–15K salary cut.

Masters in Political Science — $12K/year

Use the same approach to dedicate one day per week to volunteering or working on a political campaign. Decide to read one book per week from the Georgetown Political Science department's required first-year curriculum.

MBA — $30K per year

Commit to spending $2,500 per month on testing different "muses" intended to be sources of automated income. See *The 4-Hour Workweek* or Google "muse examples Ferriss" as a starting point.

And Overall

Commit, within financial reason, to action instead of theory.

Learn to confront the challenges of the real world, rather than resort to the protective womb of academia. You can control most of the risks, and you can't imagine the rewards.

Resources

For the fellow tech nerds among you, here are a few resources for learning about angel investing, founding tech companies, or picking the right startup to work for:

Venture Deals by Brad Feld and Jason Mendelson

Venture Hacks (venturehacks.com), co-created by Naval Ravikant (page 546) and Babak "Nivi" Nivi. Free how-to content on just about any facet of this game imaginable. Some terms and norms may be out of date, but that's less than 20% of the content, and the game theory and strategy is spot on.

AngelList, also co-founded by Naval and Nivi. Great for finding deals, seeing who's investing in what, and finding jobs at fast-growing startups. I'm an advisor to AngelList, and you can see my entire portfolio at **angel.co/tim**

**"Losers have goals.
Winners have systems."**

SCOTT ADAMS

Scott Adams (TW: @SCOTTADAMSSAYS, BLOG.DILBERT.COM) is the creator of the *Dilbert* comic strip, which has been published in 19 languages in more than 2,000 newspapers in 57 countries. He is the best-selling author of *How to Fail at Almost Everything and Still Win Big*, *God's Debris*, and *The Dilbert Principle*.

Spirit animal: Toy Australian shepherd

BEHIND THE SCENES

>>> Scott's mother gave birth to his little sister while under hypnosis, which was offered as an option by her doctor. She did not take any painkillers, did not feel pain, and was awake the entire time.

>>> Naval Ravikant (page 546) regularly credits Scott's short blog post "The Day You Became a Better Writer" for improving his writing.

LESSER-KNOWN CARTOONS HE READS AND ENJOYS

F Minus
Pearls Before Swine

THE SIX ELEMENTS OF HUMOR

Scott believes there are six elements of humor: naughty, clever, cute, bizarre, mean, and recognizable. You have to have at least two dimensions to succeed.

"Let me give you an example. Cute is usually kids and dogs, and bizarre is just anything that's out of place. If you know your cartoon history, you will know that *The Far Side* used primarily the dimension of putting something out of place. So you'd have an animal talking.

"As soon as the animal's talking, he's got one dimension. He's basically starting a race, and he's already ahead of you if you're the cartoonist who's sitting there saying, 'I think I'll do a comic about anything, the world is my canvas.' He's got the bizarre, and then he'll have the animal say something, often in the framing or the type of mood that a human would. That's the 'recognizable' part.

"Take a look at the best comic strip of all time, that I think nearly everyone in the world would say, *Calvin and Hobbes*. There's a talking tiger that is both bizarre and cute. So he took *The Far Side* one dimension further as a starting point. The moment you start reading *Calvin and Hobbes*, you already have cute because his drawing is amazing. He's got double cute. He's got a child and an animal, and it's a cool animal. So he starts that, before he even writes a joke. So then, if he has the kid doing something naughty — also, anything bad happening to anybody ('mean') — that's of course one of the dimensions. . . ."

SOMETIMES, YOU STILL NEED TO SLEEP ON IT

"Because I had this character, Dilbert, and he was the type of guy who would be a loner, I wanted to give him a dog just so there was somebody to interact with. And I wanted the name of the dog to have some correspondence with Dilbert. And so Dogbert's original name was Dildog."

TIM: "Did the name Dildog make it to print?"

SCOTT: "No, I wisely decided that was not a good commercial decision, at least not for newspapers because they're all aggressively rated G."

"SYSTEMS" VERSUS "GOALS"

Scott helped me refocus, to use his language, on "systems" instead of "goals." This involves choosing projects and habits that, even if they result in "failures" in the eyes of the outside world, give you transferable skills or relationships. In other words, you choose options that allow you to inevitably "succeed" over time, as you build assets that carry over to subsequent projects.

Fundamentally, "systems" could be thought of as asking yourself, "What persistent skills or relationships can I develop?" versus "What short-term goal can I achieve?" The former has a potent snowball effect, while the latter is a binary pass/fail with no consolation prize. Scott writes about this extensively in his book *How to Fail at Almost Everything and Still Win Big: Kind of the Story of My Life*. Here's one real-world example:

"When I first started blogging, my future wife often asked about what my goal was. The blogging seemed to double my workload while promising a 5% higher income that didn't make any real difference in my life. It seemed a silly use of time. I tried explaining that blogging was a system, not a goal. But I never did a good job of it. I'll try again here.

"Writing is a skill that requires practice. So the first part of my system involves practicing on a regular basis. I didn't know what I was practicing for, exactly, and that's what makes it a system and not a goal. I was moving from a place with low odds (being an out-of-practice writer) to a place of good odds (a well-practiced writer with higher visibility).

"The second part of my blogging system is a sort of R&D for writing. I write on a variety of topics and see which ones get the best response. I also write in different 'voices.' I have my humorously self-deprecating voice, my angry voice, my thoughtful voice, my analytical voice, my half-crazy voice, my offensive voice, and so on. Readers do a good job of telling me what works and what doesn't.

"When the *Wall Street Journal* took notice of my blog posts, they asked me to write some guest features. Thanks to all of my writing practice, and my knowledge of which topics got the best response, the guest articles were highly popular. Those articles weren't big moneymakers either, but it all fit within my system of public practice.

"My writing for the *Wall Street Journal*, along with my public practice on the blog, attracted the attention of book publishers, and that attention turned into a book deal. And the book deal generated speaking requests that are embarrassingly lucrative. So the payday for blogging eventually arrived, but I didn't know in advance what path it would take. My blogging has kicked up dozens of business opportunities over the past years, so it could have taken any direction."

TF: My podcast was never intended to be a business. I was burned out after *The 4-Hour Chef*, which was nearly 700 pages, and I wanted a casual but creative break from big projects. Since I enjoyed being interviewed by Joe Rogan, Marc Maron, *Nerdist*, and other podcasting heavies, I decided to try long-form audio for six episodes. If I didn't enjoy it after six, I would throw in the towel and walk. My rationale: Worst-case scenario, the experience would help me improve my interviewing, force me to refine my questions, and eliminate verbal tics, all of which would help later projects. One or two episodes wouldn't give me sufficient practice for a hockey stick in the learning curve, so I somewhat arbitrarily chose six episodes as a test run. Roughly 200 episodes later, here we are.

ON THE ODD EFFECTIVENESS OF AFFIRMATIONS

I believe the devil is in the details with this bullet, so it's longer than normal. It's one of those things that *shouldn't* work but nevertheless appears to improve the odds. I tested Scott's approach in my own life after a live Tony Robbins event, which I detail more on page 449. For now, here is Scott's origin story:

"Let me say first [that I don't believe] that if you say your affirmations, something magic will happen, and the universe will change in some [non-scientific] way. . . . What I have said is that I've used the technique, and I got a certain experience, which I'll be happy to share, and then I tell the story. . . .

"I'm in my 20s. I was taking a course in hypnosis to learn how to become a professional hypnotist and get certified. One day [this woman in my class] said, 'You've got to try this thing called affirmations. I read about it in a book, but I don't remember the name of the book.' So I can't tell you here, because she didn't tell me. And she said, 'It works like this.'

"**All you do is you pick a goal and you write it down 15 times a day in some specific sentence form, like 'I, Scott Adams, will become an astronaut,' for example. And you do that every day.** Then it will seem as if the universe just starts spitting up opportunities. It will look to you like these are coincidences, and whether they are or not is less relevant than the fact that they seem to pop up.

"So I, being my rational self, am saying: That seems like a terrible waste of time. There's no science behind that, blah, blah, blah. She convinced me, partly because she was a member of Mensa, that she wasn't dumb.

"The two affirmations that are notable were: First, I said I would become a number-one best-selling author. This was before I'd ever written a book, and I'd never taken a class in writing, except a 2-day course in business writing, and that was it. *The Dilbert Principle* became the number-one best-selling book.

"There was a period . . . where I lost my voice [beginning in 2005 due to to spasmodic dysphonia]. I couldn't speak for three and a half years. . . . That was the next time I used affirmations. And the affirmation was: I, Scott Adams, will speak perfectly. Now, I realize I don't speak perfectly, but when we get to that story you'll see that there's more to it."

TIM: "How exactly are you practicing these affirmations?"

SCOTT: "I'll tell you exactly how I did it, but then I'll also tell you that I'm positive the exact method doesn't matter. I think what matters is the degree of focus and the commitment you have to that focus. Because the last affirmation I mentioned was primarily done in my head while driving, but continuously for years, about 3 years. At first, the way I did it back in those times was I used a pencil or a pen and a piece of paper, and I wrote the same sentence 15 times, once a day, I think. Here's why I think it seems to work, and there are several possibilities. One is something I learned long ago, and I forget who coined it but have you ever heard the phrase 'reticular activation'? It's basically the idea that it's easy to hear your own name spoken in a crowd.

"You'll hear background noise *blah, blah, blah,* 'Tim Ferriss,' *blah, blah, blah.* And you think, how did I hear that one thing in this whole bunch of crowd noise? Basically, your brain isn't capable of processing everything in its environment, or even coming close. So the best it can do is set up these little filters. And the way it sets its filters is by what you pay attention to. It's what you spend the most energy on. . . . That's how you set your filter. So your filter is automatically set for your name, because that's the thing that matters most to you.

"But you can use these affirmations, presumably—this is just a hypothesis—to focus your mind and your memory on a very specific thing. And that would allow you to notice things in your environment that might have already been there. It's just that your filter was set to ignore, and then you just tune it through this memory and repetition trick until it widens a little bit to allow some extra stuff in. Now, there is some science to back that. . . .

"Eventually I decided to start the affirmation, I, Scott Adams would become a famous cartoonist. The odds of becoming a famous cartoonist—I think about 2,000 people submit packages to the big syndicates, the people who give you the big contract, your big break. They might pick a half dozen. Of those half dozen, most of them will not make it after a year or two, so it's very rare. In fact, *Dilbert* was probably the biggest breakout, or one of the biggest, in 20 years."

PREDICTING TRUMP — WHAT YOU CAN LEARN

On September 22, 2015, Scott Adams correctly predicted on my podcast that 10 months later, Donald Trump would be the Republican nominee. At the time, this was considered laughable. Scott based this on what he considered Trump's hypnosis abilities and media savvy, not his policies. This might seem like old news, but there are actionable lessons in what Scott noticed:

"Take the debate where he [Trump] came in as the under-prepared buffoon who was going to blow himself up. And Megyn Kelly of Fox News decided that, yes, that's exactly what was going to happen, and she started right out with the 'Did you say all these bad things about women?' quote. Now, every other politician would have been smeared off the stage by that, because it wouldn't matter what he said back. . . .

"The logical answer, maybe somebody [would've] said, 'Oh, that was taken out of context,' or whatever, which is what people usually say, and it usually is. But the public isn't going to hear that. They're just going to hear the feeling that they felt when Megyn Kelly said that person's name [plus] bad to women.

"That's really the beginning and the end of the thinking for, let's say, at least

20% of the public; about the same 20% that can easily be hypnotized, coincidentally. But what did Trump do? As soon as that question came up, he semi-interrupted her and he said, 'Only Rosie O'Donnell.' That, my friend, is hypnosis. He took an anchor that everybody could visualize, and his core audience already had a negative impression. Their negative impression of Rosie O'Donnell almost certainly was bigger, stronger, more visual and more important than whatever Megyn Kelly just said. . . .

"She showed him four kings and he beat her hand, and he did it without even trying, and he did it with a method which is well understood. It's a negotiating technique. You throw down an anchor, you divert everybody. Instead of becoming this sexist, which he could have been on day one, he became the straight talker.

"Now, I know you follow the headlines so you know what happened next. Roger Ailes of Fox News weighed in to say, 'We need to make peace with Donald Trump because this is getting out of hand,' and Donald Trump made peace with him. How do you interpret that? I'll tell you how I interpret it. I interpret it as Donald Trump just bought Fox News without paying a freaking penny. Because if they want him to appear on [their] show, that's up to him, and he proved he doesn't need them."

TF: At this point, I asked Scott about a clever line Trump often uses to shut down journalists, which is a quick interjection of "Check your facts, [insert journalist name]." *- creates ?*

SCOTT: "'Check your facts' is what I call the 'high ground maneuver.' It's the same thing Jobs did when he explained away Antennagate just by saying, 'All smart phones have problems. We're trying to make our customers happy.' He made a national story go away in less than 30 seconds with those two sentences."

MORNING "FLOODING" — LISTENING TO THE BODY INSTEAD OF THE MIND

To minimize decisions, Scott wakes up, pushes a button for coffee, and has the same breakfast every morning: a chocolate–peanut butter flavor Clif Builder's 20-gram protein bar. The next step is exposing himself to new information to generate ideas for his comic strip:

"There's a process where once you clear your mind, you have to flood it.

You may use different words for this, but I know you do it. So you empty it, and then you flood it with new input that's not the old input. So I'm looking at the news, I'm looking at stuff I haven't seen. I'm not looking at yesterday's problem for the fifth time. I'm looking at a new problem, I'm thinking of a new idea. But then you've got to find out where in that flood is the little piece that's worth working with. **That's where I use the body model.** I kind of cycle through all this stuff.

"The model is: Your brain can't find good contact, not directly in an intellectual sense. Obviously, the brain's involved, but what I mean is that as **I'm thinking of these ideas and they're flowing through my head, I'm monitoring my body; I'm not monitoring my mind. And when my body changes, I have something that other people are going to care about, too.**"

TF: B.J. Novak (page 378) has expressed something very similar. This bodily reaction—an involuntary half-chuckle, a rush of adrenaline, a surge of endorphins, a sharp change of emotions, etc.—can act as a metal detector for good material. It takes practice, but it works.

ON DIVERSIFICATION FOR STRESS MANAGEMENT

The below came from me asking, "What advice would you give your 30-year-old self?":

"My 30-year-old self wouldn't have access to medical marijuana, so I'd have a limited canvas with which to paint. I've always made it a top priority since I was a teenager—and had tons of stress-related medical problems—to make that job one: to learn how to not have stress. **I would consider myself a world champion at avoiding stress at this point in dozens of different ways. A lot of it is just how you look at the world, but most of it is really the process of diversification.** I'm not going to worry about losing one friend if I have a hundred, but if I have two friends I'm really going to be worried. I'm not going to worry about losing my job because my one boss is going to fire me, because I have thousands of bosses at newspapers everywhere. One of the ways to not worry about stress is to eliminate it. I don't worry about my stock picks because I have a diversified portfolio. Diversification works in almost every area of your life to reduce your stress."

DILBERT HARDWARE — WHAT SCOTT DRAWS ON
Wacom Cintiq tablet

THE LOGIC OF THE DOUBLE OR TRIPLE THREAT
On "career advice," Scott has written the following, which is slightly trimmed for space here. This is effectively my mantra, and you'll see why I bring it up:

> If you want an average, successful life, it doesn't take much planning. Just stay out of trouble, go to school, and apply for jobs you might like. But if you want something extraordinary, you have two paths: 1) Become the best at one specific thing. 2) Become very good (top 25%) at two or more things.
>
> The first strategy is difficult to the point of near impossibility. Few people will ever play in the NBA or make a platinum album. I don't recommend anyone even try.
>
> The second strategy is fairly easy. Everyone has at least a few areas in which they could be in the top 25% with some effort. In my case, I can draw better than most people, but I'm hardly an artist. And I'm not any funnier than the average standup comedian who never makes it big, but I'm funnier than most people. The magic is that few people can draw well and write jokes. It's the combination of the two that makes what I do so rare. And when you add in my business background, suddenly I had a topic that few cartoonists could hope to understand without living it.
>
> I always advise young people to become good public speakers (top 25%). Anyone can do it with practice. If you add that talent to any other, suddenly you're the boss of the people who have only one skill. Or get a degree in business on top of your engineering degree, law degree, medical degree, science degree, or whatever. Suddenly you're in charge, or maybe you're starting your own company using your combined knowledge.
>
> Capitalism rewards things that are both rare and valuable. You make yourself rare by combining two or more "pretty goods" until no one else has your mix. . . . At least one of the skills in your mixture should involve communication, either written or verbal. And it could be as simple as learning how to sell more effectively than 75% of the world. That's one. Now add to that whatever your passion is, and you have two, because that's

[handwritten margin note: 2 Qualiti_ combined]

the thing you'll easily put enough energy into to reach the top 25%. If you have an aptitude for a third skill, perhaps business or public speaking, develop that too.

It sounds like generic advice, but you'd be hard-pressed to find any successful person who didn't have about three skills in the top 25%.

TF: Marc Andreessen (page 170) long ago referred to the above double-/triple-threat concept, citing Scott's writing, as "even the secret formula to becoming a CEO. All successful CEOs are like this." He reiterated that you could also cultivate this in school by getting unusual combinations of degrees, like engineering + MBA, law degree + MBA, or undergrad physics + economics.

SHAUN WHITE

Shaun White (TW/FB/IG: @SHAUNWHITE, SHAUNWHITE.COM) is a professional snowboarder and skateboarder. Among his many feats, he is a two-time Olympic gold medalist and holds the X Games record for gold medals at 15 (as well as the highest overall medal count at 23). Shaun has earned the number-two spot on *BusinessWeek*'s list of the 100 Most Powerful and Marketable Athletes. He is the majority owner of the Air + Style event series, which has been called "a combination of Coachella and the X Games."

BEHIND THE SCENES

>> Shaun was born with a heart defect called the Tetralogy of Fallot. Several of the valves in his heart leaked, which required multiple open-heart surgeries to fix. In his childhood, he would pass out from overexertion on the soccer field.

>> My podcast episode with Shaun was recorded live to a sold-out crowd at The Troubadour in L.A., where Guns N' Roses played the gig that first got them signed to Geffen.

∗ What's your self-talk just before dropping into an Olympic run?
"I say, 'At the end of the day, **who cares? What's the big deal?** I'm here, I'm going to try my best, and I'm going to go home, and my family's there. . . . Even though my whole world's wrapped up in this, who cares?'"
    TF: The "and I'm going to go home, and my family's there" is a line he adopted from Andre Agassi, one of his mentors. Shaun and I both love and recommend Andre's autobiography, *Open.*

OVERCOMING PEER PRESSURE, PLUS THE VALUE OF "STUPID" GOALS
"There was an amazing situation where I was in Japan at this competition called the Toyota Big Air, and I was a wild-card entry. I was paying my travel to get there. My mom flew out with me. We're paying for the hotel, we're paying for the food, all these things. All the other riders were invited [and had flights and hotels covered]. When they got there, they got paid per diem [daily compensation] money to show up, and then there's a big prize purse of $50K.

"Everyone went out that night and partied like crazy, and I was a kid, so I was at the hotel with my mom. They show up hungover to the event, and they're like, 'You know, the jump's just lame' — because they're snowboarders, so — 'It's not cool, and we don't want to compete today. We're just gonna do a demo, and we're all going to split the money.' I'm doing the quick math and I think, 'Man, this doesn't even cover our flights out.' And so I said, 'I don't want to do it. I don't want to split the money.'

"They hazed me and said, 'Oh, you're all about the money . . .' and I just sat there: 'I'm riding really well today. I'm not doing it.' They had a big picture of all the riders' faces and they're drawing dollar signs on my eyes. I was like 15.

That was intimidating. My heroes making jabs at me, and man, I won. . . . It was $50K and a car. I was like, 'Oh my God! What do we do?'"

TIM: "What were the sources of that strength in the face of that type of peer pressure? That's unusual for a 15-year-old, especially when you're being faced by your idols who are suddenly throwing darts at you. Did that come from your parents? Or is it just something that you've always had, or is there a different answer?"

SHAUN: "I'd put in the work, I'd put in the time, I felt like I was the best rider, and these guys had their travel paid to get there. . . . I just thought, you know what? This is my day, and I'm not going to let them ruin it. I'd worked toward this goal. You know, I usually set goals. **Every single season I set a goal . . . it's usually two goals. It's something very serious and something funny, something stupid.**"

TIM: "Like what? What would be an example of each?"

SHAUN: "You're going to [laugh] — it's ridiculous. One of them was to win the Olympics, and then one of them was to see how many cars I could win. Because, at the time, the automotive industries were just handing out cars. I was on a roll, and I think by the end of the run I had nine cars. There was a Suzuki Sidekick and this Volvo, and a Jeep, and these random cars. . . . I ended up donating them at the end, because I would've had to pay taxes on them and all these things."

TIM: "Do you still set goals like that?"

SHAUN: "I do, yeah. They're always random, man. The Vancouver Olympics — I can't believe I'm telling you this — my goals were, again, to win the Olympics, and then the other goal was to wear [some] pants, and the pants that I had made were American flag pants. Just follow me . . . I saw this photo of Axl Rose wearing something similar. They were probably a little snugger and shorter. I was like, 'I can't pull that off, but I can make some pants like that.' It was just this stupid goal, like, 'Man, if I won, maybe I can get on the cover of *Rolling Stone* or something like that. . . .'

"But that's what's fun, as it takes a lot of the pressure off. Winning the Olympics is a very big goal, it's a very stressful goal to have. So it's nice to have something else to offset it. Everything was so serious at the time and that was just my way of dealing with it."

TF: Shaun got the *Rolling Stone* cover wearing the American flag pants.

ON BEING AN "OUTLIER"

Sometimes, being outside of the known hotspots is a huge advantage — something Malcolm Gladwell (page 572) explores in his book *Outliers*. The following story from Shaun also reminded me of Richard Betts's logic for choosing restaurants on page 565:

"I was reading [*Outliers*] and I was amazed by the story about the hockey players and this kind of anomaly in the system. I started applying that to my own life and thought, 'Well, people would think I was at a disadvantage growing up in Southern California. Well, I don't find that a disadvantage at all. It was probably sunny and nice out the majority of the year or the winter season.' Our winters aren't like somewhere in Colorado or Vermont. So the number of days I could actually go ride was probably, I don't know, double or triple the amount of someone growing up somewhere else.

"Then, at the same time, the person who was building the parks at Bear Mountain and Snow Summit Resort [in Southern California] — it was this small mountain — so [the management] was like, 'Oh, yeah, do what you want,' and this guy was building these amazing jumps, this amazing half pipe. He now builds all of the courses for the world's best events. That's where he got his start, at these mountains.

"You know they weren't going to let him go to Aspen and tear up the groomer trail or whatever. Also, the half pipe had a T-bar, like a tow rope, on it. So I was thinking, 'Wow, the number of days now that I'm riding because it's sunny, and the number of runs I'm getting because I don't have to unstrap and hike back up.' I would just do my trick, get back on the chair, and go back up. I realized, 'I'm packing in months of training in these small windows, compared to someone else who lives in Vermont or something, where it's well below freezing and they are hiking the pike. They're tired.'

"You know, when you're cold, it's frightening to go, 'Okay, I'm going to try this flip.' No, you're not. It's super-intimidating now, it's cold, and you want to go home and get warm. I was in these conditions where the snow was soft, I had some guy building the best terrain around, and so . . . a lot of fun things that I was able to apply to my life from that book."

TAKE THE GIG AND LOOK FOR OTHER DOORS TO OPEN

"Music was a strange one, just because no one else in my family is musical in the slightest. . . . I won a guitar at a snowboard contest and I thought, 'Wow, what if I could just be at a party somewhere and play one song?' and one song turned into 'Okay, I'm now training to be a guitar player. . . .'

"I play lead guitar in a band called Bad Things. It's composed of mostly friends of mine from the neighborhood I grew up in and some amazingly talented guys I met in L.A. We started making our own songs, and we got offered some gigs, and there was one moment where we got invited to go to Lollapalooza. And I was like, 'Man, this will be heavy.'"

[**TF:** At this point in the story, I said "Wow . . ." in a hushed tone.]

"Just wait . . . it was for *the kids' stage.* So I said, 'You know what would be so punk rock? If we just go and play that kids' stage.' Because I don't think I should be on the main stage. Just because I'm in the group does not mean that we should be given those scenarios. So we show up, and we did our thing. We had a really great show for the kids. Then the most amazing thing happened. It was like out of a movie. The main act on the Grove stage at Lollapalooza decided they weren't going to play. They put a big sign out that said, 'Our art will not be displayed here.' Their fans completely demolished their gear and all this craziness ensued.

"They [the organizers] looked around, like, 'We need a band to play the main stage.' And I said, 'We're a band.' Literally, 'We're a band.' It was crazy. They said, 'You, come with us.' I thought, 'Oh my God, this is our moment, we gotta do this.' And so we played one of the most incredible sets we've ever had. We rose to the occasion. We had this amazing set, and just like anyone who picks up a guitar and dreams of being on stage, you dream of that moment you're walking off stage and everyone is cheering for one more song. And the best moment of that—I look at my buddies, and they're just like, 'Do we even have another song? We don't have another one.' [The organizer] said, 'Play the first one again.'"

FIFTY SHADES OF CHICKEN

That's the title of Shaun's "most-gifted" book. Totally serious. I assumed it would be a complete joke, but it has nearly 700 reviews on Amazon and a 4.8-star average.

THE LAW OF CATEGORY

"In the world of ideas, to name something is to own it.
If you can name an issue, you can own the issue."

—**Thomas L. Friedman**

I constantly recommend that entrepreneurs read *The 22 Immutable Laws of Marketing* by Al Ries and Jack Trout, whether they are first-time founders or serial home-run hitters launching a new product. "The Law of the Category" is the chapter I revisit most often, and I've included a condensed version below. It was originally published in 1993, so some of the "today" references are dated, but the principles are timeless.

The Law of the Category

What's the name of the third person to fly the Atlantic Ocean solo?

If you didn't know that Bert Hinkler was the second person to fly the Atlantic, you might figure you had no chance at all to know the name of the third person. But you do. It's Amelia Earhart.

Now, is Amelia known as the third person to fly the Atlantic Ocean solo, or as the first woman to do so?

After Heineken became a big success, the people at Anheuser-Busch could have said, "We should bring in an imported beer, too." But they didn't. Instead they said, "If there's a market for a high-priced imported beer, maybe there's a market for a high-priced domestic beer." And so they started to promote Michelob, the first high-priced domestic beer, which shortly thereafter out-sold Heineken two to one. (Actually, Anheuser-Busch also brought in an imported beer, Carlsberg, which has a very good reputation in Europe. In the United States, however, the me-too Carlsberg never went anywhere.)

Miller Lite was the first domestic light. It took an importer 5 years to say, "If there's a market for a domestic light beer, maybe there's a market for an imported light beer." The result was Amstel Light, which became the largest-selling imported light beer.

If you didn't get into the prospect's mind first, don't give up hope. Find a new category you can be first in. It's not as difficult as you might think.

After IBM became a big success in computers, everybody and his brother jumped into the field. Burroughs, Control Data, General Electric, Honeywell, NCR, RCA, Sperry. Snow White and the seven dwarfs, they were called.

Which dwarf grew up to become a worldwide powerhouse, with 126,000 employees and sales of $14 billion, a company often dubbed "the second largest computer company in the world"? None of them. The most successful computer company of the seventies and eighties, next to IBM, was Digital Equipment Corporation. IBM was first in computers. DEC was first in *minicomputers*.

Many other computer companies (and their entrepreneurial owners) became rich and famous by following a simple principle: If you can't be first in a category, set up a new category you can be first in.

Tandem was first in fault-tolerant computers and built a $1.9 billion business. So Stratus stepped down with the first fault-tolerant minicomputer.

Are the laws of marketing difficult? No, they are quite simple. Working things out in practice is another matter, however.

Cray Research went over the top with the first supercomputer. So Convex put two and two together and launched the first mini supercomputer.

Sometimes you can also turn an also-ran into a winner by inventing a new category. Commodore was just another manufacturer of home personal computers that wasn't going anywhere until it positioned the Amiga as the first multimedia computer.

There are many different ways to be first. Dell got into the crowded personal computer field by being the first to sell computers by phone.

When you launch a new product, the first question to ask yourself is not "How is this new product better than the competition?" but "First what?" In other words, what category is this new product first in?

Charles Schwab didn't open a better brokerage firm. He opened the first discount broker.

This is counter to classic marketing thinking, which is brand oriented: How do I get people to prefer my brand? Forget the brand. Think categories. Prospects are on the defensive when it comes to brands. Everyone talks about why their brand is better. But prospects have an open mind when it comes to categories. Everyone is interested in what's new. Few people are interested in what's better.

When you're the first in a new category, promote the category. In essence, you have no competition. DEC told its prospects why they ought to buy a minicomputer, not a DEC minicomputer.

In the early days, Hertz sold rent-a-car service. Coca-Cola sold refreshment. Marketing programs of both companies were more effective back then.

———————

TF: Much like DEC and "minicomputers," I created the term "lifestyle design" and debuted it in *The 4-Hour Workweek*. Here's how it first appeared, with a few paragraphs removed:

> The New Rich (NR) are those who abandon the deferred-life plan
> [save and retire after 20–40 years] and create luxury lifestyles in the
> present using the currency of the New Rich: time and mobility. This
> is an art and a science we will refer to as Lifestyle Design (LD). . . .
> $1,000,000 in the bank isn't the fantasy. The fantasy is the lifestyle of
> complete freedom it supposedly allows. The question is then, How
> can one achieve the millionaire lifestyle of complete freedom without
> first having $1,000,000?

Tools and principles follow, like geoarbitrage, email triage, luxury travel workaround, and "mini-retirements" (another term I created), etc.

"Lifestyle design" represented a new and concise label for something that previously required a few sentences. I made no attempt to trademark or protect it. Instead, I propagated it as widely as possible as quickly as possible, seeded it in media interviews, conference keynotes, articles, and elsewhere. I wanted it to enter the popular vernacular, and to have organic communities of "lifestyle designers" sprout up online and all over the world. Once *The 4-Hour Workweek* was parodied by Jay Leno and *The Office*, it had arrived. The side effect was that — at least for the first year — whenever "lifestyle design" was used or defined by someone, my name or *The 4-Hour Workweek* were mentioned as well. This was because I owned the mindshare, the mental "category," not the trademark. Now, of course, it's out in the wild, all grown up, and has taken on a life of its own. At the time of this writing, there are ~14.6 million or ~585K Google search results for "lifestyle design," depending on whether you omit or use quotation marks.

> **"** I don't create art to get
> high-dollar projects, I do
> high-dollar projects so
> I can create more art. **"**

CHASE JARVIS

Chase Jarvis (TW/FB/IG: @CHASEJARVIS, CREATIVELIVE.COM) is the CEO of CreativeLive and one of the most commercially successful photographers in the world. He is the youngest person ever to be named a Hasselblad Master, Nikon Master, and ASMP Master. Chase has photographed for Nike, Apple, Columbia Sportswear, REI, Honda, Subaru, Polaroid, Lady Gaga, Red Bull, and many more. He is known for a hyperkinetic style and emphasis on sports and portraiture. CreativeLive is an online learning platform that broadcasts live, high-definition classes to more than 2 million students in 200 countries. All classes are free to watch live and can be purchased for later viewing. Teachers include Pulitzer Prize winners and business luminaries.

Spirit animal: Dragonfly

BEHIND THE SCENES

>>> Chase and Rick Rubin (page 502) were the two people who first got me to meditate consistently.

>>> Chase is also the first person to introduce me to a Moscow Mule (spicy ginger beer, vodka, lime juice).

>>> On our first visit to the White House, he was repeatedly yelled off the lawn by security, as he was finding optimal angles for selfies. I legitimately thought he was going to get Tasered. For the rest of the day, I would shout "GET OFF THE GRASS!" whenever he stepped on grass around D.C., and he'd jump like a cat seeing a cucumber (Google it. Worth the price of this book).

"CREATIVITY IS AN INFINITE RESOURCE. THE MORE YOU SPEND, THE MORE YOU HAVE."

This was Chase paraphrasing a quote from Maya Angelou and discussing how creativity and meditation are similar.

ON HIS FIRST SALE

"The first sale came about because I grew up skiing and snowboarding, and I was very familiar with the subject. I got in with a good crowd [of athletes] and had photographs of people on next year's equipment, because I knew the manufacturers and reps. If you have the right pictures of the right people on the right equipment, then the manufacturers come knocking. . . . The manufacturers saw my work, got in touch, and I ended up licensing — not selling outright — but licensing an image for $500 and a pair of skis.

"I think I was probably making $10 an hour at the time. I thought to myself, 'Wait a minute. I just sold that for $500 from going skiing for a couple of days with my buddies. I'd like to replicate that, so what did I do? What worked and what didn't?' . . . I just started doing that over and over, and upping the ante every time."

ON GOING PREMIUM FROM DAY ONE

"The way that I hacked the system was setting my first hired, day-rate gig at several thousand dollars a day. I pushed myself to a point that was incredibly uncomfortable and required myself to deliver at the highest level. I charged accordingly because I had done the work, done the research, and knew what the top guys and gals were getting. I put myself in that caliber right away. . . . I set it at $2,000 to $2,500 a day.

"They [the first contract prospect] said, 'Okay, well it's a six-day shoot.' . . . In my head, I'm shitting myself doing the math. It's more than I made last year, but I'm going to make it next week. They said, 'That sounds fine. We may need to add an extra day. . . .'

"I said 'I'll get back to you on that' [to play it cool], and I felt like I was going to go throw up in the bathroom. There were some stakes there . . . it was an indicator of where I wanted to go. I knew I wanted to be a top price point. I wanted to do less work, and do high-end stuff. Now, I don't want to pretend I didn't do a shitload. This is like a 10-year, overnight success program . . . I was eating, breathing, sleeping photography, [and then] **when I was able to start to monetize my craft, I did so at a very high price point.** Little note: If someone ever says 'yes' that quickly, you didn't ask for enough."

TF: Chase and I share many philosophies, including this one. I didn't accept advertisers for the podcast until I had 100K+ downloads per episode, as measured at the industry-standard 6 weeks post-publication. Why? Novice podcasters (which I was), bloggers, and artists of all types get too distracted in nascent stages with monetization. For podcasting: In the first 3 to 9 months, you should be honing your craft and putting out increasingly better work. "Good content is the best SEO," as Robert Scoble originally told me.

You have fundamentally two choices, and the majority of people choose Option A.

Option A: You can waste 30 to 50% of your time persuading a few small sponsors to commit early, then stall at 30K downloads per episode because you're neglecting the creative. Things are even worse if you get mired in the world of sketchy affiliate deals.

Option B: You can play the long game, wait 6 to 12 months until you have a critical mass, then get to 300K downloads per episode and make more than 10 times per episode with much larger brands who can afford to scale with you as you grow. Haste makes waste. In this case, it can easily make the difference between $50K per year and more than $1 million per year.

AMPLIFY YOUR STRENGTHS RATHER THAN FIX YOUR WEAKNESSES

"Everything is a remix, but what is your version of the remix? Say I have a relationship with a bunch of celebrities, so I might be able to get a photograph of them that no one else could because they were on my couch playing PlayStation. . . . The point is thinking about, 'What is the unique mojo that I bring, and how can I try and amplify that?' Amplify your strengths rather than fix your weaknesses.

"If you're not the best person at capturing something visually, but you're a good storyteller, you have your visual art, then you have an incredible narrative to go with it. When you go into art galleries — and I don't have the budget for it, but I'm a classical-type guy — you'll see stuff on the wall for $10 million, and you can't figure out what it is. You read the plaque next to it and you're like, 'That's a damn good story. I see how they're selling these things.'"

DIFFERENT, NOT JUST BETTER

"I took a lot of cues from Andy Warhol, Jean-Michel Basquiat [he took graffiti off the street and brought it into the gallery], and Robert Rauschenberg [large-scale guy, crazy mixed media], the artists in New York in the 1950s, 1960s, and 1970s because they were hackers. . . . [Some of them] were making art about making art. They were reinventing the game while they were playing it.

"If I look across and everyone else is doing X, how do you zig when everyone else is zagging? The way that I zigged when everyone else was zagging in photography was I chronicled my exploits of learning my craft. . . . It was 10 years before it was cool to be transparent, and I was actually vilified for sharing trade secrets."

SPECIALIZATION IS FOR INSECTS (AS HEINLEIN WOULD SAY)*

"I was told my whole career: You have to specialize, specialize. I 'specialized' in pursuing the things that interested me. I talked a lot about action sports, but then I also talked about fashion, break dancing, and all kinds of different cul-

---

*From *Time Enough for Love*: "A human being should be able to change a diaper, plan an invasion, butcher a hog, conn a ship, design a building, write a sonnet, balance accounts, build a wall, set a bone, comfort the dying, take orders, give orders, cooperate, act alone, solve equations, analyze a new problem, pitch manure, program a computer, cook a tasty meal, fight efficiently, die gallantly. Specialization is for insects."

tural stuff. I've made TV shows, shot commercials, done ad campaigns, created startups, and [made] the first iPhone app that shared images to social networks. I historically would have been called a dilettante, but to be able to touch all of these things [is to] find out that they ultimately inform one another."

(Reminiscent of Scott Adams's career advice on page 269.)

SHOW YOUR WORK

Both Chase and Derek Sivers (page 184) are big fans of the book *Show Your Work* by Austin Kleon.

DAN CARLIN

Dan Carlin (TW/FB: @HARDCOREHISTORY, DANCARLIN.COM) is the host of my absolute favorite podcast, *Hardcore History*, as well as *Common Sense*. Jocko Willink (page 412) is also a huge fan of *Hardcore History*. Tip: Start with "Wrath of the Khans."

ON NOT DOING WHAT YOU'RE QUALIFIED TO DO

"If I've learned anything from podcasting, it's **don't be afraid to do something you're not qualified to do**."

TF: This is a common thread throughout this book. Kamal Ravikant, Naval Ravikant's (page 546) brother, told me how Naval once said to him (paraphrased): "If I had always done what I was 'qualified' to do, I'd be pushing a broom somewhere." As I've also heard said, "Amateurs built the Ark, professionals built the *Titanic*." Dan preemptively disarms potential criticism of his credentials by saying in nearly every episode, "Keep in mind that I'm no historian, but . . ."

THE ORIGIN OF *HARDCORE HISTORY*

"I used to tell my stories that I've told my whole life, and I was telling them around the dinner table. My mother-in-law said to me, because I was already doing one podcast on current events [*Common Sense*], 'Why don't you do a podcast on the stuff you're talking about here at dinner?' I said I couldn't do that. I said, 'It's history, and I'm not qualified to talk about history. I don't have a doctorate, I'm not a historian.' And she said, 'I didn't realize you had to have a doctorate to tell stories.' I thought about that for a bit. . . . Most of the great historians from the non-modern era didn't have doctorates, either. They're just storytellers, too. As long as I'm not purporting to be a historian, and as long as I'm using their work . . . I will tell you the [historical] controversy, and then I will say, 'Here is what historian A says about it, and here's what historian B says about it.' I've been surprised how much the listeners like to hear about what's called 'historiography,' which is the process of how history gets written and made and interpreted. They love hearing that! So you'll actually talk about the different theories. I'm not making this stuff up. I'm using the experts to tell you a story."

TF: Dan builds shows around his answer(s) to "What's weird about this story?" when reading various and often conflicting historical accounts.

"COPYRIGHT YOUR FAULTS"

"I always was heavily 'in the red,' as they say, when I was on the radio. . . . I yelled so loud, and I still do, that the meter just jumps up into the red. They would say, 'You need to speak in this one zone of loudness, or you'll screw up the radio station's compression.' After a while, I just started writing liners [intros others would read for him] for the big-voice guy: 'Here's Dan Carlin, he talks so loud . . .' or whatever.

"That's my style. 'I meant to do that. As a matter of fact, if you do it, you're imitating me.' So it's partly taking what you already do and saying, 'No, no, this isn't a negative. This is the thing I bring to the table, buddy. I copyrighted that. I talk real loud, and then I talk really quietly, and if you have a problem with that, you don't understand what good style is.' **Just copyright your faults, man.**"

✱ Advice to your 25- or 30-year-old self?

"I remember coming out of the television station where I was a TV reporter. I was working the night shift. I had just worked on some stories all day, and I was just thoroughly unsatisfied with them by the time they hit the air. I remember walking out of the station around midnight. It was up on the top of this mountain, a beautiful place. I remember looking out and just saying, 'Oh, my God, when am I going to like this? When am I going to really be happy with the work that I'm churning out?' I look back on that all the time . . . if I could go back and just tell myself, **'Don't stress about it, it's all going to work out in the end.'** Wouldn't any of us like to know that? Just tell me it's all going to be okay, and I can get by in my 20s. The 20s were really hard for me. . . . If you could have just said, 'Stop worrying, it's all going to be okay,' . . . I would have saved a ton of emotional stress and worry. I'm a natural-born worrier. **Although, if you had told me that, I might have relaxed so much that [my current] reality might never have occurred. So that's why you can't go back in the time machine and step on the butterfly — you'll screw up everything.** So I won't go back and tell myself that, Tim, because I'll screw up my future."

RAMIT SETHI

Ramit Sethi (TW/IG: @RAMIT, IWILLTEACHYOUTOBERICH.COM) graduated from Stanford University in 2005 with bachelor's and master's degrees in technology, psychology, and sociology. He grew his personal finance blog to more than 1 million readers per month, then turned this college side project into a multi-million-dollar business with more than 30 employees. Some of his weeks now break $5 million in revenue. In a finance space saturated by "gurus" of dubious credentials, Ramit has always been willing to share real numbers.

Spirit animal: Common swift

BEHIND THE SCENES

>>> Ramit and I often laugh about how we are blessed and cursed with scammy-sounding book titles. *I Will Teach You to Be Rich* and *The 4-Hour Workweek* are about as bad as it gets. Easy to remember, hard to live down.

>>> Every few years for the last 20 years, Ramit has read *Iacocca: An Autobiography* by Lee Iacocca and William Novak.

A MAN CALLED "ASS"

"My actual birth name was Amit, which is a much more common Indian name. About 2 days after I was born, my dad woke up, rolled over, and told my mom, 'We cannot name him Amit because his initials will be ASS.' And the best part is, like true immigrants—my parents are from India—they went to the hospital, and they didn't want to pay the $50 change fee, so they told them that they had forgotten to add an R and they got it for free. Thanks, Mom and Dad."

TF: On a related note, I recently got this text from Ramit: "Btw I think I told you how my sisters wanted to get a dog for 15 years. We couldn't because my dad is allergic. Only . . . we found out he's not. He just lied to us because he hates pets."

ARE YOU J. CREW?

"We send millions of emails a month with multiple-million [combinatorial variants] of email funnels, and we generate roughly 99% of our revenue through email.

"[My emails] look like plain emails. . . . I am not J. Crew. J. Crew is selling a brand, so their emails have to be beautiful. My emails look like *I* am writing to *you* because I want to be your friend . . . at scale. That is why my emails appear to be really simple. Behind the scenes, there is a lot of stuff going on, but they appear . . . like I just jotted you a note."

TF: One of the reasons I put off using email newsletters for years was perceived complexity. I didn't want to have to craft beautiful templates and ship out gorgeous, magazine-worthy missives. Ramit convinced me to send plain-text email for my *5-Bullet Friday* newsletter, which became one of the most powerful parts of my business within 6 months.

SOME OF TOOLS OF HIS TRADE

Infusionsoft: Complete sales and marketing automation software for small businesses, with a particular focus on "funnels"

Visual Website Optimizer: A/B testing software for marketers

ADVICE FROM A MENTOR

"Tactics are great, but tactics become commoditized."

TF: If you understand principles, you can create tactics. If you are dependent on perishable tactics, you are always at a disadvantage. This is why Ramit studies behavioral psychology and the elements of persuasion that appear hardwired. One of his most-gifted books is *Age of Propaganda* by Anthony Pratkanis and Elliot Aronson, and his favorite copywriting book is an oldie: *The Robert Collier Letter Book*, originally published in 1931.

"INDIAN PEOPLE DO NOT GET PUNCHED IN THE FACE, DUDE. THEY DO NOT GET IN FIGHTS. WE ARE DOING SPELLING BEES."

For some godforsaken reason, I asked Ramit, "Do you remember the last time you were punched in the face?" He answered with the above.

1,000 TRUE FANS

"['1,000 True Fans' by Kevin Kelly] was one of the seminal articles that inspired me to really build amazing material, rather than just recycling what else was out there. I knew that if I had 1,000 true fans, then not only would I be able to live doing the things I wanted, but I would be able to turn that into 2,000, 5,000, 10,000 — and that is exactly what happened.

"In terms of getting my first 1,000 true fans, you can look at my posts. They tend to be very, very long [and definitive]. In some cases, 15, 20, 25 pages long. . . . If your material is good, if it is engaging, there is almost no maximum you can write. . . . My point is not 'write longer.' It is 'do not worry about space.'

"Second, I cannot recommend guest posting enough. I did one for you ['The Psychology of Automation'] — that probably took me 20 to 25 hours to write. It was very detailed. It included video, all kinds of stuff, and to this day a lot of the people I meet, I ask, 'How did you hear about me?' and they say, 'Oh, through Tim Ferriss.'"

TF: For the launch of *The 4-Hour Workweek,* I used this same guest posting strategy on Gigaom, Lifehacker, and other sites.

"I GIVE AWAY 98% OF MY MATERIAL FOR FREE AND, THEN, MANY OF MY FLAGSHIP COURSES ARE EXTREMELY EXPENSIVE. IN FACT, 10 TO 100 TIMES WHAT MY COMPETITORS CHARGE."

TF: I have mirrored Ramit's approach to pricing and selling. I rarely sell high-ticket items, but when I do, I charge 10 to 100 times what "competitors" might. In general, I split my content in a very binary fashion: free or ultra-premium.

"Free" means that 99% of what I do is free to the world (e.g., podcast, blog) or nearly free (books). I write on topics that A) I enjoy and want to learn more about, and that B) I think will attract intelligent, driven, and accomplished people. This is what allows ultra-premium.

Ultra-premium means:

>> Once in a blue moon, I offer a high-priced and very limited product or opportunity, such as an event with 200 seats at $7.5K to $10K per seat. I can sell out a scarce, ultra-premium opportunity within 48 hours with a single blog post, as I did with my "Opening the Kimono" (OTK) event in Napa. Of course, then you have to overdeliver. My measurement of customer satisfaction? The Facebook group established for attendees is still active . . . *5 years* later.

>> I use the network and contacts I've built through "free" to find excellent non-content opportunities, such as early-stage tech investing. I found Shopify, for instance, via my fans on Twitter while updating *The 4-Hour Workweek.* I started advising Shopify when they had ~10 employees. Now they have more than 1,000 and are a publicly traded company (SHOP). Fans on social media recommended Duolingo to me when it was in private beta-testing, and I invested in the first round of financing. Now, they have 100 million users and are the world's most popular language-learning software.

An openness to indirect paths means I don't obsess over selling my "content," and I never have. My network, partially built through writing, is my net worth. If you want to increase your income 10x instead of 10%, the best opportunities are often seemingly out of left field (e.g., books → startups).

CHECKLISTS

Ramit and I are both obsessed with checklists and love a book by Atul Gawande titled *The Checklist Manifesto*. I have this book on a shelf in my living room, cover out, as a constant reminder. Atul Gawande is also one of Malcolm Gladwell's (page 572) favorite innovators. Ramit builds checklists for as many business processes as possible, which he organizes using software called Basecamp. Google "entrepreneurial bus count" for a good article on why checklists can save your startup.

✱ Who do you think of when you hear the word "successful"?

"I think of a guy I recently met named Mark Bustos. He has an awesome Instagram account (@markbustos) and is a very high-end hairdresser in New York. He works at a top salon, and on the weekend, he goes and he cuts the hair of homeless people around New York. He records it, and he writes about their stories. I think it is so amazing that he is at the top of game as a hairdresser, working with celebrity clients and things like that, and then on the weekend — on his one day off — he goes around and is of service to people who ordinarily would never have the chance to get their hair cut, especially by somebody like him."

✱ Two people Ramit has learned from (or followed closely) in the last year

Jay Abraham and Charlie Munger.

TF: Jay Abraham is one of Daymond John's (page 323) mentors and the author of *Getting Everything You Can Out of All You've Got*, which is one of Ramit's most-gifted books. I often recommend Jay's work to people who ask about how to structure "JVs," or joint ventures.

IT'S BEEN A LONG TIME . . . AND YOU ARE FAT

"If you are overweight and you get off the plane [in India], the first thing your family is going to say is 'Wow, you got fat.'"

TF: If you want to be this brutally honest in the U.S., I suggest first reading my friend A.J. Jacobs's *Esquire* piece titled "I Think You're Fat."

1,000 TRUE FANS — REVISITED

I have recommended Kevin Kelly's "1,000 True Fans" to literally millions of people. Many guests in this book have done the same. "If you only read one article on marketing, make it this one" is my common wording. Here's a highly simplified synopsis: **"Success" need not be complicated. Just start with making 1,000 people extremely, extremely happy.**

Kevin's original piece has grown outdated in a few places, so he was kind enough to write up a newer summary of core concepts for readers of this book.

Since I first read the original nearly 10 years ago, I've tested his concepts across dozens of businesses, many of which are now multi-billion-dollar companies. I've added some of my core learnings and recommendations at the end.

Enter Kevin

I first published this idea in 2008, when it was embryonic and ragged, and now, 8 years later, my original essay needs an update—by someone other than me. Here I'll simply restate the core ideas, which I believe will be useful to anyone making things, or making things happen. —KK

To be a successful creator, you don't need millions. You don't need millions of dollars or millions of customers, clients, or fans. To make a living as a craftsperson, photographer, musician, designer, author, animator, app maker, entrepreneur, or inventor you need only 1,000 true fans.

A *true fan* is defined as "a fan who will buy anything you produce." These diehard fans will drive 200 miles to see you sing; they will buy the hardback *and* paperback *and* audio versions of your book; they will purchase your next figurine, sight unseen; they will pay for the "best-of" DVD version of your free YouTube channel; they will come to your chef's table once a month; they will buy the superdeluxe reissued hi-res box set of your stuff even though they have the low-res version. They have a Google Alert set for your name; they bookmark the eBay page where your out-of-print editions show up; they come to your openings. They have you sign their copies; they buy the T-shirt, and the mug, and the hat; they can't wait till you issue your next work. They are true fans.

If you have roughly 1,000 fans like this (also known as superfans), you can make a living—if you are content to make a living, but not a fortune.

Here's how the math works. You need to meet two criteria: First, you have to create enough each year that you can earn, on average, $100 profit from each true fan. That is easier to do in some arts and businesses than others, but it is a good creative challenge in every area because it is always easier and better to give your existing customers more, than it is to find new fans.

Second, you must have a direct relationship with your fans. That is, they must pay you directly. You get to keep all of their support, unlike the small percentage of their fees you might get from a music label, publisher, studio, retailer, or other intermediate. If you keep the full $100 from each true fan, then you need only 1,000 of them to earn $100K per year. That's a living for most folks.

1,000 customers is a whole lot more feasible to aim for than a million fans. Millions of paying fans is just not a realistic goal to shoot for, especially when you are starting out. But 1,000 fans is doable. You might even be able to remember 1,000 names. If you added one new true fan per day, it'd only take a few years to gain 1,000. True fanship is doable. Pleasing a true fan is pleasurable and invigorating. It rewards the artist to remain true, to focus on the unique aspects of their work, the qualities that true fans appreciate.

The number 1,000 is not absolute. Its significance is in its rough order of magnitude—3 orders less than a million. The actual number has to be adjusted for each person. If you are able to only earn $50 per year per true fan, then you need 2,000. (Likewise, if you can sell $200 per year, you need only 500 true fans.) Or you many need only $75K per year to live on, so you adjust downward. Or if you are a duet, or have a partner, then you need to multiply by 2 to get 2,000 fans, etc.

Another way to calculate the support of a true fan is to aim to get one day of their wages per year. Can you excite or please them sufficiently to earn what they make from one day's labor? That's a high bar, but not impossible for 1,000 people worldwide.

And of course, not every fan will be super. While the support of 1,000 true fans may be sufficient for a living, for every single true fan, you might have 2 or 3 regular fans. Think of concentric circles with true fans at the center and a wider circle of regular fans around them. These regular fans may buy your creations occasionally, or may have bought only once. But their ordinary purchases expand your total income. Perhaps they bring in an additional 50%. Still, you want to focus on the superfans because the enthusiasm of true fans can increase the patronage of regular fans. **True fans are not only the direct source of your income, but also your chief marketing force for the ordinary fans.**

Fans, customers, patrons have been around forever. What's new here? A couple of things. While direct relationships with customers was the default mode in old times, the benefits of modern retailing meant that most creators in the last century did not have direct contact with consumers. Often even the publishers, studios, labels, and manufacturers did not have such crucial information as the names of their customers. For instance, despite being in business for hundreds of years, no New York book publisher knew the names of their core and dedicated readers. For previous creators, these intermediates (and there was often more than one) meant you need much larger audiences to have a success. With the advent of ubiquitous peer-to-peer communication and payment systems—also known as the web today—everyone has access to excellent tools that allow anyone to sell directly to anyone else in the world. So a creator in Bend, Oregon, can sell and deliver a song to someone in Kathmandu, Nepal, as easily as a New York record label (maybe even more easily). This new technology permits creators to maintain relationships so that the customer can become a fan, and so that the creator keeps the total amount of payment, which reduces the number of fans needed.

This new ability for the creator to retain the full price is revolutionary, but a second technological innovation amplifies that power further. A fundamental virtue of a peer-to-peer network (like the web) is that the most obscure node is only one click away from the most popular node. In other words, the most obscure, under-selling book, song, or idea is only one click away from the best-selling book, song, or idea. Early in the rise of the web, the large aggregators of content and products, such as eBay, Amazon, Netflix, etc., noticed that the total sales of *all* the lowest-selling obscure items would equal, or in some cases exceed, the sales of the few best-selling items. Chris Anderson (my successor at *Wired*) named this effect "the Long Tail," for the visually graphed shape of the sales distribution curve: a low, nearly interminable line of items selling only a few copies per year that form a long "tail" for the abrupt vertical beast of a few bestsellers. But the area of the tail was as big as the head. With that insight, the aggregators had great incentive to encourage audiences to click on the obscure items. They invented recommendation engines and other algorithms to channel attention to the rare creations in the long tail. Even web search companies like Google, Bing, and Baidu found it in their interests to reward searchers with the obscure because they could sell ads in the long tail as well. The result was that the most obscure became less obscure.

If you live in any of the 2 million small towns on Earth, you might be the only one in your town to crave death metal music, or get turned on by whispering, or want a left-handed fishing reel. Before the web, you'd never have a way to satisfy that desire. You'd be alone in your fascination. But now, satisfaction is only one click away. Whatever your interests as a creator are, your 1,000 true fans are one click from you. As far as I can tell there is *nothing*— no product, no idea, no desire— without a fan base on the Internet. Everything made or thought of can interest at least one person in a million— it's a low bar. Yet if even only one out of a million people were interested, that's potentially 7,000 people on the planet. That means that *any* 1-in-a-million appeal can find 1,000 true fans. The trick is to practically find those fans, or, more accurately, to have them find you.

One of the many new innovations serving the true fan creator is crowdfunding. Having your fans finance your next product is genius. Win-win all around. There are about 2,000 different crowdfunding platforms worldwide, many of them specializing in specific fields: raising money for science experiments, bands, or documentaries. Each has its own requirements and a different funding model, in addition to specialized interests. Some platforms require "all-or-nothing" funding goals; others permit partial funding; some raise money for completed projects; some, like Patreon, fund ongoing projects. Patreon supporters might fund a monthly magazine, or a video series, or an artist's salary.

The most famous and largest crowdfunder is Kickstarter, which has raised $2.5 billion for more than 100,000 projects. The average number of supporters for a successful Kickstarter project is 290 funders — far less than 1,000. That means if you have 1,000 true fans, you can do a crowdfunding campaign, because by definition a true fan will become a Kickstarter funder. (Although the success of your campaign is dependent on what you ask of your fans).

The truth is that cultivating 1,000 true fans is time-consuming, sometimes nerve-wracking, and not for everyone. Done well (and why not do it well?) it can become another full-time job. At best, it will be a consuming and challenging part-time task that requires ongoing skills. There are many creators who don't want to deal with fans, and honestly should not. They should just paint, or sew, or make music, and hire someone else to deal with their superfans. If that is you, and you add someone to deal with fans, a helper will skew your formula, increasing the number of fans you need, but that might be the best mix. If you go that far, then why not "subcontract" out dealing with fans to the middle people — the labels and studios and publishers and retailers? If they work for you, fine, but remember, in most cases they would be even worse at this than you would.

The mathematics of 1,000 true fans is not a binary choice. You don't have to go this route to the exclusion of another. Many creators, including me, will use direct relations with superfans in addition to mainstream intermediaries. I have been published by several big-time New York publishers, I have self-published, and I have used Kickstarter to publish to my true fans. I chose each format depending on the content and my aim. But in every case, cultivating my true fans enriches the route I choose.

The takeaway: 1,000 true fans is an alternative path to success other than stardom. Instead of trying to reach the narrow and unlikely peaks of platinum bestseller hits, blockbusters, and celebrity status, you can aim for direct connection with 1,000 true fans. On your way, no matter how many fans you actually succeed in gaining, you'll be surrounded not by faddish infatuation, but by genuine and true appreciation. It's a much saner destiny to hope for. And you are much more likely to actually arrive there.

Some Thoughts from Tim

Kevin distinguishes between "making a living" and "making a fortune," which is an important starting point for the discussion. However, it's worth noting that these aren't necessarily mutually exclusive. Creating 1,000 true fans is also how you create massive hits, perennial mega-bestsellers, and worldwide fame (be careful what you wish for). Everything big starts small and focused (see Peter Thiel, page 232). 1,000 true fans is step #1, whether you want a $100K per year business or the next Uber. I've seen this with all of my fastest-growing and most successful startups. They start laser-focused on 100 to 1,000 people, *niche-ing* down as necessary with their messaging and targeting (demographically, geographically, etc.) to get to a manageable and cost-effectively reachable number.

So, you may ask yourself, "Why aim for a mere $100K when I can try to build a billion-dollar business?" Two reasons: 1) Aiming for the latter from the outset often leads to neglecting the high-touch 1,000 true fans who act as your most powerful unpaid marketing force for "crossing the chasm" into the mainstream. If you don't build that initial army, you're likely to fail. 2) Do you really want to build and manage a big company? For most people, it's not a fun experience; it's an all-consuming taskmaster. There are certainly ace CEOs who thread the needle and enjoy this roller coaster, but they are outliers. Read *Small Giants* by Bo Burlingham for some fantastic examples of companies that choose to be the best rather than the biggest.

And, as Kevin noted, the number of your true fans can actually be far fewer than 1,000. This is particularly true if you A) produce content that attracts a niche but well-heeled group, and then B) invite and look for indirect revenue opportunities not based on onsite transactions (e.g., paid speaking, investment opportunities, consulting). These can be far more lucrative than most advertising, tip jars, and the like.

One reasonably common critique of "1,000 True Fans" comes from musicians, for instance, who say something along the lines of, "But I can only sell an album for $10, and I can only produce one per year. That's only $10K and not enough to live on. '1,000 True Fans' doesn't work." Scores of book writers have a similar argument, but it's flawed. Remember, a *true* true fan will buy *whatever you put out.* If they refuse to purchase above $10, you haven't done the work to find and cultivate real true fans. If you have true fans, it's your responsibility to consider (and test) higher-priced, higher-value options outside of the $10 paradigm. Don't be locked in the pricing model of the incumbents. In 2015, Wu-Tang Clan sold a single bespoke album at auction—in a handcrafted silver and nickel box made by British-Moroccan artist Yahya—to one person for $2 million. There are a lot of options between $10 and $2 million. See my "free or ultra-premium" approach on page 290, which has provided me with complete creative and financial freedom.

You do not have to sacrifice the integrity of your art for a respectable income. You just need to create a great experience and charge enough.

Not sure what to charge? Perhaps you should figure out your Target Monthly Income (TMI) for your ideal lifestyle and work backward. For examples and a simple worksheet exercise, visit fourhourworkweek.com/tmi

HACKING KICKSTARTER

How to Raise $100K in 10 Days

The below is written by Mike Del Ponte, one of the founders of Soma, a startup I advise (FB/IG/TW: @somawater, drinksoma.com). He raised $100K on Kickstarter in 10 days, and I asked him to share some of the best tools and tricks you can use to replicate his success.

Note that "VA" in the below refers to "virtual assistant," which he finds through Upwork or Zirtual.

Enter Mike

How many times have you dreamt of launching a new product, only to let your dream fall to the wayside?

I don't have the money to even get started! What if it fails?

In the past, these excuses held some weight, as bringing a new product to market could be incredibly expensive. Oftentimes, you had to prototype, build, and then hope the world wanted what you were selling. If not, you could end up with a warehouse full of debt: unsellable inventory.

Now, there are new options. Crowdfunding platforms like **Kickstarter** and **Indiegogo** allow you to introduce (test) a new product before you start manufacturing, removing a huge amount of risk. If people like what you're proposing, you can pull in thousands or even millions of dollars to fund your dream. At the very worst, you were able to test your idea without investing much time or money.

But planning and running a Kickstarter campaign is often done in a haphazard fashion.

To prepare for ours, we didn't want to leave anything to chance, so we interviewed 15 of the top-earning Kickstarter creators.

I've worked with PR firms that charge $20K a month and spend 3 months planning a launch. Follow our advice — based on what we learned — and there's a good chance you'll get better results without spending anything.

Using virtual assistants, growth-hacking techniques, and principles from Tim's books, we raised more than $100K in less than 10 days. Having accomplished our goal with almost 30 days to spare, we were able to relax for the holidays.

Here are a just few of the non-obvious keys we learned.

Find the MED for Kickstarter Traffic

If you want to raise a lot of money on Kickstarter, you need to drive a lot of traffic to your project. And you want that traffic to be comprised of prospective backers of your project. Applying the concept of MED ("minimum effective dose" from *The 4-Hour Body*), we knew we needed to discover and focus on the best traffic sources.

My friend Clay Hebert is a Kickstarter expert. One of the things he taught me is a simple trick using bit.ly tracking. Bit.ly is a link shortening service used by millions of people . . . and Kickstarter. If you add a + to the end of any bit.ly URL, you can see stats related to that link. For example: Here are stats for the shortlink Kickstarter generated for our campaign: http://kck.st/VjAFva+

[**TF:** This will blow your mind. Go to any Kickstarter project, click on Share, and pick a social network, like Twitter. A pre-populated tweet will appear with a shortlink. Copy and paste the link alone into a new tab, add + to the end, and hit Return. Voilà.]

To discover the top referral sources, we gave our VA a list of Kickstarter projects similar to ours and asked her to list the referrers for each project. Based on this data, we decided to focus all of our attention on just two goals:

1. Getting coverage on the right blogs

2. Activating our networks to create buzz on Facebook, Twitter, and email

We knew that if we did this, we would be listed in Kickstarter's Popular

Projects sections, which is how you get people who are browsing Kickstarter to check out and back your project.

Find Relevant Bloggers Using Google Images

Start by looking at who covered Kickstarter projects similar to yours. You can do this by using a simple Google Images hack. If you drag and drop any image file into the search bar at **images.google.com**, you'll be shown every website that has ever posted that image. Pretty cool, huh?

Here's the process your VA will use:

» Find 10 Kickstarter projects similar to yours, and for each, do the following:

  → Right-click and save-to-desktop 2 to 3 images.

  → Drag and drop each image file from your desktop into the Google Images search bar.

  → Review blogs listed on the results page to see which might be relevant to your project.

» Fill out the following fields in a Media List spreadsheet which you create: publication, URL, first and last name of the writer, and links to relevant posts by that writer.

» You now have dozens of blogs that have a high probability of relevance, all neatly organized in a spreadsheet. Your VA can find more sites like the ones in your media list by searching SimilarSites.com.

Research Site Traffic on SimilarWeb.com or Alexa.com

Bigger is not always better, but it is helpful to know the size of each blog's readership. Have your VA research how many unique monthly visitors each blog has and add that data to your spreadsheet. **TF:** I personally use the SimilarWeb Chrome extension.

Identify Relationships on Facebook

This may be the most important part of your PR efforts. For us, 8 out of 10 valuable blog posts resulted from relationships. When we pitched a blogger without a relationship, less than 1% even responded. With introductions, our success rate was over 50%.

How do you identify relationships? Facebook. Have your VA log in to your Facebook account, search for bloggers in your media list, and add mutual friends to your spreadsheet. You can also search on professional networks like LinkedIn.

Use the Right Tools

TextExpander allows you to paste any saved message — whether it's a phone number or a two-page email — into any document or text field, simply by typing an abbreviation. This is extremely helpful for repetitive outreach. It's a must-have app that probably saved us 1 to 2 hours a day in typing.

One tool that we did not use, but should have, is **Boomerang**, a Gmail plug-in that allows you to schedule emails. We crafted emails to our influencers and in-the-know friends the day of our launch, using TextExpander, then slightly customized each one. What we should have done is written and saved these personalized emails a few days before we launched. That way, we could have scheduled them to be automatically sent by Boomerang the second we launched. This would have freed up many valuable hours on launch day.

TF: For perhaps 10 additional tips, as well as a half dozen email templates that Soma used for their PR outreach and launch (this alone could save you more than 100 hours), visit **fourhourworkweek.com/kickstarter**

> **"**Occasionally, a good idea comes to you first, if you're lucky. Usually, it only comes after a lot of bad ideas.**"**

ALEX BLUMBERG

Alex Blumberg (TW: @ABEXLUMBERG, GIMLETMEDIA.COM) is CEO and cofounder of Gimlet Media, makers of *Reply All*, *StartUp*, *Mystery Show*, and many other blockbuster podcasts. He is an award-winning radio journalist. Prior to Gimlet, he was a producer for *This American Life* and the co-founder of *Planet Money*. I featured Alex twice on my podcast, first as an interview, then second in an excerpt from his 21-lesson CreativeLive course, *Power Your Podcast with Storytelling*.

Why is an audio storyteller in Wealthy? Remember what I wrote in How to Use This Book (page xix): Questions are your pickaxes. Good questions are what open people up, open new doors, and create opportunities.

Spirit animal: Otter

IN GENERAL — ASK THE DUMB QUESTION EVERYONE ELSE IS AFRAID TO ASK

"Often, there's a very basic, very dumb question at the center of a story that no one's asking. One of the biggest stories I ever did, 'The Giant Pool of Money,' was predicated on just such a dumb question: 'Why are the banks loaning money to people who can't possibly pay it back?' **Asking the right dumb question is often the smartest thing you can do.**"

(Malcolm Gladwell also discusses this on page 573.)

IN PARTICULAR — USE THE RIGHT QUESTIONS AND PROMPTS

For Alex, good "tape" (interviews) must have stories as a primary ingredient, not uninformative yes-or-no answers. How does Alex elicit what he would call "authentic moments of emotion"? How do you get people to recount? To naturally tell funny stories? How do you make their lines memorable — concrete and specific — not abstract and general? Alex has spent more than 20 years thinking about this and testing different approaches.

Alex generally tries to cover three bases: setting (e.g., where, when, who, what), emotions, and details. Here are some specific phrases that he uses, which I've borrowed, and you'll notice that pseudo-commands are sometimes more effective than questions:

Prompts to Elicit Stories (Most Interviewers Are Weak at This)

"Tell me about a time when . . ."

"Tell me about the day [or moment or time] when . . ."

"Tell me the story of . . . [how you came to major in X, how you met so-and-so, etc.]"

"Tell me about the day you realized ___ . . ."

"What were the steps that got you to ___ ?"

"Describe the conversation when . . ."

TF: I often use the last with people who, at some point, were considering leaving a job to start a company. I'll say, "Describe the conversation when you first mentioned to your wife/husband that you wanted to drop this lucrative career in X and start your own company." It has never failed to get a good story.

Follow-Up Questions When Something Interesting Comes Up, Perhaps in Passing

"How did that make you feel?"

"What do you make of that?"

TF: I will often say, "Explain that a bit more . . ." or "What did you learn from that?"

General-Use Fishing Lures

"If the old you could see the new you, what would the new you say?"

"You seem very confident now. Was that always the case?"

"If you had to describe the debate in your head about [X decision or event], how would you describe it?"

TF: I often adapt the last to something like "When you do X [or "When Y happened to you"], what does your internal self-talk sound like? What do you say to yourself?"

SOME OF ALEX'S TOOLS
Field Recording

Audio-Technica AT8035 shotgun microphone

TASCAM DR-100mkII recorder

Sony MDR-7506 headphones

XLR cable(s)

Software

Avid Pro Tools for editing

Chartbeat for analytics

THE PODCAST GEAR I USE

Since I'm constantly asked about my podcast gear setup, and I think everyone should try starting a podcast at least once for the learning, this chapter delivers the goods.

Audio can be infinitely complex, but you can keep it simple. As Morgan Spurlock (page 221) might say, "Once you get fancy, fancy gets broken." My suggestion is to start with recording phone interviews via Skype. It allows you to test-drive podcasting extremely cheaply, and it allows you to cheat: to refer to questions, notes, and cheat sheets in Evernote or another program while speaking. It takes the pressure off. In-person interviews are much harder to set up, harder to do well, and technically easier to screw up.

Below is my "minimum effective dose" for producing a podcast that won't get laughed off the Internet. I still use all of these tools. For clickable links to all, visit fourhourworkweek.com/podcastgear

In-Person Interviews

>>> **Zoom H6 6-track portable recorder:** For in-person recording, I use the H6 with simple stage mics (below). For recording 2- to 4-person interviews, it's better than the older H4n model. Pro tip: ALWAYS put in new batteries for every important interview. I use simple earbuds for sound checks.

>>> **Shure SM58-LC cardioid vocal microphone:** Thanks to Bryan Callen (page 483) for introducing me to these. I've tried all sorts of fancy lavalier mics, booms, etc. For the money, nothing beats these old-school stage mics for in-person podcasting. You could throw them

against a wall and they'd probably be fine. Some people use mic stands to hold them, but I do not. I prefer to have guests hold them, as they're less likely to lean away. Sound levels (volume) are therefore more consistent, requiring less fussing in post-production.

>>> **XLR 3-pin microphone cable (6 feet):** To connect the Shure SM58-LC microphone to the H6 Zoom recorder. Don't cut corners here. In my limited experience, if anything is going to go wrong (and undetected until too late), it'll be a loose fitting on one of these.

>>> **Bluecell 5-pack of microphone windscreen foam covers:** These minimize the clicks, pops, and other noises picked up from vocals, as well as background noises and actual wind. Brand doesn't matter much here.

Phone/Skype Interviews

>>> **Ecamm Call Recorder for Skype:** This is used for recording "phoners" via Skype. I haven't found any software that blows me away, but this gets the job done. I've used it for more than 50% of my podcast interviews. Zencastr also gets good reviews but sometimes requires a lot of hard drive space on the part of your interviewee.

>>> **Audio-Technica ATR2100-USB cardioid dynamic USB/XLR microphone:** This is my go-to travel mic for all phone interviews. It can also be used for recording intros, sponsor reads, etc., with QuickTime. I often mail guests this mic via Amazon Prime if they need one, as it has the best bang-for-the-buck value I've found. Be sure to use a foam ball windscreen or "pop filter."

>>> **Yellowtec iXm:** I use this mic for last-minute travel recording and post-production intros. It is an amazing all-in-one mic, which allows you to record without a Zoom or laptop. It automatically corrects levels and — quite frankly — produces the best audio of all the various mics I own. I use it for my intros ("Welcome to another episode of *The Tim Ferriss Show . . .*") and sponsor reads, which I record separately from the interviews. If I'm traveling but *might* need a mic, I

stick this in my backpack. This bad boy is pricey, but I love the quality and convenience.

Post-Production and Editing

⫸ **Whatever:** I edited perhaps 20 of my first 30 episodes using Garage-Band, despite disliking it. Why? Because I could learn it quickly, and it forced me to keep the podcast format dead simple. Fancy nonsense wasn't possible for a Luddite like me, nor for the software, and that's what I wanted: a positive constraint. If GarageBand appears too amateur for your first 1 to 3 episodes, I'd bet money 99% of you will quit by episode 5. Most would-be podcasters quit because they get overwhelmed with gear and editing. Much like Joe Rogan, I decided to record and publish entire conversations (minimizing post-production), not solely highlights.

⫸ **Keep it simple:** Here are a few options my editors/engineers have used: Audacity (free), Ableton, Sound Studio, and Hindenburg. If I were to learn another piece of editing software, I would likely choose Hindenburg.

⫸ **Auphonic:** I often use Auphonic.com to finalize and polish my podcasts after editing on the above. It's a web-based audio post-production mastering tool, designed to help you improve the overall audio quality of your podcast.

THINGS I DON'T USE

To date, I have not used any pre-amps, mixers, or other hardware. It would marginally improve things, but I haven't found the additional complexity, added luggage, and risk of mechanical failure worth it.

ED CATMULL

Ed Catmull (TW: @EDCATMULL, PIXAR.COM) is, along with Steve Jobs and John Lasseter, co-founder of Pixar Animation Studios. He is current president of Pixar and Walt Disney Animation Studios. Ed has received five Academy Awards and has contributed to many important developments in computer graphics as a computer scientist. He is the author of *Creativity, Inc.*, which *Forbes* has written, ". . . just might be the best business book ever written."

LITTLE-KNOWN FACT

In 1995, also the last year that *Calvin and Hobbes* ran, I bought my first stock
— Pixar.

WE ALL BEGIN WITH SUCK

"We had to [start over internally] with *Toy Story 2*. We had to do it with
Ratatouille . . . [since] all our films, to begin with, suck."

    TIM: "Why do you say that? Just that the rough draft is always really rough?"

    ED: "This is the big misconception that people have, that [in the beginning]
a new film is the baby version of the final film, when in fact the final film bears
no relationship to what you started off with. What we've found is that the first
version always sucks. I don't mean this because I'm self-effacing or that we're
modest about it. I mean it in the sense that they really do suck."

**THE INCREDIBLE STRATEGIC AND PREDICTIVE POWER
OF STEVE JOBS**

"We went public one week after [*Toy Story*] went out. . . . Steve Jobs's logic was
that while he wanted us to go public — and he had some reasons for it which
we were skeptical of, to be honest — he wanted to do it after the film came out
to demonstrate for people that, in fact, a new art form was being born, and that
was worth investing in. . . ."

    TIM: "This is an itch that I have to scratch, but what were his reasons for the
IPO that people were skeptical of?"

    ED: "We're now making the first film. To then become a public company,
for the rest of us, because none of us had ever even been in a public company,
let alone knowing what it means, [we thought]: This could be a major distraction. . . . There was the view of 'Let's make some films and prove our worth and
get that under our belt before we go public,' but Steve had a different logic. He
said, 'Right now, we have a three-picture deal with Disney.' The financial [prof-
it-sharing] terms of the deal, while they were as good as we could have gotten under the circumstances, once we [became] a successful company, then our
share of the profits was actually pretty small.

"So Steve wanted to renegotiate the deal, and all of us had a very good relationship with Disney. But Steve said at the end of 3 years, if we then split off
as a separate company and we're no longer with Disney, we will be their worst

nightmare, because they will have helped launch a successful competitor. . . . All of this is before it happened, so we're guessing what's going to happen. But this is Steve prognosticating, because he now believes the film is going to be a big success.

"So he said, 'What will happen is, as soon as the film is out, Michael Eisner will realize that he's helped create a competitor, so he will want to renegotiate, and if we renegotiate, then what we want is to be 50/50 partners.'

"I should say right there, that's a different Steve than years before, where Steve sort of shot for the fences and tried to get almost everything for himself. He now has reached the point where he said that is not a good place to be. A good place to be is a 50/50 partnership. It's like a good standing. It's a high road to take. But if we're 50/50 partners, it also means that we have to put up half the money. Well, Pixar doesn't have any money."

TIM: "Right. You need a war chest."

ED: "So we needed a war chest. So if we go public, we will get a war chest. Then, when we renegotiate, we can come in and go for the kind of deal which is a 50/50 deal. So the film came out, and within a few months, Steve got the call from Michael Eisner saying let's renegotiate. So Steve says, 'Okay, we want it to be 50/50.' All of that happened as Steve predicted it would. For me, it was rather amazing. Wow, he completely called it correctly."

IF YOU CAN'T READ IT, TRY LISTENING TO IT

"My brain works differently. It turns out I am unable to read poetry. . . . Reading poetry, within a few seconds, shuts my brain down.

"All of this came about because there was a new translation of *The Iliad*, by Robert Fagles, and it was in verse form. The thing is, I couldn't read it. So this woman at a dinner said: 'Don't read it, listen to it.' I bought the tape and I listened to it, and I found I was completely enthralled. I was surprised by the fact that the story was orally transmitted 2,800 years ago in a different language to a different culture. It was meant for oral transmission, of course, because it had that rhythm to it."

FAVORITE LECTURES FROM THE TEACHING COMPANY

For several years, Ed listened to Teaching Company lectures every day during his commute:

"They've got them on economics, Shakespeare, and so forth. The thing that had the greatest impact on me was the whole suite of world history. . . . Although, I must admit there was one that was around the time of King Henry VIII, **the Tudors and the Stuarts**. I was so blown away with that that as soon as I listened to it, I listened to it again."

TO BECOME AN ARTIST, LEARN TO SEE

Ed wanted to be an animator in high school and did well in art. Near his freshman year of college, however, he didn't see a path to the level required to be a Disney animator, so he switched to physics. Many people think is this incongruous and unrelated. He disagrees:

"Most people to this day think of them as so radically different from each other. But I want to posit a different way to look at it. It comes from what I think is a fundamental misunderstanding of art on the part of most people. Because they think of art as learning to draw or learning a certain kind of self-expression. **But in fact, what artists do is they learn to see.**"

MEDITATION

Ed practices vipassana meditation for 30 to 60 minutes per day in one session. He got started after visiting the Symbol of Man Center, which is Tibetan.

✳ Most-gifted or recommended book?

"I would say there are certain children's books I've given a few times, like *One Monster After Another* by Mercer Mayer. I love that book."

TRACY DiNUNZIO

Tracy DiNunzio (TW: @TRACYDINUNZIO, TRADESY.COM) is a killer. She's the founder and CEO of Tradesy, which has taken off like a rocket ship. She's raised $75 million from investors including Richard Branson, Kleiner Perkins, and yours truly, and board members include the legendary John Doerr. Tradesy is on a mission to make the resale value of anything you own available on demand. Their tagline is "Cash in on your closet."

Spirit animal: Bee

"WHEN YOU COMPLAIN, NOBODY WANTS TO HELP YOU"

"I was born with spina bifida, which is a congenital birth defect where your vertebrae don't form around your spinal cord. This is likely attributed to my dad's exposure to Agent Orange when he was in Vietnam. . . . I did a lot of painting when I was recovering from surgeries, so I had to use interesting techniques, like crawling on the floor to make the painting because I couldn't stand up. [As a coping mechanism] I tried complaining and being bitter. It didn't work. It was just terrible. . . . Stephen Hawking actually has the best quote on this and also [a] legitimate story. . . . [He] has the right to complain probably more than anybody. He says that, **'When you complain, nobody wants to help you,'** and it's the simplest thing and so plainly spoken. Only he could really say that brutal, honest truth, but it's true, right? **If you spend your time focusing on the things that are wrong, and that's what you express and project to people you know, you don't become a source of growth for people, you become a source of destruction for people.** That draws more destructiveness.

"Because I was thinking about how I was in pain and talking about how I was in pain, it started a momentum that went in a negative direction in my life. At one point, probably 2006 to 2007, I just decided to put myself on a 'complaining diet,' where I said, 'Not only am I not going to say anything negative about the situation I'm in, but I'm not going to let myself *think* anything negative about it.' . . . It took a long time and I wasn't perfect at it, but . . . not only did replacing those thoughts helped me start moving my life in a better direction, where I wasn't obsessing about what was wrong, . . . it also made me not feel physical pain as much, which is very liberating and kind of necessary if you want to do anything."

PICK THE RIGHT AUDIENCE TO SUCK IN FRONT OF

"If anybody is going to go out and pitch investors, my advice is to make your first 10 meetings with investors that you don't really want funding from, because you're probably going to suck in the beginning. I sucked for a really long time."

TF: Even Jerry Seinfeld bombs with early material (see the *Comedian* documentary), so he develops it at small venues. Nike tests a lot of their new products and campaigns in places like New Zealand before getting on the big stage in the United States. I was turned down 27 times when pitching *The 4-Hour Work-week* to New York City publishers. Fortunately, you often only need one publisher, one lead investor, one X. Book your A list for after your first 10 pitches.

PHIL LIBIN

Phil Libin (TW: @PLIBIN, EVERNOTE.COM) is the co-founder and executive chairman of Evernote. Evernote has roughly 150 million users, and I personally use it at least 10 times a day. It is my external brain for capturing all the information, documents, online articles, lists, etc., in my life. It was used to capture all the research for this book. Phil is also a managing director at General Catalyst, a venture capital firm that has invested in companies such as Airbnb, Snapchat, Stripe, and Warby Parker. Phil's roster of mentors blows my mind, as evidenced in this profile.

Spirit animal: Octopus

* Who's the first person who comes to mind when you think of the word "successful"?

"The first *thing* that popped into my mind when you said 'successful' was [the] iPhone. . . . I guess I don't really think of people as 'successful.' . . . Tons of people deserve to be successful because they're supersmart and interesting and work hard, but they just haven't had the luck."

* Must-watch documentary

The Gatekeepers (2012) features interviews with all of the living heads of the Shin Bet, the Israeli security agency, who talk frankly about life, war, and peace. The motto of the Shin Bet is "Magen veLo Yera'e," literally "the unseen shield," or "defender who shall not be seen."

JEFF BEZOS ON QUESTIONING ASSUMPTIONS

"Basically, every time I talk to Bezos [Jeff Bezos, founder of Amazon.com], it changes my life. . . . [For example,] I've spent my entire life thinking that I want to go to Mars . . . it was on *The Brady Bunch*. I thought this was the best thing ever.

"At some point, if I structure my life correctly, maybe I'll get to go. I think it's just so important for humanity to be able to do that . . . and I talked to Elon [Musk] a couple of times and was vastly inspired by everything that he and SpaceX are doing. . . .

"I ran into Jeff Bezos a bit later and was saying I just got to talk with Elon, and I'm superexcited about Mars. I really hope that one day I can go. And Bezos looks at me and goes, 'Mars is stupid.' And I say, 'What?' He says, 'Once we get off of the planet, the last thing we want to do is go to another gravity.'

"Bezos said, 'The whole point, the reason this is so hard to get off the earth, is to defeat gravity the first time. Once we do that, why would you want to go to Mars? We should just live on space stations and mine asteroids and everything is much better than being on Mars.' And in 30 seconds, he had completely changed the course of my life, because he's totally right."

MIKITANI ON NECESSARY REINVENTION — THE RULE OF 3 AND 10

Phil considers Hiroshi Mikitani, the founder and CEO of Rakuten, one of the most impressive people in the world. Almost 90% of Japan's Internet population is registered with Rakuten, the country's largest online marketplace. Mikitani taught Phil "the rule of 3 and 10."

"[This effectively means] that every single thing in your company breaks every time you roughly triple in size.

"He was the first employee at Rakuten, and now they've got 10,000 or more. He said when you're just one person, everything kind of works. You sort of figure it out. And then, at some point, you have three people, and now, things are kind of different. Making decisions and everything with three people is different. But you adjust to that. Then, you're fine for a while. You get to 10 people, and everything kind of breaks again. You figure that out, and then you get to 30 people and everything is different, and then 100 and then 300 and then 1,000.

"His hypothesis is that everything breaks at roughly these points of 3 and 10 [multiples of 3 and powers of 10]. And by 'everything,' it means everything: how you handle payroll, how you schedule meetings, what kind of communications you use, how you do budgeting, who actually makes decisions. Every implicit and explicit part of the company just changes significantly when it triples.

"His insight is [that] a lot of companies get into trouble because of this. When you're a quickly growing startup, you get into huge trouble because you blow right through a few of these triplings without really realizing it. And then, you turn around, and you realize . . . we're at 400 people now, but some of our processes and systems we set in place when we were 30. . . . You should constantly, perpetually be thinking about how to reinvent yourself and how to treat the culture.

"Big companies get in trouble for exactly the opposite reason. Let's say you get to 10,000 people in your company and, theoretically, you figured out how to run things at 10,000. Well, your next big point isn't until 30,000. But you're probably not going to get the 30,000 ever, or certainly not within a few years. It might take a decade or more for a company to go from 10,000 to 30,000. But no one feels like waiting around for a decade or more to reinvent themselves, and so big companies are constantly pushing all of these bullshit innovation initiatives because they feel like they have to do something. But they're not actually connected to any fundamental change in the company."

TF: Have you outgrown your systems or beliefs? Is it time that you upgraded? Or, on a personal level, as Jerry Colonna, executive coach to some of the biggest tech stars in Silicon Valley, would ask: **"How are you complicit in creating the conditions you say you don't want?"**

CHRIS YOUNG

Chris Young (TW: @CHEFCHRISYOUNG, CHEFSTEPS.COM) is an obsessive tinkerer, inventor, and innovator. His areas of expertise range from extreme aviation to mathematics and apocalyptic-scale BBQs. Above all, he is one of the clearest thinkers I know.

Chris is the principal co-author of the genre-redefining six-volume work *Modernist Cuisine*. Chris was also the founding chef of Heston Blumenthal's Fat Duck experimental kitchen, the secret culinary laboratory behind the innovative dishes at one of the best restaurants in the world. Prior to becoming a chef, he completed degrees in theoretical mathematics and biochemistry. He is now the CEO of ChefSteps, based above Pike Place Market in Seattle, Washington.

Spirit animal: Frigate

BEHIND THE SCENES

» Matt Mullenweg (page 202) and I have visited Chris's lab many times. Search "Ferriss aerated green apple sorbet" to see video of me resembling Puff the Magic Dragon.

» Off hours, Chris is training to break a world record in unpowered gliding. Target location: Patagonia.

» Chris was my go-to scientist for the "Scientist" section of *The 4-Hour Chef*, and several of his recipes led me to a live cooking demo with Jimmy Fallon.

» Chris is good friends with science-fiction writer Neal Stephenson, who's penned several of my all-time favorites, including *Snow Crash* and *Cryptonomicon*. Many guests in this book recommend both *Snow Crash* and *The Diamond Age* (Seth Godin, page 237, and Kelly Starrett, page 122). Every year, Chris and Neal have the Annual Loudness Fest in Neal's backyard, where they build outrageous machines and cooking contraptions: "It wasn't a big deal that we dug a 6' x 6' x 6'-deep pit in his backyard and turned it into a Jacuzzi to sous-vide cook a 300-pound pig," Chris says. "Each year after that for the next 5 years, it had to be more over-the-top, more outlandish, more ludicrously dangerous. Dangerous in the sense of maybe the neighbors' houses will burn down, maybe somebody will be killed by spilling concrete, maybe somebody will be burned to cinders because we're cooking with magma, that kind of thing."

✻ **What would you put on a billboard?**
"'It all worked out anyway,'" placed outside of his high school. "High school was not a great time for me."

"THE INTERESTING JOBS ARE THE ONES THAT YOU MAKE UP."
His dad, a very successful entrepreneur, gave Chris advice when he was a freshman or sophomore in high school:
"I distinctly remember him saying not to worry about what I was going to do because **the job I was going to do hadn't even been invented yet. . . . The**

interesting jobs are the ones that you make up. That's something I certainly hope to instill in my son: Don't worry about what your job is going to be. . . . Do things that you're interested in, and if you do them really well, you're going to find a way to temper them with some good business opportunity."

"WHAT INTERESTING THING ARE YOU WORKING ON? WHY IS THAT INTERESTING TO YOU? WHAT'S SURPRISING ABOUT THAT? IS ANYBODY ELSE THINKING ABOUT THIS?"

These are common questions from Heston Blumenthal, the former executive chef of The Fat Duck, the then–#1 ranked restaurant in the world. Chris explains: "I've never seen somebody as curious as him, who could talk to just about anyone else about whatever it was they did. He would pose questions like the above to anyone about anything, whether they were psychologists, sports trainers, chefs, writers, or otherwise."

This made me smile. I met Heston once in the early 2000s at a book signing inside a culinary school in San Francisco. I sheepishly approached him and asked, "What is your favorite way to cook beans? I'm embarrassed to ask, but I have a lot of trouble getting them right." He perked up, looked me straight in the eyes, and said, "You know, people don't know how complex beans can be," asked perhaps a dozen clarifying questions, then proceeded to give me a 5-minute master's degree in cooking beans. I've been a fanboy since.

"IF YOU HAD $100 MILLION, WHAT WOULD YOU BUILD THAT WOULD HAVE NO VALUE TO OTHERS IN COPYING?"

Gabe Newell, the billionaire co-founder of video game development and distribution company Valve, has largely funded Chris's company ChefSteps. He's been a huge supporter, but only after asking questions that stretch Chris's brain:

"So Gabe goes, 'If I gave you $100 million, what would you guys go build? That by building it, there's no value for anyone copying?' I'll give you an example. When Intel goes to build a new chip fabricator, it's billions and billions of dollars, and there's no value in anybody else copying it, because not only do they have to spend even more billions to catch up, but they have to spend more billions to learn everything else Intel knows about this, and then they have to be 10 times better for anyone to want to switch. So it's just a waste of everyone's time [to attempt copying]."

TF: One of the top 10 venture capitalists I know uses a variant of this litmus test as his measurement of "disruptive": For each $1 of revenue you generate, can you cost an incumbent $5 to $10? If so, he'll invest. As a related aside, one of my favorite business-related PDFs floating around the Internet is "Valve: Handbook for New Employees" from Gabe's company. As Chris put it: "It's the only HR document you will ever knowingly want to read."

THE ACCIDENTAL JEDI MIND TRICK

Chris got his first line cook job by accidentally appealing to the chef's (William Belickis's) ego. He had been *staging* (interning) and wanted to make the jump to full-timer:

"At the end of service, William was really gracious. He sat down with me in the dining room, and he had a glass of wine. He offered me a glass. He said, 'You know, now's probably not really a great time. I'm not sure I have the work for you.' Being very earnest, I said, 'I totally understand. Is there anybody in town you'd recommend would be a good place for me to work? I'm really committed to doing this. I really want to see what it's about.'

"And what I didn't realize at the time, was that was probably the perfect thing to have said to William, because William had an enormous ego and he was just not going to be capable of bringing himself to say anybody else in town was any good at all. So you could just see him sort of sputtering. 'Well, really there's no one. I think I'm probably the right person to teach you. So why don't you come back on Tuesday?'"

HOLD THE STANDARD

Chris mentioned that by the time he arrived at The Fat Duck, Heston no longer yelled at people, but "he signaled disappointment in other ways . . . he really pushed you, the team, everyone else to strive for excellence all the time." I asked him to give me an example. Here's his response, shortened for space:

"The order came on for [quail jelly], and I saw that they weren't fully set up. I tried to float the langoustine cream on top anyway, and I sent them out to the pass knowing that they weren't perfect. Those things came back like a boomerang. Heston just came around the corner holding them in his hand and just goes, 'Chris.' He's looking at me, and he's looking at the dish, and he's looking at me, and he's looking at the dish, and . . . 'Not a chance.' Puts it back. I just remember the withering look — like if I ever did that again, don't show up again. I remember the lesson because he said, 'We can do something else. If it's not ready, we're not going to send it out, and just hope they don't notice that it's not that good. We'll fix it. We'll do something else, but don't try to slip by something that you know is below the standard.' You only need that lesson once. That wasn't the standard, and you know what the standard is. **Hold the standard. Ask for help. Fix it. Do whatever's necessary. But don't cheat.**"

TIM: "But how do you manage the fine line between insisting on high standards and simply being an overbearing asshole?" [Chris now manages a company of 50+ employees.]

CHRIS: "The first thing is, on a good day, I will try to step back and say, '**What context does this person even have, and have I provided appropriate context?**' . . . Given all the context they had, maybe I would've made the same decision, or I could imagine somebody else making the same decision. So increasingly, I try to think about: 'What context and visibility do I have and what do they have? **Am I basically being unfair because I'm operating from a greater set of information?**'"

THE ANTI-BULLSHIT MANUAL

One of the books that Chris has found himself gifting a lot is an out-of-print book on thermodynamics called *The Second Law*. "It was written by an Oxford physical chemistry professor named P.W. Atkins. That book is just a phenomenal, casual, infographic-laden read on how the world works from an energy perspective. I found that so incredibly useful in trying to understand how to do something, how to make something work, whether something's even possible. It's frequently my bullshit detector."

✳ **Who do you think of when you hear the word "successful"?**
Chris says his father and Winston Churchill. Of the latter:

"There's a great series of books, *The Last Lion* by William Manchester, on Winston Churchill. The third volume actually just came out a few years ago posthumously. But the first two, which really only got up to his life at the outbreak of World War II, didn't even touch on everything that happened after World War II started. I just remember thinking, [even before he did what we associate him with]: He was a best-selling author by 20, he'd fought in wars, he was one of the highest-paid writers, and he was an important member of Parliament."

DAYMOND JOHN

Daymond John (TW/FB/IG: @TheSharkDaymond, DaymondJohn.com) is CEO and founder of FUBU, which Daymond grew from his original $40 budget into a $6 billion lifestyle brand. He is a Presidential Ambassador for Global Entrepreneurship and appears on ABC's *Shark Tank*. Daymond is the recipient of more than 35 industry awards, including *Brandweek*'s Marketer of the Year, *Advertising Age*'s Marketing 1000 Award for Outstanding Ad Campaign, and Ernst & Young's New York Entrepreneur of the Year Award. He is the best-selling author of three books, including *The Power of Broke*.

Spirit animal: Mongoose

"If you go out there and start making noise and making sales, people will find you. Sales cure all. You can talk about how great your business plan is and how well you are going to do. You can make up your own opinions, but you cannot make up your own facts. Sales cure all."

"Five days a week, I read my goals before I go to sleep and when I wake up. There are 10 goals around health, family, business, etc., with expiration dates, and I update them every 6 months."

"My parents always taught me that my day job would never make me rich. It'd be my homework."

"I don't care if you're my brother — if we go play football, I'm gonna try to crack your head open. It doesn't mean that I don't love you. It doesn't mean that I don't respect you."

✳ What is the best or most worthwhile investment you've made? It could be an investment of money, time, energy, or otherwise.
"The best investment was when I took the time to be a foot messenger for First Boston while I was in high school. I was running around the entire city of Manhattan and came across all different types of people. Some were completely miserable high-profile executives. Others were extremely happy entry-level employees. I had never had this sort of exposure in my life, and it completely opened up my eyes to opportunity."

✳ Do you have any quotes that you live your life by or think of often?
"Money is great servant but a horrible master."

✳ Most-gifted or recommended books?
Think and Grow Rich, Who Moved My Cheese?, Blue Ocean Strategy, Invisible Selling Machine, The Richest Man in Babylon, and *Genghis Khan and the Making of the Modern World.*

TF: That last Genghis Khan book has been recommended to me by several billionaires.

NOAH KAGAN

Noah Kagan (TW/IG: @NOAHKAGAN, SUMOME.COM) was the #30 employee at Facebook, #4 at Mint.com (sold to Intuit for $170 million), and is the Chief Sumo (founder) at SumoMe, which offers free tools to help grow website traffic. To keep things extra spicy, he's become a taco connoisseur and has created four separate products that have generated more than 7 figures. Noah was my co-teacher in the "Starting a Business" episode of *The Tim Ferriss Experiment*.

TAKE THE COFFEE CHALLENGE

For would-be entrepreneurs (he calls them "wantrapreneurs"), or entrepreneurs who've grown a little too comfortable, Noah has a recommendation—ask for 10% off of your next few coffees. "Go up to the counter and order coffee. If you don't drink coffee, order tea. If you don't drink tea, order water. I don't care. Then just ask for 10% off. . . . The coffee challenge sounds kind of silly, but the whole point is that—in business and in life—you don't have to be on the extreme, but you have to ask for things, and you have to put yourself out there."

Spirit animal: Chipmunk

IMPROVE TOOLS AT THE "TOP OF THE FUNNEL"

Aim to optimize upstream items that have cascading results downstream. For instance, look for technical bottlenecks (choke points) that affect nearly everything you do on a computer. What are the things that, if defunct or slow, render your to-do list useless? Here are two of Noah's simple recommendations that I've implemented:

>>> Increase the speed of your track/mouse pad. Go into Settings or Systems Preferences and double your current speed. This takes less than 30 seconds to do.

>>> Invest in the best router you can afford. Noah currently uses the ASUS RT-AC87U Wireless-AC2400 dual band gigabit router. Kevin Rose (page 340) and others use Eero technology to improve WiFi throughout their homes.

* Related — "What is the best or most worthwhile investment you've made?"
Lasik surgery.

APPS/SOFTWARE TO TEST

Facebook News Feed Eradicator: Need to focus? Save yourself from FB and your lesser self.

ScheduleOnce (get the $99 a year option): This can eliminate the never-ending "How about next Tuesday or Thursday at 10 a.m.?" back-and-forth that eats your life.

FollowUp.cc: For automating email follow-ups and reminders. I use a close cousin called Nudgemail, in combination with Boomerang. You'll never have to remember to follow up with anyone ever again.

QUICK GMAIL TRICK

Noah and I both use the Gmail "+" trick all the time. Let's say your email address is bob@bobsmith.com. After signing up for services or newsletters, how can you tell who's sharing your email, or contain the damage if someone discovers your login email? Companies get hacked all the time. Just use + as cheap insurance. If you append + and a word to the beginning, messages will still get delivered to your inbox. Signing up for Instacart, for instance? You could use bob+insta@bobsmith.com. I use this, or benefit from it, on a daily basis.

DON'T TRY AND FIND TIME. SCHEDULE TIME.

On Tuesdays from 10 a.m. to 12 noon, Noah schedules nothing but "Learning." This is a great reminder that, for anything important, you don't find time. It's only real if it's on the calendar. My Wednesdays from 9 a.m. to 1 p.m. are currently blocked out for "Creation"—writing, podcast recording, or other output that creates a tangible "after" product. I turn off WiFi during this period to be as non-reactive as possible. (See Neil Strauss, page 347, and Ramit Sethi, page 287.)

A SHARED OBSESSION

The book *Surely You're Joking, Mr. Feynman!* by Richard P. Feynman: "If you ever meet me in person, I have an extra copy because it's just that amazing."

* **What is the worst advice you see or hear given in your trade or area of expertise?**
"That you should prioritize growing your social following (Instagram, FB, Twitter, Snapchat, YouTube). Grow things that you can fully control that directly affect sales, like your email list. 'Likes' don't pay the bills. Sales do."

* **Who are three people or sources you've learned from — or followed closely — in the last year?**
Andrew Chen (Growth team at Uber), Tomasz Tunguz (venture capitalist and software as a service [SaaS] expert), Jonathan Siegel (chairman of Earth Class Mail)

FOR HIRING WELL — "WHO?" IS OFTEN MORE IMPORTANT THAN "WHAT?"

"The *Who* book [by Geoff Smart, Randy Street] is a condensed version of *Topgrading*, and I learned of it at Mint, where the founder was using it."

TF: I now recommend this book to all of my startup founders, who have, in turn, recommended it to others.

THE CLASSICS FOR COPYWRITING

Noah is known for his copywriting skills, and he recommends two resources: *The Gary Halbert Letter* (also *The Boron Letters*) and *Ogilvy on Advertising*.

✱ Noah's best purchase of $100 or less

The NutriBullet, a tiny blender with removable cup attached, which he gifts regularly. Just blend, drink, and rinse out. No cleaning required. Noah has a $500 Vitamix blender but has stopped using it entirely, in favor of the more convenient $79.99 NutriBullet.

NO SHAME, NO GAIN — INSTAGRAM INCENTIVES

Not long ago, Noah gained 40 pounds of muscle in ~6 months. One motivational trick he used was loading his Instagram feed with images and videos that killed his excuses. I now do the same. Too old? Too bulky? Too busy? There is someone who can call you on your BS. Here are a few accounts from my personal feed (@timferriss):

@matstrane: This 53-year-old makes me cringe for complaining about my age. He started training at age 48.

@gymnasticbodies (Coach Sommer, page 9): Most of their students started gymnastics as sedentary adults.

@arboonell: Amelia Boone (page 2), the toughest woman I've ever met. She's a full-time power attorney at Apple and the only 3-time winner of World's Toughest Mudder, a 24-hour race.

@bgirlmislee: This breakdancer and stuntwoman hits power moves that were considered "impossible" for women in the 1990s (e.g., one-armed hopping handstands).

@jessiegraffpwr: Female Ninja Warrior competitor. Her grip strength makes my forearms weep tears of weakness.

@jujimufu: "Muscle-bound" anabolic acrobat who performs capoeira aerials, full splits, and other craziness. Strong and flexible are not mutually exclusive. He's also hilarious.

KASKADE

Kaskade (TW/FB/IG: @KASKADE, KASKADEMUSIC.COM) is widely considered one of the "founding fathers" of Progressive House music. He's been voted America's Best DJ twice by *DJ Times*, headlined Coachella four times, and been nominated for a Grammy five times.

HOW DID YOU GET YOUR FIRST GEAR?

"I hit a local club owner up in Utah, and I asked, 'What's your worst night that you have? What's the slowest night?' and he said, 'Monday. I'm not even open.' I said, 'Dude, let me come down on Monday night.' This is a bar that had opened in the 1940s and had all of its original decor. It's called Club Manhattan. It's an amazing place in the basement. Anyway, the owner says, 'I'll give you a cut of the door. You have your friends come in, invite some people, and we'll see what happens.' It turned out the night was a smash. I did it for 5 years, and I ended up doing two nights a week. It was Monday, and then I took on a Thursday . . . I was working at a clothing store trying to support myself going to school, and I quit after the first week. . . . It started clicking, and then, when I was making enough money, I started to buy my first studio equipment."

PUT THE BIG STONES IN FIRST

"When I can, I travel with my family. I'm married and I have three children, so I'm always trying to figure out, 'How can I make this work?' You know, putting the stones in the bucket. What's really important here, and how can I fill the bucket with the things that are really important to me?"

TF: This visual metaphor was first taught to me by a college professor, and it's a great way to think about priorities. Paraphrasing my teacher: "Imagine you have a large glass jar. Next to it, you have a few large rocks, a small pile of marble-sized pebbles, and a pile of sand. If you put in the sand or pebbles first, what happens? You can't fit the big rocks in. But if you add the big rocks, then the medium-sized pebbles, and only then the sand, it all fits." In other words, the minutiae fit around the big things, but the big things don't fit around the minutiae.

REMEMBER WHO YOU ARE

"Every time I left the house, my dad would always say, **'Remember who you are.'** Now that I am a father, this is a very profound thing to me. At the time I was like, 'Dad, what the hell? You're so weird. Like I'm gonna forget who I am? What are you saying?' Now, I'm like, 'Gosh, that guy was kind of smart.'"

∗ **Favorite festivals?**

Kaskade loves Coachella, but he also mentioned Electric Zoo in New York. "It's in Randall's Island and you're looking at the skyline while you're playing."

∗ **Iconic albums to start with?**

Daft Punk *Homework* (*Discovery* is also great, but he's a bigger fan of *Homework*)

Any Kraftwerk album

"Frustration is a matter of expectation."

LUIS VON AHN

Luis von Ahn (TW: @LuisvonAhn, duolingo.com) is a computer science professor at Carnegie Mellon University and the CEO of Duolingo, a free language learning platform with more than 100 million users. It is the most popular way to learn languages in the world, and I met him as an investor in their first round of financing. Previously, Luis was known for inventing CAPTCHAs, being a MacArthur Fellow ("genius grant" recipient), and selling two companies to Google in his 20s. Luis has been named one of the Brilliant 10 by *Popular Science* magazine and one of the 100 Most Creative People in Business by *Fast Company* magazine.

Spirit animal: Owl

CATCHING CHEATERS IN HIS CLASS WITH "GOOGLE TRAPS" AT CARNEGIE MELLON

"There was one [problem in an assignment] that was called Giramacristo's Puzzle. I made that word up beforehand. I made sure there was no such thing on Google. I made a website that had the right solution, but it recorded everybody's IP address. And at CMU you can figure out their dorm from their IP address. So I could figure out which person was actually checking. It turns out, that time, out of the 200 students, about 40 Googled for the answer, and that was fun. I used to do all kinds of things like that. The students were all usually scared of almost everything being a trick. [I would just say, 'If you just confess, you get a 0 on the assignment,' and people confess.] I would do that in the first one or two assignments, and then afterward, they would learn not to cheat."

THE ORIGIN OF DUOLINGO'S GREEN OWL MASCOT AND LOGO

"We were just getting started with Duolingo, and we had hired a Canadian company to help with our branding. . . . It's called silverorange. They made the Firefox logo, for example. We love working with them, and in one of our first meetings about the branding of the company, my co-founder Severin [Hacker] said, 'You know, I don't know much about design, and I don't particularly care. But I'll tell you this: I hate the color green. I hate it.'

"We all thought it would be hilarious if our mascot was a green thing, and so that's why it's green. It is literally that we are playing a joke on our co-founder. Ever since then, every day of his life, he has to see this. He shouldn't have said that."

THE VALUE OF "I DON'T UNDERSTAND"

"My PhD advisor [at Carnegie Mellon was] a guy named Manuel Blum, who many people consider the father of cryptography [encryption, etc.]. He's amazing and he's very funny. I learned a lot from him. When I met him, which was like 15 years ago, I guess he was in his 60s, but he always acted way older than he actually was. He just acted as if he forgot everything. . . .

"I had to explain to him what I was working on, which at the time was CAPTCHA, these distorted characters that you have to type all over the Internet. It's very annoying. That was the thing I was working on [later acquired by Google], and I had to explain it to him. It was very funny, because usually

I would start explaining something, and in the first sentence he would say, 'I don't understand what you're saying,' and then I would try to find another way of saying it, and a whole hour would pass and I could not get past the first sentence. He would say, 'Well, the hour's over. Let's meet next week.' This must have happened for months, and at some point I started thinking, 'I don't know why people think this guy's so smart.' Later, [I understood what he was doing]. This is basically just an act. Essentially, I was being unclear about what I was saying, and I did not fully understand what I was trying to explain to him. He was just drilling deeper and deeper and deeper until I realized, every time, that there was actually something I didn't have clear in my mind. He really taught me to think deeply about things, and I think that's something I have not forgotten."

TF: This week, try experimenting with saying "I don't understand. Can you explain that to me?" more often. (See Malcolm Gladwell's mention of his father on page 573.)

BUILDING A STARTUP OUTSIDE OF SILICON VALLEY

"It's pretty amazing how when you're talking to people [from Silicon Valley at industry events], it really does seem like the average tenure of a person in one of these [startup] companies is like a year and half. . . . Whereas for us [in Pittsburgh], people really don't leave. Because in terms of startups, we're not exactly the only game in town — that's unfair to say — but there aren't very many games in town."

TF: I've had successful exits from founders based in every place from Oklahoma and Colorado (Daily Burn) to Ottawa, Canada (Shopify). From a recruiting standpoint, not only is Shopify one of the major go-to tech companies in Eastern Canada, but they also don't have a lot of attrition. People are settled in Ottawa, and they're not getting poached by Facebook, Google, Uber. These families don't want to move to San Francisco, and Shopify therefore doesn't need to enter a bloodbath of bidding wars.

Think you're doomed because you're outside of the epicenter of your industry? See if you can find benefits, as there might be some non-obvious advantages.

THE CANVAS STRATEGY

"Great men have almost always shown themselves as ready
to obey as they afterwards proved able to command."

—Lord Mahon

If you want great mentors, you have to become a great mentee. If you want to lead, you have to first learn to follow. Ben Franklin, legendary NFL coach Bill Belichick, and many of the historical figures you think of as "leaders" followed a single strategy in their early days. I used the same strategy to build my network. It also explains how my first book hit the tipping point, and it can be credited for my success in tech investing.

Ryan Holiday (TW/FB/IG: @RYANHOLIDAY, RYANHOLIDAY.NET) calls it the "canvas strategy," and he's a master practitioner himself. A strategist and writer, Ryan dropped out of college at 19 to apprentice under Robert Greene, author of *The 48 Laws of Power*, and became director of marketing for American Apparel at 21. His current company, Brass Check, has advised clients like Google, TASER, and Complex, as well as many best-selling authors. Holiday has written four books, most recently *Ego Is the Enemy* and *The Obstacle Is the Way*, which has developed a cult following among NFL coaches, world-class athletes, political leaders, and others around the world. He lives on a small ranch outside Austin, Texas.

Enter Ryan

In the Roman system of art and science, there existed a concept for which we have only a partial analog. Successful businessmen, politicians, or rich playboys would subsidize a number of writers, thinkers, artists, and performers. More than just being paid to produce works of art, these artists performed a number of tasks in exchange for protection, food, and gifts. One of the roles was that of an *anteambulo* — literally meaning "one who clears the path." An *anteambulo* proceeded in front of his patron anywhere they traveled in Rome, making way, communicating messages, and generally making the patron's life easier. The famous epigrammist Martial fulfilled this role for many years, serving for a time under the patron Mela, a wealthy businessman and brother of the Stoic philosopher and political advisor Seneca. Born without a rich family, Martial also served under another businessman named Petilius. As a young writer, he spent most of his day traveling from the home of one rich patron to another, providing services, paying his respects, and receiving small token payments and favors in return.

Here's the problem: Like most of us with our internships and entry-level positions (or later on, publishers or bosses or clients), Martial absolutely hated every minute of it. He seemed to believe that this system somehow made him a slave. Aspiring to live like some country squire — like the patrons he serviced — Martial wanted money and an estate that was all his own. There, he dreamed, he could finally produce his works in peace and independence. As a result, his writing often drags with a hatred and bitterness about Rome's upper crust, from which he believed he was cruelly shunted.

For all his impotent rage, what Martial couldn't see was that it was his unique position as an outsider to society that gave him such fascinating insight into Roman culture that it survives to this day. Instead of being pained by such a system, what if he'd been able to come to terms with it? What if — *gasp* — he could have appreciated the opportunities it offered? Nope. It seemed to eat him up inside instead.

It's a common attitude that transcends generations and societies. The angry, unappreciated genius is forced to do stuff she doesn't like, for people she doesn't respect, as she makes her way in the world. *How dare they force me to grovel like this! The injustice! The waste!*

We see it in recent lawsuits, in which interns sue their employers for pay. We see kids more willing to live at home with their parents than to submit to something they're "overqualified" to work for. We see it in an inability to meet anyone else on their terms, an unwillingness to take a step back in order to potentially take several steps forward. *I will not let them get one over on me. I'd rather we both have nothing instead.*

It's worth taking a look at the supposed indignities of "serving" someone else. Because in reality, not only is the apprentice model responsible for some of the greatest art in the history of the world — everyone from Michelangelo to Leonardo da Vinci to Benjamin Franklin has been forced to navigate such a system — but if you're going to be the big deal you think you are going to be, isn't this a rather trivial, temporary imposition?

When someone gets his first job or joins a new organization, he's often given this advice: Make other people look good and you will do well. Keep your head down, they say, and serve your boss. Naturally, this is not what the kid who was chosen over all the other kids for the position wants to hear. It's not what a Harvard grad expects — after all, they got that degree precisely to avoid this supposed indignity.

Let's flip it around so it doesn't seem so demeaning: It's not about kissing ass. It's not about making someone *look* good. It's about providing the support so that others can *be* good. The better wording for the advice is this: Find canvases for other people to paint on. Be an *anteambulo*. Clear the path for the people above you and you will eventually create a path for yourself.

When you are just starting out, we can be sure of a few fundamental realities: 1) You're not nearly as good or as important as you think you are; 2) you have an attitude that needs to be readjusted; 3) most of what you think you know or most of what you learned in books or in school is out of date or wrong.

There's one fabulous way to work all of that out of your system: Attach yourself to people and organizations who are already successful, subsume your identity into theirs, and move both forward simultaneously. It's certainly more glamorous to pursue your own glory — though hardly as effective. Obeisance is the way forward.

That's the other effect of this attitude: It reduces your ego at a critical time in your career, letting you absorb everything you can without the obstructions that block others' vision and progress.

No one is endorsing sycophancy. Instead, it's about seeing what goes on from the inside, and looking for opportunities for someone *other than yourself.* Remember that *anteambulo* means clearing the path — finding the direction someone already intended to head and helping them pack, freeing them up to focus on their strengths. In fact, making things better rather than simply looking as if you are.

Many people know of Benjamin Franklin's famous pseudonymous letters written under names like Silence Dogwood. "What a clever young prodigy," they think, and miss the most impressive part entirely: Franklin wrote those letters, submitted them by sliding them under the print-shop door, and received absolutely no credit for them until much later in his life. In fact, it was his brother, the print-shop owner, who profited from their immense popularity, regularly running them on the front page of his newspaper. Franklin was playing the long game, though — learning how public opinion worked, generating awareness of what he believed in, crafting his style and tone and wit. It was a strategy he used time and again over his career — once even publishing in his competitor's paper in order to undermine a third competitor — for Franklin saw the constant benefit in making other people look good and letting them take credit for your ideas.

Bill Belichick, the four-time Super Bowl–winning head coach of the New England Patriots, made his way up the ranks of the NFL by loving and mastering the one part of the job that coaches disliked at the time: analyzing film. His first job in professional football, for the Baltimore Colts, was one he volunteered to take without pay — and his insights, which provided ammunition and critical strategies for the game, were attributed exclusively to the more senior coaches. He thrived on what was considered grunt work, asked for it, and strove to become the best at precisely what others thought they were too good for. "He was like a sponge, taking it all in, listening to everything," one coach said. "You gave him an assignment and he disappeared into a room and you didn't see him again until it was done, and then he wanted to do more," said another. As you can guess, Belichick started getting paid very soon.

Before that, as a young high school player, he was so knowledgeable about the game that he functioned as a sort of assistant coach even while playing the game. Belichick's father, himself an assistant football coach for Navy, taught him a critical lesson in football politics: If he wanted to give his coach feedback or question a decision, he needed to do it in private and self-effacingly so as not to offend his superior. He learned how to be a rising star without threatening or alienating anyone. In other words, he had mastered the canvas strategy.

You can see how easily entitlement and a sense of superiority (the trappings of ego) would have made the accomplishments of either of these men impossible. Franklin would never have been published if he'd prioritized credit over creative expression — indeed, when his brother found out, he literally beat him out of jealousy and anger. Belichick would have pissed off his coach and then probably been benched if he had one-upped him in public. He certainly wouldn't have taken his first job for free, and he wouldn't have sat through thousands of hours of film if he cared about status. Greatness comes from humble beginnings; it comes from grunt work. It means you're the least important person in the room — until you change that with results.

There is an old saying, "Say little, do much." What we really ought to do is update and apply a version of that to our early approach. Be *lesser*, do *more*. Imagine if for every person you met, you thought of some way to help them, something you could do for them? And you looked at it in a way that entirely benefited them and not you? The cumulative effect this would have over time would be profound: You'd learn a great deal by solving diverse problems. You'd develop a reputation for being indispensable. You'd have countless new relationships. You'd have an enormous bank of favors to call upon down the road.

That's what the canvas strategy is about — helping yourself by helping others. Making a concerted effort to trade your short-term gratification for a longer-term payoff. Whereas everyone else wants to get credit and be "respected," you can forget credit. You can forget it so hard that you're *glad* when others get it instead of you — that was your aim, after all. Let the others take their credit on credit, while you defer and earn interest on the principal.

The *strategy* part of it is the hardest. It's easy to be bitter, like Martial. To hate even the thought of subservience. To despise those who have more means, more experience, or more status than you. To tell yourself that every second not spent doing your work, or working on yourself, is a waste of your gift. To insist, *I will not be demeaned like this.*

Once we fight this emotional and egotistical impulse, the canvas strategy is easy. The iterations are endless.

>> Maybe it's coming up with ideas to hand over to your boss.

>> Find people, thinkers, up-and-comers to introduce to each other. Cross wires to create new sparks.

>> Find what nobody else wants to do and do it.

>> Find inefficiencies and waste and redundancies. Identify leaks and patches to free up resources for new areas.

>> Produce more than everyone else and give your ideas away.

In other words, discover opportunities to promote their creativity, find outlets and people for collaboration, and eliminate distractions that hinder their progress and focus. It is a rewarding and infinitely scalable power strategy. Consider each one an investment in relationships and in your own development.

The canvas strategy is there for you at any time. There is no expiration date on it either. It's one of the few that age does not limit — on either side, young or old. You can start at any time — before you have a job, before you're hired and while you're doing something else, or if you're starting something new or find yourself inside an organization without strong allies or support. You may even find that there's no reason to ever stop doing it, even once you've graduated to heading your own projects. Let it become natural and permanent; let others apply it to you while you're too busy applying it to those above you.

Because if you pick up this mantle once, you'll see what most people's egos prevent them from appreciating: The person who clears the path ultimately controls its direction, just as the canvas shapes the painting.

KEVIN ROSE

Kevin Rose (TW/IG: @KEVINROSE, THEJOURNAL.EMAIL) is one of the best stock pickers in the startup world. He can predict even non-tech trends with stunning accuracy. He co-founded Digg, Revision3 (sold to Discovery Communications), and Milk (sold to Google). He was subsequently a general partner at Google Ventures, where he was part of the investment team that funded companies such as Uber, Medium, and Blue Bottle Coffee. He is now CEO of Hodinkee, the world's leading online wristwatch marketplace and news site. He is one of Bloomberg's Top 25 Angel Investors and one of *Time*'s Top 25 Most Influential People on the Web. He has a popular monthly newsletter called *The Journal*.

Kevin is a close friend and we have a regular(ish) video show together called *The Random Show*, so named because the content and publication schedule are extremely erratic. This profile is also meant to be somewhat random. Why does he get special treatment? Because he was the first-ever guest on my podcast.

He's in Wealthy because of the next piece on page 343, which focuses on his investment approach.

Spirit animal: Inchworm

BACK STORY AND RANDOM BITS

» Kevin loves tea. So much so that he has a tattoo on the inside of his left bicep of the Chinese emperor Shennong (literally "divine farmer"), considered the discoverer of tea. Two of his favorite, easy-to-find teas are both from Red Blossom Tea Company: Tung Ting dark roast oolong, and, for something milder, Silver Needle white tea.

» He was my guest for episode #1 of *The Tim Ferriss Show*, which didn't have a name at the time. He suggested TIMTIMTALKTALK (long story), and tens of thousands of fans still use that nickname on social media. Damn you, KevKev.

» The worst question I asked him was "If you could be a breakfast cereal, what breakfast cereal would you choose and why?" We were drinking wine, and things got messy.

» In 2012, Kevin and his wife, neuroscientist Darya Pino Rose, spent three weeks in Japan with me and my then-girlfriend. One night after dinner, I casually walked up to my ex on the sidewalk and put my hand in her back pocket, right on her ass. "Oh, hi, TimTim," Darya said casually. It was her ass. The two ladies looked identical from the back: same hair, same build, same waist. Sorry, KevKev!

» Kevin is the only person I've ever seen spiral throw a raccoon. It was attacking his dog, and the footage was captured on security cameras from two angles. It's now on YouTube (search "Kevin Rose raccoon") and looks like CGI.

» Our favorite bone broth is one and the same—chicken broth with turmeric and ginger from the walk-up window of Brodo in New York City.

CONTENDING WITH ONLINE TROLLS

Kevin is a pro at psychologically dealing with online nonsense. I was amped up over some persistent, anonymous commenter in 2009, and Kevin asked me two simple questions that I've often thought about since:

"Do people you respect or care about leave hateful comments on the Internet?" (No.)

"Do you really want to engage with people who have infinite time on their hands?" (No.)

＊ One of his favorite tools for habit tracking and behavioral modification
Way of Life app.

HACKING BLOOD SUGAR

Several months ago, I received a text from Kevin stating "I found the grail" with a screenshot of his Dexcom continuous glucose monitor showing his levels at 79mg/dL (which is healthily low) after consuming two beers, a pork chop with honey glaze, 4 slices of corn bread with honey and butter, and a side order of potato gnocchi.

What was the "grail"? 25 mg of acarbose (¼ pill) with food. He learned this trick from Peter Attia (page 59), who I introduced him to.

GUT INVESTING

Kevin is a rare double threat as an investor: he is excellent at investing in both early-stage tech (Series Seed or A) and publicly-traded stocks. Most who are good at one are terrible at the other.

When I ask him about either, he often asks me variants of the following questions:

"Do you understand it?"

"Do you think they'll be dominant and growing 3 years from now?"

"Do you think this technology will be more or less a part of our lives in 3 years?"

He's made dozens of spectacular investments based on his own answers to these questions, plus an added dimension: emotional response. One might dismiss talk of "gut" with a wave of the hand, but, as they say, "once you're lucky, twice you're good." Kevin has replicated his success over and over again.

There are many technically complex approaches to investing, covered ad nauseam elsewhere. Here is one alternative perspective with doesn't get as much airplay.

Enter Kevin

Just before heading out on stage at a tech conference, TechCrunch founder J. Michael Arrington asked me, "You've invested in a lot of great startups, how do you pick your companies?" I responded, "I trust my gut." He seemed unsatisfied and told me, "You've got to come up with something better than that."

I've always admired the tech investors who construct a big, overarching thesis to frame their investment philosophy. "Software is eating the world," "the bottom-up economy," and "investing in thunder lizards," to name a few.

This type of theme investing is a great strategy for funds, but it never really applied to me as an individual angel investor.

For me, the decision to invest in a startup comes after following a process that is heavily weighted towards EQ (emotional quotient). This process starts with exploring the idea emotionally. Should it pass that hurdle, I then do traditional due diligence, using objective data to validate the entrepreneurs' assumptions around the quantifiable aspects of the business.

So, how does one explore an idea emotionally?

When evaluating a new product, I take the novel features (not every feature) and exhaustively play out how they might impact the emotions of the consumers who use them. After that, I take the same features and consider how they might evolve over time.

Let's take, for example, my notes around Twitter (which led to my investment in 2008). I was intrigued by a handful of novel features:

Tweeting — Quick public sharing.

Emotional reaction: Typing 140 characters is quicker and easier than starting a blog. The fear and time associated with writing a long post is nonexistent. Updates can be done through text, no computer needed (remember, this was before "apps"). This could be a huge draw for non-technical celebrities.

Following — A new contrarian concept that allowed users to follow people they didn't know. While this seems commonplace today, at the time it flipped the more popular bidirectional friendship model on its head.

Emotional reaction: Building a following base feels like a game or competition. Users will encourage their friends and fans to follow, bringing in additional users. This "game" of bringing in your friends and fans is free marketing for Twitter. Following forces public sharing as default. This gives fans a deeper connection with people they admire but do not know. [**TF:** Twitter also used a "Top 100" most-followed list early on to pour gasoline on competition.]

Syndication of content.

Emotional reaction: Users are beginning to use the nomenclature "RT" to indicate a "retweet" (this was common practice before the official retweet feature was developed). This ad hoc feature allows users to syndicate messages beyond their social graph, giving a user's message increased visibility. The real-time nature of Twitter allows news stories to break faster than traditional media (even at the time, my startup, Digg).

In allowing myself to feel these features through the eyes of the users, I can get a sense of the excitement around them.

This type of thinking can also be applied to larger industry trends.

My colleague and friend David Prager was one of the first owners of the Tesla Model S. The second he received the car he graciously allowed all of his friends to test-drive it. What stuck with me most was not the car, but the sound it made. When he dropped me off, he slammed on the acceleration pedal and was whisked up a large San Francisco hill. All I heard was the electric swish/hum of acceleration. For me, this was like so many sci-fi movies I had seen growing up — it sounded like the future.

A few days later, I remember hearing a large city bus trying to climb the same hill. The diesel engine was rattling and struggling, almost as if it were out of shape, fighting for its next breath.

It was clear to me that while consumer adoption would be slow, with technological advances in energy storage (only a matter of time), electric vehicles would be the future of this industry.

These feelings led to me take a position in the company back when it was largely unfashionable.

I've actually used this framework more to help me steer clear of bad investments than to find good ones. In evaluating my meetings over the last calendar year, I met with an average of 18 companies before I found one worthwhile of investment. That's a lot of saying "no."

For example, the current incarnation of virtual reality gear doesn't pass my test. Units are large, clunky, require insanely expensive computers, and setup is a mess. The experience, while fun, isn't an order of magnitude better than traditional gaming.

So, as of right now, I've avoided VR investments. At some point (years out), the right mixture of power, size, price, and reality technology will combine into a device that will likely see mass adoption. But as of right now, I'm a pass.

[**TF:** Kevin did call the explosion of augmented reality (AR) months before Pokémon Go exploded, emphasizing that AR and VR are not the same thing. He was bullish on AR and very bearish on VR.]

It's important to note: I'm also a believer in objective data and using it to inform decisions, especially in later rounds of financing. But in the early stage, at the seed of an idea, the bet is largely based on the quality of the team and the emotional connection you feel with the product.

Many fellow investors believe the gut shouldn't be trusted, and chalk up success using it to dumb luck. Certainly, creative intuition varies from person to person. There is no magic formula here. But I do believe we can think of gut intuition as a tool that can be called upon when evaluating ideas with very little data, such as startups that have yet to launch.

NEIL STRAUSS

Neil Strauss (TW: @NEILSTRAUSS, NEILSTRAUSS.COM) has written eight *New York Times* bestsellers, including *The Game* and *The Truth*. He's also been an editor at *Rolling Stone* and a staff writer for the *New York Times*. On top of that, he's built highly profitable companies. Even if you never want to write, his thinking can be applied nearly everywhere.

Spirit animal: Blobfish

DON'T ACCEPT THE NORMS OF YOUR TIME

"I was talking with this billionaire friend of mine, and I was saying, 'I'd really like to write a book about the way your mind works.' He was [commenting on] the difference between someone who isn't a billionaire and a billionaire.... He said, **'The biggest mistake you can make is to accept the norms of your time.'** Not accepting norms is where you innovate, whether it's with technology, with books, with anything. So, not accepting the norm is the secret to really big success and changing the world."

✱ Related book recommendation for artists

Life Is Elsewhere by Milan Kundera; "I think it's an analogy for that choice we all have in life: Are you going to fulfill your potential? Or, are you just going to give into the peer pressure of the moment and become nothing?"

✱ Neil's best purchase of $100 or less

"Freedom [app]. I have no vested interest in this, but there is this one computer program that's probably saved my life. It's my favorite program in the world. It says: 'How many minutes of freedom do you want?' You put in whatever it is — '120 minutes of freedom.' And then, you are completely locked off of your Internet, no matter what, for that amount of time. So, as soon as I sit down to write, the first thing I do is I put on Freedom, because if you're writing and you want to research something, you research something, and then you get stuck in the clickbait rabbit hole. What you can do is save all of the things you want to research, and just research them when that time expires. You'll find it so much more efficient."

TF: Neil and I, and many other writers, use "TK" as a placeholder for things we need to research later (e.g., "He was TK years old at the time."). This is common practice, as almost no English words have TK in them (except that pesky Atkins), making it easy to use Control-F when it's time to batch-research or fact-check.

EDIT FOR YOU, YOUR FANS, THEN YOUR HATERS

Neil edits his writing in three phases. Paraphrased:

First, I edit for me. (What do I like?)

Second, I edit for my fans. (What would be most enjoyable and helpful to my fans?)

Third, I edit for my haters. (What would my detractors try and pick apart, discredit, or make fun of?)

Neil elaborates on the last: "I always use Eminem as an example. You can't really criticize Eminem, because [in his songs] he impersonates the critics and then answers them.... There's nothing that people have said about him that [isn't] already answered or accomplished in some self-aware way. So, I really want to answer the critics—their questions, their critiques—in a way that is still fun and entertaining. [That's] the idea of 'hater-proofing' it."

TF: "Hater-proofing" can take many forms, whether making fun of yourself ("I know this is laughably contradictory, but...") or bringing up a likely criticism and addressing it head on (e.g., "Some people might understandably say... [criticism]."). Seneca does a fantastic job of the latter in *The Moral Letters of Lucilius*, and Scott Adams (page 261) used a similar technique in his novel *God's Debris*.

> "Writer's block does not actually exist.... Writer's block is almost like the equivalent of impotence. It's performance pressure you put on yourself that keeps you from doing something you naturally should be able to do."

WRITER'S BLOCK IS LIKE IMPOTENCE

This is a common refrain from seasoned journalists. Whether it's ideas (see James Altucher, page 246) or writing, the key is temporarily dropping your standards.

One of the best pieces of advice I've received for writing was a mantra: "Two crappy pages per day." A more experienced author related it back to IBM, who was *the* 800-pound gorilla across several different industries a few decades ago. Their salespeople were known for being incredibly effective and smashing records. How did IBM develop that? In some ways, by doing the opposite of what you'd expect. For instance, IBM made the quotas really low. They wanted the salespeople to not be intimidated to pick up the phone. They wanted the sales-people to build momentum and then overshoot their quotas and goals. This is exactly what happened. Translated to writing, I was told my goal should be "two crappy pages a day." That's it. If you hit two crappy pages, even if you never use them, you can feel "successful" for the day. Sometimes you barely eke out two pages, and they are truly terrible. But at least 50% of the time, you'll produce perhaps 5, 10, or even — on the rare miracle day — 20 pages. Draft ugly and edit pretty.

BE VULNERABLE TO GET VULNERABILITY

Neil is a seasoned interviewer and taught me a golden key early on: Open up and be vulnerable with the person you're going to interview *before* you start. It works incredibly well. Prior to hitting record, I'll take 5 to 10 minutes for ban-ter, warmup, sound check, etc. At some point, I'll volunteer personal or vulner-able information (e.g., how I've hated being misquoted in the past, and I know the feeling; how I'm struggling with a deadline based on external pressures, etc.). This makes them much more inclined to do the same later. Sometimes, I'll instead genuinely ask for advice but not interrupt things, along the lines of "You're so good at X, and I'm really struggling with Y. I want to respect your time and do this interview, of course, but someday I'd love to ask you about that."

Listeners often ask me, "How do you build rapport so quickly?" The above is part one.

Part two, I preemptively address common concerns during those 5 to 10 minutes. I've been fucked by media in the past, and I want my guests to know A) I know how terrible that is; and B) my interview is a safe space in which to be open and experiment. Among other points that I cover:

>> This isn't a "gotcha" show, and it's intended to make them look good.

>> I ask, "Let's flash forward to a week or month after this interview comes out. What would make it a home run for you? What does 'suc-cessful' look like?"

>> I ask, "Is there anything you'd prefer not to talk about?"

≫ Much like *Inside the Actors Studio* (I hired their senior researcher to read my transcripts and help me improve), the guest has "final cut." The recording isn't live (99% of the time), and we can delete anything they like. If they think of something the following morning, for instance, we can clip it out.

≫ I'll say, "I always suggest being as raw and open as possible. My fans love tactical details and stories. We can always cut stuff out, but I can't add interesting stuff in later."

✱ Three people or sources you've learned from — or followed closely — in the last year?
Rick Rubin, Laird Hamilton, Gabby Reece, and Elmo (Elmo due to watching along with his baby boy).

TF: Neil introduced me to Rick, who then introduced me to Laird and Gabby. Elmo won't return my calls.

✱ Do you have any quotes that you live your life by or think of often?

"Be open to whatever comes next." — John Cage

"No matter what the situation may be, the right course of action is always compassion and love." (paraphrased from one of his teachers, Barbara McNally)

> **"**I only do email responses
> to print interviews
> Because these people love to
> put a twist to your words
> To infer that you said something
> fucking absurd**"**
> — *lyrics from Fort Minor's "Get Me Gone"*

MIKE SHINODA

Mike Shinoda (TW: @MIKESHINODA, MIKESHINODA.COM) is best known as the rapper, principal songwriter, keyboardist, rhythm guitarist, and one of the two vocalists (yes, all that) of Linkin Park, which has sold more than 60 million albums worldwide and earned two Grammy awards in the process. Mike has collaborated with everyone from Jay Z to Depeche Mode, and he's also the lead rapper in his side project, Fort Minor. As if that's not enough, he's also provided artwork, production, and mixing for all the projects mentioned above. I first met Mike when I interviewed him for BlogWorld & New Media Expo in 2008.

Spirit animal: Snow leopard

I'm a big fan of Fort Minor, and the lyrics on the previous page take on special meaning once you've been bitten. Nearly everyone in this book has been misquoted in media. It's usually the product of a phone interview, and the fallout can be disastrous. To the interviewer, it's just another piece that'll hopefully get clicks and shares. For you, it could be a confusing mess that haunts your Wikipedia forever.

Mike elaborated in our conversation: "I don't feel like the people are necessarily being deceitful. It's just realizing that everybody's got their own agenda. Even a music magazine is not interviewing you because they love music, right? Their day to day is 'We need ad dollars, we need clickthrough. . . .' If you have a 40-word sentence that chops down to 7, [and] it's really titillating, [it doesn't matter if] it has nothing to do with anything you said in your interview. It's just clickbait, [but] they'll absolutely go for that because that's what their business is built on."

TF: The moral of the story is, whenever possible, do print/text interviews via email. A paper trail will give you evidence and recourse if people misbehave. But what if you can't keep it to the inbox? What if you can't (or don't want to) dodge phone calls? My approach has evolved over the years, but it now checks two boxes: avoiding the pain of wasted time, and not getting misquoted or misrepresented.

The pain is blocking out 1 to 3 hours for a print piece interview, but ending up with a single sentence as a quote. The remaining 99% of the Q&A never sees the light of day. Even if the journalist records the call (a step in the right direction), I've never been able to use their audio, as they have a boss who has a boss who has a boss. This situation burns time and makes me sad. So how to fix?

Easy, you record it on your side — which doubles as a way to cover your ass and combat any malicious intent — by saying, "Great to connect! What I usually do for phoners is record it on my side as a backup [via Skype using Ecamm Call Recorder; Zencastr also works well] and then email you a Dropbox link afterward. I assume that's cool?" If they agree, then you're not breaking the law by recording, and everything is hunky-dory. If they don't agree, that's a red flag and you should abort. Missing any one media opportunity won't kill you, but a terrible misquote can persist like an incurable disease.

These days, I typically broach the "I might want to put the full audio on my podcast after your piece runs, which I've done before. I assume that's cool?"

before I agree to interviews. Trading 2 hours (don't forget email follow-ups, fact-checking, etc.) for a potential one-line mention in any text piece isn't otherwise worth it. But when the trade works . . . it can be beautiful. One of my most popular "inbetweenisodes" for the podcast was with journalist and hilarious satire writer Joel Stein of *Time* (TW: @thejoelstein), who killed. It was great for both of us.

WHAT ARE THEIR INCENTIVES?

It's always smart, before starting any collaboration, to ask yourself, "What are their incentives and the timelines of their incentives? How do they measure 'success'? Are we aligned?" Don't make short-term all-or-nothing bets on gimmicks, if you're playing the long game. There will often be pressure from people who are thinking about a promotion next quarter, not your career in 1 to 10 years. Mike shared a story about advice Linkin Park got from their label in the very beginning:

"And they tell us things like, 'Well, you guys need a gimmick. We want to dress Joe in a lab coat and a cowboy hat. And Chester, you should kick a shoe off at every show.' It was stupid record-company stuff that sounds like something out of a movie like *This Is Spinal Tap*. But it was absolutely true, and these were real suggestions. I imagine that if you [reminded them now] they'd say, 'Oh, no, I was totally joking.' I assure you they were not joking."

The band agreed amongst themselves to stick to their guns, and they offered their label two choices: shelve us, or let us do what we know how to do. It worked. I've "missed" many great financial opportunities predicated on gimmicks. As Thomas Huxley famously said, "It is far better for a man to go wrong in freedom than to go right in chains." If you're good, you'll have more than one chance.

SHORT AND SWEET

* Little-known fact

We're both huge fans of Hayao Miyazaki animated films. In fact, *Princess Mononoke* was one of the main inspirations behind Linkin Park's video for "In the End." And since you asked, my favorite museum in the world is the Ghibli Museum in Tokyo, created in the "Mitaka Forest" by Miyazaki.

* Lesser-known bands Mike introduced me to

Royal Blood: I like "Figure It Out" and use it for writing.

Doomriders: "Come Alive" is for headbangers and reminiscent of Danzig. Best suited for workouts or piñata-smashing.

* Both Mike and Justin Boreta of The Glitch Mob (page 356) use Ableton Live for editing

Boreta uses Universal Audio plug-ins to emulate all of the outboard gear that you could buy. Ira Glass of *This American Life* also uses Ableton for live performances.

* Who do you think of when you hear the word "successful"?

Mike thought of Rick Rubin (page 502), not only for songwriting and producing, but also for life lessons.

JUSTIN BORETA

Justin Boreta is a founding member of The Glitch Mob (TW/IG: @THE GLITCHMOB, THEGLITCHMOB.COM). Their last album, *Love Death Immortality*, debuted on the Billboard charts as the #1 Electronic Album, #1 Indie Label, and #4 Overall Digital Album. The Glitch Mob is an artist-owned group, so it's a true self-made startup. Their music has been featured in movies like *Sin City: A Dame to Kill For*, *Edge of Tomorrow*, *Captain America: The First Avenger*, and *The Amazing Spider-Man*. Their remix for "Seven Nation Army" by The White Stripes is featured in the most-viewed video game trailer of all time, *Battlefield 1*.

* Do you live your life by any quotes?

"Be the silence that listens." — Tara Brach

"Life should not be a journey to the grave with the intention of arriving safely in a pretty and well preserved body, but rather to skid in broadside in a cloud of smoke, thoroughly used up, totally worn out, and loudly proclaiming 'Wow! What a Ride!'" — Hunter S. Thompson, *The Proud Highway: Saga of a Desperate Southern Gentleman, 1955–1967*

JUSTIN: "I have a reminder on Hunter S. Thompson's birthday each year. This one in particular reminds me to not take myself so seriously and to have fun with the process. I also keep a handful of blank pages in my morning jour-

Spirit animal: Giant squid

nal to build a quote section over the course of the journal (pulling quotes from reading, podcasts, etc.). That way, I can easily refer back to it and flip through when looking for some insight."

* If you could take one album, one book, and one luxury item to a desert island, what would they be?

Aphex Twin's *Selected Ambient Works*, *The Unbearable Lightness of Being*, and a Chemex for coffee.

* One of Justin's favorite artists — Boards of Canada

"It's very droney, beautiful music, and their albums, for me, are like a familiar old friend that I can revisit over and over again."

* Best advice ever received?

"It's something my father told me when I was very, very little, I was probably 5 or 6, and that was, **'Don't force it.'** It's seemingly such a simple thing. . . . I think that for the creative process, that's really our guiding light. . . . [Trying to force a square peg into the round hole] very rarely has the intended results, whether it's something creative, or in life in general. . . ."

TF: The question I ask whenever I'm straining for extended periods is, "What would this look like if it were easy?"

* What is the worst advice you see or hear given in your trade or area of expertise?

"There's a lot of bad advice thrown around about getting inspired and searching for a revelation. Like Chuck Close says, 'Inspiration is for amateurs — the rest of us just show up and get to work. And the belief that things will grow out of the activity itself and that you will — through work — bump into other possibilities and kick open other doors that you would never have dreamt of if you were just sitting around looking for a great 'art idea.'"

* If you could give your 20-year-old self one piece of advice, what would it be?

"'Chill out. Calm down.' I feel like myself and other people I know that are in their early- to mid-20s get really wound up about things having to be a certain way. It doesn't matter as much as you think it does."

TIM: "Yeah, that's the truth. Will you remember this in 10 years? Probably not."

JUSTIN: "No. People don't even remember a tweet 12 minutes later."

SHORT AND SWEET

* What are three people or sources you've learned from — or followed closely — in the last year?

"*Nautilus* magazine, *Brain Pickings*, Esther Perel."

* What is the best or most worthwhile investment you've ever made?

"After being laid off from my job, I decided to switch paths and dive into music headfirst. I maxed out a credit card to buy my first pair of pro studio monitors (speakers): Genelec 8040A. Monitors are arguably the most important studio purchase you will make. I still use this same pair today."

* Podcast recommendation

Radiolab "In The Dust of This Planet": The episode explores why a little-known academic treatise suddenly ended up appearing in pop culture (in *True Detective* and fashion magazines, on one of Jay Z's jackets, etc.).

* Morning routine

Every morning, Justin does 20 minutes of Transcendental Meditation followed by outdoor kettlebell swings with 24 kg (53 lbs). I do exactly the same thing 2 to 3 times per week, aiming for 50 to 75 repetitions of two-handed swings per *The 4-Hour Body*.

* Music for sleep

Justin listens to Max Richter's *From Sleep*, a composed album with a shortened version on Spotify. "I put it on very quietly as I am starting my bedtime routine, so it usually ends 15 to 20 minutes after I'm asleep. Or I will use the Sonos sleep timer, if I'm at home. It started to have this Pavlovian knockout effect after a while, if I use it every day, like a lullaby. If that's too much melody, there's an artist called Mute Button that has high-quality, long-field recordings. The gentle rain sounds plus sleep timer are fantastic. I find it great to drown out hotel sounds when traveling."

SCOTT BELSKY

Scott Belsky (TW: @SCOTTBELSKY, SCOTTBELSKY.COM) is an entrepreneur, author, and investor. He is a venture partner at Benchmark, a venture capital firm based in San Francisco. Scott co-founded Behance in 2006 and served as CEO until Adobe acquired Behance in 2012. Millions of people use Behance to display their portfolios, as well as track and find top talent across the creative industries. He is an early investor and advisor in Pinterest, Uber, and Periscope, among many other fast-growing startups.

Spirit animal: Polar bear

* What do you believe that others think is insane?

"It is essential to get lost and jam up your plans every now and then. It's a source of creativity and perspective. The danger of maps, capable assistants, and planning is that you may end up living your life as planned. If you do, your potential cannot possibly exceed your expectations."

* How has a "failure" set you up for later success?

"The hardest decisions to make in business are those that disappoint people you care about. One of the biggest mistakes I made in the early days of Behance was doing too many things. We had multiple products in market, multiple business lines, and our energy was divided across too many things. Finally, about 5 years into the business, it all came to a head. We were running out of time and needed to focus on one thing. I shut down a number of projects including our popular task-management application and disappointed thousands of customers. But doing so allowed our team to focus on building a product that ultimately reached many millions of creative people around the world.

"From this experience I learned what legendary writers call 'killing your darlings'—the plot points and characters that detract from a novel. **Sometimes you need to stop doing things you love in order to nurture the one thing that matters most.**"

* The worst advice you hear being given out often?

"'Look for patterns.' As an entrepreneur and investor, I am surrounded by people who try to categorize and generalize the factors that make a company successful. . . . Most people forget that innovation (and investing in innovation) is a business of exceptions.

"It's easy to understand why most investors rely on pattern recognition. It starts with a successful company that surprises everyone with a new model. Perhaps it is Uber and on-demand networks, Airbnb and the sharing economy, or Warby Parker and vertically integrated e-commerce. What follows is endless analysis and the mass adoption of a playbook that has already been played. . . . Sure, [those companies] may create a successful derivative, but they won't change the world.

"I try to learn from the past without being inspired by it. My big question is always, 'What did they try, and why did it work?' When I hear stories of success and failure, I look for the little things that made a big difference. **What conventional wisdom was shunned?** . . . I avoid using a past success as a proxy for the future. After all, the dirty little secret is that every success was almost a failure. Timing and uncontrollable circumstances play more of a role than any of us care to admit.

"Perhaps the greatest lesson from the past is how important it is to be inspired by things that surprise us. When I come across a quirky business model in an unpopular space, I try to find a fascinating thread worth pulling. I challenge myself to stop comparing what I learn to the past. If you only look for patterns of the past, you won't venture far."

✴ Advice to your 30-year-old self?

"In the wrong environment, your creativity is compromised. At 30, I assumed my strengths would always be with me regardless of where I applied them. I was wrong. Truth is, your environment matters."

✴ What would you put on a billboard?

"'It's not about ideas, it's about making ideas happen.' I'd put it on every college campus in the world. In our youth, we are wonderfully creative and idealistic. . . . **Truth is, young creative minds don't need more ideas, they need to take more responsibility with the ideas they've already got.**"

HOW TO EARN YOUR FREEDOM

In thinking of "wealth," it's easy to obsess over accumulation. This is natural, but it's not always helpful. Oftentimes, finances aren't the primary constraint holding us back. Starting in 2004, I traveled the world for roughly 18 months. The lessons learned formed the basis for much of my first book, *The 4-Hour Workweek*. On my journey—from the back alleys of Berlin to the hidden lakes of Patagonia—I had next to nothing: one backpack and one tiny suitcase. I took only two books with me. One was *Walden* by Henry David Thoreau (naturally), and the other was *Vagabonding: An Uncommon Guide to the Art of Long-Term World Travel* by Rolf Potts (TW: @rolfpotts, rolfpotts.com).

I penciled a list of dream destinations on the inside cover of *Vagabonding* when I first bought it, including places like Stockholm, Prague, Paris, Munich, Berlin, and Amsterdam. The list went on. Using Rolf's roadmap and tips, I checked them all off. I was able to explore many of them for 2 to 3 months at a time at my own pace, unrushed and unworried. It was a dream come true. Reading it over and over again during my travels, I realized: Travel isn't just for changing what's outside, it's for reinventing what's inside.

Enter Rolf

Of all the outrageous throwaway lines that one hears in movies, there is one that stands out for me. It doesn't come from a madcap comedy, an esoteric science-fiction flick, or a special-effects-laden action thriller. It comes from

Spirit animal: Hermit crab

Oliver Stone's *Wall Street*, when the Charlie Sheen character — a promising big shot in the stock market — is telling his girlfriend about his dreams.

"I think if I can make a bundle of cash before I'm 30 and get out of this racket," he says, "I'll be able to ride my motorcycle across China."

When I first saw this scene on video a few years ago, I nearly fell out of my seat in astonishment. After all, Charlie Sheen or anyone else could work for 8 months as a toilet cleaner and have enough money to ride a motorcycle across China. And, if they didn't yet have their own motorcycle, another couple months of scrubbing toilets would earn them enough to buy one when they got to China.

The thing is, most Americans probably wouldn't find this movie scene odd. For some reason, we see long-term travel to faraway lands as a recurring dream or an exotic temptation, but not something that applies to the here and now. Instead — out of our insane duty to fear, fashion, and monthly payments on things we don't really need — we quarantine our travels to short, frenzied bursts. In this way, as we throw our wealth at an abstract notion called "lifestyle," travel becomes just another accessory — a smooth-edged, encapsulated experience that we purchase in the same way we buy clothing and furniture.

Not long ago, I read that nearly 250,000 short-term monastery and convent-based vacations had been booked and sold by tour agents the previous year. Spiritual enclaves from Greece to Tibet were turning into hot tourist draws, and travel pundits attributed this "solace boom" to the fact that "busy overachievers are seeking a simpler life."

What nobody bothered to point out, of course, is that purchasing a package vacation to find a simpler life is kind of like using a mirror to see what you look like when you aren't looking into the mirror. All that is really sold is the romantic notion of a simpler life, and — just as no amount of turning your head or flicking your eyes will allow you to unselfconsciously see yourself in the looking-glass — no combination of 1-week or 10-day vacations will truly take you away from the life you lead at home.

Ultimately, this shotgun wedding of time and money has a way of keeping us in a holding pattern. The more we associate experience with cash value, the more we think that money is what we need to live. And the more we associate money with life, the more we convince ourselves that we're too poor to buy our freedom. With this kind of mindset, it's no wonder so many Americans think extended overseas travel is the exclusive realm of students, counterculture dropouts, and the idle rich.

In reality, long-term travel has nothing to do with demographics—age, ideology, income—and everything to do with personal outlook. Long-term travel isn't about being a college student—it's about being a student of daily life. Long-term travel isn't an act of rebellion against society—it's an act of common sense within society. Long-term travel doesn't require a massive "bundle of cash"; it requires only that we walk through the world in a more deliberate way.

This deliberate way of walking through the world has always been intrinsic to a time-honored, quietly available travel tradition known as "vagabonding."

Vagabonding involves taking an extended time-out from your normal life —6 weeks, 4 months, 2 years—to travel the world on your own terms.

But beyond travel, vagabonding is an outlook on life. Vagabonding is about using the prosperity and possibility of the information age to increase your personal options instead of your personal possessions. Vagabonding is about looking for adventure in normal life, and normal life within adventure. Vagabonding is an attitude—a friendly interest in people, places, and things that makes a person an explorer in the truest, most vivid sense of the word.

Vagabonding is not a lifestyle, nor is it a trend. It's just an uncommon way of looking at life—a value adjustment from which action naturally follows. And, as much as anything, vagabonding is about time—our only real commodity— and how we choose to use it.

Sierra Club founder John Muir (an ur-vagabonder if there ever was one) used to express amazement at the well-heeled travelers who would visit Yosemite only to rush away after a few hours of sightseeing. Muir called these folks the "time-poor"—people who were so obsessed with tending their material wealth and social standing that they couldn't spare the time to truly experience the splendor of California's Sierra wilderness. One of Muir's Yosemite visitors in the summer of 1871 was Ralph Waldo Emerson, who gushed upon seeing the sequoias, "It's a wonder that we can see these trees and not wonder more." When Emerson scurried off a couple hours later, however, Muir speculated wryly about whether the famous transcendentalist had really seen the trees in the first place.

Nearly a century later, naturalist Edwin Way Teale used Muir's example to lament the frenetic pace of modern society. "Freedom as John Muir knew it," he wrote in his 1956 book *Autumn Across America*, "with its wealth of time, its unregimented days, its latitude of choice . . . such freedom seems more rare, more difficult to attain, more remote with each new generation."

But Teale's lament for the deterioration of personal freedom was just as hollow a generalization in 1956 as it is now. As John Muir was well aware, vagabonding has never been regulated by the fickle public definition of lifestyle. Rather, it has always been a private choice within a society that is constantly urging us to do otherwise.

———————

There's a story that comes from the tradition of the Desert Fathers, an order of Christian monks who lived in the wastelands of Egypt about 1,700 years ago. In the tale, a couple of monks named Theodore and Lucius shared the acute desire to go out and see the world. Since they'd made vows of contemplation, however, this was not something they were allowed to do. So, to satiate their wanderlust, Theodore and Lucius learned to "mock their temptations" by relegating their travels to the future. When the summertime came, they said to each other, "We will leave in the winter." When the winter came, they said, "We will leave in the summer." They went on like this for over 50 years, never once leaving the monastery or breaking their vows.

Most of us, of course, have never taken such vows — but we choose to live like monks anyway, rooting ourselves to a home or a career and using the future as a kind of phony ritual that justifies the present. In this way, we end up spending (as Thoreau put it) "the best part of one's life earning money in order to enjoy a questionable liberty during the least valuable part of it." We'd love to drop all and explore the world outside, we tell ourselves, but the time never seems right. Thus, given an unlimited amount of choices, we make none. Settling into our lives, we get so obsessed with holding on to our domestic certainties that we forget why we desired them in the first place.

Vagabonding is about gaining the courage to loosen your grip on the so-called certainties of this world. Vagabonding is about refusing to exile travel to some other, seemingly more appropriate time of your life. Vagabonding is about taking control of your circumstances instead of passively waiting for them to decide your fate.

Thus, the question of how and when to start vagabonding is not really a question at all. Vagabonding starts now. Even if the practical reality of travel is still months or years away, vagabonding begins the moment you stop making excuses, start saving money, and begin to look at maps with the narcotic tingle of possibility. From here, the reality of vagabonding comes into sharper focus as you adjust your worldview and begin to embrace the exhilarating uncertainty that true travel promises.

In this way, vagabonding is not a merely a ritual of getting immunizations and packing suitcases. Rather, it's the ongoing practice of looking and learning, of facing fears and altering habits, of cultivating a new fascination in people and places. This attitude is not something you can pick up at the airport counter with your boarding pass; it's a process that starts at home. It's a process by which you first test the waters that will pull you to wonderful new places.

Earning your freedom, of course, involves work — and work is intrinsic to vagabonding for psychic reasons as much as financial ones.

To see the psychic importance of work, one need look no further than people who travel the world on family money. Sometimes referred to as "trustafarians," these folks are among the most visible and least happy wanderers in the travel milieu. Draping themselves in local fashions, they flit from one exotic travel scene to another, compulsively volunteering in local political causes, experimenting with exotic intoxicants, and dabbling in every non-Western religion imaginable. Talk to them, and they'll tell you they're searching for something "meaningful."

What they're really looking for, however, is the reason why they started traveling in the first place. Because they never worked for their freedom, their travel experiences have no personal reference — no connection to the rest of their lives. They are spending plenty of time and money on the road, but they never spent enough of themselves to begin with. Thus, their experience of travel has a diminished sense of value.

Thoreau touched on this same notion in *Walden*. "Which would have advanced the most at the end of a month," he posited, "the boy who had made his own jackknife from the ore which he had dug and smelted, reading as much as would be necessary for this — or the boy who had . . . received a Rodgers' pen-knife from his father? Which would be most likely to cut his fingers?"

At a certain level, the idea that freedom is tied to labor might seem a bit depressing. It shouldn't be. For all the amazing experiences that await you in distant lands, the "meaningful" part of travel always starts at home, with a personal investment in the wonders to come.

On a practical level, there are countless ways to earn your travels. On the road, I have met vagabonders of all ages, from all backgrounds, and walks of life. I've met secretaries, bankers, and policemen who've quit their jobs and are taking a peripatetic pause before starting something new. I've met lawyers, stockbrokers, and social workers who have negotiated months off as they take their careers to new locations. I've met talented specialists — waiters, web designers, strippers — who find they can fund months of travel on a few weeks of work. I've met musicians, truck drivers, and employment counselors who are taking extended time off between gigs. I've met semi-retired soldiers and engineers and businessmen who've reserved a year or two for travel before dabbling in something else. Some of the most prolific vagabonders I've met are seasonal workers — carpenters, park service workers, commercial fishermen — who winter every year in warm and exotic parts of the world. Other folks — teachers, doctors, bartenders, journalists — have opted to take their very careers on the road, alternating work and travel as they see fit. Before I got into writing, a whole slew of "anti-sabbaticals" (landscaping, retail sales, temp work) earned me my vagabonding time.

"I don't like work," says Marlow in Joseph Conrad's *Heart of Darkness*, "but I like what is in the work — the chance to find yourself." Marlow wasn't referring to vagabonding, but the notion still applies. Work is not just an activity that generates funds and creates desire: It's the vagabonding gestation period, wherein you earn your integrity, start making plans, and get your proverbial act together. Work is a time to dream about travel and write notes to yourself, but it's also the time tie up your loose ends. Work is when you confront the problems you might otherwise be tempted to run away from. Work is how you settle your financial and emotional debts — so that your travels are not an escape from your real life, but a discovery of your real life.

———

Now, some of you might think, "That sounds fantastic, but I only get 2 weeks of vacation time per year."

The good news is, as citizens of a stable, prosperous democracy, any one of us has the power to create our own free time.

To actualize this power, we merely need to make strategic use (if only for a few weeks for months) of a time-honored personal freedom technique, popularly known as "quitting." And, despite its pejorative implication, quitting need not be as reckless as it sounds. Many people are able to create vagabonding time through "constructive quitting" — that is, negotiating with their employers for special sabbaticals and long-term leaves of absence.

And even leaving your job in a more permanent manner need not be a negative act — especially in an age when work is likely to be defined by job specialization and the fragmentation of tasks. Whereas working a job with the intention of quitting might have been an act of recklessness 100 years ago, it is more and more often becoming an act of common sense in an age of portable skills and diversified employment options. Keeping this in mind, don't worry that your extended travels might leave you with a "gap" on your résumé. Rather, you should enthusiastically and unapologetically include your vagabonding experience on your résumé when you return. List the job skills travel has taught you: independence, flexibility, negotiation, planning, boldness, self-sufficiency, improvisation. Speak frankly and confidently about your travel experiences — odds are, your next employer will be interested and impressed (and a wee bit envious).

As Pico Iyer pointed out, the act of quitting "means not giving up, but moving on; changing direction not because something doesn't agree with you, but because you don't agree with something. It's not a complaint, in other words, but a positive choice, and not a stop in one's journey, but a step in a better direction. Quitting — whether a job or a habit — means taking a turn so as to be sure you're still moving in the direction of your dreams."

In this way, quitting should never be seen as the end of something grudging and unpleasant. Rather, it's a vital step in beginning something new and wonderful.

"I talk to CEOs all the time, and I say, 'Listen, the day before something is truly a breakthrough, it's a crazy idea. If it wasn't a crazy idea, it's not a breakthrough; it's an incremental improvement. So where inside of your companies are you trying crazy ideas?'**"**

PETER DIAMANDIS

Dr. Peter H. Diamandis (TW: @PETERDIAMANDIS, DIAMANDIS.COM) has been named one of the World's 50 Greatest Leaders by *Fortune* magazine. Peter is founder and executive chairman of the XPRIZE Foundation, best known for its $10 million Ansari XPRIZE for private spaceflight. Today the XPRIZE leads the world in designing and operating large-scale global competitions to solve market failures. He is also the cofounder (along with J. Craig Venter and Bob Hariri) and vice chairman of Human Longevity, Inc. (HLI); and the co-founder and executive chairman of Planetary Resources, a company designing spacecraft to prospect near-Earth asteroids for precious materials (seriously). He is the author of books including *Bold* and *Abundance*, which have endorsements from Bill Clinton, Eric Schmidt, and Ray Kurzweil, among others.

Spirit animal: Eagle

BEHIND THE SCENES

>>> I've heard more power players describe Peter as a "force of nature" than any other person, except for Tony Robbins, a friend of Peter's.

>>> Peter is one of those guys who, every time you meet them, leave you shaking your head and (productively) asking, "What the fuck am I doing with my life?!" He recently asked me, "What's your moon-shot?" leading me to re-explore many of the questions and concepts in this profile.

"A PROBLEM IS A TERRIBLE THING TO WASTE."

This is highly related to the "scratch your own itch" thread that pops up throughout this book. Peter expands: "I think of problems as gold mines. The world's biggest problems are the world's biggest business opportunities."

"WHEN 99% OF PEOPLE DOUBT YOU, YOU'RE EITHER GRAVELY WRONG OR ABOUT TO MAKE HISTORY."

"I saw this the other day, and this comes from Scott Belsky [page 359], who was a founder of Behance."

"THE BEST WAY TO BECOME A BILLIONAIRE IS TO HELP A BILLION PEOPLE."

Peter co-founded Singularity University with Ray Kurzweil. In 2008, at their founding conference at NASA Ames Research Center in Mountain View, California, Google co-founder Larry Page spoke. Among other things, he underscored how he assesses projects:

"I now have a very simple metric I use: Are you working on something that can change the world? Yes or no? The answer for 99.99999% of people is 'no.' I think we need to be training people on how to change the world."

ORIGINS OF THE XPRIZE AND "SUPERCREDIBILITY"

"The fact of the matter is I read this book, *The Spirit of St. Louis*, that my good friend Gregg Maryniak gave me . . . and then I thought, 'Hey, if I can create a prize [Lindbergh crossed the Atlantic to win a prize], maybe I can motivate teams to build private spaceships and that's the means to get my ass into space.'

"I start noodling on this as I'm reading the book. 10 million bucks is enough money. I'm going to call it the 'XPRIZE' because I had no idea who was going to put up the $10 million. The 'X' was going to represent the name of the person who would eventually put up the money, as a variable to be replaced. So, I'm scrambling for it back then, $100 here, $1,000 there, getting the seed money to get this going. I end up in St. Louis where an amazing man, Al Kerth, says, 'I will help you raise some seed money,' and he was driven and connected with my passion, my commitment to this.

"Long story short, over the course of a year and a lot of worn out kneepads, I end up raising a half a million dollars in $10K and $20K checks, and then our fundraising stalls.

"We make the very bold decision that we're going to announce this $10 million prize anyway with no money in place . . . [and] how you announce a big bold idea to the world really matters. . . . We all have a line of credibility around ideas. We judge them constantly.

"If you announce it below the line of credibility, people dismiss it out of hand, and then we have this line of supercredibility. If you announce it above the line of supercredibility, people say, 'Wow, when's it going to happen? How can I be involved?'

"[So, it's] May of 1996. I have half a million dollars. I decide to spend all of it on this launch event, and we do it under the Arch of St. Louis. On the dais, I don't have one astronaut, I've got 20 astronauts standing on stage with me. I've got the head of NASA, the head of the FAA, and the Lindbergh family with me onstage announcing this $10 million prize. Did I have any money? No. Did I have any teams registered to compete? No. But around the world, it was front-page news this $10 million prize was [on]. . . .

"I'm thinking, 'Who wouldn't want to pay $10 million after a person did it? It's paid only on success.' The challenge is, 150 CEOs later, over the next 5 years between 1996 and 2001, everyone's turning me down.

"I finally meet the Ansari family. There's a lot more detail here. Listen, the fact of the matter is there were many times at 3 a.m. when I was tempted to give up, and it was only because I was being driven by my own massively transformative purpose that kept me going, and we're here today having this conversation because I did not give up. I'll leave it at that."

TIM: "I love that story, and I think what I'd love to underscore, as much for myself as anyone else, is that you also had the public accountability. . . ."

PETER: "I burned my ships, dude."

TIM: "Who was the hardest person to convince to be on that stage with you?"

PETER: "Oh, the head of NASA, for sure."

TIM: "What was the pitch? How did you convince him?"

PETER: "The pitch was, 'Listen, wouldn't you want entrepreneurs around the world to be working on new technologies so that this is off your balance sheet?'"

TF: Peter is a master pitchman. I've seen some greats, and he's right at the top. One of the books he recommends for cultivating dealmaking ability is actually a children's book and a 10-minute read: *Stone Soup*. "It's a *children's* story that is the best MBA degree you can read. Between [the concept of] supercredibility and *Stone Soup*, [you have a great foundation]. If you're an entrepreneur in college or 60 years old and building your 20th company, *Stone Soup* is so critically important."

MORNING ROUTINES

Peter stretches during his morning shower:

"It's mostly my lower body, and then I'll go through a breathing exercise as well, and [an] affirmational mantra. . . . [The breathing exercise] is an accelerated deep breathing just to oxygenate and stretch my lungs. There are two elements that tie very much to human longevity. It's strange. . . . One is those people who floss and, second, those people who have a higher VO$_2$ max."

TF: Peter's breathing exercise focuses on expanding the lungs with fast, large inhales. His affirmational mantra, which he repeats a number of times, is "I am joy. I am love. I am gratitude. I see, hear, feel, and know that the purpose of my life is to inspire and guide the transformation of humanity on and off the Earth."

Peter's breathing is similar to some of Wim Hof's exercises (page 41), which I now do in a cold shower (state "priming" per Tony Robbins, page 210), right after my morning meditation.

As for the flossing-longevity connection, Peter is the first to admit this might be correlation instead of causation: People anal retentive enough to floss regularly probably have other habits that directly contribute to longer life.

PRE-BED ROUTINES

Before bed, Peter always reviews his three "wins of the day." This is analogous to the 5-Minute Journal p.m. review that I do (page 146).

ON GETTING OUT OF FUNKS

TIM: "To get out of that 2-day funk [after one of his early startups failed], what does the self-talk look like? I mean, what is the ritual that you use?"

PETER: "The self-talk, in all honesty, was probably more like 2 weeks than 2 days. It's going back to **'Why do I believe this is important?'** It's, **'Look how far I've taken it so far.'** It's a matter of reminding yourself what your purpose in life is, right? What you're here for. If you haven't connected with what your purpose and mission in life is, then forget anything I've said. That is the number-one thing you need to do: Find out what you need to be doing on this planet, why you were put here, and what wakes you up in the mornings."

HOW TO FIND YOUR DRIVING PURPOSE OR MISSION

Peter recommends Tony Robbins's Date with Destiny program, which he feels helps people improve their "operating system." This is how he developed his affirmational mantra. Peter also poses the following three questions:

"What did you want to do when you were a child, before anybody told you what you were supposed to do? What was it you wanted to become? What did you want to do more than anything else?

"If Peter Diamandis or Tim Ferriss gave you $1 billion, how would you spend it besides the parties and the Ferraris and so forth? If I asked you to spend $1 billion improving the world, solving a problem, what would you pursue?

"Where can you put yourself into an environment that gives maximum exposure to new ideas, problems, and people? Exposure to things that capture your 'shower time' [those things you can't stop thinking about in the shower]?" [Peter recommends environments like Singularity University.]

TF: Still struggling with a sense of purpose or mission? Roughly half a dozen people in this book (e.g., Robert Rodriguez) have suggested the book *Start with Why* by Simon Sinek.

THE BENEFITS OF THINKING 10X VERSUS 10%

"I interviewed Astro Teller [for my book *Bold*]. Astro is the head of Google X (now called 'X'), Google skunkworks. . . . He says, 'When you go after a *moonshot* — something that's 10 times bigger, not 10% bigger — a number of things happen. . . .'

"First of all, when you're going 10% bigger, you're competing against everybody. Everybody's trying to go 10% bigger. When you're trying to go 10 times bigger, you're there by yourself. For me, [take asteroid mining as an example]. I don't have a lot of asteroid mining competition out there, or prospecting. Or take human longevity, trying to add 40 years in healthy lifespan with HLI. There are not a lot of companies out there [attempting this].

"The second thing is, when you are trying to go 10 times bigger, you have to start with a clean sheet of paper, and you approach the problem completely differently. I'll give you my favorite example: Tesla. How did Elon start Tesla and build from scratch the safest, most extraordinary car, not even in America, but I think in the world? It's by not having a legacy from the past to drag into the present. That's important.

"The third thing is when you try to go 10 times bigger versus 10% bigger, it's typically not 100 times harder, but the reward is 100 times more."

MORE EXCELLENT QUESTIONS FROM PETER

"One of the questions is: 'Is there a grand challenge or a billion-person problem that you can focus on?'

"Three to five *billion* new consumers are coming online in the next 6 years. Holy cow, that's extraordinary. What do they need? What could you provide for them, because they represent tens of trillions of dollars coming into the global economy, and they also represent an amazing resource of innovation. So I think about that a lot, and I ask that.

"The other question I ask is, 'How would you disrupt yourself?' One of the most fundamental realizations is that every entrepreneur, every business, every company will get disrupted. I've had the honor of talking with Jeff Immelt, the CEO of GE, in his leadership team meetings. The same thing for Muhtar Kent, chairman and CEO of Coca-Cola, and for Cisco and for many companies. I ask them, 'How will you disrupt yourself, and how are you trying to disrupt yourself? If you're not, you're in for a real surprise.' Find the smartest 20-somethings in your company. I don't care if they're in the mail room or where they are. Give them permission to figure out how they would take down your company."

PETER'S LAWS

Peter has a set of rules that guide his life. His 28 Peter's Laws have been collected over decades. Here are some of my favorites:

Law 2: When given a choice . . . take both.

Law 3: Multiple projects lead to multiple successes.

Law 6: When forced to compromise, ask for more.

Law 7: If you can't win, change the rules.

Law 8: If you can't change the rules, then ignore them.

Law 11: "No" simply means begin again at one level higher.

Law 13: When in doubt: THINK.

Law 16: The faster you move, the slower time passes, the longer you live.

Law 17: The best way to predict the future is to create it yourself. (adopted from Alan Kay)

Law 19: You get what you incentivize.

Law 22: The day before something is a breakthrough, it's a crazy idea.

Law 26: If you can't measure it, you can't improve it.

SOPHIA AMORUSO

Sophia Amoruso (TW/IG: @SOPHIAAMORUSO, GIRLBOSS.COM) is the founder and executive chairman of Nasty Gal, a global online destination for both new and vintage clothing, shoes, and accessories. Founded in 2006, Nasty Gal was named Fastest Growing Retailer in 2012 by *Inc.* magazine, thanks to its 10,160% three-year growth rate.

Sophia has been called "fashion's new phenom" by *Forbes* magazine, and she has become one of the most prominent and iconic figures in retail. She recently founded the #Girlboss Foundation, which awards financial grants to women in the worlds of design, fashion, and music. Sophia's first book, *#GIRLBOSS*, is a *New York Times* bestseller and has been published in 15 countries.

JUMPING AND BUILDING A PLANE ON THE WAY DOWN

"I like to make promises that I'm not sure I can keep and then figure out how to keep them. I think you can will things into happening by just committing to them sometimes. . . . I had started to leave feedback for my customers on eBay saying [things like], 'Hey, coming soon, nastygalvintage.com.' [Not long after, I realized], 'Oh, shit, I better build a website. I better actually do this.' So I figured it out, launched the website, and when I launched the website, eBay decided to suspend me around the same time. It was not a transition, it was literally: 'I'm going to try this website thing, and I hope I can go back to eBay if it doesn't work out.' It became apparent pretty quickly that that wasn't going to be an option. I got suspended for leaving the URL in the feedback for the customers."

A DAY THAT ENDS WELL . . .

TIM: "When you were CEO of the company, on a day when you look back and you're like, 'Fuck yeah, I kicked ass today,' what did the first 60 to 90 minutes of your day look like, or what were your morning routines?"

SOPHIA: **"A day that ends well is one that started with exercise.** That's for sure."

✳ Who do you think of when you hear the word "successful"?

"I just really want people to remember that they're capable of doing everything that the people they admire are doing. Maybe not everything, but — **don't be so impressed.** I guess that's where my head goes. . . . There's no reason that you can't have the things that the people you admire have. 'Success' sells this kind of ultimate destination when — even though I've accomplished something, and you [Tim] have accomplished something — I told you I was crying last night. It's not like, 'I'm done, I've arrived' or anything like that."

✳ Advice to your 30-year-old self?

"It doesn't get any easier . . . the challenges are bigger with bigger things."

"A good comedy operates the exact same way a good mystery operates. [Which is] the punchline is something that is right in front of your face the whole time and you never would have put your finger on it."

B.J. NOVAK

B.J. Novak (TW: @BJNOVAK, LI.ST) is best known for his work on NBC's Emmy Award–winning comedy series *The Office* as an actor, writer, director, and executive producer. He has appeared in films such as Quentin Tarantino's *Inglourious Basterds* and Disney's *Saving Mr. Banks*. He is the author of the acclaimed short story collection *One More Thing* and the #1 *New York Times* bestseller *The Book with No Pictures*, which has more than 1 million copies in print. Last but not least, he is co-founder of li.st, a new way to create and discover lists about anything and everything.

Spirit animal: Seagull

"ANY TIME I'M TELLING MYSELF, 'BUT I'M MAKING SO MUCH MONEY,' THAT'S A WARNING SIGN THAT I'M DOING THE WRONG THING."

Looking back at his career, B.J. noticed that he could have stalled in a number of places. Instead, he became very well known for *The Office* and other mega-successes. How did he repeatedly choose the right fork in the road? He attributes a lot of it to heeding the above rule of thumb.

If you find yourself saying, "But I'm making so much money" about a job or project, pay attention. "But I'm making so much money," or "But I'm making good money" is a warning sign that you're probably not on the right track or, at least, that you shouldn't stay there for long. Money can always be regenerated. Time and reputation cannot.

GETTING VIPS WHEN YOU'RE A NOBODY

One of B.J.'s extracurricular activities as a Harvard undergrad was putting on a show called *The B.J. Show* with another kid conveniently named B.J. During their senior year, the two B.J.s decided to put on a show, and thought to invite Bob Saget to perform. They'd heard that the wholesome *Full House* star was, in fact, a really filthy standup comic.

But how could two no-name kids get a massive celebrity to come for free?

B.J. Novak (henceforth "B.J.") came up with two ideas. The first was to "honor" Bob at the *Harvard Lampoon*, hoping that he would agree to perform in order to receive an award. The second part of the pitch was that all the proceeds of the show would go to charity. This approach was so successful that B.J. used it repeatedly later in life: When possible, always give the money to charity, as it allows you to interact with people well above your pay grade.

B.J. cold-called Saget's management, pitched all this, and it worked like a charm. He talked to Saget's manager (who later became B.J.'s manager). Saget came to Boston with Jonathan Katz, the creator of *Raising Dad* (their new show at the time), they liked B.J.'s edgy writing style, and they offered him a job on their staff.

GET THE LONG-TERM GOAL ON THE CALENDAR BEFORE THE SHORT-TERM PAIN HITS

The first time B.J. tried standup comedy at an open-mic night in L.A., it was a disaster. It took him 3 months to work up the courage to get back on stage. B.J.

advises first-time comics to book their first week of shows (open mic commitments) in advance, so they can't quit after the first performance. He learned that you can't make each night a referendum on whether to continue or not. "I was really bad for a while, but let's say you do 20 jokes and 3 of them get pity laughs — well, those are the 3 you keep. And then, after a while, 1 of them always does well — well, that's your opener. And now 2 of them do well — well, you have a closer. . . . It evolves that way."

TF: Schedule (and, if possible, pay for) things in advance to prevent yourself from backing out. I've applied this to early morning AcroYoga sessions, late-night gymnastics training, archery lessons, etc. Make commitments in a high-energy state so that you can't back out when you're in a low-energy state.

TO GO BIG, AIM SMALL (AND FOR TECH, IF YOU CAN)

B.J. said it was bizarre when *The Office* became so successful because they weren't aiming for a huge national success. They were just trying to achieve "cult status" with a small and loyal following. One factor that made a difference: the launch of the Apple iTunes store. Their cult following was very young and tech-savvy, which made them a huge hit on the iTunes store, even though they weren't a huge hit on NBC at that point. *The Office* was one of the first shows to be an online hit, and it created one of the first viral drivers for a primetime TV show.

TF: Once again, see "1,000 True Fans" (page 292). By design, *The 4-Hour Workweek* benefited from the launch of Twitter at the SXSW conference circa 2007, where I gave a keynote presentation. I was deliberately aiming for tech early adopters. I've done this for each book launch since, embracing different technologies that are uncrowded but gaining influence quickly (e.g., Product Hunt, BitTorrent Bundles).

ON WORKING WITH STEVE CARELL

B.J. once brought a bunch of jokes to Steve Carell, who said, "These just feel like jokes to me." For Steve, comedy was a by-product of authenticity. This is the difference between a kid who knows he's cute and one who doesn't (the one who knows he's cute isn't cute).

THE IMPORTANCE OF THE "BLUE SKY" PERIOD

The season writing process for *The Office* began with the Blue Sky Period, which was B.J.'s favorite part of every year.

For 2 to 4 weeks, the writers' room banter was each person asking, "What if . . . ?" over and over again. Crazy scenarios were encouraged, not penalized. Every idea, no matter what, was valid during this period. The idea generation and filtering/editing stages were entirely separate. As B.J. explained, "To me, everything is idea and execution and, if you separate idea and execution, you don't put too much pressure on either of them."

"I CONSIDER BEING IN A GOOD MOOD THE MOST IMPORTANT PART OF MY CREATIVE PROCESS."

B.J. typically spends the first few hours of his day "powering up" and getting in a good mood, until he gets an idea he's excited about, or until he has so much self-loathing and caffeine that he has to do something about it. (See Paulo Coelho, page 511.)

It can take B.J. hours of walking, reading newspapers over coffee, listening to music, etc., before he hits his stride and feels he can write, his zone generally occurring between 11 a.m. and 2 p.m. Says B.J., "I find that being in a good mood for creative work is worth the hours it takes to get in a good mood."

He added, "I read the book *Daily Rituals*, and I am demoralized by how many great people start their day very early." For lifelong night owls like me, it's nice to know that *when* you get started each day seems to matter less than learning how to get started consistently, however your crazy ass can manage it.

NO ARTISANAL ASPIRIN

Every day, B.J. has the same coffee: a venti-size, black Pike Place coffee from Starbucks. He has found that brewing his own coffee at home is too unpredictable, and is "like getting artisanal Tylenol." He wants a standard dose of caffeine.

IF HE TAUGHT A COMEDY WRITING COURSE

P.J. O'Rourke, one of the big *National Lampoon* editors, said that if he ever taught writing or English, he would assign parodies, because you really learn something when you attempt to parody it. B.J. would therefore assign parodies of literature that students were reading and studying in other classes. This would open them up. Mischief is critical in comedy.

AND FOR SCREENWRITING SPECIFICALLY . . .

These are the screenplays B.J. would have students study:

Casablanca broke the form from its time period, and now it is the form.

Pulp Fiction completely breaks the form chronologically.

Ferris Bueller narrates the movie to the camera.

The Naked Gun will do anything for a laugh.

Adaptation completely comments on itself and breaks all of the rules.

LEARN HOW TO PERSUADE (AND LAUGH)

B.J. likes and recommends two podcasts related to debating, the second of which is completely farcical: *Intelligence Squared* and *The Great Debates*.

SHOEBOXES OF CAHIERS

B.J. uses a Moleskine Cahier notebook for jotting notes down throughout the day. He likes it because it is much thinner than a standard Moleskine notebook, so it's easier to carry around, and he has a feeling of accomplishment when he finishes one. He orders different colors, and he also buys huge batches of shape stickers. Any time he starts a new notebook, he writes his name and phone number on the first page and puts a sticker in the top left of the book, which lets him know which notebook he is currently using. He doesn't date them, which can be problematic, but he feels the lack of dates aids the creative process in some capacity. He keeps the untranscribed notebooks in a white box, and he uses a red box for those he has already transcribed to his computer.

✶ **B.J.'s playlist for working**

"Morning Becomes Eclectic" radio program, which has commercial-free new music from 9 a.m. to 12 noon every weekday.

Sirius XM #35 — Indie music

"Early Blues" Pandora station

* Who do you think of when you hear the word "successful"?

Shakespeare, because he made things that were moving, permanent, and popular.

* Most-gifted books

The Oxford Book of Aphorisms by John Gross because it contains the most brilliant one-liners in history. You can spend hours on a page, or you can just flip through it.

B.J. also recommended *Daily Rituals* by Mason Currey for anyone who would enjoy seeing the daily routines of legends like Steve Jobs, Charles Darwin, and Charles Dickens. "It is so reassuring to see that everyone has their own system, and how dysfunctional a lot of them are." Small world: I actually produced the audiobook version of *Daily Rituals*.

* Advice to his younger self

B.J. was very anxious during the first season of *The Office* because he was always trying to write something extra on the side that he never had time to finish. He really didn't stop to enjoy the incredible, once-in-a-lifetime experience of *The Office*. B.J. wishes he had told himself back then that it was a very special time in his life, and that he should own it and enjoy it, instead of being so nervous, for what ended up being no reason at all.

"And you know what I also tell people all the time? If Will Smith isn't in a movie for 3 years, you're not walking around saying, 'Where's Will Smith?' Nobody's paying attention to anyone else at all. You think everyone is, but they're not. **So take as long as you want if you're talented. You'll get their attention again if you have a reason to."**

* Favorite documentaries

Catfish — "It's a cliché, but it's a brilliant, generation-defining documentary."

To Be and to Have — "This is a beautiful and simple film about a one-room school in France, and what happens over the course of one year."

The Overnighters — "This covers oil exploration in North Dakota, which has become perhaps bigger than the Gold Rush in the 1800s, due to the process of 'fracking.'"

HOW TO SAY "NO" WHEN IT MATTERS MOST

"The wisdom of life consists in the elimination of non-essentials." —**Lin Yutang**

"Discipline equals freedom."—**Jocko Willink** (page 412)

This chapter will teach you how to say "no" when it matters most.

It will also explain how I think about investing, overcoming "fear of missing out" (FOMO), and otherwise reducing anxiety.

Last, it's also about how to kill the golden goose when the goose is no longer serving you.

I'll dig into one specifically hard decision — deciding to say "no" to startup investing, which is easily the most lucrative activity in my life. Even if you don't view yourself as an "investor" — which you are, whether you realize it or not — the process I used to get to "no" should be useful.

Caveat for any investing pros reading this:

>>> I realize there are exceptions to every "rule" I use. Most of this post is as subjective as the fears I felt.

>>> My rules might be simplistic, but they've provided a good ROI and the ability to sleep. Every time I've tried to get "sophisticated," the universe has kicked me in the nuts.

>>> Many startup investors use diametrically opposed approaches and do very well.

» There are later-stage investments I've made (2 to 4x return deals) that run counter to some of what's below (e.g., aiming for more than 10x), but those typically involve a discount to book value, due to distressed sellers or some atypical event.

» Many concepts are simplified to avoid confusing a lay audience.

The Road to No

So, Why Did I Decide to Tap Out and Shift Gears?

Below are the key questions I asked to arrive at this cord-cutting conclusion. I revisit these questions often, usually every month. I hope they help you remove noise and internal conflict from your life.

Are You Doing What You're Uniquely Capable of, What You Feel Placed Here on Earth to Do? Can You Be Replaced?

I remember a breakfast with Kamal Ravikant (the brother of Naval, page 546). Standing in a friend's kitchen downing eggs, lox, and coffee, we spoke about our dreams, fears, obligations, and lives. Investing had become a big part of my net worth and my identity. Listing out the options I saw for my next big move, I asked him if I should raise a fund and become a full-time venture capitalist (VC), as I was already doing the work but trying to balance it with 5 to 10 other projects. He could sense my anxiety. It wasn't a dream of mine; I simply felt I'd be stupid not to strike while the iron was hot.

He thought very carefully in silence and then said: "I've been at events where people come up to you crying because they've lost 100-plus pounds on the Slow-Carb Diet. You will never have that impact as a VC. If you don't invest in a company, they'll just find another VC. You're totally replaceable."

He paused again and ended with, "Please don't stop writing."

I've thought about that conversation every day since.

For some people, being a VC is their calling and they are the Michael Jordan–like MVPs of that world. They should cultivate that gift. But if I stop investing, no one will miss it. In 2015, that much was clear. There have never been more startup investors, and—right along with them—founders basing "fit" on highest valuation and previously unheard-of terms. There are exceptions, of course, but it's crowded. If I exit through the side door, the startup party will roll on uninterrupted.

Now, I'm certainly not the best writer in the world. I have no delusions otherwise. People like John McPhee and Michael Lewis make me want to cry into my pillow.

BUT . . . if I stop writing, perhaps I'm squandering the biggest opportunity I have, created through much luck, to have a lasting impact on the greatest number of people. This feeling of urgency was multiplied 100-fold in the 2 months preceding the decision, as several close friends died in accidents no one saw coming. Life is short. Put another way: A long life is far from guaranteed. Nearly everyone dies before they're ready.

I was tired of being interchangeable, no matter how lucrative the game. Even if I end up wrong about the writing, I'd curse myself if I didn't give it a shot.

Are you squandering your unique abilities? Or the chance to find them in the first place?

How Often Are You Saying "Hell, Yeah!"?

Philosopher-programmer Derek Sivers (page 184) is one of my favorite people.

His incisive thinking has always impressed me, and his "hell, yeah!" or "no" philosophy has become one of my favorite rules of thumb. From his blog:

> Those of you who often over-commit or feel too scattered may appreciate a new philosophy I'm trying: If I'm not saying "HELL YEAH!" about something, then I say no. Meaning: When deciding whether to commit to something, if I feel anything less than "Wow! That would be amazing! Absolutely! Hell yeah!" — then my answer is no. When you say no to most things, you leave room in your life to really throw yourself completely into that rare thing that makes you say, "HELL YEAH!" We're all busy. We've all taken on too much. Saying yes to less is the way out.

To become "successful," you have to say "yes" to a lot of experiments. To learn what you're best at, or what you're most passionate about, you have to throw a lot against the wall.

Once your life shifts from pitching outbound to defending against inbound, however, you have to ruthlessly say "no" as your default. Instead of throwing spears, you're holding the shield.

From 2007 to 2009 and again from 2012 to 2013, I said yes to way too many "cool" things. Would I like to go to a conference in South America? Write a time-consuming guest article for a well-known magazine? Invest in a startup that five of my friends were in? "Sure, that sounds kinda cool," I'd say, dropping it in the calendar. Later, I'd pay the price of massive distraction and overwhelm. My agenda became a list of everyone else's agendas.

Saying yes to too much "cool" will bury you alive and render you a B-player, even if you have A-player skills. To develop your edge initially, you learn to set priorities; to maintain your edge, you need to defend against the priorities of others.

Once you reach a decent level of professional success, lack of opportunity won't kill you. It's drowning in "kinda cool" commitments that will sink the ship.

These days, I find myself saying "Hell, yes!" less and less with new startups. That's my cue to exit stage left completely, especially when I can do work I love (e.g., writing) with $\frac{1}{10}$ the energy expenditure.

I need to stop sowing the seeds of my own destruction.

How Much of Your Life Is Making Versus Managing?
How Do You Feel About the Split?

One of my favorite time-management essays is "Maker's Schedule, Manager's Schedule" by Paul Graham of Y Combinator fame. Give it a read.

As investor Brad Feld and many others have observed, great creative work isn't possible if you're trying to piece together 30 minutes here and 45 minutes there. Large, uninterrupted blocks of time — 3 to 5 hours minimum — create the space needed to find and connect the dots. And one block per week isn't enough. There has to be enough slack in the system for multi-day, CPU-intensive synthesis. For me, this means at least 3 to 4 mornings per week where I am in "maker" mode until at least 1 p.m.

If I'm reactive, maker mode is impossible. Email and texts of "We're over-committed but might be able to squeeze you in for $25K. Closing tomorrow. Interested?" are creative kryptonite.

I miss writing, creating, and working on bigger projects. "Yes" to that means "no" to any games of whack-a-mole.

What Blessings in Excess Have Become a Curse?
Where Do You Have Too Much of a Good Thing?

In excess, most things take on the characteristics of their opposite. Thus:

Pacifists become militants. Freedom fighters become tyrants. Blessings become curses. Help becomes hindrance. More becomes less.

To explore this concept more, read up on Aristotle's golden mean.

In my first 1 to 2 years of angel investing, my basic criteria were simple (and complement those on page 250 in Real-World MBA):

» Consumer-facing products or services

» Products I could be a dedicated "power user" of, products that scratched a personal itch

» Initial target demographic of 25- to 40-year-old tech-savvy males in big U.S. cities like S.F., NYC, Chicago, L.A., etc. (allowed me to accelerate growth/scaling with my audience)

» Less than $10 million pre-money valuation

» Demonstrated traction and consistent growth (not doctored with paid acquisition)

» No "party rounds" — crowded financing rounds with no clear lead investor. Party rounds often lead to poor due diligence and few people with enough skin in the game to really care.

Checking these boxes allowed me to add a lot of value quickly, even as relatively cheap labor (i.e., I took a tiny stake in the company).

My ability to help spread via word of mouth, and I got what I wanted: great "deal flow." Deals started flowing in en masse from other founders and investors.

Fast forward to 2015, and great deal flow was paralyzing the rest of my life. I was drowning in inbound.

Instead of making great things possible in my life, it was preventing great things from happening. I'm excited to go back to basics, and this requires cauterizing blessings that have become burdens.

Why Are You Investing, Anyway?

For me, the goal of "investing" has always been simple: **to allocate resources (e.g., money, time, energy) to improve quality of life**. This is a personal definition, as yours likely will be.

Some words are so overused as to have become meaningless. If you find yourself using nebulous terms like "success," "happiness," or "investing," it pays to explicitly define them or stop using them. Answering "What would it look like if I had ___ ?" helps clarify things. **Life favors the specific ask and punishes the vague wish.**

So, here "investing" means to allocate resources (e.g., money, time, energy) to improve quality of life.

This applies to both the future and the present. I am willing to accept a *mild and temporary* 10% decrease in current quality of life for a *high-probability* 10x return, whether the ROI comes in the form of cash, time, energy, or otherwise. That could be a separate book, but conversely:

An investment that produces a massive financial ROI but makes me a complete nervous mess, or causes insomnia and temper tantrums for a long period of time, is NOT a good investment.

I don't typically invest in public stocks for this reason, even when I know I'm leaving cash on the table. My stomach can't take the ups and downs, but — like drivers rubbernecking to look at a wreck — I seem incapable of ignoring the charts. I will compulsively check Google News and Google Finance, despite knowing it's self-sabotage. I become Benjamin Graham's Mr. Market. As counterexamples, friends like Kevin Rose (page 340) and Chris Sacca (page 164) have different programming and are comfortable playing in that arena. They can be rational instead of reactive.

One could argue that I should work on my reactivity instead of avoiding stocks. I'd agree on tempering reactivity, but I'd disagree on fixing weaknesses as a primary investment (or life) strategy.

All of my biggest wins have come from leveraging strengths instead of fixing weaknesses. Investing is hard enough without having to change your core behaviors. Don't push a boulder uphill just because you can.

Public market sharks will eat me alive in their world, but I'll beat 99% of them in my little early-stage startup sandbox. I live in the middle of the informational switch box and know the operators.

From 2007 until recently, I paradoxically found startup investing very low-stress. Ditto with some options trading. Though high-risk, I do well with binary decisions. In other words, I do a ton of homework and commit to an investment that I cannot reverse. That "what's done is done" aspect allows me to sleep well at night, as there is no buy-sell choice for the foreseeable future. I'm protected from my lesser, flip-flopping self. That has produced more than a few 10x to 100x ROI investments.

In the last two years, however, things have changed.

As fair-weather investors and founders have flooded the "hot" tech scene, it's become a deluge of noise. Where there were once a handful of micro VCs, for instance, there are now hundreds. Private equity firms and hedge funds are betting earlier and earlier. It's become a crowded playing field. Here's what that meant for me personally:

>>> I received 50 to 100 pitches per week. This created an inbox problem, but it gets worse, as . . .

>>> Many of these are unsolicited "cold intros," where other investors will email me and CC 2 to 4 founders with, "I'd love for you to meet A, B, and C" without asking if they can share my email address.

>>> Those founders then "loop in" other people, and it cascades horribly from there. Before I know it, 20 to 50 people I don't know are emailing me questions and requests. As a result, I've had to declare email bankruptcy twice in the last 6 months. It's totally untenable.

Is there a tech bubble? That question is beyond my pay grade, and it's also beside the point. Even if I were guaranteed there would be no implosion for 3 to 5 years, I'd still exit now. Largely due to communication overload, I've lost my love for the game. On top of that, the marginal minute now matters more to me than the marginal dollar (a lesson learned from Naval Ravikant).

But why not cut back 50%, or even 90%, and be more selective? Good question. That's next ...

Are You Fooling Yourself with a Plan for Moderation?

"The first principle is that you must not fool yourself, and you are the easiest person to fool." — **Richard P. Feynman**

Where in your life are you good at moderation? Where are you an all-or-nothing type? Where do you lack a shut-off switch? It pays to know thyself.

The Slow-Carb Diet from *The 4-Hour Body* succeeds where other diets fail for many reasons, but the biggest is this: It accepts default human behaviors versus trying to fix them. Rather than say "don't cheat" or "you can no longer eat X," we plan weekly "cheat days" (usually Saturdays) in advance. People on diets will cheat regardless, so we mitigate the damage by regularly scheduling it and limiting it to 24 hours.

Outside of cheat days, slow carbers keep "domino foods" out of their homes. What are domino foods? Foods that *could* be acceptable if humans had strict portion control, but that are disallowed because practically none of us do. Common domino foods include:

Chickpeas
Peanut butter
Salted cashews
Alcohol

Domino triggers aren't limited to food. For some people, if they play 15 minutes of *World of Warcraft*, they'll play 15 hours. It's 0 or 15 hours.

For me, startups are a domino food.

In theory, "I'll only do one deal a month" or "I'll only do two deals a quarter" sounds great, but I've literally NEVER seen it work for myself or any of my angel investor friends. Zero. Sure, there are ways to winnow down the pitches. Yes, you can ask any VC who introduces a deal, "Is this one of the top 1 to 2 entrepreneurs you know?" and reject any "no"s. But what if you commit to two deals a quarter and see two great ones the first week? What then? If you invest in those two, will you be able to ignore every incoming pitch for the next 10 weeks? Not likely.

For me, it's all-or-nothing. I can't be half pregnant with startup investing. Whether choosing 2 or 20 startups per year, you have to filter them from the total incoming pool.

If I let even one startup through, another 50 seem to magically fill up my time (or at least my inbox). I don't want to hire staff for vetting, so I've concluded I must ignore all new startup pitches and intros.

Know where you can moderate and where you can't.

You Say "Health Is #1" . . . But Is It Really?

After contracting Lyme disease and operating at ~10% capacity for 9 months in 2014, I made health #1. Prior to Lyme, I'd worked out and eaten well, but when push came to shove, "health #1" was negotiable. Now, it's literally #1. What does this mean?

If I sleep poorly and have an early morning meeting, I'll cancel the meeting last-minute if needed and catch up on sleep. If I've missed a workout and have a conference call coming up in 30 minutes? Same. Late-night birthday party with a close friend? Not unless I can sleep in the next morning. In practice, strictly making health #1 has real social and business ramifications. That's a price I've realized I MUST be fine with paying, or I will lose weeks or months to sickness and fatigue.

Making health #1 50% of the time doesn't work. It's absolutely all-or-nothing. If it's #1 50% of the time, you'll compromise precisely when it's most important not to.

The artificial urgency common to startups makes mental and physical health a rarity. **I'm tired of unwarranted last-minute "hurry up and sign" emergencies and related fire drills. It's a culture of cortisol.**

Are You Over-Correlated?

[**NOTE:** Two investor friends found this section slow, as they're immersed in similar subjects. Feel free to skip if it drags on, but I think there are a few important concepts for novices in here.]

"Correlated" means that investments tend to move up or down in value at the same time.

As legendary hedge fund manager Ray Dalio told Tony Robbins (page 210): "It's almost certain that whatever you're going to put your money in, there will come a day when you will lose 50% to 70%." It pays to remember that if you lose 50%, you need a subsequent 100% return to get back to where you started. That math is tough.

So, how to de-risk your portfolio?

Many investors "rebalance" across asset classes to maintain certain ratios (e.g., X% in bonds, Y% in stocks, Z% in commodities, etc.). If one asset class jumps, they liquidate a part of it and buy more of lower performing classes. There are pros and cons to this, but it's common practice.

From 2007 to 2009, during the Real-World MBA that taught me to angel invest (page 250), less than 15% of my liquid assets were in startups. But most startups are illiquid. I commonly can't sell shares until 7 to 12 *years* after I invest, at least for my big winners to date. What does that mean? In 2015, startups comprised more than 80% of my assets. Yikes!

Since I can't take chips off the table, the simplest first step for lowering stress was to stop investing in illiquid assets.

I sold large portions of liquid stocks — mostly early startup investments in China (e.g., Alibaba) — to help get me to "sleep at night" levels, even if they were lower than historical highs of the last 6 to 12 months. **Beware of anchoring to former high prices (e.g., "I'll sell when it gets back to X price per share . . .").** I only have 1 to 2 stock holdings remaining.

Some of you might suggest hedging startup investments with short positions, and I'd love to, but it's not my forte, and it's easy to get yourself into legal issues if done haphazardly.

The best approximation to a "hedge" that I've seen in the typically bull-market-dependent VC world is investing in businesses like Uber, which A) have a lot of international exposure (like U.S. blue chips), and B) could be considered macroeconomically counter-cyclical. For instance, it's conceivable a stock market correction or crash could simultaneously lead fewer people to buy cars and/or more people to sign up as Uber drivers to supplement or replace their jobs. Ditto with Airbnb and others that have more variable than fixed costs compared to incumbents (e.g., Hilton).

What's the Rush? Can You "Retire" and Come Back?

I'm in startups for the long game. In some capacity, I plan to be doing this 20 years from now.

Here's the reality: If you're spending your own money, or otherwise not banking on management fees, you can wait for the perfect pitches, even if it takes years. It might not be the "best" approach, but it's more than enough. To get rich beyond your wildest dreams, it isn't remotely necessary to bet on a Facebook or Airbnb every year. If you get a decent bet on ONE of those non-illusory, real-business unicorns every 10 years, or if you get 2 to 3 investments that turn $25K into $2.5 million, you can retire and have an outrageously wonderful quality of life. Many would argue that you need to invest in 50 to 100 startups to find that one lottery ticket. I think it's possible to narrow those odds quite a bit (Peter Thiel on page 232 would likely agree), and a lot of it is predicated on maintaining stringent criteria; ensuring you have an informational, analytical, or behavioral advantage; and TIMING.

Most of my best investments were made during the "Dot-com Depression" of 2008–2009 (e.g., Uber, Shopify, Twitter, etc.), when only the hardcore remained standing on a battlefield littered with startup bodies. In lean times, when startups no longer grace magazine covers, founders are those who cannot help but build companies. LinkedIn in 2002 is another example.

Now, of course, great companies are still built during "frothy" periods. The froth just makes my job and detective work 10 times harder, and the *margin of safety* becomes much narrower.

Think of the "margin of safety" as wiggle room.

Warren Buffett is one of the most successful investors of the 20th century and a self-described "value investor." He aims to buy stocks at a discount (below intrinsic value), so that even with a worst-case scenario, he can do well. This discount is referred to as the "margin of safety," and it's the bedrock principle of some of the brightest minds in the investing world (e.g., Seth Klarman). It doesn't guarantee a good investment, but it allows room for error. Back to the startup world . . .

I want each of my investments, if successful, to have the ability to return my "entire fund," which is how much capital I've earmarked for startups over two years, for instance. This usually means potential for a minimum 10x return. That 10x minimum is an important part of my recipe that allows margin for screwups.

For the fund-justifying ROI to have a snowball's chance in hell of happening, I must A) know basic algebra to ensure my investment amounts (check sizes) permit it, and B) avoid companies that seem overpriced, where the 10x price is something the world has never seen before.

If you throw low-due-diligence Hail Marys everywhere and justify it with "they could be the next Uber!", you will almost certainly be killed by 1,000 slow-bleeding $25K paper cuts. Despite current euphoria, applying something like Pascal's wager to startups is a great way to go broke.

Good Startup Investors Who Suggest Being "Promiscuous" Are Still Methodical

It's popular in startup land to talk about "moonshots," the impossibly ambitious startups that will either change the world or incinerate themselves into stardust.

I'm a fan of funding ballsy founders (which includes women, such as Tracy DiNunzio, page 313), and I want many moonshots to be funded, but here's the reality of my portfolio: As I've signed the investment docs for every big success I've had, I've always thought, "I will never lose money on this deal."

The "this will be a home run or nothing" deals usually end up at nothing. I'm not saying such deals can't work, but I try not to specialize in them.

These days, the real unicorns aren't the media darlings with billion-dollar valuations. Those have become terrifyingly passé. The unicorns are the high-growth startups with a reasonable margin of safety.

Fortunately, I'm not in a rush, and I can wait for the tide to shift.

If you simply wait for blood in the streets, for when true believers are the only ones left, you can ensure that intrinsically driven founders are at least half of your meetings.

It might be morbid, but it's practical. If you're investing for life, don't rush. Timing often overrides technique.

Are You Having a Breakdown or a Breakthrough? A Short How-To Guide

"Make your peace with the fact that saying 'no' often requires trading popularity for respect." —**Greg McKeown**, *Essentialism*

If you're suffering from a feeling of overwhelm, it might be useful to ask yourself two questions:

1. In the midst of overwhelm, is life not showing me exactly what I should subtract?

2. Am I having a *breakdown* or a *breakthrough*?

As Marcus Aurelius and Ryan Holiday (page 334) would say, "The obstacle is the way." This doesn't mean seeing problems, accepting them, and leaving them to fester. Nor does it mean rationalizing problems into good things. To me, it means using pain to find clarity. If pain is examined and not ignored, it can show you what to excise from your life.

For me, step one is always the same: Write down the 20% of activities and people causing 80% or more of your negative emotions.

My step two is doing a "fear-setting" exercise on paper (page 463), in which I ask and answer, "What is really the worst that could happen if I stopped doing what I'm considering? And so what? How could I undo any damage?"

Allow me to share a real-world example: a transcript of the journal page that convinced me to write this and kickstart an extended startup vacation.

The questions in my mind were: "What is really the worst that could happen if I stopped angel investing for a minimum of 6 to 12 months? Do those worst-case scenarios really matter? How could I undo any potential damage? Could I do a 2-week test?"

As you'll notice, I made lists of the *guaranteed* upsides versus *speculative* downsides. If we define "risk" as I like to—the likelihood of an irreversible negative outcome—we can see how stupid (and unnecessarily painful) all my fretting and procrastination was. All I needed to do was put it on paper.

Hit snooze 4–5 times, so up at ~10:15 instead of 8:33. The anxiety is mostly
   related to email and startups: new pitches, new intros, etc.
Do a 2-week test where "no" to ALL cold intros and pitches?
Why am I hesitant? For saying "no" to all:

PROS:

—*100% guaranteed anxiety reduction*
—*Feeling of freedom*
—*Less indecision, less deliberation, far more bandwidth for CREATING,*
   for READING, for PHYSICAL [TRAINING], for EXPERIMENTS

CONS (i.e., why not?):

—*Might find the next Uber (<10% chance)*
—*Who cares? Wouldn't materialize for 7–9 years minimum. If Uber pops*
   (IPO), it won't matter.
—*Not get more deals. But who cares?*
      *Dinner with 5 friends fixes it.
      *One blog post [for sourcing from readers] fixes it.
      *NONE of my best deals (Shyp, Shopify, Uber, Twitter, Facebook,
      Alibaba, etc.) came from cold intros from acquaintances.

If try 2 weeks, how to ensure successful:

—*I don't even see [new] startup emails.*
—*No con-calls. [Cite] "con-call vacation" → push to email or EOD*
   [end-of-day review with assistant].
—*Offer [additional] "office hours" on Fridays [for existing portfolio]?*

I ultimately realized: If I set up policies to avoid new startups for 2 weeks, the systems will persist. I might as well make it semi-permanent and take a real "startup vacation."

   Now it's your turn: What do *you* need a vacation from?

My Challenge to You: Write Down the "What Ifs"

"I am an old man and I have known a great many troubles, but most of them never happened." —**Mark Twain**

"He who suffers before it is necessary suffers more than is necessary."
—**Seneca**

Tonight or tomorrow morning, think of a decision you've been putting off, and challenge the fuzzy "what ifs" holding you hostage.

If not now, when? If left at the status quo, what will your life and stress look like in 6 months? In 1 year? In 3 years? Who around you will also suffer?

I hope you find the strength to say "no" when it matters most. I'm striving for the same, and only time will tell if I pull it off. So far, it's turned out better than I ever could have imagined.

What will I spend my time on next? More crazy experiments and creative projects, of course. Things are going to get nuts.

But more important—how could *you* use a new lease on life?

To surf every day, like the attorney in *The 4-Hour Workweek* who quit the rat race to build his own business paradise in Brazil? To travel with your family around the world for more than 1,000 days? To learn languages or work remotely in more than 20 countries while building a massive business? It's all possible. I know because those are all case studies from my readers. It can all be done. The options are practically limitless.

So start by writing them down. Dig into your fears, and you'll often find that the mental monsters are harmless scarecrows. Sometimes, it just takes a piece of paper and a few questions to create a breakthrough.

What do you have to lose? Chances are, next to nothing.

3

WISE

"The struggle ends when the gratitude begins."

— *Neale Donald Walsch*

"There is no way to happiness — happiness is the way."

— *Thich Nhat Hanh*

"What you seek is seeking you."

— *Rumi*

"[At the end of life,] you can let a lot of the rules that govern our daily lives fly out the window. Because you realize that we're walking around in systems in society, and much of what consumes most of our days is not some natural order. We're all navigating some superstructure that we humans created."

BJ MILLER

BJ Miller (TW: @ZENHOSPICE, ZENHOSPICE.ORG) is a palliative care physician at the University of California at San Francisco and an advisor to the Zen Hospice Project in San Francisco. He thinks deeply about how to create a dignified, graceful end of life for his patients.

He is an expert in death. Through that, he's learned how we can dramatically improve our own lives, often with very small changes. He has guided or been involved with ~1,000 deaths, and he's spotted patterns we can all learn from. BJ is also a triple amputee due to an electrocution accident in college. His 2015 TED talk, "What Really Matters at the End of Life," was among the top 15 most viewed TED talks of 2015.

"DON'T BELIEVE EVERYTHING THAT YOU THINK."

This was BJ's answer to "what would you put on a billboard?" He wasn't sure of the source but attributed it to a bumper sticker. By the end of this profile, you'll see how BJ loves this type of absurdity.

STARGAZING AS THERAPY

"**When you are struggling with just about anything, look up. Just ponder the night sky for a minute** and realize that we're all on the same planet at the same time. As far as we can tell, we're the only planet with life like ours on it anywhere nearby. Then you start looking at the stars, and you realize that the light hitting your eye is ancient, [some of the] stars that you're seeing, they no longer exist by the time that the light gets to you. Just mulling the bare-naked facts of the cosmos is enough to thrill me, awe me, freak me out, and kind of put all my neurotic anxieties in their proper place. A lot of people — when you're standing at the edge of your horizon, at death's door, you can be much more in tune with the cosmos."

TF: Ed Cooke (page 517) does something surprisingly similar, and I've started doing "star therapy" every night that I can. The effects are disproportionate to the effort.

DELIGHTING IN PERISHABILITY

The following is BJ's answer to "What $100 or less purchase has most positively impacted your life in recent memory?"

"I would probably point to a beautiful pinot noir from Joseph Swan up in Sonoma County. It's like the artwork of Andy Goldsworthy, or anyone who delights in anything ephemeral. The charm in a bottle of wine, the craft, all the work that goes into it . . . actually delighting in the fact that it's perishable and goes away I find really helpful. I've gotten a lot of miles out of a beautiful bottle of wine, not just for the taste and the buzz, but the symbolism of delighting in something that goes away."

HERE'S A GOOD REASON TO QUESTION YOUR "I CAN'TS"

Be patient with this and read the whole thing. It's worth it. Scuderia motorcycle dealership in San Francisco also aided BJ with his seemingly outrageous mission.

TIM: "I hate to focus on something perhaps superficial, but you just said 'riding your motorcycle' in passing. Now, I apologize if this sounds like a weird question, but you have three limbs that have been damaged [effectively amputated]. How do you ride a motorcycle?"

BJ: "You know, this was sort of a long dream that recently came true."

TIM: "Congratulations. I mean, it's fantastic. I'm just so curious about the logistics."

BJ: "Thank you. Well, it's interesting you ask. The man who helped make this dream come true, Randy, ended up being my patient and our resident at Zen Hospice Project not too long after he converted my motorcycle. So there's a lot to this story, my friend.

"I love two wheels. I love the gyroscopic lifestyle. I love the feeling of it, and I've always loved riding bicycles. I'd always wanted to get on a motorcycle. But I kept going to shops, people would look at me, and I could never find a mechanic who was willing to take it on and try to help make it happen.

"A fellow named Mert Lawwill, who's an old motorcycle racing champion — sort of legendary in that world — happens to live around here [Northern California] in Tiburon. I don't know what inspired Mert, but he's a machinist himself and a handy fella, and in his retirement, he got into the business of building a prosthetic component that lends itself very well to mounting an arm onto a bicycle or a motorcycle.

"So, the first piece of this puzzle was discovering Mert's invention and getting a hold of it myself, which allowed me to get my prosthetic arm attached to a handlebar in a very functional way."

TIM: "How are the hand controls modified?"

BJ: "Randy figured out . . . Aprilia made a model, the Mana, that is clutchless. This is essentially an automatic transmission. So do away with the clutch and gear changes. That's a huge piece of the puzzle out of the way. Then Randy figured out a way to splice the brakes, front and rear in a certain ratio, into a single lever. So I'm doing nothing with my prosthetic feet except holding onto the bike. I'm doing nothing with my prosthetic arm except for holding onto the bike. All the action is in my right hand. Brakes are one lever, and then Randy built this box and moved all the controls — the turn signals, horn, and all that stuff — over to the right side of the bike at a good distance for my thumb to reach them. I have throttle, brake lever, and then the turn signal box all going with one hand."

TIM: "That's so awesome."

BJ: "That's it, you know. Away you go!"

TIM: "I just have to pause here for a second and just ask everyone listening: What bullshit excuses do you have for not going after whatever it is that you want? Please, write in, tell us on social media why these are real excuses with #bullshit afterwards. Oh my God, man, that's such a great story."

THE MIRACLE OF A SNOWBALL

BJ described waking up in a burn unit after being electrocuted in college and losing three limbs:

"A burn unit is a particular place. A gruesome place. The pain that the patients are going through is gut-wrenching. Working in a burn unit is very difficult. People usually don't last in a burn unit very long as a clinician. The thing that often kills burn victims after they've survived the initial trauma is infection, so burn units are incredibly sterile environments. Everyone's gowned up, masked, and gloved. For the first several weeks, I could only have one person in my room at a time.

"You're cut off from everything. There's no day or night. There was no window in my room. Even when people are at your bedside, there's all this garb in between you and them. You have no relationship to the natural world. You can touch nothing. You're also in a fair amount of pain, of course, which does not necessarily reward your paying attention to anything. It's not fun.

"So that was November. At some point in December — maybe it was early January — there were two nurses in particular I felt very close to, and it may have been one of them [who brought me the snowball]. [One was named] Joi Varcardipone. It may have been Joi. It was snowing outside and I didn't know that.

"She had the bright idea of smuggling in a snowball to me so I could feel snow. Man, it was just stunning. What a simple little thing, right? But she put it in my hand, and just feeling the contrast of that cold snow on my sort of crisp, burnt skin — the obnoxious, inflamed skin — and watching it melt and watching the snow become water, the simple miracle of it, was just a stunner for me. It really made it so palpable that we as human beings, as long as we're in this body, are feeling machines. If we're cut off, if our senses are choked off, we are choked off. It was the most therapeutic moment I could imagine.

"I would never have guessed this. First of all, the sensation, just holding that snowball. But also the implied, inherent perspective that it helped me have. *That everything changes.* Snow becomes water. It's beautiful because it changes. Things are fleeting. It felt so beautiful to be part of this weird world in that moment. I felt part of the world again, rather than removed from it. It was potent."

THE POWER OF BEARING WITNESS AND LISTENING

I asked BJ, "If you were brought in as a physician or mentor to someone who had just suffered nearly identical injuries to yours, what would your conversation look like? Or what resources, reading, or otherwise would you point them to?" He replied with:

"I think I've gotten in trouble when I've tried to come in with some predetermined idea of advice-giving. Oftentimes, that's not really what's needed. It's more just the camaraderie and bearing witness. So to answer your question, when I do go into folks' rooms, I'm there and I'll avail myself to any questions they have. But I think most of the power of the visit is just visiting, just being together and sharing this awkward body."

TF: Since chatting with BJ, I've noticed how this applies in many areas. To "fix" someone's problem, you very often just need to empathically listen to them. Even on social media or my blog, I've realized that people *knowing* you're listening—valuing them, collectively—is more important than responding to everyone. For instance, I sometimes put a period before readers' names when I reply to someone on Twitter (e.g., ".@Widgett, that's a good question. The answer is . . ."), so that everyone sees the reply. Even though I can't respond to everyone, it shows I'm paying attention to blog comments and @ replies. It's a simple "I see you."

∗ **If an introverted hospice patient were to say, "Give me one to three things that I can watch, do, absorb, look at, etc., without human interaction," what would your answer be?**
"I guess I'd put a picture book of Mark Rothko paintings in front of them. I would put probably any music by Beethoven into their ears. And I probably would reserve that third thing for staring into space."

✳ Favorite documentary?

"*Grizzly Man.* Any piece of art where I'm not sure whether to sob or laugh hysterically — I love that feeling. Where you just go in either direction, and you're not even sure which is the correct emotion. You're simultaneously attracted and repulsed by something. That was my experience watching that film, so I think it's an amazing piece of filmmaking."

SOMETIMES COOKIES ARE THE BEST MEDICINE

For hospice patients at death's door, big existential conversations aren't always the needed medicine. One oddly powerful alternative is baking cookies together.

"Just the basic joy of smelling a cookie. It smells freaking great. [And it's like the snowball.] You're rewarded for being alive and in the moment. Smelling a cookie is not on behalf of some future state. It's great in the moment, by itself, on behalf of nothing. And this is another thing back to art. Art for its own sake. Art and music and dance. Part of its poignancy is its purposelessness, and just delighting in a wacky fact of perhaps a meaningless universe and how remarkable that is. One way for all of us to live until we're actually dead is to prize those little moments."

✳ Advice to your 30-year-old self?

"Let it go. I do mean to take life very seriously, but I need to take things like playfulness and purposelessness very seriously. . . . This is not meant to be light, but I think I would have somehow encouraged myself to let go a little bit more and hang in there and not pretend to know where this is all going. You don't need to know where it's all going."

" If you're looking for a
formula for greatness, the
closest we'll ever get, I think,
is this: Consistency driven by
a deep love of the work. **"**

" Life is a continual process of
arrival into who we are. **"**

MARIA POPOVA

Maria Popova (TW: @BRAINPICKER , BRAINPICKINGS.ORG) has written
for outlets like the *Atlantic* and the *New York Times*, but I find her most
amazing project to be BrainPickings.org. Founded in 2006 as a weekly
email to seven friends, *Brain Pickings* now gets several million readers
per month. *Brain Pickings* is Maria's one-woman labor of love — an inquiry into how to live and what it means to lead a good life. She often
reads a book a day, distilling the most timeless and meaningful wisdom
worth remembering and sharing. Her quality and output are staggering.

Spirit animal: Standard poodle

BEHIND THE SCENES

Maria has a tattoo on one forearm (much like Ryan Holiday, page 334) that says, "What to Focus On:" with a bullseye-like circle below it. In the very middle of the circle is the word "Happy." From Maria: "This is a piece by the artist Marc Johns, which I had on my wall for years. When I was going through a particularly difficult period in my life, I decided it was one of those simple, enormous truths we so easily forget, and a wonderful incantation of sorts to wake up to. To make it as inescapable as possible in beginning each day, I put it on my arm."

SOMETIMES, THE BEST "NO" IS NO REPLY

"Why put in the effort to explain why it isn't a fit, if they haven't done the homework to determine if it is a fit?" Maria could spend all day replying to bad pitches with polite declines. I think of her above policy often. Did the person take 10 minutes to do their homework? Are they minding the details? If not, don't encourage more incompetence by rewarding it. Those who are sloppy during the honeymoon (at the beginning) only get worse later. For a hilarious example of how to spot-check attention to detail, Google "David Lee Roth Ferriss." Neil Strauss (page 347) will often put at the very bottom of his job postings on Craigslist "Do not email a response, call [a phone number] and leave a voicemail with A, B, and C." Anyone who responds via email is disqualified. Don't succumb to replying to everyone out of guilt. From Maria: **"Guilt [is] interesting because guilt is the flip side of prestige, and they're both horrible reasons to do things."**

ON SAYING NO TO THE SIREN SONG OF MEDIA INQUIRIES

"Maybe appearing on CNN for two minutes will make your grandmother proud, but if the travel and the preparation and the logistics eat up 20 hours of your time so that your writing suffers [and] you will ultimately not be proud of the result, then maybe it's not worth it. Often **I think the paradox is that accepting the requests you receive is at the expense of the quality of the very work — the reason for those requests in the first place** — and that's what you always have to protect."

TF: This is precisely why I have stopped nearly all investing, speaking engagements, and interviews. Maria shared how famed neurologist and writer

Oliver Sacks (RIP) used to put a "piece of paper on the wall by his desk that simply said, in all caps, 'NO!' with an exclamation point. It was to remind himself to decline invitations that took away from his writing time."

✳ What text do you refer to again and again?

"Right now, and this answer might be different in another 9 years, the diaries of Henry David Thoreau. Speaking of this intersection of the outer world and the inner world, nobody writes more beautifully about the immutable dialog between the two than he. There is just so much — and I mean *so much* — universal timeless truth in his private reflections, on everything from the best definition of success to the perils of sitting, which he wrote about 150 years before we started saying, 'Sitting is the new smoking.'"

"All those artists and writers who bemoan how hard the work is, and oh, how tedious the creative process, and oh, what a tortured genius they are. Don't buy into it. . . . As if difficulty and struggle and torture somehow confer seriousness upon your chosen work. Doing great work simply because you love it, sounds, in our culture, somehow flimsy, and that's a failing of our culture, not of the choice of work that artists make." This reminded her of a journal entry of Thoreau's from March of 1842:

"Thoreau writes, 'The really efficient laborer will be found not to crowd his day with work, but will saunter to his task surrounded by a wide halo of ease and leisure. There will be a wide margin for relaxation to his day. He is only earnest to secure the kernels of time, and does not exaggerate the value of the husk.' Think of what a beautiful metaphor this is for not mistaking the husk — the outer accoutrements of productivity like busyness, or a full calendar, or a clever auto-responder — not mistaking those for the kernel, the core and substance of the actual work produced. And he then says, 'Those who work much, do not work hard.' I love that."

> "Ours is a culture where we wear our ability to get by on very little sleep as a kind of badge of honor that symbolizes work ethic, or toughness, or some other virtue — but really, it's a total profound failure of priorities and of self-respect."

To remind ourselves of this "profound failure," Maria, I, and at least six other guests in this book read and recommend *On the Shortness of Life* by Seneca.

MARIA'S HEADER IMAGE ON FACEBOOK, AND A GOOD RULE TO LIVE BY

"This should be a cardinal rule of the Internet (and of being human): If you don't have the patience to read something, don't have the hubris to comment on it."

NOTE-TAKING — DISTILLING THE GEMS

Maria and I have a nearly identical note-taking process for books: "I highlight in the Kindle app in the iPad, and then Amazon has this function where you can, basically, see your Kindle notes and highlights on the desktop of your computer. I copy them from that page and paste them into an Evernote file to have all of my notes on a specific book in one place. I also take a screen grab of a specific iPad Kindle page with my highlighted passage, and then email that screen grab into my Evernote email because Evernote has, as you know, optical character recognition. So, when I search within it, it's also going to search the text in that image. I don't have to wait until I finish the book to explore all my notes. . . . I love Evernote. I've been using it for many years, and I could probably not get through my day without it."

If Maria is reading a paper book and adding her notes in the margins (what she calls "marginalia"), she'll sometimes add "BL" to indicate "beautiful language." I use "PH," standing for "phrase," to indicate the same. We both create our own indices at the beginning of books on near-blank pages, like the title page. This makes review later much faster. For instance, I might have "PH 8, 12, 19, 47" to indicate the pages where I've found great turns of phrase, and I'll add in more page numbers as they pop up.

READING IN MOTION

Maria does most of her long-form reading at the gym on the iPad. Her first choice is an elliptical, where she does high-intensity interval training (HIIT). Plan B for cardio is sprints (which preclude reading, which is why they're Plan B), and Plan C is jumping rope. She travels with a weighted jump rope.

WHEN IN DOUBT, SCRATCH YOUR OWN ITCH

"When Kurt Vonnegut wrote 'Write to please just one person,' what he was really saying was write for yourself. Don't try to please anyone but yourself.... **The second you start doing it for an audience, you've lost the long game because creating something that is rewarding and sustainable over the long run requires, most of all, keeping yourself excited about it....** Trying to predict what [an audience will] be interested in and kind of pretzeling yourself to fit those expectations, you soon begin to begrudge it and become embittered — and it begins to show in the work. **It always, always shows in the work when you resent it.** And there's really nothing less pleasurable to read than embittered writing."

TF: To keep things fun for myself, I include inside jokes and *Star Wars* references in my books that only a few friends will get. In *The 4-Hour Body*, there was one line that drove copyeditors crazy: "Because I'm a man, meng." It's a long story.

✳ **Out of more than 4,600 articles on *Brain Pickings*, what are Maria's starting recommendations?**

"The Shortness of Life: Seneca on Busyness and the Art of Living Wide Rather Than Living Long"

"How to Find Your Purpose and Do What You Love"

"9 Learnings from 9 Years of *Brain Pickings*"

Anything about Alan Watts: "Alan Watts has changed my life. I've written about him quite a bit."

✳ **What is the worst advice you see or hear given in your trade or area of expertise?**

"'Follow your dreams.' It's impossible to do without self-knowledge, which takes years. You discover your 'dream' (or sense of purpose) in the very act of walking the path, which is guided by equal parts choice and chance."

✳ **Three people or sources Maria has learned from or followed closely in the last year?**

"Three writers and thinkers who I came to know through their exceptionally insightful and beautiful writing, and who have since become dear friends: memoirist, novelist, and essayist Dani Shapiro, a kind of Virginia Woolf of our day; science writer extraordinaire James Gleick; cosmologist, novelist, and science-and-society cross-pollinator Janna Levin."

* What is the best or most worthwhile investment you've made?
A very rare edition of Maurice Sendak's illustrated *Poems from William Blake's "Songs of Innocence."*

SHORT AND SWEET

"The culture of news is a culture without nuance."

* If you could guarantee that every public official or leader read one book, what would it be?
"The book would be, rather obviously, Plato's *The Republic*. I'm actually gobsmacked that this isn't required in order to be sworn into office, like the Constitution is required for us American immigrants when it comes time to gain American citizenship."

JOCKO WILLINK

Jocko Willink (FB/TW: @JOCKOWILLINK; JOCKOPODCAST.COM) is one of the scariest human beings imaginable. He is a lean 230 pounds. He is a Brazilian jiu-jitsu black belt who used to tap out 20 Navy SEALs per workout. He is a legend in the special operations world, and his eyes look *through* you more than at you. His interview with me was the first interview he ever did, and it took the Internet by storm.

Jocko spent 20 years in the U.S. Navy and commanded SEAL Team Three's Task Unit Bruiser, the most highly decorated special operations unit from the Iraq war. Upon returning to the United States, Jocko served as the officer-in-charge of training for all West Coast SEAL Teams, designing and implementing some of the most challenging and realistic combat training in the world. After retiring from the Navy, he co-founded Echelon Front, a leadership and management consulting company, and co-authored the #1 *New York Times* bestseller *Extreme Ownership: How U.S. Navy SEALs Lead and Win*. He now discusses war, leadership, business, and life in his top-rated podcast, *Jocko Podcast*. He is an avid surfer, a husband, and the father of four "highly motivated" children.

DISCIPLINE EQUALS FREEDOM

To "what would you put on a billboard?" Jocko responded: "My mantra is a very simple one, and that's 'Discipline equals freedom.'"

TF: I interpret this to mean, among other things, that you can use positive constraints to increase perceived free will and results. Freeform days might seem idyllic, but they are paralyzing due to continual paradox of choice (e.g., "What should I do now?") and decision fatigue (e.g., "What should I have for breakfast?"). In contrast, something as simple as pre-scheduled workouts acts as scaffolding around which you can more effectively plan and execute your day. This gives you a greater sense of agency and feeling of freedom. Jocko adds, "It also means that if you want freedom in life — be that financial freedom, more free time, or even freedom from sickness and poor health — you can only achieve these things through discipline."

"TWO IS ONE AND ONE IS NONE."

This is a common expression among SEALs. Jocko explains: "It just means, 'Have a backup.'" If you have two of something, you will break or lose one and end up with one remaining; if you have one, you will break or lose it and be screwed. One of my favorite Franz Kafka quotes is related: "Better to have, and not need, than to need, and not have." Where can you eliminate "single points of failure" in your life or business? Jocko adds, "And don't just have backup gear — have a backup plan to handle likely contingencies."

EXPOSING YOURSELF TO DARKNESS TO SEE THE LIGHT

"I think that in order to truly experience the light and the bright, you have to see the darkness. I think if you shield yourself from the darkness, you'll not appreciate — and fully understand — the beauty of life."

On July 4, 2016, I texted Jocko to thank him for his service. We exchanged hellos, and I asked him how he and his family were doing. He responded: "All good here. With the exception of the book I'm reading about the My Lai massacre. What a nightmare. Thankful for what we have. . . ."

All of the interviewees in this book have methods for achievement. Most who've been successful for decades also have methods to cultivate gratitude. Remembering his friends who made the ultimate sacrifice in war, Jocko is truly grateful for every sunrise, every smile, every laugh, every breath. He also delib-

erately and regularly exposes himself to the stories of those who have been subjected to horror, misfortune, and darkness. If you're open to reading a "dark"
book to help put things in perspective, *If This Is a Man* and *The Truce* (often
combined into one volume) by Primo Levi are two of my favorites. They were
recommended to me by the illusionist David Blaine, who has Levi's concentration camp number tattooed on his arm. When I asked him, "What did you learn
from the book?" he answered: "Everything."

IF YOU WANT TO BE TOUGHER, BE TOUGHER

**"If you want to be tougher mentally, it is simple: Be tougher. Don't meditate
on it."** These words of Jocko's helped one listener — a drug addict — get sober
after many failed attempts. The simple logic struck a chord: "Being tougher"
was, more than anything, a *decision* to be tougher. It's possible to immediately
"be tougher," starting with your next decision. Have trouble saying "no" to dessert? Be tougher. Make that your starting decision. Feeling winded? Take the
stairs anyway. Ditto. It doesn't matter how small or big you start. If you want to
be tougher, be tougher.

"TAKE EXTREME OWNERSHIP OF YOUR WORLD"

While Jocko was a SEAL Task Unit commander, the SEAL Commodore, who
led all SEALs on the west coast, would hold meetings with all the Task Unit
commanders to assess the needs and problems of the troops, then marshal resources to help them:

"[The SEAL Commodore] would go around the room, because he wants to
get direct feedback from the frontline leaders. These guys are my peers. He'd
ask one of the leaders, 'What do you need?' and the leader would say, 'Well, the
boots that we have are okay in the hot weather, but we're getting ready to be
in a cooler environment. We need new boots, and we need them this week before our next training block.' The Commodore would reply, 'Okay, got it.' Then
he'd ask the next person, who'd say, 'When we're out at the desert training facility and there's no Internet, our guys are disconnected. We really need to get
WiFi out there.' 'Okay, got it.' The next guy would say, 'We need more helicopter
training support, because we don't feel like we're working around helicopters
enough. We really need that.' The Commodore would agree to take care of that
as well. Eventually, he'd get to me.

"The Commodore would say: 'Jocko, what do you need?' and I would say, 'We're good, sir.' The implication is obvious: If I have problems, I'm going to handle them. I'm going to take care of them, and I'm not going to complain. I took extreme ownership of my world. The way that worked was twofold. When I did need something, it was something significant, it was something real. And when I told the Commodore, 'Hey, boss, we need this right here,' I would get it almost instantaneously because he knew that I really, truly needed it.

"You can't blame your boss for not giving you the support you need. Plenty of people will say, 'It's my boss's fault.' No, it's actually your fault because you haven't educated him, you haven't influenced him, you haven't explained to him in a manner he understands why you need this support that you need. That's extreme ownership. Own it all."

A GOOD REASON TO BE AN EARLY RISER

"I'm up and getting after it by 4:45. I like to have that psychological win over the enemy. For me, when I wake up in the morning—and I don't know why—I'm thinking about the enemy and what they're doing. I know I'm not on active duty anymore, but it's still in my head: that there's a guy in a cave somewhere, he's rocking back and forth, and he's got a machine gun in one hand and a grenade in the other. He's waiting for me, and we're going to meet. When I wake up in the morning, I'm thinking to myself: What can I do to be ready for that moment, which is coming? That propels me out of bed."

TF: This story has compelled so many listeners to start waking early that there is a #0445club hashtag on Twitter, featuring pictures of wristwatches. It's still going strong more than a year after the podcast.

POMEGRANATE WHITE TEA AND BEYOND

Jocko drinks no coffee and next-to-no caffeine. His one indulgence is occasional pomegranate white tea ("... which I believe hits your soul pretty well"). But...

"[During] my first deployment to Iraq, we did longer patrols in the vehicles, and I would have—in a series of pouches hanging in front of my seat—a flashbang grenade and then another flashbang grenade, and then a frag grenade, which is the grenade that kills people, and then another frag grenade. And then, the next three pouches were Red Bull, Red Bull, Red Bull."

TIM: "But you're an intense guy, which is meant as a compliment. What are you like on three Red Bulls?"

JOCKO: "More Jocko."

TF: Jocko doesn't want to need caffeine. On a similar note, another SEAL friend who regularly eats only one meal per day sent me the following: "I think it's hilarious when some [special operations] guys get grumpy if they don't have protein powder every 2 hours. I have a huge advantage if I can turn anything into fuel, including garbage, or go without food."

WHAT MAKES A GOOD COMMANDER?

"The immediate answer that comes to mind is 'humility.' Because you've got to be humble, and you've got to be coachable. . . . Later, when I was running training, we would fire a couple leaders from every SEAL Team because they couldn't lead. And 99.9% of the time, it wasn't a question of their ability to shoot a weapon, it wasn't because they weren't in good physical shape, it wasn't because they were unsafe. It was almost always a question of their ability to listen, open their mind, and see that, maybe, there's a better way to do things. That is from a lack of humility. . . .

"We put these guys through very realistic and challenging training, to say the least. If there are any guys who went through training when I was running it, right now they're chuckling because it was very realistic. In fact, it was borderline psychotic. We put so much pressure on these guys and overwhelmed them. A good leader would come back and say [something like one of the following], 'I lost it, I didn't control it. I didn't do a good job. I didn't see what was happening. I got too absorbed in this little tiny tactical situation that was right in front of me.' Either they'd make those criticisms about themselves, or they'd ask, 'What did I do wrong?' And when you told them, they'd nod their head, pull out their notebook, and take notes. That right there, that's a guy who's going to make it, who's going to get it right. The arrogant guys, who lacked humility, they couldn't take criticism from others — and couldn't even do an honest self-assessment because they thought they already knew everything. Stay humble or get humbled."

ON THE IMPORTANCE OF DETACHMENT

"I was probably 20 or 21 years old. I was in my first SEAL platoon. We're on an oil rig in California doing training. We'd come up on this level of this oil rig, and we've never been on an oil rig before. There's gear and boxes and stuff everywhere on these levels, and you can see through the floors because they are steel grating—not solid material. It's a complex environment. So, we come up, and we all get on this platform and, because of the complexity, everybody freezes.

"I'm kind of waiting. I'm a new guy, so I don't really feel like I should be doing anything. But then I said to myself, 'Somebody's got to do something,' so I just did what's called 'high port' with my gun: I pointed my gun up toward the air [to indicate] 'I'm not a shooter right now.' I took one step back off the line, looked around, and I saw what the picture was.

"Then I said, 'Hold left, move right.' Everybody heard it, and they did it. And I said to myself, 'Hmmm . . . that's what you need to do: step back and observe.' I realized that detaching yourself from the situation, so you can see what's happening, is absolutely critical. Now, when I talk to executives or mid-level managers, I explain to them that I'm doing that all the time.

"It sounds horrible, but it's almost like, sometimes, I'm not a participant in my own life. I'm an observer of that guy who's doing it. So, if I'm having a conversation with you and we're trying to discuss a point, I'm watching and saying [to myself], 'Wait, am I being too emotional right now? Wait a second, look at him. What is his reaction?' Because I'm not reading you correctly if I'm seeing you through my own emotion or ego. I can't really see what you're thinking if I'm emotional. But if I step out of that, now I can see the real you and assess if you are getting angry, or if your ego is getting hurt, or if you're about to cave because you're just fed up with me. Whereas, if I'm raging in my own head, I might miss all of that. So being able to detach as a leader is critical."

✴ Who do you think of when you hear the word "successful"?

"The first people who come to mind are the real heroes of Task Unit Bruiser: Marc Lee, first SEAL killed in Iraq. Mike Monsoor, second SEAL killed in Iraq, posthumously awarded the Medal of Honor after he jumped on a grenade to save three of our other teammates. And finally, Ryan Job, one of my guys [who was] gravely wounded in Iraq, blinded in both eyes, but who made it back to

America, was medically retired from the Navy, but who died from complications after the 22nd surgery to repair his wounds. Those guys, those men, those heroes, they lived, and fought, and died like warriors."

* Most-gifted or recommended books?

"I think there's only one book that I've ever given and I've only given it to a couple people. That's a book called *About Face*, by Colonel David H. Hackworth. The other book that I've read multiple times is *Blood Meridian* [by Cormac McCarthy]."

* Favorite documentaries?

"*Restrepo*, which I'm sure you've seen. [**TF:** This was co-produced and co-filmed by Sebastian Junger, the next profile.] There is also an hour-long program called 'A Chance in Hell: The Battle for Ramadi.'"

QUICK TAKES

* You walk into a bar. What do you order from the bartender?

"Water."

* What does your diet generally look like?

"It generally looks like steak."

* What kind of music does Jocko listen to?

Two samples:

> For workouts — Black Flag, *My War*, side B
> In general — White Buffalo

BEHIND THE SCENES

>>> Peter Attia (page 59) introduced me to Jocko. I once witnessed Peter interview Jocko on stage. Peter said to the crowd, "Jocko can do 70 strict pull-ups . . ." and Jocko quickly interjected with, "No, I can't do 70 pull-ups. I can do 67."

>>> Jocko is a big fan of the *Hardcore History* podcast, hosted by Dan Carlin (page 285), as am I.

» When Jocko slept at my house following our interview, my then-girlfriend woke me up the next morning at 8 a.m. with "Ummm . . . I think he's been up reading for 5 hours already. What should I do?"

» The only time I've seen Jocko's eyes bug out was when I told him that I first learned to swim in my 30s. He texted me the following while I was working on this chapter: "Thanks for putting me in this book. . . . One day I will repay you, oddly enough, by tying your feet together and your hands behind your back and making you swim/survive."

TRYING TO GET JOCKO'S SPIRIT ANIMAL

I gave this a good college try. It went on for a while. The closest I got was Jocko's wife's suggestion. She felt like his spirit animal would probably resemble Motörhead's Snaggletooth logo (worth Googling). Here's part of our text exchange:

> Also, what is your spirit animal, if you had to choose one? Could also be plant or mythological creature.

Negative.

What the hell is a "spirit animal?"

> Hahaha... Oh, you're in for a treat.

SEBASTIAN JUNGER

Sebastian Junger (TW: @SEBASTIANJUNGER, SEBASTIANJUNGER.COM) is the #1 *New York Times* best-selling author of *The Perfect Storm*, *Fire*, *A Death in Belmont*, *War*, and *Tribe*. As an award-winning journalist, he has received both a National Magazine Award and a Peabody Award. Junger is also a documentary filmmaker whose debut film, *Restrepo*, co-directed with Tim Hetherington, was nominated for an Academy Award and won the Grand Jury Prize at Sundance. *Restrepo*, which chronicles the deployment of a platoon of U.S. soldiers in Afghanistan's Korengal Valley, is widely considered to have broken new ground in war reporting. Junger has since produced and directed three additional documentaries about war and its aftermath.

"HOW DO YOU BECOME A MAN IN A WORLD THAT DOESN'T REQUIRE COURAGE?"

Elaboration: "In terms of our communities and our society at home, we [thankfully] no longer have to organize young men and prepare them for group violence so that we can survive. That's been the human norm for 2 million years, either from predators or from other humans. . . . If you don't give young men a good and useful group to belong to, they will create a bad group to belong to. But one way or another, they're going to create a group, and they're going to find something, an adversary, where they can demonstrate their prowess and their unity."

THE CALMING EFFECT OF ACTING INSTEAD OF WAITING

"The special forces guys were the opposite [of those in the non-elite divisions]. As soon as they heard they were about to experience an overwhelming attack, their cortisol levels dropped. They got super calm. The reason their cortisol levels dropped was because it was stressful for them to wait for the unknown, but as soon as they knew they were going to be attacked, they had a plan of action. They started filling sandbags. They started cleaning their rifles. They started stockpiling their ammo, getting the plasma bags ready, whatever they do before an attack. All of that busyness gave them a sense of mastery and control that actually made them feel less anxious than just waiting around on an average day in a dangerous place."

THE UPSIDE OF DISASTER

"What's very fortunate, beautiful, wonderful, and also, in a weird way, tragic about modern society, is that crisis has been removed. When you reintroduce a crisis like in the Blitz in London or an earthquake that I wrote about in Avezzano, Italy, early in the 20th century, [things change]. In Avezzano, something like 95% of the population was killed. I'm going from memory, but unbelievable casualty, just like a nuclear strike. . . . People had to rely on each other, so everyone — upper-class people, lower-class people, peasants, and nobility — sort of crouched around the same campfires. One of the survivors said, 'The earthquake gave us what the law promises but does not, in fact, deliver, which is the equality of all men.'"

> "That feeling of 'us,' it buffers many people from their psychological demons."

— Sebastian discussing why unifying disasters and crisis, like 9/11 or the World War II Blitz bombings on London, often results in dramatic *decreases* in suicide, violent crime, mental illness symptoms, etc.

THE POINT OF JOURNALISM IS THE TRUTH

"The point of journalism is the truth. The point of journalism is not to improve society. There are things, there are facts, there are truths that actually feel regressive, but it doesn't matter, because the point of journalism isn't to make everything better. It's to give people accurate information about how things are."

ON MOST "WRITER'S BLOCK" IN NONFICTION

"It's not that I'm blocked. It's that I don't have enough research to write with power and knowledge about that topic. It always means, not that I can't find the right words, [but rather] that I don't have the ammunition. . . . I don't have the goods. I have not gone into the world and brought back the goods that I'm writing about, and **you never want to solve a research problem with language**. You never want to . . . thread the needle and get through a thin patch in your research just because you're such a prose artist."

DON'T USE VERBAL CRUTCHES

"God, I really dislike laziness. . . . There are these clichés like 'the mortar slammed into the hillside.' I just don't want to read that again. Say it in an original way or don't say it. You're wasting everybody's time, including your own, if you rely on these sorts of linguistic tropes."

HIS MESSAGE AT A HIGH SCHOOL COMMENCEMENT

"You guys are programmed to succeed. The hardest thing you're ever going to do in your life is fail at something, and if you don't start failing at things, you will not live a full life. You'll be living a cautious life on a path that you know is pretty much guaranteed to more or less work. That's not getting the most out of this amazing world we live in. You have to do the hardest thing that you have not been prepared for in this school or any school: You have to be prepared to fail. That's how you're going to expand yourself and grow. As you work through that process of failure and learning, you will really deepen into the human being you're capable of being."

✴ **What advice would you give your younger self?**

"I would say to myself, 'The public is not a threat.' When you realize that we all need each other, and that we can all learn from each other, your stage fright goes away."

✴ **What would your 70-year-old self advise your current self?**

"The world is this continually unfolding set of possibilities and opportunities, and the tricky thing about life is, on the one hand having the courage to enter into things that are unfamiliar, but also having the wisdom to stop exploring when you've found something worth sticking around for. That is true of a place, of a person, of a vocation. Balancing those two things — the courage of exploring and the commitment to staying — and getting the ratio right is very hard. I think my 70-year-old self would say: 'Be careful that you don't err on one side or the other, because you have an ill-conceived idea of who you are.'"

WHAT WOULD YOU DIE FOR?

At the end of our 2-plus-hour conversation, I asked Sebastian if he had any parting thoughts.

"Who would you die for? What ideas would you die for? The answer to those questions, for most of human history, would have come very readily to any person's mouth. Any Comanche would tell you instantly who they would die for and what they would die for. In modern society, it gets more and more complicated, and when you lose the ready answer to those ancient human questions, you lose a part of yourself. You lose a part of your identity. I would ask people, 'Who would you die for? What would you die for? And what do you owe your community?' In our case, our community is our country. What do you owe your country, other than your taxes? Is there anything else you owe all of us? There's no right answer or wrong answer, but it's something that I think everyone should ask themselves."

✳ **Most-gifted or recommended book?**

At Play in the Fields of the Lord by Peter Matthiessen

BEHIND THE SCENES

» I first met Sebastian at Josh Waitzkin's (page 577) wedding, who described him via text as: "One of the leanest writers I know. So little bullshit between the muscle."

» Sebastian is a big guy and doesn't look like a runner, but he can move. He has clocked 4:12 for the mile, 9:04 for 2 miles, 24:05 for 5 miles, and 2:21 for a marathon.

» After our interview in my home, I had tea, and Sebastian took a few minutes to fire off emails from his laptop. I noticed him typing with one hand and asked him if he'd injured himself. He laughed sheepishly and explained there was no injury. As it turns out, Sebastian never learned to touch type. He has written all of his books and articles by hunting and pecking with one hand. Incredible.

MARC GOODMAN

Marc Goodman (TW: @FutureCrimes, marcgoodman.net) has spent a career in law enforcement and technology. He was appointed futurist-in-residence with the FBI, worked as a senior advisor to Interpol, and served as a street police officer. Marc heads the Future Crimes Institute, a think tank and clearinghouse that researches and advises on the security and risk implications of emerging technologies. Marc is the author of *Future Crimes: Inside the Digital Underground and the Battle for Our Connected World.*

Sprit animal: Golden retriever

PREFACE
Being wise includes knowing how to defend yourself or disappear when needed. Step one is becoming aware of the threats.

GOOGLE CAN DETERMINE WHO LIVES OR DIES
"The fact of the matter is, back in 2008 [in Mumbai], terrorists were using search engines like Google to determine who shall live and who shall die. . . . When you're sharing on Facebook, it's not just the media and marketing companies that you need to be concerned about."

HOW BUSINESS TRAVELERS OFTEN GET KIDNAPPED
Organized crime outfits are good at bribing airline employees for flight manifests (lists of passengers). They then Google each name, create a list of apparent high-value targets, and arrive early to look for the right names on limo driver signs. They pay or threaten the actual limo drivers, who leave and are replaced:

"The executive flying in from New York, San Francisco, or London would then get off the plane, see the piece of cardboard with their name on it, walk up to the person who was dressed like a limousine driver, get into a car, and get kidnapped as a result. There are actually a few people who were killed."

TF: This is why I use Uber or pseudonyms for any car service pickups around the world. By using a made-up name for your car reservation, if you see a placard with your real name on it, you know it's a set-up. If you become successful — or simply appear successful on the Internet — and travel a lot overseas, this is not paranoia.

PERSONALIZED BIOWEAPONS
Marc and I discussed how criminals (or intelligent lunatics) could use your genetic information, if it's made public or hacked:

"I'll give you a perfect example. There's a medicine called Warfarin, which is a blood thinner. There's a certain small percentage of people that have a genetic marker that makes them allergic to that, and it's deadly if taken. So that would be a perfect example. It's a common pharmaceutical that exists today, and you can't know whether or not someone is allergic to Warfarin by looking at somebody. But if [you have their genetic data], now you have that additional piece of information. You know about it, and it could be fatal."

TF: I spoke about personalized bioweapons nearly 10 years ago with a qualified former NASA scientist. These are real. To stretch your brain on this subject, read a great article of Marc's in *The Atlantic* titled "Hacking the President's DNA." If you're a potential high-profile target, you need to think defensively. CRISPR and related technologies could potentially make the near future a boom era for biological weapons. Keep your genetic data very close to your chest. Even if you use pseudonyms, I've seen companies that can produce facial features from DNA info. It's going to be practically impossible to anonymize.

* Do you have any quotes that you live your life by or think of often?
[Among others]

> "The future is already here — it's just unevenly distributed." — William Gibson

> "If we continue to develop our technology without wisdom or prudence, our servant may prove to be our executioner." — Omar N. Bradley

* What is the worst advice you see or hear given in your trade or area of expertise?
"If you have nothing to hide, then you don't have to worry about privacy, and that we must sacrifice our privacy in order to have security."

* Three people or sources you've learned from — or followed closely — in the last year?
David Brooks, "The Moral Bucket List." Nir Eyal, *Hooked.* Anything by Kevin Kelly, most recently *The Inevitable.*

SAMY KAMKAR

Samy Kamkar (TW: @SAMYKAMKAR, SAMY.PL) is one of the most innovative computer hackers in the United States. He is best known for creating the fastest-spreading virus of all time, a MySpace worm named "Samy," for which he was raided by the United States Secret Service. More recently, he created SkyJack, a custom drone that hacks into any nearby drones, allowing any operator to control a swarm of devices. He also discovered illicit mobile phone tracking by Apple iPhone, Google Android, and Microsoft Windows Phone mobile devices. His findings led to a series of class-action lawsuits against these companies and a privacy hearing on Capitol Hill.

Why is Samy in Wise? Once again, because feeling safe and enjoying your resources isn't solely about offense. It's important to have basic defenses in place. Life is a full-contact sport, and the black swans will come visiting sooner or later.

Spirit animal: Honey badger

BACK STORY

Samy was — perhaps surprisingly — one of my Obi-Wans for the "Dating Game" episode of *The Tim Ferriss Experiment* TV show. In 15 to 20 minutes, he demonstrated how he optimized and automated nearly all of his online dating in L.A. and other cities. Based on all of his data crunching, he told me shirtless pics and animals were "like crack." I didn't believe him, so we tested roughly a dozen of my preexisting profile pics alongside a new, shirtless pic of me with a kitten held over my shoulder. It was an embarrassing, ludicrous pic. Even Neil Strauss (page 502) didn't want it to win. Alas, it did.

MUSIC FOR THE ZONE

To get in the zone, Samy likes to code to AudioMolly.com, The Glitch Mob, and Infected Mushroom. Based on his recommendation, I found some of my current favorites — Pegboard Nerds ("Blackout") and David Starfire (*Karuna*) — on AudioMolly.

✱ **What advice would you give to your 20-year-old self?**
"Stop committing felonies."

TOOLS OF A HACKER

I've often asked Samy, "How can I protect myself against people like you?" The tools below address more than 90% of the most common security threats. I currently use about half of them. This chapter can be dense, so feel free to skim and return to it as a reference, if needed.

If you do nothing else, here's a 60-second precaution: Put tape or a cover over your laptop camera (and perhaps your phone) when you're not using it. Samy explained to me how simple it is to hijack cameras. It's terrifying. This could be used to surveil your house and determine when you're not home. It could also be used to catch you playing patty cake with Captain Winky. Covering it is 60 seconds well spent.

Enter Samy

How to protect your data on your computer and mobile devices, in case your systems are ever stolen or in case you're traveling abroad or across borders

- » **Use BitLocker on Windows or FileVault on OS X.** Your data will be encrypted when the machine is off or suspended. Encrypt your hard drive using "full disk encryption" in order to keep your confidential data protected in case your machine is ever lost or stolen, preventing others from extracting data from your device without the password.

- » **You'll Never Take Me Alive!** is a free tool for Windows and OS X machines so that if the machine is ever disconnected from AC power or wired Ethernet while the screen is locked [**TF: e.g., someone grabs your laptop out of a coffee shop and sprints off**], the system will go into hibernate, preventing a laptop thief from accessing your encrypted data. This requires you to be using FileVault or BitLocker disk encryption.

≫ Use a PIN on your iOS or Android device to encrypt the data locally on the device. While a PIN may seem insecure, your data is typically well protected due to the mechanisms in place to prevent brute forcing of PIN codes onto your device, and the relatively secure (though not perfect) hardware implementations of security within iOS and Android. [**TF: If on iPhone, I'd also recommend increasing your PIN from 4 to 8 characters. If someone is trying to brute-force crack your password, this takes the time required from roughly 4 to 5 days to 100+ days (iPhone: Settings → Touch ID & Passcode → Change Passcode)**]

≫ Don't ever use the same password twice! Differentiate your passwords enough that someone can't guess a password for one site by knowing the password of another. I try to use long but "simple" passwords that are easy to remember like lyrics from a song relevant to the site. A long password, even if mostly English words, is typically stronger than a short password with random characters. For casual, non-technical people, I would suggest using a program like 1Password or LastPass (or KeePass, if you want open-source) to remember all of these. Personally, I use VeraCrypt (below), but it's more involved. The difference between this and a tool like 1Password is that 1Password is built into the browser and if a vulnerability is found, the software itself has access to my passwords the next time I use it. It's unlikely to happen, but there is a small risk.

≫ **Consider using the free, cross-platform tool VeraCrypt.** If you feel you might ever be compelled to reveal a password for your computer such as at a border crossing or by "rubber hose" cryptanalysis (being beaten by a rubber hose until you squeal), you can use "hidden volumes" to hide data with two passwords, providing you plausible deniability. Such hidden volumes are encrypted disks or directories that have one password that decrypts to show various files that you placed and are comfortable with revealing, while a secondary password can decrypt the same folder containing the actual, confidential data you're protecting, with no way to prove whether there's a single password or two passwords for the volume. I personally don't use a second password for any of my encrypted drives. . . . or do I?

Detecting Malware or Software Behaving Badly on Your Computer

» A great amount of software will make outbound connections to the Internet, typically for legitimate purposes, though not necessarily. If you wish to prevent or at least learn when an application is doing this, you can use **NetLimiter on Windows** or **Little Snitch on OS X** to detect and decide to allow or block when a specific application is connecting out, and learn where it's connecting to. You can use **Wireshark** for further analysis, mentioned below.

» You can use **BlockBlock on OS X**, which notifies you if a program is trying to install itself to run upon startup, even when it's hiding itself in a nook or cranny of your system, and you have the clear option to block it if you wish. Some viruses or malware or simply annoying software will try to do this and you can decide if it should run at startup or not.

» Don't plug in any USB device that you don't trust! There are even e-cigarettes that charge over USB that carry malware. If you wish to charge something, it's safer to use a USB charger/adapter [for a wall outlet] rather than your computer.

Anonymizing Yourself on the Internet

» **Tor** is a free, cross-platform software that allows you to browse the Internet anonymously and helps you defend against network surveillance. It will help change your IP address each time you use it as well as encrypt your network communication, however the last "hop" in the chain of Tor will always be able to see your unencrypted traffic, though [it will] not be able to detect your IP address. I would trust Tor over any VPN service as no Tor node knows both your IP and what you're accessing, unlike a VPN, which could be compelled to share that data.

» When you take a picture with your smartphone, it's typically recording your GPS coordinates and other data about the picture, such as device used, into the image. This is called EXIF data and is metadata that's hidden in the image, and anyone can recover it if you send the image directly to them. You can disable storing location in phones on various platforms [**See Settings, Systems Preferences, etc. For instance, on iPhone 6: Settings → Privacy → Location Services**] or use free software after the fact to do this. Search for 'EXIF removal tool' and find a tool for your operating system or mobile platform to do this when you wish to hide your location from images.

» If you want to be particularly crafty, you can use a free app called **LinkLiar on OS X** to spoof or randomize your MAC address. A MAC address is a fixed, unique hardware identifier of the network device within your computer and never changes otherwise. I've also discovered that some large companies track MAC addresses to know the last place you've been, so it doesn't hurt to adjust it every once in a while.

Accessing Interesting Data and Controlling the Websites You Visit

» If a website is delivering images, video, or audio to your computer, that means in most cases you can download it directly, even if the site attempts to stop you. **In Chrome (similar tools exist in Firefox and Safari), you can go to View → Developer → Developer Tools, click on the Network tab, refresh the page, and see all content going across. You can then right-click any file, such as an image that the site wouldn't otherwise let you download, and click Copy Link**

Address to get the direct URL. The Elements tab is also particularly useful. [**TF:** You can also use this to easily copy and paste good quotes that some sites like to prevent you from copy and pasting.]

» Using the same Developer Tools, if a site is ever trying to force you to sign up, fill out a form you don't want to fill out, or otherwise cover the page with obtrusive windows or darkening the page, **you can use the Elements tab in the Developer Tools (mentioned above), right-click on any element in the tab, and click Remove.** Don't worry, if you remove the wrong thing, you can simply refresh the page and try again! You are only affecting the page on your own computer, but this can be a useful tool to adjust a page to your liking.

» **Google Reverse Image Search** is a surprisingly useful tool if you're ever trying to perform reconnaissance, or just learn where an image came from or where else it might be used on the Internet. Simply browse to Google Images and drag and drop the image onto the page.

Tools that Hackers Use

Though I'm not a lawyer, using these tools on a network and devices you have reign over, such as your home LAN, will likely not carry any consequence. The only way to understand the security and insecurity of your own network is to test the same tools attackers would use. I highly suggest those interested in learning use these — both the good guys and the bad guys are using these same exact tools!

» To learn about some of the starting tools a hacker, attacker, or someone just curious about security would use, I'd suggest looking at beginning tools such as Wireshark, Charles (web debugging proxy), NightHawk (ARP/ND spoofing and password sniffing), arpy (ARP spoofing), dsniff (password sniffing), and Kali Linux (penetration testing) and looking up tutorials on network intrusion, sniffing, and man-in-the-middling. Within a few minutes and with a tool like Wireshark, you can start seeing all the traffic going in and out of your computer, while tools like Nighthawk and arpy in conjunction with Wireshark can help you inspect and intercept all traffic on a network!

» To further dive into security, I'd suggest learning to program. It's easier than you think! Learning to program allows you to learn how someone might engineer something and helps you think about how you can then reverse that and exploit it, as if you had created it yourself.

GENERAL STANLEY McCHRYSTAL & CHRIS FUSSELL

Stanley McChrystal (TW: @StanMcChrystal, MCCHRYSTALGROUP
.COM) retired from the U.S. Army as a four-star general after more than 34
years of service. Former Defense Secretary Robert Gates described Mc-
Chrystal as "perhaps the finest warrior and leader of men in combat I
ever met."

From 2003 to 2008, McChrystal served as commander of Joint Special
Operations Command (JSOC), where he was credited with the death of
Abu Musab al-Zarqawi, leader of Al-Qaeda in Iraq. His last assignment
was as the commander of all American and Coalition forces in Afghanistan. He is a senior fellow at Yale University's Jackson Institute for Global
Affairs and the co-founder of McChrystal Group, a leadership consulting
firm.

Chris Fussell (TW: @FussellChris) is a former U.S. Navy SEAL officer, former aide-de-camp (right-hand man) for General McChrystal, and
a current senior executive at McChrystal Group.

Spirit animal: Chris Fussell = Middle-earth elf

"THE PURPOSE OF LIFE IS A LIFE OF PURPOSE."

This is Stan's answer to "If you could put a billboard anywhere and write anything on it, what would it say?" It is a quote from Robert Byrne.

ONE PRIMARY MEAL PER DAY

Stan rewards himself with a large dinner at night and doesn't do well with smaller meals throughout the day.

ON CREATING A "RED TEAM"

STAN: "The concept of 'red team' is designed to test a plan. What happens is, as you develop a plan—you've got a problem and you develop a way to solve that problem—you fall in love with it. You start to dismiss the shortcomings of it, simply because, I think, that's the way the mind works. . . . Sometimes you're actually skipping over real challenges to it, or vulnerabilities in it, because you just want it to work. As we describe it, **sometimes a plan can end up being a string of miracles, and that's not a real solid plan**. So red teaming is: You take people who aren't wedded to the plan and [ask them,] 'How would you disrupt this plan or how would you defeat this plan?' If you have a very thoughtful red team, you'll produce stunning results."

EVERYONE SAYS YOU'RE GREAT, BUT . . .

TIM: "I've heard stories of how you vet people for the McChrystal Group. And I've heard that you sometimes throw a statement out that people need to finish. Specifically, let's say you were interviewing Chris, you'd say, '**Everyone says Chris is great, but . . .**' and then you'd sit there in silence. Do you do that?"

STAN: "I do do that. . . . It puts a person in the position of having to try to articulate what they think the perception of them by others is. Because there is a perception, and often in the vetting process, we'll figure that out because we'll get inputs from other people. But if you asked somebody and you said, 'Everybody loves you but they don't love this about you,' or 'they'd hire you but . . .' [it accomplishes] a couple of things. **One, it forces them to come to grips with 'What is it people don't love about me?' And the second is, they've got to say it to you.** It could be very common knowledge, but if they don't have the courage to face up to it and tell somebody who's thinking about hiring them, that's a window into personality, I think."

TIM: "What are the answers that are a red flag to you, and what are the answers that are not a red flag? Or Chris, if you want to tackle . . ."

CHRIS: "I always like to flip [the usual interview approach] on its head [and say something like,] 'We're a small community. You and I haven't worked together, but I know a lot of your peers, and after this, we're going to follow up with people who like you and who don't like you. No one's perfect, and I have my naysayers just like you do. What will the people who don't hold you in highest regard say about you?'

"To me, the most important thing was that they have an answer. A) It shows the courage to be able to address it, and B) it shows self-awareness that 'I might be top peer-rated and have this great career, but there's somebody out there, and here's what they'd probably say. . . .' They'd say I was self-serving at one time, or I appear too good on paper, or I'm lazy on these types of physical training, or whatever the case may be. Show me that, if you identify it, you're working on it. I don't care what you think about it. I just want to know that you're aware of how other people view you."

✳ Who do you think of when you hear the word "successful"?

CHRIS: "I'll answer it this way, and I don't know if this gets to the exact point. I had a great mentor early on in my career give me advice that I've heeded until now, which is that you should have a running list of three people that you're always watching: someone senior to you that you want to emulate, a peer who you think is better at the job than you are and who you respect, and someone subordinate who's doing the job you did — one, two, or three years ago — better than you did it. If you just have those three individuals that you're constantly measuring yourself off of, and you're constantly learning from them, you're going to be exponentially better than you are."

STAN'S WORKOUT ROUTINE

Stan starts his workout at home, if he's at home:

- » Set of push-ups to max reps

- » 100 sit-ups, 3-minute plank, 2 to 3 minutes of yoga

- » Set of push-ups to max reps

>> 50 to 100 crunch-like crossover (legs up), 2.5-minute plank, 2 to 3 minutes of yoga

>> Set of push-ups to max reps

>> 50 to 100 crossover sit-ups (the first two variations combined), 2-minute plank, 2 to 3 minutes of yoga

>> Set of push-ups to max reps

>> 60 flutter kicks, followed by static hold; 1.5-minute plank; set of crunches; 1-minute plank; 2 to 3 minutes of yoga

STAN: "Then I'll leave my house and go to the gym, because my gym opens at 5:30. It's three blocks from my house."

TIM: "I assume we mean a.m."

STAN: "Yeah. If I get up at 4, I can do all that from 4:30 to about 5:20, then at 5:25, go down to my gym. When I get to the gym, I do four sets of pull-ups, alternated with inclined bench press and standing curls. [One-legged balance exercises are the rest break between them.] Then I'll do a few other things, and I can do all that in 30, 35 minutes. So by 6:15 or 6:20, I can be done at the gym, head back home, get cleaned up, and then start work."

WHY EXERCISE IS IMPORTANT TO STAN

Aside from the self-image and performance aspects:

"It also puts discipline in the day. I find that if the day is terrible, but I worked out, at the end of the day I'll go, 'Well, I had a good workout,' almost no matter what happens. When the *Rolling Stone* article came out, it came out at about 1:30 in the morning. I found out about it, I made a couple of calls, I knew we had a big problem, and I put my clothes on and ran for an hour. Clear my head, stretch myself. It didn't make it go away, but that is something that I do in those situations."

THREE PRACTICES FOR MENTAL TOUGHNESS

The following was in response to "What are three tests or practices from the military that civilians could use to help develop mental toughness?":

STAN: "The first is to push yourself harder than you believe you're capable of.

You'll find new depth inside yourself. The second is to put yourself in groups who share difficulties, discomfort. We used to call it 'shared privation.' You'll find that when you have been through that kind of difficult environment, that you feel more strongly about that which you're committed to. And finally, create some fear and make individuals overcome it."

TF: I think these three elements largely explain the exploding popularity of obstacle course racing like Spartan Race (see Joe De Sena, page 38) and World's Toughest Mudder (see Amelia Boone, page 2).

ADVICE TO YOUR 30-YEAR-OLD SELF?

STAN: "I think up through probably 35, I was very much a control freak, because the size of the organizations I commanded, and I was part of, were small enough where I could micromanage them. I had a fairly forceful personality, and if you worked hard and studied hard, you could just about move all the chess pieces, no problem. **Around age 35 to 40, as you get up to battalion level, which is about 600 people, suddenly, you're going to have to lead it a different way, and what you're really going to have to do is develop people. The advice I'd give to anyone young is it's really about developing people who are going to do the work.** Unless you are going to go do the task yourself, then the development time you spend on the people who are going to do that task, whether they are going to lead people doing it or whether they are actually going to do it, **every minute you spend on that is leveraged, is exponential return.**"

FOR THOSE OF US WHO SAY WE DON'T HAVE TIME TO READ . . .

Stan consumes most of his books as audiobooks, a habit acquired overseas, as print books are cumbersome to lug around on deployment. He probably now "reads" via audio 70% of the time.

STAN: "I learned to run with audiobooks. My mind will stay collected on it when I lift weights. . . . **I also have a little set of speakers in my bathroom. So I go in in the morning, and I'm listening to one book there. I turn it on and [I'll listen] while I brush my teeth, while I shave, while I put my PT clothes on, because my wife's out in the bedroom. . . .** I've found that I go through books very, very quickly, because if you're working out an hour and a half a day, you actually go through books much faster than you would if you just had reading time. . . . I tend to like sweeping history stories of an era that's 20, 30, 40 years, or big projects like the building of the Panama Canal, the building of the Boulder Dam [now known as the Hoover Dam], because they've got a beginning, middle, and end, and challenges. I will also do binge reading. I did seven or eight books on George Washington and other founding fathers, and because they're all mutually overlapping, suddenly you know more about the era, and the new one is more interesting because it's filling in holes. So I'll binge on one subject for a while, and then on another subject."

* Books to read for insight into the realities of combat?

CHRIS: "Well, a classic in the special operations community is *Gates of Fire*, by Steven Pressfield. Really highly read. . . ."

* Stan's most-gifted book

"I have probably given the most copies of a book written in 1968 by Anton Myrer, called *Once an Eagle*. It's a story of two characters, [who both] entered the military during the first World War, and it follows them up through the second World War into the postwar years."

* Stan's favorite film

The Battle of Algiers. It takes about 15 minutes to pull you in, but be patient and stick with it. I put off watching this for months, and I wish I'd watched it immediately after Stan recommended it. This documentary-style film, shot in Algiers, recreates the increasingly violent events of 1957, as occupied Algeria fought for independence from France. It humanizes both sides and is extremely relevant to current events. On top of that, it explores the good and the bad of broader human nature.

" You can tell the true character of a man by how his dog and his kids react to him. **"**

" If you don't believe in God, you should believe in the technology that's going to make us immortal. **"**

SHAY CARL

Shay Carl (TW/IG: @SHAYCARL, YOUTUBE.COM/SHAYTARDS) got his first computer at age 27. He was a manual laborer and uploaded his first YouTube video while on break from a granite countertop job. Flash forward to today:

≫ His SHAYTARDS channel now has roughly 2.5 BILLION views. Celebs like Steven Spielberg have appeared alongside Shay and his family.

≫ He co-founded Maker Studios, which sold to Disney for nearly $1 billion.

Spirit animal: Bald eagle

>>> He has been married 13 years and has 5 kids.

>>> He's lost more than 100 pounds since his overweight peak.

BEHIND THE SCENES

>>> Shay flew from Utah to California for our podcast together. In San Francisco, I roped him into a number of firsts, including AcroYoga (page 52) and getting whipped with branches at Russian baths.

>>> He is an investor in DietBet.com, which I've used with tens of thousands of fans without realizing he was involved. It forces you to put money on the line as an incentive to lose weight, and it works. Those who reach certain milestones "win" and receive a portion of the total pot. Players have lost more than 5 million pounds and DietBet has paid out more than $21 million.

"THE SECRETS TO LIFE ARE HIDDEN BEHIND THE WORD 'CLICHÉ.'"
Shay recalled being on a specific bike ride during his rapid weight-loss period: "I remember exactly where I was. I thought to myself, 'The secrets to life are hidden behind the word "cliché."' So any time you hear something that you think is a cliché, my tip to you is to perk your ears up and listen more carefully." He had heard certain phrases like "Eat more vegetables" a million times, but ignored them for years, as it all seemed too simplistic. Ultimately, it was the simple that worked. He didn't need sophisticated answers. They were right in front of him the whole time. What advice are you ignoring because you think it's trite or clichéd? Can you mine it for any testable action?

LEARNING FROM YOUR FUTURE SELF — AN EXERCISE WE BOTH USE
I asked Shay what advice he'd give his 25-year-old self, and he replied with:
"Maybe I would've said, 'Drop out of college sooner'? But I don't think I would change anything. . . . It's easy to think, 'Well, what *would* I tell my 25-year-old self?' So then I think, 'Well, if I'm 45 and I'm asked that question, what would I tell my 36-year-old self [how old Shay is currently]?'"
TF: This prompted me to share a story with him, which I'll repeat here in

brief. I never write fiction, but one of the only pieces of writing I've lost that made me sad for an extended period was fiction. I wrote a short story about going skiing, retiring to the ski lodge to sip hot chocolate and wine, and ending up seated across the table from a wise old stranger. Several hours of conversation later, this stranger turns out to be my future self. I ask him for advice and he gives me the benefit of his 20/20 hindsight. It was a fun story to write, but — and this sounds a bit weird — I also got a lot of actionable, specific advice by going through the exercise. When I put my pen down, I was somewhat puzzled and thought, "I don't know what I just did there, but it seems like a funky magic trick." I later realized that the story line is similar to a spectacular piece written by Jorge Luis Borges entitled "The Other" ("*El Otro*"). When I told Shay this story, his eyes lit up. He jumped in with:

"What you just explained is exactly what I was going to suggest. Think about how old you are right now and think about being a 10-year-older version of yourself. Then think, 'What would I probably tell myself as an older version of myself?' That is the wisdom that I think you found in that exercise. . . . [If you do this exercise and then start living the answers,] I think you're going to grow exponentially faster than you would have otherwise."

WORK WILL WORK WHEN NOTHING ELSE WILL WORK

Shay is a member of the Church of Jesus Christ of Latter-Day Saints (Mormon). On my podcast, he spoke publicly for the first time about battling and overcoming alcoholism:

"It's not easy to get better. It's tough. Our natural inclination is toward addiction and toward the things that are easy. It's easy to drink alcohol and take away the pain. It's easy to not wake up in the morning and exercise. It's easy to go through the drive-through and buy a Big Mac, right? What are you willing to do that is hard? I remember my Grandpa saying, '**Work will work when nothing else will work.**'"

HOW SHAY CURRENTLY SHOOTS VIDEO

Canon PowerShot G7 X camera and Final Cut Pro X. He thinks of his day as 3 acts and films it in thirds: morning, afternoon, evening. He captures 10 to 15 minutes total, and he never shoots for more than 2 minutes at a time.

TWO APPROACHES TO MOOD ELEVATION

Shay explained to me how posting daily videos or "vlogging" (video + blogging) was cheap therapy:

"Physiologically, I could feel my body was different. . . . Just by sitting up straight, putting a smile on my face, and faking it until you make it, you actually do feel better. There's real power in this."

TF: This inspired me to experiment with short vlogging for roughly 15 days for mood elevation. I made it as simple as possible, using my iPhone for a 10-minute Facebook Live video Q&A. I uploaded the FB videos to YouTube, and it was incredible how quickly a large repeat viewership formed, something I'd never achieved before. As both Casey Neistat (page 217) and Shay have explained to me: It's about the relationship you build, not the production quality. The effects of "acting" more upbeat seemed to last at least 2 to 3 hours.

Shay has another tactic for mood elevation, probably best used outside of the airport:

"This might sound really crazy, but I'll just look in the mirror and laugh at myself . . . break down this wall of being so pretentious about not being able to be silly. I think there's a great power in not taking things so seriously."

✱ Who comes to mind when you hear the word "successful"?

"To me, the definition of success is being cool with your parents, your grandparents [if still alive], and your kids. Being able to navigate the difficult task of dealing with each other as human beings."

CARE BEAR STARE TO $1 BILLION EXIT

"[Maker Studios] just grew like wildfire. It was the first time that you had social influencers coming together. It was like a Care Bear stare, if you will. You know how all the Care Bears get together, and once they link and they Care Bear stare, it's way stronger than just the individual Care Bear power? You get what I'm saying."

TF: What kind of first-of-a-kind group could you gather if you had a gun to your head? Rereading "The Law of Category" (page 276) and "1,000 True Fans" (page 292) might help.

* What would you put on a billboard?

"'YOU ARE GOING TO DIE!'" [**TF:** CAPS are his.]

Shay constantly reminds himself of the shortness of life and inevitability of death. I also build *memento mori* (reminders of death) into my schedule, whether reading Seneca and other stoicism, spending time with hospice caretakers, visiting graveyards (e.g., Omaha Beach), or placing the memoirs of the recently deceased cover-out in my living room.

" If you earn $68K per year, then globally speaking, you are the 1%. **"**

WILL MacASKILL

Will MacAskill (TW: @WILLMACASKILL, WILLIAMMACASKILL.COM) is an associate professor of philosophy at Lincoln College, University of Oxford. Just 29 years old, he is likely the youngest associate (i.e., tenured) professor of philosophy in the world. Will is the author of *Doing Good Better* and a co-founder of the "effective altruism" movement. He has pledged to donate everything he earns over ~$36K per year to whatever charities he believes will be most effective.

He has also co-founded two well-known nonprofits: 80,000 Hours, which provides research and advice on how you can best make a difference through your career, and Giving What We Can, which encourages people to commit to give at least 10% of their income to the most effective charities. Between them, they have raised more than $450 million in lifetime pledged donations, and are in the top 1% of nonprofits in terms of growth.

"You can't make a lousy charity good by having a low overhead."

TF: Will introduced me to GiveWell.org, a site that conducts in-depth research to determine how much nonprofits and foundations actually accomplish (in terms of lives saved, lives improved, etc.) per dollar spent. This avoids the problem of most other charity "rankers," which look at low admin and overhead costs as a flawed proxy for "efficient." Of course, if a charity is doing the wrong things, being financially lean means nothing, hence Will's quote. It's all about real-world results.

According to GiveWell.org in 2016, three of the most effective and impactful charities are:

>>> Against Malaria Foundation

>>> Deworm the World Initiative

>>> Give Directly

∗ Two of Will's philosophical role models

>>> Peter Singer, Australian moral philosopher and Ira W. DeCamp Professor of Bioethics at the University Center for Human Values at Princeton University. His most famous works are the surprisingly readable *Practical Ethics* and *Animal Liberation*.

>>> Derek Parfit, who has spent his entire life at All Souls College at Oxford, which is elite even within Oxford. Derek wrote a book called *Reasons and Persons*, which Will considers one of the most important books written in the 20th century.

"FOLLOW YOUR PASSION" IS TERRIBLE ADVICE

"I think it misconstrues the nature of finding a satisfying career and satisfying job, where the biggest predictor of job satisfaction is mentally engaging work. It's the nature of the job itself. It's not got that much to do with you. . . . It's whether the job provides a lot of variety, gives you good feedback, allows you to exercise autonomy, contributes to the wider world — Is it actually meaningful? Is it making the world better? — and also, whether it allows you to exercise a skill that you've developed."

✳ Most gifted books for life improvement and general effectiveness

Mindfulness by Mark Williams and Danny Penman. This book is a friendly and accessible introduction to mindfulness meditation, and includes an 8-week guided meditation course. Will completed this course, and it had a significant impact on his life.

The Power of Persuasion by Robert Levine. The ability to be convincing, sell ideas, and persuade other people is a meta-skill that transfers to many areas of your life. This book didn't become that popular, but it's the best book on persuasion that Will has found. It's much more in-depth than other options in the genre.

✳ Advice to your 20-year-old self?

"One is emphasizing that you have 80,000 working hours in the course of your life. It's incredibly important to work out how best to spend them, and what you're doing at the moment — 20-year-old Will — is just kind of drifting and thinking. [You're] not spending very much time thinking about this kind of macro optimization. You might be thinking about 'How can I do my course-work as well as possible?' and *micro* optimization, but not really thinking about 'What are actually my ultimate goals in life, and how can I optimize toward them?'

"An analogy I use is, if you're going out for dinner, it's going to take you a couple of hours. You spend 5 minutes working out where to go for dinner. It seems reasonable to spend 5% of your time on how to spend the remaining 95%. If you did that with your career, that would be 4,000 hours, or 2 working years. And actually, I think that's a pretty legitimate thing to do — spending that length of time trying to work out how should you be spending the rest of your life."

THE DICKENS PROCESS — WHAT ARE YOUR BELIEFS COSTING YOU?

The "Dickens Process" (sometimes called the "Dickens Pattern") is related to *A Christmas Carol*, written by Charles Dickens. It is one of the exercises I completed over several days at Tony Robbins's Unleash the Power Within (UPW) event.

My friend Navin Thukkaram is a millionaire many times over and lives a charmed life. He has been to UPW 11 times and told me, even if I missed some sessions, I could not miss the live Dickens Process. It was his main reason for attending every year. It serves as his annual upgrade and reboot. This chapter will give you a rough and simplified outline of my experience.

In *A Christmas Carol*, Scrooge is visited by the Ghosts of Christmas Past, Present, and Future. In the Dickens Process, you're forced to examine limiting beliefs — say, your top two or three handicapping beliefs — across each tense. Tony guides you through each in depth, and I recall answering and visualizing variations of:

>> What has each belief cost you in the past, and what has it cost people you've loved in the past? What have you lost because of this belief? See it, hear it, feel it.

>> What is each costing you and people you care about in the present? See it, hear it, feel it.

>> What will each cost you and people you care about 1, 3, 5, and 10 years from now? See it, hear it, feel it.

Why does this appear to work so well? I asked Tony months later, as I saw persistent personal results, and he sent me the following example via audio text:

"If they are coughing like crazy right now [from lung cancer], how do they keep smoking? They say to themselves, 'Well, I smoked for years and it was never a problem.' Or they say, 'It will get better in the future. After all, George Burns lived until 102 smoking cigars.' They find the exception to the rule because no one knows what the future is. We can make it up, we can convince ourselves it's going to be okay. Or we can remember a past time in which it was okay. That's how people get out of it.

"When we feel pain in one time zone—meaning past, present, or future—we just switch to another time zone rather than change, because change brings so much uncertainty and so much instability and so much fear to people."

The Dickens Process doesn't allow you to dodge any time zones.

Naturally, it's one thing to read about swimming, and another to go swimming. The live process took at least 30 minutes, with Tony on stage and 10,000 people in the audience. I could hear hundreds, perhaps thousands, of people crying. It was the straw that productively broke the camel's back of resistance. Confronted with vivid and painful imagery, attendees (present company included) could no longer rationalize or accept destructive "rules" in their lives. As Tony put it to me later, "There is nothing like a group dynamic of total immersion, when there is nothing around to distract you. Your entire focus is on breaking through and going to the next level, and that's what makes the Dickens Process work."

After you feel the acute pain of your current handicapping beliefs, you formulate 2 to 3 replacement beliefs to use moving forward. This is done so that "you are not pulled back into [old beliefs] by old language patterns." One of my top 3 limiting beliefs was "I'm not hardwired for happiness," which I replaced with "Happiness is my natural state." Post-event, I used Scott Adams's (page 261) affirmation approach in the mornings to reinforce it. Now, I'm well aware how cheesy this all might sound on paper. Nonetheless, I experienced a huge phase shift in my life in the subsequent 3 to 4 weeks. Roughly a year later, I can say this: I've never felt consistently happier in my entire adult life.

Perhaps it's time for you to take a temporary break from pursuing goals to find the knots in the garden hose that, once removed, will make everything else better and easier? It's incredible what can happen when you stop driving with the emergency brake on.

"Being an entrepreneur is being willing to do a job that nobody else wants to do, [in order] to be able to live the rest of your life doing whatever you want to do."

"I usually know when I'm on to something when I'm a little bit afraid of it. I go: 'Wow, I could mess this up.'"

KEVIN COSTNER

Kevin Costner (TW: @MODERNWEST) is an internationally renowned filmmaker. He is considered one of the most critically acclaimed and visionary storytellers of his generation. Costner has produced, directed, and starred in memorable films such as *Dances with Wolves*, *JFK*, *The Bodyguard*, *Field of Dreams*, *Tin Cup*, *Bull Durham*, *Open Range*, *Hatfields & McCoys*, and *Black or White*, among many others. He has been honored with two Academy Awards, two Golden Globe Awards, and an Emmy Award. He is the co-author of *The Explorers Guild*.

NEAR-DEATH CLARITY AND SHIFTING THE BURDEN

Kevin described driving to his first real audition (for a community theater production of *Rumpelstiltskin*) in an old Datsun pickup. The accelerator broke and dropped to the floor, sending his speedometer from 60 to 80. He saw brake lights up ahead:

"I had my wits about me at one point, halfway through, when I realized I didn't want to die. I threw the clutch in. There was never such a terrible whine but [it did engage]. . . . I was able to turn the key off, and I coasted to a stop, pulled over into the emergency lane, and didn't kill anybody. I jumped out of that fucking car, hopped over that fence, and hitchhiked to my audition because I wasn't going to miss it. I left it on the freeway.

"Because I had someplace I wanted to be. I had a place [where] something was going to happen . . . and, of course, nothing did. I wasn't good enough. I didn't have enough skill. I didn't really know about Rumpelstiltskin. . . . But my imagination started to burn with the possibilities.

"I started to fall in love with something. Didn't know if I was going to be able to make a living at it, but I finally got rid of the whispers in my head [from my parents], which were 'What are you going to be?' And I'd say, 'It's none of your business. I'm going to be what I want to be.'"

"When I articulated that I didn't care anymore about what anybody thought about what I did except me, **all the weight of the world came off my shoulders, and everything became possible. It shifted to everybody else [being] worried. Now they're worried. But everything for me, it shifted to a place where I felt free.**"

LET US SUPPOSE . . .

For his role in the film *JFK*, Kevin didn't want to go too far out on a limb with speculation. He wanted to protect himself and his credibility and came up with an elegant workaround:

"When I came to certain things that I was unsure about, and some other people questioned a little bit, I said, 'Oliver [Stone], I'm not comfortable saying this. I would be more comfortable saying, "Let us suppose . . . ," as opposed to "This actually happened."' Because the 'let us suppose' is framing things for people to see. Because if there's no actual eyewitness there, you go, 'Let us suppose this happened. . . .' And Oliver didn't fight that at all, to his credit. He said,

'That's fine. Let's just paint this picture because that's the picture I believe is there.'"

TAKING CHANCES

Kevin described a rare heart-to-heart conversation with his dad, who was critical of Kevin becoming an actor. By this point, Kevin was an adult and had succeeded. His dad was sitting in the bathtub:

"He looked at me and he says, **'You know, I never took a chance in my life.'** I was almost in my own *Field of Dreams* moment. There were some tears coming down. He says, 'I came out of that goddamn fucking Dust Bowl, and when I got a job, Kevin, I didn't want to lose it. I was going to hold on to that, because I knew there would always be food on the table.' And I said, 'There was. There was.' There was really kind of just an amazing moment, my dad sitting there."

"On one level, wisdom is nothing more than the ability to take your own advice. It's actually very easy to give people good advice. It's very hard to follow the advice that you know is good. . . . If someone came to me with my list of problems, I would be able to sort that person out very easily.**"**

SAM HARRIS

Sam Harris (TW: @SamHarrisOrg, samharris.org) received a degree in philosophy from Stanford University and a PhD in neuroscience from UCLA. He is the author of the best-selling books *The End of Faith*, *Letter to a Christian Nation*, *The Moral Landscape*, *Free Will*, *Lying*, *Waking Up*, and *Islam and the Future of Tolerance: A Dialogue* (with Maajid Nawaz). He also hosts the popular podcast *Waking Up with Sam Harris*.

Spirit animal: Owl

BEHIND THE SCENES

Sam and I first met in the bathroom at TED in 2010, immediately after I'd accidentally (truthfully) eaten two enormous pot brownies. I was not prepared for the THC or Sam Harris, and especially not mega-THC *and* Sam Harris.

MORNING "ROUTINE"

"What you should have in your mind is a picture of controlled chaos. These are not the smoothly oiled gears of a well-calibrated machine. This is somebody staggering out of his bedroom in search of caffeine, and he may or may not have checked his email before the whistle on the kettle blew. But I do meditate frequently and certainly try to make that every day [for 10 to 30 minutes]."

ON APPRECIATING THE RISKS OF ARTIFICIAL INTELLIGENCE

"Jaan Tallinn, one of the founders of Skype, said that when he talks to people about this issue, he asks only two questions to get an understanding of whether the person he's talking to is going to be able to grok just how pressing a concern artificial intelligence is. The first is, 'Are you a programmer?'—the relevance of which is obvious—and the second is, 'Do you have children?' He claims to have found that if people don't have children, their concern about the future isn't sufficiently well-calibrated so as to get just how terrifying the prospect of building superintelligent machines is in the absence of having figured out the control problem [ensuring the AI converges with our interests, even when a thousand or a billion times smarter]. I think there's something to that. It's not limited, of course, to artificial intelligence. It spreads to every topic of concern. To worry about the fate of civilization in the abstract is harder than worrying about what sorts of experiences your children are going to have in the future."

EXPLORING "SELF-TRANSCENDENCE"

"Buddha and countless contemplatives through the ages can attest to the experience of, for lack of a better phrase, unconditional love. That has some relationship to what I would call 'self-transcendence,' which I think is even more important. So, there's this phenomenon that's clearly deeper than any of our provincial ways of talking about it in the context of religion. There's a deeper truth of human psychology and the nature of consciousness. I think we need to explore it in terms that don't require that we lie to ourselves or to our children about the nature of reality, and that we don't indulge this divisive language of picking teams in the contest among religions. [My book *Waking Up* is] about the phenomenon of self-transcendence and the ways in which people can explore it without believing anything on insufficient evidence. One of the principal ways is through various techniques of meditation, *mindfulness* being, I think, the most useful one to adopt first. There's also the use of psychedelic drugs, which is not quite the same as meditation, but it does, if nothing else, reveal that the human nervous system is plastic in a very important way, which means your experience of the world can be radically transformed."

MINDFULNESS AND MENTAL CHATTER

"'Mindfulness' is just that quality of mind which allows you to pay attention to sights and sounds and sensations, and even thoughts themselves, without being lost in thought and without grasping at what is pleasant and pushing what is unpleasant away. . . .

"We're so deeply conditioned to be lost in thought and to have this conversation with ourselves from the moment we wake up to the moment we fall asleep. It's just chatter in the mind, and it's so captivating that we're not even aware of it. We are essentially in a dream state, and it's through this veil of thought that we go about our day and perceive our environment. But we are just talking to ourselves nonstop, and until you can break that spell and begin to notice thoughts themselves as objects of consciousness, just arising and passing away, you can't even pay attention to your breath, or to anything else, with any clarity."

✷ What is "vipassana" meditation?

"It's simply a method of paying exquisitely close and nonjudgmental attention to whatever you're experiencing anyway."

TF: Many of the guests in this book listen to Sam's guided meditations on SoundCloud or his site. Just search "Sam Harris guided meditations." Per Sam: "People find it very helpful to have somebody's voice reminding them to not be lost in thought every few seconds."

THE VALUE OF INTENSIVE MEDITATION RETREATS

"In my case, [meditation] didn't really become useful, which is to say it really didn't become true meditation, until I had sat my first one or two intensive retreats. I remember the experience clearly. I'd been very disciplined and had been sitting an hour every day in the morning for a year before I sat my first 10-day retreat. I remember looking back over that year at some point, somewhere around the middle of my first 10-day vipassana retreat, and realizing that I had just been thinking with my legs crossed every hour that I had practiced that year. This is not to say that this will be true of all of you who are practicing meditation without ever having gone on a retreat, but it's very likely true of many of you. . . . A silent retreat is a crucible where you can develop enough energy and attention to break through to another level. . . ."

ON THE POWER AND LIABILITY OF PSYCHEDELICS

In his fantastic and lengthy essay "Drugs and the Meaning of Life," Sam wrote:

"If she [my daughter] does not try a psychedelic like psilocybin or LSD at least once in her adult life, I will worry that she may have missed one of the most important rites of passage a human being can experience . . . a life without drugs is neither foreseeable nor, I think, desirable."

I asked him about these lines in our conversation, and he added:

"The caveat is that I have an increasingly healthy respect for what can go wrong on psychedelics, and wrong in a way that I think has lasting consequences. . . . I think they're still indispensable for a lot of people. They certainly seem to have been indispensable for me. I don't think I ever would have discovered meditation without having taken, in particular, MDMA, but mushrooms and LSD also played a role for me in unveiling an inner landscape that was worth exploring. . . .

"The sense of being a self riding around in your head — this feeling that everyone calls 'I' — is an illusion that can be disconfirmed in a variety of ways. . . . It's vulnerable to inquiry, and that inquiry can take many forms. The unique power and liability [of psychedelics] is that they are guaranteed to work in some way. . . .

"[Ethnobotanist Terence McKenna's] point was, well, if you teach someone to meditate or to do yoga, there's no guarantee whatsoever that something is going to happen. They could spend a week doing it. They could spend a year doing it. Who knows what's going to happen? They may just get bored and wander away, not knowing that there was a *there* there. If I give you 5 grams of mushrooms or 300 micrograms of LSD and tell you to sit on that couch for an hour, you are guaranteed to have a radical transformation of your experience. It doesn't matter who you are. A freight train of significance is going to come bearing down on you, and we just have to watch the clock, to know when it's going to happen. . . .

"If you have a good experience, you're going to realize that human life can be unutterably sublime — that it's possible to feel at home in the universe in a way that you couldn't have previously imagined. But if you have a bad experience — and the bad experiences are every bit as bad as the good experiences are good — you will have this harrowing encounter with madness. It's as pathological as it is in any lunatic who's wandering the streets, raving to himself and completely cut off from others. You can have that experience, and hopefully it goes away, and in virtually every case, it does go away. But it's still rough, and it still has consequences. Some of those consequences are good. I happen to think that it gives you a basis for compassion, in particular for people who are suffering mental illness, that you couldn't otherwise have."

USING THE SKY FOR MEDITATION

Look at the sky while meditating. "Often my meditation is in the afternoon. I often try to do it outside. If you know anything about Dzogchen, you know that Dzogchen yogis often use the sky as kind of a support for practice. You meditate with your eyes open looking at a clear sky or any place where you can see the horizon. I like to practice that way. I don't always get a chance to do it, but I find that it clears the head in a very useful way."

MORE IN AUDIO

Listen to episode #87 of *The Tim Ferriss Show* (fourhourworkweek.com/87) for Sam's thoughts on the following:

>>> What books would you recommend everyone read? (6:55)

>>> A thought experiment worth experiencing: The Trolley Problem (55:25)

CAROLINE PAUL

Caroline Paul (TW: @CAROWRITER, CAROLINEPAUL.COM) is the author of four published books. Her latest is the *New York Times* bestseller *The Gutsy Girl: Escapades for Your Life of Epic Adventure*. Once a young scaredy-cat, Caroline decided that fear got in the way of the life she wanted. She has since competed on the U.S. National Luge Team in Olympic trials and fought fires as one of the first female firefighters in San Francisco, where she was part of the Rescue 2 group. Rescue 2 members not only fight fires; they are also called upon for scuba dive searches (i.e., for bodies), rope and rappelling rescues, hazardous material calls, and the most severe car and train accidents.

BEHIND THE SCENES

» Caroline has an identical twin who was a TV superstar on *Baywatch*.

» Caroline incorporated a lot of Charles Poliquin's (page 74) techniques into her weight lifting training, after she met him through Canadian Olympic luger Andre Benoit.

"SECRETS ARE A BUFFER TO INTIMACY"

"My dad was superconservative. He voted for Nixon. He still believed that Nixon was a great president up until his death. He definitely was a true-blue Republican. I didn't tell him [I was gay] for a long time, until my sister said, 'Why are you keeping secrets? Secrets are a buffer to intimacy.' I said, 'No, he doesn't need to know,' and she said, 'It's a part of your life he's not hearing about, and you're keeping from him. Even though he might not realize it, that is keeping a distance. You need to tell him.'

"She was so right. I told him and was petrified. He was really sweet about it. He was shocked and then sort of struggled and said, 'Well, I know some gay people.' He started listing the gay people he knew. It was really cute."

COOKING AT THE FIREHOUSE

The firefighters of Rescue 2 had to take turns cooking food for the rest of the crew:

"There were three tricks. [First] I remember once, I had a guy come up to me and say, 'You just don't put any love into this meal.' I was so shocked that this big burly firefighter wanted love in his meal, and he was right, actually. I was so sullen about cooking that I didn't. He was a little indignant about that. Now, I try to put love in my meals when I cook.

"The second was to make it colorful. . . . It's very hard for me to do. Everything was kind of gray. And the third was to have three set meals that you make."

PRIDE CAN BE A TOOL

"For me, pride worked because my fear of failure was way greater than my fear of fire. I didn't often feel fear of fire, to be totally frank. I'm not trying to pretend I'm so brave. It's just that I had a bigger fear — humiliation, failure, letting down women. Pride can be a really great motivator."

✱ A book to give every graduating college student?

"I would say *The Things They Carried* by Tim O'Brien. It's a beautiful book by a writer who fought in Vietnam. That book actually got me back to reading. When you go to college, reading gets kicked out of you a little bit."

PUTTING FEAR IN LINE

In the 1990s, Caroline illegally climbed the Golden Gate Bridge, rising to ~760 feet on thin cables. She'd mentioned "putting fear in line" to me, and I asked her to dig into the specifics.

"I am not against fear. I think fear is definitely important. It's there to keep us safe. But I do feel like some people give it too much priority. It's one of the many things that we use to assess a situation. I am pro-bravery. That's my paradigm.

"Fear is just one of many things that are going on. For instance, when we

climbed the bridge, which was five of us deciding we wanted to walk u̲
cable in the middle of the night. Please don't do that, but we did. Talk about
fear — you're walking on a cable where you have to put one foot in front of the
other until you're basically as high as a 70-story building with nothing below
you and . . . two thin wires on either side.

"It's just a walk, technically. Really, nothing's going to happen unless some
earthquake or catastrophic gust of wind hits. You're going to be fine as long as
you keep your mental state intact. In those situations, I look at all the emotions
I'm feeling, which are anticipation, exhilaration, focus, confidence, fun, and
fear. Then I take fear and say, 'Well, how much priority am I going to give this?
I really want to do this.' I put it where it belongs. It's like brick laying or making
a stone wall. You fit the pieces together."

TIM: "Have you visualized the bricks? To someone who doesn't have this
practice, give a suggestion for an exercise — 'The next time you're feeling fear,
do this.' What would you advise them to do?"

CAROLINE: "I actually want someone to partition each emotion as if it's a little
separate block and then put it in a line. Once you assess your own skill and the
situation, often things change. As long as you stop and really look, I think people's lives will change kind of radically, especially for women. Women are very,
very quick to say they're scared. That's something I really want to change."

ENCOURAGING GIRLS

On common parenting differences when raising sons and daughters:

"With boys, there is an active encouragement — despite the possibility that
they could get hurt — and guiding the son to do it, often on his own. When a
daughter decides to do something that might have some risk involved, after
cautioning her, the parents are much more likely to assist her in doing it. What
is this telling girls? They're fragile and they need our help. That is acculturated
so early. So of course, by the time we're women and in the workplace or relationships, that's going to be a predominant paradigm for us: fear."

TIM: "For women who are listening and say to themselves, 'My God. She's
totally right. I was raised in a bubble of sorts. I don't want to have this default
anymore. I want to condition myself to be able to contend with fear and put it
in line.' What would you say to them?"

CAROLINE: "I would say it's time to adopt a paradigm of bravery instead of a paradigm of fear. So, when you have a boy and a girl, or a man and a woman, facing the exact same situation, there will be two emotional reactions to it that are sort of opposite. The man will be trying to access his bravery, and the woman will be accessing her fear."

TIM: "This really underscores something important. Courage takes practice. It's a skill you have to develop. I feel like a coward sometimes. We're sitting here in my house and doing this interview, and on my coffee table is a quote on a piece of driftwood [from Anaïs Nin]. It says, 'Life shrinks or expands in proportion to one's courage.' I literally have this on my coffee table so I see it every single day."

FRAGILITY IS OVERRATED

"I hope no one gets injured, but injury is not as bad as people think. To not do something because you might get injured is a terrible reason not to do something. We can get injured in anything. Just getting into your car is very dangerous. I think we should just put that in its place. Girls are often told, 'Oh, you could get hurt,' and the specter of getting hurt takes on these huge proportions. For boys, that's not emphasized. And yet, girls and boys are physically the same before puberty. They break the same, and they're as able as each other, if not girls being *more* able at that time. The fact that girls are told and treated as if they're more fragile doesn't make sense at all. It primes them to be very over-cautious...."

TF: Two of my favorite lines from Caroline's writing are from her *New York Times* Op-Ed piece titled "Why Do We Teach Girls That It's Cute to Be Scared?": "... By cautioning girls away from these experiences, we are not protecting them. We are woefully under-preparing them for life."

MY FAVORITE THOUGHT EXERCISE: FEAR-SETTING

This chapter details my process of "fear-setting," which I use constantly and schedule at least once per quarter. This is adapted from a chapter in *The 4-Hour Workweek*.

Fear-Setting and Escaping Paralysis

"Many a false step was made by standing still."

—**Fortune cookie**

"Named must your fear be before banish it you can."

—**Yoda, from *Star Wars: The Empire Strikes Back***

Rio de Janeiro, Brazil

Twenty feet and closing.

"Run! Ruuuuuuuuuun!" Hans didn't speak Portuguese, but the meaning was clear enough—haul ass. His sneakers gripped firmly on the jagged rock, and he drove his chest forward toward 3,000 feet of nothing.

He held his breath on the final step, and the panic drove him to near-unconsciousness. His vision blurred at the edges, closing to a single pinpoint of light, and then . . . he floated. The all-consuming celestial blue of the horizon hit his visual field an instant after he realized that the thermal updraft had caught him and the wings of the paraglider. Fear was behind him on the mountaintop, and thousands of feet above the resplendent green rainforest and pristine white beaches of Copacabana, Hans Keeling had seen the light.

That was Sunday.

On Monday, Hans returned to his law office in Century City, Los Angeles's posh corporate haven, and promptly handed in his 3-week notice. For nearly 5 years, he had faced his alarm clock with the same dread: I have to do *this* for another 40 to 45 years? He had once slept under his desk at the office after a punishing half-done project, only to wake up and continue on it the next morning. That same morning, he had made himself a promise: Two more times and I'm out of here. Strike number three came the day before he left for his Brazilian vacation.

We all make these promises to ourselves, and Hans had done it before as well, but things were now somehow different. He was different. He had realized something while arcing in slow circles toward the earth — risks weren't that scary once you took them. His colleagues told him what he expected to hear: He was throwing it all away. He was an attorney on his way to the top — what the hell did he want?

Hans didn't know exactly what he wanted, but he had tasted it. On the other hand, he did know what bored him to tears, and he was done with it. No more passing days as the living dead, no more dinners where his colleagues compared cars, riding on the sugar high of a new BMW purchase until someone bought a more expensive Mercedes. It was over.

Immediately, a strange shift began — Hans felt, for the first time in a long time, at peace with himself and what he was doing. He had always been terrified of plane turbulence, as if he might die with the best inside of him, but now he could fly through a violent storm sleeping like a baby. Strange indeed.

More than a year later, he was still getting unsolicited job offers from law firms, but by then had started Nexus Surf, a premier surf adventure company based in the tropical paradise of Florianopolis, Brazil. He had met his dream girl, a Carioca with caramel-colored skin named Tatiana, and spent most of his time relaxing under palm trees or treating clients to the best times of their lives.

Is this what he had been so afraid of?

These days, he often sees his former self in the underjoyed and overworked professionals he takes out on the waves. Waiting for the swell, the true emotions come out: "God, I wish I could do what you do." His reply is always the same: "You can."

The setting sun reflects off the surface of the water, providing a Zen-like setting for a message he knows is true: It's not giving up to put your current path on indefinite pause. He could pick up his law career exactly where he left off if he wanted to, but that is the furthest thing from his mind.

As they paddle back to shore after an awesome session, his clients get a hold of themselves and regain their composure. They set foot on shore, and reality sinks its fangs in: "I would, but I can't really throw it all away."

He has to laugh.

The Power of Pessimism: Defining the Nightmare

"Action may not always bring happiness, but there is no happiness without action." —**Benjamin Disraeli, former British Prime Minister**

To do or not to do? To try or not to try? Most people will vote no, whether they consider themselves brave or not. Uncertainty and the prospect of failure can be very scary noises in the shadows. Most people will choose unhappiness over uncertainty. For years, I set goals, made resolutions to change direction, and nothing came of either. I was just as insecure and scared as the rest of the world.

The simple solution came to me accidentally in 2004. At that time, I had more money than I knew what to do with, and I was completely miserable, worse than ever. I had no time and was working myself to death. I had started my own company, only to realize it would be nearly impossible to sell. Oops. I felt trapped and stupid at the same time. "I should be able to figure this out," I thought. Why am I such an idiot? Why can't I make this work?! Buckle up and stop being such a (insert expletive)! What's wrong with me? The truth was, nothing was wrong with me.

Critical mistakes made in the company's infancy would never let me sell it. I could hire magic elves and connect my brain to a supercomputer—it didn't matter. My little baby had some serious birth defects. (This turned out to be yet another self-imposed limitation and false construct. BrainQUICKEN was acquired by a private equity firm in 2009, which I discuss more in Real-World MBA on page 250.) The question then became, "How do I free myself from this Frankenstein while making it self-sustaining? How do I pry myself from the tentacles of workaholism and the fear that it would fall to pieces without my 15-hour days? How do I escape this self-made prison?" A trip, I decided. A sabbatical year around the world.

So I took the trip, right? Well, I'll get to that. First, I felt it prudent to dance around with my shame, embarrassment, and anger for 6 months, all the while playing an endless loop of reasons why my cop-out fantasy trip could never work. One of my more productive periods, for sure.

Then, one day, in my bliss of envisioning how bad my future suffering would be, I hit upon a gem of an idea. It was surely a highlight of my "don't happy, be worry" phase: Why don't I decide exactly what my nightmare would be — the worst thing that could possibly happen as a result of my trip?

Well, my business could fail while I'm overseas, obviously. Probably would. A legal warning letter would accidentally not get forwarded, and I would get sued. My business would be shut down, and inventory would spoil on the shelves while I'm picking my toes in solitary misery on some cold shore in Ireland. Crying in the rain, I imagine. My bank account would crater by 80% and certainly my car and motorcycle in storage would be stolen. I suppose someone would probably spit on my head from a high-rise balcony while I'm feeding food scraps to a stray dog, which would then spook and bite me squarely on the face. God, life is a cruel, hard bitch.

Conquering Fear = Defining Fear

> "Set aside a certain number of days, during which you shall be content
> with the scantiest and cheapest fare, with coarse and rough dress,
> saying to yourself the while: 'Is this the condition that I feared?'"
>
> **—Seneca**

Then a funny thing happened. In my undying quest to make myself miserable, I accidentally began to backpedal. As soon as I cut through the vague unease and ambiguous anxiety by defining my nightmare, the worst-case scenario, I wasn't as worried about taking a trip. Suddenly, I started thinking of simple steps I could take to salvage my remaining resources and get back on track if all hell struck at once. I could always take a temporary bartending job to pay the rent if I had to. I could sell some furniture and cut back on eating out. I could steal lunch money from the kindergarteners who passed by my apartment every morning. The options were many. I realized it wouldn't be that hard to get back to where I was, let alone survive. None of these things would be fatal — not even close. Mere panty pinches on the journey of life.

I realized that on a scale of 1 to 10, 1 being nothing and 10 being permanently life-changing, my so-called worst-case scenario might have a *temporary* impact of 3 or 4. I believe this is true of most people and most would-be "holy sh*t, my life is over" disasters. Keep in mind that this is the one-in-a-million disaster nightmare. On the other hand, if I realized my best-case scenario, or even a probable-case scenario, it would easily have a *permanent* 9 or 10 positive life-changing effect.

In other words, I was risking an unlikely and temporary 3 or 4 for a probable and permanent 9 or 10, and I could easily recover my baseline workaholic prison with a bit of extra work if I wanted to. This all equated to a significant realization: There was practically no risk, only huge life-changing upside potential, and I could resume my previous course without any more effort than I was already putting forth.

That is when I made the decision to take the trip and bought a one-way ticket to Europe. I started planning my adventures and eliminating my physical and psychological baggage. None of my disasters came to pass, and my life has been a near–fairy tale since. The business did better than ever, and I practically forgot about it as it financed my travels around the world in style for 15 months.

Q&A: Questions and Actions

"I am an old man and have known a great many troubles, but most of them never happened." —**Mark Twain**

If you are nervous about making the jump or simply putting it off out of fear of the unknown, here is your antidote. Write down your answers, and keep in mind that thinking a lot will not prove as fruitful or as prolific as simply brain-vomiting on the page. Write and do not edit — aim for volume. Spend a few minutes on each answer.

1. Define your nightmare, the absolute worst that could happen if you did what you are considering. What doubt, fears, and "what-ifs" pop up as you consider the big changes you can — or need to — make? Envision them in painstaking detail. Would it be the end of your life? What would

be the permanent impact, if any, on a scale of 1 to 10? Are these things really permanent? How likely do you think it is that they would actually happen?

2. What steps could you take to repair the damage or get things back on the upswing, even if temporarily? Chances are, it's easier than you imagine. How could you get things back under control?

3. What are the outcomes or benefits, both temporary and permanent, of more probable scenarios? Now that you've defined the nightmare, what are the more probable or definite positive outcomes, whether internal (confidence, self-esteem, etc.) or external? What would the impact of these more-likely outcomes be on a scale of 1 to 10? How likely is it that you could produce at least a moderately good outcome? Have less intelligent people done this before and pulled it off?

4. If you were fired from your job today, what would you do to get things under financial control? Imagine this scenario and run through questions 1 to 3 above. If you quit your job to test other options, how could you later get back on the same career track if you absolutely had to?

5. What are you putting off out of fear? Usually, what we most fear doing is what we most need to do. That phone call, that conversation, whatever the action might be—it is fear of unknown outcomes that prevents us from doing what we need to do. Define the worst case, accept it, and do it. I'll repeat something you might consider tattooing on your forehead: *What we fear doing most is usually what we most need to do.* As I have heard said, a person's success in life can usually be measured by the number of uncomfortable conversations he or she is willing to have. Resolve to do one thing every day that you fear. I got into this habit by attempting to contact celebrities and famous businesspeople for advice.

6. What is it costing you—financially, emotionally, and physically—to postpone action? Don't only evaluate the potential downside of action. It is equally important to measure the atrocious cost of inaction. If you don't pursue those things that excite you, where will you be in 1 year, 5

years, and 10 years? How will you feel having allowed circumstance to impose itself upon you and having allowed 10 more years of your finite life to pass doing what you know will not fulfill you? If you telescope out 10 years and know with 100% certainty that it is a path of disappointment and regret, and if we define risk as "the likelihood of an irreversible negative outcome," inaction is the greatest risk of all.

7. What are you waiting for? If you cannot answer this without resorting to the BS concept of "good timing," the answer is simple: You're afraid, just like the rest of the world. Measure the cost of inaction, realize the unlikelihood and repairability of most missteps, and develop the most important habit of those who excel and enjoy doing so: action.

"Productivity is for robots. What humans are going to be really good at is asking questions, being creative, and experiences."

KEVIN KELLY

Kevin Kelly (TW: @KEVIN2KELLY, KK.ORG) is "senior maverick" at *Wired* magazine, which he co-founded in 1993. He also co-founded the All Species Foundation, a nonprofit aimed at cataloging and identifying every living species on earth. In his spare time, he writes best-selling books, co-founded the Rosetta Project, which is building an archive of all documented human languages, and serves on the board of the Long Now Foundation. As part of the last, he's investigating how to revive and restore endangered or extinct species, including the woolly mammoth. He might be the real-world "most interesting man in the world."

BEHIND THE SCENES

I attended the very first Quantified Self meet-up on September 10, 2008, at Kevin's picturesque wood cabin-style home. From that small, 28-person gathering, "QS" has grown into a pop-culture term and international phenomenon, with organizations in more than 20 countries.

SIT, SIT. WALK, WALK. DON'T WOBBLE.

"The Zen mantra is 'Sit, sit. Walk, walk. Don't wobble.' . . . It's this idea that when I'm with a person, that's total priority. Anything else is multitasking. No, no, no, no. The people-to-people, person-to-person trumps anything else. I have given my dedication to this. If I go to a play or a movie, I am at the movie. I am not anywhere else. It's 100% — I am going to listen. If I go to a conference, I am going to go to the conference."

TF: This is very similar to Derek Siver's (page 184) "Don't be a donkey" rule. In a world of distraction, single-tasking is a superpower.

THE DEATH COUNTDOWN CLOCK

"I actually have a countdown clock that Matt Groening at *Futurama* was inspired by, and they did a little episode of *Futurama* about it. I took the actuarial tables for the estimated age of my death, for someone born when I was born, and I worked back the number of days. I have that showing on my computer, how many days. I tell you, nothing concentrates your time like knowing how many days you have left. Now, of course, I'm likely to live longer than that. I'm in good health, etc. But nonetheless, I have 6,000-something days. It's not very many days to do all the things I want to do.

"I learned something from my friend Stewart Brand [founder of the *Whole Earth Catalog*, president of the Long Now Foundation], who organized his remaining days around 5-year increments. He says any great idea that's significant, that's worth doing, for him, will last about 5 years, from the time he thinks of it, to the time he stops thinking about it. And if you think of it in terms of 5-year projects, you can count those off on a couple hands, even if you're young."

TF: One massively successful private equity investor I know uses an Excel spreadsheet to display his own death countdown clock. *Memento mori* — remember that you're going to die. It's a great way to remember to live.

✳ One manual project that every human should experience?

"You need to build your own house, your own shelter. It's not that hard to do, believe me. I built my own house."

WRITE TO GET IDEAS, NOT TO EXPRESS THEM

"What I discovered, which is what many writers discover, is that I write in order to think. I'd say, 'I think I have an idea,' but when I begin to write it, I realize, 'I have no idea,' and I don't actually know what I think until I try and write it. . . . That was the revelation."

THE PROBLEM WITH BEING NOSTRADAMUS

Kevin has an incredible track record of predicting tech innovations and trends. It's a blessing and a curse:

"The dilemma is that any true forecast about the future is going to be dismissed. Any future that is believable now is going to be wrong, and so you're stuck. If people believe it, it's wrong, and if they don't believe it, where does it get you?"

TF: One of his tools for coming up with unbelievable (yet ultimately accurate) predictions is making a list of what everyone thinks is true or will be true, and asking "What if that weren't true?" for each, brainstorming the ramifications.

CAN YOU FLIP THE DEFERRED-LIFE PLAN AND MAKE IT WORK?

"Many, many people are working very hard, trying to save their money to retire so they can travel. Well, I decided to flip it around and travel when I was really young, when I had zero money. And I had experiences that, basically, even a billion dollars couldn't have bought."

"YOU DON'T WANT 'PREMATURE OPTIMIZATION'"

"I really recommend slack. 'Productive' is for your middle ages. When you're young, you want to be prolific and make and do things, but you don't want to measure them in terms of productivity. You want to measure them in terms of extreme performance, you want to measure them in extreme satisfaction."

THE IDEAS YOU CAN'T GIVE AWAY OR KILL . . .

"I became a proponent of trying to give things away first. Tell everybody what you're doing . . . you try to give these ideas away, and people are happy, because they love great ideas. [I'll give it to them and say,] 'Hey, it's a great idea. You should do it.' I'd try to give everything away first, and then I'd try to kill everything [else]. It's the ones that keep coming back that I can't kill and I can't give away, that make me think, 'Hmmm, maybe that's the one I'm supposed to do.'"

TF: Kevin Rose (page 340) does EXACTLY the same thing. I've seen him do it dozens of times.

CREATE A NEW SLOT

"The great temptation that people have is they want to be someone else, they want to be in someone else's movie. They want to be the best rock star, and there are so many of those already that you can only wind up imitating somebody in that slot. To me, success is you make your own slot. You have a new slot that didn't exist before. That's, of course, what Jesus and many others were doing. That's really hard to do, but I think that's what I chalk up as success."

(See "The Law of Category," page 276.)

TRUE FILMS

On TrueFilms.com, Kevin has reviewed the best documentaries he's seen over decades. The counterpart book series, *True Films 3.0*, contains the 200 documentaries he feels you should see before you die, and it is available as a PDF on kk.org. Three docs we both love are *The King of Kong*, *Man on Wire*, and *A State of Mind*.

THE WORST CASE: A SLEEPING BAG AND OATMEAL

"One of the many life skills that you want to learn at a fairly young age is the skill of being an ultra-thrifty, minimal kind of little wisp that's traveling through time . . . in the sense of learning how little you actually need to live, not just in a survival mode, but in a contented mode. . . . That gives you the confidence to take a risk, because you say, 'What's the worst that can happen? Well, the worst that can happen is that I'd have a backpack and a sleeping bag, and I'd be eating oatmeal. And I'd be fine.'"

IS THIS WHAT I SO FEARED?

"Our life is frittered away by detail. . . . Simplify, simplify. . . . A man is rich in proportion to the number of things which he can afford to let alone." —**Henry David Thoreau,** *Walden*

Fear-setting (page 463) is one instrument in the toolbox of conquering fear. Another of my favorites is *fear-rehearsing*—regularly microdosing myself with the worst-case scenario as inoculation. One exchange with Jocko Willink (page 412) explains the value of planned exposure to the "bad":

TIM: "How do you prepare people and condition them, so that they can actually function when the shit starts hitting the fan?"

JOCKO: "The SEAL Teams do a very good job of desensitizing you to horrible situations so that you can deal with it when it comes."

The following is an excerpt from "On Festivals and Fasting," letter 18 from *The Moral Letters to Lucilius*, which Seneca wrote to his pupil Lucilius. The source text is the Loeb Classics translation by Richard Mott Gummere of *Seneca's Moral Letters to Lucilius, vol. 1* (Harvard University Press, 1917).

I reread letter 18 often. Half of the time, you will realize that the "horrible" isn't so horrible, and when it is, you can make it less so with repeated exposure.

After Seneca's writing, I've included a few examples of how I personally implement this:

Enter Seneca

I am so firmly determined to test the constancy of your mind [Lucilius] that, drawing from the teachings of great men, I shall give you also a lesson: Set aside a certain number of days, during which you shall be content with the scantiest and cheapest fare, with coarse and rough dress, saying to yourself the while: "Is this the condition that I feared?" It is precisely in times of immunity from care that the soul should toughen itself beforehand for occasions of greater stress, and it is while Fortune is kind that it should fortify itself against her violence. In days of peace the soldier performs maneuvers, throws up earthworks with no enemy in sight, and wearies himself by gratuitous toil, in order that he may be equal to unavoidable toil. If you would not have a man flinch when the crisis comes, train him before it comes. Such is the course which those men have followed who, in their imitation of poverty, have every month come almost to want, that they might never recoil from what they had so often rehearsed.

You need not suppose that I mean meals like Timon's, or "paupers' huts," or any other device which luxurious millionaires use to beguile the tedium of their lives. Let the pallet be a real one, and the cloak coarse; let the bread be hard and grimy. Endure all this for three or four days at a time, sometimes for more, so that it may be a test of yourself instead of a mere hobby. Then, I assure you, my dear Lucilius, you will leap for joy when filled with a pennyworth of food, and you will understand that a man's peace of mind does not depend upon Fortune; for, even when angry, she grants enough for our needs.

———————

How might you put this into practice? Here are a few things I've done repeatedly for 3 to 14 days at a time to simulate losing all my money:

>> Sleeping in a sleeping bag, whether on my living room floor or outside

>> Wearing cheap white shirts and a single pair of jeans for the entire 3 to 14 days

>> Using CouchSurfing.com or a similar service to live in hosts' homes for free, even if in your own city

>>> Eating only A) instant oatmeal and/or B) rice and beans

>>> Drinking only water and cheap instant coffee or tea

>>> Cooking everything using a Kelly Kettle. This is a camping device that can generate heat from nearly anything found in your backyard or on a roadside (e.g., twigs, leaves, paper)

>>> Fasting, consuming nothing but water and perhaps coconut oil or powdered MCT oil (see page 24 for more on fasting)

>>> Accessing the Internet only at libraries

Oddly, you might observe that you are happier after this experiment in bare-bones simplicity. I often find this to be the case.

Once you've realized — and it requires a monthly or quarterly reminder — how independent your well-being is from having an excess of money, it becomes easier to take "risks" and say "no" to things that seem too lucrative to pass up.

There is more freedom to be gained from practicing poverty than chasing wealth. Suffer a little regularly and you often cease to suffer.

> **"**If something offends you, look inward. . . . That's a sign that there's something there.**"**

WHITNEY CUMMINGS

Whitney Cummings (TW: @WHITNEYCUMMINGS, WHITNEYCUMMINGS .COM) is an L.A.-based comedian, actor, writer, and producer. She is executive producer and, along with Michael Patrick King, co-creator of the Emmy-nominated CBS comedy *2 Broke Girls*. She has headlined with comics including Sarah Silverman, Louis C.K., Amy Schumer, Aziz Ansari, and others.

Her first 1-hour standup special, *Whitney Cummings: Money Shot*, premiered on Comedy Central in 2010 and was nominated for an American Comedy Award. Her second standup special, *Whitney Cummings: I Love You*, debuted on Comedy Central in 2014 and her latest special, *Whitney Cummings: I'm Your Girlfriend*, premiered on HBO.

Spirit animal: Hummingbird

LITTLE-KNOWN FACT

Both Whitney and Josh Waitzkin (page 577) recommend the book *The Drama of the Gifted Child* by Alice Miller.

"IN ORDER FOR ART TO IMITATE LIFE, YOU HAVE TO HAVE A LIFE"

"[In intensive therapy, similar to trauma therapy,] I had to replace a negative thought with a positive thought for 28 days. I got really worried. I was talking to my therapist and a bunch of people in my program, and I said, 'I'm just really afraid that I'm not going to be as funny if I'm not as dark and in pain all the time.'

"It [turned out to be] the opposite, because I waste so much time trying to manage unhealthy relationships and having low self-esteem, and my perfectionism can be paralyzing. **Perfectionism leads to procrastination, which leads to paralysis.** I could go a couple of days without getting any writing done, because my self-esteem was too low. I didn't think I was good enough. Just these old, obsolete messages and survival instincts.

"[Doing the work and therapy] has given me so much more mental energy, physical energy. I have much more balance in my life now, and I'm much more productive and much more vulnerable. As a writer, you have to be vulnerable. Before, I was so overworked, I was such a chronic workaholic that I didn't have a life. **And in order for art to imitate life, you have to have a life.**"

TIM: "That's a really profound statement."

WHITNEY: "**For me, art was imitating art because all I was doing was working.**"

"PEOPLE-PLEASING IS A FORM OF ASSHOLERY"

Whitney wrote, produced and starred in *Whitney*, which aired on NBC from 2011 to 2013:

"I was so apologetic and afraid of people not liking me, that . . . [I] slowed down the writing process and confused employees. In the room, people would pitch jokes, and I would just say 'yes' to all of them, because I didn't want to hurt anyone's feelings. I'd have to go later and change them, and then — all of a sudden — the script comes out and their jokes aren't there, and they feel betrayed and lied to.

"When I first went in to Al-Anon [support group for addiction] I heard someone say, 'People-pleasing is a form of assholery,' which I just loved, because you're not pleasing anybody. You're just making them resentful because you're being disingenuous, and you're also not giving them the dignity of their own experience and [assuming] they can't handle the truth. It's patronizing."

TF: After this conversation with Whitney I reread *Lying* by Sam Harris. The types of "white lies" Whitney describes can be hugely destructive, and Sam makes a compelling case for stopping the use of a wide spectrum of half-truths.

> "Codependence is often used incorrectly. It's when you look to other people to decide how you are feeling."

START WITH "I LOVE YOU"

During the first few minutes of our interview at a friend's kitchen table, I noticed very faint tattoos on Whitney's arm. It turns out they were done with white ink.

"I have a white tattoo on my lower left forearm that says 'I love you,' and I don't think anyone has ever noticed it without me having to point it out.... I was struggling a little bit with patience and compassion. Again, I'm codependent. I grew up in an alcoholic home.... How we survived as children [was by exerting control whenever possible], as though 'if I could just organize my drinks in the right row, I'm going to be fine.' [As an adult] I found myself getting frustrated with people not doing things my way.... 'I don't like the way you're doing things, I don't like the way you're saying that, I don't like the way you're sitting'; just everything . . . 'Is he wearing flip-flops to work?' It was just a way to not focus on myself. **And I think ultimately, sometimes when we judge other people, it's just a way to not look at ourselves; a way to feel superior or sanctimonious or whatever. My trauma therapist said every time you meet someone, just in your head say, 'I love you' before you have a conversation with them, and that conversation is going to go a lot better.**

"It's just an interesting little trick. For 28 days, when I met someone, whether it's the lady at the DMV who's making me wait 2 hours [or someone else], I would just assume everybody is doing the best they can with what they have, which is really hard for a lot of us to accept."

IT'S ALL MATERIAL

"When I first had money—I grew up without any money—I got a car.... It was a Lexus hybrid, and the first day I got it, I filled it up with diesel fuel. I destroyed it. It was awful. I got this great joke out of it, though, a 7-minute bit that probably paid for all the damage. So now, I'm in this place where when something bad happens, I think: 'Oh, good, I can use that.'"

TF: I recently spotted a T-shirt in Manhattan that read BAD DECISIONS MAKE GOOD STORIES. Look for the silver lining, or at least consider sharing the dark lining. It might pay for your Lexus.

BREAK YOUR HEART OPEN, BUY A HOUSE

"There is a difference between getting your heart broken and getting your heart broken open. When it gets broken open, that's where the meat is. That's where you write great characters. That's how you get vulnerable, and it's important. As comedians, we pride ourselves on how tough we are, but we're porcupines. Under there, it's all marshmallow. [And] that's where the gold is. . . .

"I remember sharing in an Al-Anon meeting something that really hurt my feelings. I said: 'He did this, and then he did this . . .' and people started laughing. I realized, 'Oh, my God, this is funny because it's happened to other people, and people are relating and it's resonating.' When you tell the truth about your embarrassing moments and show your shadow, a catharsis happens, which is what laughter is. **I promise, if you just tell the truth and get your heart broken as a comedian, you will have a house.**"

THE MATERIAL IS 10% OF IT

TIM: "If you had 8 weeks to get someone ready to do 5 minutes on stage at an open mic, what would you do?"

WHITNEY: "I would get them on stage the first night [and] every night for all of the 8 weeks, whether they have material or not. . . . The material is like 10% of it. Being comfortable on stage is all of it. So I would say, just get on stage. The first year and a half, two years of standup is just getting comfortable on stage. Your material doesn't matter. . . .

"It took me a long time to realize that as soon as you get on stage, you need to address what the audience is already thinking. . . . I don't know who said this quote, but 'Comedians become comedians so they can control why people laugh at them.'

"The first couple of years, I had to address the last name Cummings in the beginning. Everyone was then like: 'Cool, we don't have to think about this anymore.' Because people were like: 'Did she just say Cummings? Is her last name Cummings?' and then they're distracted. So you have to take it off the table. 'Can we move on here? Okay, my last name is Cummings, now let's get to some other stuff.'"

TF: See Neil Strauss's related strategy for "hater-proofing" on page 348.

WHAT PISSES YOU OFF?

To develop new material:

"What I'd do first is figure out what pisses you off. So people's limitations piss you off, the airport bathrooms piss you off? What pisses you off? Comedy is, for the most part, just an obsession with injustice: This isn't fair. . . . So what pisses you off? Louis C.K. says, 'If you think about something more than three times a week, you have to write about it.'"

WHITNEY'S DEFINITION OF "LOVE"

"My definition of 'love' is being willing to die for someone who you yourself want to kill. That, in my experience, is kind of the deal."

EQUINE THERAPY

One of the most fascinating things Whitney introduced me to was equine therapy, which entails walking a horse across an enclosure with no bridle, solely using body language and intention. She did this at The Reflective Horse in the Santa Monica mountains in Southern California.

"The first thing you do is you pick a horse. There are four horses, all with various degrees of damage. She tells you about each one, and you choose your horse, which already says everything that she needs to know about you. It's like a Rorschach test. Then, the first objective is get the horse from one end of the corral to the other, which is probably half a football field.

"So I'm thinking, 'How do you get a horse with no reins from one end to the other without controlling it?' You can't use treats. I can't use charm, I can't use humor, I can't use intelligence; I can't use any of the things I rely on on a daily basis to manipulate and beguile people. Essentially, you have to use your intention.

"So, you let them know, 'We're going to the other end.' You can use words if you want. As long as you're saying something and meaning it, they're going to buy it.

"It's a way to practice being present and connected and having a consistent intention with these animals that are basically a mirror for your psyche. . . . I've almost learned [more] from that than any other book or therapy I've ever done. . . . Equine therapy is so fascinating because of what comes up, the way that we relate to horses says so much about the how we try to run businesses, marriages, relationships. It's a metaphor for everything, because the way you do anything is the way you do everything."

MAKING COFFEE LIKE A SLAVE

"I do it with almond milk and all-natural sugar. I had this woman come in and take all the carcinogens out of my house, so I'm making my own almond milk like an Amish slave these days."

DAMN, THAT NEIL GAIMAN'S GOOD

Whitney and I both love Neil Gaiman's "Make Good Art" commencement speech, which he gave at Philadelphia's University of the Arts. I've watched the video dozens of times on YouTube during rough periods. Our mutual favorite portion is "The moment that you feel that, just possibly, you're walking down the street naked, exposing too much of your heart and your mind and what exists on the inside, showing too much of yourself. That's the moment you may be starting to get it right." And, yes, I know I've mentioned this before. It bears repeating.

* **Who does Whitney think of as a standup comedy "monster," a true master?**
Bill Burr.

* **Underrated comedians to pay attention to**
   Sebastian Maniscalco (totally clean, no cursing, all performance)
   Jerrod Carmichael
   Natasha Leggero
   Tig Notaro
   Chris D'Elia
   Neil Brennan (co-creator of *Chappelle's Show* with Dave Chappelle)

" Happiness is wanting
what you have. **"**

" Penguins are basically
feathered sausages for
polar bears. **"**

BRYAN CALLEN

Bryan Callen (TW: @BRYANCALLEN, BRYANCALLEN.COM) is a world-class comic and prolific actor. He travels the globe performing standup for sold-out audiences, and regularly appears on shows like *Kingdom* and *The Goldbergs*, as well as in films such as *Warrior, The Hangover,* and *The Hangover 2*. He hosts a top iTunes podcast called *The Fighter and the Kid* with former UFC fighter Brendan Schaub (TW: @BRENDANSCHAUB).

Spirit animal: Forest hen

THE THREE THINGS YOU CAN'T FAKE

"There are three things you can't really fake: one is fighting, the second is sex, and the third is comedy. It doesn't matter who your publicist is or how famous you are, man — if you don't bring the money, it gets quiet in that room fast."

ASKING PERSONAL QUESTIONS FOR LONGEVITY IN COMEDY

"I think the way to write standup, if you want longevity in this business, at least for me, is to start by asking yourself personal questions. I write from this. I ask myself what I'm afraid of, what I'm ashamed of, who I'm pretending to be, who I really am, where I am versus where I thought I'd be. . . . If you watched yourself from afar, if you met yourself, what would you say to yourself? What would you tell you?"

IMPACTFUL BOOKS

Bryan is one of the best-read humans I know. He is voracious, and I often ask him for book recommendations. Illusionist David Blaine credits Bryan with being the first person to get him to read extensively. They met when Blaine was in theater school, and Bryan told him: "The difference between the people you admire and everybody else [is that the former are] the people who read." Here are a few of Bryan's favorites:

"I remember reading *Atlas Shrugged* and *The Fountainhead* by Ayn Rand. That's good fodder for a young man. It sets these bold, stark characters — you could even call them Christ figures — and you think to yourself, 'I want to be that.' Of course, I read Nietzsche. *On the Genealogy of Morality*, etc., where the truths and truisms are really cut and dried in a lot of ways. It's the equivalent of, I guess, intellectual red meat. But then I got into Joseph Campbell — *The Power of Myth* and *The Hero with a Thousand Faces*. Joseph Campbell was the first person to really open my eyes to [the] compassionate side of life, or of thought. . . . Campbell was the guy who really kind of put it all together for me, and not in a way I could put my finger on. . . . It made you just glad to be alive, [realizing] how vast this world is, and how similar and how different we are."

* Most-gifted or recommended books?

"You're going to think I'm plugging you, but I probably have recommended *The Art of Learning* [by Josh Waitzkin, page 577] and *The 4-Hour Body*, I'm not kidding, more than any other books."

WHAT WOULD YOU SAY IN A COLLEGE COMMENCEMENT SPEECH?

"Well, I would say that if you are searching for status, and if you are doing things because there's an audience for it, you're probably barking up the wrong tree.

"I would say, 'Listen to yourself.' Follow your bliss, and Joseph Campbell, to bring it back around, said, 'There is great security in insecurity.' We are wired and programmed to do what's safe and what's sensible. I don't think that's the way to go. I think you do things because they are just things you have to do, or because it's a calling, or because you're idealistic enough to think that you can make a difference in the world.

"I think you should try to slay dragons. I don't care how big the opponent is. We read about and admire the people who did things that were basically considered to be impossible. That's what makes the world a better place to live."

"When people seem like they are mean, they're almost never mean. They're anxious.**"**

ALAIN DE BOTTON

Alain de Botton (TW: @ALAINDEBOTTON, ALAINDEBOTTON.COM) is many things, but I think of him as a rare breed of practical philosopher. In 1997, he turned away from writing novels and instead wrote an extended essay titled *How Proust Can Change Your Life*, which became an unlikely blockbuster. His subsequent books have been described as a "philosophy of everyday life" and include *Essays in Love*, *Status Anxiety*, *The Architecture of Happiness*, *The News: A User's Manual*, and *Art as Therapy*. In 2008, Alain helped start The School of Life in London, a social enterprise determined to make learning and therapy relevant in modern culture.

DON'T ATTRIBUTE TO MALICE THAT WHICH CAN BE EXPLAINED OTHERWISE

"Wasn't it Bill Clinton who said that when dealing with anyone who's upset, he always asks, 'Has this person slept? Have they eaten? Is somebody else bugging them?' He goes through this simple checklist. . . . When we're handling babies and the baby is kicking and crying, we almost never once say, 'That baby's out to get me' or 'She's got evil intentions.'"

"SUCCESS" MUST INCLUDE PEACE

"The very word 'success' has become contaminated by our ideas of someone extraordinary, very rich, etc., and that's really unhelpful. . . . Ultimately, to be properly successful is to be at peace as well."

OFFENSE VERSUS DEFENSE

"The more you know what you really want, and where you're really going, the more what everybody else is doing starts to diminish. The moments when your own path is at its most ambiguous, [that's when] the voices of others, the distracting chaos in which we live, the social media static start to loom large and become very threatening."

DON'T EXPECT OTHERS TO UNDERSTAND YOU

"To blame someone for not understanding you fully is deeply unfair because, first of all, we don't understand ourselves, and even if we do understand ourselves, we have such a hard time communicating ourselves to other people. Therefore, to be furious and enraged and bitter that people don't get all of who we are is a really a cruel piece of immaturity."

THE PROBLEM WITH MOST MODERN PHILOSOPHERS

"Nowadays, philosophers tend to only be employed by universities. . . . When no one will pay directly for your subject matter, that's often a sign that something's gone wrong. . . . Philosophers [generally] don't tell us how to live and die anymore. There are only a few."

✳ Which philosophers would Alain suggest for practical living?

Alain's list overlaps nearly 100% with my own: Epicurus, Seneca, Marcus Aurelius, Plato, Michel de Montaigne, Arthur Schopenhauer, Friedrich Nietzsche, and Bertrand Russell.

* Most-gifted or recommended books?

The Unbearable Lightness of Being by Milan Kundera, *Essays* of Michel de Montaigne.

* Favorite documentary

The *Up* series: This ongoing series is filmed in the UK, and revisits the same group of people every 7 years. It started with their 7th birthdays (*Seven Up!*) and continues up to present day, when they are in their 50s. Subjects were picked from a wide variety of social backgrounds. Alain calls these very undramatic and quietly powerful films "probably the best documentary that exists."

TF: This is also the favorite of Stephen Dubner on page 574. Stephen says, "If you are at all interested in any kind of science or sociology, or human decision-making, or nurture versus nature, it is the best thing ever."

* Advice to your 30-year-old self?

"I would have said, 'Appreciate what's good about this moment. Don't always think that you're on a permanent journey. Stop and enjoy the view.' . . . I always had this assumption that if you appreciate the moment, you're weakening your resolve to improve your circumstances. That's not true, but I think when you're young, it's sort of associated with that. . . . I had people around me who'd say things like, 'Oh, a flower, nice.' A little part of me was thinking, 'You absolute loser. You've taken time to appreciate a flower? Do you not have bigger plans? I mean, this the limit of your ambition?' and when life's knocked you around a bit and when you've seen a few things, and time has happened and you've got some years under your belt, you start to think more highly of modest things like flowers and a pretty sky, or just a morning where nothing's wrong and everyone's been pretty nice to everyone else. . . . Fortune can do anything with us. We are very fragile creatures. You only need to tap us or hit us in slightly the wrong place. . . . You only have to push us a little bit, and we crack very easily, whether that's the pressure of disgrace or physical illness, financial pressure, etc. It doesn't take very much. So, we do have to appreciate every day that goes by without a major disaster."

LAZY: A MANIFESTO

Tim Kreider (TIMKREIDER.COM) is an essayist and cartoonist. His most recent book is *We Learn Nothing*, which I loved so much that I reached out to Tim, and we produced the audiobook together. The essay that follows is excerpted from that book. He has contributed to the *New York Times*, the *New Yorker*, *Men's Journal*, the *Comics Journal*, *Film Quarterly*, and others. His cartoons have been collected in three books by Fantagraphics. He lives in New York City in an undisclosed location on the Chesapeake Bay. He had the same cat for 19 years.

Enter Tim Kreider

If you live in America in the 21st century you've probably had to listen to a lot of people tell you how busy they are. It's become the default response when you ask anyone how they're doing: "Busy!" "*So* busy." "*Crazy* busy." It is, pretty obviously, a boast disguised as a complaint. And the stock response is a kind of congratulation: "That's a good problem to have," or "Better than the opposite."

This frantic, self-congratulatory busyness is a distinctly upscale affliction. Notice it isn't generally people pulling back-to-back shifts in the ICU, taking care of their senescent parents, or holding down three minimum-wage jobs they have to commute to by bus who need to tell you how busy they are; what those people are is not *busy* but *tired. Exhausted. Dead on their feet.* It's most often said by people whose lamented busyness is purely self-imposed: work and obligations they've taken on voluntarily, classes and activities they've "encouraged" their kids to participate in. They're busy because of their own ambition or drive or anxiety, because they are addicted to busyness and dread what they might have to face in its absence.

Almost everyone I know is busy. They feel anxious and guilty when they aren't working or doing something to promote their work. They schedule in time with their friends the way 4.0 students make sure to sign up for some extracurricular activities because they look good on college applications. I recently wrote a friend asking if he wanted to do something this week, and he answered that he didn't have a lot of time but if something was going on to let him know and maybe he could ditch work for a few hours. My question had not a preliminary heads-up to some future invitation: This *was* the invitation. I was hereby asking him to do something with me. But his busyness was like some vast churning noise through which he was shouting out at me, and I gave up trying to shout back over it.

I recently learned a neologism that, like *political correctness*, *man cave*, and *content-provider*, I instantly recognized as heralding an ugly new turn in the culture: *planshopping*. That is, deferring committing to any one plan for an evening until you know what all your options are, and then picking the one that's most likely to be fun/advance your career/have the most girls at it — in other words, treating people like menu options or products in a catalog.

Even *children* are busy now, scheduled down to the half hour with enrichment classes, tutorials, and extracurricular activities. At the end of the day they come home as tired as grownups, which seems not just sad but hateful. I was a member of the latchkey generation, and had three hours of totally unstructured, largely unsupervised time every afternoon, time I used to do everything from scouring *The World Book Encyclopedia* to making animated movies to convening with friends in the woods in order to chuck dirt clods directly into one another's eyes, all of which afforded me knowledge, skills, and insights that remain valuable to this day.

This busyness is not a necessary or inevitable condition of life; it's something we've chosen, if only by our acquiescence to it. I recently Skyped with a friend who had been driven out of New York City by the rents and now has an artist's residency in a small town in the South of France. She described herself as happy and relaxed for the first time in years. She still gets her work done, but it doesn't consume her entire day and brain. She says it feels like college — she has a circle of friends there who all go out to the café or watch TV together every night. She has a boyfriend again. (She once ruefully summarized dating in New York: "Everyone is too busy and everyone thinks they can do better.") What she had mistakenly assumed was her personality — driven, cranky, anxious, and sad — turned out to be a deformative effect of her environment, of the crushing atmospheric pressure of ambition and competitiveness. It's not as if any of us wants to live like this, any more than any one person wants to be part of a traffic jam or stadium trampling or the hierarchy of cruelty in high school; it's something we collectively force one another to do. It may not be a problem that's soluble through any social reform or self-help regimen; maybe it's just how things are. Zoologist Konrad Lorenz calls "the rushed existence into which industrialized, commercialized man has precipitated himself" and all its attendant afflictions — ulcers, hypertension, neuroses, etc. — an "inexpedient development," or evolutionary maladaptation, brought on by our ferocious intraspecies competition. He likens us to birds whose alluringly long plumage has rendered them flightless, easy prey.

I can't help but wonder whether all this histrionic exhaustion isn't a way of covering up the fact that most of what we do doesn't matter. I once dated a woman that interned at a magazine where she wasn't allowed to take lunch hours out, lest she be urgently needed. This was an entertainment magazine whose raison d'etre had been obviated when Menu buttons appeared on remotes, so it's hard to see this pretense of indispensability as anything other than a form of institutional self-delusion. Based on the volume of my email correspondence and the amount of Internet ephemera I am forwarded on a daily basis, I suspect that most people with office jobs are doing as little as I am. More and more people in this country no longer make or do anything tangible; if your job wasn't performed by a cat or a boa constrictor or a worm in a Tyrolean hat in a Richard Scarry book I'm not convinced it's necessary. Yes, I know we're all very busy, but what, exactly, is getting done? Are all those people running late for meetings and yelling on their cell phones stopping the spread of malaria or developing feasible alternatives to fossil fuels or making anything beautiful?

This busyness serves as a kind of existential reassurance, a hedge against emptiness: Obviously your life cannot possibly be silly or trivial or meaningless if you are *so busy*, completely booked, in demand every hour of the day. All this noise and rush and stress seem contrived to drown out or cover up some fear at the center of our lives. I know that after I've spent a whole day working or running errands or answering emails or watching movies, keeping my brain busy and distracted, as soon as I lie down to sleep all the niggling quotidian worries and Big Picture questions I've successfully kept at bay come crowding into my brain like monsters swarming out of the closet the instant you turn off the nightlight. When you try to meditate, your brain suddenly comes up with a list of a thousand urgent items you should be obsessing about rather than simply sit still. One of my correspondents suggests that what we're all so afraid of is being left alone with ourselves.

I'll say it: I am not busy. I am the laziest ambitious person I know. Like most writers, I feel like a reprobate who does not deserve to live on any day that I do not write, but I also feel like 4 or 5 hours is enough to earn my stay on the planet for one more day. On the best ordinary days of my life, I write in the morning, go for a long bike ride and run errands in the afternoon, and see friends, read, or watch a movie in the evening. The very best days of my life are given over to uninterrupted debauchery, but these are, alas, undependable and increasingly difficult to arrange. This, it seems to me, is a sane and pleasant pace for a day. And if you call me up and ask whether I won't maybe blow off work and check out the new American Wing at the Met or ogle girls in Central Park or just drink chilled pink minty cocktails all day long, I will say, "What time?"

But just recently, I insidiously started, because of professional obligations, to become busy. For the first time in my life I was able to tell people, with a straight face, that I was "too busy" to do this or that thing they wanted me to do. I could see why people enjoy this complaint: It makes you feel important, sought-after, and put-upon. It's also an unassailable excuse for declining boring invitations, shirking unwelcome projects, and avoiding human interaction. Except that I hated actually being busy. Every morning my inbox was full of emails asking me to do things I did not want to do or presenting me with problems that I had to solve. It got more and more intolerable, until finally I fled town to the Undisclosed Location from which I'm writing this.

Here I am largely unmolested by obligations. There is no TV. To check email I have to drive to the library. I go a week at a time without seeing anyone I know. I've remembered about buttercups, stinkbugs, and the stars. I read a lot. And I'm finally getting some real writing done for the first time in months. It's hard to find anything to say about life without immersing yourself in the world, but it's also just about impossible to figure out what that might be, or how best to say it, without getting the hell out of it again. I know not everyone has an isolated cabin to flee to. But not having cable or the Internet turns out to be cheaper than having them. And nature is still technically free, even if human beings have tried to make access to it expensive. Time and quiet should not be luxury items.

Idleness is not just a vacation, an indulgence, or a vice: It is as indispensable to the brain as vitamin D is to the body, and deprived of it we suffer a mental affliction as disfiguring as rickets. The space and quiet that idleness provides is a necessary condition for standing back from life and seeing it whole, for making unexpected connections and waiting for the wild summer lightning strikes of inspiration — it is, paradoxically, necessary to getting any work done. "Idle dreaming is often the essence of what we do," writes Thomas Pynchon in his essay on Sloth. Archimedes' "Eureka" in the bath, Newton's apple, Jekyll and Hyde, the benzine ring: history is full of stories of inspirations that came in idle moments and dreams. It almost makes you wonder whether loafers, goldbrickers, and no-accounts aren't responsible for more of the world's great ideas, inventions, and masterpieces than the hardworking.

"The goal of the future is full unemployment, so we can play. That's why we have to destroy the present politico-economic system." This may sound like the pronouncement of some bong-smoking anarchist, but it was in fact Arthur C. Clarke, who found time between scuba diving and pinball games to write *Childhood's End* and think up communications satellites. Ted Rall recently wrote a column proposing that we divorce income from work, giving each citizen a guaranteed paycheck, which sounds like the kind of lunatic notion that'll be a basic human right in about a century, like abolition, universal suffrage, and 8-hour workdays. I know how heretical it sounds in America, but there's really no reason we shouldn't regard drudgery as an evil to rid the world of if possible, like polio. It was the Puritans who perverted work into a virtue, evidently forgetting that God invented it as a punishment. Now that the old taskmaster is out of office, maybe we could all take a long smoke break.

I suppose the world would soon slide to ruin if everyone behaved like me. But I would suggest that an ideal human life lies somewhere between my own defiant indolence and the rest of the world's endless frenetic hustle. My own life has admittedly been absurdly cushy. But my privileged position outside the hive may have given me a unique perspective on it. It's like being the designated driver at a bar: When you're not drinking, you can see drunkenness more clearly than those actually experiencing it. Unfortunately the only advice I have to offer the Busy is as unwelcome as the advice you'd give the Drunk. I'm not suggesting everyone quit their jobs — just maybe take the rest of the day off. Go play some skee-ball. Fuck in the middle of the afternoon. Take your daughter to a matinee. My role in life is to be a bad influence, the kid standing outside the classroom window making faces at you at your desk, urging you to just this once to make some excuse and get out of there, come outside and play.

Even though my own resolute idleness has mostly been a luxury rather than a virtue, I did make a conscious decision, a long time ago, to choose time over money, since you can always make more money. And I've always understood that the best investment of my limited time on earth is to spend it with people I love. I suppose it's possible I'll lie on my deathbed regretting that I didn't work harder, write more, and say everything I had to say, but I think what I'll really wish is that I could have one more round of Delanceys with Nick, another long late-night talk with Lauren, one last good hard laugh with Harold. Life is too short to be busy.

CAL FUSSMAN

Cal Fussman (TW: @CALFUSSMAN, CALFUSSMAN.COM) is a *New York Times* best-selling author and a writer-at-large for *Esquire* magazine, where he is best known for being a primary writer of the *What I've Learned* feature. The *Austin Chronicle* has described Cal's interviewing skills as "peerless." He has transformed oral history into an art form, conducting probing interviews with icons who have shaped the last 50 years of world history: Mikhail Gorbachev, Jimmy Carter, Ted Kennedy, Jeff Bezos, Richard Branson, Jack Welch, Robert De Niro, Clint Eastwood, Al Pacino, George Clooney, Leonardo DiCaprio, Tom Hanks, Bruce Springsteen, Dr. Dre, Quincy Jones, Woody Allen, Barbara Walters, Pelé, Yao Ming, Serena Williams, John Wooden, Muhammad Ali, and countless others.

Born in Brooklyn, Cal spent 10 straight years traveling the world, swimming over 18-foot tiger sharks, rolling around with mountain gorillas in Rwanda, and searching for gold in the Amazon. He has also made himself a guinea pig — Cal has boxed against world champion Julio César Chávez and served as a sommelier atop the World Trade Center. He now lives with his wife, who he met while on a quest to discover the world's most beautiful beach, and his three children in Los Angeles, where he spends every morning eating breakfast with Larry King.

Spirit animal: Sponge

PREFACE

Writing this short profile was a real challenge. Cal's strength is long stories that last 10 to 15 minutes and then—*BAM!*—hit you like a tidal wave of emotion. He's a master. When I told my podcast listeners that I was doing a second interview with Cal, dozens replied with some variation of "Please just let Cal talk for 3 hours. I could listen to him tell stories forever." I highly recommend listening to both of Cal's episodes. They will make your spine tingle.

DINNER AT THE BAR, A TICKET ACROSS THE WORLD

Cal first felt like he'd hit the big time when he got a job at *Inside Sports* in New York City. There, he was able to do shots with Hunter S. Thompson and trade stories with Pulitzer Prize–winning journalists:

"I was only a kid. I was 22. Every night, everybody would go across the street to a bar called The Cowboy. At the time, I had no money. They would put out these little hors d'oeuvres, and that was where my dinner would be, if the guys with expense accounts weren't going out later. . . . *Inside Sports* wasn't a job, it was an experience. It was an event every evening. Who's coming tonight?"

Inside Sports was an artistic success but not a commercial one. It went belly up, and Cal was out of a job and largely out of money:

"I didn't know what to do, so I called up my mom and dad. I said: 'You know, I think I'm going to take some time off and travel,' and my mom, who's always really supportive, said 'Oh, Cal, that's wonderful.' Little did she know when I said it that I wasn't coming back for 10 years. But I didn't know it, either. I just bought a ticket to go over to Europe, left with a few guys, and that started a 10-year odyssey of 'Cal going around the world.'"

THE MAGIC OF GOULASH

"The trip down the aisle [on a bus or train, during his travels] was where all the stakes were. Because as I'm going down that aisle, I've got to look for an empty seat next to somebody who seems interesting. Somebody I can trust, somebody who might be able to trust me. The stakes are high because I know that at the end of that ride, wherever it was going, that person had to invite me to their home. Because I had no money to spend night after night in a hotel."

The clincher question Cal used to get free room and board around Europe as a poor traveler was: "Can you tell me: How do you make the perfect goulash?" He would purposefully sit down next to grandmas, who would then pour out their souls. After a few minutes of passionate pantomiming, people would come from around the train to help translate, no matter the country. Cal never had to worry about where he was spending the night.

"During [one dinner party a grandma threw in Hungary to feed me goulash,] one of the neighbors says, 'Have you ever tasted apricot brandy? Because nobody makes apricot brandy like my father. He lives a half an hour away. You've got to come to taste the apricot brandy.' That weekend, we're tasting apricot brandy, having a great time. Another party starts, another neighbor comes over to me. 'Have you ever been to Kiskunhalas, the paprika capital of the world? You cannot leave Hungary without visiting Kiskunhalas.' Now we're off to Kiskunhalas. I'm telling you, a single question about goulash could get me 6 weeks of lodging and meals, and that's how I got passed around the world. 10 years. *10 years.*"

AIM FOR THE HEART, NOT THE HEAD

"Lesson number one, when people ask me what [interviewing] tips would I give, is aim for the heart, not the head. Once you get the heart, you can go to the head. Once you get the heart and the head, then you'll have a pathway to the soul."

BE DIFFERENT, NOT JUST "BETTER"

Cal was able to get ~30 minutes with Mikhail Gorbachev in his prime, even after a publicist allotted him 2 and a half. How? "Go to the heart with the first question." Here's the beginning of the story:

"So the publicist leads me into the room, and at this point I'm thinking, 'Okay, if it's 2 and a half minutes, just do your best.' I look up and there he is, Gorby. He's a little older than I remember, about 77 at the time. He was in town to speak about nuclear weapons and why they should be abolished. We sit down. I'm looking at him, and I just know he's expecting my first question to be about nuclear arms, world politics, perestroika, Ronald Reagan. He's just ready. So I looked at him and I said: 'What's the best lesson your father ever taught you?' He is surprised, pleasantly surprised. He looks up and he doesn't answer. He's thinking about this. It's as if, after a little while, he's seeing this movie of his past on the ceiling, and he starts to tell me this story. It's a story about the day his dad was called to go fight in World War II. See, Gorbachev lived on a farm, and it was a long distance between this farm and the town where Gorbachev's dad had to join the other men to go off to war. . . ."

"DON'T PANIC. LET THE SILENCE DO THE WORK."

This was Cal's advice to me, when I mentioned that I sometimes panic and jump in if an interviewee freezes — seemingly stumped — after a question. Another quote that has helped me to be calm in such situations is from Krista Tippett, host of the public radio program and podcast *On Being*: "Listening is about being present, not just being quiet."

A QUESTION CAL SUGGESTS ASKING PEOPLE MORE OFTEN

"What are some of the choices you've made that made you who you are?"

"THE GOOD SHIT STICKS"

Cal once asked Harry Crews, novelist and author of *A Feast of Snakes* and *Car*, how he could remember anything, given how much booze and drugs he consumed. Harry kept no diary. His response was, "Boy, the good shit sticks." This was what Cal recalled decades later, when he lost an entire box of research notes in his basement — they'd been soaked by a rainstorm and the pages turned black. Cal's ultimate piece, written from memory and titled "Drinking at 1,300 Feet," is incredible. It won a James Beard Award, which is akin to an Oscar in the food world. One of the starting lines in the piece is: "We all know the feeling of wanting to do something so well and so badly that we try too hard and can't do it at all."

SO, YOU WANT TO WRITE A BOOK?

Cal described why he sometimes gifts Gabriel García Márquez's *One Hundred Years of Solitude* to would-be writers: "If you've never written a book and you're going to tell somebody you want to write a great book, all right. Read this and know what a great book is."

IF YOU WERE A BILLIONAIRE . . .

I asked Cal, "If you were a billionaire and could give 2 to 3 books to every graduating high school senior in the country this year, what would they be?" His answer (updated since the podcast) is: "For everyone: *How to Win Friends and Influence People* by Dale Carnegie. For females: *West with the Night* by Beryl Markham. For males: *The Right Stuff* by Tom Wolfe. That's a good start for a journey."

＊ **What would you put on a billboard?**
"LISTEN."

JOSHUA SKENES

Joshua Skenes (IG: @SAISONSF, SAISONSF.COM) has become famous for his use of fire. As chef-owner of Saison in San Francisco (three Michelin stars), he has classical training and loves his high-end Japanese Nenohi knives, but nothing captures his imagination quite like the open flame. The back of his business card sports three words, stark on ivory stock: PLAY WITH FIRE.

REMEMBER "THE GOOD SHIT STICKS"?

Josh had to embrace Cal Fussman's philosophy (page 495) when he moved his restaurant Saison in the early days. There was a sewage flood that overtook the entire restaurant the day of their move, and all of his hand-written recipe books were destroyed. Josh had to look on the bright side:

. "But, we were moving to a new space, so there was a positive spin. I thought, 'Fuck it—we're just going to start over.' It's the same thing that we started with [before opening the first time]. It's all up here [in his head]." He reinvented Saison with no original notebooks but also no baggage. It became the first restaurant in San Francisco history to earn three Michelin stars (alongside Benu).

＊ What's the best decision you've made with your new restaurant space?

"We were starting over, actually. I think the best decision I made was just to say, 'Let's really start over. **Let's just completely empty our cup here and really think about what is valuable to me now. What's honest. What's sincere about what we're doing?** Let's do that.' That's still the driver of Saison now."

＊ Most-gifted or recommended books?

   Cocktail Techniques by Kazuo Uyeda

   The Dao of Taijiquan by Tsung Hwa Jou

RICK RUBIN

Rick Rubin has been called "the most important [music] producer of the last 20 years" by MTV. Rick's résumé includes everyone from Johnny Cash to Jay Z. His metal artists include groups like Black Sabbath, Slayer, System of a Down, Metallica, Rage Against the Machine, and Linkin Park. He's worked with pop artists like Shakira, Adele, Sheryl Crow, Lana Del Rey, and Lady Gaga. He's also been credited with helping to popularize hip-hop with artists like LL Cool J, the Beastie Boys, Eminem, Jay Z, and Kanye West. And that's just the tip of the iceberg.

Spirit animal: Polar bear

BEHIND THE SCENES

» Rick agreed to do the podcast only if we did it in his excruciatingly hot barrel sauna (see page 45). I'd joined Rick a dozen times for sauna and ice bath sessions, but never with electronics. Extensive homework ensued, and I thought of everything... except for the mics. They got so scalding to the touch that we needed to wrap them in towels.

» Rick was introduced to regular sauna use by Chris Chelios, a friend and former professional hockey player. Chris had one of the longer careers of any NHL player, competing until he was 48. He played the most games of any active player in the NHL, and holds the record for most games played in the NHL by a defenseman. Chris largely credits his sports longevity, and general lack of illness, to daily sauna use.

» Rick wears a T-shirt, shorts, and flip-flops everywhere. If a restaurant requires a different dress code, he doesn't go.

» Rick and Kelly Starrett (page 122) were the first people to introduce me to the incredible ChiliPad (page 139)

» Adele effectively scrapped the first version of her *25* album based on, among other things, Rick's feedback. She "went back to the drawing board" and began again. The new and improved *25* became the world's best-selling album of 2015.

THE CLEANSING POWER OF COLD

"Often, exercise will make me feel better, meditating will make me feel better, but the ice bath is the greatest of all. It's just magic — sauna, ice, back and forth. By the end of the fourth, or fifth, or sixth round of being in an ice tub, there is nothing in the world that bothers you."

20 MINUTES OF SUN IN THE MORNING

Rick has lost more than 100 pounds since his peak weight. He has completely physically remodeled himself, can kick my ass in paddleboarding, and credits Dr. Phil Maffetone with many critical changes, including improving his circadian rhythm. Rick now typically wakes between 7:30 and 8:30 a.m., reversing a lifetime of nocturnal living. What did it? "When I was in college [at NYU], I never took a class before 3 p.m., because I knew I wouldn't go. . . . [Before meeting Dr. Maffetone] I slept with blackout blinds, and I usually didn't leave the house until the sun was setting. He said, 'From now on, when you wake up, I want you to go outside. As soon as you wake up, open the blinds, and go outside, naked if possible, and be in the sun for 20 minutes.'"

TF: I now do my morning meditation outside and shirtless whenever possible. I tried naked but nearly got kicked out of a Parisian hotel, as my "private" courtyard turned out to be shared. *Bonjour!*

"THE BEST ART DIVIDES THE AUDIENCE"

I first saw Rick's name in a cassette insert for the very first heavy metal album I bought: Slayer's *Reign in Blood*. I asked him about signing them:

"When we signed [Slayer], there was this terrible fear. . . . They were doing their first album for a major label, [and the fear was that] they were going to sell out. . . . I always liked extreme things, and they were extreme, and I wanted to maximize it. I didn't want to water it down — the idea of watering things down for a mainstream audience, I don't think it applies. I think people want things that are really passionate, and often, the best version they could be is not for everybody. . . . **The best art divides the audience.** If you put out a record, and half the people who hear it absolutely love it, and half the people who hear it absolutely hate it, you've done well, because it's pushing that boundary."

✻ Advice to your younger self?

"**To be kinder to myself, because I think I've beaten myself up a lot.** I expect a lot from myself, I'll be hard on myself, and I don't know that I'm doing anyone any good by doing that."

TIM: "Something that I struggle with is — on one hand — I don't want to beat myself up, but on the other hand, I feel like the perfectionism that I have has enabled me to achieve whatever modicum of success I've had. I've heard stories about ZZ Top and *La Futura*, and how they worked on it with you from 2008 to 2012, and they realized the value of your wanting the art to be as perfect as it could be, or the best it could be, and taking whatever time and pains necessary to make that possible. I want to be easier on myself, but I worry that if I do that, I will lose whatever magic, if there is such a thing, that enables me to do what I do."

RICK: "I think, ultimately, that's a myth. I think that your take on things is specific to you [and not dependent on perfectionism] — **it's almost like you've won the war, and to accept the fact that you've won the war: You have an audience. People are willing to hear what you are interested in, what you're interested in learning about, and what you want to share. You can do that without killing yourself. And killing yourself won't be of service, neither to you nor your audience.**"

NEED TO GET UNSTUCK? MAKE YOUR TASK LAUGHABLY SMALL

How does Rick help artists who feel stuck? "Usually, I'll give them homework — a small, doable task. I'll give you an example. There was an artist I was working with recently who hadn't made an album in a long time, and he was struggling with finishing anything. He just had this version of a writer's block. But I would give him very doable homework assignments that almost seemed like a joke. 'Tonight, I want you to write one word in this song that needs five lines, that you can't finish. I just want one word that you like by tomorrow. Do you think that you could come up with one word?'"

THE BEGINNING IS "HEART WORK," NOT "HEAD WORK"

"So much of the job is more emotion and 'heart work' than it is 'head work.' The head comes in after, to look at what the heart has presented and to organize it. But the initial inspiration comes from a different place, and it's not the head, and it's not an intellectual activity."

LEARN FROM THE GREATS, NOT YOUR COMPETITION

"Going to museums and looking at great art can help you write better songs. Reading great novels . . . seeing a great movie . . . reading poetry. . . . The only way to use the inspiration of other artists is if you **submerge yourself in the greatest works of all time.** . . . If you listen to the greatest songs ever made, that would be a better way to work through [finding] your own voice today, [rather] than listening to what's on the radio now and thinking, 'I want to compete with this.' . . . [For music,] search online for *MOJO*'s 100 Greatest Albums Ever Made, or *Rolling Stone*'s 500 Greatest Albums of All Time, or any trusted source's top 100 albums, and start listening to what are considered the greats."

✳ Who do you think of when you hear the word "successful"?

Don Wildman. "He's 82 years old, and he did 23 pull-ups on the beach the other day. He's in the Senior Olympics. He retired . . . because he wanted to spend his days enjoying life and exercising. He's one of the most inspiring, uplifting, great, successful people on so many levels."

TF: Laird Hamilton, Gabby Reece, and Brian MacKenzie also bring Don up constantly (see page 92). I highly recommend reading an *Esquire* profile of him from a few years ago titled "The World's Healthiest 75-Year-Old Man." From that piece: "Wildman officially retired in 1994, at age 61 [after selling his company to what became Bally Total Fitness], not because he'd lost his passion for the business but because having a job — even one in the fitness industry — made it difficult to snowboard 100 days a year."

THE SOUNDTRACK OF EXCELLENCE

As mentioned before, more than 80% of the world-class performers I've interviewed meditate in the mornings in some fashion.

But what of the remaining 20%? Nearly all of them have *meditation-like* activities. One frequent pattern is listening to a single track or album on repeat, which can act as an external mantra for aiding focus and present-state awareness.

Here are just a few examples:

» Alex Honnold, free solo climbing phenom: *The Last of the Mohicans* soundtrack

» Rolf Potts, author of *Vagabonding* and others: ambitones like *The Zen Effect* in the key of C for 30 minutes, made by Rolfe Kent, the composer of music for movies like *Sideways*, *Wedding Crashers*, and *Legally Blonde*

» Matt Mullenweg, lead developer of WordPress, CEO of Automattic: "Everyday" by A$AP Rocky and "One Dance" by Drake

» Amelia Boone, the world's most successful female obstacle course racer: "Tonight Tonight" by the Smashing Pumpkins and "Keep Your Eyes Open" by NEEDTOBREATHE

» Chris Young, mathematician and experimental chef: Paul Oakenfold's "Live at the Rojan in Shanghai," Pete Tong's Essential Mix

» Jason Silva, TV and YouTube philosopher: "Time" from the *Inception* soundtrack by Hans Zimmer

» Chris Sacca: "Harlem Shake" by Baauer and "Lift Off" by Jay Z and Kanye West, featuring Beyoncé. "I can bang through an amazing amount of email with the Harlem Shake going on in the background."

>>> Tim Ferriss: Currently I'm listening to "Circulation" by Beats Antique and "Black Out the Sun" by Sevendust, depending on whether I need flow or a jumpstart.

Personally, I take this repetitive Monk-ish behavior a step further.

On a book deadline, I pick 1 or 2 albums and 1 or 2 movies for late-night writing sessions, as I do my best work between 11 p.m. and 4 a.m. Polling the most prolific authors I know, more than 90% do their best work when others are sleeping, whether they start after 10 p.m. or wake up well before 6 a.m. Personally, I'll play a movie on mute in the background to avoid feeling isolated, and listen to 1 or 2 albums per session, repeating both the movie and the music over and over. This means that I've "seen" some movies literally 100-plus times, as I might play a single film 3 to 6 times per night. Toward the end of a session, when I'm getting tired, I'll also switch from default "flow" music to default "wake-up" music. Here is my filmography and discography for all of my books:

The 4-Hour Workweek
Films: *The Bourne Identity, Shaun of the Dead*
"Flow" album: *Gran Hotel Buenos Aires* by Federico Aubele
"Wake-up" album: *One-X* by Three Days Grace

The 4-Hour Body
Films: *Casino Royale, Snatch*
"Flow" album: *Luciano Essential Mix* (2009, Ibiza) featuring DeadMau5
"Wake-up" album: *Cold Day Memory* by Sevendust

The 4-Hour Chef
Films: *Babe* (Yes, the pig movie. It was the first thing that popped up for free under Amazon Prime. I watched it once as a joke and it stuck. "That'll do, pig. That'll do." Gets me every time.)
"Flow" album: "Just Jammin'" extended single track by Gramatik
"Wake-up" album: *Dear Agony* by Breaking Benjamin

Tools of Titans
Films: None! I was traveling and used people-watching at late-night cafés in Paris and elsewhere as my "movie."
"Flow" album: *I Choose Noise* by Hybrid
"Wake-up" album: *Over the Under* by Down

JACK DORSEY

Jack Dorsey (TW: @JACK) is the co-founder and CEO of Twitter, the founder and CEO of Square, and a board member of The Walt Disney Company. He received the "Innovator of the Year Award" in 2012 from the *Wall Street Journal* and was named one of the "top 35 innovators under 35" by *MIT Technology Review* in 2008.

* What book or books have you gifted most to other people?
The Old Man and the Sea, Leaves of Grass (first edition).

* If you could have a gigantic billboard anywhere, what would it say?
"Breathe."

* Do you have any quotes that you live you life by or think of often?
"I know nothing."

* What is the worst advice you see or hear given in your trade?
"Fail fast!"

* What is something you believe that other people think is crazy?
We're born with everything we'll ever need.

* Three people or sources you've learned from — or followed closely — in the last year?
Wim Hof, Rick Rubin, Rick Owens

* What are your favorite episodes of *The Tim Ferriss Show*?
Rick Rubin and Wim Hof

* What is the best or most worthwhile investment you've made?
Taking the time to walk to work every day (5 miles, 1 hour 15 minutes)

"There are only four stories: a love story between two people, a love story between three people, the struggle for power, and the journey. Every single book that is in the bookstore deals with these four archetypes, these four themes."

"The world is changed by your example, not by your opinion."

PAULO COELHO

Paulo Coelho (FB/TW: @PAULOCOELHO, PAULOCOELHOBLOG.COM) has long been one of my writing inspirations. His books, of near universal appeal, include *The Alchemist* and his most recent, *The Spy*, and have been translated into more than 70 languages. He is staggeringly consistent as a writer and averages one book every 2 years. As I type this, I am under the pressure of deadlines and often feel as Kurt Vonnegut did: "When I write, I feel like an armless, legless man with a crayon in his mouth." There is much to learn from Paulo.

BACK STORY

Few people realize that *The Alchemist*, which has sold more than 65 million copies worldwide, was originally published by a small Brazilian publisher to the tune of 900 copies. They declined to reprint it! It wasn't until after his subsequent novel *Brida* that *The Alchemist* was revived and took off.

Paulo was born in Brazil but now lives in Geneva, Switzerland, where he recorded the audio for my podcast.

WHAT DOES YOUR MORNING AND DAILY ROUTINE LOOK LIKE?

"I sit down, of course. I have the book inside of me, and I start procrastinating. In the morning, I check my emails, I check news, I check everything that I could check just to postpone, for the moment, sitting and facing myself. For 3 hours, I'm trying to tell myself, 'No, no, no. Later, later, later,' and then, one moment, I say—just not to lose face in front of myself—'I'm going to sit, and I'm going to write for half an hour.' And I do. Of course, this half an hour becomes 10 hours in a row. That's why I write my books very quickly, because I cannot stop. . . . [But] I cannot stop [procrastinating]. **Probably, this is my inner ritual. I have to feel guilty about not writing for 3 hours or 4 hours.** Then, when I'm there, I start writing and it's nonstop. . . .

"A successful writing day is a day that I suffer in the morning, and I have fun in the evening, fun by writing. [I should] not describe this as fun. It's also painful . . . I'm in a kind of trance. When I go to bed after 10 hours of working, well, the adrenaline is still circulating in my blood. It takes hours to sleep. **There is this notepad by my side, and I take notes, but I take notes only to take them out from my head. They will be useless the next day.** I never use notes that I take . . . and this has happened since I wrote my first book, *The Pilgrimage*. I cannot change this process. I wish I could sit and write and not feel guilty for 4 or 5 hours during the day. It is impossible."

TF: Even the best in the world struggle. I need to relearn this lesson often. For most writers who didn't start off as journalists (e.g., Malcolm Gladwell, Neil Strauss), writing is hard and continues to be hard. What makes it easier? Knowing that many of the "greats" are going through the same thing. It's reassuring to know that someone at the top of their game—who has seemingly beaten all of the odds—still has the daily struggle.

✳ What are the most common mistakes or weaknesses of first-time novelists?

"Keep it simple. Trust your reader. He or she has a lot of imagination. Don't try to describe things. Give a hint, and they will fulfill this hint with their own imagination. That's why I am so reluctant to sell the rights of my books for movies because there, you have everything. The [viewer] does not need to think. However, if I say like in *Aleph*, at the very beginning, 'I am in my house in the Pyrenees, and there is an oak there.' I don't need to explain my house in the Pyrenees. I only needed to put in the elements that are important: the oak, myself, and the person that I'm talking to. That's all. . . . Trust your reader. Understand that he or she can fill the empty spaces. Don't over-explain."

✳ How do you capture ideas that might help your writing?

"I strongly encourage writers not to think about writing every time they do something. Forget notebooks. Forget taking notes. Let what is important remain. What's not important goes away. When you sit down to write, there is this process of purging, this process of cleansing, where only the important things remain. It's much easier than taking notes and overloading yourself with information."

✳ What do you find helpful when you are stuck or stagnated?

"There is only one thing. When I feel stagnated, I promise myself that [even] if I don't feel inspired, I need to move forward. I need to have discipline. . . . In the middle of a book, there I am: I don't know how to continue the story, even if it's a nonfiction story. But then, I say, 'You, book, are fighting with me. Okay. I'm going to sit here, and I'm not going to leave you alone until I find my way out of this crossroads.' It may take 10 minutes. It may take 10 hours. But if you don't have enough discipline, you don't move forward. . . ."

TF: Several people in this book, including yours truly, have found Anne Lamott's book *Bird by Bird* a lifeline during book-related crises of faith. One friend was on the verge of returning his advance to the publisher and calling it quits. Instead, I loaned him my copy of *Bird by Bird*. He regained his confidence, and his book became a *New York Times* bestseller.

* Do you have a team, or researchers, who help you?

"I don't have researchers, no. No, no . . . If you overload your book with a lot of research, you're going to be very boring to yourself and to your readers. Books are not here to show how intelligent and cultivated you are. Books are out there to show your heart, to show your soul, and to tell your fans, readers: You are not alone."

WRITING PROMPTS FROM CHERYL STRAYED

Cheryl Strayed (FB: CHERYLSTRAYED.AUTHOR, TW: @CHERYLSTRAYED, CHERYLSTRAYED.COM) is the #1 *New York Times* best-selling author of *Wild*, *Tiny Beautiful Things*, *Brave Enough*, and *Torch*. Cheryl's essays have been published in *The Best American Essays*, the *New York Times*, the *Washington Post Magazine*, *Vogue*, *Salon*, *The Sun* magazine, *Tin House*, and elsewhere. She holds an MFA in fiction writing from Syracuse University and a bachelor's degree from the University of Minnesota. She lives in Portland, Oregon.

———

Every writer in this book has a slightly different process, but they all start with the same thing: a blank page.

Even if you don't consider yourself a writer (I never did), putting thoughts on paper is the best way to A) develop ideas, and B) review and improve your thinking. The benefits of even 30 minutes a week of scribbling can transfer to everything else that you do.

The following bullets are writing prompts that Cheryl has suggested when asked for assignment ideas for students who've read *Wild*. They are brilliant and make fantastic jumping-off points for any type of journaling or writing, whether Morning Pages (page 224), a blog post, the beginning of a novel, a letter to a friend, a diary entry, a screenplay, or a too-fast-too-soon Tinder message.

Try one for two pages of longhand writing. Go for uninterrupted flow, and don't stop to edit. Step one is to generate without judging. Chances are that you'll surprise yourself.

≫ Write about a time when you realized you were mistaken.

≫ Write about a lesson you learned the hard way.

≫ Write about a time you were inappropriately dressed for the occasion.

≫ Write about something you lost that you'll never get back.

≫ Write about a time when you knew you'd done the right thing.

≫ Write about something you don't remember.

≫ Write about your darkest teacher.

≫ Write about a memory of a physical injury.

≫ Write about when you knew it was over.

≫ Write about being loved.

≫ Write about what you were really thinking.

≫ Write about how you found your way back.

≫ Write about the kindness of strangers.

≫ Write about why you could not do it.

≫ Write about why you did.

ED COOKE

Ed Cooke (TW: @TEDCOOKE, MEMRISE.COM) is the CEO of Memrise and a certified Grandmaster of Memory. This means he's able to memorize and recite: A) a 1,000-digit number within an hour, B) a shuffled pack of cards within a few of minutes, and C) 10 packs of shuffled cards within an hour. Perhaps more impressive, he can quickly train others to do the same. In 2010, he was interviewed by a journalist named Joshua Foer. Under Ed's Yoda-like tutelage, in 2011, Joshua became the very next American Memory Champion. It took less than a year for Ed to transform a novice into world-class. The result was Foer's book *Moonwalking with Einstein.*

Spirit animal: Jaguar

ON THE MAGIC OF JOHANN WOLFGANG VON GOETHE

"Goethe is really cool. . . . At the age of 25, he writes a novel, which is extraordinarily brilliant [*The Sorrows of Young Werther*], about the troubles of young Goethe. It's this wonderful story of a young man who falls in love, and it doesn't really work out so well. . . . Goethe wrote this book by locking himself in a hotel room for 3 months, imagining his five best friends on different chairs, and then discussing with his imaginary friends different possibilities of plot and so on and so forth. This is an example, by the way, of that spatial separation I was talking about. [**TF:** Humans naturally remember faces, people, and locations/spaces well, so you can use them to construct mnemonic devices like the "memory palace" technique, for example.] In one's own mind, we're somehow inherently boxed in and constricted, and by imagining in different spatial locations and then iterating an idea — or novel, in this case — through perspectives, he was able to give himself five perspectives separated out, and give himself a multidimensional playground for creating a work of art . . . which, by the way, is an awesome technique."

TF: We don't need in-person mentors as often as we think. Every day, using people from this book, I will ask myself questions like "What would Matt Mullenweg do?" or "What would Jocko say?"

FEELING LIKE A LOSER (AS WE ALL DO SOMETIMES)

"When I was at school, I would lose a debating competition or discover that I was a loser in a more general sense. I had what I call, in a way, a 'mind hack.' I'd be sitting on the loo or something and I'd just think, 'Oh, everything feels terrible and awful. It's all gone to shit.' Then I'd [consider], 'But if you think about it, the stars are really far away,' then you try to imagine the world from the stars. Then you sort of zoom in and you're like, 'Oh, there's this tiny little character there for a fragment of time worrying about X.'"

TF: This is similar to the "star therapy" that BJ Miller describes on page 401. I use a combination of both each night before bed.

* **Book recommendations**

> *In Praise of Idleness and Other Essays* by Bertrand Russell
> *The Joyous Cosmology* by Alan Watts

Maxims and Reflections by Goethe: "I was traveling around the world at the age of 18, which is what people in England do between high school and university. In my coat, I had Goethe's aphorisms, his short little thoughts in my pocket. I read and reread this book.... It's actually had quite a fundamental [impact] on my life because these are his little snippets of wisdom on almost any imaginable topic, and all of them are brilliant. There are things like, 'The company of women is schooling in good manners,' or 'Boldness has genius, power, and magic.' Ones you don't remember in their precise form, but which nonetheless act as little micro filters for interpreting reality."

Touching the Rock by John Hull. This is about a man's slow descent into blindness over 20 years. "He's a kind of theologian, but he has these wonderful reflections on how he came to enjoy the world [as a blind man]. One go-to example is that rain is the best thing for blind people, because you can hear the world in three dimensions. The pattering of the raindrops on the roofs, the pavement, the lampposts, and the buildings, gives you — because of the echo — a sense of 3-D space, where most of the time your 3-D space only goes a couple of yards in front of you, and otherwise is just the void."

> "Looking somebody in the eye . . . is often the antidote for what is ailing us."

AMANDA PALMER

Amanda Palmer (TW: @AMANDAPALMER, AMANDAPALMER.NET) first rose to prominence as one half of the internationally acclaimed punk cabaret duo The Dresden Dolls. Her surprise hit TED presentation, "The Art of Asking," has been viewed more than 8 million times. She followed up with a book expanding on the lessons, titled *The Art of Asking: How I Learned to Stop Worrying and Let People Help*. I read it and upgraded my life in an afternoon of asking for help.

Spirit animal: Sloth

"JUST TAKE ON THE PAIN, AND WEAR IT AS A SHIRT"

Amanda explains how she got the nickname and stage name "Amanda Fucking Palmer":

"It was one of those things where Ben [Folds, producer of her first solo album] had someone who was a friend of a current enemy, who referred to me — every time she referred to me — as 'Amanda Fucking Palmer.' And so Ben, because we were working on a record in Nashville together for a month, as a joke, started calling me 'AFP.' . . . You lose your mind in the studio, and everything devolves into toilet humor instantly. That just became the running studio joke, and that was Ben's pet name for me, and I thought it was funny enough that I started using it myself. Then it just sort of turned into a thing. I don't even know how it turned into a thing, but I think that's a good nickname. . . . It lands on you, and then it sticks like glue."

TIM: "I love it. So you disarmed the insult by adopting it completely."

AMANDA: "Which kind of is my life philosophy."

TIM: "I love that."

AMANDA: "No, really. Just take on the pain, and wear it as a shirt."

TF: This is precisely why I regularly refer to myself a "professional dilettante" when I'm being interviewed by someone who views me as a dabbling generalist (which I probably am). By preemptively using the language of a critic, I remove some of their potential weapons.

TWO WORDS FOR CONFLICT RESOLUTION

"[My mentor's] life advice to me, when I'm going into a conflict or a difficult situation with my parents or an argument with Neil [Gaiman, her husband] is, 'Say less.' That's it. Just say less."

EXPLAINING HER EARLY SUCCESS AS A STREET PERFORMER:

"I treated every single patron like a ten-second love affair."

AMANDA'S MEDITATION PRACTICE

"Basic vipassana meditation, nothing fancy, no crazy mantras, no gods or deities, just basically sitting on the earth as a human being and paying attention to your breath and your body and letting thoughts come and go, but really trying not to be attached to the drama that comes visiting."

DROPPING ASHES ON THE BUDDHA

"One of my absolute favorite books of all time, because it changed my life, is a book called *Dropping Ashes on the Buddha*. It's by Zen Master Seung Sahn, who was a Korean Zen monk. I read it when I was maybe 24, and it's a short book: just a series of letters that this really funny, very direct, very no-bullshit Korean monk wrote back and forth with his students in the 1970s. It was one of those, 'Oh, my God, I think I get it' books. . . . I have given that book to probably 30 or 40 people, especially people who have told me that they are feeling kind of lost and/or depressed or directionless, or younger people who are at crazy crossroads in their life and need something to hang onto. If you like it, there is a companion book that was his second collection of letters, which was called *Only Don't Know*."

AIM NARROW, OWN YOUR OWN CATEGORY

The following is one of my favorite excerpts from *The Art of Asking*, which I highlighted because it beautifully showcases the "1,000 True Fans" philosophy I'm so fond of (page 292):

> Dita Von Teese, a star in the contemporary burlesque scene, once recounted something she'd learned in her early days stripping in L.A. Her colleagues — bleach-blonde dancers with fake tans, Brazilian wax jobs, and neon bikinis — would strip bare naked for an audience of 50 guys in the club and be tipped a dollar by each guy. Dita would take the stage wearing satin gloves, a corset, and a tutu, and do a sultry striptease down to her underwear, confounding the crowd. And then, though 49 guys would ignore her, one would tip her fifty dollars.
>
> That man, Dita said, was her audience.

✱ Any quotes you live by, or think of often?

"'Honor those who seek the truth, beware of those who've found it' [adapted from Voltaire]. A reminder that the path never ends and that absolutely nobody has this shit figured out."

ERIC WEINSTEIN

Eric Weinstein (TW: @ERICRWEINSTEIN) is managing director of Thiel Capital, a PhD in mathematical physics from Harvard, and a research fellow at the Mathematical Institute of Oxford University.

BEHIND THE SCENES

» This is the text from Eric that catalyzed our podcast: "Do you want to try a podcast on [the topics in our text thread] . . . psychedelics, theories of everything, and the need to destroy education in order to save it?"

» The most viral thing Eric has ever written is about *Kung Fu Panda*, his all-time favorite film ["In *Kung Fu Panda*, how does Po end up developing the capability to be an awesome Kung Fu fighter?" on Quora]. Eric has also written about professional wrestling as a metaphor for living in a constructed and false reality [see "Kayfabe" on Edge.org].

2,000–3,000 PEOPLE, NOT GENERAL FAME

This is one of the messages Eric burned into my brain last year, and it's guided many decisions since. We were sitting in a large soaking tub talking about the

Spirit animal: Mirror orchid

world (as mathematicians and human guinea pigs do in San Francisco), and he said: "General fame is overrated. You want to be famous to 2,000 to 3,000 people you handpick." I'm paraphrasing, but the gist is that you don't need or want mainstream fame. It brings more liabilities than benefits. However, if you're known and respected by 2–3K high-caliber people (e.g., the live TED audience), you can do anything and everything you want in life. It provides maximal upside and minimal downside.

GOOD QUESTION TO ASK YOURSELF WHEN TACKLING INCUMBENT COMPANIES (OR IDEAS)

"How is their bread buttered?"

"What is it that they can't afford to say or think?"

"CONSENSUS" SHOULD SET OFF YOUR SPIDEY SENSE

"Somehow, people have to learn that consensus is a huge problem. There's no 'arithmetic consensus' because it doesn't require a consensus. But there is a Washington consensus. There is a climate consensus. In general, consensus is how we bully people into pretending that there's nothing to see. 'Move along, everyone.' I think that, in part, you should learn that people don't naturally come to high levels of agreement unless something is either absolutely clear, in which case consensus isn't present, or there's an implied threat of violence to livelihood or self."

TF: I start nearly every public presentation I give with a slide that contains one quote: "Whenever you find yourself on the side of the majority, it's time to pause and reflect." — Mark Twain. This isn't just for my audience. It's also a reminder for me.

CHANGE YOUR WORDS, CHANGE YOUR WORLD

Eric has an amazing vocabulary that regularly stumps me, and we speak a lot about the culture-shaping power of language.

As mentioned in Reid Hoffman's profile (page 228), one of my favorite quotes is from Ludwig Wittgenstein: "The limits of my language mean the limits of my world." Partly as a result of my late-night jam sessions with Eric, I started experimenting with inventing new words and spreading them in pop culture This can be for shits and giggles, but sometimes it's because a serious national conversation is in need of new words. In the former category, my first was "teledultery" from a tweet on April 6, 2016:

"Proposed new word — TELEDULTERY (n.) — When a significant other secretly watches a TV series solo that you've agreed to watch together."

My second experiment, in the "serious" category, was made public in my conversation with Eric: "bigoteer."

There currently isn't much of a penalty for frivolously labeling people an "ist" (e.g., sexist, racist, misogynist, classist), despite the fact that people who are unfairly accused of such things can have their careers, marriages, etc., destroyed. This often happens with no evidence, very questionable evidence, or even strong countering evidence. The damage is hard to undo, even if there's a retraction or correction. Google and Wikipedia will, at the least, continue to have "has been accused of . . . ," which is damning ambiguity.

So, what to do? I think we can fight fire with fire. This is where "bigoteer" comes in.

Bigoteer (n) — a person who implies other people are bigots, for personal gain.

Let's say a writer takes the lazy route for cheap applause (i.e., sensationalizing for clicks) and haphazardly accuses others of being an "ist" like sexist or racist. That mudslinger could now become labeled as a "well-known bigoteer" in their own Wikipedia entry, for instance. This would create a consequence and disincentive, which I don't see currently, to acting in such a cavalier and damaging way.

Out-of-control political correctness and online lynch mobs are the end of free speech. Fight it. The world we live in is becoming a horrible "consensus reality." Don't run over the cliff.

DEFINING A "HIGH-AGENCY" PERSON

Eric said "high-agency person" in passing, and I asked him to elaborate:

"When you're told that something is impossible, is that the end of the conversation, or does that start a second dialogue in your mind, how to get around whoever it is that's just told you that you can't do something? So, how am I going to get past this bouncer who told me that I can't come into this nightclub?

How am I going to start a business when my credit is terrible and I have no experience?"

TF: Eric describes *The Martian* as "The ultimate high-agency film."

WHAT IS "CANONICAL DESIGN"?

"Well, let's look at nature. There's a great virus called T4 bacteriophage. If you look it up, it's like a lunar lander. It's really cool. The genetic material is held in a capsule called a 'capsid' that has the form of an icosahedron [20-faced poly-hedron].... It's a little crazy to think that before Plato ever existed, nature had figured out this complicated 20-sided object. But because it was so natural at a mathematical level, even if it was complex, nature found the canonical design even though there was no canonical designer.... Because it was a God-given form, it didn't need to be 'thunk up,' if you will, by any individual. Or the recent discovery of grasshoppers that use gear mechanisms for jumping. You would think we had invented gears. But, in fact, gears are such a natural idea that natural selection found it long before we did.... These forms really don't have an inventor so much as a discoverer."

∗ Most-gifted or recommended books?

"For my science friends, I tell them to read ***The Emperor of Scent***, by Chandler Burr, about my friend Luca Turin. It talks about a renegade scientist being stymied by the journal *Nature*, by various conferences, by the established research centers, and it's just a wonderful introduction to how the dissident voice is marginalized. Because Luca is such a genius of olfaction and chemistry, he's able to take a perspective, which may or may not be true, but keep pushing forward and battling. So, that's one of my favorites.

"I have another weird recommendation, which is this book ***Heraclitean Fire*** by Erwin Chargaff, who effectively shorted Watson and Crick. He told Watson and Crick that he didn't think that they were very good or very smart, and that they didn't know their chemistry. They weren't qualified to work on DNA, etc. It turned out that they got it right, and he got it wrong. When I heard that there was somebody who bet against Watson and Crick, I thought, 'Well, this is just going to be the laugh of the century,' but it turned out that just to short those guys required another genius. He writes about trying to suppress these guys and failing because they were right and he was wrong. He has enough presence of mind to struggle with it.

"These are books that I think are incredibly powerful because they talk about what it's like to be one against the many."

THE POWER OF THINKING SIDEWAYS

"Nobody really knew how to do wheeled luggage before 1989. It's hard to imagine that the whole world had their heads wedged so far up there that they couldn't think to put in these recessed wheels with a telescoping handle. And this was the invention of a guy named Robert Plath, who was a pilot for Northwest, I think. In one fell swoop, he convinced everyone that their old luggage was terrible. So even though there wasn't a lot of growth, he created the growth because nobody wanted their old luggage. You could compare these discrete brainwave innovations across fields. For example, in table tennis in the early '50s, the worst player on the Japanese team at the Bombay Table Tennis Championships was this guy Hiroji Satoh. He glued two foam expanses to both sides of a sandpaper table tennis bat, and nobody could cue off of the sounds because it changed the sound of the ball."

TIM: "Like a silencer on a gun."

ERIC: "Exactly. So if you put a suppressor on your paddle . . ."

TIM: "Suppressor. Just the fact that you used that word makes me think that you have a bunch of firearms hiding in your basement."

ERIC: "I can neither confirm nor deny. But the idea that the worst player on one of the lower-rated teams would be the undisputed champion simply through an innovation that was that profound shows you what the power of one of these ideas is. [**TF:** "These ideas" = having a "secret" as described in Peter Thiel's *Zero to One*: knowing or believing something that the rest of the world thinks is nonsense.] The power laws are just so unbelievably in your favor if you win that it makes [venturing outside the norm] worthwhile."

TIM: "Or Dick Fosbury, who went backwards over the high jump bar for the first time in the Olympics, winning gold —"

ERIC: "1968, you got it."

TIM: "Ridiculed, then mimicked, and eventually made standard."

ERIC: "[In the case of the poorly designed standard umbrella] I would, for example, immediately think about, let's say, the Japanese and their love of origami, and the mathematics of paper folding. That would be a place that I might see whether I could mine that silo of expertise for any application to the umbrella. Very often, it's a question of being the first person to connect things that have never been connected before, and something that is a commonplace solution in one area is not thought of in another."

FOR DEEP FUCKING CREATIVE WORK

TIM: "If you are trying to do deep creative work that requires a lot of synthesis, or as Naval Ravikant might say, 'orthogonal thinking,' what would your work cycle look like?"

ERIC: "I use a weird technique. I use 'coprolalia' — it sounds pornographic."

TIM: "A little bit."

ERIC: "You know the strings of obscenities that Tourette's patients involuntarily utter? [That's coprolalia.] So, I find that when we use words that are prohibited to us, it tells our brain that we are inhabiting unsafe space. It's a bit of a sign that you're going into a different mode. . . . When I'm going to do deep work, very often, it has a very powerful, aggressive energy to it. It's not easy to be around. It's very exacting, and I think I would probably look very autistic to people who know me to be social, were they ever to see me in work mode."

TIM: "How do you incite that? Do you just start trying to string together as many obscenities as possible? Like an incantation?"

ERIC: "I have my same sequence. It's like an invariant mantra that I have to say."

TIM: "Can you share it, or is that top secret?"

ERIC: "No, no. You can't share your meditation word."

TIM: "Well, just some hints, then. How long is it?"

ERIC: "It probably takes me seven seconds to say it. You [also] have to decamp from normal reality where you start thinking about [things like], 'Well, how am I negatively going to impact my neighbor?' No, this is your time. You're stealing the time. And the act of creation is itself a violent action."

TF: This odd technique does seem to quickly produce a slightly altered state. Try it — write down a precise sequence of curse words that takes 7 to 10 seconds to read. Then, before a creative work session of some type, read it quickly and loudly like you're casting a spell or about to go postal. Eric also finds late nights, around 3 a.m., to be ideal for deep creative work.

ERIC: "When the phone stops ringing, when you have no FOMO [fear of missing out] because everybody's asleep. It's a Monday night, and it's just you and an expanse of whiteboard. That's when the magic happens."

OLD HABITS DIE HARD — THE WATCH SMILE

"In almost every advertisement for wristwatches, the watches are set to 10:10. [Until you see] that, you can't really believe that it's true. But afterwards, you realize that the world has just pulled one over on you, because 10:10 looks like a smile to watch advertisers."

TIM: "Oh, I guess it's very symmetrical, isn't it?"

ERIC: "Yeah. But what's funny is that the wisdom has crept in to the point that sometimes you'll see digital watch ads, and they'll still be set to 10:10, even though it doesn't look like a smile."

ON STARTING TO USE PSYCHEDELICS AFTER AGE 40

For his entire life, Eric believed that using psychedelics was "like pouring acid on your brain and leaving it as Swiss cheese." That has changed in the last several years:

"It wasn't until I started meeting some of the most intellectually gifted people in the sciences and beyond . . . I realized that this was sort of the open secret of what I call the hallucinogenic elite, whether it's billionaires, or Nobel laureates, or inventors and coders. . . . A lot of these people were using these agents either for creativity or to gain access to the things that are so difficult to get access to through therapy and other conventional means."

"LEARNING DISABILITY" OR "TEACHING DISABILITY"?

". . . This is where we run into the trouble, which is we don't talk about *teaching disabilities*. We [only] talk about *learning disabilities*, and a lot of the kids that I want are kids who have been labeled 'learning disabled,' but they're actually super learners. They're like learners on steroids who have some deficits to pay for their superpower, and teachers can't deal with this.

"We label those kids 'learning disabled' to cover up from the fact that the economics of teaching require that one central actor, the teacher, be able to lead a room of 20 or more people in lockstep. Well, that's not a good model. I want to get as many of my dangerous [in a good way] kids out of that idiom, whether it requires dropping out of high school, dropping out of college. But not for no purpose. **Drop into something.** Start creating, building. Join a lab. Skip college."

ERIC'S "MORNING ROUTINE"

"Each morning is basically a struggle against a new day, which I view as a series of opponents who must be defeated. I'm not a morning person. So every morning I get out of bed, I'm just astounded that I've done it. . . . It was Julian Schwinger, the great Harvard physicist, I think, who was asked if he would teach the 9:00 a.m. quantum mechanics course, and he stopped for a second. The person asking said, 'Well, what's the problem, Professor Schwinger?' and he answered, 'I don't know if I can stay up that late.' "

✳ Advice to your 30-year old self?

"When I was 30, I guess I was still struggling to stay in or get out of academics. What I didn't realize is that the structure of the universities was either hitting steady state, or growing very little, or shrinking. That was not a healthy place to be, because most of the good seats in the musical chairs competition [e.g., tenured positions] had already been found in the '60s, and they had occupants. . . . I think what I needed to do was decamp and realize that technology was going to be a boom area. **And even though I wanted to do science rather than technology, it's better to be in an expanding world and not quite in exactly the right field, than to be in a contracting world where peoples' worst behavior comes out.** [In the latter,] your mind is grooved in defensive and rent-seeking types of ways. Life is too short to be petty and defensive and cruel to other people who are seeking to innovate alongside you."

PARTING ADVICE?

"What I would really like is for those of you who have been told that you're learning disabled, or you're not good at math, or that you're terrible at music, or something like that, to seek out unconventional ways of proving that wrong. Believe not only in yourselves, but that there are [ways, tools, methods] powerful enough to make things that look very difficult much easier than you ever imagined."

SETH ROGEN
& EVAN GOLDBERG

Seth Rogen (TW/FB: @SETHROGEN) is an actor, writer, producer, and director. Evan Goldberg (TW: @EVANDGOLDBERG) is a Canadian director, screenwriter, and producer. They've collaborated on films such as *Superbad* (which they first conceived of as teenagers), *Knocked Up*, *Pineapple Express*, *The Green Hornet*, *This Is the End*, *Funny People*, *Neighbors*, and *Sausage Party*. They have also written for *Da Ali G Show* and *The Simpsons*.

Spirit animal: Seth = sloth; Evan = bonobo

FUCK, FUCK, FUCK

I visited the production of *Neighbors 2* in Atlanta to observe Seth, Evan, and their team in action. One day, I sat in on a writers' room brainstorm. The script was put up on a huge screen, one person manning the keyboard. Everyone started throwing out ideas, which were typed in at hyperspeed. Evan and others said "fuck" or "fucking" at least once a sentence, and it all went on the screen. I asked afterward, "Doesn't it take a lot of time to polish the script?" to which Evan responded with a smile: **"You can always de-fuck the script later."** The important thing was to brainstorm freely and not self-edit. That came afterward.

WHY *SUPERBAD* WORKED

Superbad worked because Seth and Evan wrote about exactly what they were experiencing at the time. Evan explains, "At the time, all we knew was that we really wanted to get laid, we weren't getting laid, and we weren't supercool." It pays to write what you know.

Seth started doing standup when he was 13 years old. He adds: "That's something that came from standup comedy. There's a comic named Darryl Lenox who still performs, who is great. I remember he saw me perform. . . . I would try to mimic other comedians like Steven Wright or Seinfeld, like, 'What's the deal with Krazy Glue?' and he said: 'Dude, you're the only person here who could talk about trying to get a hand job for the first time. . . . Talk about that!'"

LESSONS FROM JUDD APATOW

EVAN: "I would say the biggest thing we learned from [Judd] is 'Don't keep stuff to yourself.' You're surrounded by smart people. Bring them in. Get other people's opinions. Share it with them. And most importantly, emotion is what matters. It's an emotional journey. . . ."

SETH: ". . . I remember one time we were filming a scene in *Knocked Up* and improvising, or maybe it was even *40-Year-Old Virgin*, and the direction he screamed at us — because he screams direction from another room a lot, which is hilarious — was, 'Less semen, more emotion!' I think that is actually a good note to apply across the board."

TIM: "You also mentioned that every character has to have a wound of some kind."

EVAN: "That's a big Judd-ism."

TF: Judd recommended they read *The Art of Dramatic Writing* by Lajos Egri (Evan: "If you're a writer, 60% of it is useless and 40% of it is gold."), which Judd said was Woody Allen's favorite writing book.

WEED FOR CREATIVE WORK

Evan and Seth are both serious marijuana connoisseurs, and they use different strains for different purposes. For writing and other creative sessions, Evan considers "Jack Herer" to be a good working weed. It's described by Leafly online as "a sativa-dominant cannabis strain that provides the perfect pairing of cerebral elevation and full-body relief."

✳ Any parting thoughts or advice?

EVAN: "In the end, *Superbad* was a success, but make no mistake, for 10 years it was a failure. And the first five drafts, if you read them, you'd [think,] 'This is the worst thing I've ever read in my life.'"

SETH: "People told us over and over again, 'I don't think anyone's going to make this movie,' and it didn't even occur to us to listen to them. It wasn't even a conversation of 'Should we stop?' We literally didn't even have that conversation. It was just like, 'Fuck those people. Let's go to the next one.'"

EVAN: "To picture Stephen King writing his first book and then being like: 'Man, I'm stumped. I'm gonna go be something else.' You just keep going."

SETH: "Blind belief in yourself."

8 TACTICS FOR DEALING WITH HATERS

Life is a full-contact sport, especially on the Internet. If you're going to step into the arena, bloody noses and a lot of scrapes are par for the course.

The sharp elbows and body checks can take many forms. Here is one of the first Amazon reviews I ever received for *The 4-Hour Workweek*, while I was still a wee lad finding his Bambi legs on the web:

"This book is mistitled. The subtitle should be 'Escape 9–5, Live Anywhere, Join the New Rich, and Become the World's Biggest Jerk.' Don't buy it. He'll probably use your money to set a Guinness Book record for the most kittens strangled in one minute."

Ah, welcome to town, kid. Want a tissue?

That was 2007. Over the last decade, I've collected a handful of rules and quotes that help me keep my sanity and reputation largely intact. Here they are:

#1 — It doesn't matter how many people don't get it. What matters is how many people do.

Even if your objective is to do the greatest good for the greatest number of people, you only need to find, cultivate, and thrill your first 1,000 diehard true fans (page 292). These people become your strongest marketing force, and the rest takes care of itself. The millions or billions who don't get it don't matter. Focus on the few who do. They are your Archimedes lever.

#2 — 10% of people will find a way to take anything personally. Expect it and treat it as math.

Particularly as you build an audience, this 10% can turn into a big number. Mentally prepare yourself before publishing anything. "Oh, I have 1,000 readers now. That means that 100 are going to respond like assholes. Not because I'm bad, not because they're bad, but because that's how the math works." If you anticipate it, it will throw you off less. On top of that, I assume that 1% of my fans are completely batshit crazy, just like the general population, which helps me handle the far scarier stuff. If you (wrongly) assume that everyone is going to respond with smiles and high-fives, you are going to get slapped, you'll respond impulsively, and you'll triple the damage. And you are not exempt from Crazy Town just because you cover non-offensive material. Here is a real, verbatim comment left on my blog: "You are showing a grave example of the white horseman to our children. Shame on you. You're an evil one who has gained the world and lost your soul." He proceeded to threaten to deliver me on Judgment Day. It became a real FBI-worthy threat! This was not in response to my post about clubbing baby seals. I don't have one. It was in response to a blog post I wrote to help raise funds for high-need public school classrooms in the U.S. (through donorschoose.org) that lack sufficient funding for books, pens, pencils, etc.

Anticipate, don't react.

#3 — When in doubt, starve it of oxygen.

Here are my three primary responses to online criticism:

>>> Starve it of oxygen (ignore it) — 90%

>>> Pour gasoline on it (promote it) — 8%

>>> Engage with trolls after too much wine (and really regret it) — 2%

I'm not going to cover option number three, but the first two are worth explaining.

The reason that you would want to starve 90% of oxygen is because doing otherwise gives your haters extra Google juice. In other words, if you reply publicly — worst-case scenario, you put something on another site with high page rank and link to the critic — all you're going to do is gift them powerful inbound links, increase traffic, and ensure the persistence and prominence of the piece. In some cases, I've had to bite my tongue for months at a time to wait for something (infuriating BS that I could easily refute) to drop off the front page or even the second page of Google results. It's very, very hard to stay silent, and it's very, very important to have that self-control. Rewatch the "Hoooold! Hooooooold!" scene from *Braveheart*.

But what about pouring gasoline on 8% of the negative? Why would anyone ever do that? First off, we must realize that not all critics are "haters." Let's look at a real-world example. Eric Karjaluoto wrote a post called "Is Tim Ferriss Acting Like an Asshole?" in response to a spec design competition I held, which had caused a firestorm. I don't agree with all of his arguments, but he did have some well-thought-through points that I felt contributed to a more interesting discussion. So I promoted his piece. For me, doing this 8% to 10% of the time accomplishes two things: It shows that I'm open to criticism, and it shows that I don't take myself too seriously. Both of these things tend to decrease the number of real haters who come out of the woodwork.

#4 — If you respond, don't *over*-apologize.

There are times to apologize when you truly screw up or speak too soon, but more often than not, acknowledgment is all that's required.

Some version of "I see you" will diffuse at least 80% of people who appear to be haters or would-be haters. They'll even sometimes do an about-face and become your strongest proponents. Just present the facts or wish them luck, and let them come to their own conclusions. I often use something along the lines of, "Thanks for the feedback. I'm always trying to improve. In the meantime, I hope you find what you're looking for."

#5 — You can't reason someone out of something they didn't reason themselves into.

#6 — "Trying to get everyone to like you is a sign of mediocrity. You'll avoid the tough decisions, and you'll avoid confronting the people who need to be confronted." — Colin Powell

#7 — "If you want to improve, be content to be thought foolish and stupid." — Epictetus

Cato of ancient Rome, who Seneca believed to be the perfect Stoic, practiced Epictetus's maxim by wearing darker robes than was customary and by wearing no tunic. He expected to be ridiculed and he was. He did this to train himself to only be ashamed of those things that are truly worth being ashamed of. To do anything remotely interesting, you need to train yourself to handle—or even enjoy—criticism. I regularly and deliberately "embarrass" myself for superficial reasons, much like Cato. This an example of "fear-rehearsing" (page 463).

#8 — "Living well is the best revenge." — George Herbert

During a tough period several years ago, Nassim Taleb of *The Black Swan* fame sent me the following aphorism, which was perfect timing and perfectly put:

"Robustness is when you care more about the few who like your work than the multitude who hates it (artists); fragility is when you care more about the few who hate your work than the multitude who loves it (politicians)."

Choose to be robust.

> **"**I really love the user-friendly quality of the word 'fuck.'**"**

MARGARET CHO

Margaret Cho (TW: @MARGARETCHO, MARGARETCHO.COM) is a polymath. She is an internationally acclaimed comic, actress, author, fashion designer, and singer-songwriter. She's on the big screen and in TV series such as *Sex and the City* and *30 Rock*. In 1999, her off-Broadway one-woman show, *I'm the One that I Want*, toured the country and was made into a best-selling book and feature film of the same name. Her first album, *Cho Dependent*, was nominated for a Grammy for best comedy album.

HOW TO HANDLE HECKLERS FROM THE STAGE

Margaret is known for being very good at shutting down hecklers. She learned a lot from the legendary Paula Poundstone:

"Really try to find out what they're trying to say. . . . It's really going deeper, and finding out **why this person has chosen to disrupt a performance that everybody has paid for, and that everybody is there for and agreed to sit for? Why did somebody want to rebel against that? I'm curious about it.** I usually give them quite a lot of time. There's the potential to create a whole show around them. . . .

"Then, I can ask them about who they're with. I can ask the person they're with [things like,] 'Why are they like that? Are they like this all the time? Is this a special thing?' You can also talk to other people around them, people who are seated next to them: 'What was this person like before the show?' or 'What were they saying? What led us to this?'"

TF: This is pure genius. Sometimes, the best way to defuse or defeat attackers is to ask short questions and keep them talking. Even a simple, "Why do you say that?" "Why do you ask?" or "Why would you say something like that?" can do the trick. Online, I'll sometimes let famous people answer my hecklers in the form of quotes. If someone is outraged over something ridiculous on social media, for instance, one of my favorite replies, especially after some wine, is: "Those who are offended easily should be offended more often" — Mae West.

ANDREW ZIMMERN

Andrew Zimmern (TW: @ANDREWZIMMERN, ANDREWZIMMERN.COM) is a three-time James Beard Award–winning TV personality, chef, writer, and teacher. As the creator, executive producer, and host of the Bizarre Foods franchise on Travel Channel (including *Bizarre Foods with Andrew Zimmern*, *Andrew Zimmern's Bizarre World*, *Bizarre Foods America* and the new *Bizarre Foods: Delicious Destinations*), Andrew has explored cultures in more than 150 countries, promoting impactful ways to think about, create, and live with food. It hasn't all been roses. Now sober for more than 20 years, Andrew was once a homeless heroin addict. He turned his life around with the help of a friend at the Hazelden clinic in Minnesota.

Spirit animal: Old and wise sea turtle

THE MOST IMPORTANT THING IS TO BE YOU, NOT YOUR INNER ACTOR

TIM: "I'm looking at some notes I took after one of our first "therapy sessions" [to help me prepare for a TV show]. . . . One of the recommendations was that the most important thing is to be you, not your inner actor. The line that really stuck with me was how 'Episode one is how you're going to have to be. . . .'"

ANDREW: "Episode one, moment one. You can never take that back. . . . I think I told you the story of episode 1, show 1 [of *Bizarre Foods*]. It was actually the pilot. I went to the Asadachi, which is a restaurant in Tokyo. The translation for the name means 'morning erections.' True. It's a *getemono* bar, the kind of place where businessmen close deals and drink a lot. . . . 'If you eat snake bile, I'll eat snake bile,' and then the deal will be done sort of thing. . . . There was a part of me that had all the funniest lines [for] making fun of their name . . . [and, sure,] you can make fun of these people. It's the easy go-to. You see people do it all the time on TV. A little voice inside my head said, 'Don't do it, because if you do that, you're going to have to come up with those lines all the time. You're going to be someone you're not. . . .' Quite frankly, the person that I am is very respectful of other cultures. 'Don't do it. Don't give into the fast, easy, cheap temptation,' which we always do. It's the easiest way. [So] all I did was walked up and turned and said some benign line and walked in the door. The moral of the story being: I didn't have to make fun of the people, make fun of their food, make fun of the name. It has turned out to be the best decision I ever made, because people always talk about the respect that I pay to other people within the show, which pleases me, and I think it's an important thing for all of us when we are travelers. [And] **it is so much less work just to be yourself.**"

❋ If you had to choose three herbs or spices to cook with for the next year?
"The world of herbs and spices is great, but before that, there are some other building blocks that I would prefer to have in my kitchen or my desert island: **hot chilies, shallots, and lemon.** . . . Sure, I can pick cumin or cilantro or things like that, but they have fairly limited use. With the lemon, chilies, and an allium or shallot, I can do anything. I can do ceaseless variations on them. . . . Salt [can act as] an acid and citrus is an acid [**TF:** Hence, some chefs say, "I use citrus like others use salt"], and there is an incredible amount of acid in all the alliums. There is an incredible amount of acid in all of the chilies. It's no secret why

those things are food-changing, food-altering, technique-inspiring ingredients to use. Much more versatile in the kitchen than basil or thyme or something like that."

FINDING THE RIGHT RECIPE FOR THE KITCHEN OR LIFE: LOOK FOR DETAILS AND DOERS

"[If you] go on the Internet, there are 20 recipes for pound cake. I go with the one that even describes to a quarter of an inch the size of the pan. Because if someone is describing that level of detail, you know they have gone through it. The person who writes a recipe that says, 'Grease the cake pan' [without specifying the size]? You know they haven't made it. It's a tip-off right away that something is wrong."

✳ *What is the best or most worthwhile investment you've made?

"The best thing I ever did, besides getting sober 25 years ago, was shelving my restaurant career in 2002, selling my shares in my restaurant, and working for free for a local radio station, magazine, and TV station in an effort to create my own media syllabus. I wanted to create a product with a massive platform, and try to make a difference in the world, and I couldn't do it without becoming a 40-year-old intern, learning everything I needed, and rebooting my career."

"Cynicism is a disease that robs people of the gift of life."

RAINN WILSON

Rainn Wilson (FB/IG/TW: @RAINNWILSON, SOULPANCAKE.COM) is best known for playing Dwight Schrute on NBC's Emmy-winning TV show *The Office*. He has also acted in *Super, Cooties, Juno, Monsters vs. Aliens*, and *The Rocker*, among other movies. He co-founded SoulPancake, a media company that seeks to tackle life's big questions. He's a board member of the Mona Foundation and co-founded Lidè Haiti, an educational initiative in rural Haiti that empowers young, at-risk women through the arts. He is the author of *The Bassoon King*.

Spirit animal: Sloth

BEHIND THE SCENES

For those of you who'd love to kick me in the face, Rainn saved you the trouble. Just search "Rainn Wilson kicking Tim Ferriss in the face." Long story.

✳ What advice would you give your 30-year-old self?

"At 30, I was a starving New York theater actor, just going around trying to get acting work, and barely making $17 grand a year doing theater. I did a bunch of side jobs. I was a 'man with a van' — I had a moving company. I think what I would talk to myself about is, 'You have to believe in your capacity.' You have to believe that your capacity is greater than you could probably imagine. To me, this is a kind of divine question. God has given us talents and faculties, and it's up to us to discover them, expand them to their maximum, and use them for maximum service in the world. I had a lot more capacity at 30 than I thought. I thought of myself as, 'Well, I could get some acting work and maybe I could do an occasional guest spot on *Law and Order* and make enough money to just get by as an actor, so I don't have to drive this damn moving van.' That was the extent of where my imagination was for myself. **So I would just say, 'Believe in yourself more deeply. You're bigger than that. Dream bigger,' I would say.**"

GETTING TO "NORMAL"

This was extremely refreshing to hear from Rainn, as I often feel the same:

"I'm in my head a lot, and it kind of sucks. . . . So there are certain tools that I have to use to get by. I've learned in my life that there are certain things I have to do to just be out of my head and get to normal. **I'm not talking about being really supereffective. Just to get to normal, I have to do meditation, I have to do some exercise.** If I can get into nature, great. If I can play some tennis, better, and acting is that same way. Acting, rehearsing, playing characters, these are the things that get me out of my head and out of analyzing every goddamn thing that comes down the pike and leaves me miserable and making really bad choices."

ON BEING THE BEST VERSION OF YOURSELF

As Oscar Wilde is thought to have said, "Be yourself. Everyone else is taken":

"I was cast in a Broadway show when I was about 29 or 30 years old. It was my first Broadway show, and I sucked. I bombed. Again, I was very in my head.

I was very stuck, cerebral, and stiff. I couldn't get out of it, and I tried and I tried, but I was just terrible at the part.

"But after I finished that show, I thought: 'You know what, fuck it. I'm never doing that again. . . . I can't. Life is too short. I'm too miserable, and I've got to be me as an actor. I have to bring who I really am as a human to my acting. So I'm offbeat and I'm odd. I'm a weirdo. I buy shirts at the thrift store, and this is who I am, and this is who I have to be.' It really changed me as an actor and as an artist. . . . I never would have had the success that I had in L.A. and on TV and film in doing odd characters if I hadn't gone through that terrible, terrible ordeal."

✳ Any final thoughts?

"I don't want to sound like a pretentious asshole, but I would ask people to dig deeper. We can make the world a better place. We can ask more of ourselves. We can do more for others. I think that our life is a journey. . . . Dig deep on your journey and the world will benefit from it."

> **"**The most important trick to be happy is to realize that **happiness is a choice that you make and a skill that you develop.** You choose to be happy, and then you work at it. It's just like building muscles.**"**

NAVAL RAVIKANT

Naval Ravikant (TW: @NAVAL, STARTUPBOY.COM) is the CEO and co-founder of AngelList. He previously co-founded Vast.com and Epinions, which went public as part of Shopping.com. He is an active angel investor and has invested in more than 100 companies, including many "unicorn" mega-successes. His deals include Twitter, Uber, Yammer, Postmates, Wish, Thumbtack, and OpenDNS. He is probably the person I call most for startup-related advice.

Spirit animal: Owl

BACK STORY

- Naval was raised poor in an immigrant family: "We came to this country [from India] when I was 9 and my brother was 11. We had very little. My mother raised us as a single mom in a studio apartment. She worked a menial job by day and then she went to school at night, so we were latchkey kids. . . . A lot of growing up was watching the ideal American lifestyle, but from the other side of the windowpane, with my nose pressed against the glass, saying, 'I want that, too. I want that for myself and my kids.' I grew up with a very dark view of the world on the other side of the tracks. . . ."

- Naval's name roughly means "new man" in Sanskrit. His son is named Neo, which means "new" in Greek, is an anagram for "one" (Naval pointed this out to me), and, of course, is well featured in *The Matrix*.

- Many years ago, Naval and I first met because he saw me hitting on his then-girlfriend (unbeknownst to me) at a coffee shop in San Francisco. He sauntered up with a huge grin and introduced himself.

- His brother Kamal is the person who convinced me to "retire" from early tech investing (page 384).

SUCCESSFUL AND HAPPY — DIFFERENT COHORTS?

"If you want to be successful, surround yourself with people who are more successful than you are, but if you want to be happy, surround yourself with people who are less successful than you are."

HANDLING CONFLICT

"**The first rule of handling conflict is don't hang around people who are constantly engaging in conflict. . . .** All of the value in life, including in relationships, comes from compound interest. People who regularly fight with others will eventually fight with you. I'm not interested in anything that's unsustainable or even hard to sustain, including difficult relationships."

THE THREE OPTIONS YOU ALWAYS HAVE IN LIFE

"In any situation in life, you only have three options. You always have three options. You can change it, you can accept it, or you can leave it. What is not a good option is to sit around wishing you would change it but not changing it, wishing you would leave it but not leaving it, and not accepting it. It's that struggle, that aversion, that is responsible for most of our misery. The phrase that I probably use the most to myself in my head is just one word: *accept*."

THE FIVE CHIMPS THEORY

"There's a theory that I call 'the five chimps theory.' In zoology, you can predict the mood and behavior patterns of any chimp by which five chimps they hang out with the most. Choose your five chimps carefully."

LESSONS FROM PHYSICS AND THE RUSSIAN MOB

"I learned [the importance of honesty] from a couple of different places. One is, when I grew up, I wanted to be a physicist and I idolized Richard Feynman. I read everything by him, technical and non-technical, that I could get my hands on. He said: 'You must never, ever fool yourself, and you are the easiest person to fool.'

"So the physics grounding is very important because in physics, you have to speak truth. You don't compromise, you don't negotiate with people, you don't try and make them feel better. If your equation is wrong, it just won't work. Truth is not determined by consensus or popularity — usually, it's quite the opposite. So I think the science background is important. A second is, I grew up around some really rough-and-tumble kids in New York, some of whom were actually in the Russian mob. I once had an encounter where I watched one of them threaten to kill the other.

"The would-be victim went and hid, and then finally, he let the aggressor into his house after the aggressor promised him: 'No, I'm not going to kill you.' Honesty was such a strong virtue between them that even when they were ready to kill each other, they would take each other's word for things. It went above everything. Even though it was honesty in a mob context, I realized how important that is in relationships."

HONESTY AS CORE FOUNDATIONAL VALUE

Here's a brief story for comedic relief, and keep in mind that we both happily live in San Francisco.

TIM: "You never hesitate to say what's on your mind. I can see how that might be misinterpreted by people who are used to polite, 'uh-huh,' nod-nod conversation. I remember once, you and I were both invited to a dinner, and there were a lot of people neither of us had met. You were standing in a group chatting over wine, and I showed up with this pretty unusual getup. I had on this turquoise long-sleeved shirt, which I never wore. I don't know if you remember this."

NAVAL: "I do not."

TIM: "I had jeans on, and these brown, odd-looking dress shoes that kind of looked like bowling shoes. You looked at me, smiled, and asked, 'Why are you dressed like a gay banker?' Then, this woman that neither of us had ever met started defending me, and I was like, 'Oh God, here we go. . . .'"

NAVAL: "The honesty thing is a core foundational value."

TIM: "In fairness, I totally did."

EMBARRASSED INTO STARTING HIS FIRST COMPANY

"I was working at this tech company called @Home Network, and I told everybody around me — my boss, my coworkers, my friends — 'In Silicon Valley, all of these other people are starting companies. It looks like they can do it. I'm going to go start a company. I'm just here temporarily. I'm an entrepreneur.' I told everybody, and I wasn't meaning to actually trick myself into it. It wasn't a deliberate, calculated thing.

"I was just venting, talking out loud, being overly honest. But I actually didn't [start a company]. This was 1996. It was a much scarier, more difficult proposition to start a company then. Sure enough, everyone started coming up to me and saying, 'What are you still doing here? I thought you were leaving to start a company?' 'Wow, you're still here. That was a while ago that you said that.' I was literally embarrassed into starting my own company."

NOW, USE THAT TECHNIQUE ON PURPOSE

"Tell your friends that you're a happy person. Then you'll be forced to conform to it. You'll have a consistency bias. You have to live up to it. Your friends will expect you to be a happy person."

90% FEAR, 10% DESIRE

"I find that 90% of thoughts that I have are fear-based. The other 10% are probably desire-based. There's a great definition I read that says, 'Enlightenment is the space between your thoughts,' which means that enlightenment isn't this thing you achieve after 30 years sitting in a corner on a mountaintop. It's something you can achieve moment to moment, and you can be a certain percentage enlightened every single day."

⁎ Naval's best $100 or less purchase?

"The teppanyaki grill. It's a little tabletop grill [search "Presto 22-inch electric griddle"]. What I learned is that for food, the freshness and quality of the food going straight from the grill to your mouth is way more important than what you do with it. For example, in most recipes, we sauce the heck out of everything, we cream it, we overprepare it, and we overprocess it because it's sitting under a heat lamp for 10 minutes."

⁎ What would you put on a billboard?

"I don't know if I have messages to send to the world, but there are messages I like to send to myself at all times. One message that really stuck with me when I figured this out is: **"Desire is a contract you make with yourself to be unhappy until you get what you want."** I don't think most of us realize that's what it is. I think we go about desiring things all day long, and then wondering why we're unhappy. So, I like to stay aware of that because then I can choose my desires very carefully. I try not to have more than one big desire in my life at any given time, and I also recognize that as the axis of my suffering. I realize that that's where I've chosen to be unhappy. I think that is an important one."

TF: Naval first encountered a variation of the above bolded text on a now-extinct blog called *Delusion Damage*.

NAVAL'S LAWS

The below is Naval's response to the question "Are there any quotes you live by or think of often?" These are gold. Take the time necessary to digest them.

"These aren't all quotes from others. Many are maxims that I've carved for myself."

→ Be present above all else.

→ Desire is suffering (Buddha).

→ Anger is a hot coal that you hold in your hand while waiting to throw it at someone else (Buddhist saying).

→ If you can't see yourself working with someone for life, don't work with them for a day.

→ Reading (learning) is the ultimate meta-skill and can be traded for anything else.

→ All the real benefits in life come from compound interest.

→ Earn with your mind, not your time.

→ 99% of all effort is wasted.

→ Total honesty at all times. It's almost always possible to be honest and positive.

→ Praise specifically, criticize generally (Warren Buffett).

→ Truth is that which has predictive power.

→ Watch every thought. (Always ask, "Why am I having this thought?")

→ All greatness comes from suffering.

→ Love is given, not received.

→ Enlightenment is the space between your thoughts (Eckhart Tolle).

→ Mathematics is the language of nature.

→ Every moment has to be complete in and of itself.

A FEW OF NAVAL'S TWEETS THAT ARE TOO GOOD TO LEAVE OUT

"What you choose to work on, and who you choose to work with, are far more important than how hard you work."

"Free education is abundant, all over the Internet. It's the desire to learn that's scarce."

"If you eat, invest, and think according to what the 'news' advocates, you'll end up nutritionally, financially, and morally bankrupt."

"We waste our time with short-term thinking and busywork. Warren Buffett spends a year deciding and a day acting. That act lasts decades."

"The guns aren't new. The violence isn't new. The connected cameras are new, and that changes everything."

"You get paid for being right first, and to be first, you can't wait for consensus."

"My one repeated learning in life: 'There are no adults.' Everyone's making it up as they go along. Figure it out yourself, and do it."

"A busy mind accelerates the passage of subjective time."

MONKEYS ON A SPINNING ROCK

On why Naval no longer has a quest for immortality:

"If you study even the smallest bit of science, you will realize that, for all practical purposes, we are nothing. We're basically monkeys on a small rock orbiting a small, backwards star in a huge galaxy, which is in an absolutely staggeringly gigantic universe, which itself may be part of a gigantic multiverse.

"This universe has been around for probably 10 billion years or more, and will be around for tens of billion years afterwards. So your existence, my existence, is just infinitesimal. It is like a firefly blinking once in the night. Nothing that we do lasts. Eventually you will fade, your works will fade, your children will fade, your thoughts will fade, this planet will fade, the sun will fade . . . it will all be gone.

"There are entire civilizations that we remember now with just one or two words like 'Sumerian' or 'Mayan.' Do you know any Sumerians or Mayans? Do you hold any of them in high regard or esteem? Have they outlived their natural lifespan somehow? No.

"If you don't believe in an afterlife, then you [should realize] that this is such a short and precious life, it is really important that you don't spend it being unhappy. There is no excuse for spending most of your life in misery. You've only got 70 years out of the 50 billion or however long the universe is going to be around."

GLENN BECK

Glenn Beck (FB/TW: @GLENNBECK, GLENNBECK.COM) hit rock bottom as an alcoholic in his 30s and restarted his life. Fast forward to 2014, *Forbes* named him to their annual Celebrity 100 Power List and pegged his earnings at $90 million for that year. This placed him ahead of people like Mark Burnett, Jimmy Fallon, Leonardo DiCaprio, and Will Smith. Glenn's platforms — including radio, television, digital (TheBlaze.com), publishing, etc. — receive somewhere between 30 and 50 million unique visitors per month.

The goal of my podcast is to push listeners outside of their comfort zones and force them to question assumptions. I regularly invite divergent thinkers who disagree with one another. This interview came about thanks to a late-night sauna session with an old friend, a mixed-race Brown University grad who is liberal in nearly every sense of the word. I casually asked him, "If you could pick one person to be on the podcast, who would it be?" He answered without a moment's hesitation. "Glenn Beck. His story is FASCINATING." And it was. . . .

THE MOST IMPORTANT LESSON GLENN LEARNED IN RADIO

"If I have to pick one, the best thing I learned, I learned by mistake. Somebody calls in [to the radio show in the early days] and said: 'Glenn Beck, you're Mr. Perfect, like you've ever done anything wrong. You just can't accept a flaw in anybody.' I stood there for a while and the room got really quiet. And I said, 'You know, let me tell you something. You don't have any idea who I even am, or the bad things that I have done. Let me tell you who I am.' And I spent about 15 minutes being unbelievably, brutally honest and laying out who I am. The worst. No apology, nothing. Just saying: 'You think you know? I've been lying to you. This is who I am.' I turned off my mic and I looked at my then-intern, the lowest producer on the ladder who's now my executive producer. I said to him, 'Mark this down on your calendar. Today is the day Glenn Beck ended his career.'

"The opposite happened. I had grown up in a world where everything was manufactured, everything was written, timed, produced perfectly. What I realized that day was people are starving for something authentic. They'll accept you, warts and all, if that's who you really are. Once you start lying to them, they're not interested. We're all alike. **So the best advice I learned by mistake, and that is: Be willing to fail or succeed on who you really are. Don't ever try to be anything else.** What you are is good enough for whatever it is you're doing."

RIGHTEOUS DOESN'T MEAN RADICAL

Glenn recounted what he learned from an old lady who, at age 16, gave a Jew a bowl of soup. It was a death sentence at the time and she was sent to Auschwitz:

"She said, 'Glenn, **remember, the righteous didn't suddenly become righteous. They just refused to go over the cliff with everybody else.**' That's all we have to do: Know what our principles — not our interests — are today. And as the world goes over the cliff, I'm not going to change my principles. Treating human beings, whether they're like me or not like me, whether they're the same religion or a different religion, with love and respect."

ON A LIFE-CHANGING CONVERSATION WITH YALE PROFESSOR WAYNE MEEKS

In his early 30s, Glenn spent a semester at Yale as a theology major and felt out of place:

"[Wayne] reached across the table, and he grabbed my hand and he said, 'You listen to me for a second, would you? You realize you belong here, right? You're okay to be here.' That endorsement, and as stupid as it seems, opened up my whole world. Because it was the first time somebody said, 'You're smart enough. You can do it.' . . . That changed my world. I wish it hadn't, in some ways. I wish it didn't mean so much to me. But I've learned from that, now in my position, to say that to people. Because there's something stupid in us that just makes us feel like we're not good enough, we're not smart enough."

GLENN'S GUIDING QUOTE

"Question with boldness even the existence of a God; because, if there be one, he must more approve of the homage of reason, than that of blindfolded fear."
— Thomas Jefferson

> **"** There's a mystic who says there's only one really good question, which is, 'What am I unwilling to feel?' **"**

TARA BRACH

Tara Brach (FB: TARABRACH, TARABRACH.COM) is a PhD in clinical psychology and one of the leading teachers of Buddhist thinking and meditation in the Western world. She is the founder of the Insight Meditation Community of Washington in Washington, D.C., and her lectures are downloaded hundreds of thousands of times each month at TARABRACH .COM.

I was first introduced to Tara by Maria Popova (page 406), who said, "[Tara] has changed my life, perhaps more profoundly than anybody in my life." I then read Tara's first book, *Radical Acceptance*, after it was recommended to me by a neuroscience PhD who worked with Adam Gazzaley (page 135). I digested 10 pages each night in the tub, and it immediately had a huge impact. So much so that I initially stopped reading after 20% to test-drive the lessons in real life. There was a lot to work with.

Spirit animal: Panther

Perhaps my favorite lesson, excerpted below, is "Inviting Mara to Tea." It relates to actively recognizing anger and other types of what we consider "negative" emotions. Rather than trying to suppress something or swat it away, we say to the emotion/ourselves, "I see you." This counterintuitively helps to dissolve or resolve the issue. For instance, if you're meditating and anger comes up, maybe the memory of some personal slight, you might silently repeat "anger, anger" to yourself and acknowledge it, which allows you to quickly return to whatever your focus is.

I've always been a fighter, and calm acknowledgment doesn't come naturally to me, which makes it all the more valuable.

Fighting emotions is like flailing in quicksand—it only makes things worse. Sometimes, the most proactive "defense" is a mental nod and wink.

––––––––––

Inviting Mara to Tea

This being human is a guest house.
Every morning a new arrival.

A joy, a depression, a meanness,
Some momentary awareness comes
as an unexpected visitor.

Welcome and entertain them all! . . .

The dark thought, the shame, the malice,
meet them at the door laughing,
and invite them in.

Be grateful for whoever comes,
because each has been sent
as a guide from beyond.
—Rumi

One of my favorite stories of the Buddha shows the power of a wakeful and friendly heart. The night before his enlightenment, the Buddha fought a great battle with the Demon God Mara, who attacked the then-bodhisattva

Siddhartha Gautama with everything he had: lust, greed, anger, doubt, etc. Having failed, Mara left in disarray on the morning of the Buddha's enlightenment.

Yet, it seems Mara was only temporarily discouraged. Even after the Buddha had become deeply revered throughout India, Mara continued to make unexpected appearances. The Buddha's loyal attendant, Ananda, always on the lookout for any harm that might come to his teacher, would report with dismay that the "Evil One" had again returned.

Instead of ignoring Mara or driving him away, the Buddha would calmly acknowledge his presence, saying, "I see you, Mara."

He would then invite him for tea and serve him as an honored guest. Offering Mara a cushion so that he could sit comfortably, the Buddha would fill two earthen cups with tea, place them on the low table between them, and only then take his own seat. Mara would stay for a while and then go, but throughout the Buddha remained free and undisturbed.

When Mara visits us, in the form of troubling emotions or fearsome stories, we can say, "I see you, Mara," and clearly recognize the reality of craving and fear that lives in each human heart. By accepting these experiences with the warmth of compassion, we can offer Mara tea rather than fearfully drive him away. Seeing what is true, we hold what is seen with kindness. We express such wakefulness of heart each time we recognize and embrace our hurts and fears.

Our habit of being a fair-weather friend to ourselves—of pushing away or ignoring whatever darkness we can—is deeply entrenched. But just as a relationship with a good friend is marked by understanding and compassion, we can learn to bring these same qualities to our own inner life.

Pema Chödrön says that through spiritual practice, "We are learning to make friends with ourselves, our life, at the most profound level possible." We befriend ourselves when, rather than resisting our experience, we open our hearts and willingly invite Mara to tea.

"The key in a restaurant, and the key in any kind of high-pressure situation, I think, is that **75% of success is staying calm** and not losing your nerve. The rest you figure out, but once you lose your calm, everything else starts falling apart fast."

SAM KASS

Sam Kass (TW: @CHEFSAMKASS, TROVEWORLDWIDE.COM) almost became a pro baseball player. Instead, he pivoted a history major from the University of Chicago into becoming the private chef for the Obamas. He then became the senior White House policy advisor for nutrition and was named #11 on *Fast Company* magazine's 2011 list of 100 Most Creative People for his work, which focused on establishing private-sector partnerships to reduce childhood obesity to just 5% by 2030. Sam was the first person in the history of the White House to have a position both in the Executive Office of the President and the Residence. He is now a founding partner of Trove, which connects businesses, organizations, and governments that are serious about making an impact on the world with the people and tools to help them achieve it.

FROM HIS FIRST SOUS-CHEF — TWO RULES FOR THE KITCHEN AND LIFE

"The first is: Never serve anything you wouldn't want to eat. Never serve crap. It's Rule Number 1. You can have a high standard on everything. Rule Number 2: When things get really busy, instead of just plowing ahead, trying to work as fast as you can, and just going through all the tickets, he always would tell me, 'Step back and come up with a plan. Look at what dishes you have, and figure out the most efficient way to cook them.' So, if you have five of one thing, don't just cook them one at a time. Get them out, prep them together, and do them together."

PROS USE ACID

"One difference between home cooks and pros is acidity level. When you think it's ready, add another lemon. Pros bump up the acidity level. It's one of the secrets. We add a little more acid, and it makes everything taste better."

THE SECRET TO GREAT EGGS

"Eggs are one of the hardest things to cook. Some of the great chefs in the world, their test for a new cook would be how to make an omelet. That would be their one master test. So, I actually like eggs all ways, but almost always soft, like a soft-boiled egg. I'll do eggs over easy or really soft scrambled eggs. The trick for soft scrambled eggs is — after you get your butter knives out — I crack the eggs straight into the pan, let them cook for a second, and then mix them up. Then, before you think they're done, take them out because they'll harden a little bit as they sit on the plate."

TF: In the last few years, I've developed a love affair with soft-boiled eggs, which can be a decadent indulgence if done right. Here's my approach: 1) Bring water to a boil. 2) Gently add eggs and set timer for exactly 5 minutes. 3) Manage the heat so it's a gentle bubbling boil, not a violent lava pit. 4) At 5 minutes, pour out the hot water and replace with cold tap water. 5) Remove, peel, and enjoy.

✳ **Advice to your younger self at college graduation?**

"'Passion' is an overstated word. I think passion develops. . . . I threw myself into food, and although I was passionate about it, it wasn't a life passion until

I combined food and nourishment with health, sustainability, politics, policy, and what we're doing to really help make sure that all people can live healthy, productive, awesome lives through the food that they're eating.

"That is what became that passion. . . . A lot of people [say], 'Find your passion.' I think passion comes from a combination of being open and curious, and of really going all-in when you find something that you're interested in."

EDWARD NORTON

Edward Norton (TW: @EdwardNorton, crowdrise.com) is an actor, filmmaker, and activist. He has been nominated for three Academy Awards for his work in *Primal Fear*, *American History X*, and *Birdman*. He has starred in scores of other films, including *Fight Club*, *The Illusionist*, and *Moonrise Kingdom*. Edward is also a serial startup founder (e.g., CrowdRise), a UN ambassador for biodiversity, a massively successful investor (e.g., early Uber), a pilot, and is deeply involved with wilderness conservation.

YOU WANT TO BE TAKEN SERIOUSLY? THEN TAKE THINGS SERIOUSLY

"[Toby Orenstein] was a great director. . . . If you're lucky, you have someone when you're young who doesn't talk down to you, who speaks to you as a serious person and exhorts you to take something seriously, to take work seriously. If a person does that in the right way, you feel elevated. As a young person, you feel like someone is saying to you, 'Hey! You want to be taken seriously? Then take things seriously. Do the work, you know? Don't coast, you know?' I'd say that's what she gave."

✳ One of Edward's recommended essays

"The Catastrophe of Success" by Tennessee Williams.

TF: One of my favorite lines from this piece is: "For me, a convenient place to work is a remote place among strangers where there is good swimming."

* Edward's favorite documentaries

Bennett Miller's *The Cruise* and Adam Curtis's films. "He's got a four-part film called *The Century of the Self*, and then a three-part series called *The Power of Nightmares*. I think those are absolutely brilliant films, dense but really eye-opening."

TF: *The Century of the Self* has been recommended to me by several podcast guests.

* Three favorite recent films?

"Of late, I'm a huge fan of the French filmmaker Jacques Audiard. I think, in the last few years, he put up a hat trick of films": *The Beat That My Heart Skipped*, *A Prophet*, and *Rust and Bone*.

TF: *A Prophet* is now one of my favorite films. If you like gangster movies, it is violently gorgeous and teaches a lot of leadership lessons.

MARLON BRANDO: REAL GENIUS VERSUS FAKED GENIUS

"One of the best stories I ever heard about young people in an acting class, and the difference between what happens to people typically and what a real, authentic kind of genius is [relates to Marlon Brando]. Harry Belafonte talked about being in an acting class with Marlon. They were both 19 or 20 years old in Greenwich Village. [The organizers of the class said,] 'Okay. One person's in his apartment, and the other one enters. You're the person who's on your couch in your apartment. Just run with it.' People were doing all kinds of forced conversations or trying to create a scenario. . . . Supposedly, Marlon sat on the couch and started reading a magazine, and whoever it was walked in his door. He looked up, jumped up, grabbed the guy by the shirt front, threw him out the door, and slammed the door. Everybody was like, 'What are you doing?' He said, 'I don't know who that fucking guy is. He just walked into my apartment. He scared the shit out of me.' You know what I mean? It's like, 'Wait a minute. Yeah, there probably wouldn't be a scene. There probably wouldn't be a conversation.'"

> **"Wine is a grocery, not a luxury."**

RICHARD BETTS

Richard Betts (TW:@YOBETTS, MYESSENTIALWINE.COM) served as the wine director at The Little Nell in Aspen from 2000 to 2008. Richard also passed the Court of Master Sommeliers' Masters Exam on his first attempt, becoming the ninth person in history ever to do so. As of this writing, there are only roughly 240 Master "somms" in the world. He is the author of *The Essential Scratch & Sniff Guide to Becoming a Wine Expert* and *The Essential Scratch & Sniff Guide to Becoming a Whiskey Know-It-All*.

THE BEGINNING OF RICHARD'S WINE ADVENTURE

Richard was on track to become a lawyer, and . . . he hated it. Many years earlier, he'd spent time in Italy. Then: "When I was in grad school in Flagstaff, I was clerking for a small environmental firm. I found it didn't matter whether you were doing environmental, or you were doing bankruptcy—it was the same Monopoly board, making the same motions, pass Park Place every time. You just traded the hat for the shoe or whatever your piece was. It's still the same game, and I found I didn't like the game. So, I was really ripe for this

Spirit animal: Spinner dolphin

moment. . . . It was about to be thesis defense weekend. My thesis was great, and I was supposed to go to law school six weeks later.

"[Instead,] I walked out of the lab, hopped over the fence, and ran across Route 66 there in Flagstaff to a small restaurant/wine store. I didn't know anything about wine. I just knew that I drank it daily in Italy and how much that meant to me. I walked in and I bought totally based on sight . . . I thought, 'I kind of recognize that label,' and I took it home, popped the cork, and poured a glass. That first smell took me back to a moment almost four years earlier when living in Italy. I specifically remembered a dinner I had at the Osteria del Cinghiale Bianco in Florence. I remembered where I sat, where my companion sat, what she ate, what she wore, what I ate, and what the waitress did right and wrong that night. All of that just came rushing back from one smell."

✴ What are a few underpriced or underrated wines?
Grenache from Rusden, Zinfandel from Turley, and Chenin Blanc from Mosse. And don't forget: "Try smelling with your mouth open, as you'll get more information."

EXPLAINING HIS "BE NICE" TATTOO, WHICH STARTED AS THE LETTER "B"

"It was a note to self to just **be** kind, **be** thoughtful, **be**nevolent . . . just be a good guy. Sometimes, I thrash about, and it's a little reminder. Note to self. It grew into 'Be nice,' plain and simple."

CULINARY SCHOOL — A POTATOES-TO-POTATOES COMPARISON

"I went and talked to a chef, and I said, 'This is what I'm thinking about . . . I'm either going to ask you for a job or I'm thinking about culinary school.' He said, 'Here's the deal. You can come here today, and you can ask me for a job, and I'll say, "Yeah, great. Here are the potatoes. Get peeling." Or you can go to culinary school, spend two more years of your life preparing, spending $30K or $40K a year in bills to be there, then, you can come to me and ask me for a job, and I'll say, "Yeah, sure. Here's a big pot of potatoes. Get peeling." Same thing.' I was like, 'Okay, I'm pretty good at math. I got this. Where are the potatoes? Let's do it.' So it was that simple."

GOING ON OFFENSE — DELIBERATELY AVOIDING THE HOTBEDS FOR BETTER ACCESS

"There were these two chefs I wanted to work for in Tucson, who are great — well regarded on a national level. Nobody wanted to move there to work with them, so [if I went,] I could get immediate access and supercharge my learning and my path. So I did. I went to that second chef, and I said, 'Hey, man, I want to work with you. This is why I'm in Arizona,' and he said, 'Great. What have you been doing?'"

TF: Richard got the job. This is very similar to the "going on offense" philosophy and decision-making of Chris Sacca (page 164), who first introduced me to Richard. Competition is overrated (see Peter Thiel, page 232), and sometimes you can you push a rock downhill instead of uphill (see Seth Godin, page 237).

DON'T WORK FOR THE AWARDS, MAKE THE AWARDS WORK FOR YOU

TIM: "What do you think financially successful people who are generally unhappy have in common?"

RICHARD: "Misplaced goals. I think chasing the financial is not the right way to do it. That first chef who gave me that first wine job, he was great. We were overlooked for a couple of things in the press, and I'm new in this food and wine world. He said, **'Look, Richard, if you work for the awards, you don't do good work. But if you do good work, the awards will come.'**"

* **Advice to your 25-year-old self?**
"**Don't be so fucking shy.** . . . Dude, I can still think of instances within the last 24 months where I think, 'Man, Richard, I wish you had been more forward. I wish you had asked for X instead of being so subtle and implying it.' I try to go for that subtle, elegant thing, which sounds really nice. I think part of that is actually being shy. Sometimes, the clues that you put outwardly are too subtle to be heard, or someone is just talking louder than you."

* **I think you're a spectacularly good teacher. If you were teaching a ninth-grade class, what would you teach?**
"Love yourself . . . You've got to love yourself before you can love others. Without it, nothing productive is going to happen, and we can all bang our heads on the wall."

MIKE BIRBIGLIA

Mike Birbiglia (TW: @BIRBIGS, BIRBIGS.COM) is a one of the busiest comedians in the world, both behind and in front of the camera. He started as a standup comic and has reached the height of his field — an international touring solo act that blends theater, film, storytelling, and standup comedy. His projects range from sold-out tours and *New York Times* bestsellers to feature film and regular appearances on public radio's *This American Life*, where he has a meaningful collaboration with host and producer Ira Glass. Most recently, he is the creator, writer, and star of the film *Don't Think Twice*.

Spirit animal: Grizzly bear

ART IS SOCIALISM, BUT LIFE IS CAPITALISM

"My wife made the observation that everyone's equal on stage, but off stage, they're completely unequal." Mike wrote down, "Art is socialism but life is capitalism," and that became a guiding principle for his film *Don't Think Twice*.

ONLY EMOTION ENDURES

Mike cork-boards his walls and pins 3x5 cards to them. One of his favorites is just three words from Ezra Pound, which Mike considers one of the best quotes for writing: "Only emotion endures."

SILENCE SOMETIMES SPEAKS LOUDER THAN WORDS

TIM: "With someone like Ira [Glass], or anyone else, is there a particular way that you elicit feedback to make it as helpful as possible?"

MIKE: "Usually, I will tell people bits and jokes over the phone, partly because they can peacefully give feedback in a way that's not judgmental. When you're face to face with somebody [and say a joke, they can] feel the pressure of 'Oh, I should laugh or I should politely respond.' On the phone, it's pretty easy to skim through stuff, and I can hear when people are interested by what's being said. Quentin Tarantino — I've read this — will call people endlessly and pitch them movies that he's working on. He says he doesn't even have to hear the laughter; he can hear in their silence what their interest level is."

WRITE IN A TRANCE AND ACT IN A TRANCE

"I try to write before my inhibitions take hold of me. I try to do 7 a.m. Because I'm an actor, as well, I always say, 'Write in a trance and act in a trance.' You don't want to think consciously about what you're putting on the page. A lot of times, I'll write in my journal as though it will never be seen by anyone, and then, more often than not, the things that I put in my secret journal are the things that I publish."

MIKE!!! YOU HAVE A MEETING WITH YOURSELF!

"Actually, this is a real quirk that I rarely admit to anyone, never mind in public. To finish the script, I found that I kept putting it off, and I was analyzing my habits. [I realized] I was putting off writing the script, but I wasn't putting off having lunch with Brian Koppelman [page 613, a mutual friend] or having lunch with my brother or whatever. . . . So I thought, 'I'm always on time, and I always show up to things, so why don't I do that for myself?' So I put a hand-written note next to my bed that said — and it has three exclamation points — 'Mike!!! You have a meeting at Café Pedlar [where I was writing] at 7 a.m. with your mind,' which is so stupid. It's so embarrassing to admit, but it worked!"

✻ Recommended podcasts

Sleep with Me: Mike falls asleep to this podcast. Mike is famous for his very real sleep disorders. He once jumped out of a second-story win-dow while sleepwalking and nearly killed himself.

Scriptnotes: This has come up with at least a half dozen guests. Legit ad-vice from legit doers.

✻ What would you put on a billboard?

"I'd put it in Times Square and it would say, 'None of these companies care about you.'"

HOW TO APPROACH CELEBRITIES (AND GET PRESIDENT OBAMA TO SAY "POO")

"I met [President Obama] 2 years ago, when my wife was pregnant. Our whole thing was, whenever we meet someone who we know doesn't care about meet-ing us, my wife and I always try and come up with a trick question that throws them off. They kind of have to answer, or have to think about it. I give this ad-vice to people. If you ever see Jimmy Fallon on the street, don't say, 'I love *The Tonight Show*!' Just say something like: 'What do you think of kiwi?' and he won't be able to not be like, 'I love kiwi!' Talk to people about a thing they didn't think they were going to talk about. Then, next thing you know, you're talking to Jimmy Fallon about kiwi and you'll have that for your life.

"So our thing with Obama, because my wife was 4 months pregnant but we hadn't told anybody yet, was 'Why don't we tell him you're pregnant?' So when we get to the front, I say, 'Mr. President, this is my wife, Jen. She's newly pregnant but don't tell anyone.' And he couldn't help it. The president of the United States couldn't help but say, 'Well, am I first to know?' And my wife says yes. She asks, 'Do you have any parenting advice?' And he says, 'Well, get some sleep.' And we're like, 'Ha-ha' because he's the president. It wasn't that funny, comically, but he's like your boss times a million. But then he got better, because he goes, 'No, actually, I've got something. When you bring him home, the poo . . .' The president said 'poo,' and the moment he said 'poo,' I thought, 'This is the greatest day of my life. I could die right now and I'd be fine.' He says, 'When you bring him home, the poo doesn't smell. It doesn't smell like adult poo. Adult poo smells bad.' Then he looked at me for affirmation, and I was like, 'Absolutely, Mr. President; adult poo does indeed smell terrible. Thank you for inviting me to the Poo Seminar 2015.'

"And he goes, 'And when you bring him home, babies crave structure in their eating and in their sleeping. Breastfeeding doesn't always work out right away. There's going to be a little bit of wonky. Don't freak out. And if the sleeping doesn't work out right away, don't freak out.' And he paused and he thought about it and he goes, 'That's actually some pretty good advice.' He complimented his own advice. I'm telling you, the best thing to do is give people questions they're not expecting."

✱ Advice to your 20-year-old self?

"I would say, **'Write everything down because it's all very fleeting.'** I would say, 'Keep a journal,' which I have but I would have been more meticulous. Then I would say, 'Don't bow to the gatekeepers at the head of, in my case, show business, but at the gate of any business or any endeavor.' **Don't bow to the gatekeepers because I think, in essence, there are no gatekeepers. You are the gatekeeper. . . .**

"**Don't waste your time on marketing, just try to get better. . . .**

"**And also, it's not about being good; it's about being great.** Because what I find, the older I get, is that a lot of people are good, and a lot of people are smart, and a lot of people are clever. But not a lot of people give you their soul when they perform."

THE JAR OF AWESOME

This was not my idea. It is thanks to an ex-girlfriend who is a real sweetheart. She made and gave me the Jar of Awesome as a gift, because I'm very good at achievement and historically not good at appreciation. Here's how it works:

There is a mason jar on my kitchen counter with JAR OF AWESOME in glitter letters on the side. Anytime something really cool happens in a day, something that made me excited or joyful, doctor's orders are to write it down on a slip of paper and put it in this mason jar. When something great happens, you think you'll remember it 3 months later, but you won't. The Jar of Awesome creates a record of great things that *actually* happened, all of which are easy to forget if you're depressed or seeing the world through gray-colored glasses. I tend to celebrate very briefly, if at all, so this pays dividends for weeks, months, or years.

The Jar of Awesome has had a tremendous impact on my quality of life. It sounds ridiculous to admit and my 20-year-old self would probably vomit, but — man — it works.

I keep the jar where I will see it constantly Each time the name catches my eye, a little voice in my head says, "Things aren't so bad, Eeyore. Perk the fuck up!" I came to realize that A) If you're serious all the time, you'll wear out before the truly serious stuff gets done; and B) if you don't regularly appreciate the small wins, you will never appreciate the big wins. They'll all fall through your fingers like sand as you obsess on the next week, the next to-do, the next thing to fix. This makes "success" a Pyrrhic victory at best.

Now, if you don't want to have a jar with "Jar of Awesome" written on it, you could just put a huge star or exclamation point on the side. However, the more serious you are in "real life," the more ridiculous I think you should make it. Who are you trying to impress? If you have kids, get them involved. Many of my fans now have their entire families developing gratitude using this simple, low-tech godsend.

Cultivate the habit of putting something in every day. Can't think of anything? "I didn't die today!" is a reliable winner. That's totally awesome compared to the alternative. Look for the good, practice finding the good, and you'll see it more often.

MALCOLM GLADWELL

Malcolm Gladwell (TW: @GLADWELL, GLADWELL.COM) is the author of five *New York Times* bestsellers. He has been named one of the 100 Most Influential People by *Time* magazine and one of *Foreign Policy*'s Top Global Thinkers. He explored how ideas spread in *The Tipping Point*, decision-making in *Blink*, the roots of success in *Outliers*, and the advantages of disadvantages in his latest book, *David and Goliath*. In his latest project, the *Revisionist History* podcast, Gladwell examines the way the passage of time changes and enlightens our understanding of the world around us.

✳ What did you have for breakfast?

"I had a cappuccino and a third of a croissant. I love croissants, but I think one should eat the absolute minimum in the morning. . . . That's one of my rules."

✳ On lapsang souchong black tea

"Some people smell it, and they just run in the opposite direction. They don't even think it's tea. There's a little coffee shop where I often go in the morning, and they have it. I think I'm one of the only people who orders it."

TF: Lapsang souchong has a very smoky, peaty flavor. It reminds one of my friends so much of whisky that he used it to cut back on drinking alcohol.

✳ How do you decide how to start a chapter or book?

"It's not a math question where there's only one answer. So, as long as you understand there is not just one good answer, it takes the pressure off. Typically, I might try out several openings. It's made easier by the fact that I don't start at the beginning. Once you don't start at the beginning, your life just gets so much simpler."

TF: Search "5 great examples of *in medias res*" for more on this approach. *In medias res* literally means "into the middle things" in Latin and refers to beginning a story (chapter, novel, movie, video game, whatever) in the middle or at the end of the narrative. I've done this with all of my previous books.

HOW MALCOLM LEARNED TO ASK QUESTIONS

His father, a mathematician, taught Malcolm to ask questions upon questions:

"My father has zero intellectual insecurities.... It has never crossed his mind to be concerned that the world thinks he's an idiot. He's not in that game. So if he doesn't understand something, he just asks you. He doesn't care if he sounds foolish. He will ask the most obvious question without any sort of concern about it.... So he asks lots and lots of 'dumb,' in the best sense of that word, questions. He'll say to someone, 'I don't understand. Explain that to me.' He'll just keep asking questions until he gets it right, and I grew up listening to him do this in every conceivable setting. [If my father had met Bernie Madoff, he] never would have invested money with him because he would have said, 'I don't understand' a hundred times. 'I don't understand how that works,' in this kind of dumb, slow voice. 'I don't understand, sir. What is going on?'"

(See Alex Blumberg, page 303.)

✳ Malcolm's role models in the public speaking world

"Niall Ferguson, the historian, gave a birthday toast, which is just the best toast I've ever heard in my life. [It was] so much better than anything I'd ever heard. It was on another level."

✳ What's bad advice that you hear being given out often?

"The worst advice that, in general, we give in America is that we terrify high school kids about their college choices. All things related to college fall under the category of bad advice. As you will find out when you listen to my rants about college [on *Revisionist History*], I think the American college system needs to be blown up and they need to start over.... Am I so inspired by what I learned during the day that I want to be talking about it at 1:00 in the morning? And do I have someone who will have that conversation with me and who will challenge me? That's it. Everything else is nonsense."

STEPHEN J. DUBNER

Stephen J. Dubner (TW: @FREAKONOMICS, FREAKONOMICS.COM) is an award-winning author, journalist, and radio and TV personality. He is best known for writing, along with the economist Steven D. Levitt, *Freakonomics*, *SuperFreakonomics*, *Think Like a Freak*, and *When to Rob a Bank*, which have sold more than 5 million copies in 35 languages. He is the host of the massively popular *Freakonomics Radio* podcast.

Spirit animal: A mid-sized mutt of very unimpressive lineage — a little shy, relatively friendly after a while, sloppy but not too wild, quite loyal, a good sleeper

A LESSER-KNOWN FAVORITE

We both absolutely love *Levels of the Game* by John McPhee, an entire book about a single tennis match between Arthur Ashe and Clark Graebner in 1968. It's a short 162 pages and the *New York Times* gushed, "This may be the high point of American sports journalism." It's Stephen's most-gifted book for adults. For kids, his most-gifted book is *The Empty Pot* by Demi.

✻ Any quotes you live by or think of often?

"Enough is as good as a feast."

WHEN TO PUT AWAY YOUR MORAL COMPASS

"If you want to solve a problem — any problem that you care enough about to want to solve — you almost certainly come to it with a whole lot of ideas about it. Ideas about why it's an important problem, what is it that bothers you exactly, who the villains are in the problem, etc.

"So if you're an environmentalist, and you believe that one of the biggest tragedies of the last 100 years is people despoiling the environment, the minute you hear about an issue that kind of abuts the environment, whether it's honeybee collapse or something having to do with air quality, your immediate moral position is, 'Well, I know exactly what the cause of that is. It's caused by people being stupid and careless and greedy' and so on.

"Now that may be true, but it also may not be true. Our point is, if you try to approach every problem with your moral compass, first and foremost, you're going to make a lot of mistakes. You're going to exclude a lot of possible good solutions. You're going to assume you know a lot of things, when in fact you don't, and you're not going to be a good partner in reaching a solution with other people who don't happen to see the world the way you do."

✻ What's the worst advice you hear often?

"'Write what you know.' Why would I want to write about what little I know? Don't I want to use writing to learn more?"

ON VETTING BRAINSTORMED IDEAS

"Some of them just turned out to not be so interesting. Some of them we didn't really believe in. Some of them turned out to be interesting and true, but they didn't have any data or stories that really illustrated them . . . **so our brainstorming was: Let's come up with as many ideas as possible, and then put them under scrutiny, and basically try to kill them off, and if they were unkillable, then we'd keep going with them.**"

✽ Three sources you've learned from or followed closely in the last year?

Online: *Marginal Revolution*, Kottke.org, and Cool Tools (by Kevin Kelly, page 470).

✽ Advice to your younger self?

"I would say it's pretty simple: 'Don't be scared.' There are a lot of things I did not do, a lot of experiences I never tried, a lot of people I never met or hung out with because I was, in some form, intimidated or scared. . . . It also plays into what psychologists call the 'spotlight effect,' [as if] everybody must be caring about what I do. And the fact is: Nobody gives a crap what I do."

JOSH WAITZKIN

Josh Waitzkin (JOSHWAITZKIN.COM) was the basis for the book and movie *Searching for Bobby Fischer*. Considered a chess prodigy, he has perfected learning strategies that can be applied to anything, including his other loves of Brazilian jiu-jitsu (he's a black belt under phenom Marcelo Garcia) and tai chi push hands (he's a world champion). These days, he spends his time coaching the world's top athletes and investors, working to revolutionize education, and tackling his new passion of paddle surfing, often nearly killing me in the process. I first met Josh after reading his book, *The Art of Learning*, and we've become dear friends.

Spirit animal: Gorilla

EMPTY SPACE

Josh has no social media, does no interviews (except my podcast, for which he often says to me, "You fuck!"), and avoids nearly all meetings and phone calls. He minimizes input to maximize output, much like Rick Rubin. Josh says: "I cultivate empty space as a way of life for the creative process."

LEARNING THE MACRO FROM THE MICRO

Josh focuses on depth over breadth. He often uses a principle nicknamed "learning the macro from the micro." This means focusing on something very small in a field (whether chess, martial arts, or elsewhere) to internalize extremely powerful macro principles that apply everywhere. This is sometimes combined with "beginning with the endgame." For instance, when Josh gave me a beginner's tutorial on chess, he didn't start with opening moves. Memorizing openings is natural, and nearly everyone does it, but Josh likens it to stealing the test answers from a teacher. You're not learning principles or strategies — you're merely learning a few tricks that will help you beat your novice friends. Instead, Josh took me in reverse, just as his first teacher, Bruce Pandolfini, did with him. The board was empty, except for three pieces in an endgame scenario: king and pawn against king. Through the *micro*, positions of reduced complexity, he was able to focus me on the *macro*: principles like the power of empty space, opposition, and setting an opponent up for *zugzwang* (a situation where any move he makes will destroy his position). By limiting me to a few simple pieces, he hoped I would learn something limitless: high-level concepts I could apply anytime against anyone. I've seen him apply this to many things, including teaching jiu-jitsu, where he can cover nearly all of the principles of jiu-jitsu by focusing on a single submission (endgame) called the "guillotine" (specifically "Marcelotine").

IF YOU'RE STUDYING MY GAME, YOU'RE ENTERING MY GAME

Josh and I spend a lot of time discussing Marcelo Garcia, 5-time world champion in Brazilian jiu-jitsu, with whom Josh owns the Marcelo Garcia Academy in New York City. Marcelo is arguably the best grappler of the last 100 years, the combined Mike Tyson, Wayne Gretzky, and Michael Jordan of his sport. Whereas most competitors are secretive about their competition prep, Marcelo routinely records and uploads his sparring sessions, his exact training for major events. Josh explains the rationale:

"[Marcelo] was visually showing these competitors what he was about to use against them at 2 weeks, 3 weeks, 4 weeks [away from competition], and his attitude about this was just completely unique: 'If you're studying my game, you're entering my game, and I'll be better at it than you.'"

TF: I often share exact under-the-hood details of how I've built the podcast, put together Kickstarter campaigns, etc. I do this because of two core beliefs. Belief #1 — It's rarely a zero-sum game (if someone wins, someone else must lose), and the more I help people with details, the more detailed help I receive. Belief #2 — If it is competitive, I'm simply offering people the details of *my* game. My attention to detail will scare off half of the people who would have tried; 40% will try it and be worse than me; 10% will try it and be better than me, but . . . see Belief #1. That 10% will often reach out to teach me what they've learned, as they're grateful for my own transparency.

REMEMBER THE LAST THREE TURNS

"I remember when I went skiing with Billy Kidd, who is one of the great Olympic downhill racers from back in the 1960s. He's an awesome dude. Now he skis out in Colorado wearing a cowboy hat . . . and he [asked] me years ago when I first skied with him, 'Josh, what do you think are the three most important turns of the ski run?' I've asked that question to a lot of people since.

"Most people will say 'the middle because it's the hardest' or 'the beginning because of momentum,' but he describes the three most important turns of a ski run as the last three before you get on the lift. It's a very subtle point. For those of you who are skiers, that's when the slope is leveled off, there's less challenge. Most people are very sloppy then . . . they have bad form. The problem is that on the lift ride up, unconsciously, you're internalizing bad body mechanics.

"As Billy points out, if your last three turns are precise, then what you're internalizing on the lift ride up is precision. So I carry this on to the guys who I train in the finance world, for example: ending the work day with very high quality, which for one thing means you're internalizing quality overnight."

TF: Thanks to Josh, I now always end training sessions on a good "rep," whether AcroYoga, gymnastics, archery, or other. For instance, even if I have

60 minutes budgeted for a workout, if I hit a fantastic "PR" (personal record) at 45 minutes, or do something new well, I pack it in. In the case of archery, I also use "blank bale" practice, where I start and end all sessions with 5 to 6 arrows shot by feel alone, eyes closed, into a target that is a mere 10 feet away. This is similar to "dry firing" with firearms. One of Josh's favorite writers, Hemingway, had a practice of ending his writing sessions mid-flow and mid-sentence. This way, he knew exactly where to start the next day, and he could reliably both end and start his sessions with confidence.

TO TURN IT ON, LEARN TO TURN IT OFF (AND VICE VERSA)

"One of my most beautiful memories of [Marcelo] is in the world championship, right before going to the semifinals. He's napping on a bleacher. Everyone's screaming and yelling, and he's asleep on the bleacher. I can't wake him up.

"He [finally] took a stumble into the ring, [and] you've never seen a guy more relaxed before going into a world championship fight. . . . He can turn it off so deeply, and man, when he goes in the ring, you can't turn it on with any more intensity than he can. His ability to turn it off is directly aligned with how intensely he can turn it on, so [I train] people to do this, to have stress and recovery undulation throughout their day.

"Interval training [often at midday or lunch break] and meditation together are beautiful habits to develop to cultivate the art of turning it on and turning it off."

THE LITTLE THINGS ARE THE BIG THINGS

"We're talking about Marcelo embodying the principle of quality in all these little ways [e.g., specific cleaning protocols for the gym, having people tidy their uniforms in class]. These little ways, you could say don't matter, but they add up to matter hugely."

TIM: "Oh, I think the little things are the big things. Because they're a reflection. This may sound clichéd, but how you do anything is how you do everything."

JOSH: "It's such a beautiful and critical principle, and most people think they can wait around for the big moments to turn it on. But if you don't cultivate 'turning it on' as a way of life in the little moments — and there are hundreds of times more little moments than big — then there's no chance in the big moments. . . . I believe that when you're not cultivating quality, you're essentially cultivating sloppiness."

"JUST GO AROUND" FOR LIFE

"Lateral thinking or thematic thinking, the ability to take a lesson from one thing and transfer it to another, is one of the most important disciplines that any of us can cultivate. From a really young age, we [my wife and I] began to cultivate this [in our toddler son, Jack] around this principle of 'go around.' The first time, we were staying in a little cottage in Martha's Vineyard in a big field, and he was trying to get in one door. He couldn't, but he could get in the other door, and I said, 'Jack, go around.' He looked at me and he went around.

"Then 'go around' became language for us, in terms of solving puzzles and in terms of any time you run into an obstacle. Working with the metaphor of 'go around' opened up this way that we could just have dialogue around connecting things — taking away a principle from one thing and applying it to something else — and we've had a lot of fun with that."

"EMBRACE YOUR FUNK"

"That's a term from my buddy, Graham Duncan [a successful manager of a 'fund of funds'], who's a dear friend of ours who's come on our surf adventures. He's a brilliant thought partner . . . you think about the entanglement of genius and madness, our brilliance and eccentricity. Understanding that entanglement is a precursor to working with anybody who's trying to be world-class at something, because the entanglement is fundamental to their being. They have to, ultimately, embrace their funk, embrace their eccentricity, embrace what makes them different, and then build on it."

WHO DO YOU PICK WHEN YOUR EGO SEEMS THREATENED?

Back in the world of combat sports and jiu-jitsu:

"It's very interesting to observe who the top competitors pick out when they're five rounds into the sparring sessions and they're completely gassed. The ones who are on the steepest growth curve look for the hardest guy there — the one who might beat them up — while others look for someone they can take a break on."

THE IMPORTANCE OF LANGUAGE ON A RAINY DAY

"One of the biggest mistakes that I observed in the first year of Jack's life was parents who have unproductive language around weather being good or bad. Whenever it was raining, you'd hear moms, babysitters, dads say, 'It's bad weather. We can't go out,' or if it wasn't, 'It's good weather. We can go out.' That means that, somehow, we're externally reliant on conditions being perfect in order to be able to go out and have a good time. So, Jack and I never missed a single storm, rain or snow, to go outside and romp in it. Maybe we missed one when he was sick. We've developed this language around how beautiful it is. Now, whenever it's a rainy day, Jack says, 'Look, Dada, it's such a beautiful rainy day,' and we go out and we play in it. I wanted him to have this internal locus of control — to not be reliant on external conditions being *just so*."

WHY YOU NEED A "DELOADING" PHASE IN LIFE

My daily journaling isn't limited to mornings. I use it as a tool to clarify my thinking and goals, much as Kevin Kelly (page 470) does. The paper is like a photography darkroom for my mind.

This chapter shares is a transcription of a real entry from October 2015.

It was written in Samovar Tea Lounge in San Francisco after a 2-hour walk and led me to re-incorporate "deloading" phases in my life. "Deloading" is a concept used in strength and athletic training, but it can be applied to many things. Let's look at the sports definition, here from the website T Nation:

> A back-off week, or deload, is a planned reduction in exercise volume or intensity. In collegiate strength-training circles, it's referred to as the unloading week, and is often inserted between phases or periods. Quoting from *Essentials of Strength Training and Conditioning*: "The purpose of this unloading week is to prepare the body for the increased demand of the next phase or period," and to mitigate the risk of overtraining.

So, how might this relate to creativity, productivity, or quality of life?

Let's start with a personal outcome: In the last 12 months, I've used deloading outside of sports to decrease my anxiety at least 50% while simultaneously doubling my income.

Deloading for business, in my case, consists of strategically taking my foot off of the gas. I alternate intense periods of batching similar tasks (recording podcasts, clearing the inbox, writing blog posts, handling accounting, etc.) with extended periods of—for lack of poetic description—unplugging and fucking around.

The unplug can still be intense (search "4-hour reality check" for an example), but you shouldn't be working on "work."

Let's dig into the journal entry, as it provides much of the reasoning. I've added some additional thoughts below it:

TUES — SAMOVAR @ 5:40PM —

The great "deloading" phase.

This is what I'm experiencing this afternoon, and it makes a Tuesday feel like a lazy Sunday morning. This is when the muse is most likely to visit.

I need to get back to the slack.

To the pregnant void of infinite possibilities, only possible with a lack of obligation, or at least, no compulsive reactivity. Perhaps this is only possible with the negative space to — as Kurt Vonnegut put it — "fart around"? To do things for the hell of it? For no damn good reason at all?

I feel that the big ideas come from these periods. It's the silence between the notes that makes the music.

If you want to create or be anything lateral, bigger, better, or *truly* different, you need room to ask "what if?" without a conference call in 15 minutes. The aha moments rarely come from the incremental inbox-clearing mentality of, "Oh, fuck . . . I forgot to . . . Please remind me to . . . Shouldn't I? . . . I must remember to . . ."

Inbox land is the land of the lost, and we all become lost.

My Tuesday experience reinforced, for me, the importance of creating large, uninterrupted blocks of time, during which your mind can wander, ponder, and find the signal amidst the noise. If you're lucky, it might even create a signal, or connect two signals (core ideas) that have never shaken hands before.

I've scheduled deloading phases in a few ways: roughly 8 a.m. to 9 a.m. daily for journaling, tea routines, etc.; 9 a.m. to 1 p.m. every Wednesday for creative output (i.e., writing, interviewing for the podcast); and "screen-free Saturdays," when I use no laptops and only use my phone for maps and coordinating with friends via text (no apps). Of course, I still use "mini-retirements" à la *The 4-Hour Workweek* a few times a year.

Deloading blocks must be scheduled and defended *more* strongly than your business commitments. The former can strengthen and inform the latter, but not vice versa.

To sum up, how can one throttle back the reactive living that has them following everyone's agenda except their own?

Create slack, as no one will give it to you. This is the only way to swim forward instead of treading water.

BRENÉ BROWN

Dr. Brené Brown (TW: @BreneBrown, brenebrown.com) is a research professor at the University of Houston Graduate College of Social Work. Brené's 2010 TEDxHouston talk, "The Power of Vulnerability," has been viewed more than 31 million times and is one of the top five most viewed TED talks in the world. She has spent the past 13 years studying vulnerability, courage, worthiness, and shame. Brené is the *New York Times* best-selling author of *Daring Greatly*, *The Gifts of Imperfection*, and *Rising Strong*.

AFRAID AND BRAVE CAN COEXIST

"This idea that we're either courageous or chicken shit is just not true, because most of us are afraid and brave at the exact same moment, all day long."

TF: This reminded me of Cus D'Amato, Mike Tyson's legendary first coach, who told his athletes the following before big fights: "The hero and the coward both feel the same thing, but the hero uses his fear, projects it onto his opponent, while the coward runs. It's the same thing—fear—but it's what you do with it that matters."

Spirit animal: Jackalope

GIVE DISCOMFORT ITS DUE

TIM: "Do you have any ask or request of my audience?"

BRENÉ: "Lean into discomfort, because I think these seemingly impossible problems that we have around race and homophobia and the environment, and just the lack of love sometimes, are not going to be solved in a comfortable way. . . . So I guess my ask would be more of a big metaphysical ask: Give vulnerability a shot. Give discomfort its due. Because I think he or she who is willing to be the most uncomfortable is not only the bravest, but rises the fastest."

TF: One of the most common Kindle highlights from *The 4-Hour Workweek* complements this: "A person's success in life can usually be measured by the number of uncomfortable conversations he or she is willing to have."

WHEN I HAD THE OPPORTUNITY, DID I CHOOSE COURAGE OVER COMFORT?

Brené flew under the radar for a long time, until she came across Theodore Roosevelt's famous "arena" quote ("The credit belongs to the man who is actually in the arena, whose face is marred by dust and sweat and blood; who strives valiantly; who errs, who comes short again and again, because there is no effort without error and shortcoming. . . ."). She decided to teach as a public figure, despite hurtful online comments and attacks.

"In that moment, what I realized is, you know what? I do want to live a brave life. I do want to live in the arena. And if you're going to live in the arena, the only guarantee is you will get your ass kicked. . . . Daring greatly is being vulnerable. So when you ask yourself, 'Did I dare greatly today?' **The big question I ask is, 'When I had the opportunity, did I choose courage over comfort?'**"

TF: This is a great question for daily review as part of a 5-Minute Journal or other evening journaling (page 146).

HOW THAT TRANSLATES TO MORE THAN 30 MILLION VIDEO VIEWS

"I went to the TED event and I experimented. I really put myself out there. I talked about my own breakdown, my spiritual awakening. I talked about having to go to therapy . . . and I remember driving home and thinking, 'I will never do that again.'"

She then watched the popularity of her video explode, now totaling more than 31 million views on TED.com and YouTube. "If I look back, my takeaway from that experience was this: **If I'm not a little bit nauseous when I'm done, I probably didn't show up like I should have shown up."**

ONE OF HER RULES FOR PUBLIC SPEAKING: HOUSE LIGHTS

"I require that the house lights are on, so I can see people's faces. I rarely allow any of my presentations to be videotaped. If they're taping you, you have to be super 'hot' [bright] under the lights, and the audience has to be dark. Then it's performance, not connection, for me."

SHAME VERSUS GUILT

"Shame is 'I am a bad person.' Guilt is 'I did something bad.' . . . Shame is a focus on self. Guilt is a focus on behavior."

TO BE TRUSTED, BE VULNERABLE

"One of the things that emerged from the data is this idea of trust and the relationship between trust and vulnerability. People always [think] you gain trust first and then you're vulnerable with people. But the truth is, **you can't really earn trust over time with people without being somewhat vulnerable [first]."**

(See Gabby Reece's advice to "go first," page 94, and Neil Strauss's pre-interview approach, page 350.)

✱ **Who do you think of when you hear the word "successful"?**
"I don't picture anybody. I picture the word 'redefine.' The word 'successful' or 'success' has been such a dangerous word in my research. **My answer is: Be clear that your ladder is leaning against the right building."**

✱ **Advice to your 30-year-old self?**
"It's okay to be afraid. **You don't have to be so scary when you're scared. . . .** The 30s are so exhausting. It's the age of perfecting, proving, pretending."

"Everything came when I completely dove in fearlessly and made the content that I needed to make as a kind of artist . . . I got out of my own way. I stopped doubting myself, and the universe winked at me when I did that, so to speak.**"**

JASON SILVA

Jason Silva (FB: JASONLSILVA; THISISJASONSILVA.COM) has been called a "Timothy Leary for the viral video age" by *The Atlantic*. He is host of *Brain Games* on National Geographic Channel. The show was the highest-rated series launch in Nat Geo's history, with an average of 1.5 million viewers for the first two episodes.

Spirit animal: Seagull

✳ What is the best or most worthwhile investment you've made?

"Investing in the editing of my videos 3 years ago, which kickstarted my career. I had left Al Gore's Current TV in 2011 and was technically unemployed: a former TV host with limited savings. Deciding to spend money on editing these videos without an income was a leap of faith. The first two videos were 'You Are a RCVR' and 'The Beginning of Infinity.' Both of these were essentially proofs of concept for what would become my signature digital media style: philosophical espresso shots. I released both on Vimeo and immediately saw excitement and interest grow in my work. I knew I was onto something. Within months, I was being invited to give speeches and was eventually asked to make a video that opened TEDGlobal 2012. From there, things took off. A few months later, National Geographic became fans of the videos and invited me to host the TV series *Brain Games,* which was a huge global hit and garnered me an Emmy nomination."

TF: I love to study the early versions of current successes. Jason is quite polished, but the hatchling stages are often amusingly rough around the edges. For instance, search "old blog of Ramit Sethi," "old blog of Gretchen Rubin," or "old blog of Tim Ferriss," or watch the first few episodes of *Wine Library TV* by Gary Vaynerchuk.

✳ What has become more important to you in the last few years and what has become less important?

"I want to build my life around flow states [the sense of being 'in the zone']."

TF: This is something Josh Waitzkin (page 577) talks about often: journaling and using tools like HRV (heart-rate variability) devices to identify the patterns and prerequisites that create peak flow states or their opposites.

BEING JADED = DEATH

"To me being jaded is almost like being dead. Nothing impresses you because you feel like you've seen it all before, and you go through life with dark lenses on . . . the curtain's closed. No light gets in, no rhapsody gets in, and to me that's death."

TF: Closely related advice from one of my own mentors: "Be a skeptic, don't be a cynic."

✻ Video and YouTube channel recommendation

"Did Shakespeare Invent Love?" by Nerdwriter.

TF: My favorite podcast is *Hardcore History* by Dan Carlin (page 285). Nerdwriter can be thought of as a short-form video complement to *HH*.

✻ Do you have any quotes that you live your life by or think of often?

"We are simultaneously gods and worms." — Abraham Maslow

✻ Advice to your 25- or 30-year-old self?

"I would encourage my younger self to just not be afraid, right? To realize that a lot of things that were — I don't want to say crippling anxieties, but — definitely ever-pervasive fears in my life growing up were unnecessary. A lot of time was wasted, a lot of energy was wasted, being worried."

TF: Across all guests, the most common answer to this question is some variation of "It's all going to be alright."

JON FAVREAU

Jon Favreau (TW: @JON_FAVREAU, FB/IG: @JONFAVREAU) burst into the acting scene with his role in *Rudy*. He established himself as a writer with the iconic cult hit *Swingers*, in which he starred. Then, Favreau made his feature film directorial debut with *Made*, which he also wrote and produced. Other directing credits include *The Jungle Book*, *Iron Man*, *Iron Man 2*, *Cowboys & Aliens*, *Elf*, *Zathura*, and *Chef*, which he wrote, produced, directed, and starred in. Lots of commas! Jon does everything.

GO FOR TRUTH, AND YOU'LL HIT FUNNY ALONG THE WAY

Before we started recording our interview in Jon's office, he mentioned the best advice he got from one of his teachers, Glenn Close: "Don't go for funny. Go for the truth, and you'll hit funny along the way."

TELL THE TRUTH. IT'S THE EASIEST THING TO REMEMBER (AND WRITE)

"Although [*Swingers*] wasn't really autobiographical, there were enough things that I could draw from. . . . What's the expression from *Glengarry Glen Ross*? 'Always tell the truth. It's the easiest thing to remember.' . . . If you're going to talk about a neighborhood, talk about the neighborhood you grew up in. Talk about the neighborhood you know. Even if it's not you, you're going to have a more consistent world that you're developing than if you're putting them on Mars, and you don't understand Mars."

Side note: Jon wrote *Swingers* in roughly 2 weeks and it was eventually made for less than $200K.

ON COOKING AND BONDING

The first time I spent a day with Jon at his house, I was immediately invited to help make beignets as part of a group (using a mix from Café du Monde in New Orleans, for those curious). Jon explains why:

"Here we were. We didn't really know each other that well. I'd read your stuff, you saw my stuff, and then lo and behold, you put some hot oil there, and the focus is no longer on each other. [It's about] keeping all your fingers. . . . There's so little overlap with most people that I meet, [which makes cooking great] because it creates this context where everybody is on equal footing, and everybody has a different skill set. It becomes a real task [where you become interdependent]. I find I have endless patience to spend time with people I don't know very well, if you're working on a really intimate cooking project. Then at the end, we all serve it together, and we really feel like we fought a war together. It's a great bonding thing."

THE POWER OF MYTH

For screenwriting, Jon recommends *The Writer's Journey* by Christopher Vogler, which he used to determine if *Swingers* was structurally correct. He is also a big fan of *The Power of Myth*, a video interview of Joseph Campbell by Bill Moyers. "With *The Jungle Book*, I really am going back and doubling down on the old myths."

TF: We recorded our podcast during the shooting of *The Jungle Book*, in his production office next to set. Months later, *The Jungle Book* was the #1 movie in the world and currently has a staggering 95% review average on Rotten Tomatoes.

LONG-TERM IMPACT TRUMPS SHORT-TERM GROSS

"Thanks to video, and later DVD and laser disc, everybody had seen this film [*Swingers*], and it had become part of our culture. That's when I learned that it's not always the movie that does the best [financially] that has the most impact, or is the most rewarding, or does the most for your career, for that matter."

ANOTHER REASON TO MEDITATE

"In the middle of [a meditation session], the idea for *Chef* hit me, and I let myself stop, which I don't usually do, and I took out a pad. I scribbled down like eight pages of ideas and thoughts, [and then I] left it alone. If I look back on it, and read those pages, it really had 80% of the heavy lifting done, as far as what [*Chef*] was about, who was in it, who the characters were, what other movies to look at, what the tone was, what music I would have in it, what type of food he was making, the idea of the food truck, the Cuban sandwiches, Cuban music . . . so it all sort of grew out from that."

TESTING THE "IMPOSSIBLE": 17 QUESTIONS THAT CHANGED MY LIFE

"Whenever you find yourself on the side of the majority, it is time to pause and reflect." —**Mark Twain**

Reality is largely negotiable.

If you stress-test the boundaries and experiment with the "impossibles," you'll quickly discover that most limitations are a fragile collection of socially reinforced rules you can choose to break at any time.

What follows are 17 questions that have dramatically changed my life. Each one is time-stamped, as they entered the picture at precise moments.

#1 — What if I did the opposite for 48 hours?

In 2000, I was selling mass data storage to CEOs and CTOs in my first job out of college. When I wasn't driving my mom's hand-me-down minivan to and from the office in San Jose, California, I was cold calling and cold emailing. "Smiling and dialing" was brutal. For the first few months, I flailed and failed (it didn't help that my desk was wedged in a fire exit). Then, one day, I realized something: All of the sales guys made their sales calls between 9 a.m. and 5 p.m. Obvious, right? But that's part one. Part two: I realized that all of the gatekeepers who kept me from the decision makers—CEOs and CTOs—also worked from

9 to 5. *What if I did the opposite of all the other sales guys, just for 48 hours?*
I decided to take a Thursday and Friday and make sales calls only from 7 to
8:30 a.m. and 6 to 7:30 p.m. For the rest of the day, I focused on cold emails. It
worked like gangbusters. The big boss often picked up the phone directly, and
I began doing more experiments with "What if I did the opposite?": What if I
only asked questions instead of pitching? What if I studied technical material,
so I sounded like an engineer instead of a sales guy? What if I ended my emails
with "I totally understand if you're too busy to reply, and thank you for reading
this far," instead of the usual "I look forward to your reply and speaking soon"
presumptive BS? The experiments paid off. My last quarter in that job, I outsold
the entire L.A. office of our biggest competitor, EMC.

#2 — What do I spend a silly amount of money on? How might I scratch my own itch?

In late 2000 and early 2001, I saw the writing on the wall: The startup I worked
for was going to implode. Rounds of layoffs started and weren't going to end. I
wasn't sure what to do, but I'd been bitten by the startup bug and intoxicated
by Silicon Valley. To explore business opportunities, I didn't do in-depth market research. I started with my credit card statement and asked myself, "What
do I spend a silly amount of money on?" Where did I spend a disproportionate
amount of my income? Where was I price *insensitive*? The answer was sports
supplements. At the time, I was making less than $40K a year and spending
$500 or more per month on supplements. It was insane, but dozens of my
male friends were equally overboard. I already knew which ads got me to buy,
which stores and websites I used to purchase goods, which bulletin boards I
frequented, and all the rest. Could I create a product that would scratch my
own itch? What was I currently cobbling together (I had enough science background to be dangerous) that I couldn't conveniently find at retail? The result
was a cognitive enhancer called BrainQUICKEN. Before everyone got fired, I
begged my coworkers to each prepay for a bottle, which gave me enough money
to hire chemists, a regulatory consultant, and do a tiny manufacturing run. I
was off to the races.

#3 — What would I do/have/be if I had $10 million? What's my real TMI?

In 2004, I was doing better than ever financially, and BrainQUICKEN was distributed in perhaps a dozen countries. The problem? I was running on caffeine, working 15-hour days, and constantly on the verge of meltdown. My girlfriend, who I expected to marry, left me due to the workaholism. Over the next 6 months of treading water and feeling trapped, I realized I had to restructure the business or shut it down — it was literally killing me. This is when I began journaling on a few questions, including "What would I want to do, have, and be if I had $10 million in the bank?" and "What's my real target monthly income (TMI)?" For the latter, in other words: How much does my dream life — the stuff I'm deferring for "retirement" — really cost if I pay on a monthly basis? (See fourhourworkweek.com/tmi) After running the numbers, most of my fantasies were far more affordable than I'd expected. Perhaps I didn't need to keep grinding and building? Perhaps I needed more time and mobility, not more income? This made me think that maybe, just maybe, I could afford to be happy and not just "successful." I decided to take a long overseas trip.

#4 — What are the worst things that could happen? Could I get back here?

These questions, also from 2004, are perhaps the most important of all, so they get their own chapter. (See "fear-setting" on page 463.)

#5 — If I could only work 2 hours per week on my business, what would I do?

After removing anxieties about the trip with fear-setting, the next practical step was removing myself as the bottleneck in my business. Alas, "how can I not be a bottleneck in my own business?" isn't a good question. After reading *The E-Myth Revisited* by Michael Gerber and *The 80/20 Principle* by Richard Koch, I decided that extreme questions were the forcing function I needed. The question I found most helpful was, "If I could only work 2 hours per week on my business, what would I do?" Honestly speaking, it was more like, "Yes, I know it's impossible, but if you had a gun to your head or contracted some horrible disease, and you *had* to limit work to 2 hours per week, what would you do to keep things afloat?" The 80/20 principle, also known as Pareto's law, is the primary tool in this case. It dictates that 80% (or more) of your desired outcomes are the result of 20% (or less) of your activities and inputs. Here are two related questions I personally used: "What 20% of customers/products/regions are producing 80% of the profit? What factors or shared characteristics might account for this?" Many such questions later, I began making changes: "firing" my highest-maintenance customers; putting more than 90% of my retail customers on autopilot with simple terms and standardized order processes; and deepening relationships (and increasing order sizes) with my 3 to 5 highest-profit, lowest-headache customers. That all led to . . .

#6 — What if I let them make decisions up to $100? $500? $1,000?

This question allowed me to take my customer service workload from 40 to 60 hours per week to less than 2 hours per week. Until mid-2004, I was the sole decision maker. For instance, if a professional athlete overseas needed our product overnighted with special customs forms, I would get an email or phone call from one of my fulfillment centers: "How should we handle this? What would you like to charge?" These unusual "edge cases" might seem like rare exceptions, but they were a daily occurrence. Dozens per week hit me, on top of everything else. The fix: I sent an email to all of my direct reports along the lines of "From this point forward, please don't contact for me with questions about A, B, or C. I trust you. If it involves less than $100, please made the decision yourself and take a note (the situation, how you handled it, what it cost) in one document, so we can review and adjust each week. Just focus on making our customers happy." I expected the worst, and guess what? Everything worked, minus a few expected hiccups here and there. I later increased the threshold to $500, then $1,000, and the "reviews" of decisions went from weekly, to monthly, to quarterly, to—once people were polished—effectively never. This experience underscored two things for me: 1) To get huge, good things done, you need to be okay with letting the small, bad things happen. 2) People's IQs seem to double as soon as you give them responsibility and indicate that you trust them.

#7 — What's the least crowded channel?

Fast-forward to December 26, 2006. I've finished writing *The 4-Hour Work-week,* and I sit down after a lovely Christmas to think about the upcoming April launch. What to do? I had no idea, so I tracked down roughly a dozen best-selling authors. I asked each questions like, "What were the biggest wastes of time and money for your last book launch? What would you never do again? What would you do more of? If you had to choose one place to focus $10,000, where would you focus?"

I heard one word repeatedly: blogs. They were apparently both very powerful and under-appreciated. My first question was, "What the hell is a blog?" My next questions were "How are people currently trying to reach bloggers?" and "What's the least crowded channel?" The people pitching bloggers were generally using email first and phone second. Even though those were my strengths, I decided to experiment with in-person meetings at conferences. Why? Because I felt my odds would be better as one out of five people in a lounge, rather than one email out of 500 emails in an overflowing inbox. I packed my bags and headed to Las Vegas for the Consumer Electronics Show in January, which had more than 150,000 attendees in 2005. It's like the Super Bowl of technology releases, where all the geeks get to play with new toys. I never even walked in the front door. I parked myself at the offsite Seagate-sponsored BlogHaus lounge, where bloggers were invited to relax, recharge their laptops, and drink free booze. I sipped alcohol, asked a lot of dumb questions, and *never* overtly pitched. I only mentioned the book if someone asked me why I was there (answer: "I just finished my first book, and I'm really nervous about the launch. I'm here to learn more about blogs and technology"). Famous tech blogger Robert Scoble later described my intricate marketing plan as "get drunk with bloggers." It worked surprisingly well.

#8 — What if I couldn't pitch my product directly?

During the 2007 book launch, I quickly found that most media rightly don't give a rat's ass about book launches. They care about stories, not announcements, so I asked myself, "What if I couldn't pitch my product directly? What if I had to sell *around* the product?" Well, I could showcase people from the book who've completely redesigned their lives (human interest); I could write about unrelated crazy experiments, but drive people to my book-focused website (Google "Geek to Freak" to see the result. It was my first-ever viral blog post); I could popularize a new term and aim for pop culture (see "lifestyle design" on page 278); I could go meta and make the launch *itself* a news item (I also did this with my video "book trailer" for *The 4-Hour Body*, as well as the BitTorrent partnership for *The 4-Hour Chef*). People don't like being sold products, but we all like being told stories. Work on the latter.

#9 — What if I created my own real-world MBA?

This kicked off in 2007 to 2008. See page 250 for full details.

#10 — Do I need to make it back the way I lost it?

In 2008, I owned a home in San Jose, California, and its value cratered. More accurately, the bank owned the home and I had an ill-conceived adjustable-rate mortgage. On top of that, I was on the cusp of moving to San Francisco. To sell would have meant a $150,000 loss. Ultimately, I picked up and moved to San Francisco, regardless, leaving my San Jose home empty.

For months, friends pressured me to rent it, emphasizing how I was flushing money down the toilet otherwise. I eventually buckled and followed their advice. Even with a property management company, regular headaches and paperwork ensued. Regret followed. One introspective night, I had some wine and asked myself: "Do I really need to make money back the same way I'm losing it?" If you lose $1,000 at the blackjack table, should you try and recoup it there? Probably not. If I'm "losing" money via the mortgage payments on an empty house, do I really need to cover it by renting the house itself? No, I decided. I could much more easily create income elsewhere (e.g., speaking gigs, consulting, etc.) to put me in the black. Humans are very vulnerable to a cognitive bias called "anchoring," whether in real estate, stocks, or otherwise. I am no exception. I made a study of this (a lot of good investors like *Think Twice* by Michael Mauboussin), and shortly thereafter sold my San Jose house at a large loss. Once my attention and mind space was freed up, I quickly made it back elsewhere.

#11 — What if I could only subtract to solve problems?

From 2008 to 2009, I began to ask myself, "What if I could only subtract to solve problems?" when advising startups. Instead of answering, "What should we do?" I tried first to hone in on answering, "What should we simplify?" For instance, I always wanted to tighten the conversion fishing net (the percentage of visitors who sign up or buy) before driving a ton of traffic to one of my portfolio companies. One of the first dozen startups I worked with was named Gyminee. It was rebranded Daily Burn, and at the time, they didn't have enough manpower to do a complete redesign of the site. Adding new elements would've been time-consuming, but removing them wasn't. As a test, we eliminated roughly 70% of the "above the fold" clickable elements on their homepage, focusing on the single most valuable click. Conversions immediately improved 21.1%. That quick-and-dirty test informed later decisions for much more expensive development. The founders, Andy Smith and Stephen Blankenship, made a lot of great decisions, and the company was acquired by IAC in 2010. I've since applied this "What if I could only subtract . . . ?" to my life in many areas, and I sometimes rephrase it as "What should I put on my *not*-to-do list?"

#12 — What might I put in place to allow me to go off the grid for 4 to 8 weeks, with no phone or email?

Though wordy, I have asked variations of this question many times since 2004. It used to end with, ". . . allow me to go on vacation for 4 to 8 weeks," but that's no longer enough. Given the spread of broadband, it's extremely easy to take a "vacation" to Brazil or Japan and still work nonstop on your business via laptop. This kind of subtle self-deception is a time bomb.

For the last 5 years, I've asked myself, in effect, "What can I put in place so that I can go completely off the grid for 4 to 8 weeks?" To entrepreneurs who are feeling burned out, this is also the question I pose most often. Two weeks isn't enough, as you can let fires erupt and then attempt to repair things when you return. Four to 8 weeks (or more) doesn't allow you to be a firefighter. It forces you to put systems and policies in place, ditch ad-hoc email-based triage, empower other people with rules and tools, separate the critical few from the trivial many, and otherwise create a machine that doesn't require you behind the driver's wheel 24/7.

Here's the most important point: The systems far outlive the vacation, and when you come home, you'll realize that you've taken your business (and life) to the next level. This is only possible if you work *on* your business instead of *in* your business, as Michael Gerber might say.

#13 — Am I hunting antelope or field mice?

I lifted this question around 2012 from former speaker of the U.S. House of Representatives, Newt Gingrich. I read about it in *Buck Up, Suck Up . . . and Come Back When You Foul Up: 12 Winning Secrets from the War Room*, written by James Carville and Paul Begala, the political strategists behind Bill Clinton's presidential campaign "war room." Here's the excerpt that stuck with me:

> Newt Gingrich is one of the most successful political leaders of our time. Yes, we disagreed with virtually everything he did, but this is a book about strategy, not ideology. And we've got to give Newt his due. His strategic ability — his relentless focus on capturing the House of Representatives for the Republicans — led to one of the biggest political landslides in American history.
>
> Now that he's in the private sector, Newt uses a brilliant illustration to explain the need to focus on the big things and let the little stuff slide: the analogy of the field mice and the antelope. A lion is fully capable of capturing, killing, and eating a field mouse. But it turns out that the energy required to do so exceeds the caloric content of the mouse itself. So a lion that spent its day hunting and eating field mice would slowly starve to death. A lion can't live on field mice. A lion needs antelope. Antelope are big animals. They take more speed and strength to capture and kill, and once killed, they provide a feast for the lion and her pride. A lion can live a long and happy life on a diet of antelope. The distinction is important. Are you spending all your time and exhausting all your energy catching field mice? In the short term it might give you a nice, rewarding feeling. But in the long run you're going to die. So ask yourself at the end of the day, "Did I spend today chasing mice or hunting antelope?"

Another way I often approach this is to look at my to-do list and ask: "Which *one* of these, if done, would render all the rest either easier or completely irrelevant?"

#14 — Could it be that everything is fine and complete as is?

Since starting deep work with "plant medicines" in 2013 (see James Fadiman, page 100), I've doubled and tripled down on cultivating more daily appreciation and present-state awareness. The above is one of the questions I ask myself. It's accompanied by complementary tools and rituals like the 5-Minute Journal (page 146), the Jar of Awesome (page 570), and thinking of "daily wins" before bed à la Peter Diamandis (page 373). To reiterate what I've said elsewhere in this book, type-A personalities have goal pursuit as default hardwiring. This is excellent for producing achievement, but also anxiety, as you're constantly future-focused. I've personally decided that achievement is no more than a passing grade in life. It's a C+ that gets you limping along to the next grade. For anything more, and certainly for anything approaching happiness, you have to want what you already have.

#15 — What would this look like if it were easy?

This question and the next both came about in 2015. These days, more than any other question, I'm asking "What would this look like if it were easy?" If I feel stressed, stretched thin, or overwhelmed, it's usually because I'm overcomplicating something or failing to take the simple/easy path because I feel I should be trying "harder" (old habits die hard).

#16 — How can I throw money at this problem? How can I "waste" money to improve the quality of my life?

This is somewhat self-explanatory. Dan Sullivan is the founder and president of a company called Strategic Coach that has saved the sanity of many serial entrepreneurs I know. One of Dan's sayings is: "If you've got enough money to solve the problem, you don't have the problem." In the beginning of your career, you spend time to earn money. Once you hit your stride in any capacity, you should spend money to earn time, as the latter is nonrenewable. It can be hard to make and maintain this gear shift, so the above question is in my regular journaling rotation.

#17 — No hurry, no pause.

This isn't a question—it's a fundamental reset. "No hurry, no pause" was introduced to me by Jenny Sauer-Klein (jennysauerklein.com), who, along with Jason Nemer (page 46), co-created AcroYoga. The expression is one of the "9 Principles of Harmony" from Breema, a form of bodywork she studied for many years. I routinely write "No hurry, no pause" at the top of my notebooks as a daily reminder. In effect, it's shorthand for Derek Sivers's story of the 45-minute versus 43-minute bike ride (page 190)—you don't need to go through life huffing and puffing, straining and red-faced. You can get 95% of the results you want by calmly putting one foot in front of the other. One former Navy SEAL friend recently texted me a principle used in their training: "Slow is smooth. Smooth is fast."

Perhaps I'm just getting old, but my definition of luxury has changed over time. Now, it's not about owning a lot of stuff. Luxury, to me, is feeling unrushed. No hurry, no pause.

So, kids, those are my questions. May you find and create many of your own.

Be sure to look for simple solutions.

If the answer isn't simple, it's probably not the right answer.

"In a blink of an eye, we'll all be gone. 100 years compared to infinity is nothing. I talk to my sister all the time. . . . [I say,] 'Girl, you better start having some fun. We're gonna be gone in a minute. You're gonna look back and say, "Shit, I should have been laughing, and now I'm dead."'"

JAMIE FOXX

Jamie Foxx (TW/IG/SC: @IAMJAMIEFOXX) is an Academy Award–winning actor, a Grammy Award–winning musician, and a world famous standup and improv comedian. He is, without a doubt, the most consummate performer and entertainer I have ever met. In the 2½ hours we spent together in his home studio, he blew my mind.

PULL-UP BARS ARE EVERYTHING

Jamie's morning workout routine, done roughly every other day, consists of:

- »» 15 pull-ups, 50 push-ups, 100 sit-ups
- »» 15 pull-ups (different grip), 50 push-ups
- »» 10 pull-ups (first grip)
- »» 10 pull-ups (second grip)

"I kept wondering how Tyrin [Turner], Caine in *Menace II Society*, was always in shape. He said: 'Man, I'm trying to tell you, the pull-up bars are everything.'"

(This is similar in its simplicity to General Stan McChrystal's workout, page 435.)

THE FIRST DAY ERIC MARLON BISHOP
USED THE NAME "JAMIE FOXX"

"I ended up going to this Evening at the Improv, the Improv in Santa Monica. I had never been there. I noticed that 100 guys would show up, and 5 girls would show up. The 5 girls would always get on the show because they needed to break up the monotony. [The producers would pick randomly from the list of people who showed up.] So I said, 'Hmmm, I got something.' I wrote down all of these unisex names on the list: Stacy Green, Tracy Brown, Jamie Foxx . . . and the guy chooses from the list. He says, 'Jamie Foxx, is she here? She'll be first.' I said, 'No, that's me.' 'Oh, okay. All right, well, you're going up. You're the fresh meat.' They were shooting Evening at the Improv, this old comedy show back in the day. He said, 'You'll be the guy we just throw up to see if you get a laugh or two. It's gonna be a tough crowd.' . . . People [in the crowd] are like, 'Who's the kid? Is he on the show? Oh, he's fresh meat. He's an amateur.' So then they started yelling my name — 'Yo, Jamie! Hey, Jamie!' — but I'm not used to the name. So now they think I'm arrogant. 'This motherfucker . . . he's not even listening to us. . . .'"

WHAT'S ON THE OTHER SIDE OF FEAR? NOTHING.

Jamie is incredibly confident. As one of his close friends described to me: "Even when things go a little south, he ALWAYS makes you feel like he has everything under control. I see a lot of people in his circle gravitate toward him for that confidence, myself included." I asked Jamie how he teaches confidence to his children, and he said that he asks his daughters to explore their fears with the question, "What's on the other side of fear?" His answer is always, "Nothing."

He elaborates: "People are nervous for no reason, because no one's gonna come out and slap you or beat you up. . . . When we talk about fear or a lack of being aggressive [holding someone back], it's in your head. Not everybody is going to be super aggressive, but the one thing that you can deal with is a person's fears. If you start early, if they are a shy person, they won't be as shy if you keep instilling those things."

TF: Look at whatever you're afraid of and ask, "What is on the other side of fear, if I push through this?" The answer is generally nothing. There are few or no negative consequences, or they're temporary. This touches upon Francis Ford Coppola's lesson that we'll explore later: Failure is not durable.

> "When you raise your kids, you're the bow, they're the arrow, and you just try to aim them in the best direction that you can, and hopefully your aim isn't too off. That's what [my grandmother] did for me."

FOR THOSE IMPERSONATORS AMONG YOU

Jamie did nearly a dozen impersonations during our interview. Here's one tip: "Start with Kermit the Frog, then add some swagger, and you got Sammy Davis Jr."

YOU ARE EITHER GREAT OR YOU DON'T EXIST

Jamie explained how disciplined Keenen Ivory Wayans was about writing jokes for *In Living Color*: "You were not allowed to come in and be half-assed. He'd pull you aside and say, 'As a black comedian, you cannot be half-assed. You're either great or you don't exist.' . . . He wrote for Eddie Murphy. He was around the greatest. He said, 'I'm around the greatest, all the time, so that's what we're gonna do.'"

TF: This applies far outside of comedy or racial lines. It's never been easier to be a "creator," and it's never been harder to stand out. Good isn't good enough.

LEARNING TO SPEAK TRUTH

"I'm 10 years old, maybe. I think I'm in the fifth grade, 1976, President Carter. The preacher started preaching about homosexuality. I don't know what it is. He's saying God made Adam and Eve, God didn't make Adam and Steve. It's Southern, it's Texas. My grandmother stood up and said, 'You stop that,' and the whole church stopped. 'What's that, Miss Talley?' Now, her words, what she said next, was very interesting. 'Let me tell you something. I've had this nursery school for 30 years, and I want to let all of you know that God makes sissies, too.' The whole place went, 'What?' She said, 'These little boys that I've watched since they could walk, they play by different music, and you stop that because you're making it hard for them to navigate.' Sits down.

"My grandmother raised those people at church. [She taught the whole community's children during the school year and] then, during the summer, you'd drop the kids off at my grandmother's house and just let her keep them. She was very powerful in that sense."

ED SHEERAN BEFORE HE BECAME FAMOUS

"A young man by the name of Ed Sheeran slept on this carpet [he points at the floor, where we were recording] for like 6 weeks, trying to get his music career going. He came over from London. He heard about a live show that I do in L.A. He said, 'I really want to do your live show, if it's possible, because I have some music that I love.' I'm thinking, 'Do my live show?' It's mostly black, you know what I'm saying? It's *music people*, really hardcore music people. They're very finicky. People who have played for Stevie Wonder. I had Miranda Lambert one night. I had Babyface. [I said,] 'This is the real shit you're talking about. I don't care about London and the accent. You gotta really come with it.' He said, 'I think I'll be okay.' . . . So I take him to my live night, 800 people there. People are playing, black folks sweating and just getting it . . . they would tear *American Idol* up. All of a sudden, Ed Sheeran gets up with a ukulele, walks out onto the stage, and the brother next to me says, 'Yo, Foxx, who the fuck is this dude right here, with the red hair and shit and the fucking ukulele?' I said, 'Man, his name is Ed Sheeran. Let's see what he does.' Within 12 minutes, he got a standing ovation."

BEFORE YOU SEARCH FAR AND WIDE . . .

Jamie played Ray Charles in the film *Ray*, for which he won an Academy Award. Before filming, the two of them played piano together:

"As we're playing, I'm on cloud nine. Then he moves into some intricate stuff, like Thelonious Monk. I was like, 'Oh shit, I gotta catch up' and I hit a wrong note. He stopped because his ears are very sensitive: 'Now, why the hell would you do that? Why you hit the note like that? That's the wrong note, man. Shit.' I said, 'I'm sorry, Mr. Charles,' and he said, 'Let me tell you something, brother. The notes are right underneath your fingers, baby. You just gotta take the time out to play the right notes. That's life.'"

BRYAN JOHNSON

Bryan Johnson (TW: @BRYAN_JOHNSON, BRYANJOHNSON.CO) is an entrepreneur and investor. He is the founder of OS Fund and Braintree, the latter of which was bought by eBay in 2013 for $800 million in cash. Bryan launched OS Fund in 2014 with $100 million of his personal capital to support inventors and scientists who aim to benefit humanity by rewriting the operating systems of life. In other words: He fuels real-world mad scientists tackling things like asteroid mining, artificial intelligence, life extension, and more. He is currently the founder and CEO of Kernel, which is developing the world's first neuroprosthesis [brain-implantable computer] to mimic, repair, and improve cognition.

BEHIND THE SCENES

» To inspire his kids, Bryan commissioned a graffiti artist to paint Gandalf the Grey and Harry Potter on one of his walls at home. They are pointing their wands skyward and above it all is the word "dream." He wants to teach them that, just as Tolkien and Rowling authored worlds using text, entrepreneurs have the ability to author their lives with companies.

» On our regular hikes in San Francisco, Bryan has asked me variations of this question several times: "What can you do that will be remembered in 200 to 400 years?"

Spirit animal: African lion

ONE OF HIS FIRST ENTREPRENEURIAL GIGS

On selling credit card processing door-to-door to retailers:

"I would say, 'Tim, if you give me 3 minutes of your time, I will give you $100 if you do not say "yes" to using my service.' Usually they would say something like, 'That is interesting . . .' and I would open my pitch book and walk them through the industry. Here are the providers, here is what they do, here is how they do it, here is what I do. I am the same as everyone else, except with me, you get honesty and transparency and great customer support. So, I became this company's number-one sales person. I broke all their sales records following this really simple formula of just selling honesty and transparency in a broken industry."

IS IT AN ITCH OR A BURN?

"I have a lot of conversations with people who want to start their own thing, and one of my favorite questions to ask is, 'Is this an itch, or is it burning?' If it is just an itch, it is not sufficient. It gets to this point of how badly you really want it. For me, I burned the boats. There was no way I was going to get a job. Failure was never an option. I had to make this work."

YOU SHOULD PROBABLY NOT DO THAT AGAIN

"One time [as a kid], I wondered — if you filled a milk gallon jug full of gasoline and you lit it on fire, what would happen? So, I took the gasoline that was otherwise used for the lawnmower, and I filled up this carton, and I went out on the street and I lit it on fire. . . . As expected, it produced quite a flame. [My mom's] green Taurus rolled around the corner, coming down the street and I thought, 'Oh, no . . .' So, in haste, I kicked over the jug and the gasoline spills onto the street and into the gutter. Now it is rolling down the gutter and there are cars [down the street]. I am imagining cars blowing up. So, I walk over to the gutter and I stomp on the gasoline to put it out, and, of course, that splashes. Now, the lawn is on fire. It is getting worse and worse. Anyway, we put the fire out and then the only thing she says to me is, 'Bryan, you probably should not do that again,' and I said, 'All right, that is fair.' That is typical of my mom."

PARENTING ADVICE — "HOW DID YOU THINK ABOUT IT?"

"So, we got on a four-wheeler 2 weeks ago — my 11- and 9-year-old and I — and I said, 'Okay, I am going to put your helmets on, I am going to give you a 2-minute lesson on how to go forward and how to go backwards, how to brake. I am going to give you some lessons — do not go into a ditch, do not go on a hillside that you will turn you over, etc. — but I am expecting you now to go out for 5 minutes and come back safely, and tell me how you did it. What were your thought processes? How did you stay safe? What were the risks you took? But I want you to do it, and I am not going with you.' . . . They came back in one piece, and it was a good experience for them to tell me 'Okay, Dad, this is how we looked at the risk, this is how we thought we might potentially get into a problem. . . .' They [even ran into a tree] going slowly . . . but they talked about it, which I thought was really helpful."

THE SHACKLETON SNIFF TEST

Ernest Shackleton had a huge impact on Bryan as a child. "He is remembered [for] the grit and how they actually overcame all the obstacles that came about during the expedition. He is hugely inspirational in my life, because I apply what I call the 'Shackleton sniff test' to everything I do. . . . I contemplate: If I go about on this endeavor, does it meet the threshold that Shackleton applied? Is this the most audacious endeavor I can possibly conceive of? What would Shackleton do?"

TF: Joe De Sena (page 38) goes through the same exercise using Shackleton as the litmus test. "That's his dude, too," as a mutual friend put it.

✴ **What is something you believe that other people think is crazy?**

"Our existence is programmable."

✴ **Do you have any quotes you live your life by or think of often?**

"Life is not waiting for the storm to pass, it's learning how to dance in the rain" [adapted from Vivian Greene].

FIVE-MONKEY GAMES

This relates to learned helplessness, which is often outdated and reinforced by others who mean well:

"At Braintree, one of the principles I consistently communicated was, 'Challenge all assumptions.' The story that I accompanied that with was: There are five monkeys in a room, and there is a basket of bananas at the top of a ladder. The monkeys, of course, want to climb the ladder to get the bananas, but every time one tries, they are all sprayed with cold water. After a few times of being sprayed by cold water, the monkeys learn to not climb up the ladder to get the bananas. . . . [The experimenters then] take one monkey out and put a new monkey in, and the new monkey sees a banana. He thinks, 'Hey, I am going to grab a banana,' but when he tries to go up the ladder, the other monkeys grab him and pull him back. . . . [The experimenters eventually] systematically pull every monkey out, and now you have five new monkeys. Any time a new monkey comes in and tries to climb the ladder, they grab the monkey and pull it back, but none of the five have ever been sprayed by cold water."

TF: This brought to mind a story from Tara Brach (page 555) that I think of often:

This is a story about a tiger named Mohini that was in captivity in a zoo, who was rescued from an animal sanctuary. Mohini had been confined to a 10-by-10-foot cage with a concrete floor for 5 or 10 years. They finally released her into this big pasture: *With excitement and anticipation, they released Mohini into her new and expensive environment, but it was too late. The tiger immediately sought refuge in a corner of the compound, where she lived for the remainder of her life. She paced and paced in that corner until an area 10-by-10 feet was worn bare of grass.* . . . Perhaps the biggest tragedy in our lives is that freedom is possible, yet we can pass our years trapped in the same old patterns.

What past limitations — real or perceived — are you carrying as baggage? Where in your life are you pacing in a 10-by-10-foot patch of grass? Where are you afraid of getting sprayed with water, even though it's never happened? Oftentimes, everything you want is a mere inch outside of your comfort zone. Test it.

BRIAN KOPPELMAN

Brian Koppelman (TW: @BRIANKOPPELMAN, BRIANKOPPELMAN.COM) is a screenwriter, novelist, director, and producer. Prior to his hit show *Billions*, which he co-created and executive produced (and co-wrote on spec), he was best known as the co-writer of *Rounders* and *Ocean's Thirteen*, as well as a producer of *The Illusionist* and *The Lucky Ones*. He has directed films such as *Solitary Man*, starring Michael Douglas. Brian also hosts *The Moment* podcast. One of my favorite episodes is with John Hamburg, who wrote and directed *I Love You, Man* and wrote *Meet the Parents*, among many others. It's like film school and an MFA in screenwriting wrapped into one conversation.

Spirit animal: Penn Jillette (a close friend)

YOU DON'T FIND TIME, YOU MAKE TIME

"I was 30 years old. I was unhappy with the life I was living when I went into this one poker club in New York City, heard the way that people spoke, saw the way they looked. I realized 'Okay, that's a movie [*Rounders*]. . . .' I went to my wife, Amy, and my best friend, Dave, and made a plan to be able to continue to work but to write this script in the mornings. Amy cleared out a storage space under our apartment. Dave and I at the time had no contacts in the movie business. We met for 2 hours every single morning. I think we took Sundays off, but other than that we didn't miss a morning. We worked for 2 hours. He was bartending, and I was going to my job [Brian had just finished law school by taking night classes and was in the record business].

"That 2 hours in the morning . . . there's a slop sink in this little storage area. Room for one chair. I'd sit on the floor, Dave would sit at the typewriter most of the time. We had a stack of books that were reading material about poker and the language of the game. We'd sit in that room and write, and then at night, we'd go to these poker clubs and try to collect data. Lines that people said, stories that they told us, character traits . . . with no thought [of whether it] was realistic or unrealistic. We didn't calculate any of it, except 'How can we write a screenplay that we believe could be the basis for a movie that would be like *Diner* was for us?' **A movie that people—at the time, I was probably thinking about guys in their 20s—would want to quote to each other.** It would be the thing that was their little secret, private movie, and that if we could do that, we'd succeeded."

TF: Khaled Hosseini wrote *The Kite Runner* in the early mornings before working as a full-time doctor. Paul Levesque (page 128) often works out at midnight. If it's truly important, schedule it. As Paul might ask you, "Is that a dream or a goal?" If it isn't on the calendar, it isn't real.

ON MORNING PAGES, WHICH BRIAN INTRODUCED ME TO

"[Every morning,] what I do is based on the Morning Pages by Julia Cameron in *The Artist's Way*. It's three longhand pages where you just keep the pen moving for three pages, no matter what. No censoring, no rereading. It's the closest thing to magic I've come across. If you really do it every day in a real disciplined practice, something happens to your subconscious that allows you to get to your most creative place. I'd say—and I know you've had this experience with other things you've given people — I've given that book to 100 people and said, 'I'm telling you, you need to do this. . . .' Of the 100 people I've given it to, maybe ten of them have actually opened the book and done the exercises. Of those ten, seven have had books, movies, TV shows, and made out successful. It's incredible. That book changed my life, even though it's very spiritual and I'm an atheist."

* **Book and podcast recommendations?**
   The War of Art by Steven Pressfield
   What Makes Sammy Run by Budd Schulberg, about how someone makes their way in Hollywood.
   The *Scriptnotes* podcast by Craig Mazin and John August. "Between them, [they] have 20 hit movie credits. Those two guys know what they're talking about. They're in the trenches making movies every day."

SOME PRACTICAL THOUGHTS ON SUICIDE

In this chapter, I'm going to talk about suicide, and why I'm still on this planet. It might seem dark, but the objective is to give hope and tools to those who need them. It's a much larger number than you might imagine.

I kept the following stories secret from my family, girlfriends, and closest friends for years. Recently, however, I had an experience that shook me — woke me up — and I decided that it was time to share everything.

So, despite the shame I might feel, the fear that is making my palms sweat as I type this, allow me to get started.

Here we go . . .

A TWIST OF FATE

"Could you please sign this for my brother? It would mean a lot to him."

There were perhaps a dozen people around me asking questions, and one fan had politely waited his turn. The ask: A simple signature.

It was Friday night, around 7 p.m., and I'd just finished a live recording of the *TWiST* podcast. There was electricity in the air. Jason Calacanis, the host and interviewer, knows how to put on a show. He'd hyped up the crowd and kept things rolling for more than 2 hours on stage, asking me every imaginable question. The venue had been packed to capacity. Now, more than 200 people were milling about, drinking wine or heading off for their weekends.

A handful of attendees had gathered near the mics to chat with me.

"Anything in particular you'd like me to say to him? To your brother?" I asked this one gent, who was immaculately dressed in a suit. His name was Silas.

He froze for a few seconds. I saw his eyes flutter. There was something unusual that I couldn't put a finger on.

I decided to take the pressure off: "I'm sure I can come up with something. Are you cool with that?" Silas nodded.

I wrote a few lines, added a smiley face, signed the book he'd brought, and handed it back. He thanked me and backed out of the crowd. I waved and returned to chatting with the others.

Roughly 30 minutes later, I had to run. My girlfriend had just landed at the airport, and I needed to meet her for dinner. I started walking toward the elevators.

"Excuse me, Tim?" It was Silas. He'd been waiting for me. "Can I talk to you for a second?"

"Sure," I said, "but walk with me."

We meandered around tables and desks to the elevator vestibule, and I hit the Down button. As soon as Silas started his story, I forgot about the elevator.

He apologized for not having an answer earlier. His younger brother—the one I signed the book for—had recently committed suicide. He was 22.

"He looked up to you," Silas explained. "He loved listening to you and Joe Rogan. I wanted to get your signature for him. I'm going to put this in his room." He gestured to the book. I could see tears welling up in his eyes, and I felt my own doing the same. He continued.

"People listen to you. Have you ever thought about talking about these things? About suicide or depression? You might be able to save someone." Now, it was my turn to stare at him blankly. I didn't know what to say.

I also didn't have an excuse. Unbeknownst to him, I had every reason to talk about suicide.

Some of my closest high school friends killed themselves.

Some of my closest college friends killed themselves.

I almost killed myself.

"I'm so sorry for your loss," I said to Silas. I wondered if he'd waited more than three hours just to tell me this. I suspected he had. Good for him. He had bigger balls than I. Certainly, I'd failed his brother by being such a coward in my writing. How many others had I failed? These questions swam in my mind.

"I will write about this," I said to Silas, awkwardly patting his shoulder. "I promise."

And with that, I got into the elevator.

INTO THE DARKNESS

"They tried to bury us. They didn't know we were seeds."

— **Mexican proverb**

There are some secrets we don't share because they're embarrassing.

Like that time I met Naval Ravikant (page 546) by accidentally hitting on his girlfriend at a coffee shop? Oops. Or the time a celebrity panelist borrowed my laptop to project a boring corporate video, and a flicker of porn popped up — à la *Fight Club* — in front of a crowd of 400 people? Another good example.

But then there are dark secrets. The things we tell no one. The shadows we keep covered for fear of unraveling our lives.

For me, 1999 was full of shadows.

So much so that I never wanted to revisit them. I hadn't talked about this traumatic period publicly until April 29, 2015 during a Reddit AMA (Ask Me Anything).

What follows is the sequence of my downward spiral. In hindsight, it's incredible how trivial some of it seems. At the time, though, it was the perfect storm.

I include wording like "impossible situation," which was reflective of my thinking at the time, not objective reality.

I still vividly recall these events, but any quotes are paraphrased. So, starting where it began . . .

>>> It's the beginning of my senior year at Princeton University. I'm slated to graduate around June of 1999. Somewhere in the next six months, several things happen in the span of a few weeks.

>>> First, I fail to make it to final interviews for McKinsey consulting and Trilogy software, in addition to others. I have no idea what I'm doing wrong, and I start losing confidence after "winning" in the game of academics for so long.

>>> Second, a long-term (for a college kid, anyway) girlfriend breaks up with me shortly thereafter. Not because of the job stuff, but because I

became insecure during that period, wanted more time with her, and was massively disruptive to her varsity sports season. What's wrong with me?

» Third, I have a fateful meeting with one of my thesis advisors in the East Asian Studies department. Having read a partial draft of my work, he presents a large stack of original research in Japanese for me to incorporate. I walk out with my head spinning—how am I going to finish this thesis (which generally run 60–100 pages or more) before graduation? What am I going to do?

It's important to note that at Princeton, the senior thesis is largely viewed as the pinnacle of your four-year undergrad career. That's reflected in its grading. The thesis is often worth around 25% of your entire departmental GPA. After the above, things unfolded as follows . . .

» I find a rescue option! In the course of language learning research for the thesis, I'm introduced to a wonderful PhD who works at Berlitz International. Bernie was his name. We have a late dinner one night on Witherspoon Street in Princeton. He speaks multiple languages and is a nerd, just like me. One hour turns into two, which turns into three. At the end, he says, "You know, it's too bad you're graduating in a few months. I have a project that would be perfect for you, but it's starting sooner." This could be exactly the solution I'm looking for!

» I chat with my parents about potentially taking a year off, beginning in the middle of my senior year. This would allow me time to finish and polish the thesis, while simultaneously testing jobs in the "real world." It seems like a huge win-win, and my parents are supportive.

» The Princeton powers that be okay the idea, and I meet with the aforementioned thesis advisor to inform him of my decision. Instead of being happy that I'm taking time to get the thesis right (what I expected), he seems furious: "So you're just going to quit?! To cop out?! This better be the best thesis I've ever seen in my life." In my stressed-out state, I hear a series of thinly veiled threats and ultimatums in the exchange that follows . . . but no professor would actually do that, right? The meeting ends with a dismissive laugh and a curt "Good luck." I'm crushed and wander out in a daze.

» Once I've regained my composure, my shock turns to anger. How could a thesis advisor threaten a student with a bad grade just because they're taking time off? I knew my thesis wouldn't be "the best thesis" he'd ever seen, so it was practically guaranteed to get a bad grade, even if I did a great job. This would be obvious to anyone, right?

» I meet with multiple people in the Princeton administration, and the response is — simply put — "He wouldn't do that." I'm speechless. Am I being called a liar? Why would I lie? What's my incentive? It seems like no one is willing to rock the boat with a senior (or tenured) professor. I'm speechless and feel betrayed. Faculty politics matter more than I do.

» I leave my friends behind at school and move off campus to work — remotely, it turns out — for Berlitz. "Remote" means I work at home by myself. This is a recipe for disaster. The work is rewarding, but I spend all of my non-work time — from when I wake to when I go to bed — looking at hundreds of pages of thesis notes and research spread out on my bedroom floor. It's an uncontainable mess.

» After 2 or 3 months of attempting to incorporate my advisor's original-language Japanese research, the thesis is a disaster. Despite (or perhaps because of) staring at paper alone for 8 to 16 hours a day, it's a Frankenstein's monster of false starts, dead ends, and research that shouldn't be there in the first place. At least half is totally unusable. I am, without a doubt, in worse shape than when I left school.

» My friends are graduating, celebrating, and leaving Princeton behind. I am sitting in a condo off campus, trapped in an impossible situation. My thesis work is going nowhere, and even if it turns out spectacular, I have (in my mind) a vindictive advisor who's going to burn me. By burning me, he'll destroy everything I've sacrificed for since high school: great grades in high school got me to Princeton, great grades in Princeton should get me to a dream job, etc. By burning me, he'll make Princeton's astronomical tuition wasted money, nothing more than a small fortune my family has pissed away. I start sleeping in until 2 or 3 p.m. I can't face the piles of unfinished work surrounding me. My coping mechanism is to cover myself in sheets, minimize time awake, and hope for a miracle.

» No miracle arrives. Then one afternoon, as I'm wandering through a Barnes and Noble with no goal in particular, I chance upon a book about suicide. It's right there in front of me on a display table. Perhaps this is the "miracle"? I sit down and read the entire book, taking copious notes into a journal, including other books listed in the bibliography. For the first time in ages, I'm excited about research. In a sea of uncertainty and hopeless situations, I feel like I've found hope: the final solution.

» I return to Princeton campus. This time, I go straight to Firestone Library to check out all of the suicide-related books on my to-do list. One particularly promising-sounding title is out, so I reserve it. I'll be next in line when it comes back. I wonder what poor bastard is reading it, and if they'll be able to return it.

It's important to mention that, by this point, I was past *deciding*. The decision was obvious to me. I'd somehow failed, painted myself into this ridiculous corner, wasted a fortune on a school that didn't care about me, so what would be the point of doing otherwise? To repeat these types of mistakes forever? To be a hopeless burden to myself and my family and friends? Fuck that. The world was better off without a loser who couldn't figure this basic shit out. What would I ever contribute? Nothing. So the decision was made, and I was in full-on planning mode.

» In this case, I'm dangerously good at planning. I have 4 to 6 scenarios all specced out, start to finish, including potential collaborators and covers when needed. And that's when I get the phone call.

» [My mom?! That wasn't in the plan.]

» I'd forgotten that Firestone Library had my family home address on file, as I'd technically taken a year of absence. This meant a postcard was mailed to my parents, something along the lines of "Good news! The suicide book you requested is now available at the library for pickup!"

» Oops (and thank fucking God).

» I'm caught on the phone with my mom, totally unprepared. She nervously asks about the book, so I think fast and lie: "Oh, no need to worry about that. Sorry! One of my friends goes to Rutgers and didn't have access to Firestone, so I reserved it for him. He's writing about depression and stuff."

» I am snapped out of my own delusion by a one-in-a-million accident. It was only then that I realize something: My death wouldn't just be about *me*. It would completely destroy the lives of those I cared about most. I imagine my mom, who had no part in creating my thesis mess, suffering until her dying day, blaming herself.

» The very next week, I decide to take the rest of my "year off" truly *off* (to hell with the thesis) and focus on physical and mental health. That's how the entire "sumo" story of the 1999 Chinese Kickboxing (Sanshou) Championships came to be, if you've read *The 4-Hour Workweek*.

» Months later, after focusing on my body instead of sitting around trapped in my head, things are much clearer. Everything seems more manageable. The "hopeless" situation seems like shitty luck but nothing permanent.

» I return to Princeton, turn in my now-finished thesis to my still-sour advisor, get chewed up in my thesis defense, and I don't give a fuck. It wasn't the best thesis he'd ever read, nor the best thing I'd ever written, but I had moved on.

Many thanks are due to a few people who helped me regain my confidence that final semester. None of them have heard this story, but I'd like to give them credit here. Among others: My parents and family (of course), Professor Ed Zschau, Professor John McPhee, Sympoh dance troupe, and my friends at the amazing Terrace Food Club. I graduated with the class of 2000 and bid good-bye to Nassau Hall. I rarely go back, as you might imagine.

[Sidenote: After graduating, I promised myself that I would never write anything longer than an email ever again. Pretty hilarious that I now write 500-plus-page books, eh?]

Given the purported jump in "suicidal gestures" at Princeton and its close cousins (e.g., Harvard appears to have 2x the national average for undergrad suicides), I hope the administration is taking things seriously. If nearly half of your student population reports feeling depressed, there might be systemic issues to fix. Left unfixed, you'll have more dead kids on your hands.

And, by the way, it's not enough to wait for people to reach out, or to request that at-risk kids take a leave of absence "off the clock" of the university to dodge liability. Perhaps regularly reach out to the entire student body to catch people before they fall? It could be as simple as an email offering help, resources, or a sympathetic ear.

OUT OF THE DARKNESS

"Being deeply loved by someone gives you strength, while loving someone deeply gives you courage . . ."

— **Lao Tzu**

First, allow me to give a retrospective analysis of my near obliteration. Then, I'll give you a bunch of tools and tricks that I still use for keeping the darkness at arm's length.

Also, some of you might also be thinking "That's it?! A Princeton student was at risk of getting a bad grade? Boo-fuckin'-hoo, man. Give me a break . . ."

But . . . that's the entire point. It's easy to blow things out of proportion, to get lost in the story you tell yourself, and to think that your entire life hinges on one thing you'll barely remember 5 or 10 years later. That *seemingly* all-important thing could be a bad grade, getting into college, a relationship, a divorce, getting fired, or a bunch of hecklers on the Internet.

So, why didn't I kill myself?

Below are the realizations that have helped me (and a few friends). They certainly won't work for everyone suffering from depression, but my hope is that they help some of you.

I. If you're in a dangerous place, call this number: (800) 273–8255. I didn't have it, and I wish I had. It's the National Suicide Prevention Lifeline. They also have live chat at suicidepreventionlifeline.org. It's available 24 hours a day, 7 days a week, in both English and Spanish.

If you're outside of the U.S., check suicide.org for a list of international hotlines.

Sometimes, it just takes one conversation with a rational person to stop a horrible, irrational decision. If you're considering ending your life, please reach out to them. If you're too embarrassed to admit that, as I was, then you can ping them "just to chat for a few minutes." Pretend you're killing time or testing different suicide hotlines for a directory you're compiling. Whatever works.

Speaking personally, I want to see the gifts *you* have to offer the world. And speaking from personal experience, believe me: This too shall pass, whatever it is.

2. I realized it would destroy other people's lives. Killing yourself can spiritually kill other people.

Your death is not perfectly isolated. It can destroy a lot, whether your family (who will blame themselves), other loved ones, or simply the law enforcement officers or coroners who have to haul your death mask–wearing carcass out of an apartment or the woods. The guaranteed outcome of suicide is NOT things improving for you (or going blank), but creating a catastrophe for others. Even if your intention is to get revenge through suicide, the damage won't be limited to your targets.

A friend once told me that killing yourself is like taking your pain, multiplying it by 10, and giving it to the ones who love you. I agree with this, but there's more to it. Beyond any loved ones, you could include neighbors, innocent bystanders exposed to your death, and people — often kids — who commit "copycat suicides" when they read about your demise. This is the reality, not the cure-all fantasy, of suicide.

If you think about killing yourself, imagine yourself wearing a suicide bomber's vest of explosives and walking into a crowd of innocents. That's effectively what it is.

Even if you "feel" like no one loves you or cares about you, you are most likely loved, and you're most definitely lovable and worthy of love.

3. There's no guarantee that killing yourself improves things!

In a tragically comic way, this was a depressing realization I came to while considering blowing my head off or getting run over. Damnation! No guarantees.

The "afterlife" could be 1,000 times worse than life at its most painful. No one knows. I personally believe that consciousness persists after physical death, and it dawned on me that I literally had *zero* evidence that my death would improve things. It's a terrible bet. At least here, in this life, we have known variables we can tweak and change. The unknown void could be Dante's *Inferno* on steroids. When we just "want the pain to stop," it's easy to forget this. You simply don't know what's behind door #3.

In our desperation, we often just don't think it through. It's kind of like the murder-suicide joke by one of my favorite comics, Demetri Martin:

"Someone who commits a murder-suicide is probably somebody who isn't thinking through the afterlife. Bam! You're dead. Bam! I'm dead. Oh shit . . . this is going to be awkward forever."

4. Tips from friends, related to #2 above.

For some of my friends (including high achievers you'd never suspect), a "non-suicide vow" is what made all the difference. Here is one friend's description:

"It only mattered when I made a vow to the one person in my life I knew I would never break it to [a sibling]. It's powerful when you do that. All of a sudden, this option that I sometimes played around in my mind, it was off the table. I would never break a vow to my brother, ever. After the vow and him accepting it, I've had to approach life in a different way. There is no fantasy escape hatch. I'm in it. In the end, making a vow to him is the greatest gift I could have given myself."

As silly as it might sound, it's sometimes easier to focus on keeping your word, and avoiding hurting someone, than preserving your own life.

And that's totally okay. Use what works first, and you can fix the rest later. If you need to disguise a vow out of embarrassment ("How would I confess that to a friend?!"), find a struggling friend and make a mutual "non-suicide vow."

Make it seem like you're only trying to protect him or her. Still too much? Make it a "mutual non-self-hurt" vow with a friend who beats himself or herself up.

Make it about them as much as you. **If you don't care about yourself, make it about other people.**

PRACTICAL GREMLIN DEFENSE

Now, let's talk day-to-day tactics.

The fact of the matter is this: if you're driven, an entrepreneur, a type-A personality, or a hundred other things, mood swings are part of your genetic hardwiring. It's a blessing and a curse.

Below are a number of habits and routines that help me. They might seem simplistic, but they keep me from careening too far off the tracks. They are my defense against the abyss. They might help you find your own. Test them, keep your favorites, and use them as a starting point:

>>> 5 Morning Rituals that Help Me Win the Day (page 143)

>>> "Productivity" Tricks for the Neurotic, Manic-Depressive, and Crazy (Like Me) (page 197)

>>> Is This What I So Feared? (page 474)

>>> The Jar of Awesome (page 570)

>>> Gymnastics Strength Training (page 14)

>>> AcroYoga (page 52)

>>> The Slow-Carb Diet (page 81)

And when in doubt or starting to slip, try these:

1. Go to the gym and move for at least 30 minutes. For me, this is 80% of the battle. When possible, I prefer an actual "How can I help you, sir?" gym to walking or a home-based workout, as the last thing I need is alone time with my head. Somehow force yourself to be around other humans.

2. Each morning, express heartfelt gratitude to one person you care about,

or who's helped or supported you. Text, message, write, or call. Can't think of anyone? Don't forget past teachers, classmates, coworkers from early in your career, old bosses, etc.

3. If you can't seem to make yourself happy, do little things to make *other* people happy. This is a very effective magic trick. Focus on others instead of yourself. Buy coffee for the person behind you in line (I do this a lot), compliment a stranger, volunteer at a soup kitchen, help a classroom on DonorsChoose.org, buy a round of drinks for the line cooks and servers at your favorite restaurant, etc. The little things have a big emotional payback, and guess what? Chances are, at least one person you make smile is on the front lines with you, quietly battling something nearly identical.

TO WRAP UP — ON THE GREEN AND THE GRAY

My "perfect storm" was nothing permanent.

But, of course, it's far from the last storm I'll face. There will be many more. The key is building fires where you can warm yourself as you wait for the tempest to pass. These fires — the routines, habits, relationships, and coping mechanisms you build — help you to look at the rain and see fertilizer instead of a flood. If you want the lushest green of life (and you do), the gray is part of the natural cycle.

You are not flawed.

You are human.

You have gifts to share with the world.

And when the darkness comes, when you are fighting the demons, just remember: I'm right there fighting with you. You are not alone. There's a large tribe around you, and thousands of them are reading this book.

The gems I've found were forged in the struggle. Never ever give up.

Much love to you and yours,
Tim

ROBERT RODRIGUEZ

Robert Rodriguez (TW: @RODRIGUEZ, ELREYNETWORK.COM) is a director, screenwriter, producer, cinematographer, editor, and musician. He is also the founder and chairman of El Rey Network, a new genre-busting cable network. There, he hosts one of my favorite interview-format shows, *The Director's Chair*.

While a student at the University of Texas at Austin, Rodriguez wrote the script for his first feature film while he was a paid subject in a clinical experiment at a drug research facility. That paycheck covered the cost of shooting. The film, *El Mariachi*, went on to win the Audience Award at the Sundance Film Festival, and became the lowest-budget movie ever released by a major studio. Rodriguez went on to write, produce, and direct many successful films, including *Desperado*, *From Dusk Till Dawn*, the *Spy Kids* franchise, *Once Upon a Time in Mexico*, *Frank Miller's Sin City*, *Machete*, and others.

Spirit animal: Great white shark

PREFACE

This is the motherlode. The stars and caffeine aligned to make this interview extremely rich, and Robert hit a home run. My personal highlight doc for this episode was a book by itself. So, please indulge me, as this one is longer than usual. It's worth it.

WHAT'S YOUR OWN "RODRIGUEZ LIST"?

The term "Rodriguez list" has come to mean writing down all of your assets and building a film around the list. It originates from Robert's approach to making *El Mariachi*, which he shot as a "test film" for himself. This "What assets might we have?" question is also asked by billionaire Reid Hoffman (page 228). Here's Robert's story:

"I just took stock of what I had. My friend Carlos, he's got a ranch in Mexico. Okay, that'll be where the bad guy is. His cousin owns a bar. The bar is where there's going to be the first, initial shootout. It's where all the bad guys hang out. His other cousin owns a bus line. Okay, there will be an action scene with the bus at some point, just a big action scene in the middle of the movie with a bus. He's got a pitbull. Okay, he's in the movie. His other friend had a turtle he found. Okay, the turtle's in the movie because people will think we had an animal wrangler, and that will suddenly raise production value.

"I wrote everything around what we had, so you never had to go search, and you never had to spend anything on the movie. The movie cost, really, nothing. [The only cost] was really just that I wanted to shoot it on film instead of video, so that it would look more expensive, and try to tell people I made it for $70K and try to sell it for $70K. [Robert spent $7K on *El Mariachi*.]

"Instead, it ended up going to Columbia and getting released. When we won Sundance, the Audience Award, my acceptance speech said, 'You're going to get a lot more entries next year. When people find out that this is the one that won, a movie made with no money and no crew, everyone's going to pick up a camera and start making their own movies.' It's been flooded with entries since then. It was a real change in the paradigm."

THE BENEFITS OF TREATING THINGS LIKE A "TEST"

"I didn't think anyone was going to see [*El Mariachi*]. It was really just a test film. That's why I did it in Spanish. I did it for the Spanish market. . . . [I figured] I'll do two or three of these things, cut them all together, take out the best portions and use it on my demo reel, and then use the money that I make to go make a real first English-language, American, independent film....

"I didn't overthink it at all. I would have treated it completely differently, had I thought I would ever even show it to anybody. Had I thought it would go to a festival and I would submit it, I would have spent ten times as much. I would have gone and borrowed money. Instead, everything was one take, even if it didn't work, because the film's so expensive. And it was a noisy camera and a soundless camera. It would make so much noise, you couldn't record sound [at the same time]. So, I had to record sound the way you're doing right now. I would shoot a take, put the camera away, get the sound out, put the mic up close.... So I got great sound, but it was out of sync. But, you kind of talk in your own rhythm. So if I say, 'Hi, my name is Robert,' you put the camera away, and now you do the audio: 'Hi, my name is Robert,' you can pretty much get it to sync.... If you look at *Mariachi*, it's [almost] all in sync.... Where it started to get out of sync, I cut away to the dog, or I cut away to a closeup. It created this really snappy editing style, but it was really just to get it back in sync because I couldn't stand it....

"There's a freedom [in] limitations. It's almost more freeing to know I've got to use only these items: turtle, bar, ranch. You're almost completely free within that."

TF: Excuses are a dime a dozen. In the case of entrepreneurship, the "I don't have" list—I don't have funding, I don't have connections, etc.—is a popular write-off for inaction. But lack of resources is often one of the critical ingredients for greatness. Jack Ma, founder of China's Alibaba Group, is worth an estimated $20 to $30 billion, and he explains the secret of his success this way: "There were three reasons why we survived: We had no money, we had no technology, and we had no plan. Every dollar, we used very carefully."

TURN WEAKNESSES INTO STRENGTHS, BUGS INTO FEATURES

"I remember on *From Dusk Till Dawn*, the film, the special effects guys put too much fire in the explosion, and the actors come running out of the building. It's in the movie. You see the building blow up, the bar at the end.... It just kept going and engulfed the whole set, and that was the first shot. We still needed to shoot lots of other stuff with it. Everyone else was freaking out, the production designer was crying. That was all their work. My assistant director comes over and he goes, 'Are you thinking what I'm thinking?' I go, 'Yeah, it looks good the way it is. It's all charred. Let's just keep shooting, we'll do the little repair that needs to be done for next week, and we'll shoot that exterior next week. But let's just keep shooting.' You use those gifts, because nothing ever goes according to plan. Sometimes I hear new filmmakers talk down about their film, and 'Oh, nothing worked and it was a disappointment.' They don't realize yet that *that's* the job. The job is that nothing is going to work at all. So you go: "How can I turn it into a positive and get something much better than if I had all the time and money in the world?" I love those experiences so much. . . . I talked to Michael Mann about this [during] *The Director's Chair*. We talked about *Manhunter* once, years ago. He didn't have money, he'd fired the effects crew.

"Some of the really cool staccato editing was to cover up the fact that they didn't have effects, and I didn't know that. I always thought it was a stylistic choice. And he says, 'No, it's because we didn't have any money or time. I had to almost cut it myself, and I was throwing ketchup on the guy between edits.' It was like, 'Oh, my God, I thought that was a brilliant stylistic choice.' I said, 'I'm going to do that for all my movies now.' I want all of them to not have enough money, not enough time, so that we're forced to be more creative. Because that's going to give it some spark that you can't manufacture. People will tap into it or they'll go: 'I don't know why I like this movie. It's kind of a weird movie, but there's something about it that makes me want to watch it again and again because it's got a life to it.' Sometimes art should be imperfect in a way."

DON'T FOLLOW THE HERD — STUMBLE INSTEAD

"It's good not to follow the herd. Go the other way. If everyone's going that way, you go this other way. You're gonna stumble, but you're also gonna stumble upon an idea no one came up with. . . .

"That way, at least it's a new frontier. I always found success by just going the opposite way. There was too much competition over there. If everyone's trying to get through that one little door, you're in the wrong place. Sometimes at a film festival when people ask, 'How do we break in?' I say, 'The problem is you're at a film festival. Nothing wrong with film festivals, but everyone else here is trying to get through that same door, and they're not all going to fit.' . . .

"So you've got to think bigger than that. There's less competition up there. I always wanted to get into TV, but instead of going and competing with every-one else trying to get in on 7 p.m. on NBC on a Friday night, [I decided to] own a network. You know how many people are trying to own a network? Nobody. When that network I got, El Rey, was up for grabs, there were 100 other appli-cants. Now, that sounds like a lot. But out of the whole country, 100? Really? How many actually had a solid business plan and a vision of something that could be implemented? Probably 5. So you're competing with the top 5 instead of the top 20,000 trying to get in on NBC on Friday or Saturday night. So I al-ways say: 'Try to look bigger. . . .'"

FAILURE IS NOT DURABLE

One of my favorite episodes of *The Director's Chair* is with Francis Ford Cop-pola (*The Godfather, Apocalypse Now,* etc.), and Robert refers later to this quote from Francis: "Failure is not necessarily durable. Remember that the things that they fire you for when you are young are the same things that they give lifetime achievement awards for when you're old."

ROBERT: "Even if I didn't sell *Mariachi,* I would have learned so much by do-ing that project. That was the idea — I'm there to learn. I'm not there to win; I'm there to learn, because then I'll win, eventually. . . .

"You've got to be able to look at your failures and know that there's a key to success in every failure. If you look through the ashes long enough, you'll find something. I'll give you one. Quentin [Tarantino] asked me, 'Do you want to do one of these short films called *Four Rooms* [where each director can create the film of their choosing, but it has to be limited to a single hotel room, and include New Year's Eve and a bellhop]?' and my hand went up right away, in-stinctively. . . .

"The movie bombed. In the ashes of that failure, I can find at least two keys of success. On the set when I was doing it, I had cast Antonio Banderas as the dad and had this cool little Mexican as his son. They looked really close to-gether. Then I found the best actress I could find, this little half-Asian girl. She was amazing. I needed an Asian mom. I really wanted them to look like a family. It's New Year's Eve, because [it] was dictated by the script, so they're all dressed in tuxedos. I was looking at Antonio and his Asian wife and thinking, 'Wow, they look like this really cool, international spy couple. What if they were spies, and these two little kids, who can barely tie their shoes, didn't know they were spies?' I thought of that on the set of *Four Rooms*. There are four of those [Spy Kids movies] now and a TV series coming.

"So that's one. The other one was, after [*Four Rooms*] failed, I thought, 'I still love short films.' Anthologies never work. We shouldn't have had four stories; it should have been three stories because that's probably three acts, and it should just be the same director instead of different directors because we didn't know what each person was doing. I'm going to try it again. Why on earth would I try it again, if I knew they didn't work? Because you figured something out when you're doing it the first time, and [the second attempt] was *Sin City*."

TIM: "Amazing."

ROBERT: "So *Spy Kids* and *Sin City* came out of [*Four Rooms*]. If you have a positive attitude, you can look back. That's why what Francis [Ford Coppola] is saying is correct. Failure isn't always durable. You can go back and you can look at it and go, 'Oh, that wasn't a failure. That was a key moment of my development that I needed to take, and I can trust my instinct. I really can'"

SETTING THE PRECEDENT: BE A "PROBLEM" EARLY

Robert has made all of his own movie posters since *Desperado*. Here's how he got there:

"The [creative] agency shows up [to shoot the movie poster]. Antonio was sick that day, and they were like, 'We're here only one day so we'll put his outfit on one of the other crew members and we'll paste his head on later.' I'm thinking, 'That's not going to look right. Nobody moves like him. Oh, geez, this is going to be awful.' So we shot our own poster on the set, the famous one of him with the gun. I saw him doing that one day on the set, and I went and took a little snapshot that would be a great poster.

"When we went to show the studio the posters, the ones the other guys did looked like DVD covers. I put mine up there, too, and Lisa Henson, the president of Columbia, looked at all of them. She looked at the one that I had and said, 'We like that one,' and I said, 'That one's mine.' She looks at me like, 'Oh shit, had I known it was you, I probably wouldn't have said that.' She goes, 'Really? Oh, we didn't know.' I'm glad I just put it up there along with the others and didn't say anything. Then that set a precedent. From then on, I could go to every studio and say, 'I do my own posters, too. So you guys can go ahead and try and make one, but we'll try and make one.'

"The key is to do it early. Do it while you're still shooting. First impression is everything. I'll cut a trailer while I'm still shooting and send it to a studio. They'll try to make their own, over and over, and they can't get that first thing they saw out of their heads, 'It's still not as good as the one we saw.'"

NOTES AT MIDNIGHT

Robert takes copious notes. He sets an alarm for midnight every night to input the day's notes into a Word document. He dates everything and stores them by year, so he can find whatever he might want later:

"I have a little alarm that goes off at midnight, because around midnight is usually a good time, and I'll write something down. Because I found that even when I just wrote some items down, I could go back and fill them in later because I would remember. . . . What kept it going is when I would go back and review the journals and realize how many life-changing things happened within a weekend. Things that you thought were spread out over 2 years were actually Friday, Saturday, Sunday, and that Monday. So many occurrences happened in chunks that could blow you away, things that kind of define you. . . .

"For anyone who is a parent, it's a must. It's a must because your children — and you — forget everything. Within a few years, they'll forget things that you think they should remember for the rest of their lives. They'll only remember it if it's reinforced. I'm a real family man, so I really love every birthday. I'll tell my kids, because they forget by the next year, what their first years were like. I'll just read through the journal entries, and it blows them away. Or they'll say: 'Hey, we should go camping again.' I go, 'Camping? Oh yeah, remember that time we went camping and I put the tent in the backyard and it had electricity going through? We had fans, and we were watching *Jonny Quest* and we were playing. . . . I must have a journal on that, and I must have video.' So year by year, I just search 'camping.' 'Oh, May 4, 1999. We went camping. It's on tape 25.' I go find the tape and show it to them. After I'd show them the tape, they didn't have to go camping again. They just relived it. . . .

"[Or] you ask your girlfriend or your wife, 'What did we do last year on your birthday?' They won't remember. A year goes by and you will not remember the details. You go back and you see the journals, it's even better the second time. You live through it again and you realize the importance of it."

YOU DON'T NEED TO KNOW. TRUST COMES FIRST.

Robert has many different "jobs" and doesn't view creativity as job-specific. It's a meta-skill. He routinely plays guitar on set and invites master painters to set to teach the actors during breaks. He believes that if you develop creativity, trust and getting started often take care of the rest:

"The technical part of any job is 10%. 90% is creativity. If you already know how to be creative, you've kind of got the battle half beat, [because] you don't need to know. You don't need to know what note specifically you're going to play when you get on stage and do your solo.

"Everybody will ask, what did you just play? And you're going to go, 'I don't know.' I asked Jimmie Vaughan: 'How do you know what you're playing just now?' 'I don't even know what I played.' . . . Ask any of the greats. I studied under a painter, Sebastian Krüger. I went all the way to Germany to watch him paint, to figure out his trick. How does he do it? Because I tried to do what he did, and it looked like garbage. He must have a special brush. He must have special paint and a special technique. So, I go and now, he starts with a mid tone, starts knocking in some highlights, a little bit on the chin, and then he goes to the eye. I ask, 'How do you know where to go next?' He says, 'Oh, I never know. It's different every time.'

"That drives me bonkers. 'What do you mean? How come I can't do that?' and I'd go sit down, and suddenly I could do it. It blows you away. So I take those lessons back and I teach my actors that. I teach my crew that. You don't need to know."

TIM: "Sorry to pause, but this is so fascinating to me. So what clicked? What was the realization when you sat down and suddenly . . . ?"

ROBERT: "You get it in your own way—thinking that you needed to know something, a trick or a process, before it would flow. If you got out of the way, it would just flow. What gives you permission to let it flow? Sometimes if you take 4 years of schooling or you study under somebody, then you've suddenly given yourself permission to let it flow. . . .

"You're just opening up the pipe and the creativity flows through. And as soon as your ego gets in the way, and you go, 'I don't know if I know what to do next' you've already put 'I' in front of it and you've already blocked it a little bit. 'I did it once, but I don't know if I can do it again.' It was never you. The best you can do is just to get out of the way so it comes through.

"When an actor comes to me and he says, 'I'm not sure I know how to play this part,' I say, 'That's beautiful because the other half's gonna show up when we're there.' They say knowing's half the battle. I think the most important is the other part — not knowing what's going to happen but trusting that it will be there when you put the brush up to the canvas. It's going to know where to go."

TIM: "So the trust comes first."

ROBERT: "The trust comes first."

LESSONS FROM DAILY CARTOONING

While at the University of Texas, Robert produced a comic strip called *Los Hooligans*:

"I used to come home and I'd have to do a strip a day, and it might take 3 or 4 hours. I would sometimes not feel like facing the blank page, so I would go lie down and try and figure out if I could create this method, where I could stare at the ceiling and it will just appear, fully formed, and then I could go and draw it. I never could get that to work. I'd be running out of time. I'd run back to the table, and I'd realize the only way to do it was by drawing. You'd have to draw and draw and draw. Then one drawing would be kind of funny or cool. 'That one's kind of neat. This one kind of goes with that.' Then you draw a couple of filler-ups and that's how it would be created. You had to actually move.

"I applied that to all my other work: filmmaking and everything. Even if I didn't know what to do, I just had to begin. For a lot of people, that's the part that keeps them back the most. They think, 'Well, I don't have an idea, so I can't start.' I know you'll only get the idea once you start. It's this totally reverse thing. You have to act first before inspiration will hit. You don't wait for inspiration and then act, or you're never going to act, because you're never going to have the inspiration, not consistently."

TF: This is also how Kevin Kelly (page 470) writes, and the sentiment reminds me of Rolf Potts (page 362): "The simple willingness to improvise is more vital, in the long run, than research."

EVEN THE PROS DON'T KNOW

"[On *The Director's Chair*, Robert Zemeckis said] he thought he was making the worst movie ever in *Forrest Gump* . . . or that he was so punchy in *Back to the Future* [that] he almost cut the 'Johnny B. Goode' sequence because he thought, 'Well, it doesn't really fit. I'm going to cut it before we even preview it.'"

TIM: "That's when his editor was like, 'Just leave it in for the screening.'"

ROBERT: "Let's just preview it. . . . He said, 'We couldn't peel people off the ceiling.' You never know. It shows that you don't know. I want people to hear those stories because when you feel like, 'Oh, I don't know if I'm doing it right. These other guys seem to know.' No, they don't know. None of them know. That's the beauty of it. You don't have to know. You just have to keep moving forward."

MORE ON CREATIVITY

"When people say: 'You do so many things. You're a musician, you're a painter, you're a composer, you're a cinematographer, you're the editor. You do so many different things.' I go, 'No, I only do one thing. I live a creative life. When you put creativity in everything, everything becomes available to you.' . . .

"[If] I'm going to get into this character's head, maybe I'll paint him first and see what he looks like visually, or musically [figure out] what he sounds like. You can work completely nonlinear that way.

"How you journal things, how you cross reference, how you present things, how you inspire your crew, how you inspire other people around you, how you inspire yourself—it's all creative. **And if you say you're not creative, look at how much you're missing out on just because you've told yourself that.** I think creativity is one of the greatest gifts that we're born with that some people don't cultivate, that they don't realize it could be applied to literally everything in their lives."

HIS PITCH TO FRANK MILLER TO GET RIGHTS FOR *SIN CITY*

"I went to Frank Miller, and I showed him this test I did for *Sin City* [based on the graphic novels]. I said, 'I know what it's like to create original characters and to not trust Hollywood, but this isn't Hollywood. This is something totally different. I made this on my own, and I'm going to offer you a deal. How about

I write the screenplay, and it will be unremarkable, because I'm going to copy it right out of your books. It's November. I'll have the screenplay by December. We'll go shoot a test in January. I'll have some actor friends come down. We'll shoot [the opening scene], I'll cut it. You'll be there, you'll direct with me. I'll do the effects, I'll do the score, I'll do the fake title sequence with all the actors we want to be in it [e.g., Bruce Willis, Mickey Rourke]. . . . And if you like what you see, we'll make a deal for the rights, and then we'll make the movie. If you don't like it, you keep it as a short film you can show your friends.'"

FUNNY QUOTE FROM HIS KIDS

"That's what my kids always say, 'Dad's not cheating. It's just creative sportsmanship,' when I beat them at a game because I bent some rule in my favor. They're entertained by that. They don't feel bad. They actually look forward to how I'm going to bend the rules."

START WITH WHY

Robert's most-gifted book is *Start with Why* by Simon Sinek.

"I realized better what I was doing when I read that book, and I gave it to people to show them how to clarify what they're doing right and what they're doing wrong.

"It's a very simple approach that they should take every day. [For instance] if you go to an actor and say, 'Hey, I'm a filmmaker and I'm making a low-budget movie, and I kind of need your name as a marquee to help sell it. I can't pay you very much, and it's going to be probably a lot of work, but if you want to be in it . . .' you're thinking about only yourself. And [the answer will be]: 'No, get the hell out of here' because all you're talking about is *what* you do and *how* you do it, which is: I make low-budget movies. Yeah, so what? It means you've got no money.

"Instead, I always start with a why. I go to them [and say], 'I love what you do. I've always been a big fan. I've got a part that you would never get. I believe in creative freedom. I don't work with the studios. I work independently. I'm the boss there. It's just me and my crew. It's very creative. Ask any of your actor friends. They'll say: Go have that experience.

"'You're just going to feel so invigorated. I shoot very quickly. Robert De Niro did *Machete* in 4 days. I'm going to shoot you out in 4 days. You'll be on your next movie for 6 months. You're on my movie for 4 days, and it's going to be the most fun you've ever had, and you'll probably get great reviews.

"'Your performance is going to be really free, because I'm going to give you that freedom. That's why I do it. How do I do it? Well, I work very independently. I have very few people on my crew, we all do multiple jobs. We do it with less money, so that we have more freedom. What is it I do? I'm an independent filmmaker. Do you want to come make this movie?' They're like, 'Yes.' Because it's all about what they can do and how it's going to fulfill them."

YOU NEVER HAVE TO BE UPSET ABOUT ANYTHING

Robert recounted a conversation with his son, who was extremely upset:

"I said, 'I'm going to tell you a secret in life: You never have to be upset about anything. Everything is for a purpose. You just failed your driver's test, and you're all pissed off. I couldn't be happier. I'd rather you fail with a teacher and take it 100 more times than go fail in front of a cop, or make that same mistake and hit somebody. . . . I can't even think of a negative reason why you failing that test is a bad thing. It's really how you look at it, and the way you look at it is so important. If you can have a positive attitude, look at it, and say, "Let me see, what I can learn from this?" . . . Why would you ever get upset about anything?' And he said, 'Wow. That makes so much sense.' You're upset because something didn't go according to plan? It might be for a good reason."

"GOOD"

by Jocko Willink, retired Navy SEAL Commander
(Full profile on page 412.)

How do I deal with setbacks, failures, delays, defeat, or other disasters? I actually have a fairly simple way of dealing with these situations. There is one word to deal with all those situations, and that is: "good."

This is something that one of my direct subordinates, one of the guys who worked for me, a guy who became one of my best friends, pointed out. He would call me up or pull me aside with some major problem or some issue that was going on, and he'd say, "Boss, we got this, that, or the other thing going wrong," and I would look at him and I'd say, "Good."

And finally, one day, he was telling me about some situation that was going off the rails, and as soon as he got done explaining it to me, he said, "I already know what you're going to say."

And I asked, "What am I going to say?"

He said, "You're going to say: 'Good.'"

He continued, "That's what you always say. When something is wrong or going bad, you just look at me and say, 'Good.'"

And I said, "Well, I mean it. Because that is how I operate." So I explained to him that when things are going bad, there's going to be some good that will come from it.

>> Oh, mission got cancelled? Good. We can focus on another one.

>> Didn't get the new high-speed gear we wanted? Good. We can keep it simple.

>> Didn't get promoted? Good. More time to get better.

» Didn't get funded? Good. We own more of the company.

» Didn't get the job you wanted? Good. Go out, gain more experience, and build a better résumé.

» Got injured? Good. Needed a break from training.

» Got tapped out? Good. It's better to tap out in training than to tap out on the street.

» Got beat? Good. We learned.

» Unexpected problems? Good. We have the opportunity to figure out a solution.

That's it. When things are going bad, don't get all bummed out, don't get startled, don't get frustrated. No. Just look at the issue and say: "Good."

Now. I don't mean to say something clichéd. I'm not trying to sound like Mr. Smiley Positive Guy. That guy ignores the hard truth. That guy thinks a positive attitude will solve problems. It won't. But neither will dwelling on the problem. No. Accept reality, but focus on the solution. Take that issue, take that setback, take that problem, and turn it into something good. Go forward. And, if you are part of a team, that attitude will spread throughout.

Finally, to close this up: If you can say the word "good," guess what? It means you're still alive. It means you're still breathing.

And if you're still breathing, that means you've still got some fight left in you. So get up, dust off, reload, recalibrate, re-engage, and go out on the attack.

And that, right there, is about as good as it gets.

SEKOU ANDREWS

Sekou Andrews (TW: @SEKOUANDREWS, SEKOUANDREWS.COM) is the most impressive poetic voice I've ever heard. I first saw him perform at TED, where he amazed me. Sekou is a schoolteacher turned two-time National Poetry Slam champion. He has presented privately for Barack Obama, Bono, Oprah Winfrey, Maya Angelou, and for many Fortune 500 companies.

TF: Since we're getting to the end (or is it the beginning?), my friends, this profile is short, sweet, and to the point. Here is just one line from Sekou's art to set the tone:

"You must want to be a butterfly so badly, you are willing to give up being a caterpillar."

Spirit animal: Black panther

CONCLUSION

"Learn the rules like a pro, so you can break them like an artist."

—**Pablo Picasso**

"Enjoy it."

—**the best answer I've heard to what I always ask close friends:**
"What should I do with my life?"

During the writing of this book, I would sit in the sauna for 20 to 30 minutes late at night to decompress, then lie in the pool on my back, looking at the stars through the silhouetted branches of the trees. Under the light of a single bulb inside the barrel sauna, I would read something poetic to wind down my brain, such as *Leaves of Grass* or, as I began at one point on a recommendation, *Zen in the Art of Archery* by Eugen Herrigel.

I had just started the practice of archery, and my routine was to take two or three breaks per day for 18 arrows each. I had textbooks and a coach on the practical side. *Zen in the Art of Archery*, on the other hand, appeared to be 80% nonsense riddle-talk and 20% genius philosophical insight.* But it provided a welcome break, a little mental stretching, and that was enough.

One morning, my researcher, who I'd brought from Canada to work on the book in person, stopped me at the refrigerator, where I was grabbing some food and cold water:

"You're so calm. How are you so calm when you have a million things flying around?"

---

*It makes a lot more sense if you've done psychedelics.

I thought about it, and he was right. There was a lot up in the air. I was on the final sprint of my book deadline, there were perhaps a dozen unexpected business fires to manage, my dog had just been badly injured, our car had died, and I had various family members and houseguests coming and going. It was a three-ring circus, and I was the plate spinner.

Historically, I'd been an anxious, short-fused mess on book deadlines. I was extremely unpleasant to be around. So what was different?

I then realized and explained to him: In the process of reading and rereading the lessons in this book, I'd absorbed much more than I'd realized. On autopilot, I was using "good" from Jocko, inviting Mara to tea like Tara Brach, looking at the stars as BJ Miller and Ed Cooke would, and putting fear in line, just as Caroline Paul did atop the Golden Gate Bridge.

I'm a list maker. It's how I keep my life in order, my world organized. What most surprised me about my calmness was that there was no list involved. I'd simply tested one or two titan one-liners or tools in my head every day, and — as Cal Fussman told me — "the good shit sticks." The things I needed at any given time kept coming to mind. The more I reread and pondered them, the more I saw the impact.

Perhaps 16 hours after the refrigerator talk, I was totally spent and ready for a good sweat and cooldown. Solo, I headed out to the barrel sauna and sat down to breathe in the smell of cedar. The perspiration slowly poured out, like the day's tension, and I reached the end of *Zen in the Art of Archery*. One passage, involving the parting comments of the Japanese master, caused me to stop for several minutes. I've slightly abridged it here:

> I must only warn you of one thing. You have become a different person in the course of these years. For this is what the art of archery means: a profound and far-reaching contest of the archer with himself. Perhaps you have hardly noticed it yet, but you will feel it very strongly when you meet your friends and acquaintances again in your own country: things will no longer harmonize as before. You will see with other eyes and measure with other measures. [It has happened to me too, and it happens to all who are touched by the spirit of this art.]

In farewell, and yet not in farewell, the Master handed me his best bow. "When you shoot with this bow you will feel the spirit of the Master near you. . . ."

This made me smile.

For the nerds among you, it made me think of the end of *Return of the Jedi*, after the Alliance defeats the Galactic Empire, when Luke Skywalker looks up into the night sky of Endor (bear with me) to see the shimmering and smiling spirit figures of Obi-Wan Kenobi, Yoda, and Anakin Skywalker.

The first two were with him all along, and all three would be with him forever.

It is my hope that when you read and reread this book, you will feel the spirit of these titans with you. No matter the hardship, challenge, or grand ambition before you, they are here.

You are not alone, and you are better than you think. As Jocko would say: Get after it.

For more mischief . . . fourhourworkweek.com/friday

THE TOP 25 EPISODES OF *THE TIM FERRISS SHOW*

Here are the top-25 most popular episodes of *The Tim Ferriss Show* as of September 2016. All episodes can be found on fourhourworkweek.com/podcast and itunes.com/timferriss

1. "Jamie Foxx on Workout Routines, Success Habits, and Untold Hollywood Stories" (episode 124)

2. "Tony Robbins on Morning Routines, Peak Performance, and Mastering Money" (episode 37)

3. "The Scariest Navy SEAL Imaginable . . . and What He Taught Me" (episode 107)

4. "Tony Robbins — On Achievement Versus Fulfillment" (episode 178)

5. "Lessons from Geniuses, Billionaires, and Tinkerers" (episode 173)

6. "Tim Ferriss Interviews Arnold Schwarzenegger on Psychological Warfare (and Much More)" (episode 60)

7. "The Secrets of Gymnastic Strength Training" (episode 158)

8. "How Seth Godin Manages His Life — Rules, Principles, and Obsessions" (episode 138)

9. "Dom D'Agostino on Fasting, Ketosis, and the End of Cancer" (episode 117)

10. "Charles Poliquin on Strength Training, Shredding Body Fat, and Increasing Testosterone and Sex Drive" (episode 91)

11. "5 Morning Rituals that Help Me Win the Day" (episode 105)

12. "Shay Carl — From Manual Laborer to 2.3 Billion YouTube Views" (episode 170)

13. "Tony Robbins on Morning Routines, Peak Performance, and Mastering Money (Part 2)" (episode 38)

14. "The Science of Strength and Simplicity with Pavel Tsatsouline" (episode 55)

15. "Dissecting the Success of Malcolm Gladwell" (episode 168)

16. "Kevin Rose" (episode 1)

17. "How to 10x Your Results, One Tiny Tweak at a Time" (episode 144)

18. "The Importance of Being Dirty: Lessons from Mike Rowe" (episode 157)

19. "The Interview Master: Cal Fussman and the Power of Listening" (episode 145)

20. "The Man Who Studied 1,000 Deaths to Learn How to Live" (episode 153)

21. "Kevin Kelly — AI, Virtual Reality, and the Inevitable" (episode 164)

22. "Dom D'Agostino — The Power of the Ketogenic Diet" (episode 172)

23. "Tools and Tricks from the #30 Employee at Facebook" (episode 75)

24. "Marc Andreessen — Lessons, Predictions, and Recommendations from an Icon" (episode 163)

25. "Tara Brach on Meditation and Overcoming FOMO (Fear of Missing Out)" (episode 94)

MY RAPID-FIRE QUESTIONS

If you ended up sitting next to a Nobel Prize winner or billionaire, what would you ask them? If you only had 2 to 5 minutes and they were willing to talk, how could you make the most of it?

Below are questions I've collected or concocted for just this hypothetical situation. Many of them are the "rapid-fire questions" that I ask nearly every guest on *The Tim Ferriss Show*. A handful are adapted from questions I picked up from guests themselves (such as Peter Thiel, page 232, and Marc Andreessen, page 170).

- » When you think of the word "successful," who's the first person who comes to mind and why?

- » What is something you believe that other people think is insane?

- » What is the book (or books) you've given most as a gift?

- » What is your favorite documentary or movie?

- » What purchase of $100 or less has most positively impacted your life in the last 6 months?

- » What are your morning rituals? What do the first 60 minutes of your day look like?

- » What obsessions do you explore on the evenings or weekends?

- » What topic would you speak about if you were asked to give a TED talk on something outside of your main area of expertise?

» What is the best or most worthwhile investment you've made? Could be an investment of money, time, energy, or other resource. How did you decide to make the investment?

» Do you have a quote you live your life by or think of often?

» What is the worst advice you see or hear being dispensed in your world?

» If you could have one gigantic billboard anywhere with anything on it, what would it say?

» What advice would you give to your 20-, 25-, or 30-year-old self? And please place where you were at the time, and what you were doing.

» How has a failure, or apparent failure, set you up for later success? Or, do you have a favorite failure of yours?

» What is something really weird or unsettling that happens to you on a regular basis?

» What have you changed your mind about in the last few years? Why?

» What do you believe is true, even though you can't prove it?

» Any ask or request for my audience? Last parting words?

THE MOST-GIFTED AND RECOMMENDED BOOKS OF ALL GUESTS

This is what you've been asking me for!

A note on formatting:

>>> **Bolded books** are "most-gifted book" answers.

>>> **Bolded** and <u>underlined books</u> are "most-gifted book" answers that did *not* appear in the podcast episode but that guests sent me afterward.

>>> Unbolded books were recommended or mentioned by the guest, but not specifically "most-gifted."

Which books came up the most? Here are the top 17 — everything with 3 or more mentions — in descending order of frequency:

1. *Tao Te Ching* by Lao Tzu (5 mentions)

2. *Atlas Shrugged* by Ayn Rand (4)

3. *Sapiens* by Yuval Noah Harari (4)

4. *Siddhartha* by Hermann Hesse (4)

5. *The 4-Hour Workweek* by Tim Ferriss (4)

6. *The Checklist Manifesto* by Atul Gawande (4)

7. *Dune* by Frank Herbert (3)

8. *Influence* by Robert Cialdini (3)

9. *Stumbling on Happiness* by Daniel Gilbert (3)

10. *Superintelligence* by Nick Bostrom (3)

11. *Surely You're Joking, Mr. Feynman!* by Richard P. Feynman (3)

12. *The 4-Hour Body* by Tim Ferriss (3)

13. The Bible (3)

14. *The Hard Thing About Hard Things* by Ben Horowitz (3)

15. *The War of Art* by Steven Pressfield (3)

16. *Watchmen* by Alan Moore (3)

17. *Zero to One* by Peter Thiel with Blake Masters (3)

Enjoy!

Adams, Scott: *Influence* (Robert B. Cialdini)

Altucher, James: ***Jesus' Son: Stories*** (Denis Johnson), *The Kite Runner; A Thousand Splendid Suns* (Khaled Hosseini), *Antifragile; The Black Swan; Fooled by Randomness* (Nassim Nicholas Taleb), *Brain Rules* (John Medina), *Outliers* (Malcolm Gladwell), *Freakonomics* (Steven D. Levitt and Stephen J. Dubner)

Amoruso, Sophia: ***The Richest Man in Babylon*** (George Samuel Clason), *No Man's Land: Where Growing Companies Fail* (Doug Tatum), *Venture Deals* (Brad Feld and Jason Mendelson), *Rilke on Love and Other Difficulties* (Rainer Maria Rilke)

Andreessen, Marc: *High Output Management; Only the Paranoid Survive* (Andrew S. Grove), *Zero to One: Notes on Startups, or How to Build the Future* (Peter Thiel with Blake Masters), *Walt Disney: The Triumph of the American Imagination* (Neal Gabler), *Schulz and Peanuts: A Biography* (David

Michaelis), *The Wizard of Menlo Park: How Thomas Alva Edison Invented the Modern World* (Randall E. Stross), *Born Standing Up: A Comic's Life* (Steve Martin), *The Hard Thing About Hard Things* (Ben Horowitz)

Arnold, Patrick: *Jack Kennedy: Elusive Hero* (Chris Matthews), *From Chocolate to Morphine: Everything You Need to Know About Mind-Altering Drugs* (Andrew Weil), *Guns, Germs, and Steel* (Jared Diamond)

Attia, Peter: ***Mistakes Were Made (but Not by Me): Why We Justify Foolish Beliefs, Bad Decisions, and Hurtful Acts*** (Carol Tavris and Elliot Aronson), ***Surely You're Joking, Mr. Feynman!*** (Richard P. Feynman), *10% Happier: How I Tamed the Voice in My Head, Reduced Stress Without Losing My Edge, and Found Self-Help That Actually Works — A True Story* (Dan Harris)

Beck, Glenn: *The Book of Virtues* (William J. Bennett), ***Winners Never Cheat*** (Jon Huntsman)

Bell, Mark: *COAN: The Man, The Myth, The Method: The Life, Times & Training of the Greatest Powerlifter of All-Time* (Marty Gallagher)

Belsky, Scott: <u>*Life's Little Instruction Book*</u> (H. Jackson Brown, Jr.)

Betts, Richard: *A Fan's Notes* (Frederick Exley), *The Crossroads of Should and Must* (Elle Luna)

Birbiglia, Mike: *The Promise of Sleep* (William C. Dement)

Blumberg, Alex: *On the Run* (Alice Goffman), *Hiroshima* (John Hersey)

Boone, Amelia: *House of Leaves* (Mark Z. Danielewski)

Boreta, Justin: <u>*Musicophilia: Tales of Music and the Brain*</u> (Oliver Sacks), <u>***Waking Up: A Guide to Spirituality Without Religion***</u> (Sam Harris), *This Is Your Brain on Music* (Daniel J. Levitin), *The Unbearable Lightness of Being* (Milan Kundera)

Brach, Tara: *The Essential Rumi* (Jalal al-Din Rumi, Coleman Barks translation), ***When Things Fall Apart: Heart Advice for Difficult Times*** (Pema

Chödrön), *The Shallows* (Nicholas Carr), *A Path with Heart: A Guide Through the Perils and Promises of Spiritual Life* (Jack Kornfield)

Brewer, Travis: *Autobiography of a Yogi* (Paramahansa Yogananda), *Be Here Now* (Ram Dass), *Conversations with God* (Neale Donald Walsch)

Brown, Brené: *The Alchemist* (Paulo Coelho)

Callen, Bryan: *Excellent Sheep* (William Deresiewicz), *Atlas Shrugged; The Fountainhead* (Ayn Rand), *The Power of Myth; The Hero with a Thousand Faces* (Joseph Campbell), *The Genealogy of Morals* (Friedrich Nietzsche), *The Art of Learning* (Josh Waitzkin), *The 4-Hour Body; The 4-Hour Workweek* (Tim Ferriss), *Bad Science, Bad Pharma: How Drug Companies Mislead Doctors and Harm Patients* (Ben Goldacre), *Fiasco: The American Military Adventure in Iraq, 2003 to 2005* (Thomas Ricks), *The Looming Tower: Al-Qaeda and the Road to 9/11; Going Clear: Scientology, Hollywood, and the Prison of Belief* (Lawrence Wright), *Symposium* (Plato)

Carl, Shay: *The Book of Mormon* (Joseph Smith Jr.), *As a Man Thinketh* (James Allen), *How to Win Friends & Influence People* (Dale Carnegie), *Think and Grow Rich* (Napoleon Hill), *The Total Money Makeover* (Dave Ramsey), *The 7 Habits of Highly Effective People* (Stephen R. Covey), *The Denial of Death* (Ernest Becker)

Catmull, Ed: *One Monster After Another* (Mercer Mayer)

Chin, Jimmy: *Musashi: An Epic Novel of the Samurai Era* (Eiji Yoshikawa and Charles Terry), *A Guide to the I Ching* (Carol K. Anthony), *Missoula: Rape and the Justice System in a College Town* (Jon Krakauer)

Cho, Margaret: *How to Be a Movie Star* (William J. Mann)

Cooke, Ed: *The Age of Wonder* (Richard Holmes), *Touching the Rock* (John M. Hull), *In Praise of Idleness: And Other Essays* (Bertrand Russell), *The Sorrows of Young Werther; Theory of Colours; Maxims and Reflections* (Johann Wolfgang von Goethe), *The Joyous Cosmology* (Alan Watts)

Cummings, Whitney: *Super Sad True Love Story* (Gary Shteyngart), *The Drama of the Gifted Child* (Alice Miller), *The Fantasy Bond* (Robert W. Firestone), *The Continuum Concept* (Jean Liedloff)

D'Agostino, Dominic: *Personal Power* (Tony Robbins), *Tripping Over the Truth* (Travis Christofferson), *The Language of God* (Francis Collins), *The Screwtape Letters* (C.S. Lewis), *Cancer as a Metabolic Disease: On the Origin, Management, and Prevention of Cancer* (Thomas Seyfried), *Ketogenic Diabetes Diet: Type 2 Diabetes* (Ellen Davis, MS and Keith Runyan, MD), *Fight Cancer with a Ketogenic Diet* (Ellen Davis, MS)

de Botton, Alain: *The Unbearable Lightness of Being* (Milan Kundera), *The Complete Essays* (Michel de Montaigne), *In Search of Lost Time* (Marcel Proust)

De Sena, Joe: *A Message to Garcia* (Elbert Hubbard), *Atlas Shrugged* (Ayn Rand), *Shōgun* (James Clavell), *The One Minute Manager* (Kenneth H. Blanchard)

Diamandis, Peter: *The Spirit of St. Louis* (Charles Lindbergh), *The Man Who Sold the Moon* (Robert A. Heinlein), *The Singularity Is Near* (Ray Kurzweil), *Atlas Shrugged* (Ayn Rand), *Stone Soup* story

DiNunzio, Tracy: *Good to Great: Why Some Companies Make the Leap . . . and Others Don't* (Jim Collins), *The Everything Store: Jeff Bezos and the Age of Amazon* (Brad Stone)

Dubner, Stephen: For adults: *Levels of the Game* (John McPhee); for kids: *The Empty Pot* (Demi)

Eisen, Jonathan: *National Geographic Field Guide to the Birds of North America* (Jon L. Dunn and Jonathan Alderfer)

Engle, Dan: *Mating in Captivity: Unlocking Erotic Intelligence* (Esther Perel), *The Cosmic Serpent* (Jeremy Narby), *Autobiography of a Yogi* (Paramahansa Yogananda)

Fadiman, James: *Pihkal: A Chemical Love Story*; *Tihkal: The Continuation* (Alexander Shulgin and Ann Shulgin)

Favreau, Jon: *The Writer's Journey* (Christopher Vogler and Michele Montez), *It Would Be So Nice If You Weren't Here* (Charles Grodin), *The 4-Hour Body* (Tim Ferriss), *The Hobbit* (J.R.R. Tolkien), *Kitchen Confidential* (Anthony Bourdain)

Foxx, Jamie: *Without Sanctuary: Lynching Photography in America* (James Allen)

Fussell, Chris: *Gates of Fire* (Steven Pressfield), *Steve Jobs*; *The Innovators* (Walter Isaacson)

Fussman, Cal: *One Hundred Years of Solitude* (Gabriel García Márquez), *Between the World and Me* (Ta-Nehisi Coates), *Speak Like Churchill, Stand Like Lincoln: 21 Powerful Secrets of History's Greatest Speakers* (James C. Humes), *A Feast of Snakes*; *Car* (Harry Crews)

Ganju, Nick: *Don't Make Me Think* (Steve Krug), *How to Measure Anything: Finding the Value of Intangibles in Business* (Douglas W. Hubbard), *How Not to Be Wrong: The Power of Mathematical Thinking* (Jordan Ellenberg), *Getting to Yes* (Roger Fisher and William Ury)

Gazzaley, Adam: *Foundation* (Isaac Asimov), *The Reality Dysfunction* (The Night's Dawn Trilogy) (Peter F. Hamilton), *Mountain Light* (Galen Rowell)

Gladwell, Malcolm: *Strangers to Ourselves: Discovering the Adaptive Unconscious* (Timothy D. Wilson), *Merchant Princes: An Intimate History of Jewish Families Who Built Great Department Stores* (Leon A. Harris), *Tinker, Tailor, Soldier, Spy*; *Little Drummer's Girl*; *The Russia House*; *The Spy Who Came in from the Cold* (John le Carré), *The Big Short: Inside the Doomsday Machine* (Michael Lewis), *The Checklist Manifesto* (Atul Gawande), all of Lee Child's books

Godin, Seth: *Makers*; *Little Brother* (Cory Doctorow), *Understanding Comics* (Scott McCloud), *Snow Crash*; *The Diamond Age* (Neal Stephenson), *Dune* (Frank Herbert), *Pattern Recognition* (William Gibson) AUDIOBOOKS: *The Recorded Works* (Pema Chödrön), *Debt* (David Graeber), *Just Kids* (Patti Smith), *The Art of Possibility* (Rosamund

Stone Zander and Benjamin Zander), *Zig Ziglar's Secrets of Closing the Sale* (Zig Ziglar), *The War of Art* (Steven Pressfield)

Goldberg, Evan: *Love You Forever* (Robert Munsch), *Watchmen; V for Vendetta* (Alan Moore), *Preacher* (Garth Ennis), *The Hitchhiker's Guide to the Galaxy* (Douglas Adams), *The Little Prince* (Antoine de Saint-Exupéry)

Goodman, Marc: *One Police Plaza* (William Caunitz), *The 4-Hour Workweek* (Tim Ferriss), *The Singularity Is Near* (Ray Kurzweil), *Superintelligence: Paths, Dangers, Strategies* (Nick Bostrom)

Hamilton, Laird: **The Bible**, *Natural Born Heroes* (Christopher McDougall), *Lord of the Rings* (J.R.R. Tolkien), *Deep Survival* (Laurence Gonzales), *Jonathan Livingston Seagull* (Richard Bach and Russell Munson), *Dune* (Frank Herbert)

Harris, Sam: *A History of Western Philosophy* (Bertrand Russell), *Reasons and Persons* (Derek Parfit), *The Last Word; Mortal Questions* (Thomas Nagel), *Our Final Invention* (James Barrat), *Superintelligence: Paths, Dangers, Strategies* (Nick Bostrom), *Humiliation; The Anatomy of Disgust* (William Ian Miller), *The Flight of the Garuda: The Dzogchen Tradition of Tibetan Buddhism* (Keith Dowman), *I Am That* (Nisargadatta Maharaj), *Machete Season: The Killers in Rwanda Speak* (Jean Hatzfeld), *God Is Not Great; Hitch-22* (Christopher Hitchens), *Stumbling on Happiness* (Daniel Gilbert), The Qur'an

Hart, Mark: *Mastery* (Robert Greene), *The Art of Learning* (Josh Waitzkin), *The 4-Hour Body* (Tim Ferriss)

Hof, Wim: *Jonathan Livingston Seagull* (Richard Bach and Russell Munson), *Siddhartha* (Hermann Hesse), The Bhagavad Gita, The Bible

Hoffman, Reid: *Conscious Business: How to Build Value Through Values* (Fred Kofman), *Sapiens* (Yuval Noah Harari)

Holiday, Ryan: *Meditations* (Marcus Aurelius), *The War of Art* (Steven Pressfield), *What Makes Sammy Run?* (Budd Schulberg), *Titan: The Life of John D. Rockefeller, Sr.* (Ron Chernow), *How to Live: Or a Life of Montaigne in One Question and Twenty Attempts at an Answer* (Sarah

Bakewell), *The Fish that Ate the Whale: The Life and Times of America's Banana King*; *Tough Jews* (Rich Cohen), *Edison: A Biography* (Matthew Josephson), *Ulysses S. Grant: Triumph over Adversity* (Brooks Simpson), *Fahrenheit 451* (Ray Bradbury)

Honnold, Alex: *A People's History of the United States* (Howard Zinn), *Sacred Economics: Money, Gift, and Society in the Age of Transition* (Charles Eisenstein)

Jarvis, Chase: *Steal Like an Artist*; *Show Your Work!* (Austin Kleon), *The 22 Immutable Laws of Marketing* (Al Ries and Jack Trout), *Trust Me, I'm Lying: Confessions of a Media Manipulator* (Ryan Holiday), *The Rise of Superman* (Steven Kotler), *Daring Greatly* (Brené Brown), *Unlabel: Selling You Without Selling Out* (Marc Eckō), *Play It Away: A Workaholic's Cure for Anxiety* (Charlie Hoehn), *Jab, Jab, Jab, Right Hook* (Gary Vaynerchuk)

John, Daymond: **Think & Grow Rich** (Napoleon Hill), **Who Moved My Cheese?** (Spencer Johnson), **Blue Ocean Strategy** (W. Chan Kim and Renée Mauborgne), **Invisible Selling Machine** (Ryan Deiss), **The Richest Man in Babylon** (George S. Clason), **Genghis Khan and the Making of the Modern World** (Jack Weatherford)

Johnson, Bryan: *A Good Man: Rediscovering My Father, Sargent Shriver* (Mark Shriver), *Man's Search for Meaning* (Viktor E. Frankl), *Siddhartha* (Hermann Hesse), *Endurance: Shackleton's Incredible Voyage* (Alfred Lansing), *Thinking, Fast and Slow* (Daniel Kahneman),

Junger, Sebastian: *At Play in the Fields of the Lord* (Peter Matthiessen), *Sapiens* (Yuval Noah Harari)

Kagan, Noah: *The Ultimate Sales Machine* (Chet Holmes), *Essentialism* (Greg McKeown), **Replay** (Ken Grimwood), *Who* (Geoff Smart and Randy Street), *Million Dollar Consulting* (Alan Weiss), *The Sales Acceleration Formula: Using Data, Technology, and Inbound Selling to Go from $0 to $100 Million* (Mark Roberge), *Smartcuts: How Hackers, Innovators, and Icons Accelerate Success* (Shane Snow), *SPIN Selling* (Neil Rackham), *Small Giants: Companies that Choose to Be Great Instead of Big* (Bo

Burlingham), *Surely You're Joking, Mr. Feynman!* (Richard P. Feynman), *Recession Proof Graduate* (Charlie Hoehn), *Ogilvy on Advertising* (David Ogilvy), *The Martian* (Andy Weir)

Kamkar, Samy: *Influence* (Robert Cialdini)

Kaskade: *Lights Out: A Cyberattack, A Nation Unprepared, Surviving the Aftermath* (Ted Koppel)

Kass, Sam: <u>Sapiens</u> (Yuval Noah Harari), **The Art of Fielding** (Chad Harbach), *Plenty; Jerusalem; Plenty More* (Yotam Ottolenghi), *The Flavor Bible: The Essential Guide to Culinary Creativity, Based on the Wisdom of America's Most Imaginative Chefs* (Karen Page and Andrew Dornenburg), *A History of World Agriculture* (Marcel Mazoyer and Laurence Roudart)

Kelly, Kevin: *The Adventures of Johnny Bunko* (Daniel Pink), *So Good They Can't Ignore You* (Cal Newport), *Shantaram* (Gregory David Roberts), *Future Shock* (Alvin Toffler), *Regional Advantage: Culture and Competition in Silicon Valley and Route 128* (AnnaLee Saxenian), *What the Dormouse Said: How the Sixties Counterculture Shaped the Personal Computer Industry* (John Markoff), The Qur'an, The Bible, *The Essential Rumi*; *The Sound of the One Hand: 281 Zen Koans with Answers* (Yoel Hoffman), *It's All Too Much: An Easy Plan for Living a Richer Life with Less Stuff* (Peter Walsh)

Koppelman, Brian: *What Makes Sammy Run?* (Budd Schulberg), *The Artist's Way Morning Pages Journal* (Julia Cameron), *The War of Art* (Steven Pressfield)

Libin, Phil: *The Clock of the Long Now* (Stewart Brand), *The Alliance* (Reid Hoffman), *The Selfish Gene* (Richard Dawkins), *A Guide to the Good Life* (William Irvine)

MacAskill, Will: *Reasons and Persons* (Derek Parfit), *Mindfulness: An Eight-Week Plan for Finding Peace in a Frantic World* (Mark Williams and Danny Penman), *The Power of Persuasion* (Robert Levine), *Superintelligence: Paths, Dangers, Strategies* (Nick Bostrom)

MacKenzie, Brian: *Tao Te Ching* (Lao Tzu), *Way of the Peaceful Warrior* (Dan Millman)

McCarthy, Nicholas: *The Life and Loves of a He Devil: A Memoir* (Graham Norton), *I Put a Spell on You: The Autobiography of Nina Simone* (Nina Simone)

McChrystal, Stanley: *Once an Eagle* (Anton Myrer), *The Road to Character* (David Brooks)

McCullough, Michael: *The Start-up of You: Adapt to the Future, Invest in Yourself, and Transform Your Career* (Reid Hoffman and Ben Casnocha), *Getting Things Done: The Art of Stress-Free Productivity* (David Allen), *The 7 Habits of Highly Effective People: Powerful Lessons in Personal Change* (Stephen R. Covey), *The Checklist Manifesto* (Atul Gawande)

McGonigal, Jane: *Finite and Infinite Games* (James Carse), *Suffering Is Optional* (Cheri Huber), *The Willpower Instinct* (Kelly McGonigal), *The Grasshopper: Games, Life, and Utopia* (Bernard Suits)

Miller, BJ: Any picture book of Mark Rothko art.

Moynihan, Brendan: *Money Game* (Adam Smith), *Once in Golconda: A True Drama of Wall Street 1920–1938* (John Brooks), *The Crowd: A Study of the Popular Mind* (Gustave Le Bon)

Mullenweg, Matt: *The Year Without Pants: WordPress.com and the Future of Work* (Scott Berkun), *How Proust Can Change Your Life* (Alain de Botton), *A Field Guide to Getting Lost* (Rebecca Solnit), *The Effective Executive; Innovation and Entrepreneurship* (Peter Drucker), *Words that Work* (Frank Luntz), *Women, Fire, and Dangerous Things* (George Lakoff), *History of the Peloponnesian War* (Thucydides), *Hard-Boiled Wonderland and the End of the World* (Haruki Murakami), *The Magus* (John Fowles), *The Everything Store* (Brad Stone), *The Halo Effect: . . . and the Eight Other Business Delusions that Deceive Managers* (Phil Rosenzweig), *Bird by Bird* (Anne Lamott), *On Writing Well* (William Zinsser), *Ernest Hemingway on Writing* (Larry W. Phillips), *The Hard*

Thing About Hard Things (Ben Horowitz), *Zero to One* (Peter Thiel), *The Art of the Start 2.0* (Guy Kawasaki), the works of Nassim Nicholas Taleb

Neistat, Casey: *It's Not How Good You Are, It's How Good You Want to Be* (Paul Arden), *The Second World War* (John Keegan), *The Autobiography of Malcolm X* (Malcolm X and Alex Haley)

Nemer, Jason: *The Prophet* (Kahlil Gibran), *Tao Te Ching* (Lao Tzu)

Norton, Edward: *Wind, Sand and Stars* (Antoine de Saint-Exupéry), *Buddhism Without Beliefs* (Stephen Batchelor), *Shōgun* (James Clavell), *The Search for Modern China; The Death of Woman Wang* (Jonathan Spence), "The Catastrophe of Success" (essay by Tennessee Williams), *The Black Swan* (Nassim Nicholas Taleb)

Novak, B.J.: *The Oxford Book of Aphorisms* (John Gross), *Daily Rituals: How Artists Work* (Mason Currey), *Easy Riders, Raging Bulls: How the Sex-Drugs-and-Rock 'N' Roll Generation Saved Hollywood* (Peter Biskind), *The Big Book of New American Humor; The Big Book of Jewish Humor* (William Novak and Moshe Waldoks)

Ohanian, Alexis: *Founders at Work: Stories of Startups' Early Days* (Jessica Livingston), *Masters of Doom: How Two Guys Created an Empire and Transformed Pop Culture* (David Kushner)

Palmer, Amanda: *Dropping Ashes on the Buddha: The Teachings of Zen Master Seung Sahn; Only Don't Know: Selected Teaching Letters of Zen Master Seung Sahn* (Seung Sahn), *A Short History of Nearly Everything* (Bill Bryson)

Paul, Caroline: *The Things They Carried* (Tim O'Brien), *The Dog Stars* (Peter Heller)

Polanco, Martin: *The Journey Home* (Radhanath Swami), *Ibogaine Explained* (Peter Frank), *Tryptamine Palace: 5-MeO-DMT and the Sonoran Desert Toad* (James Oroc)

Poliquin, Charles: *The ONE Thing* (Gary Keller and Jay Papasan), *59 Seconds: Change Your Life in Under a Minute* (Richard Wiseman), *The Checklist*

Manifesto (Atul Gawande), *Bad Science* (Ben Goldacre), *Life 101: Everything We Wish We Had Learned about Life in School — But Didn't* (Peter McWilliams)

Popova, Maria: *Still Writing* (Dani Shapiro), *On the Shortness of Life* (Seneca), *The Republic* (Plato), *On the Move: A Life* (Oliver Sacks), *The Journal of Henry David Thoreau, 1837–1861* (Henry David Thoreau), *A Rap on Race* (Margaret Mead and James Baldwin), *On Science, Necessity and the Love of God: Essays* (Simone Weil), *Stumbling on Happiness* (Daniel Gilbert), *Desert Solitaire: A Season in the Wilderness* (Edward Abbey), *Gathering Moss* (Robin Wall Kimmerer), *The Essential Scratch & Sniff Guide to Becoming a Wine Expert* (Richard Betts)

Potts, Rolf: *Leaves of Grass* (Walt Whitman), *Writing Tools: 50 Essential Strategies for Every Writer* (Roy Peter Clark), *To Show and to Tell: The Craft of Literary Nonfiction* (Phillip Lopate), *Screenplay: The Foundations of Screenwriting* (Syd Field), *Story* (Robert McKee), *Alien vs. Predator* (Michael Robbins), *The Best American Poetry* (David Lehman), the works of poets Aimee Nezhukumatathil and Stuart Dischell

Randall, Lisa: *I Capture the Castle* (Dodie Smith)

Ravikant, Naval: *Total Freedom: The Essential Krishnamurti* (Jiddu Krishnamurti), *Sapiens* (Yuval Noah Harari), *Snow Crash* (Neal Stephenson), *Poor Charlie's Almanac: The Wit and Wisdom of Charles T. Munger* (Charles T. Munger), *Siddhartha* (Hermann Hesse), *The Rational Optimist* (Matt Ridley), *V for Vendetta* (Alan Moore), *Labyrinths* (Jorge Luis Borges), *Meditations* (Marcus Aurelius), *The Book of Life: Daily Meditations with Krishnamurti* (Jiddu Krishnamurti), *Illusions* (Richard Bach), *Striking Thoughts* (Bruce Lee), *Influence* (Robert Cialdini), *Surely You're Joking, Mr. Feynman!*; *What Do You Care What Other People Think?*; *Perfectly Reasonable Deviations from the Beaten Track* (Richard P. Feynman), *Love Yourself Like Your Life Depends On It*; *Live Your Truth* (Kamal Ravikant), *Distress* (Greg Egan), *The Boys* (Garth Ennis and Darick Robertson), *Genome*; *The Red Queen*; *The Origins of Virtue*; *The Evolution of Everything* (Matt Ridley), *The Essential Writings* (Mahatma Gandhi), *The Tao of Philosophy* (Alan Watts), *The Bed of Procrustes* (Nassim Nicholas Taleb), *Fear and Loathing in Las Vegas* (Hunter S. Thompson), *The Power of Myth* (Joseph Campbell), *Tao Te Ching* (Lao Tzu), *Falling into Grace* (Adyashanti), *God's Debris* (Scott Adams), *The Origin of Consciousness in the Breakdown of the Bicameral Mind* (Julian Jaynes), *Mastering the Core Teachings of the Buddha* (Daniel M. Ingram), *The Power of Habit* (Charles Duhigg), *The Lessons of History* (Will Durant and Ariel Durant), *Too Soon Old, Too Late Smart* (Gordon Livingston), *The Prophet* (Kahlil Gibran), *The Secret Life of Salvador Dalí* (Salvador Dalí), *Watchmen* (Alan Moore)

Reece, Gabby: ***Atlas Shrugged*** (Ayn Rand), ***The Alchemist*** (Paulo Coelho)

Richman, Jessica: ***The Complete Short Stories*** (Ernest Hemingway)

Robbins, Tony: ***As a Man Thinketh*** (James Allen), ***Man's Search for Meaning*** (Viktor E. Frankl), ***The Fourth Turning;*** *Generations* (William Strauss), *Slow Sex* (Nicole Daedone), *Mindset* (Carol Dweck)

Rodriguez, Robert: ***Start with Why: How Great Leaders Inspire Everyone to Take Action*** (Simon Sinek)

Rogen, Seth: *Watchmen* (Alan Moore), ***Preacher*** (Garth Ennis), ***The Hitchhiker's Guide to the Galaxy*** (Douglas Adams), ***The Art of Dramatic Writing*** (Lajos Egri), ***The Conquest of Happiness*** (Bertrand Russell)

Rose, Kevin: ***The Miracle of Mindfulness: An Introduction to the Practice of Meditation*** (Thich Nhat Hanh), ***The Wisdom of Crowds*** (James Surowiecki)

Rowe, Mike: ***The Deep Blue Good-by;*** *Pale Gray for Guilt, Bright Orange for the Shroud; The Lonely Silver Rain, Nightmare in Pink; A Tan and Sandy Silence; Cinnamon Skin* (John D. MacDonald), *At Home: A Short History of Private Life; The Lost Continent: Travels in Small-Town America* (Bill Bryson), *A Curious Discovery: An Entrepreneur's Story* (John Hendricks)

Rubin, Rick: ***Tao Te Ching*** (Lao Tzu, translation by Stephen Mitchell), ***Wherever You Go, There You Are*** (Jon Kabat-Zinn)

Sacca, Chris: ***Not Fade Away: A Short Life Well Lived*** (Laurence Shames and

Peter Barton), ***The Essential Scratch & Sniff Guide to Becoming a Whiskey Know-It-All;*** *The Essential Scratch & Sniff Guide to Becoming a Wine Expert* (Richard Betts), *How to Get Filthy Rich in Rising Asia: A Novel* (Mohsin Hamid), *I Seem to Be a Verb* (R. Buckminster Fuller)

Schwarzenegger, Arnold: ***The Churchill Factor: How One Man Made History*** (Boris Johnson), ***Free to Choose*** (Milton Friedman), ***California*** (Kevin Starr)

Sethi, Ramit: *Age of Propaganda: The Everyday Use and Abuse of Persuasion* (Anthony Pratkanis and Elliot Aronson), *The Social Animal* (Elliot Aronson), ***Getting Everything You Can Out of All You've Got*** (Jay Abraham), ***Mindless Eating*** (Brian Wansink), ***The Robert Collier Letter Book*** (Robert Collier), *Never Eat Alone, Expanded and Updated: And Other Secrets to Success, One Relationship at a Time* (Keith Ferrazzi), *What They Don't Teach You at Harvard Business School* (Mark H. McCormack), *Iacocca: An Autobiography* (Lee Iacocca), *The Checklist Manifesto* (Atul Gawande)

Shinoda, Mike: *Becoming a Category of One: How Extraordinary Companies Transcend Commodity and Defy Comparison* (Joe Calloway), ***The Tipping Point; Blink*** (Malcolm Gladwell), *Learning Not to Drown* (Anna Shinoda), *The 4-Hour Workweek* (Tim Ferriss)

Silva, Jason: ***TechGnosis: Myth, Magic, and Mysticism in the Age of Information*** (Erik Davis), *The Rise of Superman: Decoding the Science of Ultimate Human Performance* (Steven Kotler), *The 4-Hour Workweek* (Tim Ferriss)

Sivers, Derek: *A Geek in Japan: Discovering the Land of Manga, Anime, Zen, and the Tea Ceremony* (Hector Garcia), *Awaken the Giant Within: How to Take Immediate Control of Your Mental, Emotional, Physical and Financial Destiny!* (Tony Robbins), *Stumbling on Happiness* (Daniel Gilbert), *Tricks of the Mind* (Derren Brown), *Show Your Work!* (Austin Kleon), *How to Win Friends and Influence People* (Dale Carnegie), *How to Talk to Anyone* (Leil Lowndes), *How to Make People Like You in 90 Seconds or Less* (Nicholas Boothman), *Power Schmoozing* (Terri Mandell), *Au Contraire: Figuring Out the French* (Gilles Asselin and Ruth

Mastron), *Thinking, Fast and Slow* (Daniel Kahneman), *A Guide to the Good Life: The Ancient Art of Stoic Joy* (William Irvine), *Seeking Wisdom* (Peter Bevelin)

Skenes, Joshua: *Cocktail Techniques* (Kazuo Uyeda)

Sommer, Christopher: *The Obstacle Is the Way* (Ryan Holiday), the works of Robert Heinlein

Spurlock, Morgan: **The Living Gita: The Complete Bhagavad Gita — A Commentary for Modern Readers** (Sri Swami Satchidananda)

Starrett, Kelly: *Deep Survival* (Laurence Gonzales), *The Sports Gene: Inside the Science of Extraordinary Athletic Performance* (David Epstein), *The Talent Code: Greatness Isn't Born. It's Grown. Here's How.* (Daniel Coyle), *The Diamond Age* (Neal Stephenson), *Dune* (Frank Herbert), *The Power of Habit* (Charles Duhigg), *Island of the Blue Dolphins* (Scott O'Dell)

Strauss, Neil: *On the Shortness of Life* (Seneca), **Ask the Dust** (John Fante), **Journey to the End of the Night Novel** (Louis-Ferdinand Céline), **The Painted Bird** (Jerzy Kosinski), **Meditations** (Marcus Aurelius), **Siddhartha** (Hermann Hesse), **Maxims** (François de La Rochefoucauld), **Ulysses** (James Joyce), **StrengthsFinder 2.0** (Tom Rath) (aside from Neil: Just for the coupon to take the online test), **One Hundred Years of Solitude** (Gabriel García Márquez), **Life Is Elsewhere** (Milan Kundera)

Stein, Joel: *The Body Reset Diet* (Harley Pasternak)

Tan, Chade-Meng: **What the Buddha Taught** (Walpola Rahula), **In the Buddha's Words: An Anthology of Discourses from the Pali Canon** (Bhikkhu Bodhi)

Teller, Astro: **What If?: Serious Scientific Answers to Absurd Hypothetical Questions** (Randall Munroe), **Ready Player One: A Novel** (Ernest Cline), *The Gormenghast Novels* (Mervyn Peake)

Teller, Danielle: *Oscar and Lucinda* (Peter Carey), **The Hours** (Michael Cunningham)

Thiel, Peter: **Things Hidden Since the Foundation of the World** (René Girard)

Tsatsouline, Pavel: *Psych* (Judd Biasiotto), *Paradox of Choice* (Barry Schwartz)

von Ahn, Luis: ***Zero to One*** (Peter Thiel), *The Hard Thing About Hard Things* (Ben Horowitz)

Waitzkin, Josh: *On the Road; The Dharma Bums* (Jack Kerouac), *Tao Te Ching* (Lao Tzu), *Zen and the Art of Motorcycle Maintenance* (Robert Pirsig), *Shantaram* (Gregory David Roberts), *For Whom the Bell Tolls; The Old Man and the Sea; The Green Hills of Africa* (Ernest Hemingway), *Ernest Hemingway on Writing* (Larry W. Phillips), *Mindset* (Carol Dweck), *Dreaming Yourself Awake: Lucid Dreaming and Tibetan Dream Yoga for Insight and Transformation* (B. Alan Wallace and Brian Hodel), *The Drama of the Gifted Child* (Alice Miller), *Tribe: On Homecoming and Belonging* (Sebastian Junger), *Grit: The Power of Passion and Perseverance* (Angela Duckworth), *Peak: Secrets from the New Science of Expertise* (Anders Ericsson and Robert Pool)

Weinstein, Eric: ***Heraclitean Fire: Sketches from a Life Before Nature*** (Erwin Chargaff), ***The Emperor of Scent: A True Story of Perfume and Obsession*** (Chandler Burr)

White, Shaun: ***Fifty Shades of Chicken: A Parody in a Cookbook*** (F.L. Fowler), ***Outliers: The Story of Success*** (Malcolm Gladwell), *Open: An Autobiography* (Andre Agassi)

Willink, Jocko: ***About Face: The Odyssey of an American Warrior*** (Colonel David H. Hackworth), *Blood Meridian: Or the Evening Redness in the West* (Cormac McCarthy)

Wilson, Rainn: ***The Family Virtues Guide: Simple Ways to Bring Out the Best in Our Children and Ourselves*** (Linda Kavelin Popov, Dan Popov, and John Kavelin)

Young, Chris: ***On Food and Cooking: The Science and Lore of the Kitchen*** (Harold McGee), ***Essential Cuisine*** (Michel Bras), ***The Second Law*** (P.W. Atkins), *Seveneves* (Neal Stephenson), *The Last Lion Box Set: Winston Spencer Churchill, 1874–1965* (William Manchester)

Zimmern, Andrew: *Rain and Other South Sea Stories* (W. Somerset Maugham)

FAVORITE FILMS AND TV SHOWS

Documentaries and TV series are noted in parentheses. Any entry lacking parentheses is a fictional film.

Adams, Scott: *Whitey: United States of America v. James J. Bulger* (doc)

Altucher, James: *High on Crack Street: Lost Lives in Lowell* (doc), *Hoop Dreams* (doc), *Comedian* (doc)

Amoruso, Sophia: *The Color of Pomegranates*, *Girl Boss Guerilla*

Andreessen, Marc: *Mr. Robot* (TV), *Halt and Catch Fire* (TV), *Silicon Valley* (TV)

Attia, Peter: *Pumping Iron* (doc), *The Bridge* (doc), *Bigger, Stronger, Faster* (doc)

Beck, Glenn: *Citizen Kane*

Betts, Richard: *The Breakfast Club*, *Baraka* (doc)

Birbiglia, Mike: *Tickled* (doc), *Captain Fantastic*, *Other People*, *Terms of Endearment*, *Broadcast News*, *Stop Making Sense*, *No Refunds* (Doug Stanhope comedy special)

Blumberg, Alex: *Man on Wire* (doc), *Hoop Dreams* (doc), *Magic and Bird: A Courtship of Rivals* (doc)

Boone, Amelia: *The Goonies*

Boreta, Justin: *Meru* (doc), *Grizzly Man* (doc), *Daft Punk Unchained* (doc)

Brach, Tara: *Race: The Power of an Illusion* (doc), *Breaking Bad* (TV)

Callen, Bryan: *Fed Up* (doc), Ken Burns's *Baseball* (doc), Ken Burns's *Jazz* (doc)

Carl, Shay: *Captain Fantastic, Transcendent Man* (doc), *Forks over Knives* (doc), big fan of the documentary filmmaker Morgan Spurlock

Cooke, Ed: *Withnail and I, The Armando Iannucci Shows* (TV), *Monty Python's Flying Circus* (TV), Alan Partridge (fictional personality)

Costner, Kevin: *Coney Island* (doc), *E.T. the Extra-Terrestrial, Jaws, Close Encounters of the Third Kind, The Sugarland Express, Minority Report*

Cummings, Whitney: *Buck* (doc), *Comedian* (doc)

D'Agostino, Dominic: "An Advantaged Metabolic State: Human Performance, Resilience and Health" (talk by Peter Attia at IHMC)

de Botton, Alain: *Seven Up!* From the *Up* series (doc)

De Sena, Joe: *Sugar Coated* (doc), *Food Inc.* (doc), *Finding Vivian Maier* (doc)

Diamandis, Peter: *Transcendent Man* (doc), *Tony Robbins: I Am Not Your Guru* (doc), *An Inconvenient Truth* (doc)

DiNunzio, Tracy: *The Overnighters* (doc), *The True Cost* (doc), *The Fog of War* (doc)

Dubner, Stephen: *Seven Up!* From the *Up* series (doc)

Eisen, Jonathan: *Shackleton* (TV miniseries)

Engle, Dan: *Racing Extinction* (doc), *Neurons to Nirvana* (doc), *Searching for Sugar Man* (doc)

Fussell, Chris: *Restrepo* (doc) — should be required viewing for every U.S. citizen. *The Commanding Heights* (doc) — based on Dan Yergin and Joseph Stanislaw's book of the same name. *Bush's War* (doc) — *Frontline*

Fussman, Cal: *The Walk, Cinema Paradiso, Man on Wire* (doc)

Foxx, Jamie: *The Pianist*

Ganju, Nick: *Forrest Gump*

Gazzaley, Adam: Carl Sagan's *Cosmos: A Personal Voyage* (doc)

Godin, Seth: *Man on Wire* (doc), *Exit Through the Gift Shop* (doc), *The Matrix*

Goldberg, Evan: *Die Hard, Lethal Weapon, Adaptation, The Princess Bride, The Fast and the Furious, Rejected* (short film), *Kids in the Hall* (TV), *Absolutely Fabulous* (TV), *Second City Television*

Goodman, Marc: *Ghostbusters* (1984), *WarGames, Sneakers, The Net*, any movie with Bill Murray or Dan Aykroyd in it

Hamilton, Laird: *Blackfish* (doc), *Senna* (doc), *On Any Sunday* (doc)

Harris, Sam: Recommendation to watch Christopher Hitchens, a brilliant speaker

Holiday, Ryan: *Gladiator, This Is Spinal Tap*

Honnold, Alex: *Star Wars, Gladiator*

John, Daymond: BBC's *Planet Earth*

Johnson, Bryan: *Man on Wire* (doc), *Exit Through the Gift Shop* (doc), *Cosmos* (doc)

Kagan, Noah: *Commando, The Count of Monte Cristo, The Jinx* (doc)

Kamkar, Samy: *Into Eternity* (doc), *We Live in Public* (doc), *Revenge of the Electric Car* (doc)

Kass, Sam: *Just Eat It: A Food Waste Story* (doc)

Kelly, Kevin: *Man on Wire* (doc), *The King of Kong* (doc), *A State of Mind* (doc)

Koppelman, Brian: *Fight Club, Client 9: The Rise and Fall of Eliot Spitzer* (doc), *Don't Look Back* (doc), *Roger and Me* (doc)

Libin, Phil: *Star Wars: Episode V — The Empire Strikes Back, The Lord of the Rings: The Two Towers, House of Cards* (TV), *Game of Thrones* (TV), *Top Gear* (TV)

MacAskill, Will: *Louis Theroux's Weird Weekends* (documentary series)

MacKenzie, Brian: *Spinning Plates* (doc)

McChrystal, Gen. Stanley A.: *The Battle of Algiers*

McGonigal, Jane: *Buffy the Vampire Slayer* (TV), *G4M3RS* (doc), *The King of Kong* (doc)

Miller, BJ: *Waiting for Guffman*, *The Kentucky Fried Movie*, *The Groove Tube*, *Grizzly Man* (doc)

Mullenweg, Matt: *Citizenfour* (doc), *Something from Nothing: The Art of Rap* (doc), *Jean-Michel Basquiat: The Radiant Child* (doc)

Neistat, Casey: *The Life and Death of Colonel Blimp*, *Little Dieter Needs to Fly* (doc)

Nemer, Jason: *Marley* (doc), *I Know I'm Not Alone* by Michael Franti (doc), *Happy* (doc)

Norton, Edward: *The Revenant*, *Rust and Bone*, *The Godfather*, *Goodfellas*, *A Prophet*, *The Beat That My Heart Skipped*, *Birdman*, *Biutiful*, *The French Lieutenant's Woman*, *Shōgun* (miniseries), *The Century of the Self* (doc), *The Power of Nightmares* (doc), *The Cruise* (doc)

Novak, B.J.: *Adaptation*, *Ferris Bueller's Day Off*, *Casablanca*, *Pulp Fiction*, *The Naked Gun*, *Catfish* (doc), *To Be and to Have* (doc), *The Overnighters* (doc)

Ohanian, Alexis: *Food Inc.* (doc), *Planet Earth* (doc), *Jiro Dreams of Sushi* (doc)

Palmer, Amanda: *Alive Inside: A Story of Music and Memory* (doc), *Happy* (doc), *One More Time with Feeling* (doc)

Patrick, Rhonda: *Happy People: A Year in the Taiga* (doc), *Planet Earth* (doc)

Paul, Caroline: *Maidentrip* (doc)

Polanco, Martin: *The Crash Reel* (doc), *Waste Land* (doc), *Lo and Behold: Reveries of the Connected World* (doc)

Poliquin, Charles: *The Last Samurai, Gladiator, The Imitation Game, 22 Bullets.* Also: The History Channel and documentaries from National Geographic, and Tarantino movies

Potts, Rolf: *Grizzly Man* (doc)

Reece, Gabby: *Food Inc.* (doc), *Roger and Me* (doc), *Bowling for Columbine* (doc), *Crumb* (doc)

Richman, Jessica: *The Edge*

Robbins, Tony: *Inside Job* (doc)

Rogen, Seth: *Pulp Fiction, Clerks, Rushmore, Bottle Rocket, Adaptation, The Princess Bride, Fawlty Towers* (TV), *Kids In The Hall* (TV), *Monty Python's Flying Circus* (TV), *Second City Television* (TV)

Rose, Kevin: *Anchorman: The Legend of Ron Burgundy, Inglourious Basterds, Food Inc.* (doc)

Rubin, Rick: *20,000 Days on Earth* (doc)

Sacca, Chris: *The Big Lebowski*

Schwarzenegger, Arnold: *Brooklyn Castle* (doc)

Sethi, Ramit: *Jiro Dreams of Sushi* (doc)

Shinoda, Mike: *House of Cards* (TV), *The Godfather, The Usual Suspects, Fight Club, Seven, Ninja Scroll, WALL-E, Princess Mononoke*

Silva, Jason: *Inception, The Matrix, The Truman Show, Vanilla Sky, eXistenZ, The Beach, Maidentrip* (doc)

Sivers, Derek: *Scott Pilgrim vs. the World*

Skenes, Joshua: *Chef's Table* (TV)

Sommer, Christopher: *The Legend of Tarzan*

Spurlock, Morgan: *Scanners, An American Werewolf in London, Making a Murderer* (TV), *Mr. Robot* (TV), *Enron: The Smartest Guys in the Room* (doc), *The Jinx* (doc), *Going Clear: Scientology and the Prison of Belief* (doc), *Brother's Keeper* (doc), *The Thin Blue Line* (doc), *The Fog of War* (doc), *Hoop Dreams* (doc), *Stevie* (doc), *Life Itself* (doc)

Starrett, Kelly: *On the Way to School* (doc), *Trophy Kids* (doc), *Amy* (doc), *Super Size Me* (doc), *Restrepo* (doc)

Strauss, Neil: *The Act of Killing* (doc), *Gimme Shelter* (doc), *The Fog of War* (doc)

Teller, Astro: *Fast, Cheap and Out of Control* (doc)

Thiel, Peter: *No Country for Old Men*

Tsatsouline, Pavel: *The Magnificent Seven* (1960)

von Ahn, Luis: *The Matrix, Jiro Dreams of Sushi* (doc)

Waitzkin, Joshua: *Searching for Sugar Man* (doc), *Riding Giants* (doc), *The Last Patrol* (doc)

Weinstein, Eric: *Kung Fu Panda, Rate It X* (doc)

Willink, Jocko: *Against the Odds — "A Chance in Hell: The Battle for Ramadi"* (doc), *Restrepo* (doc), *The Pacific* (TV), *Band of Brothers* (TV)

Wilson, Rainn: *Apocalypse Now, The Act of Killing* (doc)

White, Shaun: *7 Days in Hell*

Young, Chris: *Ferris Bueller's Day Off, Pulp Fiction, The Right Stuff*

Zimmern, Andrew: *Great Chefs* (TV)

ACKNOWLEDGMENTS

First, I must thank the Titans whose advice, stories, and lessons are the essence of this book. Thank you for your time and generosity of spirit. May the good you share with the world be returned to you a hundredfold. Readers, please see the thank-you list in "On the Shoulders of Giants" (page xi).

To the inimitable Arnold Schwarzenegger, thank you for the wonderfully thoughtful Foreword. Speaking as a Long Island kid raised on *Commando* and *Predator*, it's a dream come true to have you in these pages. To Daniel Ketchell and the rest of his A-Team, thank you for the great work you do, and for helping me get to know the Terminator. The more time I spend with Arnold and those around him, the more impressed I am.

To Stephen Hanselman, my agent and friend, I told you to kick me in the head next time I wanted to do a "definitive" book. Good thing you forgot. Shall we get some jazz and whiskey now?

To the entire team at Houghton Mifflin Harcourt, especially the superhuman Stephanie Fletcher and the amazing design and production team: Rebecca Springer, Emily Andrukaitis, Rachael DeShano, Jamie Selzer, Marina Padakis Lowry, Teresa Elsey, David Futado, Kelly Dubeau Smydra, Jill Lazer, Rachel Newborn, Brian Moore, Melissa Lotfy, and Becky Saikia-Wilson — you helped tame this beast and make it the ultimate playbook. Thank you for burning the midnight oil alongside me! To my publisher Bruce Nichols and his incredible team, including president Ellen Archer, my partner in crime Laurie Brown, Deb Brody, Lori Glazer, Stephanie Kim, Debbie Engel, and all members of the dedicated marketing and sales team, thank you for believing in this book and making magic happen.

To Donna S. and Adam B., thank you for holding down the fort while I was offline! The podcast wouldn't exist, and I wouldn't be able to do any of it, without you. Donna, sorry for Molly's terrorizing of Hank. I'll pay for the therapy. Adam, next time I'm at altitude, please knock the wine glass out of my hand.

To Hristo Vassilev and Jordan Thibodeau, many thanks for the research, double-checking of details, and endless support. Hristo, would you like a few hundred more Mediterranean wraps? Or calamari, perhaps? And don't forget those 20 minutes of sun in the morning. . . .

To Amelia, you are the warrior princess of redlining. Words cannot express how much your help and support meant to me. Through all the SodaStreams and lost arrows, you never wavered. Thank you, thank you, thank you. Payment in nut butters and ice cream is in process.

To Kamal Ravikant, your proofreading laughs were much-needed medicine, and your suggested edits were much-needed feedback. Thank you for being a companion on the path.

I'd be remiss to leave out the kind folks who spent many hours educating me on the details, tech, and craft of podcasting in the beginning. Many thanks, gentlemen! Listed in alphabetical order by first name (and if I forgot anyone, please let me know):

Jason DeFillippo of *Grumpy Old Geeks*
John Lee Dumas of *Entrepreneur on Fire*
Jordan Harbinger of *The Art of Charm*
Lewis Howes of *The School of Greatness*
Matt Lieber and Alex Blumberg of Gimlet Media
Pat Flynn of *Smart Passive Income*
and Rob Walch of Libsyn

Last but not least, this book is dedicated to my parents, who have guided, encouraged, loved, and consoled me through it all. I love you more than words can express.

Also by Tim Ferriss

The #1 *New York Times* Bestsellers

VISIT PRH.COM/TIMFERRISS TO READ EXCERPTS.

HARMONY

BOOKS · NEW YORK